Rows
11-21

995-
253-0609

Management

Canadian Edition

Ricky W. Griffin

Texas A & M University

Jang B. Singh

University of Windsor

HOUGHTON MIFFLIN
Boston   Toronto   Geneva, Illinois
Palo Alto   Princeton, New Jersey

1120 Birchmount Road
Scarborough, Ontario M1K 5G4
www.nelson.com
www.thomson.com

and

Houghton Mifflin Company

222 Berkeley Street
Boston, Massachusetts 02116–3764
www.management.hmcanada.com

For permission to use material from this text or product, contact us by
• Web: www.thomsonrights.com
• Phone: 1-800-730-2214
• Fax: 1-800-730-2215

Canadian Cataloguing in Publication Data
Griffin, Ricky W.
　Management

Canadian ed.
Includes bibliographical references and index.
ISBN 0-17-607400-7

1. Management. I. Singh, Jang Bahadur, 1955–　. II. Title.
HD31.G763 1999　　　658　　　C99–930961–7

Editorial Director	Michael Young
Acquisitions Editor	Tim Sellers
Marketing Manager	David Tonen
Project Editor	Mike Thompson
Production Editors	Rosalyn Steiner and Tracy Bordian
Copy Editor	Sarah Robertson
Proofreader	Marcia Miron
Art Director	Angela Cluer
Cover Design	Angela Cluer
Cover Image	Bildhuset/Photonica
Composition	Alicja Jamorski
Printer	RR Donnelley

2　3　4　03　02　01

For Emily ...
My partner and inspiration (JBS)

For Glenda ...
Always searching for life's new chapters to explore (RWG)

Brief Contents

Contents

Chapter 14: Managing Workforce Diversity in Organizations   384

Preface

A challenge for both students and instructors in principles of management courses lies in covering a vast amount of material in a limited period of time. To be effective, textbooks for such courses must be direct and concise in their treatment of the foundational elements of management. This edition of *Management* is an attempt to provide such a treatment from a Canadian perspective that is mindful of globalization and the special economic relationship that exists between Canada and the United States. Therefore, this textbook, while presenting a Canadian perspective, is not overly parochial.

Writing a survey text like *Management* poses a number of other challenges. First, because it is a survey, it has to be comprehensive. Second, it has to be accurate and objective. Third, because management is a real activity, the book has to be relevant. Fourth, it has to be timely and up-to-date. Fifth, it needs to be as interesting and engaging as possible.

In this edition, we think that these goals have been met effectively. We believe that users of this text will be drawn to the solid foundations of management theory and practice, balanced with new and exciting material. We welcome feedback from the students and instructors who use this text. Interested parties can contact us at the e-mail addresses provided at the end of this preface.

FEATURES OF THE BOOK

Integrated Coverage

Many books set certain material off from the rest of the text. This is usually done by creating a separate section at the end of the book called "emerging trends," "special challenges," or something similar. New and emerging topics and other material that does not easily fit elsewhere is then covered in that section. Unfortunately, by setting it apart this way, the material often tends to get ignored or receive minimal attention. In this edition, we have avoided the use of a separate section; if the material is really worth having in the book to begin with, it needs to be fully integrated with the core material.

Chapter Organization

This integrated approach to the subject has also resulted in a streamlined chapter organization. In Part I, "An Introduction to Management," the chapter on managing and the manager's job is followed by an examination of different schools of thought on management. Part II, "The Environmental Context of Management," contains chapters on organization–environment relationships and the ethical and global contexts of management. In Part III, "Planning and Decision Making," the chapter on managerial decision making follows the planning and strategy chapters, reflecting a logical and straightforward view of the planning process. Chapter 9, "Managing Entrepreneurship and New Venture Formation," concludes this section.

Part IV contains the chapter entitled "Managing Workforce Diversity in Organizations" (Chapter 14). Instructors interested in beefing up organizational behaviour coverage in their course should note that Part V contains chapters on employee motivation, leadership, interpersonal relations, and the management of groups and teams. In Part VI, we examine the basic elements of control (Chapter 20), quality (Chapter 21), and information technology (Chapter 22).

Material for a Brand New World of Management

Special treatment of a variety of topics especially relevant to the new world of management is interwoven throughout the book. Key examples include:

- the art and science of management (Chapter 1)
- benchmarking (Chapters 3 and 21)
- organizational culture (Chapter 3)
- NAFTA and the European Union (Chapter 5)
- entrepreneurship in Canada (Chapter 9)
- reengineering (Chapter 12)
- innovation (Chapter 12)
- goal setting theory (Chapter 16)
- charismatic leadership (Chapter 17)
- modern communication technology (Chapter 18)
- work teams (Chapter 19)
- diversity in the Canadian workplace (Chapter 14)
- the legal environment of human resource management (Chapter 13)
- financial control (Chapter 20)
- total quality management (Chapter 21)
- ISO 9000 (Chapter 21)

Basic Themes

Several key themes are prominent in this edition of *Management*. One is the global character of the field of management. Examples and cases throughout the book reinforce this. Another timely theme is quality. Although we cover quality and quality-related material in detail in Chapter 21, quality is also woven into the discussion of several topics throughout the book. Still another theme is the balance of theory and practice. Managers must have a sound basis for their decisions, but theories that provide that basis must be grounded in reality. Throughout the book we explain the theoretical frameworks that guide managerial activities, and then provide illustrations and examples of how and when those theories do and do not work. A fourth theme is that management is a generic activity not confined to large businesses. We use examples and discuss management in both large and small businesses as well as in not-for-profit organizations.

A Pedagogical System That Works

The pedagogical elements built into *Management,* Canadian Edition, should prove to be effective teaching and learning aids for students and instructors.

- *Learning objectives and a chapter outline* serve to preview key themes at the start of every chapter. *Key terms* and concepts are highlighted in boldface type, and many are defined in the margin next to where they are discussed. Effective *figures, tables,* and *photographs* help bring the material to life.

- Three kinds of questions are found at the end of every chapter, designed to test different levels of student understanding. *Questions for Review* ask students to recall specific information; *Questions for Analysis* ask students to integrate and synthesize material; *Questions for Application* ask students to apply what they've learned to their own experiences.
- We also have *video exercises* that conclude each of the six parts in the book. The video segments from CTV explore various aspects of the management process as they relate to the particular section where they are presented. The exercises in the text challenge students to think critically about the issues raised in the videos, and provide numerous points of departure for lively class discussions or homework assignments.
- Another pedagogical element in this edition is the conclusion of each chapter with a *skill development exercise* based on the managerial skills framework developed in Chapter 1. Students are able to measure their technical, interpersonal, conceptual, and diagnostic skills within various management situations and learn how they can work to improve those skills.

Applications That Keep Students Engaged

To fully appreciate the role and scope of management in contemporary society, it is important to see examples and illustrations of how concepts apply in the real world, both in Canada and internationally. We rely heavily on fully researched examples to illustrate real-world applications. They vary in length and were all reviewed for their timeliness. In order to give the widest view possible, we vary examples of traditional management roles with nontraditional roles; profit-seeking businesses with nonprofit organizations; large corporations with small businesses; and international examples with Canadian examples. Other applications include:

- *Opening incidents at the beginning of every chapter.* These brief vignettes draw the student into the chapter with a real-world scenario that introduces a particular management theme.
- *Boxed inserts.* Each chapter also contains two boxed inserts intended to briefly depart from the flow of the chapter with extensions of points made in the text. The *Managing in a Changing World* boxes highlight the nature and importance of change in organizations. They focus on how companies have dealt with new circumstances and ways of managing in an increasingly dynamic environment. Among the topics covered are technology, sociocultural standards, economic forces, and globalization. The *Environment of Management* boxes reinforce the idea that managers do not operate in a vacuum but are subject to forces in the environment within which they function. The consideration of factors such as ethics, organizational design, and the Internet are a few examples of what is covered in these boxes.
- *End-of-chapter cases.* Each chapter also concludes with a detailed case study. Both Canadian and international cases are presented.

An Effective Teaching and Learning Package

- Instructor's Manual (prepared by Ron Shay, Kwantlen University College)
- Test Bank (prepared by Brian Harrocks, Algonquin College)
- Computerized Test Bank

- PowerPoint Slides (prepared by Jim Clark, University of Lethbridge)
- Colour Transparencies (Note: Originally designed to accompany U.S. 5th edition of *Management*.)
- CTV Video Package
- Web site with information on careers, additional cases, etc.

We invite your feedback on this book. If you have any questions, suggestions, or issues to discuss, please feel free to contact us. The most efficient way to do so is by e-mail. Ricky Griffin's address is rgriffin@tamu.edu; Jang Singh's address is jang@uwindsor.ca. We look forward to hearing from you.

R.W.G
J.B.S.

Acknowledgments

Writing a textbook is a challenging but stimulating activity that brings with it a variety of rewards. An intrinsic reward that flows from this activity is the feeling that one is helping to disseminate knowledge to a variety of students from all parts of the world. Positive feedback from instructors is the greatest of rewards.

We owe enormous debts to many persons for helping us create this edition of *Management*. Our colleagues at the University of Windsor and at Texas A & M University have helped create conditions conducive to scholarly pursuits. Our secretaries, My Nhan (Windsor) and Phyllis Wasburn (Texas A & M), deserve special recognition, as do Pritee Sethi (Graduate Assistant, University of Windsor) and Roger Jaipargass (former Research Assistant, University of Windsor).

The fine team of professionals at Nelson, Thomson Learning has been instrumental in this project. Mike Thompson, Tim Sellers, Rosalyn Steiner, and Tracy Bordian played major roles in the development and creation of this edition of *Management*. Jennifer Dewey and Anita Mieznikowski were also instrumental in the development and production of this book. We are especially grateful to Michael Young, Editorial Director, Nelson, Thomson Learning.

Many reviewers have played a critical role in the evolution of this project. We gratefully acknowledge Robert Ankli, University of Guelph; Kirk L. Bailey, Ryerson Polytechnic University; Donna Bentley, N.A.I.T.; James D. Clark, University of Lethbridge; Samuel Clement, Marianopolis College; John Logan, Ryerson Polytechnic University; Susan Quinn, Mount Royal College; and Carson Rappell, Dawson College.

We would also like to thank Parbudyal Singh (McMaster University), David Van Fleet (Arizona State University-West), and Ella Van Fleet (Professional Business Associates) for contributing some of the boxes and cases. We also acknowledge the assistance of Emily Carasco in developing Chapters 13 and 14. In addition, we recognize the contributions of academics throughout the world whose research and writing we have drawn on. We are most grateful to various organizations that, directly or indirectly, have provided information used in this text.

Finally, we acknowledge with deep gratitude the support of our families: Glenda, Dustin, and Ashley (Texas); Emily, Elizabeth, and David (Windsor). We dedicate this book to them.

R.W.G.
J.B.S.

What could the people in these two images possibly have in common? These Asian women are sorting and preparing loads of fish for a wide market, while the people in aprons are discussing how to improve customer service at a Dominion Save-A-Centre grocery store in Canada. In short, both groups are involved in managing a business enterprise through effective customer service.

An Introduction to Management

Managing and the Manager's Job

OBJECTIVES

After studying this chapter, you should be able to:

- *Describe the nature of management, define management and managers, and characterize their importance to organizations.*

- *Identify and briefly explain the four basic management functions in organizations.*

- *Describe the kinds of managers found at different levels and in different areas of the organization.*

- *Identify the basic managerial roles that managers may play and the skills they need to be successful.*

- *Discuss the science and art of management and describe how people become managers.*

- *Summarize the scope of management in organizations.*

Maureen Kempston Darkes, CEO of GM Canada, believes in marketing her product by improving the company's relationship with its consumers.

General Motors (GM) of Canada Limited is one of Canada's largest and most profitable companies. Formed in 1918, with the merger of McLaughlin Motor Car Company and the Chevrolet Car Company, the company is currently engaged in the production and distribution of cars, trucks, and locomotives, as well as parts and accessories. Plants are located in Oshawa, Windsor, London, and St. Catharines (all in Ontario), and in St. Thérèse, Quebec. In 1994, Maureen Kempston Darkes was appointed president and chief executive officer of this company. The first woman to head GM Canada, she holds the highest operating post ever attained by a woman at General Motors.

Kempston Darkes, who became the president of GM Canada when the company was just emerging from a downturn, guided the company to sales of $33.6 billion in 1998 (the highest total revenue for a Canadian company that year). She has brought to the company her keen intelligence, her strong will, 22 years' experience in many of GM's operations, and a background in international trade and policy development. Since assuming office, she has emphasized a number of strategic initiatives aimed at increasing revenues. One of her top priorities has been the improvement of the company's relationship with its consumers, especially through the dealer network. She is of the view that "GM is a marketing company."

> **"GM Canada's president is a team player who is very accessible to the company's stakeholders."**

In her first year on the new job, Kempston Darkes, who was born and raised in Toronto, travelled to dealerships on the Atlantic and Pacific coasts, as well as to Saskatchewan, northern Alberta, and almost everywhere else cars were sold by GM Canada. Being the company's main salesperson is just one of the many roles played by Kempston Darkes, a lawyer by profession who once worked as a receptionist at a Ford dealership.

Keeping a keen eye on the growth and importance of the "women market," GM Canada's president has decided to make vehicles more "woman-friendly." Given that women make slightly less than half of all car purchases and influence about 80 percent of all purchasing decisions, Kempston Darkes wants to make vehicles that address women's concerns such as safety and comfort. More vehicles are now being made with side-impact barriers, antilock brakes, lower front ends to accommodate smaller statures, and lower floors to make climbing in while wearing a skirt easier. The company's president is also emphasizing the retraining of dealers, many of whom stereotype women buyers by, for example, stressing the colour of a car rather than its safety features, or ignoring women if they enter the showroom accompanied by a man.

Along with better marketing strategies, Kempston Darkes also stresses innovation and new technology, the production of high-quality vehicles, and the achievement of production and financial targets. GM Canada's president is a team player who is very accessible to the company's stakeholders. She pays close attention to GM Canada's human resources, emphasizing the importance of employees' health and safety and the need for the company to mirror the ethnic mosaic of the Canadian population.[1] ●

Maureen Kempston Darkes is clearly a manager. So, too, are Shinroku Morohashi (president of Mitsubishi Corp.), Sir David Wilson (director of the British Museum), Bobbie Gaunt (president of Ford Canada), Gord Ash (general manager of the Toronto Blue Jays), Jean Chrétien (prime minister of Canada), John Paul II (pope of the Roman Catholic Church), and Suzanne Bernard Leclair (president of Les Fourgons Transit Inc.). As diverse as they and their organizations are, all of these managers are confronted by many of the same challenges, strive to achieve many of the same goals, and apply many of the same concepts of effective management in their work.

For better or worse, our society is strongly influenced by managers and their organizations.[2] Most people in Canada are born in a hospital (an organization), educated by public and separate schools (all organizations), and buy virtually all of their consumable products and services from businesses (organizations). And much of our behaviour is influenced by various government agencies (also organizations). We define an **organization** as a group of people working together in a structured and coordinated fashion to achieve a set of goals. The goals may include such things as profit (Bombardier), the discovery of knowledge (University of Windsor), national defence (Canadian Armed Forces), the coordination of various local charities (United Way), or social satisfaction (a student club). Because they play such a major role in our lives, understanding how organizations operate and how they are managed is important.

This book is about managers and the work they do. In Chapter 1, we examine the general nature of management, its dimensions, and its challenges. We explain the concepts of management and managers, discuss the management process and present an overview of the book, and identify various kinds of managers. We describe the different roles and skills of managers, discuss the nature of managerial work, and examine the scope of management in contemporary organizations. In Chapter 2, we describe how both the practice and theory of management have evolved. As a unit, then, these first two chapters provide an introduction to the field by introducing both contemporary and historical perspectives on management.

● **organization**
A group of people working together in a structured and coordinated fashion to achieve a set of goals

Managers are responsible for the effective and efficient utilization of all resources. Suzanne Leclair founded Transit Truck Bodies in Laval, Quebec, in 1987, a company that manufactures all types of aluminum and fibreglass truck bodies according to customer specifications. As president and CEO, she oversees all aspects of this expanding company.

AN INTRODUCTION TO MANAGEMENT

There are probably as many definitions of management as there are books on the subject. Many of the definitions are relatively concise and simplistic. For example, almost a century ago Frederick Taylor defined management as "knowing exactly what you want [people] to do, and then seeing that they do it in the best and cheapest way."[3] Management, however, is a complex process—much more complex than this simple definition leads us to believe.[4] Thus we need to develop a definition of management that better captures the nature of its complexities and challenges.

Management is perhaps best understood from a resource-based perspective. As we discuss more completely in Chapter 2, all organizations use four basic kinds of inputs, or resources, from their environment: human, financial, physical, and information. Human resources include managerial talent and labour. Financial resources are the capital used by the organization to finance both ongoing and long-term operations. Physical resources include raw materials, office and production facilities, and equipment. Information resources are usable data needed to make effective decisions. Examples of resources used in four very different kinds of organizations are shown in Table 1.1.

Managers are responsible for combining and coordinating these various resources to achieve the organization's goals. A manager at Petro-Canada, for example, uses the talents of executives and drilling platform workers, profits earmarked for reinvestment, existing refineries and office facilities, and sales forecasts to make decisions regarding the amount of oil to be refined and distributed during the next quarter. Similarly, the mayor (manager) of Montreal might use police officers, a government grant (perhaps supplemented with surplus tax revenues), existing police stations, and detailed crime statistics to launch a major crime prevention program in the city.

All organizations, regardless of whether they are large or small, profit-seeking or nonprofit, use some combination of human, financial, physical, and information resources to achieve their goals. These resources, or inputs, are generally obtained from the organization's environment.

TABLE 1.1	Examples of Resources Used by Organizations			
Organization	**Human Resources**	**Financial Resources**	**Physical Resources**	**Information Resources**
Petro-Canada	Drilling platform workers Corporate executives	Profits Shareholder investments	Refineries Office buildings	Sales forecast OPEC proclamations
University of Windsor	Faculty Secretarial staff	Alumni contributions Government grants	Computers Campus facilities	Research reports Government publications
City of Montreal	Police officers Municipal employees	Tax revenue Government grants	Sanitation equipment Municipal buildings	Economic forecasts Crime statistics
Nan's Corner Grocery Store	Grocery clerks Bookkeeper	Profits Owner investment	Building Display shelving	Price lists from suppliers Newspaper ads for competitors

management
A set of activities (including planning and decision making, organizing, leading, and controlling) directed at an organization's resources (human, financial, physical, and information), with the aim of achieving organizational goals in an efficient and effective manner

efficient
Using resources wisely and in a cost-effective way

effective
Making the right decisions and successfully implementing them

manager
Someone whose primary responsibility is to carry out the management process

How do these and other managers combine and coordinate the various kinds of resources? They do so by carrying out four basic managerial functions or activities: planning and decision making, organizing, leading, and controlling. Management, then, as illustrated in Figure 1.1, can be defined as follows: **Management** is a set of activities (including planning and decision making, organizing, leading, and controlling) directed at an organization's resources (human, financial, physical, and information) with the aim of achieving organizational goals in an efficient and effective manner.

The last phrase in our definition is especially important because it highlights the basic purpose of management—to ensure that an organization's goals are achieved in an efficient and effective manner. By **efficient**, we mean using resources wisely and in a cost-effective way. For example, a firm like Toyota Motor Corp. that produces high-quality products at relatively low costs is efficient. By **effective**, we mean making the right decisions and successfully implementing them. Toyota also makes cars with the styling and craftsmanship that inspire consumer confidence. A firm could produce black-and-white console televisions very efficiently but still not succeed because black-and-white televisions are no longer popular. A firm that produces products that no one wants (or a firm that cannot sell its products) is therefore not effective. In general, successful organizations are both efficient and effective.[5]

With this basic understanding of management, defining the term manager becomes relatively simple: A **manager** is someone whose primary responsibility is to carry out the management process. In particular, a manager is someone who plans and makes decisions, organizes, leads, and controls human, financial, physical, and information resources.

Today's managers face a variety of interesting and challenging situations. The average executive works sixty hours a week, has enormous demands placed on his or her time, and faces increased complexities posed by globalization, domestic competition, government regulation, and shareholder pressure.[6] The task is further complicated by rapid change, unexpected disruptions, and both minor and major crises. The manager's job is unpredictable and fraught with challenges, but it is also filled with opportunities to make a difference.

Many of the characteristics that contribute to the complexity and uncertainty of management stem from the environment in which organizations function. For example, as shown in Figure 1.1, the resources used by organizations to create products and services all come from the environment. Thus it is critical that managers understand this environment. The *Environment of Management* box discusses how Gordon Forward at Chaparral Steel Company uses the environment to enhance the effectiveness of his firm. Part II of the text discusses the environmental context of management in detail. Chapter 3 provides a general discussion of the organizational environment and culture, and Chapters 4 and 5 address two specific aspects of the environment more fully. In particular, Chapter 4 discusses the ethical and social context of management, and Chapter 5 explores the global context of management. After reading those chapters, you will be better prepared to study the essential activities that constitute the management process.

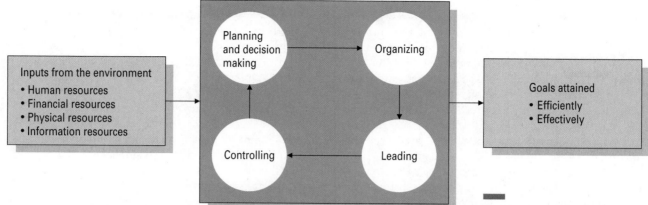

THE MANAGEMENT PROCESS

We noted earlier that management involves the four basic functions of planning and decision making, organizing, leading, and controlling. Because these functions represent the framework around which this book is organized, we introduce them here and note where they are discussed more fully. Their basic definitions and interrelationships are shown in Figure 1.2. (Note that Figure 1.2 is an expanded version of the central part of Figure 1.1.)

Basic managerial activities include planning and decision making, organizing, leading, and controlling. Managers engage in these activities to combine human, financial, physical, and information resources efficiently and effectively and work toward achieving the goals of the organization.

F I G U R E   1 . 2   The Management Process

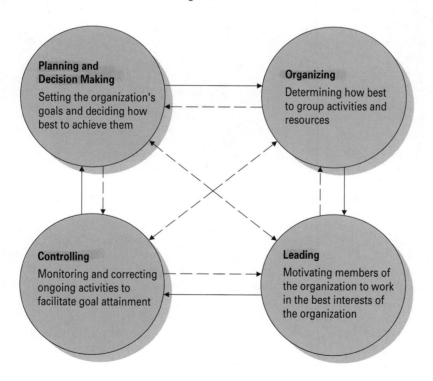

Management involves four basic activities—planning and decision making, organizing, leading, and controlling. Most managers engage in more than one activity at the same time.

Small Can Be Beautiful

When most people think of steel companies, they envision huge behemoths like USX Corporation, Bethlehem Steel Corp., Inland Steel Co., and Nippon Steel U.S.A. Inc. But one of the most effective steel companies in the world today is Chaparral Steel Company. Based in the small Texas town of Midlothian (population just over 5,000) and with a workforce of fewer than 1,000 employees, Chaparral has become the world's lowest-cost producer of steel. For example, it produces steel with only about 1.6 hours of labour per ton, versus 4.9 hours for major steel producers and 2.4 hours for other small producers like Chaparral. That cost advantage enabled Chaparral Steel to achieve sales of more than $1 billion in 1998. Obtaining these results takes an unusual work environment provided by skillful management.

Chaparral has garnered considerable attention for its success at creating just such a work environment. Its practices have been identified as necessary for global manufacturing competitiveness. Chaparral combines customer service, involvement, quality, training, and much more to achieve its record results. Its CEO, Gordon Forward, focuses on three ideas: a classless corporation that treats everyone as adults, universal education that emphasizes constantly acquiring skills necessary or useful to the organization, and autonomy or independence of action.

The classless corporation is evident at Chaparral in a variety of ways. The plant has no time clocks, and workers can set their own lunch hours and break times. They can park anywhere in the company parking lot—there are no reserved spaces. Managers and workers tend to dress casually, and the company provides free coffee.

Workers are paid a salary and a bonus. The size of the bonus depends not just on individual performance, although that is a component, but also on company profits and any new skills that the workers have acquired. Indeed, Chaparral tries to ensure that at least 85 percent of its workers are enrolled in courses at any one time. The courses vary from electronics to metallurgy to finance, but all are of value to both the individuals and the organization.

Independence of action is evident in that workers have the freedom to fail, as well as the expectation that they will speak out on issues and problems. Workers are expected to apply the knowledge they obtain in courses to solve problems or improve operations at Chaparral. This approach has paid off in a variety of ways. All workers who deal with customers are trained to perform one another's jobs so that time can be saved in responding to customer inquiries. Workers used their knowledge to develop a technology that reduced the number of passes through a system from fifty to between eight and twelve. Two maintenance workers invented a machine for strapping bundles of steel that costs only about one-fourth that of older machines. Clearly, good management can go a long way toward helping an organization become effective.

References: Brian Dumaine, "Chaparral Steel: Unleash Workers and Cut Costs," *Fortune*, May 18, 1992, p. 88; W.A. Tony, "Chaparral Steel—Management for Adults," *Iron & Steelmaker*, January 1, 1993, pp. 26–28; James Campbell Quick and David A. Gray, "Chaparral Steel Company: Bringing 'World Class Manufacturing' to Steel," *National Productivity Review*, Winter 1990, pp. 51–58; and Harold E. Edmondson, "Outstanding Manufacturing in the Coming Decade," *California Management Review*, Summer 1989, pp. 70–90; *TXI Annual Report* at: http://www.txi.com

Recall the example of Maureen Kempston Darkes discussed earlier. Kempston Darkes has created a clear set of goals that articulate what she wants GM Canada to be. She has set up an effective organization to help make that vision a reality. Kempston Darkes also pays close attention to the people who work for GM Canada. And she keeps a close eye on how well the company is performing. Each of these activities represents one of the four basic managerial functions illustrated in the figure. Setting goals is part of planning, setting up the organization is part of organizing, managing people is part of leading, and monitoring performance is part of control.

It is important to note, however, that the functions of management do not usually occur in a tidy, step-by-step fashion. Managers do not plan on Monday, make decisions on Tuesday, organize on Wednesday, lead on Thursday, and control on Friday. At any given time, a manager is likely to be engaged in several different activities simultaneously. Indeed, from one setting to another, managerial work is as different as it is similar. The similarities that pervade most settings are the phases in the management process. Important differences include the emphasis, sequencing, and implications of each phase.[7] Thus the solid lines in Figure 1.2 indicate how, in theory, the functions of management are performed. The dotted lines, however, represent the true reality of management. In the sections that follow, we explore each of these activities.

Planning and Decision Making: Determining Courses of Action

In its simplest form, **planning** means setting an organization's goals and deciding how best to achieve them. **Decision making**, a part of the planning process, involves selecting a course of action from a set of alternatives. Planning and decision making help maintain managerial effectiveness by serving as guides for future activities. For example, Paul Tellier, president and CEO of Canadian National Railway, recently established two goals for the firm: $1 billion in operating income by the turn of the century and a reduction of the operating ratio from 85 cents in 1996 to 80 cents spent for every dollar of revenue by the year 2000.[8] These goals help other managers at Canadian National Railway see that they need to emphasize revenue generation and improve efficiency. Thus the organization's goals and plans clearly help managers know how to allocate their time and resources.

Four chapters making up Part III of this text are devoted to planning and decision making. Chapter 6 examines the basic elements of planning and decision making, including the role and importance of organizational goals. Chapter 7 looks at strategy and strategic planning, which provide overall direction and focus for the organization. Chapter 8 explores managerial decision making and problem solving in detail. Finally, Chapter 9 addresses planning and decision making as they relate to the management of entrepreneurship and new venture formation, increasingly important elements of the Canadian economy. (The Appendix at the end of the book provides additional coverage of the tools managers use in planning and decision making.)

Organizing: Coordinating Activities and Resources

Once a manager has set goals and developed a workable plan, the next management function is to organize people and the other resources necessary to carry out the plan. Specifically, **organizing** involves determining how activities and resources are to be grouped. To illustrate how managers organize, consider the organization of Drypers, a small but fast-growing maker of disposable diapers. The firm is run by five executives, each of whom has specific responsibility for a major functional area such as marketing, finance, and manufacturing. Each manager hires his own employees and handles all areas of the business that relate to his area of responsibility. The five together make all the major decisions that affect the overall organization.[9]

Organizing is the subject of Part IV. Chapter 10 introduces the basic elements of organizing, such as job design, departmentalization, authority

● **planning**
Setting an organization's goals and deciding how best to achieve them

● **decision making**
Part of the planning process that involves selecting a course of action from a set of alternatives

● **organizing**
Grouping activities and resources in a logical fashion

relationships, span of control, and line and staff roles. Chapter 11 explains how managers fit these elements together to form an overall organization design. Organization change and innovation are the focus of Chapter 12. Processes associated with hiring and assigning people to carry out organizational roles are described in Chapter 13. Finally, the organization and management of workforce diversity is discussed in Chapter 14.

Leading: Managing People

leading
The set of processes used to get members of the organization to work together to further the interests of the organization

The third basic managerial function is leading. Some people consider leading to be the most important and most challenging of all managerial activities. **Leading** is the set of processes used to get people to work together to advance the interests of the organization. For example, most experts credit the leadership abilities of Laurent Beaudoin, former CEO of Bombardier, as possibly the ingredient most important to his success at the Canadian manufacturer.

Leading involves a number of different processes and activities, which are discussed in Part V. The starting point is understanding basic individual and interpersonal processes, which we focus on in Chapter 15. Motivating employees is discussed in Chapter 16, and leadership itself and the leader's efforts to influence others are covered in Chapter 17. Communication, another important part of leading, is addressed in Chapter 18. Finally, managing group and team processes is the subject of Chapter 19.

Controlling: Monitoring and Evaluating Activities

controlling
Monitoring organizational progress toward goal attainment

The final phase of the management process is **controlling**, or monitoring the organization's progress toward its goals. As the organization moves toward its goals, managers must monitor progress to ensure that it is performing in such a way as to arrive at its "destination" at the appointed time. A good analogy is that of a space mission to Mars. NASA does not simply shoot a rocket in the general direction of the planet and then look again in four months to see whether the rocket hit its mark. NASA monitors the spacecraft almost continuously and makes whatever course corrections are needed to keep it on track. Controlling helps ensure the effectiveness and efficiency needed for successful management.

The control function is explored in Part VI. First, Chapter 20 explores the basic elements of the control process, including the increasing importance of strategic control. Managing for total quality, an increasingly important concern for all organizations today, is explored in Chapter 21, along with productivity and operations management. Finally, Chapter 22 addresses the management of information and information technology, still other critical areas of organizational control. The *Managing in a Changing World* box illustrates how Harley-Davidson's managers used a variety of management functions to change their firm to improve its competitiveness in a changing marketplace.

KINDS OF MANAGERS

Earlier in this chapter we identify as managers people from a variety of organizations. Clearly, there are many kinds of managers. One point of differentiation is among organizations, as those earlier examples imply. Another point occurs within an organization. Figure 1.3 shows how managers within an organization can be differentiated by level and area.

Managers at Different Levels of the Organization

Managers can be differentiated according to their level in the organization. Although large organizations typically have a number of **levels of management**, the most common view considers three basic levels: top, middle, and first-line managers.

Top Managers Top managers make up the relatively small group of executives who manage the overall organization. Titles found in this group include president, vice president, and chief executive officer (CEO). Thus, John Cleghorn, CEO of the Royal Bank of Canada, is a top manager. An organization's top managers establish its goals, overall strategy, and operating policies. They also officially represent the organization to the external environment by meeting with government officials, executives of other organizations, and so forth. The job of a top manager is likely to be complex and varied. Top managers make decisions about such activities as acquiring other companies, investing in research and development, entering or abandoning various markets, and building new plants and office facilities.[10] They often work long hours and spend much of their time in meetings or on the telephone.[11]

● **levels of management**
The differentiation of managers into three basic categories—top, middle, and first-line

F I G U R E 1.3 Kinds of Managers by Level and Area

Levels of Management

Top managers

Middle managers

First-line managers

Marketing Finance Operations Human resources Administration Other

Areas of Management

Organizations generally have three levels of management, represented by top managers, middle managers, and first-line managers. Regardless of level, managers are also usually associated with a specific area within the organization, such as marketing, finance, operations, human resources, administration, or some other area.

Hot Harley's in Hog Heaven

Harley-Davidson's motorcycles have always been loud, fast, and gaudy. The firm dominated the world market for large motorcycles for years. Japanese competitors began to make inroads into Harley's more stable markets, however, and by the late 1970s the firm's parent, AMF, ordered management to boost output threefold. Unfortunately, without good management, this caused product quality to erode drastically, and Harley's sales soon plummeted.

In the early 1980s, Harley nearly went bankrupt. Federal tariffs were put in place to help Harley meet foreign competition, but they were set to last only until 1988. In 1987, Harley asked that the tariffs be removed. In considerably less than a decade, Harley had changed so much that the tariffs were no longer needed. Changing the organization to respond to changing conditions in markets, technology, and the like is now seen as a critical management characteristic. Harley's experience exemplifies the importance of such change.

Richard F. Teerlink, president and CEO of the Milwaukee-based motorcycle company, deserves a lot of credit for the changes at Harley. A realist with a strong personality, he had his managers look to see what was wrong and fix it. Inventory systems were streamlined so that parts arrived just when they were needed. This reduces the numbers of parts in inventory and, hence, the costs of warehousing. New manufacturing technology with integrated development processes run by computers was installed. For all of this to work, managers and workers had to learn new skills and develop different attitudes toward work, a process made easier by the threat of financial collapse and job losses.

Indeed, by 1993 Harley had a new problem. It could not maintain its high quality and increase production fast enough to meet demand. Rather than lower quality to increase production rates, Harley moved to gradually increase production while using a variety of other devices to keep customers waiting for Harleys rather than switching to competitive products.

Harley recently began to produce branded merchandise—black leather jackets, fringed leather bras, even shot glasses—that would be available only through dealers. Many Harley dealers also began to develop show rooms with antiques to lure potential customers and to ensure that those who wanted to place orders were willing to wait.

Harley Owners' Groups (HOGs) began to emerge, too. HOGs were organized in Japan, Australia, Germany, Mexico, and other countries as Harley's international sales nearly tripled from 1989 to 1993. Harley was successful in thinking globally but acting locally—that is, in developing international markets by tailoring the advertising and merchandising to local tastes and conditions. The idea was to "package" a lifestyle—HOGs, magazines, clothing, and biker rallies—to lure professionals who could afford the expensive—$10,000–$25,000 (U.S.)—machines.

These changes worked. Harley continues to ride high on its efforts but is determined not to become complacent or to lose sight of what has enabled its turnaround—focusing on changing the organization to meet the needs of customers in the changing global environment of management.

References: "Leaders of the Pack," *Machine Design*, February 21, 1994, pp. 52–60; "Born to Be Real," *Industry Week*, August 2, 1993, pp. 14–19; Gary Slutsker, "Hog Wild," *Forbes*, May 24, 1993, pp. 45–46; Kevin Kelly and Karen Lowry Miller, "The Rumble Heard Round the World: Harleys," *Business Week*, May 24, 1993, pp. 58–60; and Gary Hoover, Alta Campbell, and Patrick J. Spain (Eds.), *Hoover's Handbook 1991: Profiles of Over 500 Major Corporations* (Austin, Tex.: The Reference Press, 1990), p. 277.

Middle Managers Middle management is probably the largest group of managers in most organizations. Common middle-management titles include plant manager, operations manager, and division head. Middle managers are primarily responsible for implementing the policies and plans developed by top managers and for supervising and coordinating the activities of lower-level managers.[12] Plant managers, for example, handle inventory management,

quality control, equipment failures, and minor union problems. They also coordinate the work of supervisors within the plant.

In recent years, many organizations have thinned the ranks of middle managers to lower costs and eliminate excess bureaucracy. For example, among the literally hundreds of companies that have pared their workforces during the past decade, Alcan Aluminum Limited has cut 11,000 workers and General Motors of Canada has cut about 13,000 (more than one-third of its 1989 workforce). Even though middle managers represent only around 5 percent of an average company's workforce, they accounted for around 17 percent of total layoffs.[13] Still, middle managers are necessary to bridge the upper and lower levels of the organization and to implement the strategies developed at the top. Although many organizations have found that they can indeed survive with fewer middle managers, those who remain play an even more important role in determining how successful the organization will be.[14]

First-Line Managers First-line managers supervise and coordinate the activities of operating employees. Common titles for first-line managers are supervisor, coordinator, and office manager. A flight services manager for Air Canada is a first-line manager. He or she flies several trips a day, handles preflight instructions, oversees the flight attendants on each flight, and deals with any passenger complaints that may arise on one of the flights. Positions such as these are often the first ones held by employees who enter management from the ranks of operating personnel. In contrast to top and middle managers, first-line managers typically spend a large proportion of their time supervising subordinates.[15]

Managers in Different Areas of the Organization

Regardless of their level, managers may work in various areas within an organization. In any given firm, for example, **areas of management** may include marketing, financial, operations, human resource, administrative, and other areas.

Marketing Managers Marketing managers work in areas related to the marketing function—getting consumers and clients to buy the organization's prod-

● **areas of management**
Managers can be differentiated into marketing, financial, operating, human resource, administration, and other areas

ucts or services (be they Ford automobiles, *Maclean's* magazines, Associated Press news reports, or flights on Air Canada). These areas include new product development, promotion, and distribution. Given the importance of marketing for virtually all organizations, developing good managers in this area can be critical. Louis Gerstner, CEO of IBM, and William P. Stiritz, CEO of Ralston Purina Co., started their careers as marketing managers.[16]

Financial Managers   Financial managers deal primarily with an organization's financial resources. They are responsible for activities such as accounting, cash management, and investments. In some businesses, such as banking and insurance, financial managers are found in especially large numbers. Ron Osborne, president of Bell Canada Enterprises, Duane L. Burnham, CEO of Abbott Laboratories, and James C. Cotting, CEO of Navistar International Transportation Corp., spent much of their careers as financial managers.[17]

Operations Managers   Operations managers are concerned with creating and managing the systems that create an organization's products and services. Typical responsibilities of operations managers include production control, inventory control, quality control, plant layout, and site selection. Robert E. Allen, CEO of American Telephone & Telegraph Co. (AT&T), and James Near, CEO of Wendy's International Inc., started their careers as operations managers.[18]

Human Resource Managers   Human resource managers are responsible for hiring and developing employees. They are typically involved in human resource planning, recruiting and selecting employees, training and development, designing compensation and benefit systems, formulating performance appraisal systems, and discharging low-performing and problem employees. William J. Alley, CEO of American Brands, Inc., and Ronald Allen, CEO of Delta Air Lines, both worked in human resources management early in their careers.[19]

Administrative Managers   Administrative, or general, managers are not associated with any particular management specialty. Probably the best example of an administrative management position is that of a hospital or clinic administrator. Administrative managers tend to be generalists; they have some basic familiarity with all functional areas of management rather than specialized training in any one area. Katharine Graham, CEO of the Washington Post Co., and James Houghton, CEO of Corning Incorporated, spent much of their careers as administrative managers.[20]

Other Kinds of Managers   Many organizations have specialized management positions in addition to those already described. Public relations managers, for example, deal with the public and media for firms like Chrysler Canada and Ontario Hydro to protect and enhance the image of the organization. Research and development (R&D) managers coordinate the activities of scientists and engineers working on scientific projects in organizations such as Monsanto Company, NASA, and Merck & Co. Internal consultants are used in organizations such as The Prudential Insurance Co. of America to provide specialized expert advice to operating managers. Many areas of international management are coordinated by specialized managers in organizations like Eli Lilly and Rockwell International Corp. The number, nature, and importance of these specialized managers vary tremendously from one organization to another. As contemporary organizations continue to grow in complexity and size, the number and importance of such managers are also likely to increase.

BASIC MANAGERIAL ROLES AND SKILLS

Regardless of their level or area within an organization, all managers must play certain roles and exhibit certain skills if they are to be successful. The concept of a role, in this sense, is similar to the role an actor plays in a theatrical production. A person does certain things, meets certain needs in the organization, and has certain responsibilities. In the sections that follow, we first highlight the basic roles managers play and then discuss the skills they need to be effective.

Managerial Roles

Henry Mintzberg offers a number of interesting insights into the nature of managerial roles.[21] He closely observed the day-to-day activities of a group of CEOs by literally following them around and taking notes on what they did. From his observations, Mintzberg concluded that managers play ten different roles and that these roles fall into three basic categories: interpersonal, informational, and decisional. Table 1.2 summarizes these roles.

Interpersonal Roles There are three **interpersonal roles** inherent in the manager's job. First, the manager is often asked to serve as a *figurehead*—taking visitors to dinner, attending ribbon-cutting ceremonies, and the like. These activities are typically more ceremonial and symbolic than substantive. The manager is also asked to serve as a *leader*—hiring, training, and motivating employees. A manager who formally or informally shows subordinates how to do things and how to perform under pressure is leading. Finally, managers can have a *liaison* role. This role often involves serving as a coordinator or link between people, groups, or organizations. For example, IBM and Apple Computer recently agreed to cooperate on developing new technology. Representatives from each firm meet regularly to coordinate this new venture. Thus they are serving as liaisons for their respective companies.

● **interpersonal roles**
The roles of figurehead, leader, and liaison, which involve dealing with other people

Informational Roles The three **informational roles** identified by Mintzberg flow naturally from the interpersonal roles just discussed. The process of carrying out these roles places the manager at a strategic point to gather and disseminate information. The first informational role is that of *monitor,* one who actively seeks information that may be of value. The manager questions subordinates, is receptive to unsolicited information, and attempts to be as well informed as possible. The manager is also a *disseminator* of information, transmitting relevant information back to others in the workplace. When the roles of monitor and disseminator are viewed together, the manager emerges as a vital link in the organization's chain of communication. The third informational role focuses on external communication. The *spokesperson* formally relays information to people outside the unit or outside the organization. For example, a plant manager at Magna International may transmit information to top-level managers so that they will be better informed about the plant's activities. The manager may also represent the organization before a chamber of commerce or consumer group. Although the roles of spokesperson

● **informational roles**
The roles of monitor, disseminator, and spokesperson, which involve the processing of information

TABLE 1.2 Ten Basic Managerial Roles

Category	Role	Sample Activities
Interpersonal	Figurehead	Attending ribbon-cutting ceremony for new plant
	Leader	Encouraging employees to improve productivity
	Liaison	Coordinating activities of two project groups
Informational	Monitor	Scanning industry reports to stay abreast of developments
	Disseminator	Sending memos outlining new organizational initiatives
	Spokesperson	Making a speech to discuss growth plans
Decisional	Entrepreneur	Developing new ideas for innovation
	Disturbance handler	Resolving conflict between two subordinates
	Resource allocator	Reviewing and revising budget requests
	Negotiator	Reaching agreement with a key supplier or labour union

and figurehead are similar, there is one basic difference between them. When a manager acts as a figurehead, the manager's presence as a symbol of the organization is what is of interest. In the spokesperson role, however, the manager carries information and communicates it to others in a formal sense.

Decisional Roles   The manager's informational roles typically lead to the **decisional roles**. The information acquired by the manager as a result of performing the informational roles has a major bearing on important decisions that he or she makes. Mintzberg identified four decisional roles. First, the manager has the role of *entrepreneur*, the voluntary initiator of change. A manager at 3M Company developed the idea for the Post-it Note Pad but had to "sell" it to other skeptical managers inside the company. A second decisional role is initiated not by the manager but by some other individual or group. The manager responds to her role as *disturbance handler* by handling such problems as strikes, copyright infringements, and energy shortages.

The third decisional role is that of *resource allocator*. As resource allocator, the manager decides how resources are distributed, and with whom he or she will work most closely. For example, a manager typically allocates the funds in the unit's operating budget among the unit's members and projects. A fourth decisional role is that of *negotiator*. In this role the manager enters into negotiations

● **decisional roles**
The roles of entrepreneur, disturbance handler, resource allocator, and negotiator, which primarily relate to making decisions

with other groups or organizations as a representative of the company. For example, managers may negotiate a union contract, an agreement with a consultant, or a long-term relationship with a supplier. Negotiations may also be internal to the organization. The manager may, for instance, mediate a dispute between two subordinates or negotiate with another department for additional support.

Managerial Skills

In addition to fulfilling numerous roles, managers also need a number of specific skills to succeed. One classic study of managers identified three important types of managerial skills: technical, interpersonal, and conceptual.[22] Diagnostic skills are also prerequisites to managerial success.

Technical Skills   **Technical skills** are the skills necessary to accomplish or understand the specific kind of work being done in an organization. For example, David Packard and Bill Hewlett understand the inner workings of their company, Hewlett-Packard Co., because they were trained as engineers. Project engineers, physicians, and accountants all have the technical skills necessary for their respective professions. They each develop basic technical skills by completing recognized programs of study at colleges and universities. Then they gain experience in actual work situations, honing their skills before actually becoming R&D manager, chief of surgery, or partner in a certified public accounting firm. Similarly, the top marketing executive of any large firm probably started as a sales representative or sales manager, whereas the operations vice president was probably a plant manager at one time. Technical skills are especially important for first-line managers. These managers spend much of their time training subordinates and answering questions about work-related problems. They must know how to perform the tasks assigned to those they supervise if they are to be effective managers.

- **technical skills**
  The skills necessary to accomplish or understand tasks relevant to the organization

Interpersonal Skills   Managers spend considerable time interacting with people both inside and outside the organization. For obvious reasons, then, the manager also needs **interpersonal skills**—the ability to communicate with, understand, and motivate individuals and groups. As a manager climbs the organizational ladder, she must be able to get along with subordinates, peers, and those at higher levels of the organization. Because of the multitude of roles managers must fulfill, a manager must also be able to work with suppliers, customers, investors, and others outside of the organization. Although some managers have succeeded with poor interpersonal skills, a manager who has good interpersonal skills is likely to be more successful.

- **interpersonal skills**
  The ability to communicate with, understand, and motivate both individuals and groups

Conceptual Skills   **Conceptual skills** depend on the manager's ability to think in the abstract. Managers need the mental capacity to understand the overall workings of the organization and its environment, to grasp how all the parts of the organization fit together, and to view the organization in a holistic manner. This allows them to think strategically, to see the "big picture," and to make broad-based decisions that serve the overall organization. A few years ago, Boeing was on the verge of discontinuing its 737 aircraft line because of sliding domestic sales. Then, suddenly, one manager, Bob Norton, realized that the company needed to take a more global view of the aircraft market. By focusing on the same things that had made the 737 an earlier success in the United States, Boeing was able to reintroduce the aircraft in developing nations. Increased sales

- **conceptual skills**
  The manager's ability to think in the abstract

there have offset declines at home, and the end result is that the company has been able to maintain a highly profitable product line beyond its normal life expectancy. The conceptual skills of a single manager helped pave the way.[23]

● **diagnostic skills**
A manager's ability to visualize the most appropriate response to a situation

Diagnostic Skills   Successful managers also possess **diagnostic skills**, or skills that enable a manager to visualize the most appropriate response to a situation. A physician diagnoses a patient's illness by analyzing symptoms and determining their probable cause. Similarly, a manager can diagnose and analyze a problem in the organization by studying its symptoms and then developing a solution. For example, a manager of a plant may observe that one particular department is suffering from high employee turnover. He would diagnose the situation and perhaps decide that the turnover is caused by one of three things: dissatisfaction with pay, boring work, or a supervisor with poor interpersonal skills. After interviewing several employees, he may conclude that the problem is the supervisor. He could reassign the supervisor to a position that required less interaction with people in order to solve the turnover problem. The ability to diagnose would have enabled him to define his problem, recognize its possible causes, focus on the most direct problem, and then solve it. Diagnostic skills are also useful in favourable situations. The company may find that its sales are increasing at a much higher rate than anticipated. Possible causes might include low price, greater demand than predicted, and high prices charged by a competitor. The manager uses diagnostic skills to determine what is causing the sales explosion and how best to take advantage of it.

Of course, not every manager has equal measure of these four basic types of skills. Nor are equal measures critical. As shown in Figure 1.4, for example, the optimal skills mix tends to vary with the manager's level in the organization. First-line managers generally need to depend more on their technical and interpersonal skills and less on their conceptual and diagnostic skills. Top managers tend to exhibit the reverse combination—a greater emphasis on conceptual and diagnostic skills and a somewhat lesser dependence on technical and interpersonal skills. Middle managers require a more even distribution of skills.

Managers generally use different combinations of skills at different levels of an organization. For example, top managers rely heavily on conceptual and diagnostic skills, and first-line managers put more emphasis on technical and interpersonal skills. Middle managers are likely to rely on an equal blend of all four skills.

FIGURE 1.4   Management Skill Mixes at Different Organizational Levels

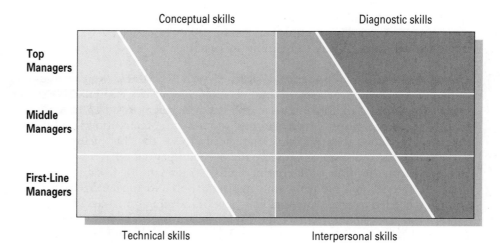

THE NATURE OF MANAGERIAL WORK

We noted earlier that managerial work does not follow an orderly, systematic progression through the workweek. Indeed, the manager's job is fraught with uncertainty, change, interruption, and fragmented activities. One study, for example, found that in a typical day CEOs are likely to spend 59 percent of their time in scheduled meetings, 22 percent doing "desk work," 10 percent in unscheduled meetings, 6 percent on the telephone, and the remaining 3 percent on tours of company facilities. (These proportions, of course, are different for managers at lower levels.)[24]

In addition, managers also perform a wide variety of tasks. In the course of a single day, for example, a manager might have to make a decision about the design of a new product, settle a complaint between two subordinates, hire a new secretary, write a report for the boss, coordinate a joint venture with an overseas colleague, form a task force to investigate a problem, and deal with a labour grievance. Moreover, the pace of the manager's job can be relentless. She may feel bombarded by mail, telephone calls, and people waiting to see her. Decisions may have to be made quickly and plans formulated with little time for reflection. In many ways, however, these characteristics of managerial work also contribute to its richness and meaningfulness. Making critical decisions under intense pressure, and making them well, can be a major source of intrinsic satisfaction. And managers are usually well paid for the pressures they bear.

The Science and the Art of Management

Given the complexity inherent in the manager's job, a reasonable question relates to whether management is a science or an art. In fact, effective management is a blend of both science and art. And successful executives recognize the importance of combining both the science and the art of management as they practise their craft.[25]

The Science of Management   Many management problems and issues can be approached in ways that are rational, logical, objective, and systematic. Managers can gather data, facts, and objective information. They can use quantitative models and decision-making techniques to arrive at "correct" decisions. And they need to take such a scientific approach to solving problems whenever possible, especially when they are dealing with relatively routine and straightforward issues. When Canadian Airlines considers entering a new market, its managers look closely at current air traffic in that market, existing competitors and fare structures, and other objective details as they formulate their plans. Technical and diagnostic skills are especially important when practising the science of management.

The Art of Management   Even though managers may try to be scientific as much as possible, they must often make decisions and solve problems on the basis of intuition, experience, instinct, and personal insights. Relying heavily on conceptual and interpersonal skills, for example, a manager may have to decide between multiple courses of action that look equally attractive. Solving unusual and nonroutine problems almost certainly requires an element of intuition and personal insight.

Becoming a Manager

How does one acquire the skills necessary to blend the science and art of management and to become a successful manager? Although there are as many variations as there are managers, the most common path involves a combination of education and experience.[26] Figure 1.5 illustrates how this generally happens.

The Role of Education   Many of you reading this book right now are doing so because you are enrolled in a management course at a college or university. Thus you are acquiring management skills in an educational setting. When you complete the course (and this book), you will have a foundation for developing your management skills in more advanced courses. A university or college degree has become almost a requirement for career advancement in business. Of the CEOs of the 1,000 largest U.S. companies, 916 have a college degree.[27] MBA degrees are also common among successful executives today. More and more foreign universities, especially in Europe, are also beginning to offer academic programs in management. In addition, many corporations pay for their managers to complete their MBA degrees through executive MBA programs. The perceived value of an MBA is shown in one finding of a 1993 poll done for *Canadian Business* magazine; of the 302 CEOs surveyed, 75 percent indicated that they would encourage their children considering a career in business to get the degree.[28] The Census of Canada revealed in 1991 (the last time the question was asked) that 28 percent of persons holding managerial positions had a BA or higher degree, compared to only 13 percent of those in nonmanagement occupations.[29]

Even after obtaining a degree, most prospective managers have not seen the end of their management education. Many middle and top managers periodically return to campus to participate in executive or management development programs (MDPs) ranging in duration from a few days to several weeks. First-line managers also take advantage of extension and continuing education programs offered by institutions of higher education. A recent innovation in extended management education is the Executive MBA program offered by many business schools, in which middle and top managers with several years of

Most managers acquire their skills as a result of education and experience. Though a few CEOs today do not hold college or university degrees, most students preparing for management careers earn college or university degrees and go on to enroll in MBA programs.

F I G U R E   1 . 5   Sources of Management Skills

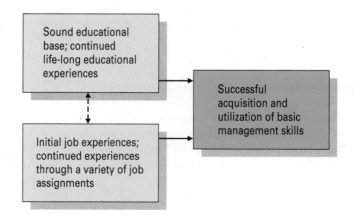

experience complete an accelerated program of study on weekends. Finally, many large companies have in-house training programs for furthering managers' education.

The primary advantage of education as a source of management skills is that a student can follow a well-developed program of study, becoming familiar with current research and thinking on management. And many university students can devote full-time energy and attention to learning. On the negative side, management education is often very general to meet the needs of a wide variety of students, and specific know-how may be hard to obtain. Further, many aspects of the manager's job can be discussed in a book but cannot really be appreciated and understood until they are experienced.

The Role of Experience   This book will help provide you with a solid foundation for enhancing your management skills. Even if you were to memorize every word in every management book ever written, however, you could not then step into a top-management position and be effective. The reason? Management skills must also be learned through experience. Most managers advanced to their present position from other jobs. By experiencing the day-to-day pressures a manager faces and by meeting a variety of managerial challenges, the individual develops insights that cannot be learned from a book.

For this reason most large companies, and many smaller ones as well, have developed management training programs for their prospective managers. People are hired from university campuses, from other organizations, or from the ranks of the organization's first-line managers and operating employees. These people are systematically assigned to a variety of jobs. Over time, the individual is exposed to most, if not all, of the major aspects of the organization. In this way the manager learns by experience. The training programs at some companies, such as Procter & Gamble, General Foods Corporation, and General Mills, are so good that other companies try to hire people who have gone through their training. Even without formal training programs, managers can achieve success as they profit from varied experiences. Of course, natural ability, drive, and self-motivation also play roles in acquiring experience and developing management skills.

Most effective managers learn their skills through a combination of education and experience. Some type of college or university degree, even if it is not in business administration, usually provides a foundation. The individual then gets his or her first job and subsequently progresses through a variety of management situations. During the manager's rise in the organization, occasional education "updates," such as management development programs, may supplement on-the-job experience. And increasingly, managers need to acquire international expertise as part of their personal development. As with general managerial skills, international expertise can also be acquired through a combination of education and experience.

THE SCOPE OF MANAGEMENT

When most people think of managers and management, they think of profit-seeking organizations. Throughout this book we use people like John Cleghorn of the Royal Bank of Canada and Laurent Beaudoin of Bombardier as examples. But we also mention examples from sports, religion, and other fields in which management is essential. Indeed, any group of two or more persons working together to achieve a goal and having human, material, financial, or informational resources at its disposal requires the practice of management.

Management in Profit-Seeking Organizations

Large Businesses   Most of what we know about management comes from large profit-seeking organizations because their survival has long depended on efficiency and effectiveness. Examples of large businesses include industrial firms (Tenneco Inc., British Petroleum Co., Toyota Motor Corp., Xerox Corp., Unilever, Magna International), commercial banks (Royal Bank of Canada, Citicorp, Bank of Montreal, Chase Manhattan Bank), insurance companies (London Life Insurance, Canada Life Assurance, Metropolitan Life Insurance Co.), retailers (Zellers, Safeway Inc., Wal-Mart Corp.), transportation companies (Air Canada, Consolidated Freightways, Laidlaw, Bombardier), utilities (Hydro-Québec, Union Gas, Canadian Utilities), communication companies (CBC, CanWest Global Communications, Rogers Communications), and service organizations (Kelly Services, Kinder-Care Learning Centers, and Century 21 Real Estate Corporation).

Small and Start-Up Business   Although many people associate management primarily with large businesses, effective management is also essential for small businesses, which play an important role in the country's economy. In fact, most of Canada's businesses are small. In some respects, effective management is more important in a small business than in a large one. A large firm such as Petro-Canada or Inco can easily recover from losing several thousand dollars on an incorrect decision, whereas a small business may ill afford even a much smaller loss. Of course, some small businesses become big ones. Compaq Computer Corporation, for example, was started by three men in 1982. By 1994 it had become the seventy-sixth largest business in the United States, with sales in excess of $7 billion (U.S.).[30]

International Management   In recent years, the importance of international management has increased dramatically. The list of U.S. and Canadian firms doing business in other countries is staggering. Exxon, for example, derives almost 75 percent of its revenues from foreign markets, and Ford Motor Co. derives more than one-third of its sales from foreign markets.[31] Other major U.S. and Canadian exporters include General Motors Corp., General Electric, Boeing, Bombardier, and Caterpillar Inc. And even numbers like Ford's are deceptive. For example, the automaker has large subsidiaries based in many European countries whose sales are not included as foreign revenue. Moreover, a number of major firms that do business in Canada have their headquarters in other countries. Firms in this category include the Royal Dutch/Shell Group (the Netherlands), Fiat S.P.A. (Italy), Nestlé SA (Switzerland), and Wal-Mart (United States). International management is not, however, confined to profit-seeking organizations. Several international sports federations (such as Little League Baseball), branches (embassies) of the federal government, and the Roman Catholic Church are established in most countries as well. In some respects, the military was one of the first multinational organizations. International management is covered in depth in Chapter 5.

International management is a growing priority for all businesses, large and small. Although Coca-Cola has long been sold around the world, the firm has recently been expanding into international markets even more aggressively. Because the U.S. soft drink market is not growing very fast, and because domestic competition is so fierce, Coke has realized that its best opportunities for expansion are in foreign markets, especially developing markets with growth potential. For example, Coke has recently started to expand its operations in Hanoi (shown here) and in Moscow.

Management in Not-for-Profit Organizations

Intangible goals such as education, social services, public protection, and recreation are often the primary aim of not-for-profit organizations. Examples include the Make-A-Wish Foundation of Canada, the Canadian Red Cross Society, Girl Guides of Canada, the International Olympic Committee, art galleries, museums, and TVOntario. Although these and similar organizations may not have to be profitable to attract investors, they must still employ sound management practices if they are to survive and work toward their goals.[32] And they must handle money in an efficient and effective way. If the Make-A-Wish Foundation of Canada were to begin to spend large portions of its contributions on administration, contributors would likely lose confidence in the organization and make their charitable donations elsewhere.

Government Organizations　The management of government organizations and agencies is often regarded as a separate specialty: public administration. Government organizations include the Canadian Radio-Television and Telecommunications Commission, Environment Canada, the National Research Council of Canada, all branches of the military, and federal and provincial prison systems. Tax dollars support government organizations, so politicians and citizens' groups are acutely sensitive to the need for efficiency and effectiveness.

Educational Organizations　Public and private schools, colleges, and universities all stand to benefit from the efficient use of resources. Government cutbacks in provinces such as Alberta and Ontario have drastically reduced the tax money available for education, forcing administrators to make tough decisions about allocating remaining resources.

Health-care Facilities   Managing health-care facilities such as clinics and hospitals is now considered a separate field of management. Here, as in other organizations, scarce resources dictate an efficient and effective approach. In recent years, many universities have established health-care administration programs to train managers as specialists in this field.

Management in Nontraditional Settings   Good management is also required in nontraditional settings to meet established goals. To one extent or another, management is practised in religious organizations, terrorist groups, student cooperatives, organized crime, street gangs, neighbourhood associations, and households. In short, as we note at the beginning of this chapter, management and managers have a profound influence on all of us.

SUMMARY OF KEY POINTS

Management is a set of activities (including planning and decision making, organizing, leading, and controlling) directed at an organization's resources (human, financial, physical, and information) with the aim of achieving organizational goals in an efficient and effective manner. A manager is someone whose primary responsibility is to carry out the management process within an organization.

The basic activities that constitute the management process are planning and decision making (determining courses of action), organizing (coordinating activities and resources), leading (managing people), and controlling (monitoring and evaluating activities). These activities are not performed on a systematic and predictable schedule.

Managers can be differentiated by level and by area. By level, we can identify top, middle, and first-line managers. Kinds of managers by area include marketing, financial, operations, human resource, administrative, and specialized managers.

Managers have ten basic roles to play: three interpersonal roles (figurehead, leader, and liaison), three informational roles (monitor, disseminator, and spokesperson), and four decisional roles (entrepreneur, disturbance handler, resource allocator, and negotiator). Effective managers also tend to have technical, interpersonal, conceptual, and diagnostic skills. The manager's job is characterized by varied, unpredictable, nonroutine, and fragmented work, often performed at a relentless pace.

The effective practice of management requires a synthesis of science and art—that is, a blend of rational objectivity and intuitive insight. Most managers attain their skills and positions through a combination of education and experience.

Management processes are applicable in a wide variety of settings, including profit-seeking organizations (large, small, and start-up businesses and international businesses) and not-for-profit organizations (government organizations, educational organizations, health-care facilities, and nontraditional organizations).

DISCUSSION QUESTIONS

Questions for Review

1. What are the four basic activities that constitute the management process? How are they related to one another?
2. Identify different kinds of managers by both level and area in the organization.
3. Briefly describe the ten managerial roles identified by Mintzberg. Give an example of each.
4. Identify the different skills of managers. Give an example of each.

Questions for Analysis

5. The text notes that management is both a science and an art. Is one of these more important than the other? Under what circumstances might one ingredient be more important than the other?
6. Recall a recent group project or task in which you have participated. Explain how each of the four basic management functions was performed.
7. Some people argue that CEOs are paid too much. Find out the pay for a CEO and discuss whether you think he or she is overpaid.

Questions for Application

8. Interview a manager from a local organization. Learn about how he or she performs each of the functions of management, the roles he or she plays, and the skills necessary to do the job.
9. Go to the library and see how many different managerial skills you can identify in the literature. Can you find ones not in the text? Share your results with the class.
10. Watch a television program that is set in an organization. Good choices include *Traders, Da Vinci's Inquest,* or *E.R.* Identify as many management functions, skills, and roles as you can.

BUILDING EFFECTIVE TECHNICAL SKILLS

Exercise Overview

Technical skills are the manager's abilities to accomplish or understand work done in an organization. More and more managers today are realizing that having the technical ability to use the Internet is an important part of communication, decision making, and other facets of their work. This exercise introduces you to the Internet and provides some practice in using it.

Exercise Background

The Internet, or "information superhighway" as it is sometimes called, is an interconnected network of information and information-based resources using computers and computer systems. Electronic mail was perhaps the first widespread application of the Internet, but applications based on "home pages" and "search engines" are increasingly popular.

A home page is a file (or set of files) created by an individual, business, or other entity. It contains whatever information its creator chooses to include. For example, a company might create a home page that includes its logo, its address and telephone number, information about its products and services, and so forth. A person looking for a job might create a home page that includes a résumé and a statement of career interests. Home pages are indexed by key words chosen by their creators.

A search engine is a system through which an Internet user can search for home pages according to their indexed key words. For example, suppose an individual is interested in knowing more about art collecting. Key words that might logically be linked to home pages related to this interest include art, artists, galleries, and framing. A search engine uses these key words to provide a listing of all home pages that are indexed to them. The user can then browse each page to see what information they contain. Popular search engines include Yahoo, Lycos, and WebCrawler.

Exercise Task

1. Visit your computer centre and learn how to access the Internet.
2. Using whichever search engine your computer centre supports, conduct a search for three or four general management-related terms (for example, management, organization, business).
3. Now select a more specific management topic and search for two or three specific topics. (If you cannot think of any terms, scan the margin notes in this book.)
4. Finally, select three or four companies and search for their home pages.

Laurent Beaudoin and Matthew Barrett: Top of Their Class

Surveys of Canada's business community taken in the last ten years repeatedly ranked Bombardier and the Bank of Montreal as two of Canada's most respected corporations, and their respective chief executive officers as two of the most admired CEOs in Canada. Bombardier's Laurent Beaudoin, a francophone accountant, joined the family business when he was 26 years old and developed it into a major multinational corporation. Bank of Montreal's Matthew Barrett, a high-school graduate from Ireland, joined the bank as a clerk and spent almost three decades working his way up to the position of CEO. In February 1999, both Barrett and Beaudoin stepped down as the CEOs of their respective corporations. While Beaudoin will serve as Bombardier's chairman, Barrett will leave a similar position at the Bank of Montreal in 1999.

Beaudoin is a prime example of the entrepreneurial drive that has transformed Quebec firms such as Bombardier and Power Corp. into very successful international enterprises. When Beaudoin assumed the presidency of Bombardier in 1964, the corporation was mainly involved in the manufacturing of snowmobiles; today Bombardier makes railcars, airplanes, and watercraft; has subsidiaries in Europe, the United States, and Mexico; and enjoys revenues of approximately $8.5 billion a year, up from $10 million in 1964. That Bombardier will continue to grow is evident in the fact that the company has a new aircraft coming on stream every year from 1997 to 2001. Moreover, it has substantial market share in most of the aircraft it produces. The preparedness of Bombardier is perhaps best exemplified by the fact that in 1997, on the day the treaty to outlaw landmines was being signed, the company had on display new airborne mine detectors: cleaning up unexploded mines around the world could be profitable.

Matthew Barrett began his banking career at the age of 18, when he obtained a job at a branch of the Bank of Montreal in London, England. Five years later, he accepted a job with the bank in Canada, moved to Montreal in 1967, and worked his way up to the CEO suite. He accomplished this by revitalizing some of the bank's worst branches and taking on a series of tough assignments. When he succeeded William Mulholland in 1990, Barrett faced the daunting task of resuscitating a demoralized institution from which many senior managers had resigned. Barrett introduced a management approach that emphasized teamwork and community involvement, a move that helped staunch the exodus of managers. His success is further reflected in the fact that the bank's share price has increased significantly and it regularly sets the pace in consumer innovations and in reducing lending rates.

That Matthew Barrett and Laurent Beaudoin, with their different backgrounds and personal styles, could gain the admiration of Canada's business community is perhaps reflective of that community's openness to diversity.

Questions

1. What are the similarities and differences between Matthew Barrett and Laurent Beaudoin?

2. What managerial roles and skills are evident in the actions of Barrett and Beaudoin?

3. Would you want to invest in the Bank of Montreal? In Bombardier? Would you want to work for Barrett? For Beaudoin? Explain your responses to each of these questions.

References: "The Sound of Two Solitudes, Applauding," *Canadian Business*, July 1993, pp. 79–81; Kenneth Kidd, "The Bombardier Express," *Report on Business Magazine*, April 1996, pp. 48–55; Peter C. Newman, *Titans: How the New Canadian Establishment Seized Power* (Toronto: Viking, 1998), pp. 374–376; "Performance 2000," *Canadian Business*, June 26/July 10, 1998, p. 138; and "Biographies: Laurent Beaudoin, Chairman of the Board and of the Executive Committee, Bombardier Inc." (http://www.bombardier.com).

CHAPTER NOTES

1. *Who's Who in Canadian Business* (Toronto: Who's Who Publishers, 1996); "Interview with Our New President, Maureen Kempston Darkes," *GM Today Magazine*, February 1995, pp. 2–5; "Power Shift Baby Boomers Have Changed the World: Now They Are Out for #1," *Canadian Business*, August, 1995, pp. 20–30; "Head of GM Canada Makes Dealerships Main Focus," *Canadian Press Newswire*, July 10, 1995; "Cars Must Reflect Women's Safety Concerns: GM President," *Canadian Press Newswire*, March 10, 1995; "Industry Finally Pays Attention to Women," *Financial Post*, February 18/20, 1995, p. A19; "General Motors of Canada Limited," *Financial Post Historical Reports* (Financial Post Data Group, 1996); "Performance 2000," *Canadian Business*, June 26/July 10, 1998, p. 138; and "Corporate Profiles: Maureen Kempston Darkes" (http://www.gmcanada.com).

2. William G. Scott and David K. Hart, *Organizational America* (Boston: Houghton Mifflin, 1979); and Page Smith, *The Rise of Industrial America* (New York: McGraw-Hill, 1984).

3. Frederick W. Taylor, *Shop Management* (New York: Harper & Row, 1903), p. 21.

4. Rosabeth Moss Kanter, "The New Managerial Work," *Harvard Business Review*, November–December 1989, pp. 85–92.

5. Fred Luthans, "Successful vs. Effective Real Managers," *The Academy of Management Executive*, May 1988, pp. 127–132.

6. Alex Taylor III, "How a Top Boss Manages His Day," *Fortune*, June 19, 1989, pp. 95–100.

7. Sumantsa Ghospal and Christopher A. Bartlett, "Changing the Role of Top Management: Beyond Structure to Process," *Harvard Business Review*, January–February 1995, pp. 86–96.

8. Don Macdonald, "Clear the Track," *Report on Business Magazine,* July 1997, pp. 28–36.

9. Brian Dumaine, "The New Non-Manager Managers," *Fortune*, February 22, 1993, pp. 80–84.

10. See Patricia Sellers, "Does the CEO Really Matter? *Fortune*, April 22, 1991, pp. 80–94.

11. Henry Mintzberg, *The Nature of Managerial Work* (New York: Harper & Row, 1973); see also Ford S. Worthy, "How CEOs Manage Their Time," *Fortune*, January 18, 1988, pp. 88–97.

12. Rosemary Stewart, "Middle Managers: Their Jobs and Behaviors," in Jay W. Lorsch (Ed.), *Handbook of Organizational Behavior* (Englewood Cliffs, N.J.: Prentice-Hall, 1987), pp. 385–391.

13. Wayne Cascio, "Downsizing: What Do We Know?" *The Academy of Management Executive*, February 1993, pp. 95–103.

14. James P. Womack and Daniel T. Jones, "From Lean Production to Lean Enterprise," *Harvard Business Review*, March–April 1994, pp. 93–103.

15. Steven Kerr, Kenneth D. Hill, and Laurie Broedling, "The First-Line Supervisor: Phasing Out or Here to Stay?" *Academy of Management Review*, January 1986, pp. 103–117; and Leonard A. Schlesinger and Janice A. Klein, "The First-Line Supervisor: Past, Present, and Future," in Lorsch (Ed.), *Handbook of Organizational Behavior*, pp. 358–369.

16. "Portrait of the Boss," *Business Week*, October 12, 1992, pp. 108–146.

17. "Portrait of the Boss."

18. "Portrait of the Boss."

19. "Portrait of the Boss."

20. "Portrait of the Boss."

21. Mintzberg, *The Nature of Managerial Work*.

22. Robert L. Katz, "The Skills of an Effective Administrator," *Harvard Business Review*, September–October 1974, pp. 90–102.

23. Andrew Kupfer, "How to Be a Global Manager," *Fortune*, March 14, 1988, pp. 52–58.

24. Mintzberg, *The Nature of Managerial Work*.

25. Gary Hamel and C.K. Prahalad, "Competing for the Future," *Harvard Business Review*, July–August 1994, pp. 122–128.

26. Walter Kiechel III, "A Manager's Career in the New Economy," *Fortune*, April 4, 1994, pp. 68–72.

27. *The Corporate Elite* (*Business Week*, Special Issue, 1990).

28. Randall Litchfield, "Can an MBA Run Your Company?" *Canadian Business*, April 1993, pp. 30–31.

29. Katherine Marshall, "The Diversity of Managers," *Perspectives*, Winter 1996, pp. 23–30.

30. "The *Fortune* 500," *Fortune*, April 18, 1994, p. 222.

31. "U.S. Corporations with the Biggest Foreign Revenues," *Forbes*, July 22, 1991, p. 286.

31. James L. Perry and Hal G. Rainey, "The Public–Private Distinction in Organization Theory: A Critique and Research Strategy," *Academy of Management Review*, April 1988, pp. 182–201; see also Ran Lachman, "Public and Private Sector Differences: CEOs' Perceptions of Their Role Environments," *Academy of Management Journal*, September 1985, pp. 671–680.

Traditional and Contemporary Issues and Challenges

2

OBJECTIVES

After studying this chapter, you should be able to:

● *Justify the importance of history and theory to management, explain the historical context of management, and discuss precursors to modern management theory.*

● *Summarize and evaluate the classical perspective on management, including scientific and administrative management, and note its relevance to contemporary managers.*

● *Summarize and evaluate the behavioural perspective on management, including the Hawthorne studies, human relations movement, and organizational behaviour, and note its relevance to contemporary managers.*

● *Summarize and evaluate the quantitative perspective on management, including management science and operations management, and note its relevance to contemporary managers.*

● *Discuss the systems and contingency approaches to management and explain their potential for integrating the other areas of management.*

● *Identify and describe contemporary management issues and challenges.*

OUTLINE

Once the dominant retailer in Canada, Eaton's has fallen on hard times. The flagship store in Toronto still attracts large crowds to its "centre."

When Eaton's applied for bankruptcy protection in March 1997, the Canadian public was stunned: an icon in Canadian business—the company that Timothy Eaton had founded in 1869—was in trouble.

Timothy Eaton's notion of "goods satisfactory or money refunded" was revolutionary in his time and partially accounted for the fact that in 1950 Eaton's accounted for more than 50 percent of department store spending in Canada. The success of the company is reflected in the estimated $1 billion real-estate holdings in its control. However, Eaton's is no longer a dominant player in the retail industry. The big question is whether the company will survive and, if so, in what form. Eaton's seems to have lost touch with consumers—a far cry from the 1950s, when Canadians saw their own values reflected in the Anglo-Saxon virtues of the company's owners whose loyalty to their staff was such that they resisted layoffs even in the Great Depression.

Timothy Eaton was succeeded by his son John Craig as president of the company, and some years later the mantle was passed on to John Craig's second son, John David. John David, who died in 1973, is said to have considered a 3 percent return on sales as adequate and to have resisted attempts to make the company more profitable. The 1990s have been especially difficult. It is estimated that from 1991 to 1996, Eaton's slashed 10 percent of its workforce of 12,000 as department stores came under attack from all sides. The advent of new forms of retailing—for example, "big box" stores such as Price Club, and "category killers" such as Business Depot Ltd.—and the entry of Wal-Mart into the Canadian marketplace have made retailing much more competitive.

Eaton's is feeling the strain. According to one estimate, the company's sales declined from $2 billion in 1990 to $1.57 billion in 1995. As Eaton's takes measures to regain lost market share and return to profitability, the big question is whether or not the Eaton's tradition in the Canadian retail industry will continue.[1] ●

> **"Eaton's is no longer a dominant player in the retail industry. The big question is whether the company will survive and, if so, in what form."**

t is critically important that all managers focus on today's competitive environment and how that environment will change tomorrow. But it is also important that they use the past as context. Managers at Eaton's are working to re-create their company, to remake it in ways that better fit today's business world. But managers also recognize the value and importance of their past. They harken back to their glory days, remember their painful declines, and will strive to avoid making the same mistakes again. History plays an important role in businesses today, and more and more managers are recognizing that the lessons of the past are an important ingredient of future success.

This chapter provides an overview of traditional management thought so that you, too, can better appreciate the importance of history in today's business world. We set the stage by establishing the historical context of management. We then discuss the three traditional management perspectives—classical, behavioural, and quantitative. Next we describe the systems and contingency perspectives as approaches that help integrate the three traditional perspectives. Finally, we introduce and discuss a variety of contemporary management issues and challenges.

THE ROLE OF THEORY AND HISTORY IN MANAGEMENT

Knowledge of both theory and history is useful to the practising manager. In this section, we establish the historical context of management and then identify important precursors to management theory.

The Importance of Theory and History

Some people question the value of history and theory. Their arguments are usually based on the assumptions that history has no relevance to contemporary society and that theory is abstract and of no practical use. In reality, however, both theory and history are important to all managers today.

Why Theory? A theory is simply a conceptual framework for organizing knowledge and providing a blueprint for action. Although some theories seem abstract and irrelevant, others appear very simple and practical. Management theories, used to build organizations and guide them toward their goals, are grounded in reality.[2] Practically any organization that uses assembly lines (such as Ford Canada, Black & Decker Corp., and Fiat S.P.A.) is drawing on what we describe later in this chapter as scientific management. Many organizations, including Kimberly-Clark Corporation, Texas Instruments Incorporated, and Seiko Time Corp., use the behavioural perspective (also introduced later) to improve employee satisfaction and motivation. And naming a large company that does not use one or more techniques from the quantitative management perspective would be difficult. For example, retailers like The Bay and Wal-Mart routinely use management science formulas to determine how many checkout stands they need to have. In addition, most managers develop and refine their own theories of how they should run their organizations and manage the behaviour of their employees.

For example, Andrew Grove, CEO of Intel Corp., has developed his own operating theory of organizations. The basis of his theory is that organizations need to become more agile and responsive to their environment. By implementing his theory, Grove has transformed Intel into just such a company. As a direct result of Grove's keen understanding of his business and his ability to implement his operating theory, Intel has become the world's largest manufacturer of semiconductors.[3]

Why History? An awareness and understanding of important historical developments are also important to contemporary managers.[4] The Hudson's Bay Co., established in 1670, has an important place in Canadian history. Understanding the historical context of management provides a sense of heritage and can help managers avoid the mistakes of others. Most courses in U.S. history devote time to business and economic developments in that country, including the Industrial Revolution, the early labour movement, and the Great Depression, and to such captains of U.S. industry as Cornelius Vanderbilt (railroads), John D. Rockefeller (oil), and Andrew Carnegie (steel). The contributions of those and other industrialists left a profound imprint on contemporary American culture.[5] Many managers are also realizing that they can benefit from a greater understanding of history in general. For example, Ian M. Ross of AT&T Bell Laboratories cites *The Second World War* by Winston Churchill as a major influence on his approach to leadership. Other books often mentioned by managers for their relevance to today's business problems include such classics as Plato's *Republic,* Homer's *Iliad,* and Machiavelli's *The Prince.*[6]

Managers at Wells Fargo & Company clearly recognize the value of history. For example, the company maintains an extensive archival library of its old banking documents and records and even employs a full-time corporate historian. As part of their orientation and training, new managers at Wells Fargo take courses to become acquainted with the bank's history.[7] Similarly, Polaroid Corp., Consolidated Edison Co. of New York, AT&T, and Navistar International Transportation Corp. have each sought to preserve information about their past and their heritage.[8] In addition, Lloyd's of London, Honda Motor Co., Nestlé Enterprises, and Unilever also pay frequent homage to their

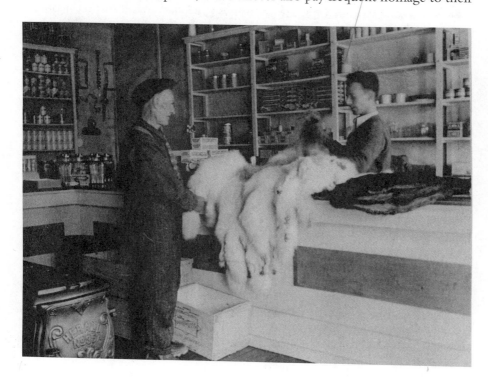

This photo, taken August 16, 1937, shows Archie White trading furs for provisions at the Hudson's Bay Company Store in Cameron Bay, NWT. The company began by royal charter in 1670 when Charles II granted a group of English merchants absolute control over the territo[ry] drained by the rivers flowing in[to] Hudson Bay. Traders bartered pelts for goods. Essentially th[e] company brought a market-oriented economy into conta[ct] with a nonmarket-oriented [economy.] In order for this trading sys[tem] to work, a variety of comp[lex] economic devices and relationships had to be se[t in] place.

historical roots. The *Managing in a Changing World* box describes how one firm, Consumers Distributing, went from being a success story to a flop, providing myriad examples of how not to conduct business in the retailing industry.

The Historical Context of Management

Management thought has been shaped over a period of centuries by three major sets of forces. These social, economic, and political forces continue to affect management theory today.[9]

Understanding Social Forces   **Social forces** are the norms and values that characterize a culture. In the early days of business, owners generally managed their own companies. As these businesses grew, however, professional managers were called in to run them, and organized labour took root. Workers in the larger organizations were often treated with disdain, and bitter strikes polarized management and labour. Vanderbilt proclaimed, "The public? The public be damned!" Such arrogance would hardly be tolerated today, but years ago it reflected the power and attitude of business in our society. The social contract between workers and the businesses they work for has changed dramatically over the years. At first, employees were paid only token wages and worked purely at the whim of their employer. Today's workers, however, have made great strides. Ideas of liberty and justice in the workplace are becoming increasingly common, workers are protected by a variety of federal and provincial laws, and organizations themselves are becoming more and more sensitive to the needs and values of workers.[10] Changes in these and other social forces have played a major role in shaping management theories in areas such as motivation, leadership, and human resource management.

Understanding Economic Forces   In similar fashion, **economic forces**—forces associated with economic systems and general economic conditions and trends—have also shaped management theory. Canada has a market economy based on the principles of private ownership of property, economic freedom, competitive markets, and a limited role for government. Most major industrial countries use similar systems. In such systems the availability of resources, the ease of acquiring those resources, and the kinds of goods and services wanted by consumers all play a role in dictating what management can do. General economic trends and the nature of the competition also greatly affect organizations. Increased global competition in recent years has also played a role. Within contemporary management theory, economic forces have affected thinking in a variety of areas, including environment analysis, strategic planning, and organization design.[11]

Understanding Political Forces   **Political forces** are the governing institutions and general governmental policies and attitudes toward business. They influence management theory in both general and specific ways. General government policies toward the regulation of business play an important role in how organizations choose to manage themselves. Management theory regarding companies in highly regulated industries like utilities, for example, varies considerably from parallel theories regarding companies like Sears and Canadian Tire in less regulated industries such as retailing. In a more specific case, legal judgments like those handed down against Exxon Corporation (for the *Valdez* oil spill) and Texaco (for interfering in a previously announced

Management

The Crash of Consumers

The story of Consumers Distributing—once a retailer with stores across Canada and a distinctive sales approach whereby customers perused catalogues, filled out order slips, and submitted them to clerks who checked product availability in an attached warehouse—provides a classic tale of how even well-informed managers using textbook methods could manage themselves out of a job.

On July 29th, 1996, Consumers Distributing Inc. [filed] for creditor protection under the Companies' [Creditors] Arrangement Act. In doing so, Consumers [joined the] ranks of other Canadian retailers (e.g., Dylex [and] w Group Inc. and Bargain Harold's Discount [who], since the early 1990s, had fallen victim to [com]petition in the retail industry. On [July 29], 1996, Consumers was forced by its [creditors into b]ankruptcy. The company had been [founded] by Jack Supp, who started in busi[ness with a c]atalogue sales operation from his [home and s]ubsequently opened showrooms [that were la]ter supplemented by the distri[bution. By] the late 1980s, Consumers [had $1.6] billion in Canada and the [U.S. It was th]e only surviving catalogue [chain in Cana]da. However, in its last [year of operation,] the chain's 217 stores [employed ? and] 2,700 part-time [staff. Sales were $? m]illion and the com[pany's losses were $?]250 million.

[What happened to Consumers] Distributing Inc.? [Why did the company's] retailing con[cept fail? One possi]ble explana[tion is ... in a] depressed [economy and competition am]ong such retailers as Wal-Mart, Canadian Tire, and Zellers, and management blunders. In the period leading up to its demise, Consumers had a high-powered team of managers, including Perry Caicco, a seasoned retail executive; Vic Steel, a former chair of Woolworths; and William Young and Guy Cogan, former consultants with Bain & Co. Support was provided by management consultants from Monitor Co. and the Tibbett & Britten Group. Consumers went public in 1969 and in 1985 was bought by Provigo of Montreal, which in 1993 sold it to a group made up of Ackermans & van Haaren of Belgium and Westbourne Management Ltd. of Toronto. Under the new arrangement, Ackermans owned 70 percent of the company's shares, Westbourne owned 11 percent, and Provigo 19 percent. The new management team resulted from the new ownership structure. While the new team seems to have attempted a textbook turnaround strategy at Consumers, it also made a number of costly blunders, including spending large sums of money in opening big box superstores and transferring resulting cash flow problems to suppliers. Sensing deepening problems, some suppliers stopped selling to Consumers while others obtained trade insurance on goods shipped to the company. Consumers' problems were compounded by mixed performance by its superstores. The company's demise was formalized on September 6, 1996.

References: Paul Brent, "Consumers Distributing Files for Creditor Protection, *Financial Post*, July 30, 1996, p. 1; "Catalogue Store Format a Bust for Consumers," *Marketing Magazine*, August 5, 1996, p. 1; John Heinzl and Marina Strauss, "Consumers Invokes CCAA," *The Globe and Mail*, July 30, 1996, pp. B1, B5; and John Lorinc, "Would You Buy This?" *Canadian Business*, December 1996, pp. 118–128.

[Pe]nzoil Co.) have major impli[cation]s. Both general and specific [tasks, li]ke environmental analysis, [plus c]ontrol.

[past] few hundred years, [sec]tion, we describe [managem]ent pioneers.

Management in Antiquity The practice of management can be traced back thousands of years. The Egyptians used the management functions of planning, organizing, and controlling when they constructed the great pyramids. Alexander the Great employed a staff organization to coordinate activities during his military campaigns. The Roman Empire developed a well-defined organizational structure that greatly facilitated communication and control. Management practices and concepts were discussed by Socrates in 400 B.C.; Plato described job specialization in 350 B.C.; and Alfarabi listed several leadership traits in A.D. 900.[12] Figure 2.1 is a simple time line showing important management breakthroughs and practices.

In spite of this history, however, management per se was not given serious attention for several centuries. One reason was that the first discipline devoted to commerce was economics. Economists generally just assumed that managerial practice was efficient and therefore focused their attention on national economic policies and other nonmanagerial aspects of business. Another reason was that very few large organizations existed until the late 1800s. When family businesses first emerged, their goal was survival—not growth or expansion. If a family could produce and sell enough to sustain itself, nothing else was needed. Finally, even though management was practised during earliest recorded history, the focus even then was not on efficiency. These early organizations were governmental, with unlimited powers of taxation and little accountability for waste.

Early Management Pioneers The serious study of management did no begin until the nineteenth century. Robert Owen (1771–1858), a British indus trialist and reformer, was one of the first managers to recognize the importanc of an organization's human resources. Until his era, factory workers were ge erally viewed in much the same way that machinery and equipment were. A f tory owner himself, Owen believed that workers deserved respect and dig He implemented better working conditions, a higher minimum working for children, meals for employees, and reduced work hours. He assume giving more attention to workers would pay off in increased output.

Management has been practised for thousands of years. For example, the ancient Babylonians used management in governing their empire, and the ancient Romans used management to facilitate communication and control throughout their far-flung territories. The Egyptians used planning and controlling techniques in the construction of their pyramids.

F I G U R E 2 . 1 Management in Antiquity

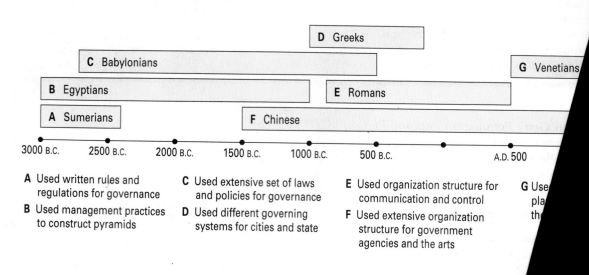

A Used written rules and regulations for governance

B Used management practices to construct pyramids

C Used extensive set of laws and policies for governance

D Used different governing systems for cities and state

E Used organization structure for communication and control

F Used extensive organization structure for government agencies and the arts

G Use
pla
th

Whereas Owen was primarily interested in employee welfare, Charles Babbage (1792–1871), an English mathematician, focused his attention on efficiencies of production. His primary contribution was his book titled *On the Economy of Machinery and Manufactures*.[13] Babbage placed great faith in the division of labour and advocated the application of mathematics to problems such as the efficient use of facilities and materials. In a sense, his work was a forerunner to both the classical and quantitative management perspectives. Nor did Babbage overlook the human element. He understood that a harmonious relationship between management and labour could serve to benefit both, and he favoured such devices as profit-sharing plans. In many ways, Babbage was an originator of modern management theory and practice.

In addition to these visionaries, a few other early pioneers deserve mention. Andrew Ure was one of the world's first professors to teach management principles, in the early seventeenth century at Anderson's College in Glasgow. Charles Dupin soon followed suit in France. Daniel McCallum developed several basic principles of management and published one of the first organization charts. In the late nineteenth century, Henry Poor wrote extensively about management inefficiencies in the railroad industry.[14]

THE CLASSICAL MANAGEMENT PERSPECTIVE

The **classical management perspective** emerged during the early years of the twentieth century. These ideas represent the first well-developed framework of management. Their emergence was a natural outgrowth of both the pioneering earlier works just noted and the evolution of large-scale business and management practices. The classical management perspective includes two different approaches to management: scientific management and administrative management.

- **classical management perspective**
Consists of two distinct branches—scientific management and administrative management

Scientific Management

Productivity emerged as a serious business problem during the first few years of this century. Business was expanding and capital was readily available, but labour was in short supply. Therefore, managers began to search for different ways to utilize existing labour more efficiently. In response to this need, experts began to focus their research on ways to improve the performance of individual workers. Their work led to the development of **scientific management**. Some of the earliest advocates of scientific management included Frederick W. Taylor (1856–1915), Frank Gilbreth (1868–1924), Lillian Gilbreth (1878–1972), Henry Gantt (1861–1919), and Harrington Emerson (1853–1931).[15] Taylor played the dominant role.

- **scientific management**
Concerned with improving the performance of individual

- **scientific management**
Concerned with improving the performance of individual workers

One of Taylor's first jobs was as a foreman at the Midvale Steel Company in Philadelphia. At Midvale he observed what he called **soldiering**—employees deliberately working at a pace slower than their capabilities. Taylor studied and timed each element of the steelworkers' jobs. He determined what each worker should be producing, and then he designed the most efficient way of doing each part of the overall task. Next he implemented a piecework pay system. Rather than paying all employees the same wage, he began increasing the pay of each worker who met and exceeded the target level of output set for his or her job.

- **soldiering**
Employees deliberately working at a slow pace

After Taylor left Midvale, he worked as a consultant for several companies, including Simonds Rolling Machine Company and Bethlehem Steel. At Simonds he studied and redesigned jobs, introduced rest periods to reduce fatigue, and implemented a piecework pay system. The results were higher quality and quantity of output and improved morale. At Bethlehem Steel, Taylor studied efficient ways of loading and unloading railcars and applied his conclusions with equally impressive results. During these experiences, he formulated the basic ideas that he called scientific management. Figure 2.2 illustrates the basic steps Taylor suggested. He believed that managers who followed his guidelines would improve the efficiency of their workers.[16]

Taylor's work had a major impact on industry. By applying his principles, many organizations achieved major gains in efficiency. Taylor was not without his detractors, however. Labour argued that scientific management was just a device to get more work from each employee and to reduce the total number of workers needed by a firm. There was a congressional investigation into Taylor's ideas, and evidence suggests that he falsified some of his findings.[17] Nevertheless, Taylor's work left a lasting imprint on business.[18] Indeed, the *Environment of Management* box describes how UPS uses many of the ideas developed from scientific management to boost productivity in its delivery business.

Frank and Lillian Gilbreth, contemporaries of Taylor, were a husband-and-wife team of industrial engineers. One of Frank Gilbreth's most interesting contributions was to the craft of bricklaying. After studying bricklayers at work, he developed several procedures for doing the job more efficiently. For example, he specified standard materials and techniques, including the positioning of the bricklayer, the bricks, and the mortar at different levels. The results of these changes were a reduction from eighteen separate physical movements to five and an increase in output of about 200 percent. Lillian Gilbreth made equally important contributions to several different areas of work, helped shape the field of industrial psychology, and made substantive contributions to the field of personnel management. Working individually and together, the Gilbreths developed numerous techniques and strategies for eliminating inefficiency. They applied many of their ideas to their family. Their experiences in raising twelve children are documented in the book and movie *Cheaper by the Dozen*.

Henry Gantt, another contributor to scientific management, was an associate of Taylor at Midvale, Simonds, and Bethlehem Steel. Later, working alone, he developed other techniques for improving worker output. One, called the Gantt chart, is still used today. A Gantt chart is essentially a means of scheduling

Frederick Taylor developed this system of scientific management, which he believed would lead to a more efficient and productive workforce. Bethlehem Steel was among the first organizations to profit from scientific management and still practices some parts of it today.

FIGURE 2.2 Steps in Scientific Management

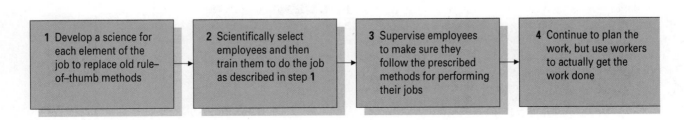

1 Develop a science for each element of the job to replace old rule-of-thumb methods

2 Scientifically select employees and then train them to do the job as described in step 1

3 Supervise employees to make sure they follow the prescribed methods for performing their jobs

4 Continue to plan the work, but use workers to actually get the work done

work and can be generated for each worker or for a complex project as a whole. Gantt also refined Taylor's ideas about piecework pay systems.

Like Taylor, the Gilbreths, and Gantt, Harrington Emerson was also a management consultant. He made quite a stir in 1910 when he appeared before the U.S. Interstate Commerce Commission to testify about a rate increase requested by the railroads. As an expert witness, Emerson asserted that the railroads could save $1 million a day by using scientific management. He was also a strong advocate of specialized management roles in organizations, believing that job specialization was as relevant to managerial work as it was to operating jobs.

Administrative Management

Whereas scientific management deals with the jobs of individual employees, **administrative management** focuses on managing the total organization. The primary contributors to administrative management were Henri Fayol (1841–1925), Lyndall Urwick (1891–1983), Max Weber (1864–1920), and Chester Barnard (1886–1961).

● **administrative management**
Focuses on managing the total organization

Henri Fayol was administrative management's most articulate spokesperson. A French industrialist, Fayol was unknown to Canadian and American managers and scholars until his most important work, *General and Industrial Management,* was translated into English in 1930.[19] Drawing on his own managerial experience, he attempted to systematize the practice of management to provide guidance and direction to other managers. Part of his thinking was expressed in fourteen principles for effective management. These principles are listed in Table 2.1. Fayol also was the first to identify the specific managerial functions of planning, organizing, leading, and controlling. He believed that these functions accurately reflect the core of the management process. Most contemporary management books (including this one) still use this framework, and practising managers agree that these functions are a critical part of their jobs.

After a career as a British army officer, Lyndall Urwick became a noted management theorist and consultant. He integrated scientific management with the work of Fayol and other administrative management theorists. He also advanced modern thinking about the functions of planning, organizing, and controlling. Like Fayol, he developed a list of guidelines for improving managerial effectiveness. Urwick is noted not so much for his own contributions as for his synthesis and integration of the work of others.

Although Max Weber lived and worked at the same time as Fayol and Taylor, his contributions were not recognized until some years had passed. Weber was a German sociologist, and his most important work was not translated into English until 1947.[20] Weber's work on bureaucracy laid the foundation for contemporary organization theory, discussed in detail in Chapter 11. The concept of bureaucracy, as we discuss later, is based on a rational set of guidelines for structuring organizations in the most efficient manner.

Chester Barnard made notable contributions to management in his book *The Functions of the Executive.*[21] The book proposes a major theory about the acceptance of authority. The theory suggests that subordinates weigh the legitimacy of a supervisor's directives and then decide whether to accept them. An order is accepted if the subordinate understands it, is able to comply with it, and views it as appropriate.

The Tightest Ship in the Shipping Business

 To many people, the scene sounds like an Orwellian nightmare: everywhere package deliverer Clay Bois goes, a supervisor follows with a stopwatch, calculating the time it takes him to walk to a customer's door (is he keeping to the standard three-feet-per-second pace?) and noting whether he knocks immediately, as he is supposed to, or whether he wastes precious seconds searching for the doorbell. To get the packages to drivers like Bois for delivery, sorters must handle 1,124 packages an hour and make a mistake less than once every two hours. Loaders are expected to fill the delivery vans at the rate of at least 500 packages per hour. What keeps these people going?

That is the secret of the United Parcel Service, the largest and most profitable transportation company in the United States. Although supervisors only occasionally ride with drivers, they have been known to goad slow drivers by asking them if they'd like a sleeping bag. The entire company is run on stopwatches, an approach that began in the 1920s when the company's founder, James E. Casey, turned to time-study engineers to help make his business 30 percent more efficient. Yet rather than create burnout and high turnover, UPS's approach has earned the company a consistently high corporate reputation, and its employee turnover rate is only 4 percent.

Much of the company's success with its workers can be attributed to what one UPS board member calls "managerial socialism." In return for their three-feet-per-second pace, UPS workers earn substantial pieces of a company that turns $700 million (U.S.) in profits per year. Attracted to UPS by its high wages, many workers stay because they like being an integral part of a team that's working hard and doing a superb job. Because the company seldom hires outside executives, drivers can often work their way up to management levels, and many retire as millionaires.

Drivers start off earning more than they could expect from other trucking companies. After ten years in the company, a middle-level manager might be earning $54,000 (U.S.) augmented by a $7,500 dividend and $14,000 in stock. Founder Casey declared that he wanted the company to be "owned by its managers and managed by its owners," and in fact most of the stock is held by 15,000 managers and supervisors, who must sell their stock to the company when they leave or retire. So people who work for the company for any length of time get the feeling of being driven not by a faceless, impersonal organization but by themselves.

The lack of status symbols at UPS promotes workers' feeling of being an equal part of an important group. Top executives battle everyone else for parking spaces, stand in the same cafeteria lines, and do their own photocopying. Not even the chair has a personal secretary. Office workers have standards as strict as those for drivers and loaders: no one is allowed to drink beverages at a desk, and everyone follows tough grooming standards, including a rule against beards and long mustaches.

Rather than seeing themselves as the drudge workers, UPS's drivers often see themselves as the company's heroes. The company, in turn, recognizes them as being, in effect, small business people, creating their own business by doing their jobs well. Workers' identification with the company is so strong that as much as 80 percent of the workforce shows up for voluntary workshops after hours.

References: "As UPS Tries to Deliver More to Its Customers, Labor Problems Grow," *The Wall Street Journal*, May 23, 1994, pp. A1, A5; "Can UPS Deliver the Goods in a New World?" *Business Week*, June 4, 1990, pp. 80–82; Kenneth Labich, "Big Changes at Big Brown," *Fortune*, January 18, 1988, pp. 56–64; and "Up to Speed: United Parcel Service Gets Deliveries Done by Driving Its Workers," *The Wall Street Journal*, April 22, 1986, p. 1.

The Classical Management Perspective Today

The contributions and limitations of the classical management perspective are summarized in Table 2.2. The classical perspective is the framework from which later theories evolved, and many of its insights still hold true today. For example, many of the job specialization techniques and scientific methods espoused by Taylor and his contemporaries are still reflected in the way that

TABLE 2.1	Fayol's Guidelines for Effective Management Practice

Henri Fayol, a French industrialist, summarized the practice of management with fourteen principles.

Division of labor	A high degree of specialization should result in efficiency. Both managerial and technical work are amenable to specialization.
Authority	Authority is needed to carry out managerial responsibilities: the formal authority to command and personal authority deriving from intelligence and experience.
Discipline	People in the organization must respect the rules that govern the organization.
Unity of command	Each subordinate should report to one and only one superior.
Unity of direction	Similar activities in an organization should be grouped together under one manager.
Subordination of individuals to the common good	Interests of individuals should not be placed before the goals of the overall organization.
Remuneration	Compensation should be fair both to employees and to the organization.
Centralization	Power and authority should be concentrated at the upper levels of the organization as much as possible.
Scalar chain	A chain of authority should extend from the top to the bottom of the organization and should be followed at all times.
Order	Human and material resources should be coordinated so that they are in the required place at the required time.
Equity	Managers should be kind and fair when dealing with subordinates.
Stability	High turnover of employees should be avoided.
Initiative	Subordinates should have the freedom to take initiative.
Esprit de corps	Teamwork, team spirit, and a sense of unity and togetherness should be fostered and maintained.

Source: From Henri Fayol, *General and Industrial Management,* Revised Edition. Copyright © 1984 by Lake Publishing Company.

many industrial jobs are designed today. Moreover, many contemporary organizations still use some of the bureaucratic procedures suggested by Weber. Also, these early theorists were the first to focus attention on management as a meaningful field of study. Several aspects of the classical perspective are also relevant to our later discussions of planning, organizing, and controlling.

TABLE 2.2	The Classical Management Perspective
General Summary	The classical management perspective had two primary thrusts. Scientific management focused on employees within organizations and on ways to improve their productivity. Noted pioneers of scientific management were Frederick Taylor, Frank and Lillian Gilbreth, Henry Gantt, and Harrington Emerson. Administrative management focused on the total organization and on ways to make it more efficient and effective. Prominent administrative management theorists were Henri Fayol, Lyndall Urwick, Max Weber, and Chester Barnard.
Period of Greatest Interest	1895 to mid-1930s; renewed interest in recent years as a means of cutting costs and increasing productivity.
Contributions	Laid the foundation for later developments in management theory.
	Identified important management processes, functions, and skills that are still recognized as such today.
	Focused attention on management as a valid subject of scientific inquiry.
Limitations	More appropriate for stable and simple organizations than for today's dynamic and complex organizations.
	Often prescribed universal procedures that are not appropriate in some settings.
	Even though some writers (such as Lillian Gilbreth and Chester Barnard) were concerned with the human element, many viewed employees as tools rather than resources.

The limitations of the classical perspective, however, should not be overlooked. These early writers dealt with stable, simple organizations; many organizations today, in contrast, are changing and complex. They also proposed universal guidelines that we now recognize do not fit every organization. A third limitation of the classical management perspective is that it slighted the role of the individual in organizations. This role was much more fully developed by advocates of the behavioural management perspective.

THE BEHAVIOURAL MANAGEMENT PERSPECTIVE

● **behavioural management perspective**
Emphasizes individual attitudes and behaviours and group processes

Early advocates of the classical management perspective essentially viewed organizations and jobs from a mechanistic point of view: that is, they essentially sought to conceptualize organizations as machines and workers as cogs within those machines. Even though many early writers recognized the role of individuals, their focus tended to be on how managers could control and standardize the behaviour of their employees. In contrast, the **behavioural management perspective** placed much more emphasis on individual attitudes and behaviours and on group processes and recognized the importance of behavioural processes in the workplace.

The behavioural management perspective was stimulated by a number of writers and theoretical movements. One of those movements was industrial psychology, the practice of applying psychological concepts to industrial settings. Hugo Munsterberg (1863–1916), a noted German psychologist, is recognized as the father of industrial psychology. He established a psychological laboratory at Harvard University in 1892, and his pioneering book *Psychology and Industrial Efficiency* was translated into English in 1913.[22] Munsterberg suggested that psychologists could make valuable contributions to managers in the areas of employee selection and motivation. Industrial psychology is still a major course of study at many colleges and universities.

Another early advocate of the behavioural approach to management was Mary Parker Follett.[23] Follett worked during the scientific management era, but quickly came to recognize the human element in the workplace. Indeed, her work clearly anticipated the behavioural management perspective and she appreciated the need to understand the role of behaviour in organizations. Her specific interests were in adult education and vocational guidance. Follett believed that organizations should become more democratic in accommodating employees and managers. Management theorists have recently come to realize that many modern management concepts such as empowerment, cross-functional work teams, and participative management were actually embedded in Mary Parker Follett's work.[24]

The Hawthorne Studies

Although Munsterberg and Follett made major contributions to the development of the behavioural approach to management, its primary catalyst was a series of studies conducted near Chicago at Western Electric's Hawthorne plant between 1927 and 1932. The research, originally sponsored by General Electric Co., was conducted by Elton Mayo and his associates.[25] Mayo was a faculty member and consultant at Harvard University. The first study involved manipulating illumination for one group of workers and comparing their subsequent productivity with the productivity of another group whose illumination was not changed. Surprisingly, when illumination was increased for the experimental group, productivity went up in both groups. Productivity continued to increase in both groups, even when the lighting for the experimental group was decreased. Not until the lighting was reduced to the level of moonlight did productivity begin to decline (and General Electric withdrew its sponsorship).

Another experiment established a piecework incentive pay plan for a group of nine men assembling terminal banks for telephone exchanges. Scientific management would have predicted that each man would try to maximize his pay by producing as many units as possible. Mayo and his associates, however, found that the group itself informally established an acceptable level of output for its members. Workers who overproduced were branded "rate busters," and underproducers were labelled "chiselers." To be accepted by the group, workers produced at the accepted level. As they approached this acceptable level of output, workers slacked off to avoid overproducing.

Other studies, including an interview program involving several thousand workers, led Mayo and his associates to conclude that human behaviour was much more important in the workplace than had been previously believed. In

The Hawthorne studies were a series of early experiments that focused on behaviour in the workplace. In one experiment involving this group of workers, for example, researchers monitored how productivity changed as a result of changes in working conditions. The Hawthorne studies and subsequent experiments led scientists to the conclusion that the human element is very important in the workplace.

the lighting experiment, for example, the results were attributed to the fact that both groups received special attention and sympathetic supervision for perhaps the first time. The incentive pay plans did not work because wage incentives were less important to the individual workers than was social acceptance in determining output. In short, individual and social processes played a major role in shaping worker attitudes and behaviour.[26]

The Human Relations Movement

The **human relations movement**, which grew from the Hawthorne studies and was a popular approach to management for many years, proposed that workers respond primarily to the social context of the workplace, including social conditioning, group norms, and interpersonal dynamics. A basic assumption of the human relations movement was that the manager's concern for workers would lead to increased satisfaction, which would in turn result in improved performance.[27] Two writers who helped advance the human relations movement were Abraham Maslow and Douglas McGregor.

In 1943, Maslow advanced a theory suggesting that people are motivated by a hierarchy of needs, including monetary incentives and social acceptance.[28] Maslow's hierarchy, perhaps the best known human relations theory, is described in detail in Chapter 16. Meanwhile, Douglas McGregor's Theory X and Theory Y model best represents the essence of the human relations movement (see Table 2.3).[29] According to McGregor, Theory X and Theory Y reflect two extreme belief sets that different managers have about their workers. **Theory X** is a relatively negative view of workers and is consistent with the views of scientific management. **Theory Y** is more positive and represents the assumptions that human relations advocates make. In McGregor's view, Theory Y was a more appropriate philosophy for managers to adhere to. Both Maslow and McGregor notably influenced the thinking of many practising managers.

The Emergence of Organizational Behaviour

Munsterberg, Mayo, Maslow, McGregor, and others have made valuable contributions to management. Contemporary theorists, however, have noted that many assertions of the human relationists were simplistic and inadequate descriptions of work behaviour. For example, the assumption that worker satisfaction leads to improved performance has been shown to have little, if any, validity.[30] If anything, satisfaction follows good performance rather than precedes it. (These issues are addressed in greater detail in Chapters 15 and 16.)

Current behavioural perspectives on management, known as **organizational behaviour**, acknowledge that human behaviour in organizations is much more complex than the human relationists realized. The field of organizational behaviour draws from a broad, interdisciplinary base of psychology, sociology, anthropology, economics, and medicine. Organizational behaviour takes a holistic view of behaviour and addresses individual, group, and organization processes.[31] These processes are major elements in contemporary management theory. Important topics in this field include job satisfaction, stress, motivation, leadership, group dynamics, organizational politics, interpersonal conflict, and the structure and design of organizations.[32] A contingency orientation also characterizes the field (discussed more fully later in this chapter). Our discussions of organizing (Chapters 10–14) and leading (Chapters 15–19) are heavily influenced by organizational behaviour.

● human relations movement
Argued that workers respond primarily to the social context of the workplace

● Theory X
A pessimistic and negative view of workers consistent with the views of scientific management

● Theory Y
A positive view of workers; it represents the assumptions that human relations advocates make

● organizational behaviour
Contemporary field focusing on behavioural perspectives on management

TABLE 2.3 Theory X and Theory Y	
Theory X Assumptions	1. People do not like work and try to avoid it.
	2. People do not like work, so managers have to control, direct, coerce, and threaten employees to get them to work toward organizational goals.
	3. People prefer to be directed, to avoid responsibility, and to want security; they have little ambition.
Theory Y Assumptions	1. People do not naturally dislike work; work is a natural part of their lives.
	2. People are internally motivated to reach objectives to which they are committed.
	3. People are committed to goals to the degree that they receive personal rewards when they reach their objectives.
	4. People will both seek and accept responsibility under favorable conditions.
	5. People have the capacity to be innovative in solving organizational problems.
	6. People are bright, but under most organizational conditions their potentials are under-utilized.

Source: Douglas McGregor, *The Human Side of Enterprise*, Copyright © 1960 by McGraw-Hill. Used with permission of the publisher.

Douglas McGregor developed Theory X and Theory Y. He argued that Theory X best represented the views of scientific management and Theory Y represented the human relations approach. He believed that Theory Y was the best philosophy for all managers.

The Behavioural Management Perspective Today

Table 2.4 summarizes the behavioural management perspective and lists its contributions and limitations. The primary contributions relate to ways in which this approach has changed managerial thinking. Managers are now more likely to recognize the importance of behavioural processes and to view employees as valuable resources instead of mere tools. On the other hand, organizational behaviour is still imprecise in its ability to predict behaviour. It is not always accepted or understood by practising managers. Hence, the contributions of the behavioural school have yet to be fully realized.

THE QUANTITATIVE MANAGEMENT PERSPECTIVE

Of the three major schools of management thought, the quantitative management perspective is the newest. The classical approach was born in the early years of this century, and the behavioural approach began to emerge in the 1920s and 1930s. The quantitative management perspective was not fully developed until World War II. During the war, managers, government officials, and scientists came together in England and the United States to help the military deploy its resources more efficiently and effectively. Led by experts like Professor P.M.S. Blackett, these groups took some of the mathematical approaches to management developed decades earlier by Taylor and Gantt and applied them to logistical problems during the war.[33] Decisions regarding

TABLE 2.4	The Behavioural Management Perspective
General Summary	The behavioural management perspective focuses on employee behaviour in an organizational context. Stimulated by the birth of industrial psychology, the human relations movement supplanted scientific management as the dominant approach to management in the 1930s and 1940s. Prominent contributors to this movement were Elton Mayo, Abraham Maslow, and Douglas McGregor. Organizational behaviour, the contemporary outgrowth of the behavioural management perspective, draws from an interdisciplinary base and recognizes the complexities of human behaviour in organizational settings.
Period of Greatest Interest	Human relations enjoyed its peak of acceptance from 1931 to the late 1940s. Organizational behaviour emerged in the late 1950s and is presently of great interest to researchers and managers.
Contributions	Provided important insights into motivation, group dynamics, and other interpersonal processes in organizations. Focused managerial attention on these same processes. Challenged the view that employees are tools and furthered the belief that employees are valuable resources.
Limitations	The complexity of individual behaviour makes prediction of that behaviour difficult. Many behavioral concepts have not yet been put to use because some managers are reluctant to adopt them. Contemporary research findings by behavioural scientists are often not communicated to practising managers in an understandable form.

troop, equipment, and submarine deployment were all solvable through mathematical analysis.

After the war, consulting firms like Arthur D. Little, Inc. and industrial firms such as E.I. Du Pont de Nemours & Co. and General Electric began to use the same techniques for deploying employees, choosing plant locations, and planning warehouses. Basically, then, this perspective is concerned with applying quantitative techniques to management. More specifically, the **quantitative management perspective** focuses on decision making, economic effectiveness, mathematical models, and the use of computers. There are two branches of the quantitative approach: management science and operations management.

Management Science

Unfortunately, the term management science appears to be related to scientific management, the approach developed by Taylor and others early in this century. But the two have little in common and should not be confused. **Management science** focuses specifically on the development of mathemat-

● **quantitative management perspective**
Applies quantitative techniques to management

● **management science**
Focuses specifically on the development of mathematical models

ical models. A mathematical model is a simplified representation of a system, process, or relationship.

At its most basic level, management science focuses on models, equations, and similar representations of reality. For example, managers at power companies use mathematical models to determine how best to route repair crews during blackouts, and banks use models to figure out how many tellers need to be on duty at particular locations at various times throughout the day. In recent years, paralleling the advent of the personal computer, management science techniques have become increasingly sophisticated. For example, automobile manufacturers Daimler-Benz and Chrysler use realistic computer simulations to study collision damage to cars. These simulations give them precise information and avoid the costs of "crashing" so many test cars.

Operations Management

Operations management is somewhat less mathematical and statistically sophisticated than management science and can be applied more directly to managerial situations. Indeed, we can think of **operations management** as a form of applied management science. Operations management techniques are generally concerned with helping the organization produce its products or services more efficiently and can be applied to a wide range of problems.[34]

For example, Loblaws Supermarkets Ltd. and Canadian Tire each use operations management techniques to manage their inventories. (Inventory management is concerned with specific inventory problems such as balancing carrying costs and ordering costs and determining the optimal order quantity.) Linear programming (which involves computing simultaneous solutions to a set of linear equations) helps Air Canada plan its flight schedules, Consolidated Freightways develop its shipping routes, and Magna International plan what automotive parts to produce at various times. Other operations management techniques include queuing theory, break-even analysis, and simulation. All of these techniques and procedures apply directly to operations, but they are also helpful in such areas as finance, marketing, and human resource management.

> **operations management**
> Concerned with helping the organization produce its products or services more efficiently

The Quantitative Management Perspective Today

Like the other management perspectives, the quantitative management perspective has made important contributions and has certain limitations. Both are summarized in Table 2.5. It has provided managers with an abundance of decision-making tools and techniques and has increased understanding of overall organizational processes. It has been particularly useful in the areas of planning and controlling. On the other hand, mathematical models cannot fully account for individual behaviours and attitudes. Some believe that the time needed to develop competence in quantitative techniques retards the development of other managerial skills. Finally, mathematical models typically require a set of assumptions that may not be realistic.

INTEGRATING PERSPECTIVES FOR MANAGERS

Recognizing that the classical, behavioural, and quantitative approaches to management are not necessarily contradictory or mutually exclusive is impor-

TABLE 2.5	The Quantitative Management Perspective
General Summary	The quantitative management perspective focuses on applying mathematical models and processes to management situations. Management science specifically deals with the development of mathematical models to aid in decision making and problem solving. Operations management focuses more directly on the application of management science to organizations. Management information systems are systems developed to provide information to managers.
Period of Greatest Interest	1940s to present.
Contributions	Developed sophisticated quantitative techniques to assist in decision making.
	Application of models has increased our awareness and understanding of complex organizational processes and situations.
	Has been very useful in the planning and controlling processes.
Limitations	Cannot fully explain or predict the behaviour of people in organizations.
	Mathematical sophistication may come at the expense of other important skills.
	Models may require unrealistic or unfounded assumptions.

tant. Even though very different assumptions and predictions are made by each of the three perspectives, each can also complement the others. Indeed, a complete understanding of management requires an appreciation of all three perspectives. The systems and contingency perspectives can help us integrate the earlier approaches and enlarge our understanding of all three.

The Systems Perspective

We briefly introduced the systems perspective in Chapter 1 in our definition of management. A **system** is an interrelated set of elements functioning as a whole.[35] As shown in Figure 2.3, by viewing an organization as a system, we can identify four basic elements: inputs, transformation processes, outputs, and feedback. First, inputs are the material, human, financial, and information resources the organization gets from its environment. Next, through technological and managerial processes, inputs are transformed into outputs. Outputs include products, services, or both (tangible and intangible); profits, losses, or both (even not-for-profit organizations must operate within their budgets); employee behaviours; and information. Finally, the environment reacts to these outputs and provides feedback to the system.

Thinking of organizations as systems provides us with a variety of important viewpoints on organizations such as the concepts of open systems, subsystems, synergy, and entropy. **Open systems** are systems that interact with their environment, whereas **closed systems** do not interact with their environment.

system
An interrelated set of elements functioning as a whole

open system
An organizational system that interacts with its environment

closed system
An organizational system that does not interact

Although all organizations are open systems, some make the mistake of ignoring their environment and behaving as though their environment is not important. This is one of the major mistakes made by Eaton's, as detailed earlier.

The systems perspective also stresses the importance of **subsystems**—systems within a broader system. For example, the marketing, production, and finance functions within Mattel Inc. are systems in their own right but are also subsystems within the overall organization. Because they are interdependent, a change in one subsystem can affect other subsystems as well. If the production department at Mattel lowers the quality of the toys being made (by buying lower-quality materials, for example), the effects are felt in finance (improved cash flow in the short run owing to lower costs) and marketing (decreased sales in the long run because of customer dissatisfaction). Managers must therefore remember that although organizational subsystems can be managed with some degree of autonomy, their interdependence should not be overlooked.

Synergy suggests that organizational units (or subsystems) may often be more successful working together than working alone. The Walt Disney Company, for example, benefits greatly from synergy. The company's movies, theme parks, television programs, and merchandise licensing programs all benefit one another. Children who enjoy a Disney movie like *The Lion King* want to go to Disney World and see the Lion King show there and buy stuffed animals of the film's characters. In Europe today, banks and insurance companies are linking up in an effort to market a wide array of financial products that each would have trouble selling on its own.[36] Synergy is an important concept for managers because it emphasizes the importance of working together in a cooperative and coordinated fashion.

Finally, **entropy** is a normal process that leads to system decline. When an organization does not monitor feedback from its environment and make appropriate adjustments, it may fail. For example, witness the problems of Studebaker and Consumers Distributing. Each of these organizations went bankrupt because it failed to revitalize itself and keep pace with changes in its environment. A primary objective of management, from a systems perspective, is to continually re-energize the organization to avoid entropy.

The Contingency Perspective

Another recent noteworthy addition to management thinking is the contingency perspective. The classical, behavioural, and quantitative approaches are considered **universal perspectives** because they tried to identify the "one best way" to manage organizations. The **contingency perspective**, in contrast, suggests that universal theories cannot be applied to organizations because each organization is unique. Instead, the contingency perspective suggests that appropriate managerial behaviour in a given situation depends on, or is contingent on, unique elements in that situation.[37] Stated differently, effective managerial behaviour in one situation cannot always be generalized to other situations. Recall, for example, that Frederick Taylor assumed that all workers would generate the highest possible level of output to maximize their own personal economic gain. We can imagine some people being motivated primarily by money—but we can just as easily imagine other people being motivated by the desire for leisure time, status, social acceptance, or any combination of these (as Mayo found at the Hawthorne plant).

A few years ago Continental Airlines hired Hollis Harris, a respected and successful executive at Delta Air Lines, to become its CEO. At the time, Delta

subsystem
A system within another system

synergy
Two or more subsystems working together to produce more than the total of what they might produce working alone

entropy
A normal process leading to system decline

universal perspective
An attempt to identify the one best way to do something

contingency perspective
Suggests that appropriate managerial behaviour in a given situation depends on, or is contingent on, a wide variety of elements

By viewing organizations as systems, managers can better understand the importance of their environment and the level of interdependence among subsystems within the organization. They must also understand how their decisions affect and are affected by other subsystems within the organization.

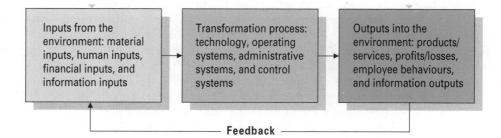

| Inputs from the environment: material inputs, human inputs, financial inputs, and information inputs | → | Transformation process: technology, operating systems, administrative systems, and control systems | → | Outputs into the environment: products/ services, profits/losses, employee behaviours, and information outputs |

Feedback

was profitable and had its costs under control. Continental, however, was losing money and its costs were not being controlled. Harris tried to manage at Continental just as he had at Delta, with relatively little concern for costs. As a result, he failed to rescue the airline from bankruptcy and was forced to resign. He made the mistake of not recognizing that he needed to manage Continental differently because it was in a different situation.

An Integrating Framework

We note earlier that the classical, behavioural, and quantitative management perspectives can be complementary and that the systems perspective and contingency perspective can help integrate them. Our framework for integrating the various approaches to management is shown in Figure 2.4. The initial premise of the framework is that before attempting to apply any specific concepts or ideas from the three major perspectives, managers must recognize the interdependence of units within the organization, the effect of environmental influences on the organization, and the need to respond to the unique characteristics of each situation. The ideas of subsystem interdependencies and environmental influences are given to us by systems theory, and the situational view of management is derived from a contingency perspective.

With these ideas as basic assumptions, the manager can use valid tools, techniques, concepts, and theories of the classical, behavioural, and quantitative

Second Cup clearly takes an open systems view to its competitive environment. It never ignores its environment and always seems on the alert for new opportunities, opening outlets in neighbourhoods and malls, or entering into alliances with hospitals and libraries. This kiosk is in the Koffler Student Centre on the downtown campus of University of Toronto.

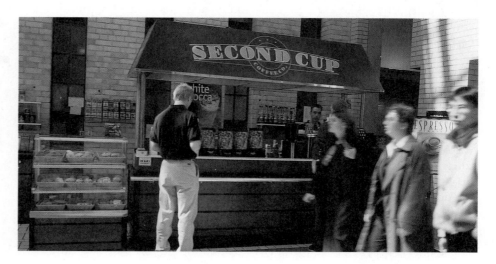

management perspectives. For example, managers can still use many of the basic techniques from scientific management. In many contemporary settings, the scientific study of jobs and production techniques can enhance productivity. But managers should not rely solely on these techniques, nor should they ignore the human element. The behavioural perspective is also of use to managers today. By drawing on contemporary ideas of organizational behaviour, the manager can better appreciate the role of employee needs and behaviours in the workplace. Motivation, leadership, communication, and group processes are especially important. The quantitative perspective provides the manager with a set of useful tools and techniques. The development and use of management science models and the application of operations management methods can help managers increase their efficiency and effectiveness.

Consider the new distribution manager of a large wholesale firm whose job is to manage one hundred truck drivers and to coordinate standard truck routes in the most efficient fashion. This new manager, with little relevant experience, might attempt to increase productivity by employing strict work specialization and close supervision (as suggested by scientific management). But doing so may decrease employee satisfaction and morale and increase turnover (as predicted by organizational behaviour). The manager might also develop a statistical formula to use route driver time more efficiently (from management science). But this new system could disrupt existing work groups and social patterns (from organizational behaviour). The manager might create even more problems by trying to impose programs and practices derived from her previous job. An incentive program welcomed by retail clerks, for example, might not work for truck drivers.

The manager should soon realize that a broader perspective is needed. Systems and contingency perspectives help provide broader solutions. Also, as the integrative framework in Figure 2.4 illustrates, applying techniques from several schools works better than trying to make one approach solve all problems. To solve a problem of declining productivity, the manager might look to scientific management (perhaps jobs are inefficiently designed or workers improperly trained), organizational behaviour (worker motivation may be low or group norms may be limiting output), or operations management (facilities may be improperly laid out or material shortages may be resulting from poor inventory management). And before implementing any plans for improvement, the manager should try to assess their effect on other areas of the organization.

Now suppose that the same manager is involved in planning a new warehouse. She will probably consider what type of management structure to create (classical management perspective), what kinds of work-group arrangements to develop (behavioural management perspective), and how to develop a network model for designing and operating the facility (quantitative perspective). As a final example, if employee turnover is too high, the manager might consider an incentive system (classical perspective), plan a motivational enhancement program (behavioural perspective), or use a mathematical model (quantitative perspective) to discover that turnover costs may actually be lower than the cost of making any changes at all.

Each of the major perspectives on management can be useful to modern managers. Before using any of them, however, the manager should recognize the situational context within which they operate. The systems and contingency perspectives serve to integrate the classical, behavioural, and quantitative management perspectives.

FIGURE 2.4 An Integrative Framework of Management Perspectives

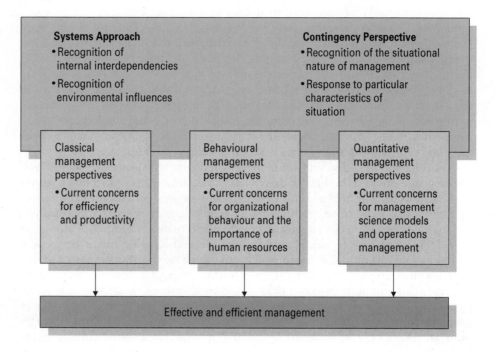

Systems Approach
- Recognition of internal interdependencies
- Recognition of environmental influences

Contingency Perspective
- Recognition of the situational nature of management
- Response to particular characteristics of situation

Classical management perspectives
- Current concerns for efficiency and productivity

Behavioural management perspectives
- Current concerns for organizational behaviour and the importance of human resources

Quantitative management perspectives
- Current concerns for management science models and operations management

Effective and efficient management

CONTEMPORARY MANAGEMENT ISSUES AND CHALLENGES

Interest in management theory and practice has heightened in recent years as new issues and challenges have emerged. No new paradigm has been formulated that replaces the traditional views, but managers continue to strive toward a better understanding of how they can better compete and lead their organizations toward improved effectiveness.[38]

Contemporary Management Theory

Several writers have attempted to develop new and imaginative management models and theories. Although it is still too early to assess the longevity of their ideas, the work of William Ouchi (the type Z model) and Thomas Peters and Robert Waterman (the excellence movement) has caught the attention of many managers.

● **Type Z model**
An attempt to integrate common business practices from the United States and Japan into one middle-ground framework

The Type Z Model The **Type Z model**, as argued by William Ouchi in 1981, is an attempt to integrate common business practices in the United States and Japan into a single middle-ground framework.[39] Ouchi suggests that there are many traditional U.S. firms (which he calls Type A companies) and a similar set of traditional Japanese companies (Type J). He argues that these firms are different along seven important dimensions: (1) length of employment, (2) mode of decision making, (3) location of responsibility, (4) speed of evaluation and promotion, (5) mechanisms of control, (6) specialization of career path, and

(7) nature of concern for the employee. For example, some Japanese firms are characterized by lifetime employment opportunities and collective decision making, whereas their American counterparts offer short-term employment and rely on individual decision making.

Ouchi also observes that a few particularly successful U.S. firms (such as Hewlett-Packard, Eastman Kodak, and Procter & Gamble) do not follow the typical Type A model. Instead, they use a hybrid, or Type Z, approach that has one characteristic from Type A (individual responsibility), three characteristics from Type J (collective decision making, slow evaluation and promotion, and holistic concern), and modified characteristics corresponding to the other three dimensions (for instance, they postulate long-term employment as opposed to short-term employment in Type A and lifetime employment in Type J).

Ouchi's ideas have been well received by practising managers. His book was on most best-seller lists for several weeks after its publication in 1981, and many organizations are trying to implement his suggestions. However, controversy has arisen about whether some of Ouchi's research was conducted as scientifically as it should have been.[40] Like many scientific breakthroughs, the Type Z model will quite likely be supplanted by more refined and valid models and theories as we begin to learn more about the international domain of management. Still, it deserves special recognition because it gave early momentum to theory development in the global arena.

The Concern for Excellence   Another popular management theory is the so-called excellence movement. Originally presented by Thomas J. Peters and Robert H. Waterman, Jr.,[41] this approach suggests that certain "excellent" companies, or those with a long-term history of success, do things in a systematic fashion that sets them apart from other firms. The basic set of characteristics that presumably lead to excellence include (1) getting things done on time; (2) staying close to the customer; (3) promoting autonomy and entrepreneurship; (4) maximizing productivity through people; (5) using a hands-on approach to managing, (6) doing what the company knows best; (7) maintaining a simple, lean organizational structure; and (8) promoting both centralization and decentralization simultaneously. Well-known firms presumed to have these characteristics include Hewlett-Packard, Eastman Kodak, Procter & Gamble, Delta Air Lines, Intel, Avon Products, Maytag, The Walt Disney Company, Dow Chemical, and Du Pont. The excellence movement has also been an important catalyst for other theorists and management scholars, although it too has been subjected to criticism.[42]

Contemporary Management Challenges

One thing that makes the manager's job exciting is the constant array of new challenges. This concluding section identifies and briefly discusses a number of contemporary challenges that confront all managers today.

The Globalization of Business   We noted in Chapter 1 that international business has become increasingly important. No longer can any organization—regardless of its size, vitality, or industry—ignore the globalization of business. Ford competes with Nissan and Volkswagen, Timex with Seiko, and Exxon with British Petroleum. Small retailers carry merchandise from around the globe. And businesses from just about any country can borrow funds from lenders in Toronto, Tokyo, or London. We explore the international challenges of managers in Chapter 5.

Quality and Productivity   Another area of interest to emerge in recent years has been quality and productivity. As they attempt to understand why Japanese and German firms have been so successful, Canadian and U.S. companies have discovered that their foreign counterparts have an edge in quality. As a result, Canadian and U.S. firms have developed renewed interest in how they can enhance the quality of their products and services. As a part of this discovery process, managers have also learned that many of their foreign competitors are producing higher-quality products with fewer resources. Hence, managers have become more and more interested in how to increase the productivity of their workers.[43] We address these issues in several chapters, especially Chapter 21.

Ownership   Ownership of business has also become a controversial subject for managers in recent years. Large institutional investors (such as pension funds and mutual funds) control major blocks of stock in many companies today. This has led to some managers feeling great pressure to produce short-term results and, consequently, not always making decisions that have only a longer-term payoff. More and more foreign firms have also taken ownership stakes in U.S. industry, a trend that is of interest to many observers. We discuss these issues in Chapters 3 and 7.

Ethics and Social Responsibility   Although ethical scandals in business are not really new, media attention focused on them in recent years has increased public sensitivity about them. Many organizations today are taking steps to enhance the ethical standards of their managers and to avoid legal or public sentiment problems. These issues are discussed in Chapter 4. Environmentalism, a related set of issues, is also addressed in that same chapter.

Workforce Diversity   Still another set of issues that managers today must confront involves workforce diversity. A wide variety of factors—globalization, immigration, an aging population, an influx of workers into new career and occupational tracks—have created workforces that are much more heterogeneous than at any time in history. Managers in every organization are finding that they must learn to be more sensitive to the needs, perceptions, and aspirations of many different kinds of workers. We discuss workforce diversity in more detail in Chapter 14.

Change   Managers also face more change today than in the past. The requirements, demands, and expectations placed on managers and their organizations are greater than ever before, as is the complexity of the environment within which they must compete. While in the past managers may have seen change as something that must be addressed periodically, it has now become a fact of everyday life for everyone in the business world.[44] We discuss change in Chapter 12, as well as highlight it in a special boxed feature called *Managing in a Changing World*.

Empowerment   Finally, managers today are also dealing with issues associated with empowerment, efforts to more fully take advantage of the organization's human resources by giving everyone more information and control over how they perform their jobs. Various techniques and methods for empowerment range from participation in decision making to the use of integrated work teams. We discuss empowerment in several places, including Chapters 3, 11, 18, and 21.

SUMMARY OF KEY POINTS

Theories are important as organizers of knowledge and as road maps for action. Understanding the historical context and precursors of management and organizations provides a sense of heritage and can also help managers avoid repeating the mistakes of others. Evidence suggests that interest in management dates back thousands of years, but a scientific approach to management has emerged only in the last hundred years. During the first few decades of this century, three primary perspectives on management emerged. These are called the classical perspective, the behavioural perspective, and the quantitative perspective.

The classical management perspective had two major branches: scientific management and administrative management. Scientific management was concerned with improving efficiency and work methods for individual workers. Administrative management was more concerned with how organizations themselves should be structured and arranged for efficient operations. Both branches paid little attention to the role of the worker.

The behavioural management perspective, characterized by a concern for individual and group behaviour, emerged primarily as a result of the Hawthorne studies. The human relations movement recognized the importance and potential of behavioural processes in organizations but made many overly simplistic assumptions about those processes. Organizational behaviour, a more realistic outgrowth of the behavioural perspective, is of interest to many contemporary managers.

The quantitative management perspective and its two components, management science and operations management, attempt to apply quantitative techniques to decision making and problem solving. These areas are also of considerable importance to contemporary managers. Their contributions have been facilitated by the tremendous increase in the use of personal computers and integrated information networks.

The three major perspectives should be viewed in a complementary, not a contradictory, light. Each has something of value to offer. The key is understanding how to use them effectively. Two relatively recent additions to management theory, the systems and contingency perspectives, appear to have great potential both as approaches to management and as frameworks for integrating the other perspectives.

Two contemporary contributions to management theory include the Type Z approach to management and the concern for excellence. Challenges facing managers today include the globalization of business, the importance of quality and productivity, ownership issues, ethics and social responsibility, workforce diversity, change, and empowerment.

DISCUSSION QUESTIONS

Questions for Review

1. Briefly summarize the classical management perspective and identify the most important contributors to each of its two branches.
2. Briefly summarize the Hawthorne studies. What are the primary conclusions reached following their completion?
3. Describe the contingency perspective and outline its usefulness to the study and practice of management.
4. What are some contemporary issues and challenges that managers must confront?

Questions for Analysis

5. What social, political, and economic conditions might have influenced the development of each of the major perspectives on management? Why?
6. Explain how a manager can use tools and techniques from each of the major management perspectives in a complementary fashion.
7. What recently published popular business books have been especially successful? Who are the prominent business leaders today whose ideas are widely accepted?

Questions for Application

8. Go to the library and locate material on Confucius. Outline his major ideas. Which seem to be applicable to management in Canada today?
9. Identify a local firm that has been in existence for a long time. Interview the current owner about the history of the firm and see if you can gain a better understanding of its current practices by knowing about its past.
10. Read a history of a company in which you are interested. Prepare for the class a brief report that stresses the impact of the firm's history on its current practices.

BUILDING EFFECTIVE DIAGNOSTIC & CONCEPTUAL SKILLS

Exercise Overview

Diagnostic skills enable a manager to visualize the most appropriate response to a situation. Conceptual skills are the manager's ability to think in the abstract. This exercise will enable you to use your diagnostic and conceptual skills to extrapolate past trends to the present to the future.

Exercise Background

Some basic consumer products have been around for decades, but others have only recently come into being. Likewise, a variety of products that were once commonplace are no longer available. Examples of such products include the automobile crank (once used to manually start car engines before electric starters were invented) and the wooden slide rule (once used to perform calculations before electronic calculators were invented).

Working alone, identify ten products or services currently available that might not exist in the next few years. Next, form small groups of four or five. Compare your individual lists and come up with a single group list that contains the ten best examples of products or services that may not exist in the future.

Exercise Task

Using the group list, respond to the questions that follow. (Your instructor will tell whether to do this exercise individually or as a group.)
1. Why might each product or service disappear?
2. Can you think of ways to prolong the existence of each product or service?
3. What advice might you give to the owner or top manager of a firm in these industries?
4. How easy or difficult was it to identify the ten requested examples? What factors made it easy or difficult?

The origins of Bombardier Inc. can be traced back to 1902 when it was incorporated, under federal law, as the Locomotive and Machine Company of Montreal Limited. Since then, the company has changed its name several times, culminating in 1978 when it was changed from Bombardier-MCW Ltd. to Bombardier Inc. Initially a small company, Bombardier now has a large and diverse manufacturing base, a reflection of how it has learned to change to suit the evolving needs of the marketplace.

One of the early prized inventions of Bombardier was the B7, a motorized vehicle that could travel over snow. The B7 enjoyed great success in the late 1930s as it met the transportation needs of a large snowbound clientele, especially those in rural and remote areas. The Second World War led to restrictions on the use of motorized vehicles and civilian snowmobile production was put on hold as the company embarked on the production of military vehicles. After the war, Bombardier reverted to the production and distribution of improved snowmobiles, but the implementation of a new snow-removal policy in the winter of 1948–49 hit the company hard and led to a reorganization of its operations. The next ten years saw the company focusing production on utility tracked vehicles for the mining, oil, and forestry sectors. The Muskeg tractor, which was first produced by Bombardier in 1953, is still sold today in modified versions throughout the world. However, it was not until the 1970s that the company intensified its diversification efforts.

The oil crisis in the early 1970s dealt a major blow to the snowmobile industry, shrinking the market from a 500,000 unit-per-year peak to approximately 100,000 units. In 1974, Bombardier entered the rail transit market with an order to supply 423 cars for the Montreal subway network. Over the years the company has become a leader in the field and has supplied, among other products, self-propelled commuter cars for Chicago, LRC trains for VIA Rail Canada, commuter train coaches for New Jersey, and subway cars for New York City.

Bombardier has also entered other countries. Recognizing the emergence of a lucrative market from a united Europe, the company intensified its industrial presence in that continent with the acquisition of Belgian, French, and British firms in the 1980s. Since then, Bombardier has expanded into many other countries, including Finland, Germany, and Mexico, in an effort to capture these markets in times of liberalizing trade.

Back in North America, the company broadened its industrial base with its plunge into the aerospace sector. The acquisition of Canadair gave Bombardier major human and technological resources needed by the company for its aerospace industrial plans. Anticipating future trends, the company launched the Canadair Regional Jet in 1989, the only 50-passenger airliner currently available in the regional air transport market. More recently, Bombardier announced plans to build the Global Express, a world-class business jet geared to meet the needs of the affluent travelling businessperson. The company is also continuously trying to improve its technological capacity and expertise, as evidenced in the development of the CL-415 turboprop amphibious aircraft, which offers greater efficiency than its predecessor, the CL-215, in fighting forest fires.

In keeping with its drive to diversify its industrial base and still be competitive in all its market segments, Bombardier initiated several innovative projects in the transportation equipment sector. These include the next generation of the New York and Paris subway rolling stock, the shuttle train cars that will transport buses and automobiles in the English Channel tunnel, and the promotion of a TGV high-speed link in the Quebec City–Windsor corridor.

A management reorganization in 1996 included the establishment of three manufacturing groups: Bombardier Aerospace, Bombardier Transportation Equipment, and Bombardier Motorized Consumer Products, each headed by a president and a chief executive officer. Two other service groups specialize in financial and real-estate services.

Today, with total assets of almost $8 billion, operating revenues of over $7 billion, and net income for the 1990s consistently over $100 million, Bombardier has become one of Canada's largest and most profitable companies. It has done so by learning from its history, keeping an eye on global trends, and adjusting to the needs of the market.

Bombardier Changes with the Times (Continued)

Questions

1. What have been the major components to Bombardier's success?

2. How does an understanding of Bombardier's history aid you in understanding its approach to management today?

3. Is Bombardier likely to be able to be as successful in the future? Why or why not?

References: *50 Years Later: A Dream with an International Reach.* (Bombardier Inc., 1996); "Flights of Fancy: Timesharing Jet Allows Executives to Enjoy the Luxury of a Private Plane, Without Its Cost or Care" *Financial Post*, Vol. 9, No. 4, p. 35; "Bombardier to Go Ahead with Stretched Version of Regional Jet" *Financial Post*, January 22, 1997, p. 7; "Bombardier Continues on Record Roll: Analyst Attributes $241.9 m Profit for Fiscal 1995 to Superb Management," *The Globe and Mail*, March 8, 1995, p. B11; "Bombardier Inc.," *Financial Post Historical Reports* (Financial Post Data Group, 1996); Bombardier Annual Reports, various years; "Bombardier Lands Lucrative New York City Transit Contract," *Canadian Press Newswire*, April 30, 1997; and "Ranking by Profits," *Report on Business Magazine*, July 1998, p. 100.

CHAPTER NOTES

1. Anne Kingston, "Rush Hour at Eaton's," *Report on Business Magazine,* May 1996, pp 46–56; and Ian McGugan, "Eaton's on the Brink," *Canadian Business,* March 1996, pp. 39–72.

2. Peter F. Drucker, "The Theory of the Business," *Harvard Business Review,* September–October 1994, pp. 95–104.

3. "Can Andy Grove Practice What He Preaches?" *Business Week,* March 16, 1987, pp. 68–69; "Intel to Motorola: Race Ya," *Business Week,* March 13, 1989, p. 42; and Gary Hoover, Alta Campbell, and Patrick J. Spain (Eds.), *Hoover's Handbook of American Business 1994* (Austin, Tex.: The Reference Press, 1993), p. 632.

4. "Why Business History?" *Audacity,* Fall 1992, pp. 7–15. See also Alan L. Wilkins and Nigel J. Bristow, "For Successful Organization Culture, Honor Your Past," *The Academy of Management Executive,* August 1987, pp. 221–227.

5. Daniel Wren, *The Evolution of Management Theory,* 4th ed. New York: Wiley, 1994); and Page Smith, *The Rise of Industrial America* (New York: McGraw-Hill, 1984).

6. Marilyn Wellemeyer, "Books Bosses Read," *Fortune,* April 27, 1987, pp. 145–148.

7. Alan M. Kantrow, (Ed.) "Why History Matters to Managers," *Harvard Business Review,* January–February 1986, pp. 81–88.

8. "Profiting from the Past," *Newsweek,* May 10, 1982, pp. 73–74.

9. For a good overview of historical management literature, see Michael T. Matteson and John M. Ivancevich (Eds.), *Management and Organizational Behavior Classics,* 5th ed. (Homewood, Ill.: Irwin), 1993.

10. William G. Scott, "The Management Governance Theories of Justice and Liberty," *Journal of Management,* June 1988, pp. 277–298.

11. Lex Donaldson, "The Ethereal Hand: Organizational Economics and Management Theory," *Academy of Management Review,* July 1990, pp. 369–381.

12. Wren, *The Evolution of Management Theory.*

13. Charles Babbage, *On the Economy of Machinery and Manufactures* (London: Charles Kinght, 1832).

14. Wren, *The Evolution of Management Theory.*

15. Wren, *The Evolution of Management Theory.*

16. Frederick W. Taylor, *Principles of Scientific Management* (New York: Harper and Brothers, 1911).

17. Charles D. Wrege and Amedeo G. Perroni, "Taylor's Pig-Tale: A Historical Analysis of Frederick W. Taylor's Pig-Iron Experiment," *Academy of Management Journal,* March 1974, pp. 6–27; and Charles D. Wrege and Ann Marie Stoka, "Cooke Creates a Classic: The Story Behind Taylor's Principles of Scientific Management," *Academy of Management Review,* October 1978, pp. 736–749.

18. Edwin A. Locke, "The Ideas of Frederick W. Taylor: An Evaluation," *Academy of Management Review,* January 1982, pp. 14–20. See also Stephen J. Carroll and Dennis J. Gillen, "Are the Classical Management Functions Useful in Describing Managerial Work?" *Academy of Management Review,* January 1987, pp. 38–51.

19. Henri Fayol, *General and Industrial Management,* trans. J. A. Coubrough (Geneva: International Management Institute, 1930).

20. Max Weber, *Theory of Social and Economic Organizations,* trans. T. Parsons (New York: Free Press, 1947); and Richard M. Weis, "Weber on Bureaucracy: Management Consultant or Political Theorist?" *Academy of Management Review,* April 1983, pp. 242–248.

21. Chester Barnard, *The Functions of the Executive* (Cambridge, Mass.: Harvard University Press, 1938).

22. Hugo Munsterberg, *Psychology and Industrial Efficiency* (Boston: Houghton Mifflin, 1913).

23. Wren, *The Evolution of Management Theory,* pp. 255–264.

24. Dana Wechsler Linden, "The Mother of Them All," *Forbes,* January 16, 1995, pp. 75–76.

25. Elton Mayo, *The Human Problems of an Industrial Civilization* (New York: Macmillan, 1933); and Fritz J. Roethlisberger and William J. Dickson, *Management and the Worker* (Cambridge, Mass.: Harvard University Press, 1939).

26. For a recent commentary on the Hawthorne studies, see Lyle Yorks and David A. Whitsett, "Hawthorne, Topeka, and the Issue of Science versus Advocacy in Organizational Behavior," *Academy of Management Review,* January 1985, pp. 21–30.

27. Barry M. Staw, "Organizational Psychology and the Pursuit of the Happy/Productive Worker," *California Management Review,* Summer 1986, pp. 40–53.

28. Abraham Maslow, "A Theory of Human Motivation," *Psychological Review,* July 1943, pp. 370–396.

29. Douglas McGregor, *The Human Side of Enterprise* (New York: McGraw-Hill, 1960).

30. Cynthia D. Fisher, "On the Dubious Wisdom of Expecting Job Satisfaction to Correlate with Performance," *Academy of Management Review,* October 1980, pp. 607–612.

31. Paul R. Lawrence, "Historical Development of Organizational Behavior," in Jay W. Lorsch (Ed.), *Handbook of Organizational Behavior* (Englewood Cliffs, N.J.: Prentice-Hall, 1987), pp. 1–9. See also Larry L. Cummings, "Toward Organizational Behavior," *Academy of Management Review,* January 1978, pp. 90–98.

32. See Gregory Moorhead and Ricky W. Griffin, *Organizational Behavior,* 4th ed. (Boston: Houghton Mifflin, 1995), for a recent review of current developments in the field of organizational behaviour.

33. Wren, *The Evolution of Management Thought,* Chapter 21.

34. For a recent review of operations management, see Everett E. Adam, Jr., and Ronald J. Ebert, *Production and Operations Management: Concepts, Models, and Behavior,* 5th ed. (Englewood Cliffs, N.J.: Prentice-Hall, 1993).

35. For more information on systems theory in general, see Ludwig von Bertalanffy, C.G. Hempel, R.E. Bass, and H. Jonas, "General Systems Theory: A New Approach to Unity of Science," I–VI *Human Biology*, Vol. 23, 1951, pp. 302–361. For systems theory as applied to organizations, see Fremont E. Kast and James E. Rosenzweig, "General Systems Theory: Applications for Organizations and Management," *Academy of Management Journal*, December 1972, pp. 447–465. For a recent update, see Donde P. Ashmos and George P. Huber, "The Systems Paradigm in Organization Theory: Correcting the Record and Suggesting the Future," *Academy of Management Review*, October 1987, pp. 607–621.

36. "European Banks, Insurance Firms Search for Synergies," *The Wall Street Journal*, April 26, 1989, p. A10.

37. Fremont E. Kast and James E. Rosenzweig, *Contingency Views of Organization and Management* (Chicago: Science Research Associates, 1973).

38. Frank Rose, "A New Age for Business?" *Fortune*, October 8, 1990, pp. 156–164; Brian Dumaine, "Payoff from the New Management," *Fortune*, December 13, 1993, pp. 103–110; and Thomas A. Stewart, "Welcome to the Revolution," *Fortune*, December 13, 1993, pp. 66–77.

39. William Ouchi, *Theory Z—How American Business Can Meet the Japanese Challenge* (Reading, Mass.: Addison-Wesley, 1981). For a recent analysis of Theory Z, see Jeremiah J. Sullivan, "A Critique of Theory Z," *Academy of Management Review*, January 1983, pp. 132–142.

40. William Bowen, "Lessons from Behind the Kimono," *Fortune*, June 15, 1981, pp. 247–250.

41. Thomas J. Peters and Robert H. Waterman, Jr., *In Search of Excellence* (New York: Harper & Row, 1982).

42. Kenneth E. Aupperle, William Acar, and David E. Booth, "An Empirical Critique of *In Search of Excellence*: How Excellent Are the Excellent Companies?" *Journal of Management*, Winter 1986, pp. 499–512; and Michael A. Hitt and R. Duane Ireland, "Peters and Waterman Revisited: The Unended Quest for Excellence," *The Academy of Management Executive*, May 1987, pp. 91–98.

43. See Tom Peters, "Restoring American Competitiveness: Looking for New Models of Organizations," *The Academy of Management Executive*, May 1988, pp. 103–109.

44. "Leaders of Corporate Change," *Fortune*, December 14, 1992, pp. 104–114.

An Introduction to Management

NEWS ITEM:
Eaton's Files for Bankruptcy Protection (1997), 1:45
Eaton's Goes Public (1998, 2:30)

Venerable Canadian department store Eaton's has fallen on troubled times. After filing for bankruptcy protection, Eaton's is attempting to restructure and redefine itself. In the process, it is changing what many Canadians have come to consider a national institution. Changes include going public with shares on the Toronto Stock Exchange, closing several stores, and trying to find a new place in the retail market.

Questions:

1. Has Eaton's been guilty of being "out of touch" with its customers and its competitors? Explain your answer from a systems perspective.
2. Are Eaton's managers on the right track? What changes in the Canadian market in recent years have necessitated these changes?

NEWS ITEM:
Banker Calls on Government to Alleviate Unemployment (1992, 2:00)

As Canadians struggled through an extremely tight employment market during the recession in the early 1990s, Matthew Barrett, recently retired Chairman of the Bank of Montreal, may have surprised many with his response. Barrett believes the government should be less concerned about attacking the deficit and should devote more money and resources to creating a stronger workforce. "We need the most comprehensive and aggressive training program in the Western world," Barrett says. "Nothing less will do."

Questions:

1. Barrett made these comments during a recession. Do you think a banker would make the same statements during strong economic times, such as the late 1990s?

2. What role do major private institutions, such as banks, have to play in the area of job training? How much responsibility should they bear?

Understanding the environment of business is somewhat akin to navigating in a complex network of moving water, land, and sky. Managers must assess their competitive environment and work to enhance the effectiveness of their business. At the same time, however, they must also be sensitive to the social and ethical context within which they work.

The Environmental Context of Management

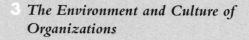

The Environment and Culture of Organizations

3

OBJECTIVES

After studying this chapter, you should be able to:

● *Discuss the nature of the organizational environment and identify the environments of interest to most organizations.*

● *Describe the external environment of organizations, identify the components of the general and task environments, and discuss their impact on organizations.*

● *Identify the components of the internal environment and discuss their impact on organizations.*

● *Identify and describe how the environment affects organizations and how organizations adapt to their environment.*

● *Discuss the importance and determinants of an organization's culture and how the culture can be managed.*

OUTLINE

IBM Canada president Khalil Barsoun helped put in place measures that returned a sagging company to profitability. By the end of 1998, the company was the leading seller of PCs in Canada.

IBM anticipated becoming a $100 billion company by 1990 and was regarded as a quintessential blue-chip corporation. However, the company started losing market share and profitability. In 1991, for the first time in its history, IBM lost money. From 1991 to 1993, the corporation lost $15.8 billion (U.S.) worldwide, with the Canadian subsidiary accounting for $125 million of the loss. "Big Blue," as the company was known, was in trouble; even its once highly regarded brand name had lost its lustre. The company had been hard hit by the microchip revolution, which saw relatively inexpensive desktop computers emerge as an alternative to its mainframes. Moreover, it was unprepared to compete with smaller and more flexible players in the desktop software and hardware markets. Big Blue had lost touch with the customer and the marketplace, but perhaps its biggest problem was that its employees were demoralized.

> **"For some analysts, 'Big Blue' has become 'The New Blue.'"**

To return to profitability, IBM Canada downsized its workforce by almost one-third (to approximately nine thousand employees) and created what it calls an "integrated decentralized organization"; approximately twenty-five businesses were formed from the original company, each focused on a different set of competitors. Moreover, the corporation embarked on a program to change its culture. It set out to change its well-known corporate discipline, which had become an impediment to the necessary process of adapting to a changing environment. The most visible part of the program was a change in the corporation's dress code from the standard blue suit that originated with IBM's founder, Thomas Watson, to a style more compatible with the informal world of personal computers. The company was making a determined effort to adapt to a changing business environment.

It did not take long to reverse the fortunes of IBM Canada. By 1995, the company had returned to profitability by getting into new markets, striking new alliances, and projecting a more friendly attitude. By the third quarter of 1998, IBM had gained the top spot in the Canadian PC market, a position it retained in the fourth quarter of that year. The morale of IBM Canada employees has apparently also improved considerably, with the company's internal system of rating employees' morale indicating an increase to 72 percent in 1995 from 56 percent in 1991. For some analysts, "Big Blue" has become "The New Blue."[1] ●

Managers at IBM made a mistake that is all too common in the business world—they lost contact with their customers and failed to recognize that their competitive environment was changing. Their marketing problems created serious problems for the computer giant. Fortunately, new management initiatives have turned things around and IBM is once again a major force in the computer market.

As we noted in Chapter 1, managers must have a deep understanding and appreciation of the environment in which they and their organizations function. Without this understanding they are like a bike without its handlebars—travelling along with no way of manoeuvring or changing direction. This chapter is the first of three devoted to the environmental context of management. After introducing the nature of the organization's environment, we describe the external and internal environments of organizations. Next we address organization–environment relationships and how these relationships determine the effectiveness of the organization. We conclude by discussing the organization's culture, another important environmental force.

THE ORGANIZATION'S ENVIRONMENT

To illustrate the importance of the environment to an organization, consider the analogy of a swimmer crossing a wide stream. The swimmer must assess the current, obstacles, and distance before setting out. If these elements are properly evaluated, the swimmer will arrive at the expected point on the far bank of the stream. But if they are not properly understood, the swimmer might end up too far upstream or downstream. The organization is like a swimmer, and the environment is like the stream. Thus, just as the swimmer needs to understand conditions in the water, the organization must understand the basic elements of its environment to properly manoeuvre among them.

● **external environment**
Everything outside an organization that might affect it

The **external environment** is everything outside an organization that might affect it. Of course, the boundary that separates the organization from its external environment is not always clear and precise. In one sense, for example, shareholders are part of the organization, but in another sense they are part of its environment. As shown in Figure 3.1, the external environment is composed of two layers: the general environment and the task environment.

● **internal environment**
The conditions and forces within an organization

An organization's **internal environment** consists of conditions and forces within the organization. Its major components include its owners, the board of directors, employees and organized labour, and the organization's culture. Of course, not all aspects of the environment are equally important for all organizations. A small, nonunion firm does not need to concern itself too much with unions, for example. A private university with a large endowment (like Harvard) may be less concerned about general economic conditions than might a Canadian university (like the University of British Columbia) that is dependent on government funding from tax revenues. Still, organizations need to fully understand which environmental forces are important and how the importance of others might increase.

● **general environment**
The set of broad dimensions and forces in an organization's surroundings that create its overall context

THE EXTERNAL ENVIRONMENT

As we just noted, an organization's external environment consists of two layers. The **general environment** of an organization is the set of broad dimensions

FIGURE 3.1 The Organization and Its Environments

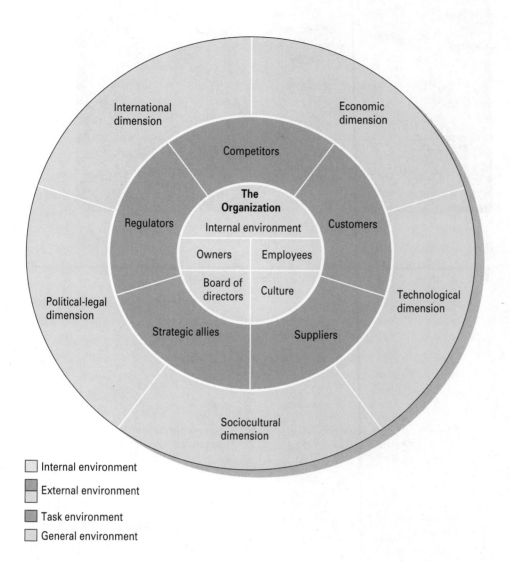

Internal environment

External environment

Task environment

General environment

Organizations have both an external and an internal environment. The external environment consists of two layers: the general environment and the task environment.

and forces in its surroundings that create its overall context. These dimensions and forces are not necessarily associated with other specific organizations. The general environment of most organizations has economic, technological, socio-cultural, political–legal, and international dimensions. The **task environment** consists of specific organizations or groups that influence an organization. The task environment includes competitors, customers, suppliers, regulators, and, increasingly, strategic allies.

● **task environment**
Specific organizations or groups that affect the organization

The General Environment

Each dimension of the general environment embodies conditions and events that have the potential to influence the organization in important ways. The dimensions constituting the general environment of Ford Motor Company of Canada are shown in Figure 3.2.

Dr. Kelvin Ogilvie, president of Acadia University, announced in 1996 that the university plans to hook up its entire student body to the Internet by 2000. Students will be provided with laptop computers and connections to the Internet.

FIGURE 3.2 Ford of Canada's General Environment

International Dimension
- International competition
- Part of Ford's extensive international operations
- Significant interest in Mazda

Economic Dimension
- High unemployment in Canada
- Growing sales in the 1990s
- Low interest rates, low inflation

Political-Legal Dimension
- Government safety standards
- Attitudes toward drunk driving
- General posture toward business regulation

Ford Motor Company of Canada

Technological Dimension
- Increased emphasis on robotics
- Improved computer-assisted design techniques
- More efficient operating systems

Sociocultural Dimension
- Growing consumer demands for quality
- Demographic shifts in number of single adults
- Unpredictable relationship between management and labour
- Varying consumer tastes

The Economic Dimension The **economic dimension** of an organization's general environment is the overall health of the economic system in which the organization operates.[2] Particularly important economic factors for business are inflation, interest rates, and unemployment, all of which affect demand for different products. During times of inflation, for example, a company pays more for resources and must raise its prices to cover the higher costs. When interest rates are high, consumers are less willing to borrow money and the company itself must pay more when it borrows. When unemployment is high, the company is able to be very selective about whom it hires, but consumer buying may decline because fewer people are working.

As shown in Figure 3.2, Ford has benefited from low inflation and interest rates, and overall consumer demand for automobiles has been strong. The economic dimension is also important to nonbusiness organizations as well. For example, during poor economic conditions, funding for universities drops and charitable organizations like the Salvation Army are asked to provide greater assistance, while their incoming contributions dwindle. Hospitals are affected by the availability of government grants.

The Technological Dimension The **technological dimension** of the general environment refers to the methods available for converting resources into products or services. Although technology is applied within the organization, the forms and availability of that technology come from the general environment. Computer-assisted manufacturing and design techniques, for example, allowed McDonnell Douglas Corp. to simulate the three miles of hydraulic tubing that run through a DC-10. The results included decreased warehouse needs, higher-quality tube fittings, fewer employees, and major time savings.[3] New innovations in robotics and other manufacturing techniques also have implications for managers. A company like Ford is clearly affected by all of these innovations. For example, technological change has affected the manner in which Ford designs, manufactures, distributes, and services cars and trucks throughout the world.

The Sociocultural Dimension The **sociocultural dimension** of the general environment includes the customs, mores, values, and demographic characteristics of the society in which the organization functions. Sociocultural processes are important because they determine the products, services, and standards of conduct that the society is likely to value. In some countries, for example, consumers are willing to pay premium prices for designer clothes. But the same clothes have virtually no market in other countries. Consumer tastes also change over time. Drinking hard liquor and smoking cigarettes are far less common in Canada today than they were just a few years ago. And sociocultural factors influence how workers in a society feel about their jobs and the organizations that employ them.

Appropriate standards of business conduct also vary across cultures. In Canada, accepting bribes and bestowing political favours in return are considered unethical. In other countries, however, payments to local politicians may be expected in return for a favourable response to common business transactions such as applications for zoning and operating permits. The shape of the market, the ethics of political influence, and attitudes in the workforce are only a few of the many ways in which culture can affect an organization. Figure 3.2 shows that Ford is clearly affected by sociocultural factors. For example, in the

● **economic dimension**
The overall health of the economic system in which the organization operates

● **technological dimension**
The methods available for converting resources into products or services

● **sociocultural dimension**
The customs, mores, values, and demographic characteristics of the society in which the organization functions

last few years there has been a shift in consumer tastes toward sports utility vehicles like Ford's popular Explorer (as well as the Nissan Pathfinder, Chevy Blazer, and Toyota 4-Runner). As a result, Ford has shifted production away from less-popular models in order to build more Explorers. IBM's lack of awareness about shifts in its sociocultural environment was a major contributor to the firm's decline in the early 1990s.

The Political-Legal Dimension   The **political-legal dimension** of the general environment refers to government regulation of business and the relationship between business and government. It is important for three basic reasons. First, the legal system partially defines what an organization can and cannot do. Although Canada is basically a free market economy, there is still major regulation of business activity.[4] Ford, for example, is subject to a growing concern in Ottawa and Washington about automobile safety standards. Air bags, side reinforcement bars, and child-restraining systems are all product changes that have been implemented in part as a result of governmental regulation.

Second, probusiness or antibusiness sentiment in government influences business activity. For example, during periods of probusiness sentiment, firms find it easier to compete and have fewer concerns about antitrust issues. On the other hand, during a period of antibusiness sentiment firms may find their competitive strategies more restricted and have fewer opportunities for mergers and acquisitions because of antitrust concerns. Finally, political stability has ramifications for planning. No company wants to set up shop in another country unless trade relationships with that country are relatively well defined and stable. Hence, Canadian firms are more likely to conduct business with England, Mexico, and the United States than with Iran and Bosnia. Similar issues are also relevant to assessments of local and provincial governments. A new mayor or premier can affect many organizations, especially small firms that do business in only one location and are susceptible to deed and zoning restrictions and property and school taxes.

The International Dimension   Yet another component of the general environment for many organizations is the **international dimension**, or the extent to which the organization is affected by or involved in businesses in other countries.[5] As we discuss more fully in Chapter 5, multinational firms such as General Electric, Boeing, Nestlé, Sony, Siemens, and Hyundai clearly affect and are affected by international conditions and markets. Specific examples relevant to Ford of Canada are noted in Figure 3.2. For example, Ford of Canada has approximately 14,600 employees while its parent company has approximately 338,000 employees worldwide. Ford sells its cars around the world. Even firms that do business in only one country may face foreign competition at home, and they may use materials or production equipment imported from abroad.

The international dimension also has implications for not-for-profit organizations. For example, the Canadian Organization for Development through Education (CODE) sends representatives to underdeveloped countries. Medical breakthroughs achieved in one country spread rapidly to others, and cultural exchanges of all kinds take place between countries. As a result of advances in transportation and communication technology in the past century, almost no part of the world is cut off from the rest. Virtually every organization is affected by the international dimension.[6]

● **political-legal dimension**
The government regulation of business and the general relationship between business and government

● **international dimension**
The extent to which an organization is involved in or affected by business in other countries

FIGURE 3.3 Ford of Canada's Task Environment

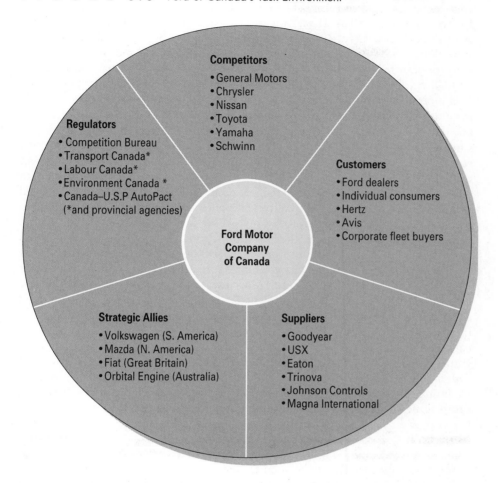

The Task Environment

Because the impact of the general environment is often vague, imprecise, and long-term, most organizations tend to focus their attention on their task environment. Whereas the task environment is also quite complex, it provides useful information more readily than does the general environment because the manager can identify environmental factors of specific interest to the organization rather than having to deal with the more abstract dimensions of the general environment. Figure 3.3 depicts the task environment of Ford Motor Company of Canada. As we note earlier, this environment consists of five dimensions. In Ford's case, competitors include other carmakers such as General Motors and Toyota; customers include Ford dealers, Hertz and other rental companies, and individual consumers; suppliers include Goodyear, USX Corporation, Magna International, TRINOVA Corporation, and Johnson Controls; and strategic allies include Volkswagen and Mazda Motor Corporation. Major regulators of Ford of Canada are Environment Canada, Transport Canada, and their respective provincial agencies.

competitor
An organization that competes with other organizations for resources

Competitors   An organization's **competitors** are other organizations that compete with it for resources. The most obvious resources that competitors vie for are customer dollars. Bata, Adidas, and Nike are competitors, as are Zehrs, A & P, and Food City. But competition also occurs between substitute products. Thus Chrysler competes with Yamaha (motorcycles) and Schwinn (bicycles) for your transportation dollars, and The Walt Disney Company, Club Med, and Carnival Cruise Lines compete for your vacation dollars. Nor is competition limited to business firms. Universities compete with trade schools, the military, other universities, and the external labour market to attract good students, and art galleries compete with each other to attract the best exhibits.[7] Organizations may also compete for different kinds of resources besides consumer dollars. For example, two totally unrelated organizations may compete to acquire a loan from a bank that has only limited funds to lend. In a large city, the police and fire departments may compete for the same tax dollars. And businesses also compete for quality labour, technological breakthroughs and patents, and scarce raw materials.

Fortunately for managers, information about competitors is often quite easily obtained. Zellers can monitor Wal-Mart's prices by reading its newspaper advertisements, for example, or by sending someone to a store to inspect price tags. Similarly, Hilton can monitor Marriott's hotel management practices by having some of its own managers check in at Marriott hotels as guests and observe how Marriott does things. Firms can also buy their competitors' products to learn more about their technology and assembly methods. This practice, called *benchmarking*, has become an important tool in quality improvement programs in recent years.[8] (We discuss benchmarking in more detail in Chapter 21.) Other kinds of information, however, may be more difficult to obtain. Ongoing research activities, new product developments, and future advertising campaigns, for example, are often closely guarded secrets.[9]

customer
Whoever pays money to acquire an organization's products or services

Customers   A second dimension of the task environment is **customers**, or whoever pays money to acquire an organization's products or services. Sometimes, however, the chain of customer transactions is not as straightforward as it seems. As consumers, for example, we do not buy a bottle of Coke from

In October 1998, Sprint Canada pulled the plug on its $20 a month flat-fee long-distance rate throughout Canada. Faced with service interruptions and overloaded lines, the company down-graded the service to 13 hours for $20 a month. Sprint Canada president Philip Bates says there has been a change in the way Canadians use their long distance with a significant increase in calling volume.

Coca-Cola. We may buy it from Beckers or 7-Eleven, which bought it from an independent bottler, which bought the syrup and the right to use the name from Coca-Cola. Customers also need not be individuals. Schools, hospitals, government agencies, wholesalers, retailers, and manufacturers are just a few of the many kinds of organizations that may be major customers of other organizations. Common sources of information about customers include market research, surveys, consumer panels, and reports from sales representatives.

Dealing with customers has become increasingly complex in recent years. New products and services, new methods of marketing, and more discriminating customers have all added uncertainty to how businesses relate to their customers. Many firms have found that focusing their advertising on specific consumer groups or regions is necessary. General Foods Corporation, for example, promotes its Maxwell House coffee differently in different regions, even though doing so costs two or three times what a single national advertising campaign would cost.[10] Pressures from consumer groups about packaging and related issues also complicate the lives of managers.

Suppliers **Suppliers** are organizations that provide resources for other organizations. Disney World buys soft-drink syrup from Coca-Cola, monorails from Daewoo, food from Sara Lee and Smucker, and paper products from Mead. Suppliers for manufacturers like Corning and Ford include the suppliers of raw materials as well as firms that sell machinery and other equipment. Another kind of supplier provides the capital needed to operate the organization. Both banks and federal lending agencies are suppliers of capital for businesses. Other suppliers, such as public and private employment agencies like Kelly Services and college placement offices, provide human resources for the organization. Still other suppliers furnish the organization's managers with the information they need to function effectively. Many companies subscribe to periodicals such as *Canadian Business, Fortune,* and *Report on Business Magazine* to help their managers keep abreast of news. Market research firms are used by some companies. And some firms specialize in developing economic forecasts and in keeping managers informed about pending legislation.

● **supplier**
An organization that provides resources for other organizations

Common wisdom used to be that a business should try to avoid depending exclusively on particular suppliers. A firm that buys all of a certain resource from one supplier may be crippled if the supplier goes out of business or is faced with a strike. This practice can also help maintain a competitive relationship among suppliers, keeping costs down.[11] The *Environment of Management* box explains how General Motors has taken an aggressive stance toward many of its major suppliers.

In recent times, however, some businesses have come to recognize that building especially strong relationships with a small set of suppliers can also pay off. Honda Motor Co. picked Donnelly Corp. to make all the mirrors for its U.S.-manufactured cars. Honda chose Donnelly because it learned enough about the firm to know that it did high-quality work and that its corporate culture and values were consistent with those endorsed by Honda. Recognizing the value of Honda as a customer, Donnelly built an entirely new plant to make the mirrors. And all this was accomplished with only a handshake. Motorola goes even further, providing its principal suppliers with access to its own renowned quality training program and evaluating the performance of each supplier as a way of helping that firm boost its own quality.[12]

When the Environment Gets Tough, GM Gets Going

Intense international competition caused the environment for automobile companies in North America to begin to deteriorate in the 1980s. In response, General Motors Corp. (GM), the world's largest industrial organization, began an extensive organizational restructuring and cost-cutting program. From a peak of nearly 900,000 employees in the mid-1980s, GM reduced its workforce to around 750,000 by the early 1990s. One important component in cost control was purchasing.

In 1991, José Ignacio López de Arriortúa came to the Detroit central offices of GM from General Motors of Europe, Ltd., to head up purchasing. By 1993, GM claimed to have saved nearly $4 billion (U.S.) in purchasing costs. Those savings enabled GM to show a profit in both 1993 and 1994 after losses in the previous three years. López's style in obtaining these spectacular results is, however, another matter. Although brilliantly effective, he managed to alienate many of GM's suppliers.

Upsetting suppliers as well as other constituencies, however, is nothing new at GM. When H. Ross Perot left GM in 1984, he charged that the top management hated customers, dealers, workers, and everyone else with whom they had to deal. When John Z. De Lorean resigned in 1974, he accused GM of lack of social responsibility.

López was not just a tough manager who had high standards; he was also a tough negotiator. He reopened numerous contracts and demanded price cuts from suppliers of up to 20 percent. This, in large part, is what soured relations with suppliers. In addition, López instituted practices that may take years to replace and that many suppliers and others believe are not good management. For example, if a part is not patented, GM may take drawings done by one potential supplier to others to see if they can produce the part for a lower cost. GM's exclusive emphasis on lowest cost has occasionally gotten the company into trouble, as when the supplier of an ashtray could not deliver acceptable quality and the introduction of the 1994 Chevrolet Caprice was delayed.

Overemphasizing a single objective was clearly not a good managerial response to the environment. Largely because of the problems developing at GM, López, in a move clouded by controversy, left GM in early 1993 to join Volkswagen AG.

References: Maryanne Keller, "Slash, Burn and So Long," *Canadian Business*, June 1, 1994, pp. 36–50; "Hardball Is Still GM's Game," *Business Week*, August 8, 1994, p. 26; and Alex Taylor III, "GM's $11,000,000,000 Turnaround," *Fortune*, October 17, 1994, pp. 54–74.

● **regulator**
A unit that has the potential to control, legislate, or otherwise influence the organization's policies and practices

● **regulatory agency**
An agency created by the government to regulate business activities

Regulators   **Regulators** are units in the task environment that have the potential to control, legislate, or influence an organization's policies and practices. There are two important kinds of regulators. The first, **regulatory agencies**, are created by the government to protect the public from certain business practices or to protect organizations from one another. Powerful government regulatory agencies include Environment Canada, the Consumers Products Directorate, the Ontario Securities Commission, Transport Canada, and the Manitoba Human Rights Commission.

Many of these agencies play important roles in protecting the rights of individuals. The Consumers Products Directorate, for example, helps ensure that consumer products are accurately labelled. The costs a firm incurs in complying with government regulations may be substantial, but these costs are usually passed on to the customer. Even so, many organizations complain that there is too much regulation at the present time. One study found that forty-eight major U.S. companies spent $2.6 billion (U.S.) in one year—over and above normal environmental protection, employee safety, and similar costs—because of stringent government regulations. On the basis of these findings, the extra costs of government regulations for all businesses in the United States have been estimated at more than \$100 billion (U.S.) per year.[13] Obviously, the impact of regulatory agencies on organizations is considerable.

Although federal regulators get a lot of publicity, the effect of provincial and local agencies is also important. For example, automobile emission laws in British Columbia aim to reduce pollution by 50 percent by 2010 and 70 percent by 2020. Not-for-profit organizations must also deal with regulatory agencies. The provinces, for example, all have departments that regulate the operation of colleges and universities.

The other basic form of regulator is the interest group. An **interest group** is organized by its members to attempt to influence organizations. Prominent interest groups include the National Action Committee on the Status of Women (NAC), Mothers Against Drunk Drivers (MADD), the National Citizens Coalition (NCC), the Canadian Federation of Independent Businesses (CFIB) and the Sierra Club of Canada. Although interest groups lack the official power of government agencies, they can exert considerable influence by using the media to call attention to their positions. MADD, for example, puts considerable pressure on alcoholic-beverage producers (to put warning labels on their products), automobile companies (to make it more difficult for intoxicated people to start their cars), local governments (to stiffen drinking ordinances), and bars and restaurants (to refuse to sell alcohol to people who are drinking too much).

● **interest group**
A group formed by its own individual members to attempt to influence business

Strategic Allies   A final dimension of the task environment is **strategic allies**—two or more companies that work together in joint ventures or other partnerships. As shown in Figure 3.3, Ford has a number of strategic allies, including Volkswagen (to make cars in South America) and Nissan (to make vans in the United States). Ford and Mazda Motor Corporation also jointly made the Probe automobile. Alliances such as these have been around for a long time, but they became popular in the 1980s and are now increasing at a rate of around 22 percent per year.[14] IBM used to shun strategic alliances but now has seventy-five active partnerships around the globe.[15]

● **strategic ally**
An organization working together with one or more other organizations in a joint venture or similar arrangement

Strategic alliances help companies get from other companies the expertise they lack. They also help spread risk. Managers must be careful, however, not to give away sensitive competitive information. For example, when Unisys Corp. entered into a strategic alliance with Hitachi, Ltd., a Japanese computer maker, it had to divulge valuable trade secrets to make the partnership work. Strategic alliances need not always involve business. Universities, for example, often work together to secure government grants. And some churches sponsor joint missionary projects.

THE INTERNAL ENVIRONMENT

As shown earlier in Figure 3.1, organizations also have an internal environment that consists of their owners, board of directors, employees, and culture (we discuss culture later in a separate section).

Owners

● **owner**
Whoever can claim property rights on an organization

The **owners** of a business are, of course, the people who have a legal property right to that business. Owners can be a single individual who establishes and runs a small business, partners who jointly own the business, individual investors who buy stock in a corporation, or other organizations. The Ford family still controls a large block of stock in Ford Motor Co., although a major share is also available for sale to other investors. Individuals who own and manage their own businesses are clearly a part of the organization's internal environment. But increasingly, so too are corporate shareholders. Until recently, shareholders of major corporations were generally happy to sit on the sidelines and let top management run their organizations. Lately, however, more and more of them are taking active roles in influencing the management of companies they hold shares in. This is especially true of owners who hold large blocks of stock. For example, a few years ago Time Warner Inc. announced that it was going to issue new stock to reduce its debt. Current shareholders were to be given first option on buying the stock, but the stock's price was not going to be known at the time options had to be exercised. Several large shareholders complained and some threatened lawsuits. Time Warner eventually backed down and cancelled its plans.[16]

Another group increasingly exerting influence is the managers of large pension funds. These enormous funds control 50 percent of the shares traded on the New York Stock Exchange and 65 percent of *Standard & Poor's 500* stocks. AT&T's pension fund, for example, exceeds $35 billion (U.S.). Pension fund managers in Canada exert similar influence. The Ontario Municipal Employees Retirement Systems pension fund, for example, exceeds $29 billion, while total assets of the Caisse de depôt et placement du Québec (established in 1965 to invest the assets of sixteen public sector funds) stood at $63.6 billion in June 1998.[17] Given the power wielded by owners (and willingness to use that power), some fear that managers are sacrificing long-term corporate effectiveness for the sake of short-term results. For example, managers at Carnation Company were afraid to increase advertising costs too much for fear of attracting the attention of institutional investors. As a result, sales declined. After Nestlé SA took over and loosened the purse strings, sales took off again.[18] Thus managers are finding that they must be considerably more concerned about owners now than in the past.

Board of Directors

Not every organization has a board of directors. Corporations, of course, are required to have them but nonincorporated businesses and many nonbusiness organizations are not. Universities, however, do have a board of governors, and most other large organizations, including hospitals and charities, have a board of trustees that serves essentially the same purpose. A corporate board of directors is elected by the shareholders and is charged with overseeing the general management of the firm to ensure that it is being run in a way that best serves the shareholders' interests.[19] Some directors, called inside directors, are also full-time employees of the firm holding top-management jobs. Outside directors, in contrast, are elected to the board for a specific purpose, such as assisting with financial management and legal issues, and are not full-time employees of the organization. Ford Motor Co. has eight board members who work for the firm, and another seven who work for other companies. Among the latter are the CEOs of Coca-Cola, Seagrams, and several other firms. The board plays a major role in helping set corporate strategy and seeing that it is implemented properly. The board also reviews all important decisions made by top management and determines compensation for top managers.

Employees

An organization's employees are also a major element of its internal environment. When managers and employees embrace the same values and have the same goals, everyone wins. When managers and employees work toward different ends, however, or when conflict and hostility pervade the organization, everyone suffers.[20] Many of the issues that we discuss in Part V, "The Leading Process," are aimed at enhancing interpersonal relationships in the organization. Of particular interest to managers today is the changing nature of Canadian workers. The workforce of tomorrow will have more women, immigrants, ethnic and visible minorities, and older people than the workforce of today. The worker of tomorrow is also expected to want more job ownership—either partial ownership in the company or at least more say in how the job is performed.[21]

The employees of many organizations are organized into labour unions. Labour relations acts require organizations to recognize and bargain with a union if that union has been legally established by the organization's employees. Presently, around 40 percent of the Canadian labour force is represented by unions. Some large organizations such as Ford, Ontario Hydro, and Bell Canada have several different unions. Even when an organization's labour force is not unionized, its managers do not ignore unions. For example, Dofasco and Wal-Mart actively avoid unionization. And even though people think primarily of blue-collar workers as union members, many white-collar workers such as government employees and teachers are also represented by unions.

ORGANIZATION—ENVIRONMENT RELATIONSHIPS

The preceding discussion identifies and describes the various dimensions of organizational environments. Because organizations are open systems, they interact with these various dimensions in many different ways. We now turn our attention to these interactions. We first discuss how environments affect organizations and then note a number of ways in which organizations adapt to their environments.

How Environments Affect Organizations

Three basic perspectives can be used to describe how environments affect organizations: environmental change and complexity, competitive forces, and environmental turbulence.[22]

Environmental Change and Complexity   James D. Thompson was one of the first people to recognize the importance of the organization's environment.[23] Thompson suggests that the environment can be described along two dimensions: its degree of change and its degree of homogeneity. The degree of change is the extent to which the environment is relatively stable or relatively

FIGURE 3.4 Environmental Change, Complexity, and Uncertainty

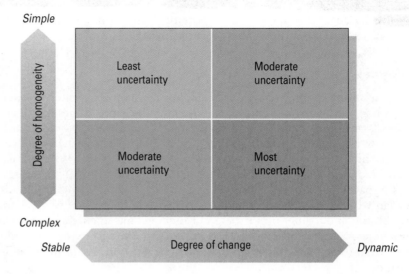

Adapted from J.D. Thompson, *Organizations in Action,* Copyright © 1967 by McGraw-Hill, Inc. Used by permission of the publisher.

● **uncertainty**
A major force caused by change and complexity that affects many organizational activities

dynamic. The degree of homogeneity is the extent to which the environment is relatively simple (few elements, little segmentation) or relatively complex (many elements, much segmentation). These two dimensions interact to determine the level of uncertainty faced by the organization. **Uncertainty**, in turn, is a driving force that influences many organizational decisions. Figure 3.4 illustrates a simple view of the four levels of uncertainty defined by different levels of homogeneity and change.

The least environmental uncertainty is faced by organizations with stable and simple environments. Although no environment is totally without uncertainty, many franchised food operations (such as Harvey's and Taco Bell) and many container manufacturers (like Par-Pak and Westra) have relatively low levels of uncertainty to contend with. Harvey's, for example, focuses on a certain segment of the consumer market, produces a limited product line, has a constant source of suppliers, and faces relatively consistent competition.

Organizations with dynamic but simple environments generally face a moderate degree of uncertainty. Examples of organizations functioning in such environments include clothing manufacturers (targeting a certain kind of clothing buyer but sensitive to fashion-induced changes) and compact disc (CD) producers (catering to certain kinds of record buyers but alert to changing tastes in music). Levi Strauss faces few competitors (Wrangler and Lee), has few suppliers and few regulators, and uses limited distribution channels. This relatively simple task environment, however, also changes quite rapidly as competitors adjust prices and styles, consumer tastes change, and new fabrics become available.

Another combination of factors is one of stability and complexity. Again, a moderate amount of uncertainty results. Ford Motor Co. faces these basic conditions. Overall, the organization must interact with a myriad of suppliers, regulators, consumer groups, and competitors. Change, however, occurs quite slowly in the automobile industry. Despite many stylistic changes, cars of today still have four wheels, a steering wheel, an internal combustion engine, a glass windshield, and many of the other basic features that have characterized cars for decades.

Finally, very dynamic and complex environmental conditions yield a high degree of uncertainty. The environment has a large number of elements, and the nature of those elements is constantly changing. Intel, Compaq, IBM, Sony, and other firms in the electronics field face these conditions because of the rapid rate of technological innovation and change in consumer markets that characterize their industry, their suppliers, and their competitors.

Competitive Forces   Although Thompson's general classifications are useful and provide some basic insights into organization–environment interactions, in many ways they lack the precision and specificity needed by managers who must deal with their environments on a day-to-day basis. Michael E. Porter, a Harvard professor and expert in strategic management, has proposed a more refined way to assess environments. In particular, he suggests that managers view the environment of their organizations in terms of **five competitive forces**.[24]

● **five competitive forces**
The threat of new entrants, competitive rivalry, substitute products, the power of buyers, and the power of suppliers

The *threat of new entrants* is the extent to which new competitors can easily enter a market or market segment. It takes a relatively small amount of capital to open a dry-cleaning service or a pizza parlour, but it takes a tremendous investment in plant, equipment, and distribution systems to enter the automobile business. Thus the threat of new entrants is fairly high for a local hamburger restaurant but fairly low for a Ford or Toyota dealership.

Competitive rivalry is the nature of the competitive relationship between dominant firms in the industry. In the soft-drink industry, Coca-Cola and Pepsico often engage in intense price wars, comparative advertising, and new-product introductions. And North American auto companies continually try to outmanoeuvre each other with warranty improvements and rebates. Local car-washing establishments, in contrast, seldom engage in such practices.

The *threat of substitute products* is the extent to which alternative products or services may supplant or diminish the need for existing products or services. The electronic calculator eliminated the need for slide rules. The advent of microcomputers, in turn, has reduced the demand for calculators as well as for typewriters and large mainframe computers. And Nutra-Sweet is a viable substitute product threatening the sugar industry.

The *power of buyers* is the extent to which buyers of the products or services in an industry have the ability to influence the suppliers. For example, a Boeing 747 has relatively few potential buyers. Only companies such as Air Canada, Canadian Airlines, and KLM Royal Dutch Airlines can purchase them; hence, they have considerable influence over the price they are willing to pay, the delivery date for the order, and so forth. On the other hand, Japanese carmakers charged premium prices for their cars in North America during the late 1970s energy crisis because if the first customer wouldn't pay the price, two more customers were waiting in line who would.

The *power of suppliers* is the extent to which suppliers have the ability to influence potential buyers. The local electric company is the only source of electricity in your community. Subject to local or provincial regulation (or both), it can therefore charge what it wants for its product, provide service at its convenience, and so forth. Likewise, even though Boeing has few potential customers, those same customers have few suppliers that can sell them a 300-passenger jet. So Boeing too has power. On the other hand, a small vegetable wholesaler has little power in selling to restaurants because if they don't like the

Environmental turbulence can often force an organization to repond to catastrophic events with little or no warning. Although organizations could have developed contingency plans for some of these crises, many of them are events that would have been hard to anticipate.

TABLE 3.1		Recent Organizational Crises

Date	Organization	Nature of Crisis
1979	Metropolitan Edison	Near meltdown at Three Mile Island nuclear power plant.
1982	Johnson & Johnson	Cyanide poisoning of Tylenol capsules results in 8 deaths.
1984	Union Carbide	Poison gas leak at plant in Bhopal, India, kills 3,000 and injures another 300,000.
1985	Jalisco	Bacteria in cheese kills 84.
1986	NASA	Space shuttle *Challenger* explodes after takeoff, killing 7 crew members.
1989	Exxon	The supertanker *Valdez* hits a rocky reef off the coast of Alaska and spills more than 10 million gallons of oil.
1989	Pacific Gas & Electric	San Francisco earthquake leaves dozens of gas leaks and millions of homes without electricity.
1992	Dow Corning	After hundreds of women file lawsuits complaining of adverse affects from the company's silicone breast implants, the Food and Drug Administration conducts an investigation resulting in a ban on the implants. Dow Corning is criticized for its handling of the disaster and announces its withdrawal from the implant-making business a month later.*
1993	Jack-in-the-Box	Tainted meat sold in Washington state restaurants kills 2 and poisons more than 400.*
1993	Pepsico	Unsubstantiated claims about sewing needles in cans of Pepsi-Cola make national headlines.*
1997	Via Rail	Passenger train derails in Biggar, Saskatchewan, killing 1 person and injuring 65 others.*
1998	Hydro-Québec	Ice storm batters Québec causing unprecedented damage to Hydro-Québec's transmission and distribution systems. More than 1 million customers are deprived of electricity, some for more than a month.*
1999	International Olympic Committee	Allegations of corruption involving the awarding of the 2002 Winter Games sparks a crisis in the world Olympic movement, including the Canadian Olympic Association.*

*Not included in original article.

Source: Suggested by Ian Mitroff, Paul Shrivastava, and Firdaus E. Udwadia, "Effective Crisis Management," *The Academy of Management Executive,* August 1987, pp. 283–292.

wholesaler has little power in selling to restaurants because if they don't like the produce, they can easily find an alternative supplier.

Environmental Turbulence Although always subject to unexpected changes and upheavals, the five competitive forces can be studied and assessed systematically, and a plan can be developed for dealing with them. At the same time, though, organizations also face the possibility of environmental change or turbulence, occasionally with no warning at all. The most common form of organizational turbulence is a crisis of some sort. Table 3.1 lists a number of crises that different organizations have had to confront in recent years.

The effects of crises like those can be devastating to an organization, especially if managers are unprepared to deal with them. For example, the tainted blood scandal that came to light in the 1990s will have a lasting effect on the Canadian Red Cross and the newly formed Canadian Blood Services. At NASA, the *Challenger* shuttle disaster paralyzed the space program for almost three years. The cost to Johnson & Johnson of the Tylenol poisonings has been estimated at $750 million (U.S.) in product recalls and changes in packaging and product design.[25] Exxon's legal problems arising from the Alaskan oil spill will not be settled for years. And Dow Corning faces long-term problems associated with its silicone gel breast implants.

Such crises affect organizations in different ways, and many organizations are developing crisis plans and teams.[26] When a Delta Air Lines plane crashed in 1988 at the Dallas–Fort Worth airport, for example, fire-fighting equipment was at the scene in minutes. Only a few flights were delayed, and none had to be cancelled. In 1987, a grocery store in Boston received a threat that someone had poisoned cans of its Campbell's tomato juice. Within six hours, a crisis team from Campbell Soup Co. removed two truckloads of juice from all eighty-four stores in the grocery chain. Still, fewer than half of the major companies in the United States have a plan for dealing with major crises.[27] The 1998 ice storm in Quebec and Eastern Ontario affected hundreds of businesses for months.

How Organizations Adapt to Their Environments

Given the myriad issues, problems, and opportunities in an organization's environments, how should the organization adapt? Obviously, each organization must assess its own unique situation and then adapt according to the wisdom of its senior management.[28] Figure 3.5 illustrates the six basic mechanisms through which organizations adapt to their environment. One of these, social responsibility, is given special consideration in Chapter 4.

Information Management One way organizations adapt to their environment is through information management. Information management is especially important when forming an initial understanding of the environment and when monitoring the environment for signs of change. Organizations use several **techniques for information management**. One is recognizing the importance of boundary spanners. A *boundary spanner* is an employee, such as a sales representative or a purchasing agent, who spends much of her time in contact with others outside the organization. Such people are in a good position to learn what other organizations are doing. All effective managers engage in *environmental scanning*, the process of actively monitoring the environment through activities such as observation and reading. Within the organization, Toronto-Dominion Bank, Canada Post, Ford, and many other firms have also

● **techniques for information management**
Recognizing the importance of boundary spanners, environmental scanning, and establishing management information systems

established elaborate *information systems* to gather and organize relevant information for managers and to assist in summarizing that information in the form most pertinent to each manager's needs (information systems are covered more fully in Chapter 22).

Strategic Response   Another way that an organization adapts to its environment is through a strategic response. Options include maintaining the status quo (for example, if its management believes that it is doing very well with its current approach), altering strategy a bit, or adopting an entirely new strategy. If the market that a company currently serves is growing rapidly, the firm might decide to invest even more heavily in products and services for that market. Likewise, if a market is shrinking or does not provide reasonable possibilities for growth, the company may decide to cut back. For example, when Tenneco's managers recently decided that oil and gas prices were likely to remain depressed for some time to come, they decided to sell the company's oil and gas business and invest the proceeds in its healthier businesses like Tenneco Automotive.[29] The *Managing in a Changing World* box describes how heavy equipment manufacturers have altered their strategy to better meet the demands of their competitive environment.

Organizations attempt to influence their environments. The most common methods for this are through information management, strategic response, mergers, takeovers, acquisitions, alliances, organization design and flexibility, and direct influence.

F I G U R E   3 . 5   How Organizations Respond to Their Environments

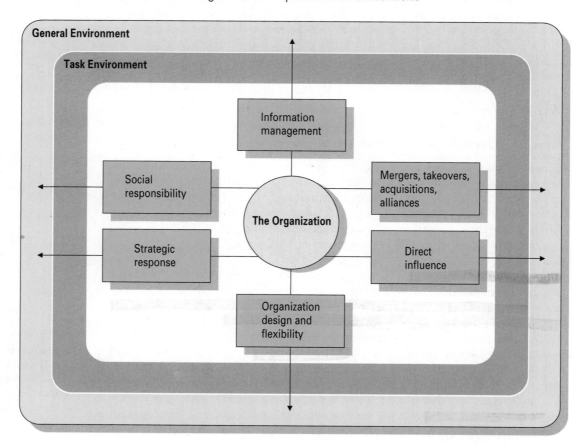

Heavy Equipment Manufacturers Adapt to Change

In the mid-1970s, more than twenty companies were manufacturing heavy equipment—the tractors used in agriculture, the bulldozers used in construction, and so forth. Today, however, just a handful remain, led by Case Corporation, Caterpillar Inc., Deere & Company, Ingersoll-Rand Company, and Kubota Corporation. These firms survived because, unlike the others, they did not ignore their environment.

For example, one important business practice that plagued the industry for years was the philosophy of maintaining vast inventories of finished goods and encouraging the dealers to do the same. Then, when demand dropped, they would just cut prices. They also did not worry too much about costs. Instead, when demand was strong, the manufacturers simply raised prices to cover their expenses. Moreover, the manufacturers gave low priority to customer service and competed against each other mostly in their domestic markets. And few of the firms in this industry paid much attention to new technology.

But now things have changed. Managers have come to realize that they can function more effectively with a much smaller inventory and less price cutting during down periods. The firms remaining in the industry have also cut their operating costs substantially. They are also paying more attention to customer service while investing in new technology. International markets are also playing a bigger role in the day-to-day operations of all equipment manufacturers.

However, the real key to success of all these firms, their top executives agree, is the fact that each has made flexibility and market responsiveness key business practices that permeate every aspect of the organizations.

References: "Heavy Equipment Gets into Gear," *Business Week*, August 5, 1996, p. 29; *Hoover's Handbook of American Business 1997* (Austin, Tex.: Hoover's Business Press, 1996), pp. 296-297; and "This Cat Keeps on Purring," *Business Week*, January 20, 1997, pp. 82–84.

Mergers, Takeovers, Acquisitions, and Alliances   A merger occurs when two or more firms combine to form a new firm. For example, Daimler–Benz and Chrysler recently merged to create a new company, Daimler–Chrysler. A takeover occurs when one firm buys another, sometimes against its will (a hostile takeover). Usually, the firm taken over ceases to exist and becomes part of the other company. For example, when AT&T took over NCR, it folded that company into its existing operations, as did Cambridge Shopping Centres when it swallowed Markborough Properties in May 1997. After an acquisition, the acquired firm often continues to operate as a subsidiary of the acquiring company. And as already discussed, in an alliance the firm undertakes a new venture with another firm. A company engages in these kinds of strategies for a variety of reasons, such as easing entry into new markets or expanding its presence in a current market.

Organization Design and Flexibility   An organization may also adapt to environmental conditions by incorporating flexibility into its structural design. For example, a firm that operates in an environment with relatively low levels of uncertainty might choose to use a design with many basic rules, regulations, and standard operating procedures. Alternatively, a firm that faces a great deal of uncertainty might choose a design with relatively few standard operating procedures, instead allowing managers considerable discretion and flexibility over management decisions. The former type, sometimes called a mechanistic organization design, is characterized by formal and rigid rules and relationships. The latter, sometimes called an organic design, is considerably more flexible and permits the organization to respond quickly to environmental change.[30] We learn much more about these and related issues in Chapter 10.

Direct Influence of the Environment   Organizations are not necessarily helpless in the face of their environments.[31] Indeed, many organizations are able to directly influence their environment in many different ways. For example, firms can influence their suppliers by signing long-term contracts with fixed prices as a hedge against inflation. Or a firm might become its own supplier. Sears, for example, owns some of the firms that produce the goods it sells, and Campbell Soup Company has started making its own soup cans.

Almost any major activity a firm engages in affects its competitors. When JVC lowers the prices of its CD players, Sony may be forced to follow suit. When London Life lowers its life-insurance rates, The Mutual Group is likely to do the same.[32] Organizations also influence their customers. One method involves creating new uses for a product, finding entirely new customers, and taking customers away from competitors. Developing new kinds of software, for example, expands the customer base of computer firms. Organizations also influence their customers by convincing them that they need something new. Automobile manufacturers use this strategy in their advertising to convince people that they need a new car every two or three years.

Organizations influence their regulators through lobbying and bargaining. Lobbying involves sending a company or industry representative to Ottawa or Washington in an effort to influence relevant agencies, groups, and committees. For example, the U.S. Chamber of Commerce lobby, the largest business lobby in the United States, has an annual budget of more than $100 million (U.S.). The automobile companies have been successful on several occasions in bargaining with the EPA to extend deadlines for compliance with pollution control and mileage standards.[33] Mobil Corporation has long attempted to influence public opinion and government action through an ongoing series of advertisements about the virtues of free enterprise. In Canada, the Business Council on National Issues (BCNI) attempts to do the same on behalf of this country's 150 largest corporations.

Most bargaining sessions between management and unions are also attempts at mutual influence. Management tries to get the union to accept its contract proposals, and unions try to get management to sweeten its offer. When unions are not represented in an organization, management usually attempts to keep them out. It was only after a bitter fight that one of Wal-Mart's Windsor, Ontario, stores was unionized in 1997—a first in the company's history. Corporations influence their owners with information contained in annual reports, by meeting with large investors, and by pure persuasion. And strategic alliance agreements are almost always negotiated through contracts. Each party tries to get the best deal it can from the other as the final agreement is hammered out.

Organizational Effectiveness

We noted in Chapter 1 the distinction between organizational effectiveness and efficiency. Efficiency involves using resources wisely and without waste, and effectiveness is doing the right things. Given the interactions between organizations and their environments, it follows that effectiveness is related to how well an organization understands, reacts to, and influences its environment.[34] Unfortunately, there is no consensus about what constitutes effectiveness. For example, an organization can make itself look extremely effective in the short term by ignoring research and development (R&D), buying cheap materials, ignoring quality control, and skimping on wages. Over time, though, the firm will no doubt falter. On the other hand, taking action consistent with a longer view such as making appropriate investments in R&D may displease investors who have a short-term outlook. Little wonder, then, that there are many different **models of organizational effectiveness**.

The *systems resource approach* to organizational effectiveness focuses on the extent to which the organization can acquire the resources it needs.[35] A manufacturer that can get raw materials during a shortage, a faculty of engineering that can hire qualified professors despite competition from industry, and a firm that can borrow at low interest rates are all effective from this perspective. They are acquiring the material, human, financial, and information resources they need to compete successfully in the marketplace.

The *internal processes approach* to organizational effectiveness deals with the internal mechanisms of the organization. It focuses on minimizing strain, integrating individuals and the organization, and conducting smooth and efficient operations.[36] An organization that focuses primarily on maintaining employee satisfaction and morale and being efficient subscribes to this view. Well-managed firms like Texas Instruments and Emerson Electric are clearly effective from this point of view.

The *goal approach* to effectiveness focuses on the degree to which an organization obtains its goals.[37] When a firm establishes a goal of increasing sales by 10 percent and then achieves that increase, the goal approach maintains that the organization is effective. How successful General Electric Co. is at its goal of being either number one or number two in every industry it enters is used by CEO Jack Welch as an indicator of effectiveness.

Finally, the *strategic constituencies approach* to organizational effectiveness focuses on the groups that have a stake in the organization.[38] The strategic constituencies of Ralston Purina, for example, include its suppliers (food producers and container manufacturers), lenders (shareholders and banks), participants (employees and managers), customers (wholesalers, retailers, and ranch cooperatives), and any others who might be influenced by the company. In this view, effectiveness is the extent to which the organization is able to satisfy the demands and expectations of all these groups.

Although these four basic models of effectiveness are not necessarily contradictory, they do focus on different things. The systems resource approach focuses on inputs, the internal processes approach focuses on transformation processes, the goal approach focuses on outputs, and the strategic constituencies approach focuses on feedback. Thus, rather than adopting a single approach, organizational effectiveness can best be understood by an integrated perspective such as the one illustrated in Figure 3.6. At the core of this unifying model is the organizational system, with its inputs, transformations, outputs, and feedback. Surrounding this core are the four basic approaches to effectiveness as well as a combined approach, which incorporates each of the other four. The basic argument is that an organization must essentially satisfy the requirements imposed on it by each of the effectiveness perspectives.

Achieving organizational effectiveness is not an easy task. The key to doing so is understanding the environment in which the organization functions. With this understanding as a foundation, managers can then chart the "correct" path

- **models of organizational effectiveness** Systems resource approach, internal processes approach, goal approach, and strategic constituencies approach

for the organization as it positions itself in that environment. If managers can identify where they want the organization to be relative to other parts of their environment, and how to best get there, they stand a good chance of achieving organizational effectiveness. On the other hand, if they pick the wrong target to aim for, or if they go about achieving their goals in the wrong way, they are likely to be less effective.

THE ORGANIZATION'S CULTURE

The **culture** of an organization is the set of values that helps its members understand what the organization stands for, how it does things, and what it considers important. Culture is an amorphous concept that defies objective measurement or observation. Nevertheless, because it is the foundation of the organization's internal environment, it plays a major role in shaping managerial behaviour.[39]

The Importance of Culture

Several years ago, executives at Levi Strauss believed that the company had outgrown its sixty-eight-year-old building. Even though everyone enjoyed its casual and relaxed atmosphere, the company needed more space. So Levi Strauss moved into a modern office building in downtown San Francisco, where its new headquarters spread over twelve floors in a skyscraper. It quickly became apparent that the change was affecting the corporate culture—and that people did not like it. Executives felt isolated, and other managers missed the informal chance meetings in the halls. Within just a few years, Strauss moved out of the skyscraper and back into a building that fosters informality. For example, there is an adjacent park area where employees converge for lunchtime conversation. Clearly, Levi Strauss has a culture that is important to everyone who works there.[40]

Culture determines the "feel" of the organization. The stereotypic image of the IBM executive is someone wearing a white shirt and dark suit. In contrast, Texas Instruments likes to talk about its "shirt-sleeve" culture, in which ties are avoided and few managers ever wear jackets. Of course, the same culture is not necessarily found throughout an entire organization. For example, the sales and marketing department may have a culture quite different from that of the operations and manufacturing department. Regardless of its nature, however, culture is a powerful force in organizations, one that can shape the firm's overall effectiveness and long-term success. Companies that can develop and maintain a strong culture, such as Hewlett-Packard and Procter & Gamble, tend to be more effective than companies that have trouble developing and maintaining a strong culture.[41]

Determinants of Culture

Where does a culture come from? Typically it develops and blossoms over a long period of time. Its starting point is often the organization's founder. For example, Timothy Eaton and James Cash Penney believed in treating employees and customers with respect and dignity. Eaton resisted trimming his payroll during the Great Depression. Employees at J.C. Penney are still called

An organization's culture plays a major role in shaping its success. Lou Bucelli, owner of CME Conference Video, a medical video production company, clearly recogizes the value of his firm's culture. He recently roped off a small section of the company's current 16,000 square feet of work space to illustrate how little space he, his partner, and his secretary had when they started the firm. The firm's first employees then sat around with newer employees in the small space and told war stories about how the firm began and how they had to struggle to get things done.

F I G U R E 3.6 A Model of Organizational Effectiveness

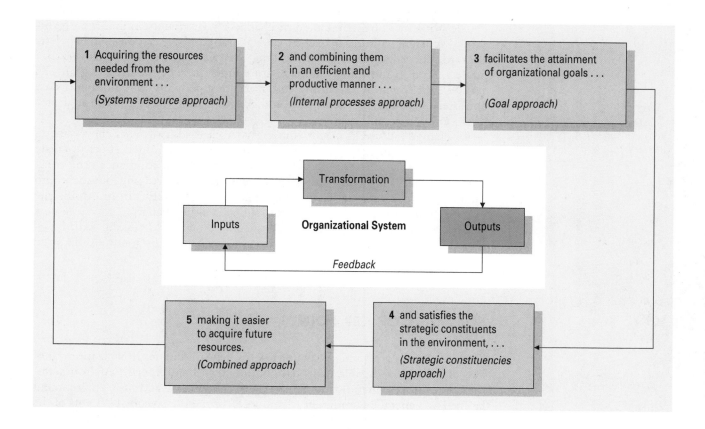

associates rather than employees (to reflect partnership), and customer satisfaction is of paramount importance. The impact of Timothy Eaton and Walt Disney is still felt in the organizations they founded. As an organization grows, its culture is modified, shaped, and refined by symbols, stories, heroes, slogans, and ceremonies. For example, an important value at Hewlett-Packard is the avoidance of bank debt. A popular story still told at the company involves a new project being considered for several years. All objective criteria indicated that HP should incur bank debt to finance it, yet Bill Hewlett and David Packard rejected it out of hand simply because "HP avoids bank debt." This story, involving two corporate heroes and based on a slogan, dictates corporate culture today.[42]

Corporate success and shared experiences also shape culture. For example, Hallmark Cards has a strong culture derived from its years of success in the greeting cards industry. Employees speak of the Hallmark family and care deeply about the company; many of them have worked at the company for years. At Navistar International, in contrast, the culture is quite weak, the management team changes rapidly, and few people sense any direction or purpose in the company. The differences in culture at Hallmark and Navistar are in part attributable to past successes and shared experiences.

The systems resource, internal processes, goal, and strategic constituencies approaches to organizational effectiveness each take a different focus on what constitutes organizational effectiveness. Thus they can be combined to create an overall integrative perspective on effectiveness

Managing Organizational Culture

How can managers deal with culture, given its clear importance but intangible nature? Essentially, the manager must understand the current culture and then decide if it should be maintained or changed.[43] By understanding the organization's current culture, managers can take appropriate actions. At Hewlett-Packard, the values represented by "the HP way" still exist. Moreover, they guide and direct most important activities undertaken by the firm. Culture can also be maintained by rewarding and promoting people whose behaviours are consistent with the existing culture and by articulating the culture through slogans, ceremonies, and so forth.

To change culture, managers must have a clear idea of what they want to create. As noted in our opening case, IBM made a determined effort to create a new culture that better reflects today's competitive environment in the computer market. One major way to shape culture is by bringing outsiders into important managerial positions. The choice of a new CEO from outside the organization is often a clear signal that things will be changing. Adopting new slogans, telling new stories, staging new ceremonies, and breaking with tradition can also alter culture. Culture can also be changed by methods discussed in Chapter 11.

SUMMARY OF KEY POINTS

Environmental factors play a major role in determining an organization's success or failure. All organizations have both external and internal environments.

The external environment is composed of general and task environment layers. The general environment is composed of the nonspecific elements of the organization's surroundings that might affect its activities. It consists of five dimensions: economic, technological, sociocultural, political-legal, and international. The effects of these dimensions on the organization are broad and gradual. The task environment consists of specific dimensions of the organization's surroundings that are very likely to influence the organization. It also consists of five elements: competitors, customers, suppliers, regulators, and strategic allies. Because these dimensions are associated with specific organizations in the environment, their effects are likely to be more direct and immediate.

The internal environment consists of the organization's owners, board of directors, employees, and culture. Owners are those who have property rights claims on the organization. The board of directors, elected by shareholders, is responsible for overseeing a firm's top managers. Individual employees and the labour unions they sometimes join are other important parts of the internal environment.

Organizations and their environments affect each other in several ways. Environmental influences on the organization can occur through uncertainty, competitive forces, and turbulence. Organizations, in turn, use information management; strategic response; mergers, takeovers, acquisitions, and alliances; organization design and flexibility; direct influence; and social responsibility to adapt to their task environments. One important indicator of how well an organization deals with its environment is its level of effectiveness. Organizational effectiveness requires that the organization do a good job of procuring resources, managing them properly, achieving its goals, and satisfying its constituencies. Adequate planning is a key determinant of effectiveness.

Culture is an especially important environmental concern for organizations. Managers must understand that culture is an important determinant of how well their organization will perform. Culture can be determined and managed in a number of different ways.

DISCUSSION QUESTIONS

Questions for Review

1. Why is an organization's environment so important? Identify and discuss each of the major dimensions of the general environment.
2. What is an organization's task environment? What are the major dimensions of that environment?
3. What are the major forces that affect organization–environment relationships? Describe those forces.
4. What is organizational effectiveness? How is it studied and assessed?

Questions for Analysis

5. Can you think of dimensions of the task environment that are not discussed in the text? Indicate their linkage to those that are discussed.
6. Some organizations come to be part-owners of other firms through mergers and acquisitions. How does the nature of partial ownership complicate the organization–environment relationship?
7. How would each dimension of an organization's task environment and internal environment assess the organization's effectiveness? Can an organization be equally effective to each of these different groups? Why or why not?

Questions for Application

8. Go to the library and research a company. Characterize its level of effectiveness according to each of the four basic models. Share your results with the class.
9. Interview a manager from a local organization about his or her organization's environments—general, task, and internal. In the course of the interview, are all of the major dimensions identified? Why or why not?
10. Outline the several environments of your college or university. Be detailed about the dimensions, and provide specific examples to illustrate how each dimension affects your institution.

BUILDING EFFECTIVE COMMUNICATION & INTERPERSONAL SKILLS

Exercise Overview

Communication skills refer to the manager's abilities to both effectively convey ideas and information to others and effectively receive ideas and information from others. Communication skills are very important when a manager is attempting to respond to or influence some element from the organization's external environment. This exercise will help you develop your communication skills as they relate to this situation.

Exercise Background

Assume that you work for a large manufacturing firm. Nine years ago, a factory owned by your company was embroiled in a major environmental disaster involving toxic waste disposal. The managers involved in the disaster, clearly your company's fault, were all fired. New procedures for dealing with waste disposal were also developed, and since that earlier situation no further problems have occurred.

The province where the factory is located is currently under fire from Environment Canada to impose tighter environmental protection regulations on a variety of industries. The province, however, cannot afford to tighten regulations out of its existing budget. A plan recently introduced in the provincial legislature calls for the imposition of a new tax on all businesses found guilty of improper waste disposal, as well as other forms of pollution, anytime during the last ten years. This tax will be used to enforce the new regulations.

At the present time it is unclear whether the tax would apply to your firm for a single year or if it will be indefinitely imposed on any firm that initially qualifies. Your boss has told you—off the record—that the firm can live with a one-time tax. But if it will remain in place for your company indefinitely, the company will close the plant. A plant closure would also have a serious negative impact on the province's economy. The boss has also placed you in charge of media relations regarding this situation.

Exercise Task

With the preceding background information as context, do the following:

1. Draft a press release stating your company's position on the potential tax.
2. Imagine that you are going to be interviewed by a reporter known to be "friendly" to your company. The reporter has agreed that you can submit potential interview questions in advance. Draft three questions and your answers to them.
3. Imagine that a reporter known to be "hostile" to your company has requested an answer. List three questions that might be asked and draft your answers to them.

Dofasco Inc. started as a small manufacturer in 1912 when Clifton W. Sherman opened a foundry in Hamilton, Ontario; it employed 150 people to make castings for the railway industry. Recognizing the market demand for other products, the company began diversifying its base in the early 1920s when it produced Canada's first steel plate. This trend continued in the 1930s with the introduction of flat rolled steel and Canada's first tinplate. In 1951, Dofasco became a fully integrated steel producer with the introduction of its first blast furnace. In 1954, it became the first mill in North America to make steel with the basic oxygen process that is now used throughout the world. All of these developments were prompted by increasing competition. Dofasco's determination to stay in front of the pack through innovative technological advances helped the company in the 1980s, when its business environment began to experience turbulence.

The economic recession of the 1980s resulted in massive financial losses for Dofasco. During this period, competition began to shift from local to global markets. As steel flooded the saturated North American market, prices plummeted. The leaner, more efficient mini-mills had a competitive advantage since they could produce small batches more cost effectively. Industry experts also cite high interest rates and a Canadian dollar that was overvalued (relative to the U.S. dollar) as factors that impaired the ability of Canadian manufacturers to compete in U.S. markets. At the same time, companies were expected to implement measures that protected the environment, a process initiated by government legislation. While these factors affected the steel industry in general, Dofasco was under further pressure to keep its employees satisfied as they compared the company with its unionized, high-wage next-door neighbour, Stelco.

Management at Dofasco realized that to prevent the company from going under, it had to continue to make decisive changes, both administrative and technological. Beginning in the late 1980s, Dofasco implemented a significant restructuring program. The company reduced its management bureaucracy from seventeen layers to five, and through a series of voluntary (e.g., early retirement) and involuntary (e.g.,

layoffs) programs, the workforce was reduced from its 1989 level of 12,300 employees to about 8,700 by 1994. In keeping with its goal of improving the competitiveness of its cost structure, the company also sold nonstrategic assets and obsolete facilities in Hamilton. Joint ventures were also initiated, including one that involved a state-of-the-art mini-mill. Between 1980 and 1995, Dofasco also improved its technological capacities, spending over $3 billion on technology improvement—a higher expenditure as a percentage of sales than incurred by almost every other steelmaker in the world.

To maintain good employee morale, Dofasco also made a number of internal changes. Compensation systems became more performance-based, benefits were increased, health and safety standards were emphasized, and new educational and training programs were introduced. The company mission became more focused on providing customers with high-quality products, offering shareholders the best investment opportunities, enhancing employees' careers and personal development, and contributing to the needs of the community and the environment.

The restructuring process was successfully completed in 1994. In 1995, Dofasco announced a $200 million expansion of its steelmaking facilities. Intended to improve efficiency, the expansion raised employee morale and marked a strategic change in direction for Dofasco. Today, the company is once again a leader in its field.

Questions

1. Describe Dofasco's external environment. What implications does that have for the company? Why?

2. Describe Dofasco's internal environment. How does that contribute to the company's competitiveness?

3. Is top management support necessary for successful change? How did Dofasco's management contribute to change?

References: "This New Age of Steel" (Dofasco, 1997); Dofasco Annual Reports, various years; interviews with Dofasco's management representatives; "Dofasco Inc.," *Financial Post Historical Reports* (Financial Post Data Group, 1996); and Naresh Agarwal and Parbudyal Singh, "Organizational Rewards for a Changing Workplace," *International Journal for Technology Management* (forthcoming).

CHAPTER NOTES

1. Gaye Emery, "Overcoming Success at IBM," *Business Quarterly*, Winter 1994, pp. 38–44; Ian McGugan, "The New Blue," *Canadian Business*, March 1994, pp. 35–36; and Tamsen Tillson, "Be It Ever So Humble," *Canadian Business* (Special Technology Issue, 1995), pp. 27–31.

2. See Vivïan Brownstein and Joseph Spiers, "The Growing Threat of Inflation," *Fortune*, January 16, 1995, pp. 66–72, and John Huey, "Waking Up to the New Economy," *Fortune*, June 27, 1994, pp. 36–46, for an overview of how current economic conditions affect business. See also Jay B. Barney and William G. Ouchi (Eds.), *Organizational Economics* (San Francisco: Jossey-Bass, 1986), for a detailed analysis of linkages between economics and organizations.

3. Robert H. Hayes and Ramchandran Jaikumar, "Manufacturing's Crisis: New Technologies, Obsolete Organizations," *Harvard Business Review*, September–October 1988, pp. 77–85.

4. "Regulation Rises Again," *Business Week*, June 26, 1989, pp. 58–59.

5. See Ricky Griffin and Michael Pustay, *International Business: A Managerial Perspective* (Reading, Mass.: Addison-Wesley, 1996), for an overview.

6. Philip M. Rosenzweig and Jitendra V. Singh, "Organizational Environments and the Multinational Enterprise," *Academy of Management Journal*, June 1991, pp. 340–361.

7. Paul Krugman, "Competitiveness: Does It Matter?" *Fortune*, March 7, 1994, pp. 109–115.

8. Jeremy Main, "How to Steal the Best Ideas Around," *Fortune*, October 19, 1992, pp. 52–56.

9. See Ian C. MacMillan, "Controlling Competitive Dynamics by Taking Strategic Initiative," *The Academy of Management Executive*, May 1988, pp. 111–118, for an interesting view of influencing competitors.

10. "National Firms Find That Selling to Local Tastes Is Costly, Complex," *The Wall Street Journal*, July 9, 1987, p. 17. See also Regis McKenna, "Marketing in an Age of Diversity," *Harvard Business Review*, September–October 1988, pp. 88–95; and William Echikson, "Luxury Steals Back," *Fortune*, January 16, 1995, pp. 112–119.

11. Susan Helper, "How Much Has Really Changed Between U.S. Automakers and Their Suppliers?" *Sloan Management Review*, Summer 1991, pp. 15–28.

12. Myron Magnet, "The New Golden Rule of Business," *Fortune*, February 21, 1994, pp. 60–64.

13. "Many Businesses Blame Governmental Policies for Productivity Lag," *The Wall Street Journal*, October 28, 1980, pp. 1, 22.

14. "More Competitors Turn to Cooperation," *The Wall Street Journal*, June 23, 1989, p. B1.

15. Jeremy Main, "The Winning Organization," *Fortune*, September 26, 1988, pp. 50–60; and update by IBM Corporate Public Relations Office, October 1994.

16. "Time Warner Feels the Force of Stockholder Power," *Business Week*, July 21, 1991, pp. 58–59.

17. Karen Howlett and Paul Waldie, "Pension Funds: The Big Kids on the Block," *The Globe and Mail*, November 14, 1998, p. B1.

18. John J. Curran, "Companies That Rob the Future," *Fortune*, July 4, 1988, pp. 84–89.

19. Idalene F. Kesner, "Directors' Characteristics and Committee Membership: An Investigation of Type, Occupation, Tenure, and Gender," *Academy of Management Journal*, March 1988, pp. 66–84; and Jeffrey Kerr and Richard A. Bettis, "Boards of Directors, Top Management Compensation, and Shareholder Returns," *Academy of Management Journal*, December 1987, pp. 645–664.

20. Marsha Sinetar, "Building Trust into Corporate Relationships," *Organizational Dynamics*, Winter 1988, pp. 73–79.

21. Louis Richman, "The New Worker Elite," *Fortune*, August 22, 1994, pp. 56–66.

22. For a recent review, see Allen C. Bluedorn, "Pilgrim's Progress: Trends and Convergence in Research on Organizational Size and Environments," *Journal of Management*, Vol. 19, No. 2, 1993, pp. 163–191.

23. James D. Thompson, *Organizations in Action* (New York: McGraw-Hill, 1967).

24. Michael E. Porter, *Competitive Strategy: Techniques for Analyzing Industries and Competitors* (New York: Free Press, 1980).

25. Ian I. Mitroff, Paul Shrivastava, and Firdaus E. Udwadia, "Effective Crisis Management," *The Academy of Management Executive*, August 1987, pp. 283–292.

26. Christine Pearson and Ian Mitroff, "From Crisis Prone to Crisis Prepared: A Framework for Crisis Management," *The Academy of Management Executive*, Vol. 7, No. 1, 1993, pp. 48–59.

27. "Getting Business to Think About the Unthinkable," *Business Week*, June 24, 1991, pp. 104–107.

28. For recent discussions of how these processes work, see Barbara W. Keats and Michael A. Hitt, "A Causal Model of Linkages Among Environmental Dimensions, Macro Organizational Characteristics, and Performance," *Academy of Management Journal*, September 1988, pp. 570–598; and Danny Miller, "The Structural and Environmental Correlates of Business Strategy," *Strategic Management Journal*, Vol. 8, 1987, pp. 55–76.

29. "Why the Street Isn't Moved by Tenneco's Big Move," *Business Week*, September 26, 1988, pp. 130–133.

30. Tom Burns and G.M. Stalker, *The Management of Innovation* (London: Tavistock, 1961).

31. Keats and Hitt, "A Causal Model of Linkages Among Environmental Dimensions, Macro Organizational Characteristics, and Performance."

32. MacMillan, "Controlling Competitive Dynamics by Taking Strategic Initiative."

33. David B. Yoffie, "How an Industry Builds Political Advantage," *Harvard Business Review*, May–June 1988, pp. 82–89.

34. Gareth Jones, *Organizational Theory and Design* (Reading, Mass.: Addison-Wesley, 1995).

35. E. Yuchtman and S. Seashore, "A Systems Resource Approach to Organizational Effectiveness," *American Sociological Review*, Vol. 32, 1967, pp. 891–903.

36. B.S. Georgopoules and A.S. Tannenbaum, "The Study of Organizational Effectiveness," *American Sociological Review*, Vol. 22, 1957, pp. 534–540.

37. Jones, *Organizational Theory and Design*.

38. Kim Cameron, "Effectiveness as Paradox," *Management Science*, May 1986, pp. 539–553.

39. Terrence E. Deal and Allan A. Kennedy, *Corporate Cultures: The Rights and Rituals of Corporate Life* (Reading, Mass.: Addison-Wesley, 1982).

40. Gurney Breckenfield, "The Odyssey of Levi Strauss," *Fortune*, March 22, 1982, pp. 110–124. See also "Levi Strauss ... at $3 Billion Plus," *Daily News Record*, October 10, 1988, p. 44.

41. Jay B. Barney, "Organizational Culture: Can It Be a Source of Sustained Competitive Advantage?" *Academy of Management Review*, July 1986, pp. 656–665.

42. "Hewlett-Packard's Whip-Crackers," *Fortune*, February 13, 1989, pp. 58–59.

43. Benjamin Schneider, Sarah K. Gunnarson, and Kathryn Niles-Jolly, "Creating the Climate and Culture for Success," *Organizational Dynamics*, Summer 1994, pp. 17–29.

The Ethical and Social Context of Management

OBJECTIVES

After studying this chapter, you should be able to:

● *Discuss the formation of individual ethics and describe three areas of special ethical concern for managers.*

● *Trace the development of the concept of social responsibility and specify to whom or what an organization might be considered responsible.*

● *Identify and describe four types of organizational approaches to social responsibility.*

● *Explain the relationship between the government and organizations regarding social responsibility.*

● *Describe some of the activities organizations may engage in to manage social responsibility.*

OUTLINE

Bre-X Minerals Ltd. CEO David Walsh spear-headed what is being called the biggest gold mine fraud of the century.

In mid-June of 1997, Price-Waterhouse, which had been appointed to monitor Bre-X Minerals Ltd. while it was under bankruptcy protection, revealed that Bre-X had established a $7 million trust fund in December 1996—a fund intended to cover the legal costs of Bre-X's top officers and directors. In December 1996, Bre-X shares were trading at more than $20 and the company was being touted as the greatest mining success in history. Why was there a need for a legal trust fund in December 1996?

While the mining activities of Bre-X were to be carried out deep in the jungles of the Indonesian island of Borneo, the company's financial activities were global but concentrated in Canada. It is for this reason that what is now being called the greatest scam of the century is associated with Canada. The story of Bre-X begins with David Walsh, a struggling Calgary-based penny-stock promoter. Some time in 1993, Walsh contacted an old acquaintance, John Felderhof. Felderhof, a geologist, told Walsh about some promising properties in Borneo and eventually Walsh was able to

> **"The company that had a market capitalization of $6 billion at its peak is now under court-approved bankruptcy protection."**

raise the $250,000 needed to purchase the site of Bre-X's operations in Busang. Walsh, Felderhof, and Michael de Guzman, another geologist, then proceeded to spearhead an operation that at one time claimed that the Busang properties contained as much as 200 million ounces of gold worth approximately $100 billion. Bre-X shares soared and in May 1996 stood at $28, after a ten-for-one stock split. (Bre-X had started out as a penny stock.)

The company's claims of a huge gold find were not challenged until March 1997, when Freeport-McMoRan Copper & Gold Inc., an American mining firm appointed by the Indonesian government to mine the Busang site, found no evidence of the huge deposits Bre-X claimed it had discovered. In fact, Freeport concluded that there was practically no gold at the Busang site. The stock market reacted to the news in dramatic fashion. On March 26th, 1997, Bre-X shares crashed (from $15.50 to $2.50), and so did the computers at the Toronto Stock Exchange. The company that had a market capitalization of $6 billion at its peak is now under court-approved bankruptcy protection. Walsh (who died in 1998), Felderhof, and de Guzman (who apparently committed suicide just before Freeport's devastating revelation) were among those who made millions by selling Bre-X shares before March 26th, 1997. Of course, many others lost millions in the Bre-X scam. [1] ●

The Bre-X episode is an unfortunate example of one of the most challenging and controversial areas that organizations must face today—their relationship with the social environment in which they function. Every society proscribes certain types of behaviours, and organizations that violate these social expectations may face consequences including public humiliation, loss of business, and legal sanctions. The ingredients that determine how an organization will respond to its social environment are the ethics of individuals within the organization and the social responsibility of the organization itself.

This chapter explores the basic issues of ethics and social responsibility in detail. We first look at individual ethics and their organizational context. Next, we expand our discussion to the more general subject of social responsibility. After we explore the relationships among businesses and the government regarding socially responsible behaviour, we examine the activities organizations sometimes undertake to be more socially responsible.

INDIVIDUAL ETHICS IN ORGANIZATIONS

● **ethics**
An individual's personal beliefs regarding what is right and wrong or good and bad

● **ethical behaviour**
Behaviour that conforms to generally accepted social norms

● **unethical behaviour**
Behaviour that does not conform to generally accepted social norms

We define **ethics** as an individual's personal beliefs about whether a behaviour, action, or decision is right or wrong.[2] Although this definition communicates the essence of ethics, three of its implications warrant additional discussion. First, note that ethics are defined in the context of the individual—people have ethics, organizations do not. Second, what constitutes ethical behaviour varies from one person to another. For example, one person who finds a twenty-dollar bill on the floor believes that it is okay to stick it in his pocket whereas another feels compelled to turn it in to the lost-and-found department. Third, although **ethical behaviour** is in the eye of the beholder, it usually refers to behaviour that conforms to generally accepted social norms. **Unethical behaviour**, then, is behaviour that does not conform to generally accepted social norms. In the sections that follow, we discuss the factors that influence

Individual beliefs about what is right or wrong—one's ethics—vary from person to person. Numerous family and peer influences, life experiences, personal values and morals, and situational factors shape our ethics. The behaviour of Garth Drabinsky, who is accused of conspiracy and securities fraud, was likely due to each of these determinants.

the formation of individual ethics and consider ethical behaviour in an organizational context.

The Formation of Individual Ethics

As Figure 4.1 shows, an individual's ethics are determined by a combination of family influences, peer influences, life experiences, personal values and morals, and situational factors.

Family Influences   People start to form ethical standards as children in response to their perceptions of the behaviour of their parents and the behaviours their parents allow them to choose. Children are more likely to adopt high ethical standards if they see that other family members adhere to these high standards and if they receive rewards for conforming, and punishment for not conforming, to them. On the other hand, if family members engage in unethical behaviours and allow children to do the same, children are likely to develop low ethical standards.

Peer Influences   As children grow and enter school, they are also influenced by peers with whom they interact every day. For example, if a child's friends engage in shoplifting, vandalism, or drug abuse, he may decide to engage in these same activities. But if the child's peers have high ethical standards and reject such behaviours, the child is likely to adopt these standards.

Life Experiences   Dozens of important individual events shape people's lives and contribute to their ethical beliefs and behaviour. These events are a normal and routine part of growing up and maturing. Both positive and negative kinds of events shape an individual's ethics. For example, if a person steals something and does not get caught, she may feel no remorse and continue to steal. But if she is caught stealing she may feel guilty enough to revise her ethical standards and not steal in the future.

Personal Values and Morals   A person's values and morals also contribute to his or her ethical standards. A person who places financial gain and personal advancement at the top of his list of priorities, for example, will adopt a personal code of ethics that promotes the pursuit of wealth. Thus he may be ruthless in efforts to gain these rewards, regardless of the costs to others. In contrast, if a person's family is his top priority, he will adopt different ethical standards.[3]

F I G U R E   4 . 1 Determinants of Individual Ethics

Individual ethics are determined by family and peer influences, experiences, values and morals, and situational factors.

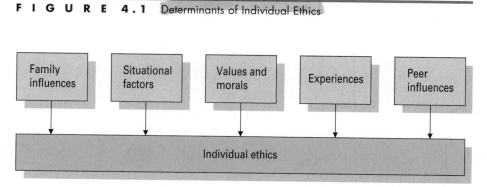

Situational Factors   Yet another determinant of an individual's ethics is situational factors that arise. Sometimes people find themselves in unexpected situations that cause them to act against their better judgment. For example, many people who steal money from their employers do so because of personal financial difficulties. Although an explanation such as this does not justify their theft, it does provide some context for understanding how people may behave unethically if they believe that they have no other choice.[4]

Managerial Ethics

- **managerial ethics**
Standards of behaviour that guide individual managers in their work

Managerial ethics are the standards of behaviour that guide individual managers in their work.[5] Although ethics can affect managerial work in any number of ways, three areas of special concern for managers are shown in Figure 4.2.

How an Organization Treats Its Employees   The behaviour of managers defines the ethical standards that determine how the organization treats its

There are three basic areas of concern for managerial ethics. These are the relationships of the firm to the employee, the employee to the firm, and the firm to other economic agents. Managers need to approach each set of relationships from an ethical and moral perspective.

F I G U R E   4 . 2   Managerial Ethics

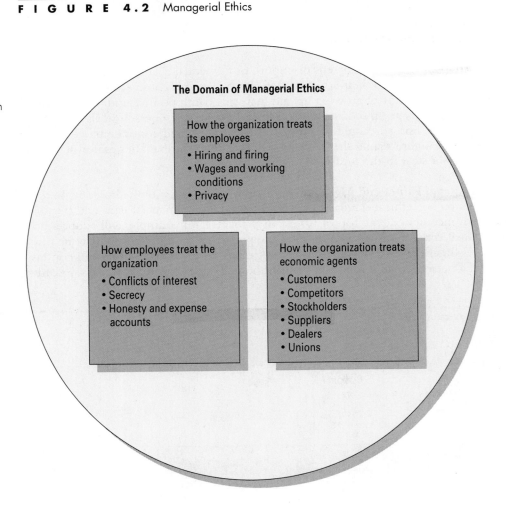

employees. This relationship includes areas such as hiring and firing, wages and working conditions, and employee privacy. For example, many people might consider it unethical for a manager to hire a family member or other close relative. Indeed, hiring or firing anyone for reasons that are not job-related represents questionable ethical practices.

Wages and working conditions, while also tightly regulated, are also areas of potential controversy. For example, a manager paying an employee less than he deserves, simply because the manager knows the employee cannot afford to quit or risk losing his job by complaining, might be considered unethical. In July 1998, the Canadian Human Rights Tribunal awarded an estimated $4 billion settlement to 200,000 (mainly female) federal government employees whom the tribunal ruled were underpaid in comparison to federal employees in male-dominated jobs. The federal government appealed the tribunal's decision, claiming that there was confusion over how to calculate pay equity awards. [6]

Finally, most observers also would agree that an organization is obligated to protect the privacy of its employees. A manager's spreading a rumour that an employee has AIDS or is having an affair with a co-worker is generally seen as an unethical breach of privacy. Likewise, the manner in which an organization responds to and addresses issues associated with sexual harassment also involves employee privacy and related rights. [7]

How Employees Treat the Organization   Numerous ethical issues also relate to how employees treat the organization, especially in regard to conflicts of interest, secrecy, and honesty in keeping expense accounts. A conflict of interest occurs when a decision potentially benefits the individual to the possible detriment of the organization. For example, if a manager in charge of selecting a new supplier accepts gifts from one supplier trying to land the account, he may award the contract to that supplier even though another one might have offered the firm a better deal. To avoid such conflicts of interest, Wal-Mart does not allow its merchandise buyers to accept meals or gifts from sales representatives. [8]

Divulging company secrets is also clearly unethical. Employees who work for businesses in highly competitive industries—electronics, software, and fashion apparel, for example—might be tempted to sell information about company plans to competitors. In late 1994, an executive at Eastman Kodak wrote a confidential memo to other managers pointing out that profit projections were not being met and implementing severe cost-control measures. Someone inside the company leaked the memo to the press; resultant media coverage of the memo caused the firm's market capitalization to plunge $1.1 billion (U.S.) in two days. [9]

A third area of concern for some organizations is expense accounts, or budgets that organizations provide to their managers for travel, entertainment, and other expenses related to doing business. Some managers have been found to routinely add or inflate meal expenses, service charges, and car mileage to their expense account reports to unethically pad their income. They also occasionally pay more than they need to for full-fare coach airline tickets (instead of buying corporate-rate discounted coach tickets) to make upgrading them to first class easier.

How the Organization Treats Other Economic Agents   Managerial ethics also come into play in the relationship between the firm and other economic agents. For example, businesses need to maintain an ethical posture toward their customers. Normal business ethics in customer relations suggest that products and services be safe; be accompanied by information about product features, uses, and limitations; and be appropriately priced.[10] The behaviour of managers toward competitors is also dictated by ethical standards. Unfair business practices (for example, pricing products low to drive a competitor out of business) and denigration of competitors (such as making false claims in advertising about a competitor's products) are examples of unethical treatment of competitors.

Similarly, ethical standards also dictate that managers be truthful with shareholders (were Bre-X managers being truthful with shareholders?).[11] Managers should also be fair and honest with suppliers, dealers, and unions. Convincing a supplier that the company needs a price break because of impending losses is unethical if the firm actually expects to make a profit.

Ethics in an Organizational Context

It is vital to note that ethical or unethical actions by particular managers do not occur in a vacuum.[12] Indeed, they most often occur in an organizational context that is conducive to them. Actions of peer managers and top managers, as well as the organization's culture, all contribute to the ethical context of the organization.

The starting point in understanding the ethical context of management is the individual's own ethical standards. Some people, for example, will risk personal embarrassment or lose their job before they would do something they considered unethical. Other people are much more easily swayed by the unethical behaviour they see around them and other situational factors, and they may be willing to commit major crimes to further their own careers or for financial gain. Organizational practices may strongly influence the ethical standards of employees. Some organizations openly permit unethical business practices as long as they are in the best interests of the firm.

If a manager becomes aware of an unethical practice and allows it to continue, she has contributed to the organizational culture that says such activity is permitted. For example, when the CEO of Beech-Nut discovered that his firm was using additives in its apple juice advertised as 100 percent pure, he decided to try to cover up the deception until the remaining juice could be disposed of. Many employees participated in his plan. When the cover-up was finally discovered, the company suffered grave damages to its reputation and had to pay several million dollars in fines. In addition, the CEO was sentenced to a jail term.[13]

The organization's environment also contributes to the context for ethical behaviour. In a highly competitive or regulated industry, for example, a manager may feel more pressure to achieve high performance. For example, the *Environment of Management* box details how managers at Kidder Peabody blamed their ethical lapses on performance pressures from parent company General Electric.

Managing Ethical Behaviour

Spurred partially by the recent spate of ethical scandals and partially from a sense of enhanced corporate consciousness about the importance of ethical and unethical behaviours, many organizations have reemphasized ethical behaviour on the part of employees.[14] This emphasis takes many forms, but any effort to enhance ethical behaviour must begin with top management. Top management establishes

GE!—Gee Whiz

General Electric Co. (GE) is a vast conglomerate that makes large household appliances, jet aircraft engines, medical equipment, and thermoplastics. GE also owns several television stations including NBC, and it is a potent force in the world of finance through its GE Capital, Employers Reinsurance, and Kidder Peabody subsidiaries.

Over the years, GE has been accused of a lot of bad things—sexism and racism in hiring, supplying faulty components to nuclear plants, cheating the Pentagon, and using PCBs in some of its plastics, just to name a few. Some of these charges have been substantiated, but others have not. But to help address the controversy, justified or not, GE created an ethics program for its employees and has established manager-directed volunteer projects to rehabilitate inner-city areas. Nevertheless, the firm's latest scandal—phony profits reported for Kidder Peabody—suggests poor management that runs deep.

When GE took over Kidder Peabody in 1989, it was suffering from an insider-trading scandal. Managers identified ensuring future integrity in the management of the firm as a number-one priority for GE. Nevertheless, GE's dual emphasis on earning profits and cutting costs was also brought to Kidder Peabody. Recent findings suggest that for three years, one individual trader reported millions of dollars in phony profits without top management, auditors, or anyone else doing anything about it. He, of course, claims that his bosses knew what he was doing; they, of course, claim that they did not.

GE hired a former Securities and Exchange Commission official to write an internal report on the Kidder Peabody problem. That report suggested that, although only a single individual committed fraud, GE's management was lax and guilty of poor judgment. The report, in turn, was also criticized by the business press for numerous omissions that suggested other problems as well. GE has removed the top executives of Kidder Peabody and replaced them with financial officers from GE. Maybe ethics will finally receive the attention it merits and GE will be able to continue its effective pursuit of its goals without having to worry about future scandals.

References: "Is Jack Welch Seeing Green?" *Business Week*, September 12, 1994, p. 33; Terence P. Paré, "Jack Welch's Nightmare on Wall Street," *Fortune*, September 5, 1994, pp. 40–48; Eric F. Coppolino, "Pandora's Poison," *Sierra*, September 1, 1994, pp. 40–45; Gary Weiss, "What Lynch Left Out," *Business Week*, August 22, 1994, pp. 60–62; "The Smoke at General Electric," *Financial World*, August 16, 1994, pp. 32–35; "Collision Course at Kidder," *Business Week*, August 8, 1994, pp. 60–61; Gary Hoover, Alta Campbell, and Patrick J. Spain (Eds.) *Hoover's Handbook of American Business 1994* (Austin, Tex.: The Reference Press, 1993), pp. 540–541; and Milton Moskowitz, Robert Levering, and Michael Chat, *Everybody's Business* (New York: Doubleday, 1990), pp. 555–559.

the organization's culture and defines what will and will not be acceptable behaviour. Some companies have also started offering employees training in how to cope with ethical dilemmas. At Boeing, for example, line managers lead training sessions for other employees, and the company also has an ethics committee that reports directly to the board of directors. The training sessions involve discussions of different ethical dilemmas that employees might face and how managers might handle those dilemmas. Chemical Bank, Xerox, and McDonnell Douglas have also established ethics training programs for their managers.[15]

Organizations are also going to greater lengths to formalize their ethical standards. Some, such as Provigo and Abitibi-Price, have prepared guidelines that detail how employees are to treat suppliers, customers, competitors, and other constituents. Others, such as Whirlpool and Hewlett-Packard, have developed formal **codes of ethics**—written statements of the values and ethical standards that guide the firms' actions. The code of ethics of Cominco Ltd., a Vancouver-based international mining and metal company, is reproduced in Figure 4.3.

● **code of ethics**
A formal, written statement of the values and ethical standards that guide a firm's

A Commitment to Ethical Business Conduct

1. The Company and its employees shall comply with all lawful requirements, both domestic and foreign, applicable to Company's business.

2. Employees shall not offer, or furnish on behalf of the Company, expensive gifts or excessive entertainment or benefits to other persons.

3. The Company's books and records must reflect, in an accurate and timely manner, all Company transactions.

4. Employees shall not use their employment status to obtain personal gain or benefit from other employees or from doing or seeking to do business with the Company.

5. The use of Company funds, goods or services as contributions to political parties, candidates, campaigns or referenda is forbidden, unless authorized by the Board of Directors.

6. All dealings between employees of the Company and public officials or other persons are to be conducted in a manner that will not compromise the integrity or question the reputation on any public official or other persons, the Company or its affiliates.

7. Employees must avoid all situations in which their personal interest conflict or might appear in conflict with their duties to the Company.

8. Unless previously published, the Company's record, reports, papers, devices, processes, plans, methods and apparatus are considered by the Company to be secret and confidential and employees are prohibited from revealing information concerning such matters without proper authorization.

9. Inside information obtained as a result of an individual's employment with the Company shall never be disclosed to others nor used for personal financial gain.

10. Employees will support and promote the Company policy to provide a work environment within which individuals are treated with respect, provided with equality of opportunity based on merit and kept free of all forms of discrimination.

Although the various matters dealt with in this Code do not cover the full spectrum of employee activities, they are indicative of the Company's commitment to the maintenance of high standards of conduct and are to be considered descriptive of the type of behaviour expected from employees in all circumstances.

Reprinted with permission Cominco Ltd. (A mining and metals company based in Vancouver.)

Of course, no code, guideline, or training program can truly make up for the quality of an individual's personal judgment about what is right behaviour and what is wrong behaviour in a particular situation. Such devices may prescribe what people should do, but they often fail to help people understand and live with the consequences of their choices. Making ethical choices may lead to very unpleasant outcomes—firing, rejection by colleagues, and the forfeiture of monetary gain, to name a few. The manager at Beech-Nut who alerted authorities to the apple juice deception eventually resigned because others thought he was a traitor to the organization. Similarly, the head of the traffic and cargo department of the Spanish subsidiary of Toronto-based Boliden Ltd. was forced into early retirement after he warned, in 1996, of an ecological disaster at the company's zinc mine. (His prediction came true in April 1998, when a dam holding toxic waste burst, spilling five million cubic metres of sludge into the Guadiamar River system and threatening the ecological balance in Donana National Park, one of the most important ecological sites in Europe.[16]) Thus managers must be prepared to confront their own consciences and weigh the options available when making difficult ethical decisions.[17]

SOCIAL RESPONSIBILITY AND ORGANIZATIONS

As we have seen, ethics relate to individuals. Organizations themselves do not have ethics, but organizations do relate to their environment in ways that often

Mining disasters have claimed many lives. The 1992 explosion at the Westray mine in Nova Scotia killed 26 miners.

involve ethical dilemmas and decisions. **Social responsibility** is the set of obligations an organization has to protect and enhance the society in which it functions.[18] The sections that follow trace historical and contemporary views of social responsibility, identify organizational constituencies, and describe the types of approaches an organization might take toward the social or environmental consequences of its practices.

Historical Views of Social Responsibility

Views of social responsibility held by organizations, the government, and the public at large have changed dramatically over the last hundred years. In particular, there have been three critical turning points in the evolution of social responsibility.[19] While these historical periods reflect developments in the United States, Canada has also been influenced by them.

The first period, called the **entrepreneurial era**, occurred in the United States during the late 1800s. The so-called Captains of Industry, including John D. Rockefeller, Cornelius Vanderbilt, J.P. Morgan, and Andrew Carnegie, were amassing fortunes and building empires in industries including oil, railroads, banking, and steel. Before their time, virtually all businesses were small, so these men were truly the first executives to control power and wield influence at a national level. Unfortunately, they often chose to abuse their power through such practices as labour lockouts, discriminatory pricing policies, kickbacks, blackmail, and tax evasion. Eventually, outcries from public officials forced the government to outlaw some business practices and restrict others. These laws were important in that they defined a relationship among business, the government, and society and indicated for the first time that business had a role to play in society beyond the pure maximization of profit.

Subtle changes in views toward social responsibility continued throughout the early part of the century, but the next turning point did not occur until the **Depression era** of the 1930s. By this time, large organizations had come to truly dominate the U.S. economy, and many people criticized them for irresponsible financial practices that led to the stock market crash of 1929. As a part of Franklin Roosevelt's New Deal, the government passed several more laws to protect investors and smaller businesses, and the Securities and Exchange Commission was created in 1934 to regulate the sales of securities and curb unfair stock market practices. As an outgrowth of these and other actions, the social responsibility of organizations was more clearly delineated. In particular, the new governmental actions insisted that organizations take an active role in promoting the general welfare of the public.

The third major turning point in social responsibility came during the **social era** of the 1960s. This period of history was characterized by a great deal of social unrest. The civil rights movement and opposition to the war in Vietnam in particular energized the public to examine the values, priorities, and goals of the United States and its allies. Government once again took a close look at organizational practices. Tighter restrictions on pollution, consumer warnings on products such as cigarettes and flammable children's clothing, and increased regulation of many other industries all grew from concerns that were raised during this period. This growing trend toward social responsibility raises two important questions: (1) exactly to whom is business responsible, and (2) who in an organization is ultimately accountable for the organization's practices? We address both these questions in the next section.

Areas of Social Responsibility

Organizations may exercise social responsibility toward their constituents, toward the natural environment, and toward the general social welfare. Social entities closer to the organization have a clear and immediate stake in what the organization does, whereas those further removed have an ambiguous and long-term stake in the organization and its practices.

Organizational Constituents   In Chapter 3, we described the task environment of organizations as those individuals, groups, or organizations that directly affect a particular organization but are not part of the organization. Another view of that same network is in terms of **organizational constituents**, or those people and organizations who are directly affected by the practices of an organization and that have a stake in its performance. Major constituents are depicted in Figure 4.4.

The interests of people who own and invest in an organization are affected by virtually anything the firm does. If the firm's managers commit criminal acts or violate acceptable ethical standards, the resulting bad press and public outcry will likely hurt the organization's profits and share prices. Organizations also have a responsibility to their creditors. If poor social performance hurts an organization's abilities to repay its debts, those creditors and their employees will also suffer.

● **Depression era**
A period of time from 1929 through the 1930s during which the public blamed business for economic problems and sought to regulate business through government to prevent such problems in the future

● **social era**
A period of great social unrest during the 1960s during which business was seen as responsible for social problems and called on to help redress those problems

● **organizational constituents**
People and organizations who are directly affected by the behaviours of an organization and who have a stake in its performance

A firm that engages in socially irresponsible practices toward some of its constituents is asking for trouble. For example, a few years ago managers at Allegheny International spent a half million dollars to buy a lavish Pittsburgh home in which to entertain clients. The firm maintained a fleet of five corporate jets so that its managers could travel anywhere at any time. While entertaining and travel are normal parts of doing business, Allegheny went too far. The company also made large loans to employees at a 2 percent interest rate. Nepotism in hiring was rampant. A close analysis of Allegheny's performance during this period suggested that it spent too much on executive perquisites, that conflicts of interest clouded executive judgment, that improper accounting methods were employed, that managers withheld information from shareholders, and that the board of directors inadequately monitored top management. Consequently, other constituents such as investors (who received lower dividends), the government (which received fewer tax dollars), the court system (which was eventually forced to deal with Allegheny's improprieties), and employees (who might have been paid higher wages under other circumstances) all were affected.[20]

On the other hand, consider Levi Strauss. The company gives 2.4 percent of its pretax earnings to social causes, treats its employees and suppliers with dignity and respect, plays an active role in important trade associations, has had no major ethical scandals, is respected by its competitors, maintains good relations with government regulatory agencies, and contributes to college and university scholarship programs. This record suggests that managers at Levi Strauss are

---

F I G U R E 4.4 Organizational Constituents

All organizations have a variety of constituents that are directly affected by the organization and that have a stake in its performance. These are people and organizations to whom an organization should be responsible.

doing an excellent job of maintaining good relations with the firm's constituents.[21]

Not all organizations do as well as Levi Strauss in attending to constituents, but most make an effort to take a socially responsible stance toward three main groups: customers, employees, and investors. Lands' End, a mail-order firm, is a good example of a company that has profited from good customer relations. Its operators are trained to be completely informed about company policies and products, to avoid pushing customers into buying unwanted merchandise, to listen to complaints, and to treat customers with respect. As a result, the company's sales have been increasing 20 percent each year.[22] Organizations that are socially responsible in their dealings with employees treat workers fairly, make them a part of the team, and respect their dignity and basic human needs.

To maintain a socially responsible stance toward investors, managers should follow proper accounting procedures, provide appropriate information to shareholders about the financial performance of the firm, and manage the organization to protect shareholder rights and investments. Insider trading, illegal stock manipulation, and withholding financial data are examples of recent wrongdoings attributed to many different businesses. Executives at Phar-Mor Inc., a Midwestern American discount retailer, kept two sets of financial records, one for public consumption and one to help them keep track of their own illegal financial transactions—personal bonuses and fraud, for example.[23]

The Natural Environment A second critical area of social responsibility relates to the natural environment. Not long ago, many organizations indiscriminately dumped sewage, waste products from production, and trash into streams and rivers, into the air, and on vacant land. Now, however, many laws regulate the disposal of waste materials. In many instances, companies themselves have become more socially responsible in their release of pollutants. Consequently, most forms of air and water pollution have decreased, although ocean dumping of sewage sludge is still widespread. Still, much remains to be done. Companies need to develop economically feasible ways to avoid contributing to acid rain and global warming; to avoid depleting the ozone layer; and to develop alternative methods of handling sewage, hazardous wastes, and ordinary garbage.[24] The Procter & Gamble Co., for example, is an industry leader in using recycled materials for containers, and Hyatt Corp. recently established a new company to help recycle waste products from its hotels.

Companies also need to develop safety policies that cut down on accidents with potentially disastrous environmental results. When one of Ashland Oil's storage tanks ruptured a few years ago, spilling more than 500,000 gallons of diesel fuel into Pennsylvania's Monongahela River, the company moved quickly to clean up the spill but was still indicted for violating U.S. environmental laws.[25] After Exxon oil tanker *Valdez* spilled millions of gallons of oil off the coast of Alaska, it adopted new and more stringent procedures to keep another disaster from happening. It remains to be seen how the disaster at Boliden's Spanish zinc mine will affect its practices.

General Social Welfare Some people believe that in addition to treating constituents and the environment responsibly, business organizations also should promote the general welfare of society. Examples include making contributions to charities, philanthropic organizations, and not-for-profit foundations and associations; supporting museums, symphonies, and public radio and television; and taking a role in improving public health and education.[26] Some people also believe that organizations should act to correct, or at least not contribute to, the political inequities that exist in the world. A well-publicized expression of this viewpoint in the late 1980s was the argument that multinational corporations should end their operations in South Africa to protest that nation's policies of apartheid.[27] Companies like Eastman Kodak and IBM responded to these concerns by selling their operations in South Africa. More recently, since that country abandoned apartheid, firms like Nike and Reebok have each started new operations in South Africa in cooperation with local black business partners.[28]

Arguments For and Against Social Responsibility

On the surface, there seems to be little disagreement about the need for organizations to be socially responsible. In truth, though, those who oppose wide interpretations of social responsibility use several convincing arguments.[29] Some of the more salient arguments on both sides of this contemporary debate are summarized in Figure 4.5 and further explained in the following sections.

Arguments For Social Responsibility   People who argue in favour of social responsibility claim that because organizations create many of the problems that need to be addressed, such as air and water pollution and resource depletion, they should play a major role in solving them. They also argue that because corporations are legally defined entities with most of the same privileges as private citizens, businesses should not try to avoid their obligations as citizens. Advocates of social responsibility point out that while governmental organizations have stretched their budgets to the limit, many large businesses

---

FIGURE 4.5   Arguments For and Against Social Responsibility

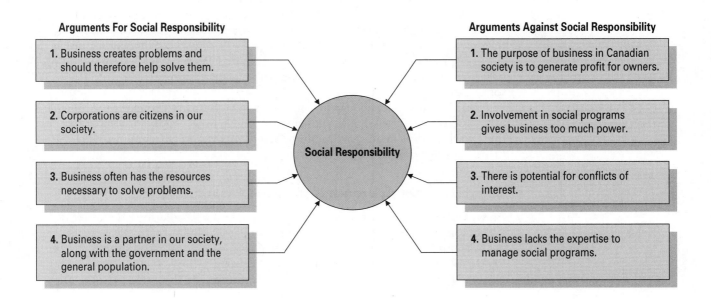

often have surplus revenues that could potentially be used to help solve social problems. For example, IBM routinely donates surplus computers to schools.

Although each of the arguments just summarized is a distinct justification for socially responsible behaviours on the part of organizations, another more general reason for social responsibility is profit itself. For example, organizations that make clear and visible contributions to society can achieve enhanced reputations and garner greater market share for their products. Although claims of socially responsible activities can haunt a company if they are exaggerated or untrue, they can also work to the benefit of both the organization and society if the advertised benefits are true and accurate. For example, during MCI's advertising campaign for its contributions to reforestation, the firm's spokesperson acknowledged that the firm was doing it to get more business. But she went on to argue that that was okay because everybody could win: the consumer would get a good product for a competitive price, the firm would increase its profits, and the natural environment would get more trees.

Arguments Against Social Responsibility Some people, including the famous economist Milton Friedman, argue that widening the interpretation of social responsibility will undermine free market economies by detracting from the basic mission of business: to earn profits for owners. For example, money that the Royal Bank of Canada or Chrysler Canada contributes to social causes or charities is money that could otherwise be distributed to shareholders as a dividend. Another objection to deepening the social responsibility of businesses points out that corporations already wield enormous power and that their activity in social programs gives them even more power.

Other arguments against social responsibility focus on the potential for conflict of interest. Suppose, for example, that one manager is in charge of deciding which local social program or charity will receive a large grant from her business. The local civic opera company (a not-for-profit organization that relies on contributions for its existence) might offer her front-row tickets for the upcoming season in exchange for her support. If opera is her favourite form of music, she might be tempted to direct the money toward the local company, when it might actually be needed more in other areas.[30]

Finally, critics argue that organizations lack the expertise to understand how to assess and make decisions about worthy social programs. Beyond the conflict of interest example just noted, how can a company truly know which cause or program is most deserving of its support? People who ask these questions also see an alarming trend on the part of organizations to tie products to social causes.

Critics of this practice fear that it will enable companies to exert too much influence over the charitable causes with which they become associated and that charities will begin to function merely as marketing agents to help the firms sell their products.[31]

Organizational Approaches to Social Responsibility

As we have seen, some people advocate a larger social role for organizations, and others argue that the role is already too large. Not surprisingly, organizations themselves adopt a wide range of positions on social responsibility. As Figure 4.6 illustrates, the four stances that an organization can take concerning its obligations to society fall along a continuum ranging from the lowest to the highest degree of socially responsible practices.

Social Obstruction   The few organizations that take what might be called a **social obstruction** approach to social responsibility usually do as little as possible to solve social or environmental problems. When they cross the ethical or legal line that separates acceptable from unacceptable practices, their typical response is to deny or cover up their actions. We note earlier Beech-Nut's attempt to hide the truth about its apple juice additives. Is this the strategy that Fortune Financial, one of Canada's largest mutual fund distributors, has chosen to follow? In April 1998, faced with an investigation by the Ontario Securities Commission (OSC), the company effectively fired its vice president of compliance before his testimony to OSC investigators. [32]

● **social obstruction**
An approach to social responsibility in which firms do as little as possible to solve social or environmental problems

Social Obligation   One step removed from social obstruction is **social obligation**, whereby the organization will do everything that is required of it legally but nothing more. Wal-Mart attempts to follow this approach when it continues to sell guns but follow all associated government regulations. This approach is most consistent with the arguments used against social responsibility just described. Managers in organizations that take a social obligation approach insist that their job is to generate profits. For example, such a firm would install pollution control equipment dictated by law, but would not install higher-quality equipment even though it might limit pollution further. Tobacco companies such as Philip Morris Incorporated take this position regarding their international marketing efforts. In the United States, they are legally required to include warnings to smokers on their products and to limit their advertising to prescribed media. Domestically they follow these rules to the letter of the law but use stronger marketing methods in countries that have no such rules. In many African countries, for example, cigarettes are heavily promoted, contain higher levels of tar and nicotine than those sold in the United States, and carry few or no health warning labels. The *Managing in a Changing World* box explores this issue in more detail.

● **social obligation**
A social responsibility stance in which an organization does everything that is required of it legally but nothing more

Social Response   A firm that adopts the **social response** approach meets its legal and ethical requirements but will also go beyond these requirements in selected cases. Such firms voluntarily agree to participate in social programs, but solicitors have to convince the organization that the programs are worthy of their support. Both Exxon and IBM, for example, will match contributions made by their employees to selected charitable causes. And many organizations will respond to requests for donations to Little League, Girl Guides, and so forth. The point, though, is that someone has to knock on the door and ask—the organizations do not proactively seek such avenues for contributing.

● **social response**
A social responsibility stance in which an organization meets its basic legal and ethical obligations and also goes beyond social obligation in selected cases

F I G U R E   4 . 6   Approaches to Social Responsibility

Degree of Social Responsibility

Social obstruction	Social obligation	Social response	Social contribution

Lowest   *Highest*

Organizations can adopt a variety of approaches to social responsibility. For example, a firm that never considers the consequences of its decisions and tries to hide its transgressions is taking a social opposition stance. At the other extreme, a firm that actively seeks to identify areas where it can help society is pursuing a social contribution approach.

Tobacco's Future

 It's no secret that smoking is unpopular today. Many businesses in Canada and the United States banish smoking to limited areas, and many others have abolished it altogether. The proportion of smokers in the Canadian population has declined from one in two in the 1960s to less than one in three today. However, a disproportionate number of the poorest Canadians smoke. The number of smokers (as a percentage of the U.S. population eighteen years of age and older) has also been steadily declining for more than twenty years—from 37.1 percent in 1974 down to only 25 percent in 1994. The U.S. tobacco industry's political action committee (PAC) contributions to federal politicians have gone from zero to more than $3 million (U.S.) during that same period of time. A coincidence? Hardly! While there are no PACs in Canada, the tobacco lobby here is quite strong. The Canadian tobacco industry is dominated by Imperial Tobacco, which has a 68 percent share of the domestic cigarette market.

The domestic tobacco market is shrinking largely as a result of continuing reports of the health and safety dangers of smoking. Some 40,000 Canadians died in 1998 from smoking-related illnesses. In addition, the industry has also been charged with knowing of those dangers for some time. Nevertheless, the U.S. tobacco industry has massive public relations advertising campaigns; is spending huge sums on political lobbying efforts at local, state, and federal levels; and is involved in aggressive litigation in an effort to stave off the progressive decline in its basic market.

The tobacco industry has been fighting this battle for years. Filter cigarettes were introduced after the first reports in 1953 that linked smoking to cancer. Then individual companies began to diversify as the cigarette market began to shrink. Philip Morris Companies acquired Miller Brewing Company, General Foods Corporation, and Kraft General Foods; R.J. Reynolds Tobacco Co. acquired Nabisco Brands to become RJR Nabisco; and B.A.T. Industries PLC (formed from a merger of the American Tobacco Company in the United States with the Imperial Tobacco Company of Britain) has moved into and out of numerous nontobacco enterprises.

The most recent move to protect the industry's sales and profits, however, is by international expansion. Because Europe may be moving toward regulating tobacco advertising, the main markets in which the tobacco industry will want to expand are those in Asia and the Third World. Philip Morris, for instance, now derives more than half of its tobacco profits from its international sales (up from less than 30 percent in 1989), and RJR Nabisco is nearing 40 percent (up from just over 10 percent in 1989). Critics question the ethics of moving from a market with relatively informed consumers who are beginning to reject the product to another where the consumers are less knowledgeable.

References: "The Uncertain Future of Tobacco Advertising in the European Community," *Boston College International and Comparative Law*, Vol. 17, No. 1, Winter 1994, pp. 177–210; "Tobacco: Does It Have a Future?" *Business Week*, July 4, 1994, pp. 24–29; Gary Hoover, Alta Campbell, and Patrick J. Spain (Eds.), *Hoover's Handbook of American Business: Profiles of Over 500 Major U.S. Corporations* (Austin, Tex: The Reference Press, 1993), p. 436; Milton Moskowitz, Robert Levering, and Michael Chat, *Everybody's Business* (New York: Doubleday, 1990), pp. 313–322; and Rachel Duplisea, "Poor Smoke More, Study Discloses," *The Windsor Star*, July 5, 1997, p. F14.

● **social contribution**
A social responsibility stance in which an organization views itself as a citizen in a society and proactively seeks opportunities to contribute to that society

Social Contribution The highest degree of social responsibility that a firm can exhibit is the **social contribution** approach. Firms that adopt this approach take to heart the arguments in favour of social responsibility. They view themselves as citizens in a society and proactively seek opportunities to contribute. An excellent example of a social contribution is the Ronald McDonald House program undertaken by McDonald's Corp. These houses, located close to major medical centres, can be used by families for minimal cost while their sick children are receiving medical treatment nearby. This and related activities and programs exceed the social response approach—they indicate a sincere and potent commitment to improving the general social welfare.

Remember that these categories are not discrete but merely define stages along a continuum of approaches. Organizations do not always fit neatly into one category. The Ronald McDonald House program has been widely applauded, for example, but McDonald's also came under fire a few years ago for allegedly misleading consumers about the nutritional value of its food products.[33] And even though Beech-Nut took a social obstruction approach in the case we cited, many individual employees and managers at the firm have no doubt made substantial contributions to society in a number of different ways.

THE GOVERNMENT AND SOCIAL RESPONSIBILITY

Government plays an increasing part in shaping the role of organizations in contemporary society. The relationship between organizations and government is two-way, however. As Figure 4.7 shows, organizations and the government use several methods in their attempts to influence each other.

How Government Influences Organizations

The government attempts to shape social responsibility practices through both direct and indirect channels. Direct influence most frequently is manifested through regulation, whereas indirect influence can take a number of forms, most notably taxation policies.

Direct Regulation The government most often directly influences organizations through **regulation**, or the establishment of laws and rules that dictate what organizations can and cannot do. To implement legislation, the government creates special agencies to monitor and control certain aspects of business

● **regulation**
Government's attempts to influence business by establishing laws and rules that dictate what businesses can and cannot do in prescribed areas

────

Business and the government influence each other in a variety of ways. Government influence can be direct or indirect. Business influence relies on personal contacts, lobbying, PACs, and favours. Federal Express, for example, has a very active political action committee, or PAC.

F I G U R E   4 . 7   How Business and the Government Influence Each Other

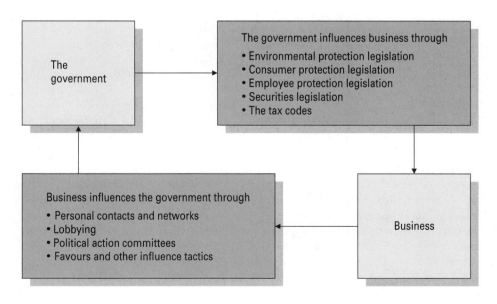

The government

The government influences business through
• Environmental protection legislation
• Consumer protection legislation
• Employee protection legislation
• Securities legislation
• The tax codes

Business influences the government through
• Personal contacts and networks
• Lobbying
• Political action committees
• Favours and other influence tactics

Business

activity. For example, Environment Canada and respective provincial agencies handle environmental issues; the Department of Consumer and Corporate Affairs handles consumer-related concerns; various human rights commissions and labour relations boards help protect employees; and securities commissions handle investor-related issues. These agencies have the power to levy fines or bring charges against organizations that violate regulations. Although these are some of the major Canadian governmental regulating agencies, many other more specialized agencies operate at both federal and provincial levels.

Indirect Regulation   Other forms of regulation are indirect. For example, the government can indirectly influence the social responsibility of organizations through its tax codes. In effect, the government can influence how organizations spend their social responsibility dollars by providing greater or lesser tax incentives. For instance, suppose that the federal government wanted organizations to spend more on training the hard-core unemployed. Parliament could then pass laws that provided tax incentives to companies that opened new training facilities. As a result, more businesses would probably do so. Of course, some critics argue that regulation is already excessive. They maintain that a free market system would eventually accomplish the same goals as regulation with lower costs to both organizations and the government.

How Organizations Influence Government

As we mentioned in Chapter 3, organizations can influence their environment in many different ways. Organizations have four main methods of addressing governmental pressures for more social responsibility.

Personal Contacts   Because many corporate executives and political leaders travel in the same social circles, personal contacts and networks offer one method of influence. A business executive may be able to contact a politician directly regarding a piece of legislation being considered.

● **lobbying**
The use of persons or groups to formally represent a company or group of companies before political bodies to influence legislation

Lobbying   **Lobbying,** or the use of persons or groups to formally represent an organization or group of organizations before political bodies, is also an effective way to influence the government. The Business Council on National Issues (BCNI) maintains an office in Ottawa and is regarded as the voice of Canadian business on public policy issues. Its long-serving president and CEO, Thomas d'Aquino, is regarded as a very effective lobbyist, and the organization itself comprises the CEOs of 150 of Canada's leading corporations.

● **political action committee (PAC)**
An organization created to solicit and distribute money to political candidates

Political Action   Corporations in Canada can legally make direct donations to political parties. Historically, at the federal level, the main beneficiaries of such contributions have been the Liberal Party and the Progressive Conservative Party. In the United States, companies themselves cannot legally make direct donations to political campaigns, so they influence the government through political action committees. **Political action committees (PACs)** are special organizations created to solicit money and then distribute it to political candidates. Employees of a firm may be encouraged to make donations to particular PACs because managers know that it will support candidates with political views similar to their own. PACs, in turn, make the contributions themselves, usually to a broad slate of state and national candidates.

Favours Finally, organizations sometimes rely on favours and other influence tactics to gain support. Although favours may be legal, they are still subject to criticism. A few years back, for example, two influential members of a U.S. House of Representatives committee attending a fundraising function in Miami were needed in Washington to finish work on a piece of legislation that Federal Express wanted passed. The law being drafted would allow the company and its competitors to give their employees standby seats on airlines as a tax-free benefit. As a favour, Federal Express provided one of its corporate jets to fly the committee members back to Washington.[34] The company was eventually reimbursed for its expenses, so its assistance was not illegal, but some people argue that such actions are dangerous because of how they might be perceived.

Bribes, blackmail, and other tactics have also been part of the arsenal businesses call on to make their wishes known to important government officials. For example, on May 1, 1998, a Quebec court found Guy Montpetit guilty of trying to buy the influence of Senator Michel Cogger. Cogger received $212,000 from the businessman to help him obtain federal funding for a factory.[35]

MANAGING SOCIAL RESPONSIBILITY

The demands for social responsibility placed on contemporary organizations by an increasingly sophisticated and educated public are probably stronger than ever. As we have seen, there are pitfalls for managers who fail to adhere to high ethical standards and for companies that try to circumvent their legal obligations. Organizations therefore need to fashion an approach to social responsibility the same way that they develop any other business strategy. That is, they should view social responsibility as a major challenge that requires careful planning, decision making, consideration, and evaluation. They may accomplish this through both formal and informal dimensions of managing social responsibility.[36]

Unions play an active social role in Canada. Large ads at busy intersections, such as this one, provided by the Canadian Auto Workers, target the imbalance between rich and poor.

Formal Organizational Dimensions

Some dimensions of managing social responsibility are a formal and planned activity on the part of the organization. Formal organizational dimensions that can help manage social responsibility are legal compliance, ethical compliance, and philanthropic giving.[37]

● **legal compliance**
The extent to which an organization complies with municipal, provincial, federal, and international laws

Legal Compliance **Legal compliance** is the extent to which the organization conforms to municipal, provincial, federal, and international laws. The task of managing legal compliance is generally assigned to the appropriate functional managers. For example, the organization's top human resource executive is generally responsible for ensuring compliance with regulations concerning recruiting, selection, pay, and so forth. Likewise, the top finance executive generally oversees compliance with securities and banking regulations. The organization's legal department is also likely to contribute to this effort by providing general oversight and answering queries managers might have concerning the appropriate interpretation of laws and regulations.

● **ethical compliance**
The extent to which an organization and its members follow basic ethical standards of behaviour

Ethical Compliance **Ethical compliance** is the extent to which the members of the organization follow basic ethical (and legal) standards of behaviour. We noted earlier that organizations have increased their activities in this area—providing training in ethics and developing guidelines and codes of conduct, for example. These activities serve as vehicles for enhancing ethical compliance. Many organizations also establish formal ethics committees, which may be asked to review proposals for new projects, help evaluate new hiring strategies, or assess a new environmental protection plan. They might also serve as a peer review panel to evaluate alleged ethical misconduct by an employee.[38]

● **philanthropic giving**
Awarding funds or gifts to charities or worthy causes

Philanthropic Giving Finally, **philanthropic giving** is the awarding of funds or gifts to charities or other social programs. Canadian universities are major recipients of corporate gifts. Government cutbacks have led to universities becoming ever more dependent on corporate funding. Several schools and buildings, such as the Joseph L. Rotman School of Management at the University of Toronto and the Odette Building at the University of Windsor, have been named in honour of major donors. Firms that engage in philanthropic giving usually have a committee of top executives who review requests for grants and decide how much and to whom money will be allocated.

Informal Organizational Dimensions

In addition to these formal dimensions for managing social responsibility, there are also informal ones. Two of the more effective ways to clarify the organization's approach are to provide appropriate leadership and culture and to allow for whistle blowing.

Organization Leadership and Culture Leadership practices and organization culture can go a long way toward defining the social responsibility stance an organization and its members will adopt. For example, Johnson & Johnson executives for years provided a consistent message to employees that customers, employees, communities where the company did business, and shareholders were all important—and primarily in that order. Thus when packages of poisoned Tylenol showed up on store shelves in the 1980s, Johnson & Johnson employees didn't need to wait for orders from headquarters to know what to do: they immediately pulled all the packages from shelves before any other customers could buy them.[39] By contrast, the message sent to Beech-Nut employees by the actions of their top managers communicates much less regard for social responsibility.

Whistle Blowing   **Whistle blowing** is the disclosure by an employee of illegal or unethical conduct on the part of others within the organization. How an organization responds to this practice often indicates its stance toward social responsibility.[40] Whistle blowers may have to proceed through a number of channels to be heard, and they may even get fired for their efforts. Many organizations, however, welcome their contributions. A person who observes questionable behaviour typically first reports the incident to his or her boss. If nothing is done, the whistle blower may then inform higher-level managers or an ethics committee, if one exists. Eventually, the person may have to go to a regulatory agency or even the media to be heard.[41] For example, the apple juice scandal at Beech-Nut started with a whistle blower. A manager in the firm's R&D department began to suspect that its apple juice was not "100% pure." His boss, however, was unsympathetic, and when the manager went to the president of the company, he too turned a deaf ear. Eventually, the manager took his message to the media, which publicized the incident. This eventually led to a criminal investigation.

● **whistle blowing**
The disclosing by an employee of illegal or unethical conduct on the part of others within the organization

Evaluating Social Responsibility

Any organization that is serious about social responsibility must ensure that its efforts are producing the desired benefits. Essentially this requires applying the concept of control to social responsibility. Many organizations now require current and new employees to read their guidelines or code of ethics and then sign a statement agreeing to abide by it. An organization should also evaluate how it responds to instances of questionable legal or ethical conduct. Does it follow up immediately? Does it punish those involved? Or does it use delay and cover-up tactics? Answers to these questions can help an organization form a picture of its approach to social responsibility.

Additionally, some organizations occasionally conduct corporate social audits.[42] A **corporate social audit** is a formal and thorough analysis of the effectiveness of the firm's social performance. The audit is usually conducted by a task force of high-level managers from within the firm. It requires that the organization clearly define all its social goals, analyze the resources it devotes to each goal, determine how well it is achieving the various goals, and make recommendations about which areas need additional attention. Unfortunately, such audits are not conducted often because they are expensive and time consuming. Indeed, most organizations probably could do much more to evaluate the extent of their social responsibility than they do.

● **corporate social audit**
A formal and thorough analysis of the effectiveness of a firm's social performance

SUMMARY OF KEY POINTS

Ethics are an individual's personal beliefs about what constitutes right and wrong behaviour. Ethics are formed by family and peer influences, life experiences, personal values and morals, and situational factors. Important areas of ethical concern for managers are how the organization treats its employees, how employees treat the organization, and how the organization treats other economic agents. The ethical context of organizations consists of each manager's individual ethics and messages sent by organizational practices. Organizations use leadership, culture, training, codes, and guidelines to help them manage ethical behaviour.

Social responsibility is the set of obligations an organization has to protect and enhance the society in which it functions. Views of social responsibility have developed from the entrepreneurial era through the Depression era, the social era, and to the present time. Organizations may be considered responsible to their constituents, to the natural environment, and to the general social welfare. Even so, organizations present strong arguments both for and against social responsibility. The approach an organization adopts toward social responsibility falls along a continuum of lesser to greater commitment: social obstruction, social obligation, social response, and social contribution.

Government influences organizations through regulation, which is the establishment of laws and rules that dictate what businesses can and cannot do in prescribed areas. Organizations, in turn, rely on personal contacts, lobbying, political action committees (in the United States), and favours to influence the government.

Organizations use three types of activities to formally manage social responsibility: legal compliance, ethical compliance, and philanthropic giving. Leadership, culture, and allowing for whistle blowing are informal means for managing social responsibility. Organizations should evaluate the effectiveness of their socially responsible practices as they would any other strategy.

DISCUSSION QUESTIONS

Questions for Review

1. What are ethics? How are an individual's ethics formed?
2. Summarize the basic historical views of social responsibility.
3. What are the arguments for and against social responsibility?
4. How does the government influence organizations? How do organizations influence the government?

Questions for Analysis

5. What is the relationship between the law and ethical behaviour? Can illegal behaviour possibly be ethical?
6. How are the ethics of an organization's CEO related to social responsibility?
7. How do you feel about whistle-blowing activity? If you were aware of a criminal activity taking place in your organization, and if reporting it might cost you your job, what would you do?

Questions for Application

8. Refresh your memory about the Exxon *Valdez* oil spill. Evaluate the social responsibility dilemmas facing the company. For example, if Exxon had pledged unlimited resources to the cleanup, would this have been fair to the company's shareholders?
9. Research the social responsibility activities of ten large companies. What is your personal assessment of each?

10. Review the arguments for and against social responsibility. On a scale of 1 to 10, rate the validity and importance of each point. Use these ratings to develop a position regarding how socially responsible an organization should be. Now compare your ratings and position with those of two of your classmates. Discuss your respective positions, focusing primarily on disagreements.

BUILDING EFFECTIVE DECISION-MAKING SKILLS

Exercise Overview

Decision-making skills refer to the manager's ability to correctly recognize and define problems and opportunities and to then select an appropriate course of action to solve problems and capitalize on opportunities. Many decisions made by managers have an ethical component. This exercise will help you appreciate the potential role of ethics in making decisions.

Exercise Background

Read and reflect on each of the following scenarios:

1. You are the top manager of a major international oil company. Because of a recent oil spill by another firm, all the companies in the industry have been subjected to close scrutiny regarding the safety of various work practices. Your safety manager has completed a review and informed you that your firm has one potential problem area. The manager estimates the probability of a problem within the next five years as being about 3 percent. The costs of fixing things now would be about $1.5 million. However, should you do nothing and a problem develop, the costs will be $10 million, plus your firm will receive a lot of bad publicity.

2. You manage a small fast-food restaurant. The owner has just informed you that you need to cut your payroll by 20 hours per week. You have determined that the most feasible option is to lay off one of two workers. One is a retired woman who works part-time for you. She lives on a fixed income, is raising three grandchildren, and really needs the money she earns from this job. The other is a college student who also works part-time. He is one year away from getting his degree and must work to pay his tuition and fees.

3. You have decided to donate $1,000 to a worthy cause in your neighbourhood on behalf of the small business you own. Based on your own research, you have learned that the groups and charities most in need of funds are a local homeless shelter, a youth soccer league, an abortion clinic, and a tutoring program for illiterate adults.

Exercise Task

With the background information above as context, do the following:

1. Make a decision between the two courses of action for scenario one.
2. Decide which of the two employees to terminate in scenario two.
3. Decide where to donate your money in scenario three.
4. What role did your own personal ethics play in making each of these decisions?
5. Compare your decisions with those of a classmate and discuss why any differences arose.

Ethics in Cosmetics

The Body Shop was founded by Anita Roddick in England in 1976. In 1979, Margot Franssen and her sister opened the first Canadian Body Shop in Toronto's Yorkville district. This company retails skin and hair care products that are inspired by natural ingredients and traditional practice, and produced, as the company claims, without any cruelty to animals. The cosmetics industry has long depended on animal testing for product development, so The Body Shop's philosophy marked a radical departure from traditional practice.

Since its initial opening, The Body Shop Canada has gone on to develop a network of more than one hundred franchise and company-owned stores across Canada and the northeast United States. By the 1990s, retail sales had reached approximately $100 million annually. However, it is not the company's profitability that has captured the imagination of the world, but rather its professed humanitarian and philosophical ideals.

The cosmetics industry has been viewed by many as one that exploits women, tortures animals, pollutes the environment, and bases its promotional efforts entirely on exaggerated statements and claims. The Body Shop maintains that its philosophy and practices are quite different. It has emphasized the use of ingredients that do not threaten endangered species or spaces; encouraged women to participate in its businesses (approximately 95 percent of its Canadian franchisees are women); and promoted investment, trade, and sustainable development in developing countries.

In keeping with its trade-not-aid ideal and its philosophy of giving back to the communities from which it receives its profits, The Body Shop Canada has initiated a number of projects and programs worldwide. For instance, the company has developed a hair conditioner made from Brazilian nut oil. The nuts are supplied by an Indian tribe in northern Brazil. The company sent two anthropologists to study the tribe so that trade could proceed without disturbing indigenous culture. As part of a project in Nepal, The Body Shop Canada has taught the locals how to make paper (which the company buys) from renewable resources such as banana skins. This plant is operating at a profit, one-quarter of which is left in the community to be spent on local improvement projects.

The Body Shop also professes a high degree of social responsibility. Its store windows across Canada are used as platforms for educational purposes three times a year to draw attention to social and environmental issues. Every Body Shop store sends its staff out on community projects of the store's staff choosing at a rate of four hours per store per week. The company's ideals have won it numerous accolades. In 1991, The Body Shop Canada received a Financial Post Environment Award for its commitment to operating in an environmentally responsible manner. The Body Shop has also been named as one of the "100 Best Companies to Work for in Canada" for its attention to employee development and workplace atmosphere.

In 1994, The Body Shop's image suffered a serious blow when the Minneapolis-based *Business Ethics* magazine criticized the company for exaggerating its charitable contributions, its trade with developing countries, and its environmental record. However, as many analysts note, The Body Shop may be discovering that companies that tout their political correctness are likely to be judged by higher standards than other companies. Recently, its U.S. stores have also experienced financial losses, a situation not uncommon with many idealistic companies. Such losses were due partly to press attacks on its image.

The Body Shop seems to have weathered the storm and is continuing with its espoused policies. In late 1996, the company teamed up with Ben and Jerry's in a promotional campaign to sell vanilla ice cream. The vanilla beans come from the Costa Rican rain forests, which is consistent with the policy of both companies of purchasing product ingredients from indigenous vendors rather than from multinational corporations. Some redemption was also gained when a recent United Nations Environmental Program report gave The Body Shop the highest score in the chemical industry for its environmental reports.

Ethics in Cosmetics (Continued)

Questions

1. What approach to social responsibility and business ethics does The Body Shop take? Do you agree with this approach? Why or why not?

2. The Body Shop is a privately held company. Could a publicly held company adopt such an approach? Why or why not?

3. What factors in its environment have led The Body Shop to adopt its philosophical approach? From your own assessment and knowledge of this company, do you think its approach is hypocritical? Explain.

References: Sean Mehegan, "Body Shop, Ben and Jerry's to Unite PC Images for Vanilla Focus," *Brandweek*, Vol. 37, September 16, 1996, p. 4; Mark Sarner and Janice Nathanson, "The Six Ps of Social Marketing: Companies Can Better Society While Boosting Profits," *Marketing*, Vol. 101, September 9, 1996, pp. 14–15; Andrew Davidson, "Anita Roddick," *Management Today*, March 1996, pp. 42–44; "Storm in a Bubble Bath," *The Economist*, Vol. 332, September 3, 1994, p. 56; and Margot Frannsen, "Beyond Profits," *Business Quarterly*, Autumn 1993, pp. 15–20.

CHAPTER NOTES

1. Brian Hutchinson, "The Prize," *Canadian Business,* March 1997, pp. 26–72; Janet McFarland and Paul Waldie, "Bre-X Report Reveals Legal Fund," *The Globe and Mail,* June 12, 1997, pp. B1, B23; Anthony Spaeth, "The Scam of the Century," *Time,* May 19, 1997, pp..34–39; and Jennifer Wells, "The Bre-X Bust," *Maclean's,* April 7, 1997, pp. 50–54.

2. See Thomas M. Garrett and Richard J. Klonoski, *Business Ethics,* 3rd ed. (Englewood Cliffs, N.J.: Prentice-Hall, 1990), for a review of the different meanings of the word *ethics.*

3. Steven Grover, "Lying, Deceit, and Subterfuge: A Model of Dishonesty in the Workplace," *Organization Science,* August 1993, pp. 474–483.

4. See Thomas M. Jones, "Ethical Decision Making by Individuals in Organizations: An Issue-Contingent Model," *Academy of Management Journal,* June 1991, pp. 366–395.

5. Thomas Donaldson and Thomas W. Dunfee, "Toward a Unified Conception of Business Ethics: An Integrative Social Contracts Theory," *Academy of Management Review,* Vol. 19, No. 2, 1994, pp. 252–284.

6. Daniel Leblanc, "Bell Pay Equity Ruling a Setback for Ottawa," *The Globe and Mail,* November 18, 1998, p. A1.

7. Anne Fisher, "Sexual Harassment—What to Do," *Fortune,* August 21, 1993, pp. 84–88.

8. John Huey, "Wal-Mart—Will It Take Over the World?" *Fortune,* January 30, 1989, pp. 52–61.

9. "Loose Lips Sink Stock Prices," *Business Week,* October 31, 1994, p. 52.

10. Patricia Sellers, "Getting Customers to Love You," *Fortune,* March 13, 1989, pp. 38–49.

11. Eric Abrahamson and Choelsoon Park, "Concealment of Negative Organizational Outcomes: An Agency Theory Perspective," *Academy of Management Journal,* Vol. 37, No. 5, 1994, pp. 1302–1334.

12. Linda Klebe Trevino, "Ethical Decision Making in Organizations: A Person-Situation Interactionist Model," *Academy of Management Review,* July 1986, pp. 601–617; and Bart Victor and John B. Cullen, "The Organizational Bases of Ethical Work Climates," *Administrative Science Quarterly,* Vol. 33, 1988, pp. 101–125.

13. "What Led Beech-Nut Down the Road to Disgrace," *Business Week,* February 22, 1988, pp. 124–128.

14. Alan Richter and Cynthia Barnum, "When Values Clash," *HR Magazine,* September 1994, pp. 42–45.

15. "Businesses Are Signing Up for Ethics 101," *Business Week,* February 15, 1988, pp. 56–57; and "Ethics on the Job: Companies Alert Employees to Potential Dilemmas," *The Wall Street Journal,* July 14, 1986, p. 17.

16. Alan Freeman, "Engineer Predicted Spanish Disaster," *The Globe and Mail,* May 2, 1998, p. A10.

17. Sir Adrian Cadbury, "Ethical Managers Make Their Own Rules," *Harvard Business Review,* September–October 1987, pp. 69–73.

18. Jerry W. Anderson, Jr. "Social Responsibility and the Corporation," *Business Horizons,* July–August 1986, pp. 22–27.

19. See Archie Carroll, *Business and Society: Ethics and Stakeholder Management* (Cincinnati: Southwestern 1989), for a review of the evolution of social responsibility.

20. "Big Trouble at Allegheny," *Business Week,* August 11, 1986, pp. 56–61.

21. Edwin M. Epstein, "The Corporate Social Policy Process: Beyond Business Ethics, Corporate Social Responsibility, and Corporate Social Responsiveness," *California Management Review,* Spring 1987, pp. 99–114.

22. "A Mail-Order Romance: Lands' End Courts Unseen Customers," *Fortune,* March 13, 1989, pp. 44–45.

23. "Chicanery at Phar-Mor Ran Deep, Close Look at Discounter Shows," *The Wall Street Journal,* January 20, 1994, pp. A1, A6.

24. Ann Reilly Dowd, "Environmentalists Are on the Run," *Fortune,* September 19, 1994, pp. 91–100; and Kathleen Dechant and Barbara Altman, "Environmental Leadership: From Compliance to Competitive Advantage," *The Academy of Management Executive,* Vol. 8, No. 3, 1994, pp. 7–15.

25. "Ashland Just Can't Seem to Leave Its Checkered Past Behind," *Business Week,* October 31, 1988, pp. 122–126.

26. Nancy J. Perry, "The Education Crisis: What Business Can Do," *Fortune,* July 4, 1988, pp. 71–81.

27. Anthony H. Bloom, "Managing Against Apartheid," *Harvard Business Review,* November–December 1987, pp. 49–56.

28. "The Color of Money Is Starting to Change," *Business Week,* March 14, 1994, p. 42.

29. For discussions of this debate, see Abby Brown, "Is Ethics Good Business?" *Personnel Administrator,* February 1987, pp. 67–74; Jean B. McGuire, Alison Sundgren, and Thomas Schneeweis, "Corporate Social Responsibility and Firm Financial Performance," *Academy of Management Journal,* December 1988, pp. 854–872; "Business Ethics for Sale," *Newsweek,* May 9, 1988, p. 56; Kenneth E. Aupperle, Archie B. Carroll, and John D. Hatfield, "An Empirical Examination of the Relationship Between Corporate Social Responsibility and Profitability," *Academy of Management Journal,* June 1985, pp. 446–463; and Margaret A. Stroup, Ralph L. Neubert, and Jerry W. Anderson, Jr., "Doing Good, Doing Better: Two Views of Social Responsibility," *Business Horizons,* March–April 1987, pp. 22–25.

30. Andrew Singer, "Can a Company Be Too Ethical?" *Across the Board,* April 1993, pp. 17–22.

31. "Doing Well by Doing Good," *Business Week,* December 5, 1988, pp. 53–57.

32. Karen Howlett, "Fortune Financial Parts Ways with Head of Compliance," *The Globe and Mail,* April 30, 1998, p. B9.

33. "Fast-Food Chains Draw Criticism for Marketing Fare as Nutritional," *The Wall Street Journal,* April 6, 1987, p. 23.

34. "How to Win Friends and Influence Lawmakers," *Business Week,* November 7, 1988, p. 36.

35. "Businessman Found Guilty in Cogger Çase," *The Globe and Mail,* May 2, 1998, p. A5.

36. Steven L. Wartick and Philip L. Cochran, "The Evolution of the Corporate Social Performance Model," *Academy of Management Review,* October 1985, pp. 758–769; Jerry W. Anderson, Jr., "Social Responsibility," *Business Horizons,* July–August 1986, pp. 22–27; and Epstein, "The Corporate Social Policy Process: Beyond Business Ethics, Corporate Social Responsibility, and Corporate Social Responsiveness."

37. Anderson, "Social Responsibility and the Corporation."

38. Lynn Sharp Paine, "Managing for Organizational Integrity," *Harvard Business Review,* March–April 1994, pp. 106–115.

39. "Unfuzzing Ethics for Managers," *Fortune,* November 23, 1987, pp. 229–234.

40. Marcia P. Miceli and Janet P. Near, "Whistleblowing: Reaping the Benefits," *The Academy of Management Executive,* Vol. 8, No. 3, 1994, pp. 65–74.

41. Janelle Brinker Dozier and Marcia P. Miceli, "Potential Predictors of Whistle-Blowing: A Prosocial Behavior Perspective," *Academy of Management Review,* October 1985, pp. 823–836; and Janet P. Near and Marcia P. Miceli, "Retaliation Against Whistle Blowers: Predictors and Effects," *Journal of Applied Psychology,* February 1986, pp. 137–145.

42. Samuel B. Graves and Sandra A. Waddock, "Institutional Owners and Corporate Social Performance," *Academy of Management Journal,* Vol. 37, No. 4, 1994, pp. 1034–1046.

The Global Context of Management

5

OBJECTIVES

After studying this chapter, you should be able to:

● *Describe the nature of international business, including its meaning, recent trends, managing internationalization, and managing in an international market.*

● *Discuss the structure of the global economy and how it affects international management.*

● *Identify and discuss the environmental challenges inherent in international management.*

● *Describe the basic issues involved in competing in a global economy, including organization size and the management challenges in a global economy.*

OUTLINE

The Nature of International Business
  The Meaning of International Business
  Trends in International Business
  Managing the Process of Internationalization
  Managing in an International Market
The Structure of the Global Economy
  Mature Market Economies and Systems
  Developing Economies
  Other Economies
Environmental Challenges of International
    Management
  The Economic Environment
  The Political–Legal Environment
  The Cultural Environment
Competing in a Global Economy
  Globalization and Organization Size
  Management Challenges in a Global Economy

Global markets provide great opportunities for many firms today. Unilever, based jointly in London and Rotterdam, is aggressively pursuing new markets around the world. This billboard in New Delhi is promoting Unilever's Close-Up toothpaste.

Unilever is one of the world's most international businesses. It was also one of the first to look beyond its own borders for growth opportunities. William and James Lever founded the business in England in 1885. Their initial product was Sunlight, the world's first packaged and branded laundry soap. By the turn of the century, the Lever Brothers were selling soap in Europe, Australia, South Africa, and the United States.

In 1930, Lever Brothers merged with the Margarine Union, a Dutch enterprise, to form Unilever. For tax purposes, the new firm maintained dual headquarters in London and Rotterdam. Top executives and a co-chair reside in the two cities, each controlling exactly half the authority in the firm.

Today, Unilever's brands are among the most widely recognized and successful in the world. The list of Unilever products and brands includes Lipton Tea, Ragu spaghetti sauces, Bertolli olive oil, Wishbone salad dressings, Dove soap, Lever 2000 deodorant soap, Surf and Wisk detergents, Aim and Close-Up toothpastes, Breyers ice cream, Pond's and Vaseline lotions, Q-Tips cotton swabs, Calvin Klein fragrances, and Elizabeth Arden cosmetics.

> **"Losing a fight over market dominance isn't just a blow to the corporate ego, it means forgoing hundreds of millions of dollars in sales that may never be recovered."—John Campbell, financial analyst**

Unilever is a dominant force in virtually every major market outside the United States. For example, it's the world leader in margarine, controls 90 percent of the detergent market in Chile, and is a major player in India, Europe, and Pacific Asia. In the year ended December 1996, Unilever Canada's revenue of $1.5 billion was ranked 45th among this country's private companies. Breyers ice cream is the world's biggest selling frozen dessert, and Pepsodent is the best selling toothpaste outside the United States.

But inside the United States is a different story. Although Unilever (its U.S. operation is still called Lever Brothers) is clearly an important player in the U.S. market, it always seems to come up short against its arch rival Procter & Gamble. Indeed, it was P&G's introduction of Tide, the first synthetic detergent, in 1946 that ended Unilever's dominance in the U.S. market. And P&G more recently got its product Liquid Tide on the market before Unilever got its Liquid All out.

Even though Unilever continues to struggle in the United States, it is still going full steam ahead in other markets. For example, it launched thirty new products in Brazil in 1992 alone, and sales there topped $2.2 billion (U.S.). It introduced twice that number of products in India in 1993, achieving new product sales of $1.3 billion (U.S.). To strengthen its market position in China, on January 18th, 1999, Unilever announced its intention to acquire Mountain Cream, a Chinese ice cream business. Clearly, then, even though the firm can't quite seem to figure out how to outsmart Procter & Gamble, it has little trouble succeeding in the rest of the world.[1] ●

Source of Quotation: John Campbell, financial analyst, in reference to Unilever, quoted in *Business Week*, July 4, 1994, p. 55.

The economic battles between Unilever and Procter & Gamble, in the North American market as well as the rest of the world, are not unique. Firms from across the globe are entering new markets, taking on new challenges, and forming alliances with other firms. And all for the same reason—to compete more effectively in the global business environment. To be successful today, managers must understand the global context within which they function. This holds true regardless of whether the manager runs one of *Report on Business Magazine*'s Top 1000 companies or a small independent manufacturing concern.

This chapter explores the global context of management. We start by describing the nature of international business. We then discuss the structure of the global market in terms of different economies and economic systems. The basic environmental challenges of management are introduced and discussed next. We then focus on issues of competition in a global economy. Finally, we conclude by characterizing the managerial functions of planning, organizing, leading, and controlling as management challenges in a global economy.

THE NATURE OF INTERNATIONAL BUSINESS

As you prepared breakfast this morning, you may have plugged in a coffee pot manufactured in Asia and perhaps ironed a shirt or blouse made in Taiwan with an iron made in Mexico. The coffee you drank was probably made from beans grown in South America. To get to school, you may have driven a Japanese car. Even if you drove a Ford or Chevrolet, some of its parts were engineered or manufactured abroad. Perhaps you didn't drive a car to school but rather rode a bus (manufactured by Daimler-Benz, a German company, or by Volvo, a Swedish company) or a motorcycle (manufactured by Honda, Kawasaki, Suzuki, or Yamaha—all Japanese firms).

Our daily lives are strongly influenced by businesses from around the world. But we aren't unique in this respect. People living in other countries have much the same experience. They drive Fords in Germany, use Compaq and IBM computers in Japan, eat McDonald's hamburgers in France, drink Labatt's beer in El Salvador, and snack on Mars candy bars in England. They drink Pepsi and wear Levi Strauss jeans in China. The Japanese buy Eastman Kodak film and use American Express credit cards. People around the world buy Air Canada or Canadian Airlines tickets and fly on planes made by Boeing. Their buildings are constructed with Caterpillar machinery, their factories are powered by General Electric engines, and they buy Mobil oil.

In truth, we have become part of a global village and have a global economy where no organization is insulated from the effects of foreign markets and competition.[2] Indeed, more and more firms are reshaping themselves for international competition and discovering new ways to exploit markets in every corner of the world.[3] Failure to take a global perspective is one of the biggest mistakes managers can make. Thus we start laying the foundation of our discussion by introducing and describing the basics of international business.

The Meaning of International Business

There are many different forms and levels of international business. Although the lines that distinguish one from another are perhaps arbitrary, we identify four levels of international activity that can be used to differentiate organizations.[4] These are illustrated in Figure 5.1. A **domestic business** acquires essen-

● **domestic business**
A business that acquires all of its resources and sells all of its products or services within a single country

FIGURE 5.1 Levels of International Business Activity

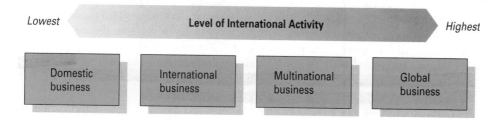

tially all of its resources and sells all of its products or services within a single country. Although most small businesses are essentially domestic in nature, as are some banks, retailers, agricultural enterprises, and service firms, few, if any, large domestic businesses are left in the world today.

Indeed, today most large firms are either international or multinational operations. An **international business** is one that is primarily based in a single country but that acquires some meaningful share of its resources or revenues from other countries. Sears fits this description. Most of its stores are in the United States, for example, and the retailer earns around 93 percent of its revenues from its U.S. operations, with the remaining 7 percent coming from Sears stores in Canada and Mexico. At the same time, however, many of the products it sells, such as tools and clothing, are made abroad.[5]

A **multinational business** has a worldwide marketplace from which it buys raw materials, borrows money, and manufactures its products and to which it subsequently sells its products. Ford Motor Co. is an excellent example of a multinational company. It has design and production facilities around the world. One of its newest models, the Ford Contour, was jointly designed by European and U.S. teams, for example, and is sold with only minor variations in dozens of foreign markets. Ford makes and sells other cars in Europe that are never seen in North America. Ford cars are designed, produced, and sold for individual markets, wherever they are and without regard for national boundaries.[6] Multinational businesses are often called *multinational enterprises* or *MNEs*.[7]

The final form of international business is the global business. A **global business** is one that transcends national boundaries and is not committed to a single home country. Although no business has truly achieved this level of international involvement, Nestlé comes close. Nestlé is based in Vevey, Switzerland; has a German CEO; and gets more than 98 percent of its revenues and has more than 95 percent of its assets outside of Switzerland. The firm has ten general managers, only five of whom are Swiss. About the only things that make Nestlé a Swiss firm are that its headquarters are in Switzerland and Swiss investors still own more than one-half of the firm's stock.[8]

Trends in International Business

To understand why and how these different levels of international business have emerged, we must briefly look to the past. In the years immediately after World War II, the United States was by far the dominant economic force in the world. Most of the industrialized countries in Europe had been devastated during the war. Many Asian countries, especially Japan, had fared no better.

• international business
A business that is primarily based in a single country but acquires some meaningful share of its resources or revenues (or both) from other countries

• multinational business
A business that has a worldwide marketplace from which it buys raw materials, borrows money, and manufactures its products and to which it subsequently sells its products

• global business
A business that transcends national boundaries and is not committed to a single home country

There were few passable roads, few standing bridges, and even fewer factories dedicated to the manufacture of peacetime products. And those regions less affected by war-time destruction—Canada, Latin America, and Africa—had not yet developed the economic muscle to threaten the economic preeminence of the United States. Businesses in war-torn countries like Germany and Japan had no choice but to rebuild from scratch. They were in the unfortunate but eventually advantageous position of having to rethink every facet of their operations, including technology, production, finance, and marketing. Although recovery in these countries took many years, it eventually occurred, and their economic systems were subsequently poised for growth.

Canada is not isolated from global competition or the global marketplace. A few simple numbers will help tell the story of international trade and industry. Exports from Canada in 1997 totalled $301 billion while imports into Canada totalled $277 billion.[9] The United States is by far Canada's largest source of imports and destination for its exports. Moreover, in 1998, of the 12,725 foreign-owned companies in Canada, 6,819 were American.[10] From 1985 to 1997, the stock of foreign direct investment in Canada more than doubled, from $90 billion to $188 billion.[11] At the same time, direct investment abroad by Canadian-owned corporations such as Bombardier and Seagram reached $194 billion in 1997.[12] These numbers reflect today's reality of increasing globalization. The days when firms could safely ignore the rest of the world and concentrate on only their domestic market are gone forever. Now businesses must be concerned with the competitive situations they face in environments both at home and abroad.

Managing the Process of Internationalization

Managers should also recognize that their global context dictates two related but distinct sets of challenges. One set of challenges must be confronted when an organization chooses to change its level of international involvement. For example, a firm that wants to move from being an international to a multinational business has to manage that transition. The other set of challenges occurs when the organization has achieved its desired level of international involvement and must then function effectively within that environment. This section highlights the first set of challenges, and the next section introduces the second set of challenges. When an organization makes the decision to increase its level of international activity, it can adopt one of several alternative strategies.[13] The most basic ones are shown in Figure 5.2.

Importing and Exporting   Importing or exporting (or both) is usually the first type of international business in which a firm gets involved. **Exporting**, or making the product in the firm's domestic marketplace and selling it in another country, can involve both merchandise and services. Firms in North America routinely export grain to the former Soviet Union, gas turbines to Saudi Arabia, locomotives to Indonesia, blue jeans to Great Britain, and diapers to Italy. **Importing** is bringing a good, service, or capital into the home country from abroad. For example, automobiles (Mazda, Volkswagen, Mercedes-Benz, Ferrari), stereo equipment (Sony, Bang & Olufsen, Sanyo), and wine (Riunite, Dom Perignon, Black Tower) are imported into Canada.

An import/export operation has many advantages. It is the easiest way of entering a market with a small outlay of capital. Because the products are sold "as is," they need not be adapted to the local conditions, and little risk is

● **exporting**
Making a product in the firm's domestic marketplace and selling it in another country

● **importing**
Bringing a good, service, or capital into the home country from abroad

FIGURE 5.2 The Process of Internationalization

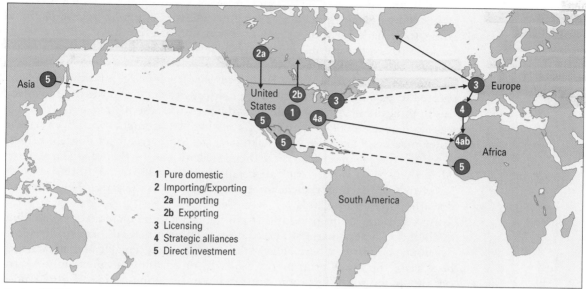

1 Pure domestic
2 Importing/Exporting
  2a Importing
  2b Exporting
3 Licensing
4 Strategic alliances
5 Direct investment

Source: *World Investment Report*, 1998, "Trends and Developments," p. 36. Geneva: UNCTAD. Reprinted by permission.

involved. But there are also disadvantages. For instance, imports and exports are subject to taxes, tariffs, and transportation expenses. Furthermore, because the products are not adapted to local conditions, they may not meet the needs of a large segment of the market. Finally, some products may be restricted and thus can be neither imported nor exported.

The process of internationalization can be managed with different strategies. These include importing and exporting, licensing, joint ventures/strategic alliances, and direct investment.

With the signing of the North American Free Trade Agreement (NAFTA), a potential $7 trillion market of 377 million people was created. NAFTA will eliminate all tariffs and other barriers to trade between Canada, United States, and Mexico and will provide for a totally free trade area by 2009. Above, former prime minister Brian Mulroney signs the agreement in Ottawa, while former trade minister Michael Wilson looks on.

licensing
An arrangement whereby one company allows another company to use its brand name, trademark, technology, patent, copyright, or other assets in exchange for a royalty based on sales

Licensing   A company may prefer to arrange for a foreign company to manufacture or market its products under a licensing agreement. **Licensing** is an arrangement whereby a firm allows another company to use its brand name, trademark, technology, patent, copyright, or other assets. In return, the licensee pays a royalty, usually based on sales. Factors that lead to this decision include excessive transportation costs, government regulations, and home production costs. When Kirin Brewery, Japan's largest producer of beer, wanted to expand its international operations, it feared that the time involved in shipping the beer from Japan would cause it to lose its freshness. Kirin has therefore entered into a number of licensing arrangements with breweries in other markets. These brewers make beer according to strict guidelines provided by the Japanese firm, and then package and market it as Kirin Beer. They then pay a royalty back to Kirin for each case sold. Molson produces Kirin in Canada under such an agreement, and the Charles Wells brewery does the same in England.[14]

An advantage of licensing is that profitability can be increased by extending the brand into new markets. This strategy is frequently used for entry into less-developed countries where older technology is still acceptable and, in fact, may be state of the art. A primary disadvantage of licensing is inflexibility. A firm can tie up control of its product or expertise for a long period of time. And if the licensee does not develop the market effectively, the licensing firm can lose profits. A second disadvantage is that licensees can take the knowledge and skill that they have been given access to for a foreign market and exploit them in the licensing firm's home market. When this happens, what used to be a business partner becomes a business competitor.

strategic alliance
A cooperative arrangement between two or more firms for mutual benefit

joint venture
A special type of strategic alliance in which the partners share in the ownership of an operation on an equity basis

Strategic Alliances   In a **strategic alliance**, two or more firms jointly cooperate for mutual gain.[15] For example, Ford and Volkswagen share a warehousing, maintenance, and distribution centre in South America. The two partners share equally in the cost of maintaining the facility, but otherwise each functions autonomously. A **joint venture** is a special type of strategic alliance in which the partners actually share ownership of a new enterprise. General Mills and Nestlé recently formed a new company called Cereal Partners Worldwide. The purpose of CPW is to produce and market cereals. General Mills supplies the technology and proven formulas, and Nestlé provides its international distribution network. The two partners share equally in the new enterprise. Strategic alliances have enjoyed a tremendous upsurge in the past few years. In most alliances, each party provides a portion of the equity or the equivalent in physical plant, raw materials, cash, or other assets. The proportion of the investment then determines the percentage of ownership in the venture.[16]

Strategic alliances have both advantages and disadvantages. For example, they can allow quick entry into a market by taking advantage of the existing strengths of participants. Japanese automobile manufacturers employed this strategy to enter the U.S. market by using the already established distribution systems of U.S. automobile manufacturers. Strategic alliances are also an effective way of gaining access to technology or raw materials. And they allow the firms to share the risk and cost of the new venture. One major disadvantage of this approach lies with the shared ownership of joint ventures. Although it reduces the risk for each participant, it also limits the control and the return that each firm can enjoy.

Direct Investment Another level of commitment to internationalization is direct investment. **Direct investment** occurs when a firm headquartered in one country builds or purchases operating facilities or subsidiaries in a foreign country. The foreign operations then become wholly owned subsidiaries of the firm. Eastman Kodak recently made a direct investment when it built a new research laboratory in Japan. Similarly, Ford's plants in Germany and Unilever's distribution centres in Canada represent direct investments. On a worldwide basis foreign direct investment inflows in 1997 reached $600 billion, an increase of 19 percent from 1996.[17]

A major reason many firms make direct investments is to capitalize on lower labour costs. That is, the goal is often to transfer production to locations where labour is cheap. Japanese businesses have moved much of their production to Thailand because labour costs are much lower there than in Japan. Many firms are using maquiladoras for the same purpose. **Maquiladoras** are light assembly plants built in northern Mexico close to the U.S. border. The plants are given special tax breaks by the Mexican government, and the area is populated with workers willing to work for very low wages. More than one thousand plants in the region employ 300,000 workers, and more are planned. The plants are owned by major corporations, primarily from the United States, Japan, South Korea, and major European industrial countries. This concentrated form of direct investment benefits the country of Mexico, the companies themselves, and workers who might otherwise be without jobs. Some critics argue, however, that the low wages paid by the maquiladoras amount to little more than slave labour.[18]

Like the other approaches for increasing a firm's level of internationalization, direct investment carries with it a number of benefits and liabilities. Managerial control is more complete, and profits do not have to be shared as they do in joint ventures. Purchasing an existing organization provides additional benefits in that the human resources, plant, and organizational infrastructure are already in place. Acquisition is also a way to purchase the brand-name identification of a product. This could be particularly important if the cost of introducing a new brand is high. For example, Ford indicated it will retain the Volvo name after it acquired the Volvo car division in January 1999. Notwithstanding these advantages, the company is now operating a part of itself entirely within the borders of a foreign country. The additional complexity in the decision making, the economic and political risks, and so forth may outweigh the advantages that can be obtained by international expansion.

Of course, we should also note that these approaches to internationalization are not mutually exclusive. Indeed, most large firms use all of them simultaneously. MNEs and global businesses have a global orientation and worldwide approach to foreign markets and production. They search for opportunities all over the world and select the best strategy to serve each market. In some settings, they may use direct investment, in others licensing, in others strategic alliances; in still others they might limit their involvement to exporting and importing. The advantages and disadvantages of each approach are summarized in Table 5.1.

Managing in an International Market

Even when a firm is not actively seeking to increase its desired level of internationalization, its managers are still responsible for seeing that it functions effectively within whatever level of international involvement the organization has achieved. In one sense, the job of a manager in an international business

● **direct investment**
When a firm headquartered in one country builds or purchases operating facilities or subsidiaries in a foreign country

● **maquiladora**
A light assembly plant built in northern Mexico close to the U.S. border that is given special tax breaks by the Mexican government

Approach to Internationalization	Advantages	Disadvantages
Importing or exporting	1. Small cash outlay 2. Little risk 3. No adaptation necessary	1. Tariffs and taxes 2. High transportation costs 3. Government restrictions
Licensing	1. Increased profitability 2. Extended profitability	1. Inflexibility 2. Helps competitors
Strategic alliance/ joint ventures	1. Quick market entry 2. Access to materials and technology	1. Shared ownership (limits control and profits)
Direct investment	1. Enhances control 2. Existing infra-structure	1. Complexity 2. Greater economic and political risk 3. Greater uncertainty

may not be that much different from the job of a manager in a domestic business. Each may be responsible for acquiring resources and materials, making products, providing services, developing human resources, advertising, or monitoring cash flow.

In another sense, however, the complexity associated with each of these activities may be much greater for managers in international firms. Rather than buying raw materials from sources in Alberta, British Columbia, and Ontario, an international purchasing manager may buy materials from sources in Peru, India, and Spain. Rather than training managers for new plants in Quebec, Manitoba, and Nova Scotia, the international human resource executive may train new plant managers for facilities in China, Mexico, and Scotland. And instead of developing a single marketing campaign for Canada, an advertising director may be working on promotional efforts in France, Brazil, and Japan.

The most important question that any manager trying to be effective in an international market must address is whether to focus on globalization or regionalism.[19] A global thrust requires that activities be managed from an overall global perspective as part of an integrated system. Regionalism, on the other hand, involves managing within each region with less regard for the overall organization. In reality, most larger MNEs manage some activities globally (for example, finance and manufacturing) and others locally (such as human resource management and advertising). We explore these approaches more fully later.

THE STRUCTURE OF THE GLOBAL ECONOMY

Managers seeking to operate in a global environment must better understand the structure of the global economy. Although each country, and indeed many regions within any given country, is unique, we can still note some basic similarities and differences. We describe three different elements of the global economy: mature market economies and systems, developing economies, and other economies.[20]

Mature Market Economies and Systems

A **market economy** is based on the private ownership of business and allows market factors such as supply and demand to determine business strategy. Mature market economies include Canada, the United States, Japan, the United Kingdom, France, Germany, and Sweden. These countries have several things in common. For example, they tend to employ market forces in the allocation of resources. They also tend to be characterized by private ownership of property, although there is some variance along this dimension. France, for example, has a relatively high level of government ownership among the market economies.

Canadian managers have relatively few problems operating in market economies. Many of the business "rules of the game" that apply in Canada, for example, also apply in Germany or England. And consumers there often tend to buy the same kinds of products. For these reasons when Canadian firms seek to expand geographically, they often begin operations in some other market economy. Although the task of managing an international business in an industrial market country is somewhat less complicated than operating in some other type of economy, it still poses some challenges. Perhaps foremost among them is that the markets in these economies are typically quite mature. Many industries, for example, are already dominated by large and successful companies. Thus competing in these economies poses a major challenge.[21]

The map in Figure 5.3 highlights three relatively mature market systems. **Market systems** are clusters of countries that engage in high levels of trade with each other. One mature market system is North America. The United States, Canada, and Mexico are major trading partners with one another; more than 70 percent of Mexico's exports go to the United States, and more than 65 percent of what Mexico imports goes to the United States. Canada and the United States are each other's largest trading partners. During the last several years, these countries have negotiated a variety of agreements to make trade even easier. The most important of these, the **North American Free Trade Agreement**, or **NAFTA**, eliminates many of the trade barriers—quotas and tariffs, for example—that existed previously.[22]

Another mature market system is Europe. Until recently, Europe was two distinct economic areas. The eastern region consisted of Communist countries such as Poland, Czechoslovakia, and Rumania. These countries were characterized by government ownership of business and greatly restricted trade. In contrast, western European countries with traditional market economies have been working together to promote international trade for decades. In particular, the **European Union** (or **EU** as it is often called) has long been a formidable market system. The formal members of the EU are Denmark, the United Kingdom, Portugal, the Netherlands, Belgium, Spain, Ireland, Luxembourg, France, Germany, Italy, and Greece. For years these countries followed a basic plan that led to the elimination of most trade barriers in 1992. The European situation has recently grown more complex, however. Communism has collapsed in most eastern countries, and they are trying to develop market economies. They also want greater participation in trade with

● **market economy**
An economy based on the private ownership of business and that allows market factors such as supply and demand to determine business strategy

● **market system**
A cluster of countries that engage in high levels of trade with one another

● **North American Free Trade Agreement (NAFTA)**
An agreement between the United States, Canada, and Mexico to promote trade with one another

● **European Union (EU)**
The first and most important international market system

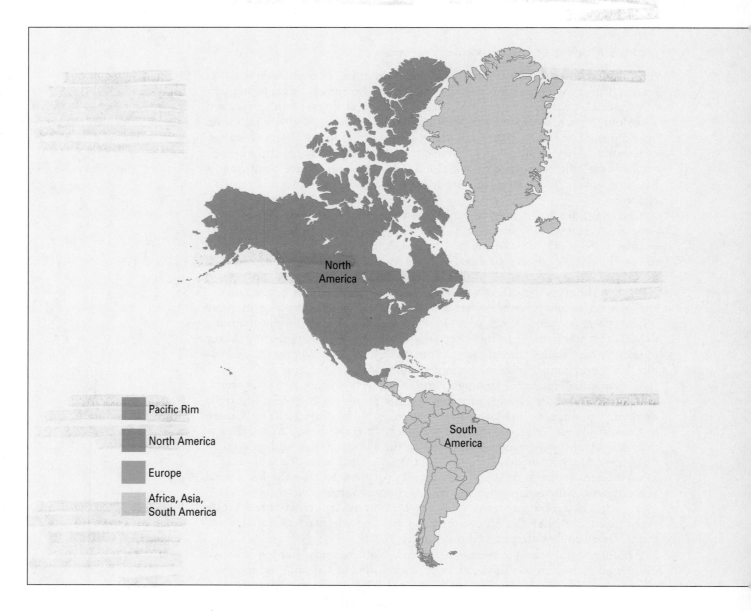

Pacific Rim

North America

Europe

Africa, Asia,
South America

the western European countries. In some ways the emergence of the East has slowed and complicated business activities in the West. Long-term, however, the new markets in the East are likely to make Europe an even more important part of the world economy.

● **Pacific Asia**
A market system located in Southeast Asia

Yet another mature market system is **Pacific Asia**. As shown in Figure 5.3, this market system includes Japan, China, Thailand, Malaysia, Singapore, Indonesia, South Korea, Taiwan, Hong Kong, the Philippines, and Australia. Whereas Japan has been a powerhouse for years, Taiwan, Hong Kong, Singapore, and South Korea have recently become major economic forces

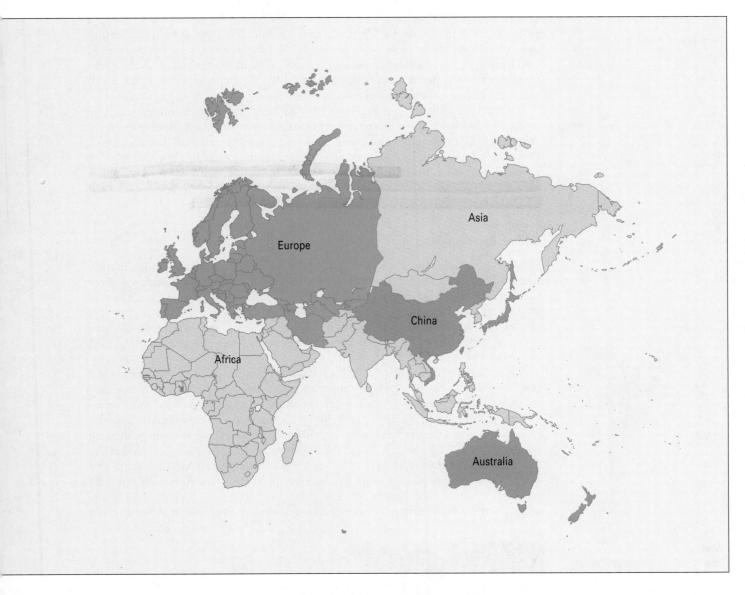

themselves. Trade among these nations is on the rise, and some Asian govern-ments have started discussing an economic community much like the EU.[23]

Developing Economies

In contrast to the highly developed and mature market economies just described, other countries have what are termed **developing economies**. These economies are relatively underdeveloped and immature. They are gen-erally characterized by weak industry, weak currency, and relatively poor con-sumers. The governments in these countries, however, are actively working to

● **developing economies**
Underdeveloped, immature economies characterized by weak industry, weak currency, and poor consumers

strengthen their economies by opening their doors to foreign investment and promoting international trade. Some of these countries have only recently adopted market economies, whereas others still use a command economy.

Even though it is technically part of Pacific Asia, the People's Republic of China is largely underdeveloped. India is also showing signs of becoming a major market in the future. Vietnam has also become a potentially important market. Many of the countries in South America and Africa are only now developing in an economic sense. And the various states and republics that make up the Confederation of Independent States (the former Soviet Union) are also viewed as developing economies.[24]

The primary challenges presented by the developing economies to those interested in conducting international business there are the lack of wealth on the part of potential consumers and the underdeveloped infrastructure. Developing economies have enormous economic potential, but much of it remains untapped. Thus international firms entering these markets often have to invest heavily in distribution systems, in training consumers how to use their products, and in providing living facilities for their workers.

Other Economies

Some economic systems around the world defy classification as either mature markets or developing economies. One major area that falls outside of these categories is the oil-exporting region generally called the Middle East. The oil-exporting countries present mixed models of resource allocation, property ownership, and the development of infrastructure. These countries all have access to major amounts of crude oil, however, and thus are important players in the global economy.

These countries include Iran, Iraq, Kuwait, Saudi Arabia, Libya, Syria, and the United Arab Emirates. High oil prices in the 1970s and 1980s created enormous wealth in these countries. Many of them invested heavily in their infrastructures. Whole new cities were built, airports were constructed, and the population was educated. As oil prices have fallen, many of the oil-producing countries have been forced to cut back on these activities. Nevertheless, they are still quite wealthy. The per capita incomes of the United Arab Emirates and Qatar, for example, are among the highest in the world. Although the oil-producing nations have great wealth, they provide great challenges to managers. Political instability (as evidenced by the Persian Gulf War in 1991 and the

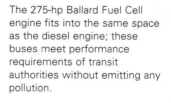

The 275-hp Ballard Fuel Cell engine fits into the same space as the diesel engine; these buses meet performance requirements of transit authorities without emitting any pollution.

U.S.-led attack on Iraq in late 1998) and tremendous cultural differences, for example, combine to make doing business in the Middle East both very risky and very difficult.

Other countries pose risks to business of a different sort. Politically and ethnically motivated violence, for example, still characterizes some countries. Foremost among these are Peru, El Salvador, Turkey, Colombia, and Northern Ireland.[25] Cuba presents special challenges because of its insulation from the outside world. With the fall of Communism, some experts believe that Cuba will eventually join the ranks of the market economies. If this is so, Cuba's strategic location will quickly make it an important business centre.

ENVIRONMENTAL CHALLENGES OF INTERNATIONAL MANAGEMENT

We noted earlier that managing in a global context both poses and creates additional challenges for the manager. As illustrated in Figure 5.4, three environmental challenges in particular warrant additional exploration at this point: the economic environment, the political–legal environment, and the cultural environment of international management.[26]

The Economic Environment

Every country is unique and creates a unique set of challenges for managers trying to do business there. However, three aspects of the economic environment in particular can help managers anticipate the kinds of economic challenges they are likely to face in working abroad.

Economic System The first of these is the economic system used in the country. As we described earlier, most countries today are moving toward market economies. In a mature market economy, managers must always consider the importance of the freedom of choice. Consumers are free to make decisions about which products they prefer to purchase, and firms are free to

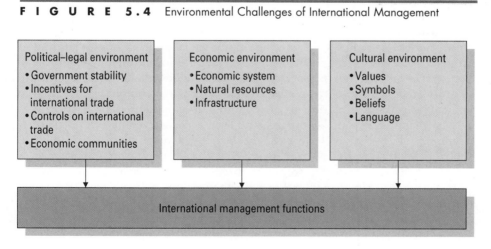

FIGURE 5.4 Environmental Challenges of International Management

Political–legal environment
- Government stability
- Incentives for international trade
- Controls on international trade
- Economic communities

Economic environment
- Economic system
- Natural resources
- Infrastructure

Cultural environment
- Values
- Symbols
- Beliefs
- Language

International management functions

Managers functioning in a global context must be aware of several environmental challenges. Three of the most important include economic, political–legal, and cultural challenges.

decide what products and services to provide. As long as both the consumer and the firm are free to decide to be in the market, then supply and demand determine which firms and which products are available.

A related characteristic of market economies that is relevant to managers concerns the nature of property ownership. There are two pure types—complete private ownership and complete public ownership. In systems with private ownership, individuals and organizations—not the government—own and operate the companies that conduct business. In systems with public ownership, the government directly owns the companies that manufacture and sell products. Few countries have pure systems of private ownership or pure systems of public ownership. Most countries tend toward one extreme or the other, but usually a mix of public and private ownership exists. The *Managing in a Changing World* box illustrates how recent shifts in the Japanese economy are affecting how businesses function there.

Natural Resources Another important aspect of the economic environment in different countries is the availability of natural resources. A very broad range of resources are available in different countries. Some countries, like Japan, have few resources of their own. Japan is thus forced to import all of the oil, iron ore, and other natural resources it needs to manufacture products for its domestic and overseas markets. Canada, in contrast, has enormous natural resources and is a major producer of oil, natural gas, coal, iron ore, copper, and other metals and materials that are vital to the development of a modern economy.

One natural resource that is particularly important in the modern global economy is oil. As we noted earlier, a small set of countries in the Middle East, including Saudi Arabia, Iraq, Iran, and Kuwait, controls a very large percentage of the world's total known reserves of crude oil. Access to this single natural resource has given these oil-producing countries enormous clout in the international economy. One of the more controversial global issues today involving natural resources is the Brazilian rain forest. Brazilian developers and farmers are clearing vast areas of rain forest, arguing that it's their land and they can do what they want with it. Many environmentalists, however, fear that the deforestation is wiping out entire species of animals and may so alter the environment as to affect weather patterns around the world.

● **infrastructure**
The schools, hospitals, power plants, railroads, highways, ports, communication systems, air fields, and commercial distribution systems of a country

Infrastructure Yet another important aspect of the economic environment of relevance to international management is infrastructure. A country's **infrastructure** comprises its schools, hospitals, power plants, railroads, highways, ports, communication systems, air fields, commercial distribution systems, and so forth. Canada has a highly developed infrastructure. For example, its educational system is modern, roads and bridges are well developed, and most people have access to medical care. Overall, Canada has a relatively complete infrastructure sufficient to support most forms of economic development and activity.

Many countries, on the other hand, lack a well-developed infrastructure. Some countries do not have enough electrical generating capacity to meet demand. Such countries often schedule periods of time during which power is turned off. These planned power failures reduce power demands but can be an enormous inconvenience to business. In the extreme, when a country's infrastructure is greatly underdeveloped, firms interested in beginning business may have to build an entire township, including housing, schools, hospitals, and perhaps even recreation facilities, to attract a sufficient overseas workforce.

Finance Changes in Japan

 Economic conditions led to a drastic reduction of Japanese asset prices in the 1990s. The fall in asset prices, in turn, dramatically reduced the wealth of Japanese banks and life insurance companies. As their wealth was reduced, the banks had to cut back on their international financial activity, which greatly slowed Japan's progress toward becoming an economic and financial superpower. In addition, this reduced role of the banks and insurance companies opened the way for a lot of entrepreneurial activity among Japanese credit unions and other financial intermediaries.

Tsu Credit Union, for instance, eliminated many very costly services to its customers, such as sending someone to pick up customers' deposits. In addition, it was able to reduce the number of employees and get rid of a fleet of cars and motor scooters. Because this action drastically reduced costs, Tsu Credit Union was able to offer its borrowers the lowest interest rates in Japan from a credit union. That makes its customers very happy. The traditional way of doing business is thus giving way to more modern approaches and providing a far more competitive atmosphere for lending and borrowing in Japan.

Credit unions aren't the only businesses that are breaking traditions in Japan. Business traditions are being shattered in such diverse industries as taxicabs, electrical components, and software. Kyoto-based MK Corp., for example, which operates a taxicab fleet, bowling alleys, and gas stations, has struck out on its own rather than adhere to traditional competitive agreements. Run by a Korean immigrant, MK fitted out its drivers in special uniforms and pushed for fare reductions while other companies tried to get hikes. When ridership fell at other taxi companies in 1993, it went up at MK.

Nemic-Lambda, which makes electric power converters, also broke with tradition by recently naming a Malaysian, Peter Hii, to a top executive position. In addition, Nemic has altered the way jobs are done and installed an extensive computerized network for its employees that is regarded as a model for other companies. Masayoshi Son, the CEO of Softbank, a software distribution and system integration firm, is another young Japanese entrepreneur who is developing new ways of doing business. Clearly, Japan's rigid, tradition-bound business system is beginning to change, perhaps substantially.

References: "Trashing Tradition: Some Maverick Firms in Japan Are Changing Its Business Climate," *The Wall Street Journal*, April 29, 1994, pp. A1, A5; Michio Hamaji, "Credit in Japan: May the Fittest Survive," *Business Credit*, May 1, 1994, p. 25; "Follow That Taxi," *Look Japan*, June 12, 1993, p. 18; "The Rock of Nemic-Lambda," *Malaysian Business*, April 1, 1993, p. 45; and Alan M. Webber, "Japanese-Style Entrepreneurship," *Harvard Business Review*, January 1992, pp. 92–98.

The Political–Legal Environment

Yet another environmental challenge facing the international manager is the political–legal environment in which he or she will do business. Four important aspects of the political–legal environment of international management are government stability, incentives for multinational trade, controls on international trade, and the influence of economic communities on international trade.

Government Stability   Stability can be viewed in two ways—as the ability of a given government to stay in power against other opposing factions in the country and as the permanence of government policies toward business. A country that is stable in both respects is preferable because managers have a higher probability of successfully predicting how government will affect their business. Civil war in countries such as Yugoslavia has made it virtually impossible for international managers to predict what government policies are likely to be and whether the government will be able to guarantee the safety of international workers. Consequently, international firms have been very reluctant to invest in Yugoslavia.

In many countries—Canada, the United States, Great Britain, and Japan, for example—changes in government occur with very little disruption. In other countries—Cambodia, Argentina, and Greece, for example—changes are likely to be chaotic. Even if a country's government is stable, the risk remains that the policies adopted by that government might change. In some countries, foreign businesses may experience **nationalization** (to be taken over by the government) with little or no warning. For example, a few years ago the government of Peru nationalized Perulac, a domestic milk producer owned by Nestlé, because of a local milk shortage.

Incentives for International Trade

Another facet of the political environment is incentives to attract foreign business. For example, the French government sold land to The Walt Disney Company far below its market value and agreed to build a connecting freeway in exchange for the company's agreeing to build its Euro Disneyland theme park outside of Paris.[27]

Such incentives can take a variety of forms. Some of the most common include reduced interest rates on loans, construction subsidies, and tax incentives. Less developed countries tend to offer different packages of incentives. In addition to lucrative tax breaks, for example, they can also attract investors with duty-free entry of raw materials and equipment, market protection through limitations on other importers, and the right to take profits out of the country. They may also have to correct deficiencies in their infrastructures, as just noted, to satisfy the requirements of foreign firms.

Controls on International Trade

A third element of the political environment that managers need to consider is the extent to which there are controls on international trade. In some instances, the government of a country may decide that foreign competition is hurting domestic trade. To protect domestic business, such governments may enact barriers to international trade. These barriers include tariffs, quotas, export restraint agreements, and "buy national" laws.

A **tariff** is a tax collected on goods shipped across national boundaries. Tariffs can be collected by the exporting country, countries through which goods pass, and the importing country. Import tariffs, which are the most common, can be levied to protect domestic companies by increasing the cost of foreign goods. Japan charges U.S. tobacco producers a tariff on cigarettes imported into Japan as a way to keep their prices higher than the prices charged by domestic firms. Tariffs can also be levied, usually by less developed countries, to raise money for the government.

Quotas are the most common form of trade restriction. A quota is a limit on the number or value of goods that can be traded. The quota amount is typically designed to ensure that domestic competitors will be able to maintain a certain market share. Honda is allowed to import 425,000 autos each year into the United States. This quota is one reason Honda opened manufacturing facilities in that country. The quota applies to cars imported into the United States, but Honda can make as many cars within the United States as it wants because they are not considered imports. **Export restraint agreements** are designed to convince other nations to voluntarily limit the volume or value of goods exported to a particular country. They are, in effect, export quotas. Japanese steel producers voluntarily limit the amount of steel they send to the United States each year.

● **nationalization**
To be taken over by the government

● **tariff**
A tax collected on goods shipped across national boundaries

● **quota**
A limit on the number or value of goods that can be traded

● **export restraint agreement**
An accord reached by governments in which countries voluntarily limit the volume or value of goods they export and import from one another

"Buy national" legislation gives preference to domestic producers through content or price restrictions. Several countries have this type of legislation. Brazil requires that Brazilian companies purchase only Brazilian-made computers. The United States requires that the Department of Defense purchase military uniforms manufactured only in the United States, even though foreign uniforms are half the price. Mexico requires that 50 percent of the parts of cars sold in Mexico be manufactured in Mexico.

Economic Communities Just as government policies can either increase or decrease the political risk facing international managers, trade relations between countries can either help or hinder international business. Relations dictated by quotas, tariffs, and so forth can hurt international trade. There is currently a strong movement around the world to reduce many of these barriers. This movement takes its most obvious form in international economic communities.

An international **economic community** is a set of countries that agrees to markedly reduce or eliminate trade barriers among its member nations. The first, and in many ways still the most important, of these economic communities is the European Union (EU), discussed earlier. The passage of NAFTA, as also noted earlier, represents perhaps the first step toward the formation of a North American economic community. Other important economic communities include the Latin American Integration Association (Bolivia, Brazil, Colombia, Chile, Argentina, and other South American countries) and the Caribbean Common Market (Guyana, the Bahamas, Belize, Jamaica, Antigua, Barbados, and eleven other countries). The *Environment of Management* box provides more details about doing business under NAFTA.

● **economic community**
A set of countries that agrees to markedly reduce or eliminate trade barriers among its member nations (a formalized market system)

The Cultural Environment

Another environmental challenge for the international manager is the cultural environment and how it affects business. A country's culture includes all the values, symbols, beliefs, and language that guide behaviour.

Values, Symbols, and Beliefs Cultural values and beliefs are often unspoken; they may even be taken for granted by those who live in a particular country. Cultural factors do not necessarily cause problems for managers when the cultures of two countries are similar. Difficulties can arise, however, when there is little overlap between the home culture of a manager and the culture of the country in which business is to be conducted. For example, most Canadian managers find the culture and traditions of the United States familiar. The people of both countries speak the same language and share strong ties, and there is a history of strong commerce between the two countries. When Canadian managers begin operations in Japan or the People's Republic of China, however, most of those commonalities disappear.[28]

Even when the cultures of two countries are similar, there is still substantial room for misunderstanding and embarrassment. For example, when someone from the United Kingdom says that he is going to (1) knock you up, (2) take a lift, (3) check under your bonnet, and (4) put the telly in the boot, he has told you that he will (1) wake you up in the morning, (2) take an elevator, (3) check under the hood of your car, and (4) put a television set in the car's trunk.

Things become even more complicated when the cultures are truly different. In Japanese, for example, the word *hai* (pronounced "hi") means "yes." In

"Afta" NAFTA

The North American Free Trade Agreement (NAFTA), which came into effect January 1, 1994, created a free trade zone between Canada, Mexico, and the United States. Executives in the automobile, heavy equipment, and hotel industries praised the agreement and its early impact, especially in Mexico. Others, particularly in Canada, have been far more cautious. Although NAFTA clearly has expanded trade and tourism among the three countries (the United States and Canada have the world's largest and most extensive trading partnership), numerous businesses are learning that the existence of a free trade zone does not mean that there is no governmental regulation within that zone. Indeed, some are finding that the enforcement of terms of the agreement may create even more red tape for doing business across borders.

Retailers expanding operations into Mexico, for instance, have run into frequent rules, regulations, and communication problems that have slowed down those expansion activities. Kmart had one construction site in Mexico City closed for a day and a half while it confirmed to Mexican officials that it had conducted the required environmental impact studies for the building. Rehiring the workers and getting construction going again at full capacity took a total of eight days. Radio Shack found the problems surrounding growth into Mexico significant enough that it drastically slowed the expansion plans of its strategic alliance with Mexican retailer Grupo Gigante. Originally it planned to have two hundred stores by 1995, but by mid-1994 it had only forty-nine stores opened.

But Wal-Mart had one of the most telling experiences of all. Wal-Mart formed a strategic alliance with Cifra, Mexico's largest retailer, to open Supercenters in Mexico City, Monterrey, and Guadalajara as well as Sam's Clubs in these and other cities. When government inspectors visited the Mexico City store, however, they ordered it shut because thousands of products were improperly labelled or lacked instructions in Spanish. By quick action and the help of the U.S. ambassador, Wal-Mart was able to get the store opened in only twenty-four hours, but the experience taught Wal-Mart a valuable lesson. Labelling must be in Spanish and denote the country of origin, content, instructions, and, in certain cases, an import permit number. Wal-Mart claimed that many of the products were obtained from a Mexican supplier, but regulators pointed out that the ultimate responsibility lies with the retailer.

NAFTA has also allowed corporations to take unprecedented action against governments. For example, in a recent controversial case, Ethyl Corporation of Richmond, Virginia, sued the Canadian government over its banning of the fuel additive MMT. In an out-of-court settlement, the Canadian government withdrew the ban, apologized, and paid the corporation $20 million.

References: "NAFTA: A Green Light for Red Tape," *Business Week*, July 25, 1994, p. 48; "NAFTA Already Looks Frayed at the Northern Border," *Business Week*, April 11, 1994, pp. 28–29; Lisa Renstrom, "Hotelier Lauds NAFTA Passage," *Hotel and Motel Management*, January 10, 1994, pp. 8, 29; Tom Buckley, "Mexican Dealer Eager for NAFTA," *Automotive News*, January 31, 1994, pp. 62+; "Caterpillar Sees Free-Trade Boon," *The New York Times*, September 21, 1993, p. D1; Martha H. Peak, "Mexican Miracle: How the U.S. Can Profit from NAFTA," *Management Review*, March 1993, pp. 10–11; and Jill McEachern and Chris Shaw, "MMT–NAFTA's Potentially Lethal Legacy: Lifting the MMT Ban Is Not Justified by Lack of Scientific Proof," *CCA Monitor*, November, 1998, ⟨http://www.policyalternatives.ca⟩

conversation, however, this word is used much like people in Canada use "uh–huh"; it moves a conversation along or shows the person you are talking to that you are paying attention. So when does "hai" mean "yes" and when does it mean "uh–huh"? This turns out to be a relatively difficult question to answer. When a Canadian manager asks a Japanese manager if he agrees to some trade arrangement, the Japanese manager is likely to say "hai"—which may mean "yes, I agree," "yes, I understand," or "yes, I am listening." Many North American managers become very frustrated in negotiations with the Japanese because they believe that the Japanese continue to raise issues that have already been settled (the Japanese managers said "yes"). What many of these managers fail to recognize is that "hai" does not always mean "yes" in Japan.

Cultural differences between countries can have a direct impact on business practice. For example, the religion of Islam teaches that people should not make a living by exploiting the misfortune of others and that making interest payments is immoral. This means that in Saudi Arabia there are no businesses that provide auto-wrecking services to tow stalled cars to the garage (because that would be capitalizing on misfortune), and in the Sudan banks cannot pay or charge interest. Given these cultural and religious constraints, automobile towing and banking don't seem to hold great promise for international managers in those particular countries.

Some cultural differences between countries can be even more subtle and yet have a major impact on business activities. For example, in Canada most managers clearly agree about the value of time. Most Canadian managers schedule their activities very tightly and then adhere to their schedules. Other cultures don't put such a premium on time. In the Middle East, managers do not like to set appointments, and they rarely keep appointments set too far into the future. Canadian managers interacting with managers from the Middle East might misinterpret the late arrival of a potential business partner as a negotiation ploy or an insult, when it is rather a simple reflection of different views of time and its value.

Language   Language itself can be an important factor. Beyond the obvious and clear barriers posed by people who speak different languages, subtle differences in meaning can also play a major role. For example, Imperial Oil of Canada markets gasoline under the brand name Esso. When the firm tried to sell its gasoline in Japan, it learned that Esso means "stalled car" in Japanese. The Chevrolet Nova was not selling well in Latin America and General Motors executives couldn't understand why until it was brought to their attention that, in Spanish, *no va* means "it doesn't go." The colour green is used extensively in Muslim countries, but it signifies death in some other countries. The colour associated with femininity in North America is pink, but in many other countries yellow is the most feminine colour.

COMPETING IN A GLOBAL ECONOMY

Competing in a global economy is both a major challenge and opportunity for businesses today. The nature of these challenges depends on a variety of factors, including the size of the organization. In addition, international management

The euro coin contains the French motto "Liberty, Equality, Fraternity" on one side. The coins will start circulating on January 1, 2002, and will provide a common currency for all European Union member countries.

also has implications for the basic functions of planning, organizing, leading, and controlling.

Globalization and Organization Size

Although organizations of any size can compete in international markets, there are some basic differences in the challenges and opportunities faced by MNEs, medium-size organizations, and small organizations.

Multinational Organizations   The large MNEs have long since made the choice to compete in a global marketplace. In general, these firms take a global perspective. They transfer capital, technology, human resources, inventory, and information from one market to another. They actively seek new expansion opportunities wherever feasible. MNEs tend to allow local managers a great deal of discretion in addressing local and regional issues. At the same time, each operation is ultimately accountable to a central authority. Managers at this central authority (for example, headquarters or a central office) are responsible for setting the overall strategic direction for the firm, making major policy decisions, and so forth. MNEs need senior managers who understand the global economy and who are comfortable dealing with executives and government officials from a variety of cultures. Table 5.2 lists the world's largest multinational enterprises, almost all of which do business in Canada.

Medium-Size Organizations   Many medium-size businesses remain primarily domestic organizations. But they still may buy and sell products made abroad and compete with businesses from other countries in their own domestic market. Increasingly, however, medium-size organizations are expanding into foreign markets as well. For example, Molex Incorporated is a medium-size firm based in Chicago that manufactures electronic connectors. Its recent annual sales have been between $300 and $400 million (U.S.). The firm operates several plants in Japan and derives more than one-half of its sales from Pacific Asia.[29] In contrast to MNEs, medium-size organizations doing business abroad are much more selective about the markets they enter. They also depend more on a few international specialists to help them manage their foreign operations.

Small Organizations   More and more small organizations are finding that they can benefit from the global economy. Some, for example, serve as local suppliers for MNEs. A dairy farmer who sells milk to Carnation Company, for example, is actually transacting business with Nestlé. Local parts suppliers also have been successfully selling products to the Toyota and GM plants in Canada. Beyond serving as local suppliers, some small businesses also buy and sell products and services abroad. For example, the Collin Street Bakery, based in Corsicana, Texas, ships fruitcakes around the world. In 1993, the firm shipped 160,000 pounds of fruitcake to Japan.[30] Most small businesses rely on simple importing or exporting operations (or both) for their international sales. Thus only a few specialized management positions are needed. Collin Street Bakery, for example, has one local manager who handles international activities. Mail-order activities within each country are subcontracted to local firms in each market.

T A B L E 5 . 2 The World's Top 25 TNCs, Ranked by Foreign Assets, 1996
Billions of dollars (U.S.) and number of employees

Ranking by Foreign assets	Transnationality index	Corporation	Country	Industry[b]	Assets Foreign	Assets Total	Sales Foreign	Sales Total	Employment Foreign	Employment Total	Transnationality index (percent)
1	83	General Electric	United States	Electronics	82.8	272.4	21.1	79.2	84,000	239,000	30.7
2	32	Shell, Royal Dutch[c]	United Kingdom/Netherlands	Petroleum/expl./ref./dist.	82.1	124.1	71.1	128.3	79,000	101,000	66.6
3	75	Ford Motor Company	United States	Automotive	79.1	258.0	65.8	147.0	[e]	371,702	37.7
4	22	Exxon Corporation	United States	Petroleum expl./ ref./dist.	55.6	95.5	102.0	117.0	[e]	79,000	72.7
5	85	General Motors	United States	Automotive	55.4	222.1	50.0	158.0	221,313	647,000	30.3
6	52	IBM	United States	Computers	41.4	81.1	46.6	75.9	121,655	240,615	54.3
7	79	Toyota	Japan	Automotive	39.2	113.4	51.7	109.3	34,837	150,736	35.0
8	49	Volkswagen Group	Germany	Automotive	[d]	60.8	41.0	64.4	123,042	260,811	55.3
9	71	Mitsubishi Corporation	Japan	Diversified	[d]	77.9	50.2	127.4	3,819	8,794	41.4
10	38	Mobil Corporation	United States	Petroleum expl./ref./dist.	31.3	46.4	53.1	80.4	22,900	43,000	62.3
11	3	Nestlé SA	Switzerland	Food	30.9	34.0	42.0	42.8	206,125	212,687	95.3
12	2	Asea Brown Boveri (ABB)	Switzerland/Sweden	Electrical equipment	[d]	30.9	32.9	33.8	203,541	214,894	96.1
13	47	Elf Aquitaine SA	France	Petroleum expl./ref./dist.	29.3	47.5	26.6	44.8	41,600	85,400	56.6
14	14	Bayer AG	Germany	Chemicals	29.1	32.0	25.8	31.4	94,375	142,200	79.9
15	34	Hoechst AG	Germany	Chemicals	28.0	35.5	18.4	33.8	93,708	147,862	65.6
16	57	Nissan Motor Co., Ltd.	Japan	Automotive	27.0	58.1	29.2	53.8	[e]	135,331	50.4
17	74	FIAT Spa	Italy	Automotive	26.9	70.6	19.8	51.3	90,390	237,865	38.2
18	8	Unilever	Netherlands/United Kingdom	Food	26.4	31.0	45.0	52.2	273,000	304,000	87.1
19	70	Daimler-Benz AG	Germany	Automotive	[d]	65.7	44.4	70.6	67,208	290,029	41.9
20	11	Philips Electronics N.V.	Netherlands	Electronics	24.5	31.7	38.9	40.9	216,000	262,500	84.9
21	9	Roche Holding AG	Switzerland	Pharmaceuticals	24.5	29.5	12.6	12.9	39,074	48,972	87.0
22	56	Siemens AG	Germany	Electronics	24.4	56.3	38.4	62.6	176,000	379,000	50.4
23	36	Alcatel Althom Cie	France	Electronics	23.5	48.4	24.6	31.6	118,820	190,600	62.9
24	40	Sony Corporation	Japan	Electronics	23.5	45.8	32.8	45.7	95,000	163,000	60.5
25	19	Total SA	France	Petroleum expl./ref./dist.	[d]	30.3	25.8	34.0	[e]	57,555	75.8

[a] The index of transnationality is calculated as the average of three ratios: foreign assets to total assets, foreign sales to total sales, and foreign employment to total employment.

[b] Industry classification for companies follows the United States Standard Industrial Classification as used by the United States Securities and Exchange Commission (SEC).

[c] Foreign sales are outside Europe whereas foreign employment is outside United Kingdom and the Netherlands.

[d] Data on foreign assets are either suppressed to avoid disclosure or they are not available. In case of nonavailability, they are estimated on the basis of the ratio of foreign to total sales, foreign to total employment, or similar ratios.

[e] Data on foreign employment are either suppressed to avoid disclosure or they are not available. In case of nonavailability, they are estimated on the basis of the ratio of foreign to total sales, foreign to total assets, or similar ratios.

Source: *World Investment Report 1998: Trends and Determinants*, Table II.1, p. 36 (Geneva: UNCTAD, 1998).

Management Challenges in a Global Economy

The management functions that constitute the framework for this book—planning, organizing, leading, and controlling—are just as relevant to international managers as to domestic managers. International managers need to have a clear view of where they want their firm to be in the future, they have to organize to implement their plans, they have to motivate those who work for them, and they have to develop appropriate control mechanisms.[31]

Planning in a Global Economy   To effectively plan in a global economy, managers must have a broad-based understanding of both environmental issues and competitive issues. They need to understand local market conditions and technological factors that will affect their operations. At the corporate level, executives need a great deal of information to function effectively. What markets are growing? What markets are shrinking? What are our domestic and foreign competitors doing in each market? They must also make a variety of strategic decisions about their organization. For example, if a firm wishes to enter the market in France, should it buy a local firm there, build a plant, or seek a strategic alliance? Critical issues include understanding environmental circumstances, the role of goals and planning in a global organization, and how decision making affects the global organization. We note special implications for global managers as we discuss planning in Chapters 6 through 9.

Organizing in a Global Economy   Managers in international businesses must also attend to a variety of organizing issues. For example, General Electric Co. has operations scattered around the globe. The firm has made the decision to give local managers a great deal of responsibility for how they run their business. In contrast, many Japanese firms give managers of their foreign operations relatively little responsibility. As a result, those managers must frequently travel back to Japan to present problems or get decisions approved. Managers in an international business must address the basic issues of organization structure and design, managing change, and dealing with human resources. We address the special issues of organizing the international organization in Chapters 10 through 14.

Leading in a Global Economy   We noted earlier some of the cultural factors that affect international organizations. Individual managers must be prepared for these and other factors as they interact with people from different cultural backgrounds. Supervising a group of five managers, each of whom is from a different province in Canada, is likely to be much simpler than supervising a group of five managers, each of whom is from a different culture. Managers must understand how cultural factors affect individuals, how motivational processes vary across cultures, the role of leadership in different cultures, how communication varies across cultures, and the nature of interpersonal and group processes in different cultures. In Chapters 15 through 19 we note special implications for international managers that relate to leading and interacting with others.

Controlling in a Global Economy   Finally, managers in international organizations must also be concerned with control. Distances, time zone differences, and cultural factors also all play a role in control. For example, in some cultures close supervision is seen as being appropriate, and in other cultures it is not. Likewise, executives in Canada and Japan may find communicating vital information to one another difficult because of the time zone differences. Basic control issues for the international manager revolve around operations management, productivity, quality, technology, and information systems. These issues are integrated throughout our discussion of control in Chapters 20 through 22.

SUMMARY OF KEY POINTS

International business has grown to be one of the most important features of the world's economy. Learning to operate in a global economy is an important challenge facing many managers today. Businesses can be primarily domestic, international, multinational, or global in scope. Managers need to understand both the process of internationalization as well as how to manage within a given level of international activity.

To compete in the global economy, managers must understand its structure. Mature market economies and systems dominate the global economy today. North America, the European Union, and Pacific Asia are especially important. Developing economies in Eastern Europe, Latin America, and Africa as well as the People's Republic of China, India, and Vietnam may play bigger roles in the future. The oil-exporting economies in the Middle East are also important.

Many of the challenges of management in a global context are unique issues associated with the international environmental context. These challenges reflect the economic, political–legal, and cultural environments of international management.

Basic issues of competing in a global economy vary according to whether the organization is a MNE, a medium-size organization, or a small organization. In addition, the basic managerial functions of planning, organizing, leading, and controlling must all be addressed in international organizations.

DISCUSSION QUESTIONS

Questions for Review

1. Describe the four basic levels of international business activity. Do you think any organization will achieve the fourth level? Why or why not?
2. Summarize the basic structure of the global economy. What are the major changes occurring within that structure today?
3. Briefly note some of the basic environmental challenges of international management.
4. What are some of the competitive differences for MNEs, medium-size organizations, and small organizations?

Questions for Analysis

5. An organization seeking to expand its international operations must monitor several different environments. Which aspect of each environment is likely to have the greatest impact on decisions involved in such a strategic move? Why?

6. Are there any industries that might not be affected by the trend toward international business? If so, which ones? If there are none, why are there none?

7. You are the CEO of an up-and-coming toy company and have plans to go international soon. What steps must you take to carry out that strategy? What areas must you stress in your decision-making process? How will you organize your company?

Questions for Application

8. Identify a local company that does business abroad. Interview an executive in that company. Why did the company go international? What major obstacles did it face? How successful has that decision been? Share your findings with the class.

9. Go to the library and find some information about the European Union's move toward a relaxation of trade barriers. What do you think will be the effect of that relaxation? What will be some of the difficulties? Do you think that relaxing trade barriers is a good idea? Explain why or why not.

10. Many organizations fail to allow for cultural and language differences when they do business with other countries. For example, Pepsi was introduced into Asia with the slogan "Come alive with Pepsi." The slogan, however, was translated as "Bring your ancestors back from the dead with Pepsi." Go to the library and locate mistakes made by other companies entering foreign markets. What did they do wrong? How could they have prevented their mistakes?

BUILDING EFFECTIVE COMMUNICATION SKILLS

Exercise Overview

Communication skills refer to the manager's ability to both effectively convey ideas and information to others and effectively receive ideas and information from others. International managers have additional communication complexities due to differences in language, time zones, and so forth. This exercise enables you to enhance your communication skills by demonstrating the impact of different time zones.

Exercise Background

Assume that you are a manager in a large multinational firm. Your office is located in Vancouver. You need to arrange a conference call with several other managers to discuss an upcoming strategic change by your firm. The other managers are located in New York, London, Rome, Moscow, Tokyo, Singapore, and Sydney.

Exercise Task

Using the preceding information, do the following:
1. Determine the time zone differences in each of these cities.
2. Assuming that people in each city work from 8:00 a.m. to 5 p.m. (local time), determine the optimal time for your conference call. That is, what time would minimize the number of people who are inconvenienced?
3. Now assume that you need to visit each office in person. You need to spend one full day in each city. Use the Internet to review airline schedules, take into account differences in time zones, and develop an itinerary.

"Going global" is one of today's hottest business trends. But amidst the hundreds of large multinationals boldly developing strategies for crossing new borders and entering new markets rests a firm that was "global" when most businesses were focused exclusively on their own domestic markets. The firm? Nestlé, a Swiss-based food processor that had international operations almost from its inception in 1866.

Just how global is Nestlé? The firm has factories in 74 of the world's 193 countries. And it sells milk, coffee, and/or chocolate bars in all of the rest! Indeed, even though Nestlé has no sales agents or distribution systems in North Korea, merchants there somehow manage to get Nestlé products on their shelves. Ninety-seven percent of Nestlé's employees are based outside of Switzerland. A recent United Nations study ranked Nestlé as having the highest level of international exposure of any business in the world. And year in and year out, Nestlé increases its market share, revenues, and profits.

So what is the key to the firm's success? Nestlé executives stress four basic operating principles. First, the firm thinks long term, rather than focusing on short-term profitability. Second, Nestlé believes in decentralization. Third, the firm sticks to what it knows best. And fourth, it recognizes the value of adapting to local tastes.

Long-term thinking shows up in many of Nestlé's decisions. For example, the firm recently paid what many observers might consider to be exorbitant prices for Perrier and Rowntree, a British-based candy maker. But Nestlé contends that although it would have obviously preferred to pay less, it nevertheless paid what it had to pay to get these prized businesses. It can afford to take this stance because investors do not expect to see a quick return. Instead, managers argue that these acquisitions will pay dividends for decades to come.

Decentralization is also a fundamental policy at Nestlé. Local managers are left alone to make decisions as they see fit. Their only reporting requirement is a one-page summary of their operations to Nestlé headquarters in Vevey, Switzerland, every quarter. Indeed, these reports cannot exceed one page in length! Somewhat more detail is required on

an annual basis, but even then the reporting requirements are far lower than in virtually any other multinational corporation.

Nestlé also believes in sticking with what it does best—food processing and marketing. Whereas many other large multinationals have dabbled in far-ranging investments, Nestlé has maintained a remarkable focus on its core businesses—infant formula, powdered milk, coffee, chocolates, soups, bottled water, ice cream, cereal, and pet foods. Each of these businesses is either number one or two in worldwide market share. Indeed, its only significant operation outside of foods is a 26.3 percent investment in the cosmetics firm L'Oreal.

But even though Nestlé keeps its eye on foods, it also recognizes the importance of adapting to local tastes. For example, it stresses instant coffee in Europe and brewed coffees in the United States, both because of local tastes. Similarly, Europeans prefer soups containing meat chunks, while Japanese consumers prefer broth with no meat. Therefore, Nestlé uses different soup recipes for the products it sells in these markets.

So where does it end? Nestlé argues that it still has significant growth opportunities. For example, Nestlé gets only about 2 percent of its revenues from the Middle East, and executives see plenty of room for growth throughout the region. Moreover, there are also many more different foods and food groups for Nestlé to develop. So the future, as they say, seems to be bright for the Swiss giant.

Questions

1. Nestlé almost makes it seem easy. If so, why don't more firms follow the same recipe for success?

2. Do you see any hazards or problems in Nestlé's future?

3. Can you think of circumstances in which Nestlé's basic operating guidelines might conflict with one another?

References: "All Over the Map," *The Wall Street Journal*, September 26, 1996, p. B1; and *Hoover's Handbook of World Business 1997* (Austin, Tex.: Hoover's Business Press, 1996), pp. 352–353.

CHAPTER NOTES

1. "Unilever's Struggle for Growth," *Business Week*, July 4, 1994, pp. 54–56; Alan Chai, Alta Campbell, and Patrick J. Spain (Eds.), *Hoover's Handbook of World Business 1993* (Austin, Tex.: The Reference Press, 1993), p. 484; "Unilever to Acquire Chinese Ice Cream Business (http://www.unilever.com); and "Top Private Companies," *Report on Business Magazine*, July 1998, pp. 137–146.

2. See Ricky W. Griffin and Michael Pustay, *International Business* (Reading, Mass.: Addison-Wesley, 1996), for an overview of international business.

3. Richard M. Steers and Edwin L. Miller, "Management in the 1990s: The International Challenge," *The Academy of Management Executive*, February 1988, pp. 21–22; David A. Ricks, Brian Toyne, and Zaida Martinez, "Recent Developments in International Management Research," *Journal of Management*, June 1990, pp. 219–254.

4. For a more complete discussion of forms of international business, see Arvind Phatak, *International Dimensions of Management*, 3rd ed. (Boston: Kent, 1992).

5. Gary Hoover, Alta Campbell, and Patrick J. Spain (Eds.), *Hoover's Handbook of American Business 1994* (Austin, Tex.: The Reference Press, 1993), p. 956.

6. Alex Taylor III, "The New Golden Age of Autos," *Fortune*, April 4, 1994, pp. 50–66.

7. John H. Dunning, *Multinational Enterprises and the Global Economy* (Wokingham, Eng.: Addison-Wesley, 1993); and Christopher Bartlett and Sumantra Ghoshal, *Transnational Management* (Homewood, Ill.: Irwin, 1992).

8. "Borderless Management," *Business Week*, May 23, 1994, pp. 24–26.

9. "Imports and Exports of Goods on a Balance-of-Payments Basis" (http://www.statcan.ca)

10. Mark MacKinnon, "Foreign Ownership Is on the Rise," *The Globe and Mail*, February 1, 1999, p. B1, B7.

11. "Foreign Direct Investment to Canada" (http://www.stategis.ic.ca)

12. "Canadian Direct Investment Abroad" (http://www.strategis.ic.ca.)

13. John D. Daniels and Lee H. Radebaugh, *International Business*, 7th ed. (Reading, Mass.: Addison-Wesley, 1995).

14. "Creating a Worldwide Yen for Japanese Beer," *Financial Times*, October 7, 1994, p. 20.

15. Kenichi Ohmae, "The Global Logic of Strategic Alliances," *Harvard Business Review*, March–April 1989, pp. 143–154.

16. Jeremy Main, "Making Global Alliances Work," *Fortune*, December 17, 1990, pp. 121–126.

17. UNCTAD, *World Investment Report 1998: Trends and Determinants* (Geneva: United Nations, 1998), p.1.

18. "The Magnet of Growth in Mexico's North," *Business Week*, June 6, 1988, pp. 48–50; "Will the New Maquiladoras Build a Better Mañana?" *Business Week*, November 14, 1988, pp. 102–106.

19. Allen J. Morrison, David A. Ricks, and Kendall Roth, "Globalization versus Regionalism: Which Way for the Multinational?" *Organizational Dynamics*, Winter 1991, pp. 17–29.

20. Griffin and Pustay, *International Business*.

21. "New Worlds to Conquer," *Business Week*, February 28, 1994, pp. 50–52.

22. Louis S. Richman, "How NAFTA Will Help America," *Fortune*, April 19, 1993, pp. 95–101.

23. John J. Curran, "China's Investment Boom," *Fortune*, March 7, 1994, pp. 116–124. See also Louis Kraar, "The Growing Power of Asia," *Fortune*, October 7, 1991, pp. 118–131.

24. Rahul Jacob, "India Gets Moving," *Fortune*, September 5, 1994, pp. 100–104; and "In the New Vietnam, Baby Boomers Strive for Fun and Money," *The Wall Street Journal*, January 7, 1994, pp. A1, A5.

25. "Where Killers and Kidnappers Roam," *Fortune*, September 23, 1991, p. 8.

26. Daniels and Radebaugh, *International Business*.

27. "Fans Like Euro Disney But Its Parents' Goofs Weigh the Park Down," *The Wall Street Journal*, March 10, 1994, p. A1.

28. "Firms Address Worker's Cultural Variety," *The Wall Street Journal*, February 10, 1989, p. B1.

29. "You Don't Have to Be a Giant to Score Big Overseas," *Business Week*, April 13, 1987, pp. 62–63; see also Edmund Faltermayer, "Competitiveness: How U.S. Companies Stack up Now," *Fortune*, April 18, 1994, pp. 52–64.

30. "Famous Bakery Keeps Business Thriving," *Corsicana Daily Sun*, June 9, 1991, p. 1C; new data obtained in personal correspondence with the company.

31. Stratford Sherman, "Are You as Good as the Best in the World?" *Fortune*, December 13, 1993, pp. 95–96.

The Environmental Context of Management

NEWS ITEM:
Bre-X "Winners" (1996, 7:00)

Just before the Bre-X phenomenon was found out to be a fraud, this report showed how "gold fever" had taken over the small Alberta town of St. Paul. Many residents have cashed in their RRSPs in order to invest in the Indonesian gold mine. At one point, the reporter makes the poignant observation that investors are still just millionaires "on paper."

Questions:

1. The Bre-X saga was a classic example of investor fraud. Was there any way that Bre-X shareholders could have proceeded differently, to protect themselves?
2. Should the stockbrokers take any responsibility for the stock-buying "frenzy" that occured in St. Paul, or were investors simply victems of their own greed?

NEWS ITEM:
Garth Drabinsky Steps Down From Livent (1998, 2:00)

Canadian theatre impresario Garth Drabinsky announces that he is relinquishing some of his control of Livent. The demotion of Drabinsky was the first indication that the mogul was headed for trouble; he was soon accused of mismanagement and fraud concerning the finances of the company.

Questions:

1. Drabinsky tried to be a "hands on" manager, handling many details of his operation. What impact do you think this had on the culture at Livent?
2. What environmental challenges led to the need for new management at Livent?
   Do you interpret Drabinsky's comments as "damage control"?

NEWS ITEM:
The Cost of the Ice Storm (1998, 2:30)

Many farms and businesses in eastern Ontario and parts of Quebec are assessing the damage caused by the ice storm and attempting to cope. Insurance claims in Ontario alone number 10,000, and will make it the most costly natural disaster in Canadian history for insurers, although many business people are discovering that they are not covered.

The Environmental Context of Management (Continued)

Questions:

1. To what extent should the government get involved in compensating business for losses due to natural disasters? Are businesses at fault for not securing proper insurance?
2. What sorts of economic spin-offs might be generated by the $1 billion rebuilding program facing Ontario and Quebec?

Managers must make decisions and develop strategies for steering their organizations through an ever-changing competitive landscape. Even on a local level, managers make decisions, plan, and promote entrepreneurship in their quest for improved organizational performance.

Planning and Decision Making

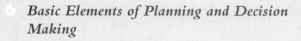

6

OBJECTIVES

After studying this chapter, you should be able to:

● *Summarize the function of decision making and the planning process.*

● *Discuss the purpose of organizational goals, identify different kinds of goals, discuss who sets goals, and describe how to manage multiple goals.*

● *Identify different kinds of organizational plans, note the time frames for planning, discuss who plans, and describe contingency planning.*

● *Discuss how tactical plans are developed and executed.*

● *Describe the basic types of operational plans used by organizations.*

● *Identify the major barriers to goal setting and planning, how organizations overcome those barriers, and how to use MBO to implement plans.*

OUTLINE

Israel Asper, executive chairman of CanWest Global Communications, has bought majority control of The Sports Network and The Discovery Channel in a deal worth $875 million.

One of the great paradoxes of business today is that sometimes managers can confidently decide what they and their organization need to do and be exactly right. At other times, however, they can just as confidently decide what to do and then be wrong. In the final analysis, success of plans is heavily dependent on how well managers read the future. In reading the future, current information is crucial. Take the example of Winnipeg-based CanWest Global Communications Corporation, a company that started with one station in Winnipeg in 1975 and is today the largest private-sector broadcaster in Canada, with operations in Australia, Great Britain, New Zealand, and Chile. In 1997, CanWest's profit of $141.8 million made it Canada's most profitable broadcasting corporation that year. Moreover, CanWest continues to grow, acquiring control in January 1999 of NetStar Communications, the parent company of The Sports Network and The Discovery Channel. Part of the success of CanWest is due to the timing of its entry into the broadcasting business and the information available to guide its planning. On average Canadians watch

> "The vision of CanWest's founder, Israel Asper, has transformed the company from a one-station operation in Winnipeg into a significant global player in the broadcasting industry."

approximately three and a half hours of prime-time television per day. Media companies compete to gain large audiences and sell advertising to corporations that are interested in selling their products to viewers. When CanWest entered the business in 1975, the Canadian networks were following the formula of building stations in local markets. CanWest took advantage of the fact that the Canadian Radio-television and Telecommunications Commission (CRTC) allowed broadcasters to use transmitters and other technology to send signals into local markets, thus eliminating the need for local stations. CanWest reaches more viewers with fewer stations than those broadcasters burdened with the old formula.

A second advantage CanWest enjoys is its focus on offering hit series such as *Seinfeld* (while it was in production) and *Frasier* during prime time. Such programs attract viewers week after week. One week in December 1995, CanWest's Global won the top ten spots in the ratings in the Toronto–Hamilton region, which is Canada's top television market.

Even CanWest has not been successful in all its ventures. For example, while the company's operations in Australia and New Zealand are profitable, its station in Chile did not do as well. Nevertheless, the vision of CanWest's founder, Israel Asper, has transformed the company from a one-station operation in Winnipeg into a significant global player in the broadcasting industry.[1] ●

Decision making is the lifeblood of organizations. Managers continually make decisions that determine successes and failures for their firms. One of the riskiest decisions facing many managers today is whether to enter such potentially lucrative but complex markets as Russia, China, and India. McDonald's has recently made the decision to enter the Russian market. These bakers are making hamburger buns at McDonald's McComplex, a giant production and distribution centre the fastfood king has opened near Moscow.

Although both the original investors and the current managers at CanWest tried to predict and understand the future of their business, they have not always succeeded. The original investors, for example, probably wish that they had maintained a stake in what has become the most profitable broadcasting corporation in Canada. And current managers, regardless of what they think they know about the broadcasting business, still make an occasional error about viewers' tastes and preferences in a given market. Fortunately, the clear and unambiguous goals set by CanWest's owner help keep the firm decidedly on track. Moreover, the firm succeeds far more often than it fails.

As we noted in Chapter 1, planning and decision making constitute the first managerial function that organizations must address. This chapter is the first of four that explore the planning process in detail. We begin by briefly relating decision making and planning and then explaining the planning process that most organizations follow. We then discuss the nature of organizational goals and introduce the basic concepts of planning. Next we discuss tactical and operational planning more fully. Finally, we conclude with a discussion of how to manage the goal-setting and planning processes.

DECISION MAKING AND THE PLANNING PROCESS

Decision making is the cornerstone of planning. Consider, for example, that the original plan to enter the broadcasting business, CanWest's acquisition of its first station in Winnipeg, and the acquisition of stations in the United Kingdom and New Zealand all reflect decisions people make. Thus decision making is the catalyst that drives the planning process. An organization's goals follow from decisions made by various managers. Likewise, deciding on the best plan for achieving particular goals also reflects a decision to adopt one course of action as opposed to others. We discuss decision making per se in Chapter 8. Our focus here is on the planning process itself. As we discuss goal setting and planning, however, keep in mind that decision making underlies every aspect of setting goals and formulating plans.

The planning process itself can best be thought of as a generic activity. All organizations engage in planning activities, but no two organizations plan in exactly the same fashion. Figure 6.1 is a general representation of the planning process that many organizations attempt to follow.[2] But although most firms follow this general framework, each also has its own nuances and variations.

As Figure 6.1 shows, all planning occurs within an environmental context. If managers do not understand this context, they are unable to develop effective plans. Thus understanding the environment is essentially the first step in planning. The three previous chapters covered many of the basic environmental issues that affect organizations and how they plan. With this understanding as a foundation, managers must then establish the organization's mission. The mission outlines the organization's purpose, premises, values, and directions. Flowing from the mission are parallel streams of goals and plans. Directly following the mission are strategic goals. These goals and the mission help determine strategic plans. Strategic goals and plans are primary inputs for developing tactical goals. Tactical goals and the original strategic plans help shape tactical plans. Tactical plans, in turn, combine with the tactical goals to shape opera-

F I G U R E 6.1 The Planning Process

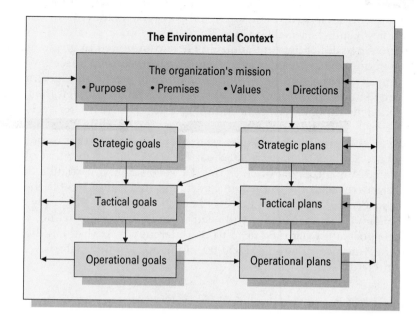

The planning process takes place within an environmental context. Managers must develop a complete and thorough understanding of this context to determine the organization's mission and develop its strategic, tactical, and operational goals and plans.

tional goals. These goals and the appropriate tactical plans determine operational plans. Finally, goals and plans at each level can also be used as input for future activities at all levels. This chapter discusses goals and tactical and operational plans. Chapter 7 covers strategic plans.

ORGANIZATIONAL GOALS

Goals are critical to organizational effectiveness, and they serve a number of purposes. Organizations can also have several different kinds of goals, all of which must be appropriately managed. And a number of different kinds of managers must be involved in setting goals.

Purposes of Goals

Goals serve four important purposes.[3] First, they provide guidance and a unified direction for people in the organization. Goals can help everyone understand where the organization is going and why getting there is important. Several years ago Jack Welch, CEO of General Electric Co., set a goal that every business owned by the firm will be either number-one or number-two in its industry. This goal helps set the tone for decisions made by GE managers.

Second, goal-setting practices strongly affect other aspects of planning. Effective goal setting promotes good planning, and good planning facilitates future goal setting. The success of CanWest demonstrates how setting goals and developing plans to reach them are complementary activities. The strong growth goal encourages managers to plan for expansion by looking for new market opportunities, for example. Similarly, they must also always be alert for competitive threats and new ideas that will help facilitate future expansion.

Third, goals can serve as a source of motivation to employees of the organization. Goals that are specific and moderately difficult can motivate people to work harder, especially if attaining the goal is likely to result in rewards.[4] When Stanley Gault became CEO of Rubbermaid Incorporated, he set a goal of increasing sales 15 percent annually. He also promised to give employees more say in how the company was run and bigger rewards for success. Workers in the company were galvanized into actions aimed at meeting the goal, and they succeeded in meeting it for eight years straight.[5] After Gault left the firm, the goal remained and Rubbermaid continues to surpass it year after year.

Finally, goals provide an effective mechanism for evaluation and control. This means that performance can be assessed in the future in terms of how successfully today's goals are accomplished. For example, suppose that officials of the United Way set a goal of collecting $250,000 from a particular community. If midway through the campaign they have raised only $50,000, they know that they need to change or intensify their efforts. If they raise only $100,000 by the end of their drive, they will need to carefully study why they did not reach their goal and what they need to do differently next year. On the other hand, if they succeed in raising $265,000, evaluations of their efforts will take on an entirely different character.

Kinds of Goals

Organizations establish many different kinds of goals. In general, these goals vary by level, area, and time frame. Figure 6.2 provides examples of each type of goal for a fast-food chain.

mission
A statement of an organization's fundamental purpose

strategic goal
A goal set by and for top management of the organization

tactical goal
A goal set by and for middle managers of the organization

operational goal
A goal set by and for lower-level managers of the organization

Level   Goals are set for and by different levels within an organization. As we noted earlier, the four basic levels of goals are the mission and strategic, tactical, and operational goals. An organization's **mission** is a statement of its "fundamental, unique purpose that sets a business apart from other firms of its type and identifies the scope of the business's operations in product and market terms."[6] Table 6.1 identifies the basic components of a typical corporate mission statement and provides an example of each component taken from actual mission statements.

Strategic goals are goals set by and for top management of the organization. They focus on broad, general issues. For example, Quebec-based Biochem Pharma, with a market capitalization of $3.5 billion at the end of 1998, recently set a strategic goal of transforming itself from a research boutique (firms that license out their discoveries) into an integrated drug company capable of competing with multinational drug companies like Glaxo and Merck.[7] **Tactical goals** are set by and for middle managers. Their focus is on how to operationalize actions necessary to achieve the strategic goals. One tactical goal at Sony was to acquire a firm in the entertainment industry; the goal was realized when Sony bought Columbia Pictures. **Operational goals** are set by and for lower-level managers. Their concern is with shorter-term issues associated with the tactical goals. An operational goal for Sony might be target level of market share for a new electronics device. (Some people use the words *objective* and *goal* interchangeably. When they are differentiated, however, the term *objective* is usually used instead of *operational goal*.)

Area   Organizations also set goals for different areas. The restaurant chain shown in Figure 6.2 has goals for operations, marketing, and finance. Hewlett-

FIGURE 6.2 Kinds of Organizational Goals for a Regional Fast-Food Chain

Organizations develop many different types of goals. A regional fast-food chain, for example, might develop goals at several different levels and for several different areas.

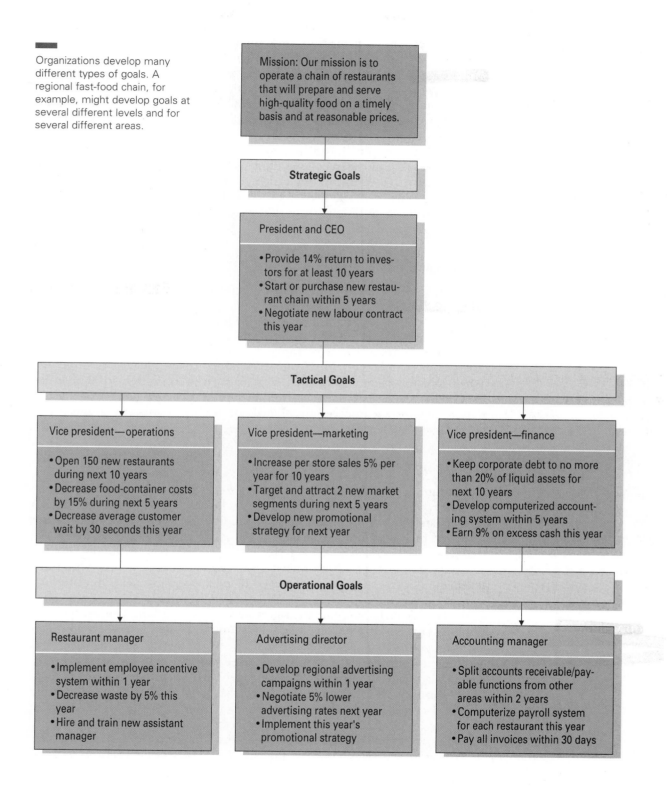

Mission: Our mission is to operate a chain of restaurants that will prepare and serve high-quality food on a timely basis and at reasonable prices.

Strategic Goals

President and CEO

- Provide 14% return to investors for at least 10 years
- Start or purchase new restaurant chain within 5 years
- Negotiate new labour contract this year

Tactical Goals

Vice president—operations

- Open 150 new restaurants during next 10 years
- Decrease food-container costs by 15% during next 5 years
- Decrease average customer wait by 30 seconds this year

Vice president—marketing

- Increase per store sales 5% per year for 10 years
- Target and attract 2 new market segments during next 5 years
- Develop new promotional strategy for next year

Vice president—finance

- Keep corporate debt to no more than 20% of liquid assets for next 10 years
- Develop computerized accounting system within 5 years
- Earn 9% on excess cash this year

Operational Goals

Restaurant manager

- Implement employee incentive system within 1 year
- Decrease waste by 5% this year
- Hire and train new assistant manager

Advertising director

- Develop regional advertising campaigns within 1 year
- Negotiate 5% lower advertising rates next year
- Implement this year's promotional strategy

Accounting manager

- Split accounts receivable/payable functions from other areas within 2 years
- Computerize payroll system for each restaurant this year
- Pay all invoices within 30 days

Packard routinely sets production goals for quality, productivity, and so forth. By keeping activities focused on these important areas, HP has managed to remain competitive against organizations from around the world.[8] Human resource goals might be set for employee turnover and absenteeism. 3M and Rubbermaid set goals for product innovation. 3M, for example, has a goal of generating at least 10 percent of its revenues each year from new products.[9]

Time Frame   Organizations set goals across different time frames. In Figure 6.2, three goals are listed at the strategic, tactical, and operational levels. The first is a long-term goal, the second an intermediate-term goal, and the third a short-term goal. Some goals have an explicit time frame (e.g., open 150 new restaurants during the next ten years) and others have an open-ended time horizon (e.g., maintain 10 percent annual growth). Finally, we should also note that the meaning of different time frames varies by level. For example, at the strategic level, long-term often means ten years or longer, intermediate term around five years or so, and short-term around one year. But two or three years may be long-term at the operational level, and short-term may mean a matter of weeks or even days.

Responsibilities for Setting Goals

Who sets goals? The answer is actually quite simple: all managers should be involved in the goal-setting process. Each manager, however, generally has responsibilities for setting goals that correspond to his or her level in the organization. The mission and strategic goals are generally determined by the board of directors and top managers. Top and middle managers then work together to establish tactical goals. Finally, middle and lower-level managers are jointly responsible for operational goals. Many managers also set individual goals for themselves. These goals may involve career paths, informal work-related goals outside the normal array of official goals, or just about anything of interest or concern to the manager.

Managing Multiple Goals

Organizations set many different kinds of goals and sometimes experience conflicts or contradictions among goals. Nike had problems with inconsistent goals a few years ago. The firm was producing high-quality shoes (a manufacturing goal) but they were not particularly stylish (a marketing goal). As a result, the company lost substantial market share when Reebok International started making shoes that were both high quality and fashionable. When Nike management recognized and corrected the inconsistencies, Nike regained its industry standing.[10]

● **optimizing**
Balancing and reconciling possible conflicts among goals

To address such problems, managers must understand the concept of optimizing. **Optimizing** involves balancing and reconciling possible conflicts between goals. Because goals may conflict with one another, the manager must look for inconsistencies and decide whether to pursue one goal to the exclusion of another or to find a mid-range target between the extremes.[11] American Express Company, for example, has long had a goal of maintaining good relations with the banks that sell its traveller's cheques. However, the company began offering its own customers products and services previously available only from banks. An example is the Optima True Value credit card, with terms and uses similar—and in some ways better—to Visa's and

TABLE 6.1	Components of Corporate Mission Statements

Component	Example
Target customers and markets	"We believe our first responsibility is to the doctors, nurses, and patients, to mothers and all others who use our products." (Johnson & Johnson)
Principal products or services	"AMAX's principal products are molybdenum, coal, iron ore, copper, lead, zinc, petroleum and natural gas, potash, phosphates, nickel, tungsten, silver, gold, and magnesium." (Amax Inc.)
Geographic domain	"We are dedicated to the total success of Corning Glass Works as a worldwide competitor." (Corning Incorporated)
Core technologies	"Control Data is in the business of applying microelectronics and computer technology in two general areas: computer-related hardware; and computer-enhancing services, which include computation, information, education, and finance." (Control Data Corporation)
Concern for survival, growth, and profitability	"In this respect, the company will conduct its operations prudently, and will provide the profits and growth which will assure Hoover's ultimate success." (Hoover Universal, Inc.)
Company philosophy	"It's all part of the Mary Kay philosophy—a philosophy based on the golden rule. A spirit of sharing and caring where people give cheerfully of their time, knowledge, and experience." (Mary Kay Cosmetics)
Company self-concept	"Hoover Universal is a diversified, multi-industry corporation with strong manufacturing capabilities, entrepreneurial policies, and individual business unit autonomy." (Hoover Universal, Inc.)
Desired public image	"To share the world's obligation for the protection of the environment." (Dow Chemical)

An organization's mission statement can have a variety of components. Basic components include target customers and markets; principal products or services; geographic domain; core technologies; concern for survival, growth and profitability; company philosophy; company self-concept; and desired public image.

Source: John A. Pearce II and Fred David, *The Academy of Management Executive,* May 1987. Republished with permission of Academy of Management, Briar Cliff Manor, NY, via Copyright Clearance Centre, Inc.

MasterCard's but with a lower interest rate. Not surprisingly, this changed American Express's relationship with banks. A few stopped carrying American Express traveller's cheques. Officials at American Express hope that the extra profits earned by Optima will offset the lost business from the banks that begin to push competitors' traveller's cheques.[12]

ORGANIZATIONAL PLANNING

Given the clear link between organizational goals and plans, we now turn our attention to various concepts and issues associated with planning itself. In particular, this section identifies kinds of plans, time frames for planning, who is responsible for planning, and contingency planning.

Kinds of Organizational Plans

Organizations establish many different kinds of plans. At a general level, these include strategic, tactical, and operational plans.

Strategic Plans   Strategic plans are the plans developed to achieve strategic goals. More precisely, a **strategic plan** is a general plan outlining decisions of resource allocation, priorities, and action steps necessary to reach strategic goals.[13] These plans are set by the board of directors and top management, generally have an extended time horizon, and address questions of scope, resource deployment, competitive advantage, and synergy. We discuss strategic planning further in Chapter 7.

Tactical Plans   A **tactical plan**, aimed at achieving tactical goals, is developed to implement specific parts of a strategic plan. Tactical plans typically involve upper and middle management and, compared with strategic plans, have a

● **strategic plan**
A general plan outlining decisions of resource allocation, priorities, and

● **tactical plan**
A plan aimed at achieving tactical goals and developed to implement parts of a strategic plan

What constitutes "long" in long-range planning varies dramatically across industries. To help information technology firms better understand long-range prospects for their industry, investors have created Interval, a think tank devoted to helping forecast the future of information technology. These employees of Interval are modelling interactions in a home to better understand how people can use information technology away from work.

somewhat shorter time horizon and a more specific and concrete focus. Thus tactical plans are concerned more with actually getting things done than with deciding what to do. Tactical planning is covered in detail in a later section.

Operational Plans An **operational plan** focuses on carrying out tactical plans to achieve operational goals. Developed by middle and lower-level managers, operational plans have a short-term focus and are relatively narrow in scope. Each one deals with a fairly small set of activities. We also cover operational planning in more detail later.

● **operational plan**
Focuses on carrying out tactical plans to achieve operational goals

Time Frames for Planning

As we previously noted, strategic plans tend to have a long-term focus, tactical plans an intermediate-term focus, and operational plans a short-term focus. The sections that follow address these time frames in more detail.

Long-Range Plans A **long-range plan** covers many years, perhaps even decades. Large firms like General Motors Corp. and Exxon Corporation routinely develop plans for ten- to twenty-year intervals. GM executives, for example, have a pretty good idea today about new car models that they plan to introduce for at least a decade in advance. The time span for long-range planning varies from one organization to another. For our purposes, we regard any plan that extends beyond five years as long-range. Managers of organizations in complex, volatile environments face a special dilemma. These organizations probably need a longer time horizon than do organizations in less dynamic environments, yet the complexity of their environment makes long-range planning difficult. Managers at these companies therefore develop long-range plans but also must constantly monitor their environment for possible changes.[14] The *Environment of Management* box explores how Hitachi uses long-range planning to compete successfully in a volatile industry.

● **long-range plan**
A plan that covers many years, perhaps even decades; common long-range plans are for five years or more

Intermediate Plans An **intermediate plan** is somewhat less tentative and subject to change than is a long-range plan. Intermediate plans usually cover periods from one to five years and are especially important for middle and first-line managers. Thus they generally parallel tactical plans. For many organizations intermediate planning has become the central focus of planning activities.[15] Philip Morris Incorporated developed a long-range plan for diversifying away from the tobacco industry. The firm bought General Foods Corporation after two years of planning, and its recent purchase of Kraft General Foods grew from an intermediate plan developed about a year earlier. Thus, although long-range planning guided Philip Morris's actions, intermediate plans actually defined those actions.[16]

● **intermediate plan**
A plan that generally covers from one to five years

Short-Range Plans A manager also develops a **short-range plan,** which has a time frame of one year or less. Short-range plans greatly affect the manager's day-to-day activities. There are two basic kinds of short-range plans. An **action plan** operationalizes any other kind of plan. For example, when the CEO of Philip Morris made the actual decision to buy Kraft, lawyers and top managers worked through the weekend on the proposal so that it could be delivered to Kraft's CEO the following Monday.[17] Their actions and accomplishments were action plans that flowed logically from a decision made by their CEO. A **reaction plan**, in turn, is a plan designed to allow the company

● **short-range plan**
A plan that generally covers a span of one year or less

● **action plan**
A plan used to operationalize any other kind of plan

HITACHI

Hitachi, which means "rising sun" in Japanese, began making electric motors during World War I. Since then it has become Japan's largest electronics and electrical products company. It is a leading producer of semiconductors, mainframe computers, TVs and VCRs, wire, special steels, locomotives, turbines, steel mills, robots, and generators among other products. A leader in research and development, it runs its factories as independent profit centres. Through carefully developed planning systems, Hitachi, Ltd., has earned a strong reputation in engineering and design.

Hitachi spends an enormous amount on research and development—generally among the highest in Japan. It has created numerous laboratories to develop new ideas and products. Hitachi has a Central Research Lab in Tokyo, an Energy Research Lab, a Device Development Centre, and a Systems Development Lab. The Advanced Research Laboratory (ARL) was established in 1985. Located away from other facilities to create an independent and innovative atmosphere, it has proved its worth many times. The idea was to support pure scientific research that other units of the organization could someday convert to practical products. That research is not limited to electronics, either; biological work is as much a part of the effort as are other fields of science.

The work of these laboratories coupled with a flexible, decentralized organizational structure and a con-glomeration of products and services enabled Hitachi to be among the first in multimedia products. Workstations with video and audio transmission and reception capabilities have been developed. The optical capabilities involved in that work have been extended into the medical field through optical storage devices, digitized X-rays, computerized tomography (CT) scans, and magnetic resonance imaging (MRI).

Hitachi's long-range planning enabled it to successfully deal with the declining mainframe computer market by developing operating systems and products and services for other markets in the late 1980s and early 1990s. Employees were moved from declining product lines to expanding ones and executive pay, including that of the president, was cut to save costs. That sort of responsiveness has enabled Hitachi to remain one of the world's largest and most successful firms.

References: S. Asai, "Basic Research in a Japanese Electronics Corporation," *Advanced Materials*, May 1, 1994, p. 343; Jean S. Bozman, "Hitachi Moving to Client/Server," *Computerworld*, April 18, 1994, p. 39; "Inside Hitachi," *Business Week*, September 28, 1992, pp. 92–100; Gary Hoover, Alta Campbell, Alan Chai, and Patrick J. Spain (Eds.), *Hoover's Handbook of World Business 1993* (Austin, Tex.: The Reference Press, 1993), p. 204; and Toru Nishikawa, "New Product Planning at Hitachi," *Long Range Planning*, August 1, 1989, p. 20.

● **reaction plan**
A plan developed to react to an unforeseen circumstance

to react to an unforeseen circumstance. When Kraft received the takeover bid from Philip Morris, its managers had to decide whether to accept the terms, fight the offer, or propose some other alternative. Any of these constitutes a reaction plan—the firm's reacting to a condition created by its environment. In fact, reacting to any form of environmental turbulence, as described in Chapter 3, is a form of reaction planning.

Responsibilities for Planning

We earlier noted briefly who is responsible for setting goals. We can now expand that initial perspective a bit and examine more fully how different parts of the organization participate in the overall planning process. All managers engage in planning to some degree. Marketing sales managers develop plans for target markets, market penetration, and sales increases. Operations managers plan cost-cutting programs and better inventory control methods. As a general rule, however, the larger an organization becomes, the more the primary planning activities become associated with groups of managers rather than with individual managers.[18]

Planning Staff   Some large organizations develop a professional planning staff. Tenneco, General Motors, General Electric, Caterpillar, Raytheon, NCR, Ford, and Boeing all have planning staffs.[19] And although the planning staff was pioneered in the United States, foreign firms like Nippon Telegraph & Telephone have also started using them. [20] Organizations might use a planning staff for a variety of reasons. In particular, a planning staff can reduce the workload of individual managers, help coordinate the planning activities of individual managers, bring to a particular problem many different tools and techniques, take a broader view than individual managers, and go beyond pet projects and particular departments.

Planning Task Force   Organizations sometimes use a planning task force to help develop plans. Such a task force often comprises line managers with a special interest in the relevant area of planning. The task force may also have members from the planning staff if the organization has one. A planning task force is most often created when the organization wants to address a special circumstance. For example, when Electronic Data Systems (EDS) decided to expand its information management services to Europe, managers knew that the firm's normal planning approach would not suffice, and top management created a special planning task force. The task force included representatives from each of the major units within the company, the corporate planning staff, and the management team that would run the European operation. Once the plan for entering the European market was formulated and implemented, the task force was eliminated.[21] EDS has since been quite successful in the European region.

Board of Directors   Among its other responsibilities, the board of directors establishes the corporate mission and strategy. In some companies, the board takes an active role in the planning process. In other companies, the board selects a competent chief executive and delegates planning to that individual.

Chief Executive Officer   The chief executive officer (CEO) is usually the president or the chair of the board of directors. The CEO is probably the single most important individual in any organization's planning process. The CEO plays a major role in the complete planning process and is responsible for implementing the strategy. The board and the CEO, then, assume direct roles in planning. The other organizational components involved in the planning process have more of an advisory or consulting role.

Executive Committee   The executive committee is usually composed of the top executives in the organization working together as a group. Committee members usually meet regularly to provide input to the CEO on the proposals that affect their own units and to review the various strategic plans that develop from this input. Members of the executive committee are frequently assigned to various staff committees, subcommittees, and task forces to concentrate on specific projects or problems that might confront the entire organization at some time in the future.

Line Management   The final component of most organizations' planning activities is line management. Line managers are those persons with formal authority and responsibility for the management of the organization. They play an important role in an organization's planning process for two reasons. First, they are a valuable source of inside information for other managers as plans are formulated and implemented. Second, the line managers at the middle and lower levels of the organization usually must execute the plans developed by top management. Line management identifies, analyzes, and recommends program alternatives, develops budgets and submits them for approval, and finally sets the plans in motion.

Contingency Planning

● **contingency planning**
The determination of alternative courses of action to be taken if an intended plan is unexpectedly disrupted or rendered inappropriate

Another important type of planning is **contingency planning**, or the determination of alternative courses of action to be taken if an intended plan of action is unexpectedly disrupted or rendered inappropriate.[22] Consider, for example, Starbucks' (a chain of coffee stores) plans for building one hundred new stores a year. Howard Schultz, Starbucks' CEO, realizes that a shift in the economy might call for a different rate of expansion. Therefore, he likely has two contingency plans based on extreme positive or negative economic shifts. First, if the economy begins to expand beyond some specific level (contingency event), then (contingency plan) the rate of the company's growth will increase from one hundred to a higher number of new stores per year. Second, if inflation increases substantially or the economy experiences a downturn, the expansion rate may drop from one hundred to seventy-five new stores per year. Starbucks would therefore have specified two crucial contingencies (expansion or inflation in the economy outside the tolerable range) and two alternative plans (increased or decreased growth).

The mechanics of contingency planning are shown in Figure 6.3. In relation to an organization's other plans, contingency planning comes into play at four action points. At action point 1, management develops the basic plans of the organization. These may include strategic, tactical, and operational plans. As part of this development process, managers usually consider various contingency events. Some management groups even assign someone the role of devil's advocate to ask "But what if ..." about each course of action. A variety of contingencies are usually considered.

At action point 2, the plan that management chooses is put into effect. The most important contingency events are also defined. Only the events that are likely to occur and whose effects will have a substantial impact on the organization are used in the contingency-planning process. Next, at action point 3, the company specifies certain indicators or signs that suggest that a contingency event is about to take place. A bank might decide that a 2 percent drop in interest rates should be considered a contingency event. An indicator might be two consecutive months with a drop of .5 percent in each. As indicators of contingency events are being defined, the contingency plans themselves should also be developed. Examples of contingency plans for various situations are delaying plant construction, developing a new manufacturing process, and cutting prices.

After this stage, the managers of the organization monitor the indicators identified at action point 3. If the situation dictates, a contingency plan is implemented. Otherwise the primary plan of action continues in force. Finally,

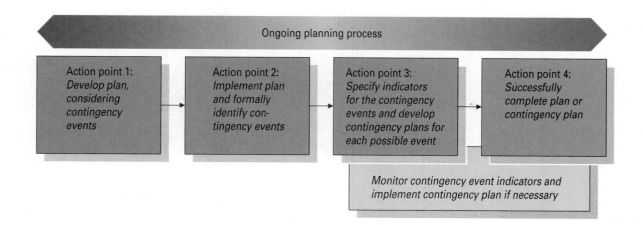

action point 4 marks the successful completion of either the original or a contingency plan.

Contingency planning is becoming increasingly important for most organizations and especially for those operating in particularly complex or dynamic environments. Few managers have such an accurate view of the future that they can anticipate and plan for everything. Contingency planning is a useful technique for helping managers cope with uncertainty and change.[23]

Most organizations develop contingency plans. These plans specify alternative courses of action to be taken if an intended plan is unexpectedly disrupted or rendered inappropriate.

TACTICAL PLANNING

As we noted earlier, tactical plans are developed to implement specific parts of a strategic plan. You have probably heard the saying about winning the battle but losing the war. Tactical plans are to battles what strategy is to a war: an organized sequence of steps designed to execute strategic plans. Strategy focuses on resources, environment, and mission, whereas tactics focus primarily on people and action.[24] Figure 6.4 identifies the major elements in developing and executing tactical plans.

Developing Tactical Plans

Although effective tactical planning depends on many factors that vary from one situation to another, we can identify some basic guidelines. First, the manager needs to recognize that tactical planning must address a number of tactical goals derived from a broader strategic goal.[25] An occasional situation may call for a stand-alone tactical plan, but most of the time tactical plans flow from and must be consistent with a strategic plan.

For example, when Roberto Goizueta became CEO of Coca-Cola, he developed a strategic plan for carrying the firm into the twenty-first century. As part of developing the plan, Goizueta identified a critical environmental threat—considerable unrest and uncertainty among the independent bottlers who packaged and distributed Coca-Cola's products. To simultaneously

F I G U R E 6.4 Developing and Executing Tactical Plans

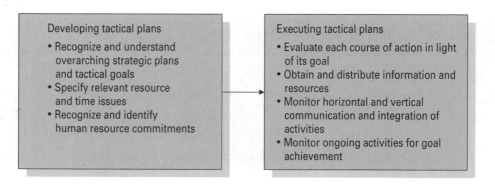

Developing tactical plans
- Recognize and understand overarching strategic plans and tactical goals
- Specify relevant resource and time issues
- Recognize and identify human resource commitments

Executing tactical plans
- Evaluate each course of action in light of its goal
- Obtain and distribute information and resources
- Monitor horizontal and vertical communication and integration of activities
- Monitor ongoing activities for goal achievement

counter this threat and strengthen the company's position, Coca-Cola bought several large independent bottlers and combined them into one new organization called Coca-Cola Enterprises. Selling half of the new company's stock reaped millions in profits while still effectively keeping control of the enterprise in Coca-Cola's hands. Thus the creation of the new business was a tactical plan developed to contribute to the achievement of an overarching strategic goal.[26] Following Mr. Goizueta's death in 1997, Coca-Cola managers had in place a comprehensive and logical set of plans with which to implement his vision of the firm.

Second, although strategies are often stated in general terms, tactics must specify resources and time frames. A strategy can call for being number-one in a particular market or industry, but a tactical plan must specify precisely what activities will be undertaken to achieve that goal.[27] Consider the Coca-Cola example again. Another element of its strategic plan involves increased worldwide market share. To facilitate additional sales in Europe, managers developed tactical plans for building a new plant in the south of France to make soft-drink concentrate and for building another canning plant in Dunkirk. Building these plants represents a concrete action involving measurable resources (i.e., funds to build the plants) and a clear time horizon (i.e., a target date for completion).[28]

Finally, tactical planning requires the use of human resources. Managers involved in tactical planning spend a great deal of time working with other people. They must be in a position to receive information from others in and outside the organization, process that information in the most effective way, and then pass it on to others who might make use of it. Coca-Cola executives have been intensively involved in planning the new plants, setting up the new bottling venture noted earlier, and exploring a joint venture with Cadbury Schweppes in the United Kingdom. Each activity has required considerable time and effort from dozens of managers. One manager, for example, crossed the Atlantic twelve times while negotiating the Cadbury deal.

Executing Tactical Plans

Regardless of how well a tactical plan is formulated, its ultimate success depends on the way it is carried out. Successful implementation, in turn, depends on the astute use of resources, effective decision making, and insightful steps to ensure that the right things are done at the right time and in the right ways. A manager can see an absolutely brilliant idea fail because of improper execution.

Proper execution depends on a number of factors. First, the manager needs to evaluate every course of action in light of the goal it is intended to reach. Next, he or she needs to make sure that each decision maker has the information and resources necessary to get the job done. Vertical and horizontal communication and integration of activities must be present to minimize conflict and inconsistent activities. And finally, the manager must monitor ongoing activities derived from the plan to make sure that they are achieving the desired results. This monitoring typically takes place within the context of the organization's ongoing control systems.

For example, when managers at The Walt Disney Company developed a new strategic plan aimed at spurring growth and profits, one tactical plan developed to stimulate growth was to build a theme park dedicated to U.S. history. The first announced location for the park, outside Washington D.C., was eventually abandoned following a barrage of protests from local residents, but Disney continues its search for a location for the park. Although building this park is a big undertaking, it is still a tactical plan within the overall strategic plan focusing on growth.

OPERATIONAL PLANNING

Another critical element in effective organizational planning is the development and implementation of operational plans. The *Managing in a Changing World* box highlights the use of operational planning by Cott Corp. Operational plans are derived from tactical plans and are aimed at achieving operational goals. Thus operational plans tend to be narrowly focused, have relatively short time horizons, and involve lower-level managers. The two most basic forms of operational plans and specific types of each are summarized in Table 6.2.

Single-Use Plans

A **single-use plan** is developed to carry out a course of action that is not likely to be repeated in the future. As Disney proceeds with its expansion plans on the West Coast, it will develop numerous single-use plans for individual rides, attractions, and hotels. The two most common forms of single-use plans are programs and projects.

● **single-use plan**
Developed to carry out a course of action that is not likely to be repeated in the future

Programs   A **program** is a single-use plan for a large set of activities. It might consist of identifying procedures for introducing a new product line, opening a new facility, or changing the organization's mission. A few years ago, Black & Decker bought General Electric's small-appliance business. The deal involved the largest brand-name switch in history: 150 products were converted from GE to the Black & Decker label. Each product was carefully studied, redesigned, and reintroduced with an extended warranty. A total of 140 steps were used for each product. It took three years to convert all 150 products over to Black & Decker. The total conversion of the product line was a program.

● **program**
A single-use plan for a large set of activities

TABLE 6.2 Types of Operational Plans

Plan	Description
Single-use plan	Developed to carry out a course of action not likely to be repeated in the future
Program	Single-use plan for a large set of activities
Project	Single-use plan of less scope and complexity than a program
Standing plan	Developed for activities that recur regularly over a period of time
Policy	Standing plan specifying the organization's general response to a designated problem or situation
Standard operating procedure	Standing plan outlining steps to be followed in particular circumstances
Rules and regulations	Standing plans describing exactly how specific activities are to be carried out

● **project**

A single-use plan of less scope and complexity than a program

Projects   A **project** is similar to a program but is generally of less scope and complexity. A project may be a part of a broader program, or it may be a self-contained single-use plan. For Black & Decker, the conversion of each of the 150 products was a separate project in its own right. Each product had its own manager, its own schedule, and so forth. Projects are also used to introduce a new product within an existing product line or to add a new benefit option to an existing salary package. The Indiana Jones ride at Disneyland is the culmination of a project.

Standing Plans

● **standing plan**

Developed for activities that recur regularly over a period of time

Whereas single-use plans are developed for nonrecurring situations, a **standing plan** is used for activities that recur regularly over a period of time. Standing plans can greatly enhance efficiency by routinizing decision making. Policies, standard operating procedures, and rules and regulations are three kinds of standing plans.[29]

● **policy**

A standing plan that specifies the organization's general response to a designated problem or situation

Policies   As a general guide for action, a policy is the most general form of standing plan. A **policy** specifies the organization's general response to a designated problem or situation. For example, McDonald's Corp. has a policy that it will not grant a franchise to an individual who already owns another fast-food restaurant. Similarly, Starbucks' stance of not franchising its coffee stores represents a policy. Likewise, a university admissions office might establish a policy that admission will be granted only to applicants with a minimum high-school average mark of 70 percent and a ranking in the top quarter of their

Cott Finds Niche

In the fiscal year ended January 25, 1997, Cott Corp. reported revenue of $1.35 billion, a slight gain over the previous year. The company's net income also increased to $34 million from a loss of $29 million the previous year. In the fiscal year ended January 27, 1990, Cott had annual sales of only $31 million.

Cott Corp., Canada's largest private-label soft-drink bottler, produces colas under such names as President's Choice, WPOP, Sam's America Choice, and Virgin Cola. Retailers that carry Cott's colas and other soft drinks include Wal-Mart, Britain's Sainsbury, France's Promodes, and Japan's Ito-Yokada. By the first quarter of 1995, Cott had gained 27 percent of supermarket cola sales in Britain. Largely as a result of Cott's sales, by 1994, private-label soda sales in Canada reached 28 percent of soft-drink sales in supermarkets.

Cott was a New England family-owned regional brand of soft drinks that, in the 1950s, attracted the attention of a Montreal clothier, Harry Pencer, who obtained the Canadian rights to the name. He quickly realized that if Cott were to succeed, it had to include a cola in its product line. However, Cott's cola was not very good, so Pencer got RC Cola to make a cola for Cott that was initially sold at Loblaws stores in Canada.

While Cott's profits in relation to sales are below the industry average, the company has succeeded in gaining market share while competing with such giants as Pepsi and Coke. It has found a niche in the private-label market, providing products that retailers call "shielding" items. Shielding works as follows. A well-known brand is advertised at a discount price to bring traffic to a store where a less familiar product is displayed at a lower price. The store makes more money selling the less familiar brand at a lower price than the better-known brand at a discount price.

So while Coke and Pepsi may be focusing on heavy advertising to sell their products, Cott's $3.99 per case of twenty-four seems to be an effective marketing tool. However, Cott's planning must address the lagging return on sales.

References: Don Angus, "Nicol Wants to Energize Cott's Beverages," *Advertising Age*, September 26, 1994, p. 37; "Earnings Summary," *Financial Post*, April 5, 1997, p. 39; "Fizz Bang," *The Economist*, July 1, 1995, p. 63; and Joel Millman, "Rich Niche," *Forbes*, May 25, 1992, p. 116.

---

high–school classes. Admissions officers may routinely deny admission to applicants who fail to reach these minimums. A policy is also likely to describe how exceptions are to be handled. The university's policy statement, for example, might create an admissions appeals committee to evaluate applicants who do not meet minimum requirements but may warrant special consideration.

Standard Operating Procedures   Another type of standing plan is the **standard operating procedure**, or **SOP**. An SOP is more specific than a policy in that it outlines the steps to be followed in particular circumstances. The admissions clerk at the university, for example, might be told that when an application is received, he or she should (1) set up a file for the applicant; (2) add test–score records, transcripts, and letters of reference to the file as they are received; and (3) give the file to the appropriate admissions director when it is complete. Gallo Vineyards in California has a three hundred–page manual of standard operating procedures. This planning manual is credited with making Gallo one of the most efficient wine operations in the United States.[30] McDonald's has SOPs explaining exactly how Big Macs are to be cooked, how long they can stay in the warming rack, and so forth.

Rules and Regulations   The narrowest of the standing plans, **rules and regulations** describe exactly how specific activities are to be carried out. Rather

● **standard operating procedure (SOP)**
A standing plan that outlines the steps to be followed in a particular circumstance

● **rules and regulations**
Describe exactly how specific activities are to be carried out

than guiding decision making, rules and regulations actually take the place of decision making in various situations. Each McDonald's restaurant has a rule prohibiting customers from using its telephones, for example. The university admissions office might have a rule stipulating that if an applicant's file is not complete two months before the beginning of a semester, the student cannot be admitted until the next semester. Of course, in most organizations a manager at a higher level can suspend or bend the rules.

Rules and regulations and SOPs are similar in many ways. They are both relatively narrow in scope, and each can serve as a substitute for decision making. An SOP typically describes a sequence of activities, however, whereas rules and regulations focus on one activity. Recall our examples: the admissions-desk SOP consisted of three activities, whereas the two-month rule related to one activity only. In an industrial setting, the SOP for orienting a new employee could involve enrolling the person in various benefit options, introducing him or her to co-workers and supervisors, and providing a tour of the facilities. A pertinent rule for the new employee might involve when to come to work each day.

MANAGING GOAL-SETTING AND PLANNING PROCESSES

Obviously, all of the elements of goal setting and planning discussed to this point involve managing these processes in some way or another. In addition, however, because major barriers sometimes impede effective goal setting and planning, knowing how to overcome some of the barriers is important.

Barriers to Goal Setting and Planning

Several circumstances can serve as barriers to effective goal setting and planning; the more common ones are listed in Table 6.3.

Inappropriate Goals   Inappropriate goals come in many forms. Paying a large dividend to shareholders may be inappropriate if it comes at the expense of research and development. Goals may also be inappropriate if they are unattainable. If Chrysler were to set a goal of selling more cars than General Motors next year, people at the company would probably be embarrassed because achieving such a goal would be impossible. Goals may also be inappropriate if they place too much emphasis on either quantitative or qualitative measures of success. Some goals, especially those relating to financial areas, are quantifiable, objective, and verifiable. Other goals, such as employee satisfaction and development, are difficult if not impossible to quantify. Organizations are asking for trouble if they put too much emphasis on one type of goal to the exclusion of the other.

Improper Reward System   In some settings, an improper reward system acts as a barrier to goal setting and planning. For example, people may inadvertently be rewarded for poor goal-setting behaviour or go unrewarded or even be punished for proper goal-setting behaviour. Suppose that a manager sets a goal of decreasing turnover next year. If turnover is decreased by even a fraction, the manager can claim success and perhaps be rewarded. In contrast, a manager

who attempts to decrease turnover by 5 percent but actually achieves a decrease of only 4 percent may receive a smaller reward because of her or his failure to reach the established goal. And if an organization places too much emphasis on short-term performance and results, managers may ignore longer-term issues as they set goals and formulate plans to achieve higher profits in the short term.

Dynamic and Complex Environment   The nature of an organization's environment can also be a barrier to effective goal setting and planning. Rapid change, technological innovation, and intense competition can each increase the difficulty of an organization's accurately assessing future opportunities and threats. For example, when an electronics firm like IBM develops a long-range plan, it tries to take into account how much technological innovation is likely to occur during that interval. But forecasting such events is extremely difficult. During the early boom years of personal computers, data were stored primarily on floppy disks. Because these disks had a limited storage capacity, hard disks were developed. Whereas the typical floppy disk can hold hundreds of pages of

TABLE 6.3 Barriers to Goal Setting	
Major barriers	Inappropriate goals
	Improper reward system
	Dynamic and complex environment
	Reluctance to establish goals
	Resistance to change
	Constraints
Overcoming the barriers	Understanding the purposes of goals and planning
	Communication and participation
	Consistency, revision, and updating
	Effective reward systems

As part of managing the goal-setting and planning processes, managers must understand the barriers that can disrupt them. Managers must also know how to overcome the barriers.

information, a hard disk can store thousands of pages. Today computers increasingly store information on optical disks that hold millions of pages. The manager attempting to set goals and plan in this rapidly changing environment faces a truly formidable task.

Reluctance to Establish Goals   Another barrier to effective planning is the reluctance of some managers to establish goals for themselves and their units of responsibility. The reason for this reluctance may be lack of confidence or fear of failure. If a manager sets a goal that is specific, concise, and time related, then whether he or she attains it is obvious. Managers who consciously or unconsciously try to avoid this degree of accountability are likely to hinder the organization's planning efforts. Pfizer, a large pharmaceutical company, ran into problems because its managers did not set goals for research and development. Consequently, the organization fell further and further behind because managers had no way of knowing how effective their R&D efforts actually were.[31] In contrast, the CEO of Nike, Philip Knight, showed no lack of confidence or fear of failure when he announced a goal of doubling the firm's annual revenues to $12 billion (U.S.) by the year 2001.[32]

Resistance to Change   Another barrier to goal setting and planning is resistance to change. Planning essentially involves changing something about the organization. As we see in Chapter 12, people tend to resist change. Avon Products almost drove itself into bankruptcy because it insisted on continuing a policy of large dividend payments to its shareholders. When profits started to fall, managers resisted cutting the dividends and started borrowing to pay them. The company's debt grew from $3 million (U.S.) to $1.1 billion in eight years. Eventually, managers were forced to confront the problem and cut dividends.[33]

Constraints   Constraints that limit what an organization can do are another major obstacle. Common constraints include a lack of resources, government restrictions, and strong competition. For example, Owens-Corning Fiberglass Corp. recently took on an enormous debt burden as part of its fight to avoid a takeover by Wickes Companies. The company now has such a large debt that it has been forced to cut back on capital expenditures and research and development. And those cutbacks have greatly constrained what the firm can plan for the future.[34] Time constraints are also a factor. It's easy to say, "I'm too busy to plan today; I'll do it tomorrow." Effective planning takes time, energy, and an unwavering belief in its importance.

Overcoming the Barriers

Fortunately, there are several guidelines for making goal setting and planning effective. Some of the guidelines are also listed in Table 6.3.

Understand the Purposes of Goals and Plans   One of the best ways to facilitate goal-setting and planning processes is to recognize their basic purposes. Managers should also recognize that there are limits to the effectiveness of setting goals and making plans. Planning is not a panacea that will solve all of an organization's problems; nor should planning be considered an iron-clad set of procedures to be followed at any cost. And effective goals and planning do not necessarily ensure success; adjustments and exceptions are to be expected as time passes. For example, Coca-Cola followed a logical and rational approach to setting goals and planning a few years ago when it decided to introduce a new formula to combat Pepsi's increasing market share. But all the plans proved to be wrong as consumers rejected the new version of Coca-Cola. Managers quickly reversed the decision and reintroduced the old formula as Coca-Cola Classic.

Interestingly, Coca-Cola has a larger market share today than before. Thus, even though careful planning resulted in a big mistake, the company came out ahead in the long run.[35]

Communication and Participation   Although goals and plans may be initiated at high levels in the organization, they must also be communicated to others in the organization. Everyone involved in the planning process should know what the overriding organizational strategy is, what the various functional strategies are, and how they are all to be integrated and coordinated. People responsible for achieving goals and implementing plans must have a voice in developing them from the outset. These individuals almost always have valuable information to contribute, and because they will be implementing the plans, their involvement is critical: people are usually more committed to plans that they have helped shape. Even when an organization is somewhat centralized or uses a planning staff, managers from a variety of levels in the organization should be involved in the planning process. Ford has demonstrated leadership in this area. Managers from all levels of the organization, and even operating employees, are given a large voice in how things are done.

Consistency, Revision, and Updating   Goals should be consistent both horizontally and vertically. Horizontal consistency means that goals should be consistent across the organization, from one department to the next. Vertical consistency means that goals should be consistent up and down the organization—strategic, tactical, and operational goals must agree with one another. Because goal setting and planning are dynamic processes, they must also be revised and updated regularly. Many organizations are seeing the need to revise and update on an increasingly frequent basis. Citicorp, for example, has used a three-year planning horizon for developing and providing new financial services. That cycle has been cut to two years, and the bank hopes to reduce it to one year very soon.

Effective Reward Systems   In general, people should be rewarded both for establishing effective goals and plans and for successfully achieving them. Because failure sometimes results from factors outside the manager's control, however, people should also be assured that failure to reach a goal will not necessarily bring punitive consequences. Frederick Smith, founder and CEO of Federal Express (now called FedEx), has a stated goal of encouraging risk. Thus when Federal Express lost $233 million (U.S.) on an unsuccessful new service called ZapMail, no one was punished. Smith believed that the original idea was a good one but was unsuccessful for reasons beyond the company's control.

Using Management by Objectives to Implement Plans

A widely used method for managing the goal-setting and planning processes concurrently to ensure that both are done effectively is **management by objectives**, or **MBO**. We should also note, however, that while many firms use this basic approach, they frequently tailor it to their own special circumstances

● **management by objectives (MBO)**
The process of collaborative goal setting by a manager and subordinate; the extent to which goals are accomplished is a major factor in evaluating and rewarding the subordinate's performance

and use a special term or name for it. For example, Tenneco uses an MBO system but calls it the Performance Agreement System.

The Nature and Purpose of MBO   The purpose of MBO is to give subordinates a voice in the goal-setting and planning processes and to clarify for them exactly what they are expected to accomplish in a given time span. Thus MBO is concerned with goal setting and planning for individual managers and their units or work groups.[36]

The MBO Process   The basic mechanics of the MBO process are shown in Figure 6.5. The MBO process is described here from an ideal perspective. In any given organization the steps of the process are likely to vary in importance and may even take a different sequence. As a starting point, however, most managers believe that if an MBO program is to be successful, it must start at the top of the organization. Top managers must communicate why they have adopted MBO, what they think it will do, and that they have accepted and are committed to MBO. Employees must also be educated about what MBO is and what their role in it will be. Having committed to MBO, managers must implement it in a way that is consistent with overall organizational goals and plans. The idea is that goals established at the top will systematically cascade down throughout the organization.

Although establishing the organization's basic goals and plans is extremely important, collaborative goal setting and planning are the essence of MBO. The collaboration involves a series of distinct steps. First, managers tell their subordinates what organizational and unit goals and plans top management has established. Then managers meet with their subordinates on a one-to-one basis to arrive at a set of goals and plans for each subordinate that both the subordinate and the manager have helped develop and to which both are committed. Next the goals are refined to be as verifiable (quantitative) as possible and to specify a time frame for their accomplishment. The goals should also be written. Furthermore, the plans developed to achieve the goals need to be as clearly stated as possible and directly relate to each goal. Managers must play the role of counsellors in the goal-setting and planning meeting. For example, they must ensure that the subordinate's goals and plans are attainable and workable and that they will facilitate both the unit's and the organization's goals and plans. Finally, the meeting should spell out the resources that the subordinate will need to implement his or her plans and work effectively toward goal attainment.

Conducting periodic reviews as subordinates are working toward their goals is advisable. If the goals and plans are for a one-year period, meeting quarterly to discuss progress may be a good idea. At the end of the period, the manager meets with each subordinate again to review the degree of goal attainment. They discuss which goals were met and which were not met in the context of the original plans. The reasons for both success and failure are explored, and the employee is rewarded on the basis of goal attainment. In an ongoing MBO program, the evaluation meeting may also serve as the collaborative goal-setting and planning meeting for the next time period.

The Effectiveness of MBO   A large number of organizations, including General Motors, Investors Group, Du Pont, Boeing, Caterpillar, Westinghouse Electric Corp., and Gilette, all use some form of MBO. As might be expected, MBO has both strengths and weaknesses. A primary benefit of MBO is improved employee motivation. By clarifying exactly what is expected, by

FIGURE 6.5 The MBO Process

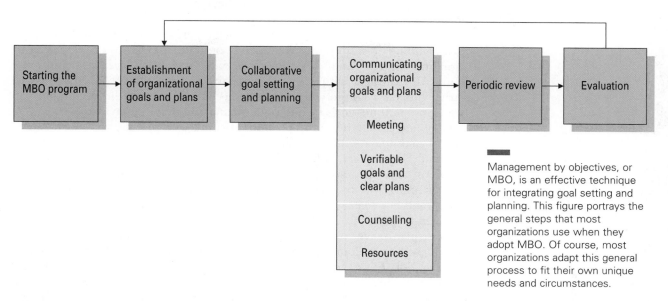

Management by objectives, or MBO, is an effective technique for integrating goal setting and planning. This figure portrays the general steps that most organizations use when they adopt MBO. Of course, most organizations adapt this general process to fit their own unique needs and circumstances.

allowing the employee a voice in determining expectations, and by basing rewards on the achievement of those expectations, organizations create a powerful motivational system for their employees.

Communication is also enhanced through the process of discussion and collaboration. And performance appraisals may be done more objectively, with less reliance on arbitrary or subjective assessment. MBO focuses attention on appropriate goals and plans, helps identify superior managerial talent for future promotion, and provides a systematic management philosophy that can have a positive effect on the overall organization. MBO also facilitates control. The periodic development and subsequent evaluation of individual goals and plans helps keep the organization on course toward its own long-run goals and plans.

On the other hand, MBO occasionally fails because of poor implementation. Perhaps the major problem that can derail an MBO program is lack of top-management support. Some organizations decide to use MBO, but then its implementation is delegated to lower management. This limits the program's effectiveness because the goals and plans cascading throughout the organization may not actually be the goals and plans of top management and because others in the organization are not motivated to accept and become committed to them. Another problem with MBO is that some firms overemphasize quantitative goals and plans and burden their systems with too much paperwork and record keeping. Some managers will not or cannot sit down and work out goals and plans with their subordinates. Rather, they "suggest" or even "assign" goals and plans to people. The result is resentment and a lack of commitment to the MBO program.[37]

SUMMARY OF KEY POINTS

The planning process is the first basic managerial function that organizations must address. With an understanding of the environmental context, managers develop a number of different types of goals and plans. Decision making is the underlying framework of all planning because every step of the planning process involves a decision.

Goals serve four basic purposes: to provide guidance and direction, to facilitate planning, to inspire motivation and commitment, and to promote evaluation and control. Kinds of goals can be differentiated by level, area, and time frame. All managers within an organization need to be involved in the goal-setting process. Managers need to pay special attention to the importance of managing multiple goals through optimizing and other approaches.

Goals are closely related to planning. The major types of plans are strategic, tactical, and operational. Plans are developed across a variety of time horizons, including long-range, intermediate, and short-range time frames. Essential people in an organization responsible for effective planning are the planning staff, planning task forces, the board of directors, the CEO, the executive committee, and line management. Contingency planning helps managers anticipate and plan for unexpected changes.

After plans have been developed, the manager must address how they will be achieved. This often involves tactical and operational plans. Tactical plans are at the middle of the organization and have an intermediate time horizon and moderate scope. Tactical plans are developed to implement specific parts of a strategic plan. They must flow from strategy, specify resource and time issues, and commit human resources. Tactical plans must be effectively executed.

Operational plans are at the lower levels of the organization, have a shorter time horizon, and are narrower in scope. Operational plans are derived from a tactical plan and are aimed at achieving one or more operational goals. Two major types of operational plans are single-use and standing plans. Single-use plans are designed to carry out a course of action that is not likely to be repeated in the future. Programs and projects are examples of single-use plans. Standing plans are designed to carry out a course of action that is likely to be repeated several times. Policies, standard operating procedures, and rules and regulations are all examples of standing plans.

There are several barriers to effective goal setting and planning. These include inappropriate goals, an improper reward system, a dynamic and complex environment, reluctance to establish goals, resistance to change, and various constraints. Methods for overcoming these barriers include understanding the purposes of goals and plans; communication and participation; consistency, revision, and updating; and an effective reward system. One particularly useful technique for managing goal setting and planning is management by objectives, or MBO. MBO is a process of collaborative goal setting and planning.

DISCUSSION QUESTIONS

Questions for Review

1. Describe the nature of organizational goals. Be certain to include both the purposes and kinds of goals.
2. What is contingency planning? Is being flexible about your plans the same as contingency planning? Why or why not?
3. What is tactical planning? What is operational planning? What are the similarities and differences between them?

4. What are the barriers to goal setting and planning? How can they be overcome? Can you think of any ways to overcome the barriers other than the ways identified in the text?

Questions for Analysis

5. Almost by definition, organizations cannot accomplish all of their goals. Why?
6. Which kind of plan—tactical or operational—should an organization develop first? Why? Does the order of development really make a difference as long as plans of both types are made?
7. Think of examples of each type of operational plan you have used at work, in your school work, or even in your personal life.

Questions for Application

8. Interview the head of the department in which you are majoring. What kinds of goals exist for the department and for the members of the department? Share your findings with the rest of the class.
9. Interview a local small-business manager about the time frames for planning that he or she uses. How do your results compare with what you might have expected from the presentation in the textbook?
10. Interview a college or university official to determine the use of single-use and standing plans at your institution. How were these plans developed?

BUILDING EFFECTIVE CONCEPTUAL SKILLS

Exercise Overview

Conceptual skills refer to a person's abilities to think in the abstract. This exercise will help you develop your conceptual skills by relating your own personal goals and plans across various time frames.

Exercise Background

Most people have a general idea of what they want their future to be like. However, few people actually take the time to formulate specific goals and plans for their future. To do so might provide a useful blueprint for achieving those goals and also help people better understand the likelihood of various goals actually coming to fruition.

Exercise Task

With the preceding background information as context, do the following:
1. Make a list of ten goals that you want to achieve in ten years. These goals might relate to work, family, or anything else you see as important.
2. Make a list of five-year goals that you must meet to be at the halfway point in achieving your long-term goals.
3. Repeat the list for each of the next five years.
4. Evaluate the likelihood of actually being able to achieve the one-year goals, the five-year goals, and the ten-year goals.
5. How might this process be similar to and different from a manager doing the same thing for business goals?

Campbell Soup Co. began in 1869 as a food canning and preserving business. Quality was a watchword from the beginning, and Campbell soon built a solid reputation as a dependable and effective enterprise. The company really took off in 1897, however, when one of its chemists discovered how to "condense" soup by removing most of the water. This condensing process allowed the company to begin selling soup in smaller and more efficient packaging options, with the consumer reconstituting the soup by adding water at home.

Campbell continued to grow slowly and steadily, and the Campbell brand name became one of the most recognized in the United States. Indeed, pop artist Andy Warhol's 1960 print illustrating a can of Campbell soup became an icon. But although the company has always performed solidly, it never really took off with periods of rapid growth and was always seen as being an underachiever in international markets.

In the late 1980s, the firm's board of directors grew tired of its less-than-spectacular performance and decided to take drastic action. The firm concluded that there was no prime leadership candidate among Campbell's existing top managers and thus decided to look outside for help. After an extensive search, the board hired David Johnson away from Gerber Products Co. to take over as CEO and gave him a mandate to shake the firm out of the doldrums.

Johnson's efforts have resulted in dramatically improved performance. The key to the turnaround, he says, is that he focuses everything the firm does on a single overriding goal—to continually increase net earnings faster than competitors. Johnson believes that returns to shareholders is the single most important criterion of effectiveness, so he thinks it only appropriate to keep the goal of net earnings central to the firm's operations. Indeed, scoreboards comparing Campbell's earnings gains with other food processing companies are scattered throughout the company—in its corporate offices, in its factories, and in its warehouses and distribution centres. The idea is to continually remind employees of what the firm's CEO sees as important.

Of course, Johnson relies on other goals as well, but they are all developed to support the overarching goal of earnings growth. For example, he sets goals each quarter for growth in earnings per share, profitability, and overall revenue growth. He also stresses market share growth. For example, Campbell sells 80 percent of the canned soup in the United States; Johnson wants to increase the share to 90 percent.

Johnson also stresses international growth. Even though the firm is doing well in its home market, international sales are still disappointing. Johnson concedes that Campbell will be hard-pressed to catch entrenched market leaders such as Nestlé and Heinz in Europe, but thinks that Asia, a market just awakening to processed foods, represents a major opportunity for the firm. Consequently, Campbell Soup has several joint ventures underway in Asia and is investing heavily in plants and distribution networks throughout the region. Campbell Soup Canada is the company's largest soup business outside the United States.

To really motivate his team, Johnson (who became chair of the board in 1997 and was succeeded as CEO by Dale Morrison) has tied financial incentives to goal attainment. Indeed, the top twelve hundred managers at Campbell all have significant bonus potential tied to reaching and exceeding Johnson's yearly goals. He also requires the firm's three hundred most senior executives to hold substantial amounts of company stock, usually one-half to three times their annual salary. Johnson argues that this financial stake will reinforce their commitment to only doing things that are in the long-term best interests of shareholders, since they themselves have a lot riding on Campbell's stock performance.

Questions

1. What roles are goals playing at Campbell Soup today?

2. What kinds of plans does Campbell Soup need to develop in order to meet its goals?

3. What problems might Campbell encounter in the future as a result of its emphasis on meeting financial goals?

References: Linda Grant, "Stirring It up at Campbell," *Fortune*, May 13, 1996, pp. 80–86; "Changing Tastes Dent Campbell's Canned-Soup Sales," *The Wall Street Journal*, April 28, 1998, pp. B1, B23; and Campbell Soup Company, Annual Report, 1998 (http://campbellsoup.com).

CHAPTER NOTES

1. David Berman, "Channel Changer," *Canadian Business*, September 1995, pp. 46–52; Trevor Cole, "Revenge of the Ratings King," *Report on Business Magazine*, May 1996, pp. 58–70; Andrea Mandel-Campbell, "CanWest's Golden Global Touch Falters in Chile's Tough TV Market," *Marketing*, June 24, 1996, p. 8; "The Rise of a TV Empire," *Maclean's*, February 1, 1999, p. 60; and "The Top 1000," *Report on Business Magazine*, July 1998, p. 102.

2. This framework is inspired by numerous sources: George Steiner, *Top Management Planning* (New York: Macmillan, 1969); John E. Dittrich, *The General Manager and Strategy Formulation* (New York: Wiley, 1988); Henry Mintzberg, "Crafting Strategy," *Harvard Business Review*, July–August 1987, pp. 66–75; Michael E. Porter, *Competitive Advantage* (New York: Free Press, 1985); and Charles W.L. Hill and Gareth R. Jones, *Strategic Management: An Analytical Approach*, 3rd ed. (Boston: Houghton Mifflin, 1995).

3. Max D. Richards, *Setting Strategic Goals and Objectives*, 2nd ed. (St. Paul, Minn.: West, 1986).

4. Shawn Tully, "Why to Go for Stretch Targets," *Fortune*, November 14, 1994, pp. 145–158.

5. Carol Davenport, "America's Most Admired Corporations," *Fortune*, January 30, 1989, pp. 68–94.

6. John A. Pearce II and Fred David, "Corporate Mission Statements: The Bottom Line," *The Academy of Management Executive*, May 1987, p. 109.

7. Sarah Scott, "First, Take $300 Million," *Report on Business Magazine*, December 1998, p. 92.

8. "How H-P Used Tactics of the Japanese to Beat Them at Their Game," *The Wall Street Journal*, September 8, 1994, pp. A1, A6.

9. "The Drought Is Over at 3M," *Business Week*, November 7, 1994, pp. 140–141.

10. "Nike Catches Up with the Trendy Frontrunner," *Business Week*, October 24, 1988, p. 88.

11. Jeffrey B. Vancouver, Roger E. Millsap, and Patricia A. Peters, "Multilevel Analysis of Organizational Goal Congruence," *Journal of Applied Psychology*, Vol. 79, No. 5, 1994, pp. 666–679.

12. "Visa, American Express and MasterCard Vie in Overseas Strategies," *The Wall Street Journal*, February 15, 1994, pp. A1, A5.

13. See Charles Hill and Gareth Jones, *Strategic Management*, 3rd ed. (Boston: Houghton Mifflin, 1995).

14. H. Donald Hopkins, "Long-Term Acquisition Strategies in the U.S. Economy," *Journal of Management*, Vol. 13, No. 3, 1987, pp. 557–572.

15. Ronald Henkoff, "How to Plan for 1995," *Fortune*, December 31, 1990, pp. 70–79.

16. "Hamish Maxwell's Big Hunger," *Business Week*, October 31, 1988, pp. 24–26; and Ronald Henkoff, "Deals of the Year," *Fortune*, January 30, 1989, pp. 162–170.

17. "Hamish Maxwell's Big Hunger."

18. Hill and Jones, *Strategic Management*.

19. Peter Lorange and Balaji S. Chakravarthy, *Strategic Planning Systems*, 2nd ed. (Englewood Cliffs, N.J.: Prentice-Hall, 1989).

20. Carla Rapoport, "The World's Most Valuable Company," *Fortune*, October 10, 1988, pp. 92–104.

21. Richard I. Kirkland, Jr., "Outsider's Guide to Europe in 1992," *Fortune*, October 24, 1988, pp. 121–127.

22. K. A. Froot, D. S. Scharfstein, and J. C. Stein, "A Framework for Risk Management," *Harvard Business Review*, November–December 1994, pp. 91–102.

23. See Donald C. Hambrick and David Lei, "Toward an Empirical Prioritization of Contingency Variables for Business Strategy," *Academy of Management Journal*, December 1985, pp. 763–788.

24. James Brian Quinn, Henry Mintzberg, and Robert M. James, *The Strategy Process* (Englewood Cliffs, N.J.: Prentice-Hall, 1988).

25. Vasudevan Ramanujam and N. Venkatraman, "Planning System Characteristics and Planning Effectiveness," *Strategic Management Journal*, Vol. 8, No. 2, 1987, pp. 453–468.

26. Gary Hector, "Yes, You *Can* Manage Long Term," *Fortune*, November 21, 1988, pp. 64–76; and John Huey, "The World's Best Brand," *Fortune*, May 31, 1993, pp. 44–54.

27. Mintzberg, "Crafting Strategy," pp. 66–75.

28. Huey, "The World's Best Brand."

29. Thomas L. Wheelon and J. David Hunger, *Strategic Management and Business Policy*, 5th ed. (Reading, Mass.: Addison-Wesley, 1995).

30. Jaclyn Fierman, "How Gallo Crushes the Competition," *Fortune*, September 1, 1986, pp. 23–31.

31. John J. Curran, "Companies That Rob the Future," *Fortune*, July 4, 1988, pp. 84–89.

32. "The Swoosh Heard 'Round the World," *Business Week*, May 12, 1997, pp. 76–80.

33. Curran, "Companies That Rob the Future."

34. Curran, "Companies That Rob the Future."

35. Hector, "Yes, You *Can* Manage Long Term."

36. Stephen J. Carroll and Henry L. Tosi, *Management by Objectives* (New York: Macmillan, 1973); and A.P. Raia, *Managing by Objectives* (Glenview, Ill.: Scott, Foresman, 1974).

37. See Jack N. Kondrasuk, "Studies in MBO Effectiveness," *Academy of Management Review*, July 1981, pp. 419–430, for a review of the strengths and weaknesses of MBO.

Managing Strategy and Strategic Planning

OBJECTIVES

After studying this chapter, you should be able to:

- *Discuss the components of strategy, types of strategic alternatives, and the distinction between strategy formulation and strategy implementation.*

- *Describe how to use SWOT analysis in formulating strategy.*

- *Identify and describe various alternative approaches to business-level strategy formulation.*

- *Describe how business-level strategies are implemented.*

- *Identify and describe various alternative approaches to corporate-level strategy formulation.*

- *Describe how corporate-level strategies are implemented.*

Wendy's purchase of Tim Hortons created a complete fast-food menu. This represents an example of related diversification, a popular form of corporate strategy.

Along Canadian highways and elsewhere, consumers are witnessing close cooperation between fast-food outlets: Harvey's and Second Cup; Wendy's and Tim Hortons. The latter relationship is much closer than it may appear to the average consumer.

Tim Hortons, founded in 1964, was named for a well-known Canadian NHL defenceman and is a Canadian institution. Tim Horton and Ronald Joyce co-founded the company, but Horton was killed in a car accident in 1974. Today, the company has more than 1,500 outlets in Canada, making it Canada's largest fast-food chain in terms of outlets and second only to McDonald's in terms of sales. Tim Hortons sells doughnuts, bagels, muffins, croissants, and cinnamon buns, but coffee brings in 40 percent of its sales revenue. Its outlets are open twenty-four hours a day, but business is brisker in the morning and late evening.

> **"Along Canadian highways and elsewhere, consumers are witnessing close cooperation between fast-food outlets."**

Wendy's, the number-three burger chain in the United States, was named for the daughter of its founder, Dave Thomas. Founded in 1968, the company grew rapidly in the 1980s. Today, Wendy's has more than 5,200 stores, up from 3,500 in 1991, with 245 of these in Canada. The company's products, although higher priced, are perceived to be of higher quality than those of fast-food chains such as McDonald's. Wendy's does not open until after breakfast and business is brisker at lunch and dinnertime.

The lack of a breakfast menu at Wendy's and Tim Hortons's almost exclusive breakfast and dessert menu suggest that a combination of the companies' offerings would create a complete fast-food menu. This must have been the logic behind Wendy's 1995 acquisition of Tim Hortons. The $630 million purchase was financed through 16.5 million Wendy's shares. The deal gave Ronald Joyce, one of Tim Hortons co-founders, 12.6 percent of Wendy's shares, making him the company's largest shareholder and providing him with a spot on its board of directors.

The acquisition, while creating a complete fast-food menu for Wendy's, also created an opportunity for Tim Hortons to expand in the United States. By the end of 1997, there were eighty Tim Hortons outlets in operation in the United States, up from just a handful before the acquisition.[1] ●

he actions taken by Tim Hortons and Wendy's reflect one of the most critical functions that managers perform for their businesses: strategy and strategic planning. Just as consumers buy things they need, Wendy's has bought Tim Hortons. Its acquisition of Tim Hortons represents a strategic action taken by the firm to better protect its competitive position.

This chapter discusses how organizations manage strategy and strategic planning. We begin by examining the nature of strategic management, including its components and alternatives. We then describe the kinds of analyses needed for firms to formulate their strategies. Next we examine how organizations first formulate and then implement business-level strategies, followed by a parallel discussion at the corporate-strategy level.

THE NATURE OF STRATEGIC MANAGEMENT

A **strategy** is a comprehensive plan for accomplishing an organization's goals. **Strategic management**, in turn, is a way of approaching business opportunities and challenges—it is a comprehensive and ongoing management process aimed at formulating and implementing effective strategies. Finally, **effective strategies** are those that promote a superior alignment between the organization and its environment and the achievement of strategic goals.[2]

The Components of Strategy

In general, a well-conceived strategy addresses three areas: distinctive competence, scope, and resource deployment. A **distinctive competence** is something the organization does exceptionally well. (We discuss distinctive competencies more fully later.) One distinctive competence of Wal-Mart in its Canadian operations is the level of convenience it offers its customers. The retailer attracts the one-stop shopper by offering twice as many products per store as its nearest rival, Zellers. This is one of several factors contributing to Wal-Mart's success in Canada.[3]

The **scope** of a strategy specifies the range of markets in which an organization will compete. Seagram Company Ltd., before its acquisition of Universal Studios, had essentially restricted its scope to the beverage business. Some organizations, called *conglomerates*, compete in dozens or even hundreds of markets.

A strategy should also include an outline of the organization's projected **resource deployment**—how it will distribute its resources across the areas in which it competes. Raytheon, for example, has used profits from its large defence-contracting business to support growth in its publishing (D.C. Heath) and appliance (Amana, Speed Queen, and Caloric) businesses. The company could have chosen to reinvest those profits in its defence businesses and let the other units stand alone. Instead, it chose a different deployment.[4]

Types of Strategic Alternatives

Most businesses today also develop strategies at two distinct levels. These levels provide a rich combination of strategic alternatives for organizations. The two general levels are business strategies and corporate strategies. **Business-level strategy** is the set of strategic alternatives that an organization chooses from as it conducts business in a particular industry or a particular market. Such alternatives help the organization focus its competitive efforts for each industry or

● **strategy**
A comprehensive plan for accomplishing an organization's goals

● **strategic management**
A comprehensive and ongoing management process aimed at formulating and implementing effective strategies; it is a way of approaching business opportunities and challenges

● **effective strategy**
A strategy that promotes a superior alignment between the organization and its environment and the achievement of strategic goals

● **distinctive competence**
An organizational strength possessed by only a small number of competing firms

● **scope**
When applied to *strategy,* it specifies the range of markets in which an organization will compete

● **resource deployment**
How an organization distributes its resources across the areas in which it competes

● **business-level strategy**
The set of strategic alternatives that an organization chooses from as it conducts business in a particular industry or market

Harrison McCain, CEO of the giant McCain Foods Company, heads a wholly family-owned private corporation in New Brunswick. The company has turned P.E.I and New Brunswick potatoes into enormously successful "seasoned spirals," among other products. The company makes extensive use of marketing research in the form of taste tests to determine whether proposed new products will appeal to consumers.

market in a targeted and focused manner. For example, Imasco has one business strategy for Imperial Tobacco, another for Canada Trust, and yet another for Shoppers Drug Mart.

Corporate-level strategy is the set of strategic alternatives that an organization chooses from as it manages its operations simultaneously across several industries and several markets.[5] As we discuss later, most large companies today compete in a variety of industries and markets. Thus, although they develop business-level strategies for each industry or market, they also develop an overall strategy that helps define the mix of industries and markets that are of interest to the firm. Imasco's decision in 1997 to sell Hardee's Food Systems Inc. reflects its corporate strategy.[6] Future decisions to buy or launch new brands or businesses, as well as decisions about markets where Imasco consciously chooses to compete, are also elements of corporate strategy.

Strategy Formulation and Implementation

Drawing a distinction between strategy formulation and strategy implementation is also instructive. **Strategy formulation** is the set of processes involved in creating or determining the strategies of the organization, whereas **strategy implementation** is the methods by which strategies are operationalized or executed within the organization. The primary distinction is along the lines of

● **corporate-level strategy**
The set of strategic alternatives that an organization chooses from as it manages its operations simultaneously across several industries and several markets

● **strategy formulation**
The set of processes involved in creating or determining the strategies of the organization; it focuses on the content of strategies

● **strategy implementation**
The methods by which strategies are operationalized or executed within the organization; it focuses on the processes through which strategies are achieved

content versus process: **the formulation stage determines what the strategy is, and the implementation stage focuses on how the strategy is achieved.**

Sometimes the process of formulating and implementing strategies is rational, systematic, and planned. This approach is often referred to as a **deliberate strategy**—a plan that is chosen and implemented to support specific goals.[7] Texas Instruments (TI) is a company that excels at formulating and implementing deliberate strategies. TI uses a planning process that assigns most senior managers two distinct responsibilities: an operational, short-term responsibility and a strategic, long-term responsibility. Thus one manager may be responsible for both increasing the efficiency of semiconductor operations over the next year (operational, short term) and investigating new materials for semiconductor manufacture in the twenty-first century (strategic, long term). TI's objective is to help managers make short-term operational decisions while keeping in mind longer-term goals and objectives.

Other times, however, organizations use an **emergent strategy**—a pattern of action that develops over time in an organization in the absence of missions and goals, or despite missions and goals.[8] Implementing emergent strategies involves allocating resources even though an organization has not explicitly chosen its strategies. 3M has at times benefited from emergent strategies. The invention of invisible tape, for instance, provides a good example. Entrepreneurial engineers working independently took the invention to their boss, who concluded that it did not have major market potential because it was not part of an approved research and development plan. Only when the product was evaluated at the highest levels in the organization was it accepted and made part of 3M's product mix. Of course, 3M's Scotch tape became a major success, despite the fact that it arose outside of the firm's established practices. 3M now counts on emergent strategies to help expand its numerous businesses.[9]

USING SWOT ANALYSIS TO FORMULATE STRATEGY

The starting point in formulating strategy is usually SWOT analysis. **SWOT** is an acronym that stands for strengths, weaknesses, opportunities, and threats. As shown in Figure 7.1, SWOT analysis is a careful evaluation of an organization's internal strengths and weaknesses as well as its environmental opportunities and threats. In SWOT analysis, the best strategies accomplish an organization's mission by (1) exploiting an organization's opportunities and strengths while (2) neutralizing its threats and (3) avoiding (or correcting) its weaknesses.

Evaluating an Organization's Strengths

Organizational strengths are skills and capabilities that enable an organization to conceive of and implement its strategies. Different strategies call on different skills and capabilities. For example, Matsushita Electric has demonstrated strengths in manufacturing and selling consumer electronics under the brand name Panasonic. Matsushita's strength in electronics does not ensure success, however, if the firm expands into insurance, swimming-pool manufacture, or retail. Different strategies such as these require different organizational

---

● deliberate strategy
A plan of action that an organization chooses and implements to support its mission and goals

● emergent strategy
A pattern of action that develops over time in an organization in the absence of mission and goals, or despite

● SWOT
An acronym that stands for strengths, weaknesses, opportunities, and threats

● organizational strength
A skill or capability that enables an organization to conceive of and implement its strategies

F I G U R E 7.1 Using SWOT Analysis to Formulate Strategy

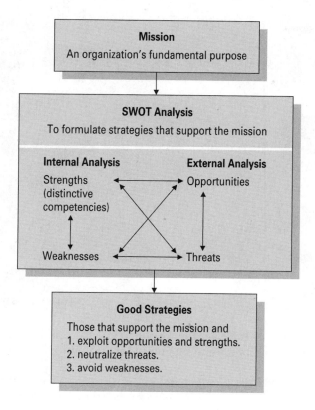

strengths. SWOT analysis divides organizational strengths into two categories: common strengths and distinctive competencies.

Common Organizational Strengths   A **common strength** is an organizational capability possessed by a large number of competing firms. For example, all major film studios possess common strengths in lighting, sound recording, set and costume design, and makeup. *Competitive parity* exists when large numbers of competing firms are able to implement the same strategy. In this situation, organizations generally attain only average levels of performance. Thus a film company that exploits only its common strengths in choosing and implementing strategies is not likely to go beyond average performance.

Distinctive Competencies   A distinctive competence is a strength possessed by only a small number of competing firms. Distinctive competencies are rare among a set of competitors. George Lucas's well-known company Industrial Light and Magic (ILM), for example, has brought the cinematic art of special effects to new heights. Some of ILM's special effects can be produced by no other organization; these rare special effects are thus ILM's distinctive competencies. Organizations that exploit their distinctive competencies often obtain a *competitive advantage* and attain above-normal economic performance.[10] Indeed, a main purpose of SWOT analysis is to discover an organization's dis-

● **common strength**
A skill and capability held by numerous competing firms

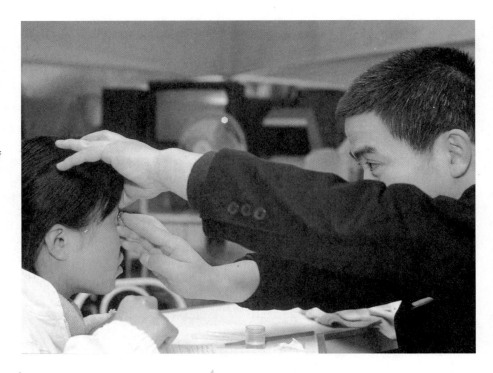

Evaluating an organization's opportunities and threats is an important part of strategy formulation. A few years ago, managers at Bausch & Lomb recognized that the billions of people in China represented a vast untapped market for contact lenses. The firm took early and aggressive steps to position itself in the Chinese market (opening a factory, for example, and teaching opticians to fit lenses) and today dominates the market in China.

tinctive competencies so that the organization can choose and implement strategies that exploit its unique organizational strengths.

Imitation of Distinctive Competencies An organization that possesses distinctive competencies and exploits them in the strategies it chooses can expect to obtain a competitive advantage and above-normal economic performance. However, its success will lead other organizations to duplicate these advantages. **Strategic imitation** is the practice of duplicating another firm's distinctive competence and thereby implementing a valuable strategy.

Although some distinctive competencies can be imitated, others cannot be. When a distinctive competence cannot be imitated, strategies that exploit these competencies generate sustained competitive advantages. A **sustained competitive advantage** is a competitive advantage that exists after all attempts at strategic imitation have ceased.[11]

A distinctive competence might not be imitated for three reasons. First, the acquisition or development of the distinctive competence may depend on unique historical circumstances that other organizations cannot replicate. Caterpillar, for example, obtained a sustained competitive advantage when the U.S. Army granted it a long-term contract. The Army felt obligated to offer this long-term contract because of the acute international construction requirements created by World War II. Caterpillar's current competitors, including Komatsu and John Deere Co., cannot re-create these circumstances.

Second, a distinctive competence might be difficult to imitate because its nature and character might not be known or understood by competing firms. The Procter & Gamble Co., for example, considers that its sustained competitive advantage is based on its manufacturing practices. Large sections of Procter & Gamble's plants are screened off to keep this information secure. Industrial Light & Magic also refuses to disclose how it creates some of its special effects.

● **strategic imitation**
The practice of duplicating another organization's distinctive competence and thereby implementing a valuable strategy

● **sustained competitive advantage**
A competitive advantage that exists after all attempts at strategic imitation have ceased

Finally, a distinctive competence can be difficult to imitate if it is based on complex social phenomena, like organizational teamwork. Competing organizations may know that a firm's success is directly traceable to the teamwork among its managers but, because teamwork is a difficult thing to create, may not be able to imitate this distinctive competence.

Evaluating an Organization's Weaknesses

Organizational weaknesses are skills and capabilities that do not enable an organization to choose and implement strategies that support its mission. An organization has essentially two ways of addressing weaknesses. First, it may need to make investments to obtain the strengths required to implement strategies that support its mission. Second, it may need to modify its mission so that it can be accomplished with the skills and capabilities that the organization already possesses. The *Environment of Management* box describes how DEC's organizational weaknesses contributed to poor performance.

Sony has invested heavily to overcome its weaknesses and accomplish its mission, which is to become an integrated consumer electronics company. To fulfill its goals in video electronics, Sony needed access to recently released films and television shows. Because the firm had no in-house video production capabilities, it had to rely on film and video work produced by other organizations. Sony addressed this weakness by purchasing Columbia Pictures, thereby acquiring high-quality in-house film and television-show production capability.[12]

In practice, organizations have a difficult time focusing on weaknesses, in part because organization members are often reluctant to admit that they do not possess all the skills and capabilities needed. Evaluating weaknesses also calls into question the judgment of managers who chose the organization's mission in the first place and who failed to invest in the skills and capabilities needed to accomplish it. Organizations that fail either to recognize or overcome their weaknesses are likely to suffer from competitive disadvantages. An organization has a **competitive disadvantage** when it is not implementing valuable strategies that are being implemented by competing organizations. Organizations with a competitive disadvantage can expect to attain below-average levels of performance.

Evaluating an Organization's Opportunities and Threats

Whereas evaluating strengths and weaknesses focuses attention on the internal workings of an organization, evaluating opportunities and threats requires analyzing an organization's environment. **Organizational opportunities** are areas that may generate higher performance. **Organizational threats** are areas that increase the difficulty of an organization's performing at a high level. Porter's five forces model of the competitive environment, as discussed in Chapter 3, can be used to characterize the extent of opportunity and threat in an organization's environment.

Recall that Porter's five forces are level of rivalry, power of suppliers, power of customers, threat of substitutes, and threat of new entrants. In general, when the level of rivalry, the power of suppliers and customers, and the threat of substitutes and new entrants are all high, an industry has relatively few opportuni-

● **organizational weakness**
A skill and capability that does not enable an organization to choose and implement strategies that support its mission

● **competitive disadvantage**
A situation in which an organization is not implementing valuable strategies that are being implemented by competing organizations

● **organizational opportunity**
An area in the environment that, if exploited, may generate high performance

● **organizational threat**
An area in the environment that increases the difficulty of an organization's achieving high performance

DEC's Strategy

The importance of an organization's strategy has probably never been more clearly evident than in the attempt at recovery of DEC (Digital Equipment Corp.), once the second-largest computer company in the United States. After an extremely profitable performance during the 1980s, DEC began losing money in 1991 (and continued to perform poorly until it was acquired by Compaq in 1998) because it failed to deal adequately with its organizational weaknesses. Management counted on massive layoffs (estimates suggest that from 50,000 to 60,000 people were terminated over a three-year period) and a restructuring of the organization to turn DEC around, but some analysts had their doubts.

Those doubts arose largely from comments and questions by customers. The new CEO had decided to focus DEC's direct customer contact on its one thousand largest customers, forcing seven thousand small customers to deal with wholesalers rather than with DEC. Customers seemed to be constantly asking what DEC's strategy was. Customers did not seem particularly concerned about new products such as the amazingly fast and powerful RISC (reduced instruction set computing) chip. Rather, customers were asking what DEC's mission was and what business it saw itself as really being involved in. Was it a software company, a hardware company, a computer consulting company, a provider of computer expertise in all areas, or something else?

A move to divide DEC into autonomous minicompanies organized by customer type was designed to answer those questions. The intent was to separate low-margin products and high-margin services and to present a clear image to each group of customers. Marketing experts were hired to assist in establishing a clear customer focus to this new organization, and worldwide sales operations were organized by industry. A strong expansion of sales in Asia in 1994 suggested that these moves might have been working, and DEC began to place greater emphasis on developing its Asian operations. However, domestic sales continued to be weak, and the company was taken over by Compaq in June 1998.

References: "Rebuilding DEC," *Forbes*, August 15, 1994, pp. 44–45; "Desperate Hours at DEC," *Business Week*, May 9, 1994, pp. 26–29; Lori Valigra, "Digital Equipment Corp: Asia Sales Lead Revival," *Asian Business*, April 1994, pp. 14–15; "How DEC's 'Minicompanies' Led to Major Losses," *Business Week*, February 7, 1994, p. 32; Tim Clark, "CEO Palmer Hits Ground Running," *Business Marketing*, August 1993, p. 14; and "Where Is DEC Going?" *Forbes*, January 7, 1991, pp. 41–42.

ties and numerous threats. Firms in these types of industries typically have the potential to achieve only normal economic performance. On the other hand, when the level of rivalry, the power of suppliers and customers, and the threat of substitutes and new entrants are all low, then an industry has numerous opportunities and relatively few threats. These industries hold the potential for above-normal performance for organizations in them.[13]

FORMULATING BUSINESS-LEVEL STRATEGIES

A number of frameworks have been developed for identifying the major strategic alternatives that organizations should consider when choosing their business-level strategies. Three important classification schemes are Porter's generic strategies, the Miles and Snow typology, and strategies based on the product life cycle.

TABLE 7.1 Porter's Generic Strategies

Strategy Type	Definition	Examples
Differentiation	Distinguish products or services	Rolex (watches) Mercedes-Benz (automobiles) Nikon (cameras) Cross (writing instruments) Hewlett-Packard (hand-held calculators)
Overall cost leadership	Reduce manufacturing and other costs	Timex Hyundai Kodak BIC Texas Instruments
Focus	Concentrate on specific regional market, product market, or group of buyers	Longines Fiat, Alpha Romeo Polaroid Waterman Pens Fisher Price

Michael Porter has proposed three generic strategies. These strategies, called differentiation, overall cost leadership, and focus, are each presumed to be widely applicable to many different competitive situations.

Porter's Generic Strategies

According to Michael Porter, organizations may pursue a differentiation, overall cost leadership, or focus strategy at the business level.[14] Table 7.1 summarizes each of these strategies. An organization that pursues a **differentiation strategy** seeks to distinguish itself from competitors through the quality of its products or services. Firms that successfully implement a differentiation strategy are able to charge more than competitors because customers are willing to pay more to obtain the extra value they perceive. Rolex pursues a differentiation strategy. Rolex watches are handmade of gold and stainless steel and are subjected to strenuous tests of quality and reliability. The firm's reputation enables it to charge thousands of dollars for its watches. Other firms that use differentiation strategies are Mercedes-Benz, Nikon, Cross, and Hewlett-Packard.

An organization implementing an **overall cost leadership strategy** attempts to gain a competitive advantage by reducing its costs below the costs of competing firms. By keeping costs low, the organization is able to sell its products at low prices and still make a profit. Timex uses an overall cost leadership strategy. For decades, this firm has specialized in manufacturing relatively simple, low-cost watches for the mass market. The price of Timex watches, starting around $29.95 (U.S.), is low because of the company's efficient high-volume manufacturing capacity. Other firms that implement overall cost leadership strategies are Hyundai, Eastman Kodak, Bic, and Texas Instruments.

A firm pursuing a **focus strategy** concentrates on a specific regional market, product line, or group of buyers. This strategy may have either a differentiation focus, whereby the firm differentiates its products in the focus market, or an overall cost leadership focus, whereby the firm manufactures and sells its products at low cost in the focus market. In the watch industry, Longines follows a focus differentiation strategy by selling highly jewelled watches to wealthy female consumers. Fiat follows a focus cost leadership strategy by selling its

● **differentiation strategy**
A strategy in which an organization seeks to distinguish itself from competitors through the quality of its products or services

● **overall cost leadership strategy**
A strategy in which an organization attempts to gain a competitive advantage by reducing its costs below the costs of competing firms

● **focus strategy**
A strategy in which an organization concentrates on a specific regional market, product line, or group of buyers

automobiles only in Italy and in selected regions of Europe; Alpha Romeo uses focus differentiation to sell its high-performance cars in these same markets. Fisher-Price uses focus differentiation to sell electronic calculators with large, brightly coloured buttons to the parents of preschoolers.

The Miles and Snow Typology

A second classification of strategic options was developed by Raymond Miles and Charles Snow.[15] These authors suggested that business-level strategies generally fall into one of four categories: prospector, defender, analyzer, and reactor. Table 7.2 summarizes each of these strategies.

A firm that follows a **prospector strategy** is a highly innovative firm that is constantly seeking out new markets and new opportunities and is oriented toward growth and risk taking. Over the years, 3M has prided itself on being one of the most innovative major corporations in the world. Employees at 3M are constantly encouraged to develop new products and ideas in a creative and entrepreneurial way. This focus on innovation has led 3M to develop a wide range of new products and markets.

Rather than seeking new growth opportunities and innovation, a company that follows a **defender strategy** concentrates on protecting its current markets, maintaining stable growth, and serving current customers. MacMillan Bloedel (MacBlo), Canada's largest forest products company, is currently using this approach: it has adopted a less aggressive, less entrepreneurial style of management and has chosen to defend its market share in the industry. While MacBlo tries to compensate for lost sales in Asia by trying to increase sales in Western Europe, for example, it has chosen to concentrate on its core business and will even close its research and development division in Burnaby, British Columbia.[16]

A business that uses an **analyzer strategy** combines elements of prospectors and defenders. Most large companies use this approach because they want to both protect their base of operations and create new market opportunities. IBM uses analyzer strategies. Whenever IBM introduces a new computer system, for example, it develops procedures that help its existing customers move from the older system to the new system. In this way IBM maintains its customer base. However, IBM also tries to create new markets. Its line of personal computers represents an effort to expand beyond its traditional product base of mainframe computers. IBM also has invested in biotechnology, superconductivity technology, and other innovative projects.

Finally, a business that follows a **reactor strategy** has no consistent strategic approach; it drifts with environmental events, reacting to but failing to anticipate or influence those events. Not surprisingly, these firms usually do not perform as well as organizations that implement other strategies. Although most organizations would deny using reactor strategies, Kmart Canada during the 1990s was clearly a reactor—a strategy that ultimately led to the company being absorbed by Hudson's Bay Co. in 1998.

Strategies Based on the Product Life Cycle

The **product life cycle** is a model that shows how sales volume changes over the life of products. Understanding the four stages in the product life cycle helps managers recognize that strategies need to evolve over time. As Figure 7.2 shows, the cycle begins when a new product or technology is first introduced. In this *introduction stage*, demand may be very high and sometimes outpaces the

prospector strategy
A strategy in which the firm encourages creativity and flexibility and is often decentralized

defender strategy
A strategy in which the firm focuses on lowering costs and improving the performance of current products

analyzer strategy
A strategy in which the firm attempts to maintain its current businesses and to be somewhat innovative in new businesses

reactor strategy
A strategy in which a firm has no consistent approach to strategy

product life cycle
A model that portrays how sales volume for products changes over the life of products

TABLE 7.2 The Miles and Snow Typology

Strategy Type	Definition	Examples
Prospector	Is innovative and growth oriented, searches for new markets and new growth opportunities, encourages risk taking	3M
Defender	Protects current markets, maintains stable growth, serves current customers	MacMillan Bloedel
Analyzer	Maintains current markets and current customer satisfaction with moderate emphasis on innovation	IBM
Reactor	No clear strategy, reacts to changes in the environment, drifts with events	Kmart Canada Consumers Distributing

The Miles and Snow Typology identifies four strategic types of organizations. Three of these—the Prospector, the Defender, and the Analyzer—can each be effective in certain circumstances. The fourth type—the Reactor—represents an ineffective approach to strategy.

firm's ability to supply the product. At this stage, managers need to focus their efforts on "getting product out the door" without sacrificing quality. Managing growth by hiring new employees and managing inventories and cash flow are also concerns during this stage. When Snapple was first introduced, its sales were so great that most stores ran out of inventory before their shelves could be restocked.

During the *growth stage*, more firms begin producing the product, and sales continue to grow. Important management issues include ensuring quality and delivery, and beginning to differentiate an organization's product from competitors' products. Entry into the industry during the growth stage may threaten an organization's competitive advantages; thus strategies to slow the entry of competitors are important.

After a period of growth, products enter a third phase. During this *mature stage*, overall demand growth for a product begins to slow down and the number of new firms producing the product begins to decline. The number of established firms producing the product may also begin to decline. This period of maturity is essential if an organization is going to survive in the long run. Product differentiation concerns are still important during this stage of the product life cycle, but keeping costs low and beginning the search for new products or services are also important strategic considerations.

In the *decline stage*, demand for the product or technology decreases, the number of organizations producing the product drops, and total sales drop. Demand often declines because all those who were interested in purchasing a particular product have already done so. Organizations that fail to anticipate the decline stage in earlier stages of the life cycle may go out of business. Those that differentiate their product, keep their costs low, or develop new products or services may do well during this stage.

Managers can use the framework of the product life cycle—introduction, growth, maturity, and decline—to plot strategy. For example, management may decide on a differentiation strategy for a product in the introduction stage and a prospector approach for a product in the growth stage. By understanding this cycle and where a particular product falls within it, managers can develop more effective strategies for extending product life.

F I G U R E   7 . 2   The Product Life Cycle

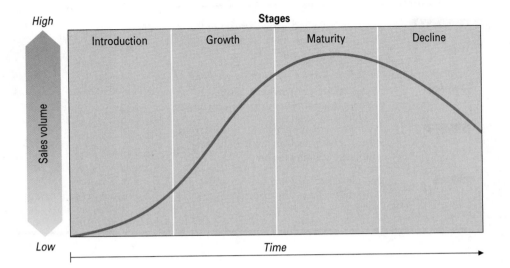

IMPLEMENTING BUSINESS-LEVEL STRATEGIES

As noted earlier, after business strategies are formulated, they must then be implemented. To do this effectively, managers must integrate the activities of several different functions. *Marketing* and *sales*, for example, are used to promote products or services and the overall public image of the organization (often through various types of advertising), price products or services, directly contact customers, and make sales. *Accounting* and *finance* control the flow of money both within the organization and from outside sources to the organization, and *manufacturing* creates the organization's products or services. Organizational *culture*, as discussed in Chapter 3, also helps firms implement their strategies.

Implementing Porter's Generic Strategies

Differentiation and cost leadership can each be implemented via these basic organizational functions. (Focus is implemented via the same approaches, depending on which one it is based.)

Differentiation Strategy   In general, to support differentiation, marketing and sales must emphasize the high-quality, high-value image of the organization's products or services. Neiman-Marcus, a department store for financially secure consumers, has excelled at using marketing to support its differentiation strategy. People do not go to Neiman-Marcus just to buy clothes or to shop for home electronics. Instead, a trip to Neiman-Marcus is advertised as a "total shopping experience." Customers who want to shop for $3,000 dog houses, $50,000 mink coats, and a $7,000 exercise machine recognize that the store caters to their needs.[17] Other organizations that have used their marketing function to implement a differentiation strategy include Roots Canada Ltd.,

Kellogg

The breakfast cereal market began to change during the 1980s. Fad cereals based on movie and comic figures such as Batman and the Ninja Turtles came and went, earning sizable sales. Private-label brands began to take over market share based on low prices. Industry leader Kellogg Co. saw its market share slipping from 42 percent in 1986 to less than 34 percent by mid-1994. A new strategy clearly seemed necessary.

During the early 1990s, other giant cereal companies such as General Mills, Quaker Oats, Ralston Purina Co., and Kraft General Foods (Post) began to move their strategies away from marketing and toward research. Companies cut prices, offered fewer coupons (except to boost the entry of new lines), and developed in the laboratories new products or new variations of existing products. They also began to use co-branding, in which two or more companies enter into a joint venture to share recipes.

Kellogg seemed to defy conventional wisdom. It acted counterintuitively by aggressively advertising and promoting its existing brands to take advantage of brand loyalty, including a huge television promotion in the fall of 1993. Even riskier, in response to overall increasing costs and increasing grain costs because of flooding in 1993, Kellogg raised prices. But by raising prices without adding value, Kellogg was taking a big risk in this increasingly competitive market—a risk that had not paid off as of 1994 since its market share fell.

Kellogg, however, did introduce yet another Rice Krispies version to try to bolster that line, which was struggling. It also joined forces with ConAgra in 1994 to try to gain back market share with a new multigrain adult cereal line. Healthy Choice From Kellogg's cereal was introduced in 1994 and seemed successful. Weak performance in early 1994, however, led to a management shakeup as the head of Kellogg's European operations became president of Kellogg North America. It was hoped that he could bring the same success to North American operations as he was able to bring to European ones. However, Kellogg appears to be having difficulty regaining market share. Following a 7 percent increase in 1995, Kellogg's net sales have since fluctuated: a 5 percent drop in 1996 was followed by a 2 percent increase in 1997 and a 1 percent drop in the first nine months of 1998. In January 1999, John Cook was appointed president of Kellogg North America and will oversee Kellogg's markets in Canada and the United States.

References: "The Nervous Faces Around Kellogg's Breakfast Table," *Business Week*, July 18, 1994, p. 33; Bob Ferguson, "Cereal Science," *Brandweek*, May 2, 1994, pp. 28–36; Karen Benezra, "Kellogg, ConAgra to Walk Up Cereal Aisle," *Brandweek*, March 14, 1994, p. 8; "What Price Brand Loyalty?" *Fortune*, January 10, 1994, pp. 103–104; Julie Liesse, "Kellogg's Prices Go Up, Up, Up," *Advertising Age*, August 9, 1993, pp. 1, 29; Malia Boyd, "A Case for Incentives," *Incentive*, November 1993, pp. 100–101; Kellogg Company, Annual Report, 1997 (http://www.kelloggs.com); and Kellogg Company (http://biz.yahoo.com).

Birks Jewellers, and Mercedes–Benz. The *Managing in a Changing World* box discusses how Kellogg Co. has tried to implement a differentiation strategy.

The function of accounting and finance in a business that is implementing a differentiation strategy is to control the flow of funds without discouraging the creativity needed to constantly develop new products and services to meet customer needs. If keeping track of and controlling the flow of money become more important than determining how money and resources are best spent to meet customer needs, then no organization, whether high-technology firm or fashion designer, will be able to implement a differentiation strategy effectively. In manufacturing, a firm implementing a differentiation strategy must emphasize quality and meeting specific customer needs, rather than simply reducing costs. Manufacturing may sometimes have to keep inventory on hand so that customers will have access to products when they want them. Manufacturing also may have to engage in costly customization to meet customer needs.

The culture of a firm implementing a differentiation strategy, like the firm's other functions, must also emphasize creativity, innovation, and response to customer needs. Marks and Spencer's culture puts the needs of customers ahead of all other considerations. This British firm offers a complete guarantee on merchandise. Dissatisfied customers may return clothes for a full refund or exchange, no questions asked. The priority given to customer needs at the mail-order firm Lands' End is typical of an organization that is successfully implementing a differentiation strategy.[18]

Overall Cost Leadership Strategy To support cost leadership, marketing and sales are likely to focus on simple product attributes and how these product attributes meet customer needs in a low-cost and effective manner. These organizations are very likely to engage in advertising. Throughout this effort, however, emphasis is on the value that an organization's products provide for the price, rather than on the special features of the product or service. Advertising for Bic pens ("Writes first time, every time"), Timex watches ("Takes a licking and keeps on ticking"), and Zellers ("The lowest price is the law") helps these firms implement cost leadership strategies.

Proper emphasis in accounting and finance is also pivotal. Because the success of the organization depends on having costs lower than the competitors', management must take care to reduce costs wherever possible. Tight financial

A researcher examines a 320-year-old Douglas fir in Canada's temperate rain forest. Forestry is one industry in Canada where the defender strategy has occasionally been implemented.

and accounting controls at Wal-Mart and Price/Costco Canada have helped these organizations implement cost leadership strategies. Manufacturing typically helps with large runs of highly standardized products. Products are designed both to meet customer needs and to be easily manufactured. Manufacturing emphasizes increased volume of production to reduce the per unit costs of manufacturing. Organizations such as Toshiba Corporation (a Japanese semiconductor firm) and Texas Instruments have used this type of manufacturing to implement cost leadership strategies.

The culture of organizations implementing cost leadership strategies tends to focus on improving the efficiency of manufacturing, sales, and other business functions. Managers in these organizations are almost fanatical about keeping their costs low. Wal-Mart appeals to its customers to leave shopping carts in its parking lot with signs that read "Please—help us keep *your* costs low." Fujitsu Electronics, in its Tokyo manufacturing facilities, operates in plain, unpainted cinder-block and cement facilities to keep its costs as low as possible.

Implementing Miles and Snow's Strategies

Similarly, a variety of issues must be considered when implementing any of Miles and Snow's strategic options. (Of course, no organization would purposefully choose to implement a reactor strategy.)

Prospector Strategy　An organization implementing a prospector strategy is innovative, seeks new market opportunities, and takes numerous risks. To implement this strategy, organizations need to encourage creativity and flexibility. Creativity helps an organization perceive, or even create, new opportunities in its environment; flexibility enables it to change quickly to take advantage of these new opportunities. Organizations often increase creativity and flexibility by adopting a decentralized organization structure. An organization is decentralized when major decision-making responsibility is delegated to middle- and lower-level managers.

Johnson & Johnson links decentralization with a prospector strategy. Each of the firm's different businesses is organized into a separate unit, and the managers of these units hold full decision-making responsibility and authority. Often these businesses develop new products for new markets. As the new products develop and sales grow, Johnson & Johnson reorganizes so that each new product is managed in a separate unit.[19]

Defender Strategy　An organization implementing a defender strategy attempts to protect its market from new competitors. It tends to downplay creativity and innovation in bringing out new products or services and focus its efforts instead on lowering costs or improving the performance of current products. Often a firm implementing a prospector strategy will switch to a defender strategy. This happens when the firm successfully creates a new market or business and then attempts to protect its market from competition. An example is MacMillan Bloedel in 1998. As noted earlier, this forest products company, faced with reduced demand for lumber in Asian countries facing economic problems, turned to other markets in Europe and China where the competition is very strong, while at the same time increasing the focus on its core business. This behaviour suggests a defender strategy.[20]

Analyzer Strategy　　An organization implementing an analyzer strategy attempts to maintain its current business and to be somewhat innovative in new businesses. Because the analyzer strategy falls somewhere between prospector strategy (with focus on innovation) and defender strategy (with focus on maintaining and improving current businesses), the attributes of organizations implementing the analyzer strategy tend to be similar to both of these other types of organizations. They have tight accounting and financial controls and high flexibility, efficient production and customized products, and creativity and low costs. Organizations maintain these multiple and contradictory processes with difficulty.

One organization that has been able to successfully balance the need for innovation with the need to maintain current businesses is Procter & Gamble (P&G). As a major food products company, P&G has established numerous brand-name products, such as Crest toothpaste, Tide laundry detergent, and Sure deodorant. P&G must continue to invest in its successful products to maintain financial performance. But P&G must also encourage the development of new products and brand names. In this way, it can continue to expand its market presence and have new products to replace those whose market falls off. Through these efforts, P&G can continue to grow.

FORMULATING CORPORATE-LEVEL STRATEGIES

Most large organizations are engaged in several businesses, industries, and markets. Each business or set of businesses within such an organization is frequently referred to as a *strategic business unit,* or *SBU*. An organization such as Bombardier operates several different businesses, making and selling products such as passenger rail vehicles, snowmobiles, and aircraft and providing services such as commercial and industrial financing, mortgage financing, and consumer financing. Bombardier organizes these businesses into five SBUs. Even organizations that sell only one product may operate in several distinct markets. McDonald's Corp. sells only fast food, but it competes in markets as diverse as Canada, the United States, Europe, Russia, Japan, and South Korea.

Decisions about which businesses, industries, and markets an organization will enter, and how to manage these different businesses, are based on an organization's corporate strategy. The most important strategic issue at the corporate level concerns the extent and nature of organizational diversification. **Diversification** describes the number of different businesses that an organization is engaged in and the extent to which these businesses are related to one another. There are three types of diversification strategies: single-product strategy, related diversification, and unrelated diversification.[21]

Single-Product Strategy

An organization that pursues a **single-product strategy** manufactures just one product or service and sells it in a single geographic market. The WD-40 Company, for example, manufactures only a single product, WD-40 spray lubricant, and sells it in just one market, North America. WD-40 has considered broadening its market to Europe and Asia, but it continues to centre all manufacturing, sales, and marketing efforts on one product.

● **diversification**
The number of different businesses that an organization is engaged in and the extent to which these businesses are related to one another

● **single-product strategy**
A strategy in which an organization manufactures just one product or service and sells it in a single geographic market

T A B L E   7 . 3   Bases of Relatedness in Implementing Related Diversification

Bases of Relatedness	Examples
Similar technology	Philips, BCE
	Westinghouse, Digital
Common distribution and marketing skills	George Weston, RJR Nabisco
	Proctor & Gamble
Common brand name and reputation	Disney, Universal
Common customers	Merck, IBM, Shaw Communications

Firms that implement related diversification can do so using any number of bases of relatedness. Four frequently used bases of related uses for diversification are similar technology, common distribution and marketing skills, common brand name and reputation, and common customers.

The single-product strategy has one major strength and one major weakness. By concentrating its efforts so completely on one product and market, a firm is likely to be very successful in manufacturing and marketing the product. Because it has staked its survival on a single product, the organization works very hard to make sure that the product is a success. Of course, if the product is not accepted by the market or is replaced by a new one, the firm will suffer. This happened to slide-rule manufacturers when electronic calculators became widely available and to companies that manufactured only black-and-white televisions when colour televisions became available.

Related Diversification

Given the disadvantage of the single-product strategy, most large businesses today operate in several different businesses, industries, or markets. If the businesses are somehow linked, that organization is implementing a strategy of **related diversification**.

Bases of Relatedness   Organizations link their different businesses, industries, or markets in different ways. Table 7.3 gives some typical bases of relatedness. In organizations such as Philips, a European consumer electronics company, a similar type of electronics technology underlies all the businesses. At BCE, communications technology links Bell Canada, BCE Mobile, Bell Canada International, and Nortel. A common computer design technology links Compaq's various computer products and peripherals..

Organizations such as George Weston Ltd., RJR Nabisco, and Procter & Gamble operate multiple businesses related by a common distribution network (grocery stores) and common marketing skills (advertising). Disney and Universal rely on strong brand names and reputations to link their diverse businesses, which include movie studios and theme parks. Pharmaceutical firms such as Merck Frosst Canada Inc. sell numerous products to a single set of customers: hospitals, doctors, patients, and drugstores. Similarly, Shaw Communications Inc., which is currently known for its cable systems in British Columbia, Alberta, Saskatchewan, Manitoba, and Ontario, is preparing to offer its customers various services associated with digital communications. For

● **related diversification**
A strategy in which an organization operates in several businesses that are somehow linked with one another

example, Shaw's 2000 kilometre fibre-optic cable network will allow it to offer optimum Internet service.[22]

Advantages of Related Diversification   Pursuing a strategy of related diversification has three primary advantages. First, it reduces an organization's dependence on any one of its business activities and thus reduces economic risk. Even if one or two of a firm's businesses lose money, the organization as a whole may still survive because the healthy businesses will generate enough cash to support the others.[23]

Second, by managing several businesses at the same time, an organization can reduce the overhead costs associated with managing any one business. In other words, if the normal administrative costs required to operate any business, such as legal services and accounting, can be spread over a large number of businesses, then the overhead costs *per business* will be lower than they would be if each business had to absorb all costs itself. Thus the overhead costs of businesses in a related diversified firm are usually lower than those of similar businesses that are not part of a larger corporation.[24]

Third, related diversification allows an organization to exploit its strengths and capabilities in more than one business. When organizations do this successfully, they capitalize on synergies, which are complementary effects that exist among their businesses. *Synergy* exists among a set of businesses when the businesses' economic value together is greater than their economic value separately. Disney is skilled at creating and exploiting synergies. Its hit movie *The Lion King* earned over $300 million (U.S.) in box office revenues. In addition, Disney earned hundreds of millions more from the sales of licensed *Lion King* toys, clothing, and video games. *The Lion King* stage show at Disney World attracts more guests to the park, and the video sold 20 million copies during the first week of its release. And people who bought the video were treated to a preview of the next Disney animated blockbuster, *Pocahontas*.

Unrelated Diversification

Firms that implement a strategy of *unrelated diversification* operate multiple businesses that are not logically associated with one another. For example, Imasco owns Imperial Tobacco, Canada Trust, Shoppers Drug Mart, and Genstar Development Company. Unrelated diversification was a very popular strategy in the 1960s and early 1970s. During this time, several conglomerates like ITT grew by acquiring literally hundreds of other organizations and then running these numerous businesses as independent entities. Even if there are important potential synergies between their different businesses, organizations that are implementing a strategy of unrelated diversification do not attempt to exploit these possible synergies.

In theory, unrelated diversification has two advantages. First, a business that uses this strategy should have stable performance over time. During any given period, if some businesses owned by the organization are in a cycle of decline, others may be in a cycle of growth. Unrelated diversification is also thought to have resource allocation advantages. Every year, when a corporation allocates capital, people, and other resources among its various businesses, it must evaluate information about the future of those businesses so that it can place its resources where they have the highest return potential. Given that it owns the businesses in question and thus has full access to information about the future of those businesses, a firm implementing unrelated diversification should be able to allocate capital to maximize corporate performance.

Despite these presumed advantages, research suggests that unrelated diversification usually does not lead to high performance for a number of reasons. First, corporate-level managers in such a company usually do not know enough about the unrelated businesses to provide helpful strategic guidance or to allocate capital appropriately. To make strategic decisions managers must have complete and subtle understanding of a business and its environment. Because corporate managers often have difficulty fully evaluating the economic importance of investments for all the businesses under their wing, they tend to concentrate only on a business's current performance. This narrow attention at the expense of broader planning eventually hobbles the entire organization.

Second, because organizations that implement unrelated diversification fail to exploit important synergies, they are at a competitive disadvantage compared to organizations that use related diversification. Universal Studios has been at a competitive disadvantage relative to Disney because its theme parks, movie studios, and licensing divisions are less integrated and therefore achieve less synergy.

For these reasons, almost all organizations have abandoned unrelated diversification as a corporate-level strategy. ITT sold off numerous businesses and now concentrates on a core set of related businesses and markets. In Canada, Toronto-based Jannock Limited has sold its interests in sugar and electrical parts in order to concentrate on its core business of building supplies.[25] Large corporations that have not concentrated on a core set of businesses eventually have been acquired by other companies and then broken up. Research suggests that these organizations are actually worth more when broken up into smaller pieces than they are when joined.[26]

IMPLEMENTING CORPORATE-LEVEL STRATEGIES

In implementing a diversification strategy, organizations face two important questions. First, how will the organization move from a single product strategy to some form of diversification? Second, once the organization diversifies, how will it manage diversification effectively?

Becoming a Diversified Firm

Most organizations do not start out completely diversified. Rather, they begin operations in a single business, pursuing a particular business-level strategy. Success in this strategy then creates resources and strengths that the organization can use in related businesses.

Internal Development of New Products   Some firms diversify by developing their own new products and services within the boundaries of their traditional business operations. Honda followed this path to diversification. Relying on its traditional strength in the motorcycle market, over the years Honda learned how to make fuel-efficient, highly reliable small engines. Honda began to apply its strengths in a new business: manufacturing small, fuel-efficient cars for the Japanese domestic market. These vehicles were first sold in North America in the late 1960s. Honda's success in North American exports led the company to increase the size and improve the performance of its cars. Over the years, Honda has introduced automobiles of increasing quality, culminating in the Acura line of luxury cars. While diversifying into the market for automobiles, Honda also applied its engine-building strengths to produce a line of all-terrain vehicles, portable electric generators, and lawn mowers. In each case, Honda was able to parlay its strengths and resources into successful new businesses.[27]

Replacement of Suppliers and Customers   Firms can also become diversified by replacing their former suppliers and customers.[28] A company that stops buying supplies (either manufactured goods or raw materials) from other companies and begins to provide its own supplies has diversified through **backward vertical integration**. Campbell Soup Co. once bought soup cans from several different manufacturers, but later began manufacturing its own cans. In fact, Campbell is currently one of the largest can-manufacturing companies in the world, although almost all the cans it makes are used in its soup operations.

An organization that stops selling to one customer and sells instead to that customer's customers has diversified through **forward vertical integration**. Companies that own factory outlet stores illustrate how forward vertical integration can be used to diversify operations. One such example is Samsonite's store in Stratford, Ontario. Samsonite has not, however, abandoned its customers in the retail industry.

Mergers and Acquisitions   Another common way for businesses to diversify is through mergers and acquisitions—that is, through purchasing another organization. Such a purchase is called a **merger** when the two organizations being combined are approximately the same size. It is called an **acquisition** when one of the organizations involved is considerably larger than the other. Organizations engage in mergers and acquisitions partly to diversify through vertical integration by acquiring former suppliers or former customers. In 1996, there were 1,185 mergers and acquisitions in Canada: these transactions had a total value of $75 billion.[29] The volume of deals in 1997 was 1,100, with a value of $100 billion. The volume of deals in 1998 remained the same, but their value in just the first ten months of that year was 30 percent higher than in 1997.[30]

Most organizations use mergers and acquisitions to acquire complementary products or complementary services, which are products or services linked by a common technology and common customers. Wendy's acquisition of Tim Hortons was undertaken for just this reason. The objective of most mergers and acquisitions is the creation or exploitation of synergies. Synergy can reduce the combined organizations' costs of doing business; it can increase revenues; and it may open the way to entirely new businesses for the organization to enter.[31]

Managing Diversification

However an organization implements diversification—whether through internal development, vertical integration, or mergers and acquisitions—it must monitor and manage its strategy. The two major tools for managing diversification are (1) organization structure and (2) portfolio management techniques. How organization structure can be used to manage a diversification strategy is discussed in detail in Chapter 11. **Portfolio management techniques** are methods that diversified organizations use to make decisions about what businesses to engage in and how to manage these multiple businesses to

Margin glossary

● **backward vertical integration**
An organization's beginning the business activities formerly conducted by its suppliers

● **forward vertical integration**
An organization's beginning the business activities formerly conducted by its customers

● **merger**
The purchase of one firm by another firm of approximately the same size

● **acquisition**
The purchase of a firm by a firm that is considerably larger

● **portfolio management technique**
A method that diversified organizations use to determine which businesses to engage in and how to manage these businesses to maximize corporate performance

FIGURE 7.3 The BCG Matrix

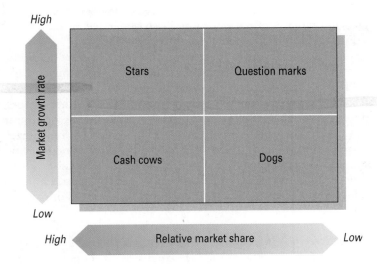

The BCG matrix helps managers develop a better understanding of how different strategic business units contribute to the overall organization. By assessing each SBU on the basis of its market growth rate and relative market share, managers can make decisions about whether to commit further financial resources to the SBU or to sell or liquidate it.

Source: *Perspectives,* No. 66, "The Product Portfolio." Adapted by permission from The Boston Consulting Group, Inc., 1970.

maximize corporate performance.[32] Two important portfolio management techniques are the BCG matrix and the GE Business Screen.

BCG Matrix   The **BCG** (for Boston Consulting Group) **matrix** provides a framework for evaluating the relative performance of businesses in which a diversified organization operates. It also prescribes the preferred distribution of cash and other resources among these businesses.[33] The BCG matrix uses two factors to evaluate an organization's set of businesses: the growth rate of a particular market and the organization's share of that market. The matrix suggests that fast-growing markets in which an organization has the highest market share are more attractive business opportunities than slow-growing markets in which an organization has small market share. Dividing market growth and market share into two categories (low and high) creates the simple matrix shown in Figure 7.3.

The matrix classifies the types of businesses that a diversified organization can engage in as dogs, cash cows, question marks, and stars. *Dogs* are businesses that have a very small share of a market that is not expected to grow. Because these businesses do not hold much economic promise, the BCG matrix suggests that organizations either should not invest in them or should consider selling them as soon as possible. *Cash cows* are businesses that have a large share of a market that is not expected to grow substantially. These businesses characteristically generate high profits that the organization should use to support question marks and stars. (Cash cows are "milked" for cash to support businesses in markets that have greater growth potential.) *Question marks* are businesses that have only a small share of a quickly growing market. The future performance of these businesses is uncertain. A question mark that is able to capture increasing amounts of this growing market may be very profitable. On the other hand, a question mark unable to keep up with market growth is likely to have low profits. The

● **BCG matrix**
A method of evaluating businesses relative to the growth rate of their market and the organization's share of the market

BCG matrix suggests that organizations should carefully invest in question marks. If their performance does not live up to expectations, question marks should be reclassified as dogs and divested. *Stars* are businesses that have the largest share of a rapidly growing market. Cash generated by cash cows should be invested in stars to ensure their preeminent position.

ITT invested profits from its cash cows in stars and new acquisitions and became one of the largest organizations in the world during the 1970s. However, ITT's performance in the 1980s reflects the main weakness of the BCG matrix technique: it may be too narrowly focused. Other factors besides market growth and market share determine the performance of a business. By relying so closely on the BCG matrix, ITT failed to recognize several promising opportunities in businesses that it had classified as dogs or cash cows. Other organizations recognized these opportunities and took advantage of them. Recently, ITT has explicitly abandoned the BCG matrix and no longer regards its businesses as dogs or cash cows simply on the basis of market growth and market share.

GE Business Screen   In response to the narrow focus of the BCG matrix, General Electric (GE) developed the **GE Business Screen**—a more sophisti-

● **GE Business Screen**
A method of evaluating businesses along two dimensions: (1) industry attractiveness and (2) competitive position; in general, the more attractive the industry and the more competitive the position, the more an organization should invest in a business

The GE Business Screen is a more sophisticated approach to portfolio management. As shown here, several different factors combine to determine a business's competitive position and the attractiveness of its industry. These two dimensions, in turn, can be used to classify businesses as winners, question marks, average businesses, losers, or profit producers. Such a classification enables managers to more effectively allocate the organization's resources across various business opportunities.

FIGURE 7.4   The GE Business Screen

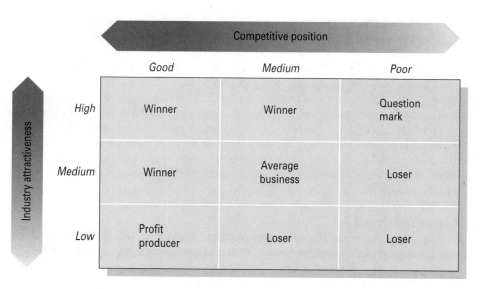

Competitive position

1. Market share
2. Technological know-how
3. Product quality
4. Service network
5. Price competitiveness
6. Operating costs

Industry attractiveness

1. Market growth
2. Market size
3. Capital requirements
4. Competitive intensity

Reprinted by permission from p. 32 of *Strategy Formulation: Analytical Concepts,* 1st edition, by C.W. Hofer and D. Schendel; Copyright © 1978. Reprinted with permission of South Western College Publishing, a division of International Thomson Publishing.

cated approach to managing diversified business units. The Business Screen is a portfolio management technique that can also be represented in the form of a matrix. Rather than focusing solely on market growth and market share, however, the GE Business Screen considers industry attractiveness and competitive position. These two factors are divided into three categories, to make the nine-cell matrix shown in Figure 7.4.[34] These cells, in turn, classify business units as winners, losers, question marks, average businesses, or profit producers.

As Figure 7.4 shows, both market growth and market share appear in a broad list of factors that determine the overall attractiveness of an industry and the overall quality of a firm's competitive position. Other determinants of an industry's attractiveness (in addition to market growth) include market size, capital requirements, and competitive intensity. In general, the greater the market growth, the larger the market, the smaller the capital requirements, and the less the competitive intensity, the more attractive an industry will be. Other determinants of an organization's competitive position in an industry (besides market share) include technological know-how, product quality, service network, price competitiveness, and operating costs. In general, businesses with large market share, technological know-how, high product quality, a quality service network, competitive prices, and low operating costs are in a favourable competitive position.

Think of the GE Business Screen as a way of applying SWOT analysis to the implementation and management of a diversification strategy. The determinants of industry attractiveness are similar to the environmental opportunities and threats in SWOT analysis, and the determinants of competitive position are similar to organizational strengths and weaknesses. By conducting this type of SWOT analysis across several businesses, a diversified organization can decide how to invest its resources to maximize corporate performance.

In general, organizations should invest in winners and in question marks (where industry attractiveness and competitive position are both favourable), should maintain the market position of average businesses and profit producers (where industry attractiveness and competitive position are average), and should sell losers.

SUMMARY OF KEY POINTS

A strategy is a comprehensive plan for accomplishing the organization's goals. Strategic management is a comprehensive and ongoing process aimed at formulating and implementing effective strategies. Effective strategies address three organizational issues: distinctive competence, scope, and resource deployment. Most large companies have both business-level and corporate-level strategies. Strategy formulation is the set of processes involved in creating or determining the strategies of an organization. Strategy implementation is the process of executing strategies.

SWOT analysis considers an organization's strengths, weaknesses, opportunities, and threats. Using SWOT analysis, an organization chooses strategies that support its mission and (1) exploit its opportunities and strengths, (2) neutralize its threats, and (3) avoid its weaknesses. Common strengths cannot be ignored, but distinctive competencies hold the greatest promise for superior performance.

A business-level strategy is the plan an organization uses to conduct business in a particular industry or market. Porter suggests that businesses may formulate a differentiation strategy, an overall cost leadership strategy, or a focus strategy at this level. According to Miles and Snow, organizations may choose one of four business-level strategies: prospector, defender, analyzer, or reactor. Business-level strategies may also take into account the stages in the product life cycle.

Strategy implementation at the business level takes place in the areas of marketing, sales, accounting and finance, and manufacturing. Culture also influences strategy implementation. Implementation of Porter's generic strategies requires different emphases in each of these organizational areas. Implementation of Miles and Snow's strategies affects organization structure and practices.

A corporate-level strategy is the plan an organization uses to manage its operations across several businesses. A firm that does not diversify is implementing a single-product strategy. An organization pursues a strategy of diversification when it operates a set of businesses that are somehow linked. Related diversification reduces the financial risk associated with any particular product, reduces the overhead costs of each business, and enables the organization to create and exploit synergy. An organization pursues a strategy of unrelated diversification when it operates a set of businesses that are not logically associated with one another.

Strategy implementation at the corporate level addresses two issues: how the organization will go about its diversification and the way that an organization is managed once it has diversified. Businesses accomplish this in three ways: developing new products internally, replacing suppliers (backward vertical integration) or customers (forward vertical integration), and engaging in mergers and acquisitions. Organizations manage diversification through the organization structure that they adopt and through portfolio management techniques. The BCG matrix classifies an organization's diversified businesses as dogs, cash cows, question marks, or stars according to market share and market growth rate. The GE Business Screen classifies businesses as winners, losers, question marks, average businesses, or profit producers according to industry attractiveness and competitive position.

DISCUSSION QUESTIONS

Questions for Review

1. What are the two main types of strategic alternatives available to an organization?
2. How does a deliberate strategy differ from an emergent strategy?
3. List and describe Porter's generic strategies and the Miles and Snow typology of strategies.
4. What is the difference between a single-product strategy, a related diversification strategy, and an unrelated diversification strategy?

Questions for Analysis

5. Common strengths among firms cannot give one firm a competitive advantage. Does this mean that an organization should ignore its common strengths in choosing and implementing its strategies? Why or why not?

6. Suppose that an organization does not have any distinctive competencies. If the organization is able to acquire some distinctive competencies, how long are these strengths likely to remain distinctive competencies? Why?

7. Suppose that an organization moves from a single-product strategy to a strategy of related diversification. How might the organization use SWOT analysis to select attributes of its current business to serve as bases of relatedness among its newly acquired businesses?

8. For decades now, Ivory Soap has advertised that it is 99% pure. Ivory has refused to add deodorants, facial creams, or colours to its soap. It also packages its soap in plain paper wrappers—no foil or fancy printing. Is Ivory implementing a product differentiation, low cost, focus strategy, or some combination? Explain your answer.

Questions for Application

9. Interview a manager and categorize the business- and corporate-level strategies of his or her organization according to Porter's generic strategies, the Miles and Snow typology, and extent of diversification.

10. Is implementing a differentiation strategy always going to improve an organization's performance? Give three real-world examples in which differentiation did not seem to improve an organization's performance, and describe why it did not. What do these "errors" have in common?

BUILDING EFFECTIVE CONCEPTUAL SKILLS

Exercise Overview

Conceptual skills refer to the manager's ability to think in the abstract. This exercise gives you some experience in using your conceptual skills on real business opportunities and potential.

Exercise Background

Many successful managers have at one time or another had an idea for using an existing product for new purposes or in new markets. For example, Arm & Hammer Baking Soda (a food product used in cooking) is now also widely used to absorb odours in refrigerators. Commercials advise consumers to simply open a box of Arm & Hammer and place it in their refrigerator. This promotion has led to a big increase in sales of the baking soda.

In other situations, managers have extended product life cycles of products by taking them into new markets. The most common example today involves products that are becoming obsolete in more industrialized countries and introducing them in less industrialized countries.

Exercise Task

Apply your conceptual skills by doing each of the following:
1. Make a list of ten simple products that have relatively straightforward purposes (for example, a pencil, which is used for writing).
2. Try to identify two or three alternative uses for each product (for example, a pencil can be used as a splint for a broken finger in an emergency).
3. Evaluate the market potential for each alternative product use as high, moderate, or low (for example, the market potential for pencils as splints is probably low).
4. Form small groups of two or three members each and pool your ideas. Each group should choose two or three ideas to present to the class.

Contrasting Strategies: Zellers versus Wal-Mart

Hudson's Bay Company, incorporated in 1670, is one of Canada's oldest and most established companies. For the first two hundred years, the company's business consisted entirely of trading in furs, moving away from the Bay and into the interior of Canada with a network of routes spread out over the north and west. Since then, Hudson's Bay Co. has acquired a number of other businesses and in the process has diversified its base. Today, the company is engaged in department store merchandising through retail outlets situated across Canada. One of its retailers is Zellers (the other is The Bay), which became a wholly owned subsidiary of Hudson's Bay in 1981.

Up to the mid-1990s, Zellers dominated the discount merchandising sector in Canada. With approximately three hundred stores across the country, located in all ten Canadian provinces, the company became a household name, its television advertising jingle sung by kids. Zellers' main strategy over the years has been to maintain prices that are lower than its competitors', emphasizing high volume of sales rather than high profit margins on items. With its competition practically beaten, Zellers' customer service took a back seat and it was not unusual to find its staff uncaring and the stores very unkempt. Further, the stores were sometimes out of stock of advertised items, with rows of empty shelves in almost every department—a cardinal sin in the competitive discount retail environment.

In 1994, U.S. giant discount retailer Wal-Mart entered Canada with a buyout of the Woolco store chain. Wal-Mart's strategy has also been to maintain low prices. However, unlike Zellers, the company has also put considerable emphasis on customer service and product availability. With an advanced computerized system, the company has been able to maintain a good record of its inventory, thus maximizing its in-stock availability. Wal-Mart also established more spacious stores, with an average of 122,000 square feet compared to Zellers' average of approximately 75,000 square feet at the time of Wal-Mart's entry.

Zellers' initial strategy to combat its new foe was the initiation of a price war in an effort to maintain its market share and retain its image as the discounter with the lowest prices. As many analysts noted, this move was destined to fail, thanks to Wal-Mart's deeper pockets. The "price war" strategy had an almost immediate impact on profit margins and Zellers' bottom line. In 1993, a year before Wal-Mart's entry into the Canadian retail scene, Zellers posted a profit of $256 million. In 1994, Zellers' profits dipped for the first time in a decade, to $216 million, and in 1997 the company lost $90 million.

Zellers has begun to rethink its strategies on a number of fronts. It is now focusing on style while lessening the intensity of the price war and pushing for improved profit margins, with a focus primarily on "soft goods" such as clothing. With 75 percent of its shoppers female, the company is expanding into toiletries, cosmetics, and fragrances. Zellers has also begun offering items Wal-Mart does not, thus ensuring more flexibility in pricing. It has also renovated many of its stores, emphasizing more open aisles. New Zellers Plus stores have wider aisles and new attractions such as a complete home entertainment centre and a full-scale paint department. These store are also much larger, pushing the average stores size to approximately 82,000 square feet.

The company also replaced some of its top executives. From 1996 to 1998, it changed presidents four times, with George Heller moving into the position in February 1998 just prior to Zellers' purchase of Kmart Canada. The operations of the two companies were merged under the Zellers name.

In the meantime, Wal-Mart has continued its aggressive expansion into Canada and now has over 130 stores countrywide. It has been unwavering in its commitment to customer service, a strategy that still seems to be lacking at Zellers. Many analysts believe that Zellers is doomed to failure, with its recent counter strategies being merely defensive and following the lead set by Wal-Mart. Only time will tell.

Questions

1. As CEO of Zellers, what strategies would you use to improve Zellers' profitability?

2. Are there similarities between the strategies employed by Zellers and Wal-Mart and those discussed in this chapter? Explain your response.

3. What is your prediction for Zellers' future? Explain your response.

References: Valerie Lawton, "Wal-Mart Announces Next Phase in Canadian Expansion," *Canadian Press Newswire*, March 19, 1997; "Wal-Mart Has Radically Changed the Retail Scene," *Financial Post*, December 21–23, 1996, p. 41; "Zellers Issues Challenge to Wal-Mart," *Financial Post*, December 19, 1996, p. 22; "Is This Any Way to Run a Discount Store?" *Canadian Business*, September 1996, pp. 34–41; "The Bay Is No Dinosaur Chief Executive Says," *Financial Post,* June 12, 1996, p. 9; "Hudson's Bay Company," *Financial Post Historical Reports* (Financial Post Data Group, 1996); and Sean Silcoff, "Boutique Z," *Canadian Business*, May 8, 1988, pp. 62–66.

CHAPTER NOTES

1. Stacy Bradford, "Here's the Beef," *Financial World,* November 18, 1996, pp. 46–48; Matt Murray, "Wendy's to Bring Tim Hortons to U.S.," *The Globe and Mail,* April 16, 1997, p. B10; Susan Noakes, "Creating Marriages of Convenience," *Financial Post,* February 14, 1997; Richard Siklos, "Finding a Hole in the U.S. Market," *Financial Post,* March 11, 1997, p. 13; and Wendy's International Annual Report, 1997 (http://www.investquest.com).

2. For early discussions of strategic management, see Kenneth Andrews, *The Concept of Corporate Strategy,* rev. ed. (Homewood, Ill.: Dow Jones-Irwin, 1980); Igor Ansoff, *Corporate Strategy* (New York: McGraw-Hill, 1965); and E.P. Learned et al., *Business Policy* (Homewood, Ill.: Irwin, 1969).

3. Brent Hutchinson, "Merchants of Boom," *Canadian Business,* May 1997, pp. 39–48.

4. Harlan Byrne, "Raytheon Co.: In Diversifying Years Ago— 'We Did the Right Thing,'" *Barron's,* April 2, 1990, pp. 61–62.

5. For a discussion of the distinction between business- and corporate-level strategies, see Charles Hill and Gareth Jones, *Strategic Management: An Integrated Approach,* 3rd ed. (Boston: Houghton Mifflin, 1995).

6. Kenneth Kidd, "Year of the Deal," *Report on Business Magazine,* July 1997, pp. 53–59.

7. Henry Mintzberg, "Patterns in Strategy Formulation," *Management Science,* October 1978, pp. 934–948; Henry Mintzberg, "Strategy Making in Three Modes," *California Management Review,* 1973, pp. 44–53; and Henry Mintzberg, D. Raisinghani, and A. Theoret, "The Structure of Unstructured Decision Processes," *Administrative Science Quarterly,* 1976, pp. 246–275.

8. See Mintzberg, "Patterns in Strategy Formulation."

9. "The Drought Is Over at 3M," *Business Week,* November 7, 1994, pp. 140–141.

10. Jay Barney, "Firm Resources and Sustained Competitive Advantage," *Journal of Management,* June 1991, pp. 99–120.

11. Jay Barney, "Strategic Factor Markets," *Management Science,* December 1986, pp. 1231–1241.

12. Andrea Rothman, "Sony Is Out to Be the World's One-Stop Shop for Entertainment," *Business Week,* March 25, 1991, pp. 64–74.

13. See Michael Porter, *Competitive Strategy* (New York: Free Press, 1980).

14. Porter, *Competitive Strategy.*

15. Raymond E. Miles and Charles C. Snow, *Organizational Strategy, Structure, and Process* (New York: McGraw-Hill, 1978).

16. Jennifer Hunter, "Swinging the Axe," *Maclean's,* February 16, 1998, pp. 38–40.

17. E. Morley and H. Lane, "Neiman Marcus," Boston: Harvard Business School, 1974.

18. Jeff Haggin and Bjorn Kartomten, "Breaking the Rules Can Pay Off: Catalogs That Dare to Be Different May Succeed Where Followers Fail," *Catalog Age,* August 1989, pp. 73–74.

19. Kenneth Labich, "The Innovators," *Fortune,* June 6, 1988, pp. 50–64; and "At Johnson and Johnson, a Mistake Can Be a Badge of Honor," *Business Week,* September 26, 1988, pp. 126–128.

20. Jennifer Hunter, "Swinging the Axe," *Maclean's,* February 16, 1998, pp. 38–40.

21. Alfred Chandler, *Strategy and Structure: Chapters in the History of the American Industrial Enterprise* (Cambridge, Mass.: MIT Press, 1962); Richard Rumelt, *Strategy, Structure, and Economic Performance* (Cambridge, Mass.: Division of Research, Graduate School of Business Administration, Harvard University, 1974); and Oliver Williamson, *Markets and Hierarchies* (New York: Free Press, 1975).

22. Peter Verburg, "Who Taught J.R.?" *Canadian Business,* June 1997, pp. 82–91.

23. See Chandler, *Strategy and Structure,* and Yakov Amihud and Baruch Lev, "Risk Reduction as a Managerial Motive for Conglomerate Mergers," *Bell Journal of Economics,* 1981, pp. 605–617.

24. Chandler, *Strategy and Structure;* and Williamson, *Markets and Hierarchies.*

25. Kenneth Kidd, "Year of the Deal," *Report on Business Magazine,* July 1997, pp. 53–59.

26. See Jay Barney and William G. Ouchi, *Organizational Economics* (San Francisco: Jossey-Bass, 1986), for a discussion of the limitations of unrelated diversification.

27. James Cook, "We Are the Target," *Forbes,* April 7, 1986, pp. 54, 56; and Alex Taylor III, "Here Come Japan's New Luxury Cars," *Fortune,* August 2, 1989, pp. 62–66.

28. Richard D'Aveni and David Ravenscroft, "Economies of Integration versus Bureaucracy Costs: Does Vertical Integration Improve Performance?" *Academy of Management Journal,* Vol. 37, No. 5, pp. 1167–1206.

29. Kenneth Kidd, "Year of the Deal."

30. Rob Ferguson, "Mega Merger Urges Grow," *The Toronto Star,* December 1, 1998, pp. D1, D6.

31. Terence Pare, "The New Merger Boom," *Fortune,* November 28, 1994, pp. 95–106.

32. Michael Lubatkin and Sayan Chatterjee, "Extending Modern Portfolio Theory into the Domain of Corporate Diversification: Does It Apply?" *Academy of Management Journal,* Vol. 37, No. 1, 1994, pp. 109–136.

33. See Barry Hedley, "A Fundamental Approach to Strategy Development," *Long Range Planning,* December 1976, pp. 2–11; and Bruce Henderson, "The Experience Curve— Reviewed. IV: The Growth Share Matrix of the Product Portfolio," *Perspectives,* No. 135 (Boston: Boston Consulting Group, 1973).

34. Michael G. Allen, "Diagramming G.E.'s Planning for What's WATT," in R. J. Allio and M. W. Pennington (Eds.), *Corporate Planning: Techniques and Applications* (New York: AMACOM, 1979). Limits of this approach are discussed in R.A. Bettis and W.K. Hall, "The Business Portfolio Approach: Where It Falls Down in Practice," *Long Range Planning,* March 1983, pp. 95–105.

Managerial Decision Making and Problem Solving

Objectives

After studying this chapter, you should be able to:

● *Define decision making and discuss types of decisions and decision-making conditions.*

● *Discuss rational perspectives on decision making, including the steps in decision making.*

● *Describe the behavioural nature of decision making.*

● *Discuss group decision making, including the advantages and disadvantages of group decision making and how it can be more effectively managed.*

Outline

A company can often expand by taking advantage of customers' familiarity with their existing products.

Well-defined seminal moments in the histories of most companies usually determine their future successes and failures. A good case in point is Kimberly-Clark Corporation. Indeed, two critical decisions coming twenty years apart have indelibly defined the company's current competitive strategies and its future directions.

In the mid-1970s Kimberly basically had its feet planted firmly in two disparate businesses. Its core business was forestry products—trees and paper—and pulp-making operations, and it was here that the company had committed most of its capital. But most of the firm's profits came from its disposable tissue business. Indeed, the name "Kleenex" was virtually synonymous with Kimberly-Clark and has almost become a generic term for facial tissues.

Company officials determined that their strategy was a barrier to future growth— low growth and low profits in the forestry businesses constrained expansion in those markets. Moreover, these operations were requiring so much capital that the company lacked the resources to fuel growth in other areas. Consequently, Kimberly management made the decision to sell off major portions of the forestry operations and use the funds this step generated to expand into consumer products such as disposable diapers and paper towels.

"Every morning I look in the mirror and ask how I can beat the hell out of P&G [Procter & Gamble]. And I want every one of my employees to do the same."

Over the course of the next several years, therefore, Kimberly sold one forestry business after another and carefully and calculatedly launched a variety of new products. Unfortunately, however, Kimberly found it tough competing against the entrenched industry giant Procter & Gamble. Its vast size and sophisticated distribution network prevented competitors such as Kimberly from gaining significant market share. At the same time, Procter & Gamble was also beginning to move into the facial tissue market, putting Kleenex in a vulnerable position.

The next major watershed event for the firm occurred in 1995 when its managers made the decision to buy Scott Paper Company for $9.4 billion (U.S.). This acquisition gave Kimberly-Clark new market share in a number of different markets. For example, Kimberly's share of the bathroom tissue market jumped from 5 percent to 31 percent, and its share of the home paper towel market more than tripled to 18 percent.

Even more important, the Scott acquisition gave Kimberly major positions in several foreign markets. Scott was the dominant tissue products company in Mexico, for example, enjoying near-monopoly status. Kimberly was also now able to use its new clout to compete with Procter & Gamble on a more even basis. Indeed, their international competition has produced some interesting twists and turns.

For example, when Kimberly entered the French market in 1994, ruthless price cutting between the two giants inadvertently pushed their largest French competitor, Peaudouce, to the edge of bankruptcy. Its saviour? Kimberly-Clark. And the next year, the same scenario was played out in Argentina, with Kimberly-Clark again landing the wounded domestic competitor. Kimberly-Clark is clearly making its presence felt. In early 1999, the company announced that improved results in Europe, higher earnings in tissue businesses in North America, and strong growth in Latin America and professional health care combined to push its earnings for the fourth quarter of 1998 to an all-time record. And it all started with a decision to sell some trees and make more tissue.[1] ●

Source of Quotation: Wayne Sanders, Kimberley–Clark chief executive, quoted in *Forbes*, March 24, 1997, p. 100.

The opening incident portrays two significant decisions made by Kimberly-Clark executives that have essentially reshaped the entire character of their firm. In addition to the two decisions highlighted here, they have made many other decisions, some also very important (such as package design and colour choices for tissue products), and others of perhaps relatively low importance (such as exact numbers of tissues to put in a box of Kleenex). Some experts believe that decision making is the most basic and fundamental of all managerial activities.[2] Thus we discuss it here in the context of the first management function, planning. Keep in mind, however, that although decision making is perhaps most closely linked to planning, it is also part of organizing, leading, and controlling.

We begin our discussion by exploring the nature of decision making. We then describe rational perspectives on decision making. Behavioural aspects of decision making are then introduced and described. We conclude with a discussion of group decision making.

THE NATURE OF DECISION MAKING

Senior managers at Canadian National Railway (CN) recently made the decision to dig a $200 million tunnel under the St. Clair River to link its route from Eastern Canada with the U.S. industrial heartland. At about the same time, a manager of purchasing with CN made a decision to purchase a batch of locomotive wheels: CN buys 40,000 pairs of wheels per year. Each of these examples includes a decision, but the decisions differ in many ways. Thus as a starting point in understanding decision making, we must first explore the meaning of *decision making* as well as types of decisions and conditions under which decisions are made.[3]

Decision Making Defined

Decision making can refer to either a specific act or a general process. **Decision making** per se is the act of choosing one alternative from among a set of alternatives. The decision-making process, however, is much more than this. One step of the process, for example, is that the person making the decision must recognize that a decision is necessary and identify the set of feasible alternatives before selecting one. Hence, the **decision-making process** includes recognizing and defining the nature of a decision situation, identifying alternatives, choosing the "best" alternative, and putting it into practice.[4]

The word "best" implies effectiveness. Effective decision making requires that the decision maker understand the situation driving the decision. Most people would consider an effective decision to be one that optimizes some set of factors such as profits, sales, employee welfare, and market share. In some situations, though, an effective decision may be one that minimizes loss, expenses, or employee turnover. It may even mean selecting the best method for going out of business, laying off employees, or terminating a contract.

We should also note that managers make decisions about both problems and opportunities. For example, making decisions about how to cut costs by 10 percent reflects a problem—an undesired situation that requires a solution. But decisions are also necessary in situations of opportunity. Learning that the firm is earning higher-than-projected profits, for example, requires a decision. Should the extra funds be used to increase shareholder dividends, reinvested in current operations, or used to expand into new markets?

● **decision making**
The act of choosing one alternative from among a set of alternatives

● **decision-making process**
Recognizing and defining the nature of a decision situation, identifying alternatives, choosing the "best" alternative, and putting it into practice

Of course, it may take a long time before a manager can know if the right decision was made. For example, Jack Welch, CEO of General Electric, took an enormous gamble a few years ago by trading his company's consumer-electronics business to Thomson, a French company, for its medical-equipment business. At the time of the exchange, GE held 23 percent of the U.S. colour-television market and 17 percent of the U.S. VCR market. Moreover, it was the only serious consumer-electronics business left in the United States and was generating enormous profits. Welch, however, believed that the medical-equipment business held even more promise for growth and profits. Analysts believe that the "winner" of the exchange will not be known until at least the turn of the century.[5]

Types of Decisions

Managers must make many different types of decisions. In general, however, most decisions fall into one of two categories: programmed and nonprogrammed.[6] A **programmed decision** is one that is fairly structured or recurs with some frequency (or both). For example, suppose that a manager of a distribution centre knows from experience that she needs to keep a thirty-day supply of a particular item on hand. She can then establish a system whereby the appropriate quantity is automatically reordered whenever the inventory drops below the thirty-day requirement. Likewise, the CN purchasing manager made a decision to place an order for a batch of wheels—a routine decision based on historical data indicating when wheels would be required. Many decisions regarding basic operating systems and procedures and standard organizational transactions are of this variety and can therefore be programmed.

Nonprogrammed decisions, on the other hand, are relatively unstructured and occur much less often. Consider GE's decision to exchange businesses with Thomson and CN's decision to dig a new tunnel: no business makes decisions like those on a regular basis. Managers faced with such decisions must treat each one as unique, investing enormous amounts of time, energy, and resources into exploring the situation from all perspectives. Intuition and experience are major factors in nonprogrammed decisions. Most

Programmed decisions are fairly structured and routine. Managers at Home Depot use programmed decision making to stock inventory in their stores. They know how quickly various products sell, and how long it takes suppliers to ship orders after they have been received. Thus, managers can use basic decision rules for ordering specified quantities of various products when inventory levels drop below a certain point.

repetitive, routine
- rules, SOP, policies

● **programmed decision**
A decision that is fairly structured or recurs with some frequency (or both)

complex, novel
- creative problem solving

● **nonprogrammed decision**
A decision that is relatively unstructured; occurs much less often than a programmed decision

CN Decides to Focus

Paul Tellier, chief executive officer (CEO) of Canadian National Railways (CN), sees changing the culture of CN as the most crucial aspect of his job. In 1992, when Tellier took over as CEO, CN was regarded as a bloated, inefficient Crown corporation. It had an operating loss of $840 million on revenues of $3.9 billion. Its operating ratio (the percentage of revenue spent in operating and maintaining the business) was almost 100 percent. Tellier and his team decided to focus on CN's core business—locomotives and boxcars—to cut costs and to increase revenues.

In order to achieve its objective of focusing on its core business, CN sold assets such as the CN Tower, its locomotive manufacturing operations, its telecommunications arm, and its oil and gas interests. Its cost-cutting exercise focused on downsizing. In 1992, 14,000 of the company's 36,000 employees were retrenched. There were subsequent cuts of 1,200 in 1997, 1,600 in 1998, and a projected 1,400 in 1999.

CN has also sold or abandoned more than a quarter of its 32,000 kilometres of track to deal with an oversupply of rail. The corporation also sought savings in purchasing: $1.44 billion of the $3.6 billion the company spends each year is on supplies and services, items such as photocopying, hotel expenditures, cellular phones, and wheels and axles. The company has also used technology to save money; for example, a remote-control device known as a belt pack is now used to assemble trains. However, CN's success in focusing on its core business and cutting costs has been more impressive than its revenue generation: revenues of $4.1 billion in 1998 were only $200 million more than revenues in 1992.

Overall, CN's plans are on track. The company had net income of $266 million in 1998, and in 1997 it made a profit of $1.04 billion. Moreover, its operating ratio fell to 81 percent in 1997, down from 87.3 percent a year earlier and almost 100 percent in 1992.

References: Peter Fitzpatrick, "CN Says It's Full Steam Ahead for Cost Cutting," *The Financial Post*, April 24, 1997, p. 20; Paul Kaihla, "Back on the Rails," *Maclean's*, January 13, 1997, pp. 36–38; Don Macdonald, "Clear the Track," *Report on Business Magazine*, July 1997, pp. 28–36; Vanessa Lu, "3000 CN Layoffs: How Trucks Have Derailed Transport," *The Toronto Star*, October 22, 1998, pp. A1, A31; and CN Quarterly Review: Consolidated Statement of Income, Fourth Quarter, 1998 (http://www.cn.ca).

of the decisions made by top managers involving strategy (including mergers, acquisitions, and takeovers) and organization design are nonprogrammed. So are decisions about new facilities, new products, labour contracts, and legal issues. The *Environment of Management* box discusses a number of nonprogrammed decisions at Canadian National Railway.

Decision-Making Conditions

Just as there are different kinds of decisions, there are also different conditions in which decisions must be made. Jack Welch at GE has no guarantees that the new medical–equipment business will be successful, whereas he had a pretty clear picture of how the electronics business was doing. Managers sometimes have an almost perfect understanding of conditions surrounding a decision, but at other times they have few clues about those conditions. In general, the circumstances that exist for the decision maker are conditions of certainty, risk, or uncertainty.[7] These conditions are represented in Figure 8.1.

Decision Making Under Certainty   When the decision maker knows with reasonable certainty what the alternatives are and what conditions are associated with each alternative, a **state of certainty** exists. Suppose, for example, that Singapore Airlines needs to buy five new jumbo jets. The decision is from

● **state of certainty**

A condition in which the decision maker knows with reasonable certainty what the alternatives are and what conditions are associated with each alternative

whom to buy them. Singapore has only two choices: Boeing and Airbus. Each has a proven product and will specify prices and delivery dates. The airline thus knows the alternative conditions associated with each. There is little ambiguity and relatively low chance of making a bad decision.

Few organizational decisions are made under conditions of true certainty.[8] The complexity and turbulence of the contemporary business world make such situations rare. Even the airplane purchase decision we just considered has less certainty than it appears. The aircraft companies may not be able to guarantee delivery dates so they may write cost-increase or inflation clauses into contracts. Thus the airline may not be truly certain of the conditions surrounding each alternative.

Decision Making Under Risk   A more common decision-making condition is a state of risk. Under a **state of risk**, the availability of each alternative and its potential payoffs and costs are all associated with probability estimates.[9] Suppose, for example, that a labour contract negotiator for a company receives a "final" offer from the union right before a strike deadline. The negotiator has two alternatives: to accept or to reject the offer. The risk centres on whether the union representatives are bluffing. If the negotiator accepts the offer, she avoids a strike but commits to a costly labour contract. If she rejects the contract, she may get a more favourable contract if the union is bluffing; she may provoke a strike if it is not.

On the basis of past experiences, relevant information, the advice of others, and her own intuition, she may believe that there is a 75 percent chance that the union is bluffing and a 25 percent chance that they'll back up their threats. Thus she can base a calculated decision on the two alternatives (accept or reject the contract demands) and the probable consequences of each. When making decisions under a state of risk, managers must determine the probabilities associated with each alternative. For example, if the union negotiators are committed to a strike if their demands are not met, and the company negotiator rejects their demands because she guesses they will not strike, her miscalculation will prove costly. As shown in Figure 8.1, decision making under conditions of risk is accompanied by moderate ambiguity and chances of a bad decision.[10]

● **state of risk**
A condition in which the availability of each alternative and its potential payoffs and costs are all associated with probability estimates

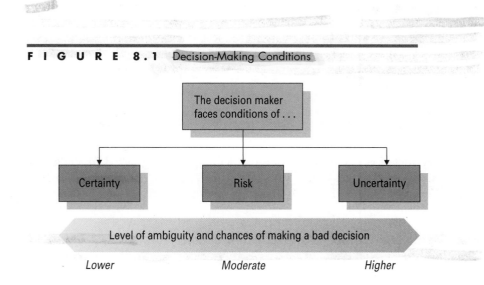

F I G U R E 8 . 1 Decision-Making Conditions

The decision maker faces conditions of . . .

Certainty   Risk   Uncertainty

Level of ambiguity and chances of making a bad decision

Lower   *Moderate*   *Higher*

Most major decisions in organizations today are made under a state of uncertainty. Managers making decisions in these circumstances must be sure to learn as much as possible about the situation and approach the decision from a logical and rational perspective.

● **state of uncertainty**
A condition in which the
decision maker does not know
all the alternatives, the risks
associated with each, or the
consequences each alternative
is likely to have

Decision Making Under Uncertainty   Most of the major decision making
in contemporary organizations is done under a **state of uncertainty**. The
decision maker does not know all the alternatives, the risks associated with
each, or the likely consequences of each alternative.[11] This uncertainty stems
from the complexity and dynamism of contemporary organizations and their
environments. Consider, for example, the decision of Nike's founders regarding
footwear. They could have decided to use existing running shoe technology to
reduce risk and avoid uncertainty. But they also saw that they would then have
fewer competitive advantages over Adidas. Thus they based their shoes on a
new waffle-type design that gave them another unique feature to highlight. But
this choice carried with it considerable uncertainty because they had no idea
how it would be received in the marketplace.

Indeed, many of the decisions already discussed—CN's decision to dig a
new tunnel and GE's decision to get out of consumer electronics—were made
under conditions of uncertainty. To make effective decisions in these circumstances, managers must acquire as much relevant information as possible and
approach the situation from a logical and rational perspective. Intuition, judgment, and experience always play major roles in the decision-making process
under conditions of uncertainty. Even so, uncertainty is the most ambiguous
condition for managers and the one most prone to error.

RATIONAL PERSPECTIVES ON DECISION MAKING

Most managers like to think of themselves as rational decision makers. And
indeed, many experts argue that managers should try to be as rational as possible in making decisions.[12]

The Classical Model of Decision Making

● **classical decision model**
A prescriptive approach to
decision making that tells
managers how they should
make decisions. It assumes that
managers are logical and
rational and that their
decisions will be in the best
interests of the organization

The **classical decision model** is a prescriptive approach that tells managers
how they should make decisions. It rests on the assumptions that managers are
logical and rational and that they make decisions that are in the best interests
of the organization. Figure 8.2 shows how the classical model views the decision-making process: (1) Decision makers have complete information about
the decision situation and possible alternatives. (2) They can effectively eliminate uncertainty to achieve a decision condition of certainty. (3) They evaluate
all aspects of the decision situation logically and rationally. As we see later, these
conditions rarely, if ever, actually exist.

Steps in Rational Decision Making

A manager who really wants to approach a decision rationally and logically
should try to follow the steps in rational decision making, listed in Table 8.1.
These steps in rational decision making help keep the decision maker
focused on facts and logic and help guard against inappropriate assumptions
and pitfalls.

Recognizing and Defining the Decision Situation   The first step in rational
decision making is recognizing that a decision is necessary—that is, there must

be some stimulus or spark to initiate the process.[13] For many decisions and problem situations, the stimulus may occur without any prior warning. When equipment malfunctions, the manager must decide whether to repair or replace it. Or when a major crisis erupts, as described in Chapter 3, the manager must quickly decide how to deal with it. As we already noted, the stimulus for a decision may be either positive or negative. A manager who must decide how to invest surplus funds, for example, faces a positive decision situation. A negative financial stimulus could involve having to trim budgets because of cost overruns.[14]

Inherent in problem recognition is the need to define precisely what the problem is. The manager must develop a complete understanding of the problem, its causes, and its relationship to other factors. This understanding comes from careful analysis of the situation. Consider the recent situation faced by Olin Pool Products. Even though Olin controlled half the market for chlorine-based pool treatment systems, its profits were slipping and it was rapidly losing market share to new competitors. These indicators provided clear evidence to General Manager Doug Cahill that something needed to be done. He went on to define the problem as a need to restore profitability and regain lost market share.[15]

Identifying Alternatives Once the decision situation has been recognized and defined, the second step is to identify alternative courses of effective action. Developing both obvious, standard alternatives and creative, innovative alternatives is generally useful.[16] In general, the more important the decision, the more attention is directed to developing alternatives. The recent decision of Eaton's to move its headquarters from the complex that bears its name in downtown Toronto came several months after the company filed for bankruptcy protection. If the problem is to choose a colour for the company softball team uniforms, less time and expertise will be brought to bear.

Although managers should seek creative solutions, they must also recognize that various constraints often limit their alternatives. Common constraints include legal restrictions, moral and ethical norms, authority constraints, or constraints imposed by the power and authority of the manager, available technology, economic considerations, and unofficial social norms. Greg Cahill at Olin identified several alternatives that might help his firm: seek a bigger firm to take control of Olin and inject new resources, buy one or more competitors to increase Olin's own size, maintain the status quo and hope that competitors stub their toes, or overhaul the organization to become more competitive.

The classical model of decision making assumes that managers are rational and logical. It attempts to prescribe how managers should approach decision situations.

F I G U R E   8 . 2   The Classical Model of Decision Making

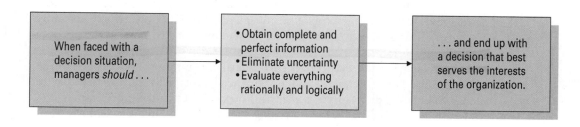

When faced with a decision situation, managers *should* . . .

- Obtain complete and perfect information
- Eliminate uncertainty
- Evaluate everything rationally and logically

. . . and end up with a decision that best serves the interests of the organization.

T A B L E 8 . 1 Steps in the Rational Decision-Making Process		
Step	**Detail**	**Example**
1. Recognizing and defining the situation	Some stimulus indicates that a decision must be made. The stimulus may be positive or negative.	A plant manager sees that employee turnover has increased by 5 percent.
2. Identifying alternatives	Both obvious and creative alternatives are desired. In general, the more important the decision, the more alternatives should be generated.	The plant manager can increase wages, increase benefits, or change hiring standards.
3. Evaluating alternatives	Each alternative is evaluated to determine its feasibility, its satisfactoriness, and its consequences.	Increasing benefits may not be feasible. Increasing wages and changing hiring standards may satisfy all conditions.
4. Selecting the best alternative	Consider all situational factors, and choose the alternative that best fits the manager's situation.	Changing hiring standards will take an extended period of time to cut turnover, so increase wages.
5. Implementing the chosen alternative	The chosen alternative is implemented into the organizational system.	The plant manager may need permission of corporate headquarters. The human resource department establishes a new wage structure.
6. Follow-up and evaluation	At some time in the future, the manager should ascertain the extent to which the alternative chosen in step 4 and implemented in step 5 has worked.	The plant manager notes that, six months later, turnover dropped to its previous level.

Although the presumptions of the classical decision model rarely exist, managers can approach decision making with rationality. By following the steps of rational decision making, managers ensure that they are learning as much as possible about the decision situation and its alternatives.

Evaluating Alternatives   The third step in the decision-making process is evaluating each of the alternatives.[17] Figure 8.3 presents a decision tree that can be used to judge different alternatives. The figure suggests that each alternative be evaluated in terms of its feasibility, its satisfactoriness, and its consequences. The first question to ask is whether an alternative is feasible. Is it within the realm of probability and practicality? For a small, struggling firm, an alternative requiring a huge financial outlay is probably out of the question. Other alternatives may not be feasible because of legal barriers. And limited human, material, and information resources may make other alternatives impractical.

When an alternative has passed the test of feasibility, it must next be examined to see how well it satisfies the conditions of the decision situation. For example, a manager searching for ways to double production capacity might consider purchasing an existing plant from another company. If closer examination reveals that the new plant would increase production capacity by only 35 percent, this alternative may not be satisfactory. Finally, when an alternative has proven both feasible and satisfactory, its probable consequences must still be assessed. To what extent will a particular alternative influence other parts of the organization? What financial and nonfinancial costs will be associated with such influences? For example, a plan to boost sales by cutting prices may disrupt cash flows, need a new advertising program, and alter the behaviour of sales representatives because it requires a different commission structure. The manager, then, must put "price tags" on the consequences of each alternative. Even an alternative that is both feasible and satisfactory must be eliminated if its consequences are too expensive for the total system. Cahill decided that being taken over would cause too great a loss of autonomy (consequences not affordable), that buying a competitor was too expensive (not feasible), and that doing nothing would not solve the problem (not satisfactory).

Selecting an Alternative

Even though many alternatives fail to pass the triple tests of feasibility, satisfactoriness, and affordable consequences, two or more alternatives may remain. Choosing the best of these is the real crux of decision making. One approach is to choose the alternative with the highest combined level of feasibility, satisfactoriness, and affordable consequences. Even though most situations do not lend themselves to objective, mathematical analysis, the manager can often develop subjective estimates and weights for choosing an alternative.

Optimization is also a frequent goal. Because a decision is likely to affect several individuals or subunits, any feasible alternative will probably not maximize all of the relevant goals. Suppose that the manager of the Toronto Blue Jays needs to select a starting centre fielder for the next baseball season. Carlos hits .350 but is not able to catch a fly ball; Joe hits only .175 but is outstanding in the field; and Alex hits .290 and is a solid but not outstanding fielder. The manager would probably select Alex because of the optimal balance of hitting and fielding. Decision makers should remember that finding multiple acceptable alternatives may be possible—selecting just one alternative and rejecting all the others may not be necessary. For example, the Jays' manager might decide that Alex will start each game, Carlos will be retained as a pinch hitter, and Joe will be retained as a defensive substitute. In many hiring decisions, the candidates remaining after evaluation are ranked. If the top candidate rejects the offer, it may be automatically extended to the number-two candidate, and, if necessary, to the remaining candidates in order. Olin Pool Products' managers selected the alternative of overhauling the organization to become more competitive.

> Managers must thoroughly evaluate all of the alternatives, which increases the chances that the alternative finally chosen will be successful. Failure to evaluate an alternative's feasibility, satisfactoriness, and consequences can lead to a wrong decision.

Implementing the Chosen Alternative

After an alternative has been selected, the manager must put it into effect. In some decision situations, implementation is fairly easy; in others, it is more difficult. In the case of a merger or acquisition, for example, managers must decide how to integrate all the activities of

FIGURE 8.3 Evaluating Alternatives in the Decision-Making Process

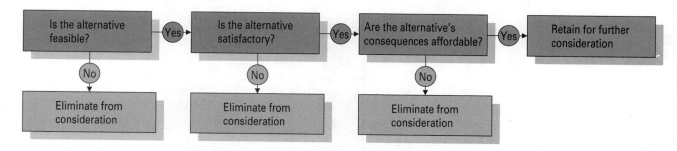

the new business, including purchasing, human resource practices, and distribution, into an organizational framework. Moreover, attention must be paid to melding the cultures of the two organizations. The merger of Loblaw and Provigo that was announced in late 1998 will entail many difficult decisions. Several such decisions will be related to the workforce of the new entity. Will there be job cuts? If so, will such reductions be obtained through layoffs or attrition? Operational plans, which we discussed in Chapter 6, are useful in implementing alternatives.

Managers must also consider people's resistance to change when implementing decisions. The reasons for such resistance include insecurity, inconvenience, and fear of the unknown. When Zellers decided to move its headquarters from Montreal to Toronto, many employees chose to resign rather than relocate. Managers should anticipate potential resistance at various stages of the implementation process. (Resistance to change is covered in Chapter 12.) Managers should also recognize that, even when all alternatives have been evaluated as precisely as possible and the consequences of each alternative weighed, unanticipated consequences are still likely. Any number of situations such as unexpected cost increases, a less-than-perfect fit with existing organizational subsystems, or unpredicted effects on cash flow or operating expenses could develop after the implementation process has begun. Greg Cahill eliminated several levels of management at Olin, combined fourteen departments into eight, gave new authority to every manager, and empowered employees to take greater control over their work.

A Provigo shopper walks out of a supermarket in the Quebec City suburb of Sainte-Foy. Toronto-based Loblaw Companies Limited announced a friendly merger with Provigo in late 1998, valued at about $1.45 billion.

Following Up and Evaluating the Results   The final step in the decision-making process requires that managers evaluate the effectiveness of their decision—that is, they should make sure that the chosen alternative has served its original purpose. If an implemented alternative appears not to be working, the manager can respond in several ways. Another previously identified alternative (the second or third choice) could be adopted. Or the manager might recognize that the situation was not correctly defined to start with and begin the process all over again. Finally, the manager might decide that the original alternative is in fact appropriate but has not yet had time to work or should be implemented in a different way.

Failure to evaluate decision effectiveness may have serious consequences. The Pentagon spent $1.8 billion (U.S.) and eight years developing the Sergeant York antiaircraft gun. From the beginning, tests revealed major problems with the weapon system, but not until it was in its final stages, when it was demonstrated to be completely ineffective, was the project scrapped.[18] In a classic case of poor decision making, managers at Coca-Cola decided to change the formula for the soft drink. Consumer response was extremely negative. In contrast to the Pentagon, however, Coca-Cola immediately reacted: it reintroduced the old formula within three months as Coca-Cola Classic. Had managers stubbornly stuck with their decision and failed to evaluate its effectiveness, the results would have been disastrous. Greg Cahill's decisions at Olin are paying big dividends—the firm's profits are back up and most of the market share it lost has been regained as well.

BEHAVIOURAL ASPECTS OF DECISION MAKING

If all decision situations were approached as logically as described in the previous section, more decisions would prove to be successful. Yet decisions are often made with little consideration for logic and rationality. Kepner-Tregoe, a Princeton-based consulting firm, estimates that U.S. companies use rational decision-making techniques less than 20 percent of the time.[19] And even when organizations try to be logical, they sometimes fail. For example, managers at Coca-Cola decided to change Coke's formula after four years of extensive marketing research, taste tests, and rational deliberation—but the decision was still wrong. On the other hand, sometimes when a decision is made with little regard for logic, it can still turn out to be correct. An important ingredient in how these forces work is the behavioural aspect of decision making.[20] The administrative model better reflects these subjective considerations. Other behavioural aspects include political forces, intuition and escalation of commitment, risk propensity, and ethics.

The Administrative Model

Herbert A. Simon was one of the first people to recognize that decisions are not always made with rationality and logic.[21] Simon was subsequently awarded the Nobel Prize in economics. Rather than prescribing how decisions should be made, his view of decision making, now called the **administrative model**, describes how decisions often actually are made. As illustrated in Figure 8.4, the model holds that managers (1) have incomplete and imperfect information, (2) are constrained by bounded rationality, and (3) tend to satisfice when making decisions.

● **administrative model**
A decision-making model that argues that decision makers (1) have incomplete and imperfect information, (2) are constrained by bounded rationality, and (3) tend to satisfice when making decisions

● **bounded rationality**
A concept suggesting that decision makers are limited by their values and unconscious reflexes, skills, and habits

● **satisficing**
The tendency to search for alternatives only until one is found that meets some minimum standard of sufficiency

---

The administrative model is based on behavioural processes that affect how managers make decisions. Rather than prescribing how decisions should be made, it focuses more on describing how they are made.

Bounded rationality suggests that decision makers are limited by their values and unconscious reflexes, skills, and habits. They are also limited by less than complete information and knowledge. Bounded rationality partially explains how U.S. auto executives allowed Japanese automakers to become so strong in the United States. For years, executives at General Motors, Ford, and Chrysler compared their companies' performance to only one another and ignored foreign imports. The foreign "threat" wasn't acknowledged until the domestic auto market had been changed forever. If managers had gathered complete information from the beginning, they might have been better able to thwart foreign competitors. Essentially, then, the concept of bounded rationality suggests that although people try to be rational decision makers, their rationality has limits.

Another important part of the administrative model is **satisficing.** This concept suggests that rather than conducting an exhaustive search for the best possible alternative, decision makers tend to search only until they identify an alternative that meets some minimum standard of sufficiency. A manager looking for a site for a new plant, for example, may select the first site she finds that meets basic requirements for transportation, utilities, and price, even though further search might yield a better location. People satisfice for a variety of reasons. Managers may simply be unwilling to ignore their own motives (such as reluctance to spend time making a decision) and therefore not be able to continue searching after a minimally acceptable alternative is identified. The decision maker may be unable to weigh and evaluate large numbers of alternatives and criteria. Also, subjective and personal considerations often intervene in decision situations.

Because of the inherent imperfection of information, bounded rationality, and satisficing, the decisions made by a manager may or may not actually be in the best interests of the organization. A manager may choose a particular location for the new plant because it offers the lowest price and best availability of utilities and transportation. Or she may choose the location because it's in a community in which she wants to live.

In summary, then, the classical and administrative models paint quite different pictures of decision making. Which is more correct? Actually, each can be used to better understand how managers make decisions. The classical model is prescriptive: it explains how managers can at least attempt to be more rational and logical in their approach to decisions. The administrative model can be used by managers to develop a better understanding of their inherent biases and limitations.[22] In the following sections, we describe more fully other behavioural forces that can influence decisions.

Political Forces in Decision Making

Political forces are another major element that contributes to the behavioural nature of decision making. Organizational politics is covered in Chapter 17, but

---

F I G U R E   8.4   The Administrative Model of Decision Making

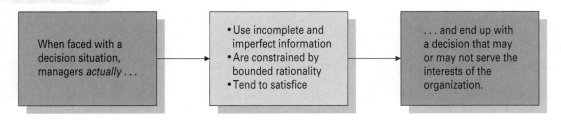

When faced with a decision situation, managers *actually*...

- Use incomplete and imperfect information
- Are constrained by bounded rationality
- Tend to satisfice

... and end up with a decision that may or may not serve the interests of the organization.

one major element of politics, coalitions, is especially relevant to decision making. A **coalition** is an informal alliance of individuals or groups formed to achieve a common goal. This common goal is often a preferred decision alternative. For example, coalitions of shareholders frequently band together to force a board of directors to make a certain decision.

Coalitions led to the formation of Unisys Corporation, a large computer firm. Sperry was once one of the world's computer giants, but a series of poor decisions put the company on the edge of bankruptcy. Two major executives waged battle for three years over what to do. One wanted to get out of the computer business altogether, and the other wanted to stay in. Finally, the manager who wanted to remain in the computer business, Joseph Kroger, garnered enough support to earn promotion to the corporation's presidency. The other manager, Vincent McLean, took early retirement. Shortly thereafter, Sperry agreed to be acquired by Burroughs Wellcome Co. The resulting combined company is called Unisys.[23]

The impact of coalitions can be either positive or negative. They can help astute managers get the organization on a path toward effectiveness and profitability, or they can strangle well-conceived strategies and decisions. Managers must recognize when to use coalitions, how to assess whether coalitions are acting in the best interests of the organization, and how to constrain their dysfunctional effects.

Intuition and Escalation of Commitment

Two other decision processes that go beyond logic and rationality are intuition and escalation of commitment to a chosen course of action.

Intuition **Intuition** is an innate belief about something without conscious consideration. Managers sometimes decide to do something because it "feels right" or they have a hunch. This feeling is usually not arbitrary, however. Rather, it is based on years of experience and practice in making decisions in similar situations. An inner sense may help managers make an occasional decision without going through a full-blown rational sequence of steps. Liz Claiborne and three partners founded Liz Claiborne, Inc. to design and sell clothes for working women. Conventional wisdom at the time suggested that they needed to build plants to make the clothing and develop a travelling salesforce to market it. Pure intuition, however, told them not to follow this "wisdom." They subcontracted production to other makers instead of building plants, and they sold their clothes to only large department and specialty store buyers willing to travel to New York. The result? Very low overhead and annual sales of more than $1 billion (U.S.).[24] Of course, all managers, but most especially inexperienced ones, should be careful not to rely on intuition too heavily. If rationality and logic are continually flaunted for what "feels right," the odds are that disaster will strike one day.

Escalation of Commitment Another important behavioural process that influences decision making is **escalation of commitment** to a chosen course of action. In particular, decision makers sometimes make decisions and then become so committed to the course of action suggested by that decision that they stay with it, even when it appears to have been wrong.[25] For example, when people buy stock in a company, they sometimes refuse to sell it even after repeated drops in price. They chose a course of action—buying the stock in anticipation of making a profit—and then stay with it even in the face of increasing losses.

● **coalition**
An informal alliance of individuals or groups formed to achieve a common goal

● **intuition**
An innate belief about something without conscious consideration

● **escalation of commitment**
A decision maker's staying with a decision even when it appears to be wrong

For years Pan American World Airways ruled the skies and used its profits to diversify into real estate and other businesses. However, with the advent of deregulation, Pan Am began to struggle and lose market share to other carriers. Since Pan Am executives still saw the company as first and foremost an airline, when they finally realized how ineffective the airlines operations had become they began to slowly sell off the firm's profitable holdings to keep the airline flying. Experts today point out that the "rational" decision would have been to sell off the remaining airline operations and concentrate on the firm's more profitable businesses. Eventually, the company was left with nothing but an ineffective and inefficient airline and then had to sell off its more profitable routes before being taken over by Delta. Had Pan Am managers made the more rational decision years earlier, chances are the firm could still be a profitable enterprise today, albeit one with no involvement in the airline industry.[26]

Thus decision makers must walk a fine line. On the one hand, they must guard against sticking with an incorrect decision too long. To do so can bring about financial decline. On the other hand, they should not bail out of a seemingly incorrect decision too soon, as did Consumers Distributing. Consumers once dominated the catalogue-shopping market in Canada. However, the company was declared bankrupt in September 1996. The bankruptcy occurred at a time when some believed that strategic moves Consumers had made in the previous five years were about to bear fruit.[27]

Risk Propensity and Decision Making

● **risk propensity**
The extent to which a decision maker is willing to gamble in making a decision

The behavioural element of **risk propensity** is the extent to which a decision maker is willing to gamble when making a decision.[28] Some managers are cautious about every decision they make. They try to adhere to the rational model and are extremely conservative in what they do. Such managers are more likely to avoid mistakes, and they infrequently make decisions that lead to big losses. Other managers are extremely aggressive in making decisions and are willing to take risks. They rely heavily on intuition, reach decisions quickly, and often risk big investments on their decisions. As in gambling, these managers are more likely than their conservative counterparts to achieve big successes with their

Consumers Distributing once dominated the catalogue-shopping market in Canada. A troubled retail economy forced it into bankruptcy in September 1996.

decisions; they are also more likely to incur greater losses. The organization's culture is a prime ingredient in fostering different levels of risk propensity.

Ethics and Decision Making

As we introduce in Chapter 4, individual ethics are personal beliefs about right and wrong behaviour. Ethics are clearly related to decision making in a number of ways.[29] For example, suppose after careful analysis a manager realizes that her company could save money by closing her department and subcontracting with a supplier for the same services. But to recommend this course of action would result in the loss of several jobs, including her own. Her own ethical standards will clearly shape how she proceeds. Indeed, each component of managerial ethics (relationships of the firm to its employees, of employees to the firm, and of the firm to other economic agents) involves a wide variety of decisions, all of which are likely to have an ethical component. A manager must remember, then, that just as behavioural processes such as politics and risk propensity affect the decisions she makes, so too do her ethical beliefs.

GROUP DECISION MAKING IN ORGANIZATIONS

In more and more organizations today, important decisions are made by groups rather than by individuals. Examples include the executive committee of Rockwell International and employee termination review teams at Honda of Canada. The *Managing in a Changing World* box discusses group decision making at Procter & Gamble. Managers can typically choose whether to have individuals or groups make a particular decision. Thus knowing about forms of group decision making and their advantages and disadvantages is important.[30]

Forms of Group Decision Making

The most common methods of group decision making are interacting groups, Delphi groups, and nominal groups.

Interacting Groups   An **interacting group** is the most common form of decision-making group. The format is simple—either an existing or a newly designated group is asked to make a decision. Existing groups might be functional departments, regular work groups, or standing committees. Newly designated groups can be ad hoc committees, task forces, or work teams. The group members talk among themselves, argue, agree, argue some more, form internal coalitions, and so forth. Finally, after some period of deliberation, the group makes a decision. An advantage of this method is that the interaction between people often sparks new ideas and promotes understanding. A major disadvantage, though, is that political processes can play too big a role.

● **interacting group**
A decision-making group in which members openly discuss, argue about, and agree on the best alternative

Delphi Groups   A **Delphi group** is sometimes used for developing a consensus of expert opinion. Developed by the Rand Corporation, the Delphi procedure solicits input from a panel of experts who contribute individually. Their opinions are combined and, in effect, averaged. Assume, for example, that the problem is to establish an expected date for a major technological breakthrough in converting coal into usable energy. The first step in using the Delphi

● **Delphi group**
A form of group decision making in which a group is used to achieve a consensus of expert opinion

procedure is to obtain the cooperation of a panel of experts. For this situation, experts might include various research scientists, university researchers, and executives in a relevant energy industry. At first, the experts are asked to anonymously predict a time frame for the expected breakthrough. The persons coordinating the Delphi group collect the responses, average them, and ask the experts for another prediction. In this round, the experts who provided unusual or extreme predictions may be asked to justify them. These explanations may then be relayed to the other experts. When the predictions stabilize, the average prediction is taken to represent the decision of the "group" of experts. The time, expense, and logistics of the Delphi technique rule out its use for routine, everyday decisions, but it has been successfully used for forecasting technological breakthroughs at Boeing, market potential for new products at General Motors, research and development patterns at Eli Lilly, and future economic conditions by the U.S. government.[31]

nominal group
A structured technique used to generate creative and innovative alternatives or ideas

Nominal Groups   Another useful group decision-making technique occasionally used is the **nominal group**. Unlike the Delphi method, where group members do not see one another, nominal group members are brought together. The members represent a group in name only, however; they do not talk to one another freely like the members of interacting groups. Nominal groups are used most often to generate creative and innovative alternatives or ideas. To begin, the manager assembles a group of knowledgeable people and outlines the problem to them. The group members are then asked to individually write down as many alternatives as they can think of. The members then take turns stating their ideas, which are recorded on a flip chart or blackboard at the front of the room. Discussion is limited to simple clarification. After all alternatives have been listed, more discussion takes place. Group members then vote, usually by rank-ordering the various alternatives. The highest-ranking alternative represents the decision of the group. Of course, the manager in charge may retain the authority to accept or reject the group decision.

Advantages of Group Decision Making

The advantages and disadvantages of group decision making relative to individual decision making are summarized in Table 8.2. One advantage of group decision making is simply that more information is available in a group setting—as suggested by the old axiom "Two heads are better than one." A group represents a variety of education, experience, and perspective. Partly as a result of this increased information, groups typically can identify and evaluate more alternatives than can one person.[32] The people involved in a group decision understand the logic and rationale behind it, are more likely to accept it, and are equipped to communicate the decision to their work groups or departments. Finally, research evidence suggests that groups may make better decisions than individuals.[33]

Disadvantages of Group Decision Making

Perhaps the biggest drawback of group decision making is the additional time and (hence) the greater expense entailed. The increased time stems from interaction and discussion among group members. If a given manager's time is worth $50 an hour, and if the manager spends two hours making a decision, the decision costs the organization $100. For the same decision, a group of five

Procter & Gamble

 The Procter & Gamble Co. (P&G) was formed by the merger of two small businesses in 1837. William Procter, a candle-maker, and James Gamble, a soapmaker, joined forces and soon became one of Cincinnati's largest businesses. With the introduction of a floating soap, Ivory, and shortening, Crisco, in 1911, P&G soon became one of the world's largest organizations. Indeed, by the early 1990s, it was number-one or -two in terms of market share in about three-fourths of the major categories in which it competed.

Early in 1993, P&G had been identified as a prime example of the type of organization that managed to stop the turnover that so many other companies were experiencing during the 1980s and 1990s. But P&G's CEO, Edwin Artzt, decided that turmoil was better than stagnation and changed all that. P&G began a massive global restructuring designed to eliminate three or more management levels and more than ten thousand jobs by 1995. The intention was to hasten decision making in everything from product development in its research and development laboratories to promotion, advertising, sales, and marketing.

Artzt believed that, although P&G was still making money, its strategic direction had become unclear. He intended to build a tougher, faster, and more globally competitive organization. He initiated value or everyday low pricing to become more competitive and to respond to increasingly price-sensitive consumers. Faster product development to beat competitors to the market and individual financial results became essential criteria in managerial evaluation. P&G redesigned almost everything about the company—the way it develops, manufactures, distributes, prices, markets, and sells its products. The intent was to tighten the distribution chain so that manufacturer, supplier, wholesaler, retailer, and customer were in much closer contact. In making these changes, P&G went by four "rules": change the tasks or the work itself, do more with less, do it right the first time to eliminate rework, and reduce costs that reduce P&G's earnings.

Additionally, P&G's team approach to decision making was modified. Artzt insisted that all teams have explicit missions and develop clear goals for individual team members to ensure that those teams were as accountable for performance as were all individuals in the P&G organization.

In September 1998, P&G, under CEO John Pepper, announced changes aimed at making the organization a global corporation. The far-reaching initiative, which has been dubbed "Organization 2005," is expected to affect P&G's organizational structure, work processes, culture, and reward structure.

References: Bill Saporito, "Behind the Tumult at P&G," *Fortune*, March 7, 1994, pp. 74–82; Judith Springer Riddle, "Procter & Gamble Sets Sweeping Employee Cuts to Stay Competitive," *Brandweek*, July 19, 1993, pp. 1, 6; William G. Ouchi and Raymond L. Price, "Hierarchies, Clans, and Theory Z: A New Perspective on Organization Development," *Organizational Dynamics*, Spring 1993, pp. 62–70; Milton Moskowitz, Robert Levering, and Michael Katz, *Everybody's Business* (New York: Doubleday, 1990), pp. 896–897; "No More Mr. Nice Guy at P&G—Not by a Long Shot," *Business Week*, February 3, 1992, pp. 130–132; and "P&G Pursues Greatest Growth Ever," P&G Corporated News Releases, September 9, 1998 (http://www.pg.com).

managers might require three hours of time. At the same $50-an-hour rate, the decision costs the organization $750. Assuming the group decision is better, the additional expense may be justified, but the fact remains that group decision making is more costly.

Group decisions may also represent undesirable compromises.[34] For example, hiring a compromise top manager may be a bad decision in the long run because he or she may not be able to respond adequately to various subunits in the organization. Sometimes one individual dominates the group process to the point where others cannot make a full contribution. This dominance may stem from a desire for power or from a naturally dominant personality. The problem is that what appears to emerge as a group decision may actually be the decision of one person.

TABLE 8.2 Advantages and Disadvantages of Group Decision Making

Advantages	Disadvantages
1. More information and knowledge are available.	1. The process takes longer, so it is costlier.
2. More alternatives are likely to be generated.	2. Compromise decisions resulting from indecisiveness may emerge.
3. More acceptance of the final decision is likely.	3. One person may dominate the group.
4. Enhanced communication of the decision may result.	4. Groupthink may occur.
5. Better decisions generally emerge.	

groupthink
A situation that occurs when a group's desire for consensus and cohesiveness overwhelms its desire to reach the best possible decision

Finally, a group may succumb to a phenomenon known as groupthink. **Groupthink** occurs when the group's desire for consensus and cohesiveness overwhelms its desire to reach the best possible decisions.[35] Under the influence of groupthink, the group may arrive at decisions that are not in the best interest of either the group or the organization but rather avoid conflict among group members. One of the clearest examples of groupthink involved the space shuttle *Challenger* disaster. As NASA was preparing to launch the shuttle, numerous problems and questions arose. At each step of the way, however, decision makers argued that there was no reason to delay and that everything would be fine. Shortly after the launch on January 28, 1986, the shuttle exploded, killing all seven crew members.

Managing Group Decision-Making Processes

Managers can do several things to help promote the effectiveness of group decision making. One is simply being aware of the pros and cons of having a group make a decision. Time and cost can be managed by setting a deadline by which the decision must be made final. Dominance can be at least partially avoided if a special group is formed just to make the decision. An astute manager, for example, should know who in the organization may try to dominate a group and can either avoid putting that person in the group or put several strong-willed people together.

To avoid groupthink, each member of the group should critically evaluate all alternatives. So that members present divergent viewpoints, the leader should not make his or her own position known too early. At least one member of the group should be assigned the role of devil's advocate. And, after reaching a preliminary decision, the group should hold a follow-up meeting wherein divergent viewpoints can be raised again if any group members wish to do so.[36] Sun Microsystems, the company that developed Java programming language, tries to avoid groupthink by having teams consider the pros and cons of each side of an issue.

SUMMARY OF KEY POINTS

Decisions are an integral part of all managerial activities, but they are perhaps most central to the planning process. Decision making is the act of choosing one alternative from among a set of alternatives. The decision-making process includes recognizing and defining the nature of a decision situation, identifying alternatives, choosing the "best" alternative, and putting it into practice. Two common types of decisions are programmed and nonprogrammed. Decisions may be made under states of certainty, risk, or uncertainty.

Rational perspectives on decision making rest on the classical model. This model assumes that managers have complete information and that they will behave rationally. The primary steps in rational decision making are (1) recognizing and defining the situation, (2) identifying alternatives, (3) evaluating alternatives, (4) selecting the best alternative, (5) implementing the chosen alternative, and (6) following up and evaluating the effectiveness of the alternative after it is implemented.

Behavioural aspects of decision making rely on the administrative model. This model recognizes that managers will have incomplete information and that they will not always behave rationally. The administrative model also recognizes the concepts of bounded rationality and satisficing. Political activities by coalitions, managerial intuition, and the tendency to become increasingly committed to a chosen course of action are all important. Risk propensity is also an important behavioural perspective on decision making. Finally, ethics also affect how managers make decisions.

To help enhance decision-making effectiveness, managers often use interacting, Delphi, or nominal groups. Group decision making in general has several advantages as well as disadvantages relative to individual decision making. Managers can adopt a number of strategies to help groups make better decisions.

DISCUSSION QUESTIONS

Questions for Review

1. Describe the nature of decision making.
2. What are the main features of the classical model of the decision-making process? What are the main features of the administrative model?
3. What are the steps in rational decision making? Which step do you think is the most difficult to carry out? Why?
4. Describe the behavioural nature of decision making. Be certain to provide some detail about political forces, risk propensity, ethics, and commitment in your description.

Questions for Analysis

5. Was your decision about what college or university to attend a rational decision? Did you go through each step in rational decision making? If not, why not?
6. Can any decision be purely rational, or are all decisions at least partially behavioural in nature? Defend your answer against alternatives.
7. Under what conditions would you expect group decision making to be preferable to individual decision making, and vice versa? Why?

Questions for Application

8. Interview a local business manager about a major decision that he or she made recently. Try to determine if the manager used each of the steps in rational decision making. If not, which were omitted? Why might the manager have omitted those steps?
9. Interview a local business manager about a major decision that he or she made recently. Try to determine if aspects of the behavioural nature of decision making were involved. If so, which were involved? Why might this have occurred?
10. Interview a department head at your college or university to determine if group decision making is used at all. If it is, for what types of decisions is it used?

Building Effective Interpersonal Skills

Exercise Overview

Interpersonal skills refer to the manager's ability to understand and motivate individuals and groups. This exercise enables you to practise your interpersonal skills in a role-playing exercise.

Exercise Background

You supervise a group of six employees who work in an indoor facility in a relatively isolated location. The company you work for has recently adopted an ambiguous policy regarding smoking. Essentially, the policy states that all company work sites are to be smoke-free unless the employees at a specific site choose differently and at the discretion of the site supervisor.

Four members of the work group you supervise are smokers. They have presented the argument that because they constitute the majority they should be allowed to smoke at work. The other two members of the group, both non-smokers, argue that the health-related consequences of secondary smoke should outweigh the preferences of the majority.

To compound the problem further, your boss wrote the new policy and is quite defensive about it—numerous individuals have already criticized the policy. You know that your boss will get very angry with you if you also raise concerns about the policy. Finally, you are personally indifferent about the issue. You do not smoke yourself, but your spouse does smoke. Secondary smoke does not bother you, and you do not have strong opinions about it. Still, you have to make a decision about what to do. You see that your choices are to (1) mandate a smoke-free environment, (2) allow smoking in the facility, or (3) ask your boss to clarify the policy.

Exercise Task

Based on the preceding background information as context, assume that you are the supervisor and do the following:

1. Assume that you have chosen option one. Write an outline that you will use to announce your decision to the four smokers.
2. Assume that you have chosen option two. Write an outline that you will use to announce your decision to the two nonsmokers.
3. Assume that you have chosen option three. Write an outline that you will use when you meet with your boss.
4. Are there other alternatives?
5. What would you do if you were actually the group supervisor?

The Quaker Oats Company began with a merger of seven millers in the late 1800s, although it didn't adopt its name until 1901. It dominated the oats market early on and has never lost that domination. Quaker diversified its product line into animal feed and some grocery items and, in 1911, bought Aunt Jemima pancake flour. During the early part of this century, then, Quaker concentrated on production and marketing and grew to be one of the larger corporations in the United States with two of the oldest brand symbols in America.

Beginning in the 1960s, Quaker management decided to pursue diversification as a strategy for growth and profits. Quaker purchased Burry Biscuit Company, the leading supplier of Girl Scout cookies, in 1962. In 1969 it bought Fisher-Price toys (and sold it in 1991); a Chicago pizza restaurant, Celeste; and a San Francisco crepe restaurant, Magic Pan (which it also later sold). In 1972, it acquired Needlecraft Corporation of America and again sold it later. In 1983, Quaker bought Stokely-Van Camp with its top brand of pork and beans and its sports beverage, Gatorade.

Quaker then decided to focus its acquisitions on food companies. In 1986, it purchased the Golden Grain Macaroni Company, makers of Rice-a-Roni and Noodle-Roni brand products. That same year Quaker purchased Anderson, Clayton & Company, producers of dog food products, including Gaines Burgers and Gravy Train. Quaker became number-one in hot cereals, pork and beans, and sports beverages and number-two in dog food.

Quaker Oats's sports beverage Gatorade had more than 85 percent of the market in 1993, but competition from new entrants such as PepsiCo's All Sport and Coke's PowerAde was increasing fast. The Gatorade unit decided to become a more aggressive marketer—introducing promotions and improving its distribution network. In addition, Gatorade introduced its SunBolt, a chilled breakfast beverage that came on the market during the summer of 1994. Quaker also began to work with Sunkist to produce a powdered beverage targeted at U.S. Club stores, and it bought Snapple (divested in 1997).

In 1994, Quaker decided to begin a restructuring effort. It combined its in-house promotion, package design, and media services divisions. About three hundred persons were let go and another fifty vacant positions were not filled, a far cry from the thousands laid off by many other companies as a result of downsizing.

One reason for this small impact from restructuring may well be the human resource policies and practices used by Quaker. Quaker offers employees several child-care services and benefits such as work flexibility to recruit and retain the best personnel it can. Those benefits grew out of an employee-developed benefits program. Fifteen persons representing as many varying demographics of its employees as possible were assembled as The Flex Team. They ranked one hundred proposed benefits and met with co-workers to check their rankings. The plan was communicated to Quaker personnel in small group meetings and a print campaign. This high-involvement approach enabled Quaker to identify problems with the plan and ensured its enthusiastic acceptance by workers.

Questions

1. What kinds of decisions are described in this case? How would you classify them in terms outlined in the chapter?

2. Are the problems and solutions in this case unique to the food products industry or could they be found in other products and situations?

3. Will Quaker be able to withstand the competition of Pepsi and Coke in the sports beverage market? Why or why not?

References: "Gatorade Is Starting to Pant," *Business Week*, April 18, 1994, p. 98; Eric Sfiligoj, "Ace of Clubs," *Beverage World*, April 1994, p. 70; Joyce E. Santora, "Employee Team Designs Flexible Benefits Program," *Personnel Journal*, April 1994, pp. 30–39; Jim Kirk, "Gatorade Stirs Morning Drink," *Brandweek*, May 23, 1994, p. 6; "Opportunities Lost," *Forbes*, July 20, 1992, pp. 70–76; Milton Moskowitz, Robert Levering, and Michael Katz, *Everybody's Business* (New York: Doubleday, 1990), pp. 20–22; "Quaker Oats Takeover Talk Goes Flat," *USA Today*, January 17, 1995, p. 3B; and "The Quaker Oats Company: A Brief History" (http://www.quakeroats.com).

Chapter Notes

1. "Kimberly-Clark Reports Fourth Quarter Earnings" (http://www.Prnewswrite.com), January 26, 1999; "The Battle of the Bottoms," *Forbes,* March 24, 1997, pp. 98–203; "Strength Ahead?" *Barrons,* July 28, 1997, p. 13; and Linda Grant, "Outmarketing P&G," *Fortune,* January 12, 1998, pp. 150–153.

2. Richard Priem, "Executive Judgment, Organizational Congruence, and Firm Performance," *Organization Science,* August 1994, pp. 421–432.

3. Paul Nutt, "The Formulation Processes and Tactics Used in Organizational Decision Making," *Organization Science,* May 1993, pp. 226–240.

4. For recent reviews of decision making, see E. Frank Harrison, *Managerial Decision Making,* 4th ed. (Boston: Houghton Mifflin, 1995).

5. Charles R. Day, Jr., "Industry's Gutsiest Decisions of 1987," *Industry Week,* February 15, 1988, pp. 33–39; and Stratford P. Sherman, "Inside the Mind of Jack Welch," *Fortune,* March 27, 1989, pp. 38–50.

6. George P. Huber, *Managerial Decision Making* (Glenview, Ill.: Scott, Foresman, 1980).

7. Huber, *Managerial Decision Making.* See also David W. Miller and Martin K. Starr, *The Structure of Human Decisions* (Englewood Cliffs, N.J.: Prentice-Hall, 1976); and Alvar Elbing, *Behavioral Decisions in Organizations,* 2nd ed. (Glenview, Ill.: Scott, Foresman, 1978).

8. Huber, *Managerial Decision Making.*

9. See Avi Fiegenbaum and Howard Thomas, "Attitudes Toward Risk and the Risk-Return Paradox: Prospect Theory Explanations," *Academy of Management Journal,* March 1988, pp. 85–106; Jitendra V. Singh, "Performance, Slack, and Risk Taking in Organizational Decision Making," *Academy of Management Journal,* September 1986, pp. 562–585; and James G. March and Zur Shapira, "Managerial Perspectives on Risk and Risk Taking," *Management Science,* November 1987, pp. 1404–1418.

10. Kenneth Froot, David Scharfstein, and Jeremy Stein, "A Framework for Risk Management," *Harvard Business Review,* November–December 1994, pp. 91–99.

11. See Richard M. Cyert and Morris H. DeGroot, "The Maximization Process Under Uncertainty," in Patrick D. Larkey and Lee S. Sproull (Eds.), *Information Processing in Organizations* (Greenwich, Conn.: JAI Press, 1984), pp. 47–61.

12. Glen Whyte, "Decision Failures: Why They Occur and How to Prevent Them," *The Academy of Management Executive,* August 1991, pp. 23–31.

13. See R.T. Lenz and Jack L. Engledow, "Environmental Analysis Units and Strategic Decision Making: A Field Study of Selected 'Leading-Edge' Corporations," *Strategic Management Journal,* Vol. 7, 1986, pp. 69–89, for a recent analysis of how decision situations are recognized.

14. William Q. Judge and Alex Miller, "Antecedents and Outcomes of Decision Speed in Different Environmental Contexts," *Academy of Management Journal,* June 1991, pp. 449–463.

15. Thomas Stewart, "How to Lead a Revolution," *Fortune,* November 28, 1994, pp. 48–61.

16. See Charles A. O'Reilly III, "The Use of Information in Organizational Decision Making: A Model and Some Propositions," in Larry L. Cummings and Barry M. Staw (Eds.), *Research in Organizational Behavior,* Vol. 5 (Greenwich, Conn.: JAI Press, 1983), pp. 103–139.

17. Carol Saunders and Jack William Jones, "Temporal Sequences in Information Acquisition for Decision Making: A Focus on Source and Medium," *Academy of Management Review,* January 1990, pp. 29–46.

18. Kenneth Labich, "Coups and Catastrophes," *Fortune,* December 23, 1985, p. 125.

19. "The Wisdom of Solomon," *Newsweek,* August 17, 1987, pp. 62–63.

20. Elbing, *Behavioral Decisions in Organizations.*

21. Herbert A. Simon, *Administrative Behavior* (New York: Free Press, 1945). Simon's ideas have been recently refined and updated in Herbert A. Simon, *Administrative Behavior,* 3rd ed. (New York: Free Press, 1976), and Herbert A. Simon, "Making Management Decisions: The Role of Intuition and Emotion," *The Academy of Management Executive,* February 1987, pp. 57–63.

22. Patricia Corner, Angelo Kinicki, and Barbara Keats, "Integrating Organizational and Individual Information Processing Perspectives on Choice," *Organization Science,* August 1994, pp. 294–302.

23. "Unisys: So Far, So Good—But the Real Test Is Yet to Come," *Business Week,* March 2, 1987, pp. 84–86; "So Far, Married Life Seems to Agree with Unisys," *Business Week,* October 3, 1988, pp. 122–126.

24. Gannes, "America's Fastest-Growing Companies." See also "Can Ms. Fashion Bounce Back?" *Business Week,* January 16, 1989, pp. 64–70.

25. Barry M. Staw and Jerry Ross, "Good Money After Bad," *Psychology Today,* February 1988, pp. 30–33; and D. Ramona Bobocel and John Meyer, "Escalating Commitment to a Failing Course of Action: Separating the Roles of Choice and Justification," *Journal of Applied Psychology,* Vol. 79, No. 3, 1994, pp. 360–363.

26. "You Snooze, You Lose," *Newsweek,* July 21, 1997, p. 50.

27. John Lorinc, "Would You Buy This?" *Canadian Business,* December 1996, pp. 118–128.

28. Kent D. Miller and Philip Bromley, "Strategic Risk and Corporate Performance: An Analysis of Alternative Risk Measures," *Academy of Management Journal,* December 1990, pp. 756–779; and Philip Bromley, "Testing a Causal Model of Corporate Risk Taking and Performance," *Academy of Management Journal,* March 1991, pp. 37–59.

29. Thomas M. Jones, "Ethical Decision Making by Individuals in Organizations: An Issue-Contingent

Model," *Academy of Management Review,* April 1988, pp. 366–395.

30. Marvin E. Shaw, *Group Dynamics—The Psychology of Small Group Behavior,* 3rd ed. (New York: McGraw-Hill, 1981); Edwin A. Locke, David M. Schweiger, and Gary P. Latham, "Participation in Decision Making: When Should It Be Used?" *Organizational Dynamics,* Winter 1986, pp. 65–79; and Nicholas Baloff and Elizabeth M. Doherty, "Potential Pitfalls in Employee Participation," *Organizational Dynamics,* Winter 1989, pp. 51–62.

31. Andre L. Delbecq, Andrew H. Van de Ven, and David H. Gustafson, *Group Techniques for Program Planning* (Glenview, Ill.: Scott, Foresman, 1975), and Michael J. Prietula and Herbert A. Simon, "The Experts in Your Midst," *Harvard Business Review,* January–February 1989, pp. 120–124.

32. Norman P.R. Maier, "Assets and Liabilities in Group Problem Solving: The Need for an Integrative Function," in J. Richard Hackman, Edward E. Lawler III, and Lyman W. Porter (Eds.), *Perspectives on Business in Organizations,* 2nd ed. (New York: McGraw-Hill, 1983), pp. 385–392.

33. James H. Davis, *Group Performance* (Reading, Mass.: Addison-Wesley, 1969).

34. Richard A. Cosier and Charles R. Schwenk, "Agreement and Thinking Alike: Ingredients for Poor Decisions," *The Academy of Management Executive,* February 1990, pp. 69–78.

35. Irving L. Janis, *Groupthink,* 2nd ed. (Boston: Houghton Mifflin, 1982).

36. Janis, *Groupthink.*

Managing Entrepreneurship and New Venture Formation

9

OBJECTIVES

After studying this chapter, you should be able to:

● *Discuss the nature of entrepreneurship.*

● *Describe the roles of entrepreneurs in society.*

● *Understand the major issues involved in choosing strategies for small firms.*

● *Discuss the structural challenges unique to entrepreneurial firms.*

● *Understand the determinants of the performance of small firms.*

● *Explain the concept of intrapreneurship and its importance to large organizations.*

OUTLINE

Hector Jacques of Jacques Whitford Group accepting his award for Atlantic Canada's entrepreneur of the year.

On September 19, 1996, Hector Jacques (pronounced "Jakes," as it is in his homeland, the former Portuguese colony of Goa in India) was named Atlantic Canada's entrepreneur of the year. Jacques is president and CEO of Jacques Whitford Group Ltd., which is headquartered in Dartmouth, Nova Scotia, and has interests in various parts of the world. The company is a privately owned, multidisciplinary firm of consulting engineers and environmental scientists with seventeen branch offices in Canada, two in Maine, one each in New Hampshire and Vermont, one in Trinidad, and joint ventures in Moscow and Buenos Aires. Jacques Whitford, established in 1972, now has a workforce of 650 and sales of more than $50 million. It is a prime example of Canadian entrepreneurial success.

The company has come a long way since Hector Jacques and Michael Whitford founded it with an initial investment of $5,000. Jacques Whitford's growth of at least 17 percent per year

> **"Jacques Whitford Group Ltd. ... is a prime example of Canadian entrepreneurial success."**

in a very competitive business environment is the result of a strategy of diversification (consulting services are provided in a wide range of areas including geotechnical engineering, environmental engineering, informational technologies) and avoidance of overreliance on government contracts.

Hector Jacques' youthful ambition was not to be an entrepreneur: he worked for other companies before co-founding Jacques Whitford. Like many of his employees, Jacques has a solid educational background. He received his general certificate of education from the University of Cambridge, his bachelor's degree in engineering from the Indian Institute of Technology, and a master's degree in engineering from the Technical University of Nova Scotia.

The success of Jacques Whitford in both local and foreign markets is particularly impressive and is reflective of the company's ability to change in response to market conditions.[1] ●

Like Hector Jacques, thousands of people all over the world start new businesses each year. And as the opening incident indicates, such businesses have an international component. Many of these people succeed in their enterprise, but many others fail. Some who fail try again, and sometimes it takes two or more failures before a new business gets under way. Henry Ford, for example, went bankrupt twice before succeeding with the Ford Motor Co.

This process of starting a new business, sometimes failing and sometimes succeeding, is part of what is called entrepreneurship, the subject of this chapter. We begin by exploring the nature of entrepreneurship. We then examine the role of entrepreneurship in the business world and discuss strategies for entrepreneurial organizations. We then describe the structure and performance of entrepreneurial organizations. Finally, we discuss the role of entrepreneurship in larger organizations, a process often called intrapreneurship.

THE NATURE OF ENTREPRENEURSHIP

entrepreneurship
The process of planning, organizing, operating, and assuming the risk of a business venture

entrepreneur
Someone who engages in entrepreneurship

small business
A business that is privately owned by one individual or a small group of individuals; it has sales and assets that are not large enough to influence its environment

Entrepreneurship is the process of planning, organizing, operating, and assuming the risk of a business venture.[2] An **entrepreneur**, in turn, is someone who engages in entrepreneurship. Hector Jacques, highlighted in our opening incident, fits this description. He is putting his own resources on the line and taking a personal stake in the success or failure of his budding enterprise. Business owners who hire professional managers to run their businesses and then turn their attention to other interests are not entrepreneurs. Although they are assuming the risk of the venture, they are not actively involved in organizing or operating it. Likewise, professional managers whose job is running someone else's business are not entrepreneurs, for they assume less-than-total personal risk for the success or failure of the business.

Entrepreneurs start small businesses. We define a **small business** as one that is privately owned by one individual, or a small group of individuals; it has sales and assets that are not large enough to influence its environment. Industry Canada defines a small business as any firm with fewer than one hundred paid employees in the manufacturing sector and fewer than fifty paid employees in all other sectors.[3]

THE ROLE OF ENTREPRENEURSHIP IN SOCIETY

The history of entrepreneurship, and of the development of new businesses, is in many ways the history of great wealth and of great failure. Some entrepreneurs have been very successful and have accumulated vast fortunes from their entrepreneurial efforts. For example, when Microsoft Corp. sold its stock to the public in 1986, Bill Gates, then just thirty years old, received $350 million (U.S.) for his share of Microsoft.[4] Today, his holdings—valued at close to $100 billion—make him one of the richest people in the world. Many more entrepreneurs, however, have lost a great deal of money. Research suggests that the majority of new businesses fail within the first three years of founding.[5] Many that last longer do so only because the entrepreneurs themselves work long hours for very little income.

Increasingly, small businesses in Canada are being spearheaded by women.[6] There are many reasons for this trend, two of which we give here. First, some women, frustrated by what they see as limited promotion opportunities in large organizations, see starting their own business as the best route to success. Some women see owning their own business as a good way to increase their flexibility vis-à-vis childrearing. Between 1975 and 1990, the self-employed female employment sector grew by 172.8 percent, the highest growth rate of all sectors in that period, while the self-employed male employment sector grew by only 50.4 percent. It is projected that there will be 680,000 self-employed women in Canada by the year 2000. The majority of women-owned businesses in Canada have gross revenues under $100,000, and 80 percent of all women-owned businesses in Canada are in the retail and wholesale trades and service industries.[7] In 1993, 31 percent of all self-employed Canadians were women—a 63 percent increase from 1975.[8] By 1997, 2.5 million people in Canada were self-employed, representing 18 percent of all workers. Of these, 34 percent were women. Figure 9.1 shows how self-employed women increased in various industries between 1991 and 1996.

The experiences of individuals who win (and lose) fortunes as a result of their entrepreneurial activities may make fascinating stories, but the vital

FIGURE 9.1 Self-Employed Women by Industry, 1991–1996*

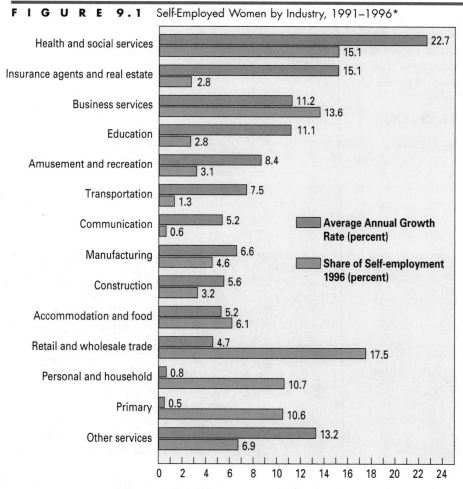

The percentage of women-owned businesses in Canada continues to grow. Although relatively few women own businesses in transportation, communication, and construction, their presence is large in social services, business services, retailing, and wholesaling.

*Based on 1991 and 1996 Census of Canada.

Source: *Small Business Quarterly Report*—Winter, 1999. Reproduced with the permission of the Minister of Public Works and Government Services Canada, 1998.

role that entrepreneurship plays in our society and our economy is even more telling. Of the 922,000 businesses (with employees) in Canada in 1993, 97 percent had fewer than fifty employees and 99 percent had fewer than one hundred employees. The 1.9 million self-employed in 1993 represented 15.4 percent of the workforce. As a percentage of the workforce, the self-employed increased roughly 33 percent between 1983 and 1993. In 1993, small and medium-sized enterprises contributed 57 percent of the private-sector gross domestic product.[9] Their vibrant, almost countless activities influence a number of economic areas, including innovation, job creation, and contributions to large businesses.[10]

Innovation

The resourcefulness and ingenuity typical of small business have spawned new industries and contributed a great many innovative ideas and technological breakthroughs to our society. Small businesses or individuals working alone invented, among other things, the personal computer, the transistor radio, the photocopying machine, the jet engine, and the instant photograph. They also gave us the pocket calculator, power steering, the automatic transmission, air conditioning, and even the nineteen-cent ballpoint pen. Some scholars believe that entrepreneurs are the driving force behind innovation in a society. As entrepreneurs seek the income and wealth associated with successful innovation, they create new technologies and products that displace older technologies and products.[11]

Job Creation

Small businesses create more new jobs than do larger businesses. Small businesses account for as much as 90 percent of all new employment in Canada each year.[12] In 1997, 73 percent of Canadian entrepreneurs expanded their workforce. In 1998, according to the Entrepreneur of the Year Institute's annual survey, 70 percent of those surveyed said they would increase staff in 1998.

Innovations such as laptop computers allow even age-old occupations such as managing a farm to be run like modern small businesses.

Those engaged in high technology have even higher expectations—83 percent reported expansion plans for 1998.[13]

The new jobs created by small businesses come in small bites. When a new restaurant opens, it may employ fifteen persons. When a new retail specialty store opens, it may employ twenty persons. Because so many new businesses are created each year, however, the cumulative impact on employment is significant.

Contributions to Large Businesses

It is primarily small businesses that supply and distribute the products of large businesses. General Motors, for example, buys materials from more than 25,000 suppliers, most of them small businesses. GM also distributes its products through small businesses—independent dealers. Likewise, an organization like Sony buys supplies from thousands of small businesses, distributes its electronic products through numerous small distributors and its movies through numerous independent movie theatres, and sells its records through independent record stores.

STRATEGY FOR ENTREPRENEURIAL ORGANIZATIONS

One of the most basic challenges facing an entrepreneurial organization is choosing a strategy. The three strategic challenges facing small firms, in turn, are choosing an industry in which to compete, emphasizing distinctive competencies, and writing a business plan.[14]

Choosing an Industry

As we discussed in Chapter 3, we can apply Michael Porter's five forces framework to estimate the average economic performance of the firms in an industry. In general, an industry characterized by high levels of rivalry, strong substitutes, a strong threat of entry, and powerful suppliers and buyers has lower return potential for firms than do industries without these characteristics.[15]

Entrepreneurs seeking to begin small-business operations should generally look to industries with favourable industry attributes. Thus, for example, entrepreneurs who start a business based on a technology with few rivals or substitutes and a low threat of entry usually earn higher rates of return than entrepreneurs who start a business without these advantages. The *Environment of Management* box explores how Cara used a twinning approach to develop what has become a very successful business today.

Examples of small businesses that chose a high-potential industry are Microsoft and Lotus, both very successful computer software companies.[16] These companies have developed personal-computer software that dominates their respective market segments (Microsoft in operating systems, Lotus in spreadsheet software). Because these firms are so dominant in their segments, there is low rivalry in their industries. Because of the skills that computer users have developed in applying these particular software packages, there are few substitutes. And because of the reputation and success of these firms, entry into these software segments is unlikely (although certainly not impossible).

An example of small businesses that begin operations in industries with low return potential is independent video rental stores. Because of the large number of video rental stores, and because all stores carry many of the same videos, rivalry in this industry is intense. Substitutes in the form of cable television, movie theatres, network television, and even books are common. Because the cost of entering this industry is relatively low (the cost of videos plus a lease and computer software), entry into the video rental business is easy. For these reasons, independent video rental operations are often marginal financial performers, although as members of national chains, video stores can be profitable.[17]

Industries in Which Small Businesses Are Strong   Small businesses tend to do well in the service, retail, and wholesale industries. Service organizations are perhaps the most common type of entrepreneurial business because they require a fairly small capital investment to start up. A chartered accountant, for example, can open a business simply by renting an office and hanging out a sign. The number of small businesses in the service industry, including video rental shops, hair salons, and tax preparation services, has significantly increased in recent years, all because the costs of the physical assets needed to start these businesses are relatively low.

Entrepreneurs are also effective in the area of specialty retailing. Specialty retailers cater to specific customer groups such as golfers, university students, and people who do their own automobile repairs. Often, the number of these special consumers is relatively small, and thus the dollar size of the market associated with these consumers is small. Although large organizations may be unwilling to enter a business where the market is so small, small businesses may be very successful in these industries.[18]

Wholesalers buy products from large manufacturers and resell them to retailers. Small businesses dominate the wholesale industry because they are often able to develop personal working relationships with several sellers and several buyers. A wholesale supplier of computer equipment may have to develop supply relationships with five or six floppy disk manufacturers, six or seven hard disk manufacturers, and five or six video screen manufacturers to have the inventory it needs to respond to the needs of its retail customers. If this wholesaler was not "independent" but instead was part of a larger electronics company, it would have supply relationships with only one supplier of floppy disks, one supplier of hard disks, and one maker of video screens. As long as end users want more supply options than this, the independent wholesaler can play an important economic role.[19]

Industries in Which Small Businesses Are Weak   Small organizations have difficulty succeeding in certain other industries. Foremost among them are industries dominated by large-scale manufacturing and agriculture, which is an industry in transition from domination by small family farms to domination by large corporate farms.

Research has shown that manufacturing costs often fall as the number of units produced by an organization increases. This relationship between cost and production is called an *economy of scale*.[20] Small organizations usually cannot compete effectively on the basis of economies of scale. As depicted in panel (a) of Figure 9.2, organizations with higher levels of production have a major cost advantage over those with lower levels of production. Given the cost positions of small and large firms when there are strong economies of scale in manufacturing,

Cara

Franchising is a system of distribution in which the right or privilege to sell a product or service is granted by a franchisor to a franchisee. Franchising is of particular appeal to conservative entrepreneurs: it is less risky than starting a business from scratch. The probability of a franchise failing is generally considerably lower than for a new independent business. The combined sales of the some sixty thousand franchisor outlets account for 40 percent of retail sales in Canada. One industry in which franchising is common is food services: McDonald's, Burger King, Pizza Hut, and KFC all have franchises in Canada. Roughly 13 percent of food service sales in Canada is accounted for by sales through franchises. A Canadian-owned franchisor that has exploited opportunities in the franchising business is Cara Operations Ltd.; the company, which owns the Harvey's and Swiss Chalet chains, ranks among the top ten franchisors in Canada in both sales and units.

In 1977, when Cara acquired the company that owned Harvey's and Swiss Chalet, franchising was only beginning to make its presence felt on the Canadian scene. The people-centred approach of Cara is thought to be different from the culture of many other franchisors. One way in which the company is similar to a number of major franchisors is that it has chosen a former franchisee to be its president. When Gabe Tsampalieros (who had previously managed a company that operated sixty Harvey's and Swiss Chalet outlets) was made president in 1996, Cara joined McDonald's, KFC, and Tim Hortons, among others, in having a president who was a former franchisee. Such a person's thorough understanding of the environment of the franchising business is obviously a major asset in the management of franchisors.

In twinning Harvey's and Swiss Chalet outlets in the 1980s, Gabe Tsampalieros had clearly seen the merits of a concept that is now common. Two significant moves Tsampalieros has made at Cara are the refocusing of the company in the food services industry and the acquisition of an interest in Second Cup Ltd. The latter action will undoubtedly allow Cara to engage in many more twinnings.

References: Rod William, "A Profile of the Food Service Sector in Canada," *Visions*, Vol. 4, No. 1, 1993, pp. 1–6; John Lorinc, "Hungry," *Canadian Business*, September 1996, pp. 104–110; and William Nickels et al., *Understanding Canadian Business*, 2nd ed. (Toronto: Irwin, 1997), p. 177.

it is not surprising that small manufacturing organizations generally do not do as well as large ones.

Interestingly, when technology in an industry changes, it often shifts the economies-of-scale curve, thereby creating opportunities for smaller organizations. For example, steel manufacturing was historically dominated by a few large companies that owned several huge facilities. With the development of mini-mill technology, however, extracting economies of scale at a much smaller level of production became possible. This type of shift is depicted in panel (b) of Figure 9.2. Point A in this panel is the low-cost point with the original economies of scale. Point B is the low-cost point with the economies of scale brought on by the new technology. Notice that the number of units needed for low costs is considerably lower for the new technology. This has allowed the entry of numerous smaller firms into the steel industry. Such entry would not have been possible with the older technology.[21]

Of course, not all manufacturing is capital-intensive. Some manufacturing can be done with minimal plant and equipment. This kind of light industry is typical of some parts of the computer industry and some parts of the plastic fabrication industry, in printing, and elsewhere. Small organizations can excel in these industries.[22]

FIGURE 9.2 Economies of Scale in Small Business Organizations

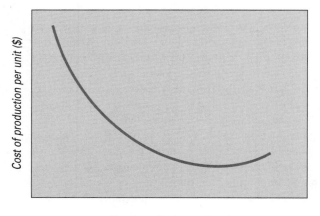

Cost of production per unit ($)

Number of units produced

Standard Economies of Scale Curve

(a)

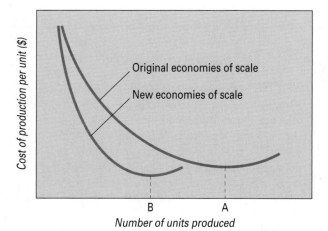

Cost of production per unit ($)

Original economies of scale

New economies of scale

B   A

Number of units produced

Change in Technology That Shifts Economies of Scale and May Make Small Business Production Possible

(b)

Small businesses sometimes find it difficult to compete in manufacturing-related industries because of the economies of scale associated with plant, equipment, and technology. As shown in (a), firms that produce a large number of units (i.e., larger businesses) can do so at a lower per unit cost. At the same time, however, new forms of technology occasionally cause the economies-of-scale curve to shift, as illustrated in (b). When this happens, smaller firms may be able to compete more effectively with larger ones, because of the drop in per unit manufacturing cost.

● **established market**
A market in which several large firms compete according to relatively well-defined criteria

Agriculture is an industry in transition. Small family farms were among the first small businesses in the world, and until recently they were among the most successful. Economies of scale and high equipment prices, however, have forced many small farmers out of business. Giant agribusiness enterprises and corporate farms are gradually replacing them. These multifarm businesses own and farm millions of hectares and are large enough to fully exploit economies of scale by purchasing and sharing the most modern farm equipment, applying the latest scientific methods in farming, and even influencing government policy to favour farmers.[23]

Emphasizing Distinctive Competencies

As we defined in Chapter 7, an organization's distinctive competencies are the aspects of business that the firm performs better than its competitors. The distinctive competencies of small business usually fall into three areas: the ability to identify new niches in established markets, the ability to identify new markets, and the ability to move quickly to take advantage of new opportunities.

Identifying Niches in Established Markets   An **established market** is one in which several large firms compete according to relatively well-defined criteria. For example, throughout the 1970s several well-known computer-manufacturing companies, including IBM, Digital Equipment Corp., and Hewlett-Packard, competed according to three product criteria: computing power, service, and price. Over the years, the computing power and quality of service delivered by these firms continued to improve, while prices (especially relative to computing power) continued to drop.

Enter Apple Computer and the personal computer. For Apple, user friendliness, not computing power, service, and price, was to be the basis of competition. Apple targeted every manager, every student, and every home as the owner of a personal computer. The major entrepreneurial act of Apple was not to invent a new technology (indeed, the first Apple computers used all standard parts) but to recognize a new kind of computer and a new way to compete in the computer industry.[24]

Apple's approach to competition was to identify a new niche in an established market. A **niche** is simply a segment of a market that is not currently being exploited. In general, small entrepreneurial businesses are better at discovering these niches than are larger organizations. Large organizations usually have so many resources committed to older, established business practices that they may be unaware of new opportunities. Entrepreneurs can see these opportunities and move quickly to take advantage of them.[25]

Identifying New Markets   Successful entrepreneurs also excel at discovering whole new markets. Discovery can happen in at least two ways. First, an entrepreneur can transfer a product or service that is well established in one geographic market to a second market. This is what Marcel Bich did with ballpoint pens, which occupied a well-established market in Europe before Bich introduced them to Canada and the United States. Bich's company, Bic Corp., eventually came to dominate the U.S. market.[26]

Second, entrepreneurs can sometimes create entire industries. For example, entrepreneurial inventions of the dry paper copying process and the semiconductor have created vast new industries. Not only have the first companies into these markets been extremely successful (Xerox and National Semiconductor, respectively), but their entrepreneurial activity has spawned the development of hundreds of thousands of other companies and hundreds of thousands of jobs. Again, because entrepreneurs are not encumbered with a history of doing business in a particular way, they are usually better at discovering new markets than are larger, more mature organizations.

Entrepreneurs are most likely to succeed if they can identify and exploit new markets. Scott Abbott, Chris Haney, John Haney, and Ed Werner, four "average Canadians," invented Trivial Pursuit, which has become the best-selling adult board game of all time. With more than 65 million games sold worldwide, it taps into our obsession with pop culture.

first-mover advantage
Any advantage that comes to a firm because it exploits an opportunity before any other firm does

First-Mover Advantages   A **first-mover advantage** is any advantage that comes to a firm because it exploits an opportunity before any other firm does. Sometimes large firms discover niches within existing markets or new markets at just about the same time as small entrepreneurial firms do but are not able to move as quickly as small companies to take advantage of these opportunities.

There are numerous reasons for this difference. For example, many large organizations make decisions slowly because each of their many layers of hierarchy has to approve an action before it can be implemented. Also, large organizations may sometimes put a great deal of their assets at risk when they take advantage of new opportunities. Every time Boeing decides to build a new model of a commercial jet, it is making a decision that could literally bankrupt the company if it does not turn out well. The size of the risk may make large organizations cautious. The dollar value of the assets at risk in a small organization, in contrast, is quite small. Managers may be willing to "bet the company" when the value of the company is only $100,000. They might be unwilling to "bet the company" when the value of the company is $1 billion.[27]

Writing a Business Plan

business plan
A document that summarizes the business strategy and structure

Once an entrepreneur has chosen an industry to compete in and determined which distinctive competencies to emphasize, these choices are usually included in a document called a business plan. In a **business plan** the entrepreneur summarizes the business strategy and how that strategy is to be implemented.[28] The very act of preparing a business plan forces prospective entrepreneurs to crystallize their thinking about what they must do to launch their business successfully and obliges them to develop their business on paper before investing time and money in it. The idea of a business plan is not new.[29] What is new is the growing use of specialized business plans by entrepreneurs, mostly because creditors and investors demand them for use in deciding whether to help finance a small business.

The plan should describe the match between the entrepreneur's abilities and the requirements for producing and marketing a particular product or service. It should define strategies for production and marketing, legal aspects and organization, and accounting and finance. In particular, it should answer three questions: (1) What are the entrepreneur's goals and objectives? (2) What strategies will the entrepreneur use to obtain these goals and objectives? (3) How will the entrepreneur implement these strategies?

Some idea of the complexity of planning a new business may be gleaned from the PERT diagram shown in Figure 9.3. The diagram shows the major steps in planning the launch of a new business. Notice that the development of a business plan consists of a set of specific activities, perhaps none of which is more pivotal than marketing research—the systematic and intensive study of all the facts, opinions, and judgments that bear on the successful marketing of a product or service.

Figure 9.3 also demonstrates the sequential nature of much strategic decision making in small businesses. For example, entrepreneurs cannot forecast sales revenues without first researching markets. The sales forecast itself is one of the most important elements in the business plan. Without such forecasts, it is all but impossible to estimate intelligently the size of a plant, store, or office or to determine how much inventory to carry or how many employees to hire.

Another important activity is financial planning, which translates all other activities into dollars. Generally, the financial plan is made up of a cash budget, an income statement, balance sheets, and a break-even chart. The most important of these statements is the cash budget because it tells entrepreneurs how much money they need before they open for business and how much money they need to keep the business operating.

STRUCTURE OF ENTREPRENEURIAL ORGANIZATIONS

With a strategy in place and a business plan in hand, the entrepreneur can then proceed to devise a structure that turns the vision of the business plan into a reality. Many of the same concerns in structuring any business, which are described in the next five chapters of this book, are also relevant to small businesses. For example, entrepreneurs need to consider organization design and develop job descriptions, organization charts, and management control systems. Small businesses do have some special concerns relating to structure, however, including the form of ownership and sources of financing, methods for starting the business, and sources of management help.

Business planning involves a number of very specific activities and events, as shown in this PERT diagram. Following a logical and systematic process such as this will enhance the chances for success.

F I G U R E 9 . 3 A PERT Diagram for Business Planning

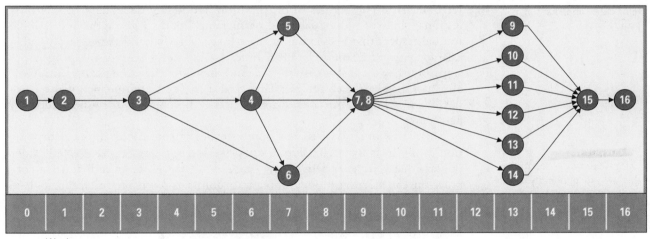

Weeks

1 Commit yourself
2 Analyze yourself
3 Choose product or service
4 Market research
5 Forecast sales revenues
6 Choose site

7 Develop production plan
8 Develop marketing plan
9 Develop organizational plan
10 Develop legal plan
11 Develop accounting plan
12 Develop insurance plan

13 Develop computer plan
14 Develop total quality management plan
15 Develop financial plan
16 Write cover letter

Source: Figure "A PERT Diagram for Business Planning" from Nicholas C. Siropolis, *Small Business Management*, Fifth Edition. Copyright © 1994 by Houghton Mifflin Company. Used by permission.

Forms of Ownership and Sources of Financing

Ownership structure specifies who possesses legal title to all of an organization's assets and who has a claim on any economic profits generated by a firm. Financing a small business involves decisions concerning the sources of capital that will be used to start the business and what claims (if any) these sources have on the organization's profits. There are a number of alternatives for both ownership structure and sources of financing, and each of them has advantages and disadvantages.[30]

Forms of Ownership   A popular form of legal ownership for many new businesses is the **sole proprietorship**, in which legal title to all assets and claims on all future economic profits are controlled by a single individual. About 75 percent of all Canadian businesses are sole proprietorships. The major advantages of a sole proprietorship are that the individual entrepreneur has total freedom in conducting business, start-up is simple and inexpensive, and business profits are taxed as ordinary income to the proprietor. The disadvantages are that the proprietor has unlimited liability (his or her personal assets are at risk to cover business debts) and the business ends when the proprietor retires or dies.

Another form of ownership is the **partnership**, in which two or more persons agree to be partners in a business, share title in the assets of the firm, be held jointly liable for a firm's debts, and share a firm's profits. The least common form of ownership, partnerships are often used by accounting, legal, and architectural firms. These types of organizations are highly dependent on the professional skills of individuals, and partnerships tend to foster the professional mutual respect that is essential in these business activities. Partnerships provide a larger pool of talent and capital to start a business than do sole proprietorships, but they are just as easy to form and they offer the same tax benefits. They also have similar disadvantages: liability and no legal continuance if the partnership is dissolved. An added difficulty may be conflict or tension between partners.

Most large organizations, and some smaller organizations, use the corporation as the basis for ownership. A **corporation** is a legal entity created under the law that is independent of any single individual. Like an individual, a corporation can borrow money, enter into contracts, own property, sue, and be sued. Its owners are the shareholders. An advantage that distinguishes the corporation from sole proprietorships and partnerships is that it is responsible for its own liabilities, so the owners have limited liability. A corporation continues to exist despite the retirement or death of any of its owners, and it can often borrow money easily. Corporations have higher start-up costs, however, and they are subject to increased regulation and double taxation (the corporation pays taxes on its profits, and then shareholders pay taxes on their dividends).

Sources of Financing   An important issue confronting all entrepreneurs is locating the money necessary to open and operate the business. Personal resources (usually savings and money borrowed from friends or family) are the most common sources of new-business financing. Personal resources are often the most important source because they reinforce the entrepreneur's personal commitment to the venture.[31] Many entrepreneurs also take advantage of various lending programs and assistance that is provided by lending institutions and government agencies.[32]

---

sole proprietorship
A form of ownership in which legal title to all assets and claims or all future profits are controlled by a single individual

partnership
A form of ownership in which two or more persons agree to be partners, share title of firm assets, be held jointly liable for firm debts, and share firm profits

corporation
A legal entity created under the law independently of any single individual for the sole purpose of business ownership and control

Another common source of funds is venture capitalists. A **venture capitalist** is someone who actively seeks to invest in new businesses. The advantage of this approach is that it gives entrepreneurs access to a large resource base with fewer restrictions than might be imposed by the government or by lending establishments. In return, however, the entrepreneur must relinquish to the venture capitalist a portion of the profits or share ownership.[33]

● **venture capitalist**
Someone who actively seeks to invest in new businesses

Methods for Starting a New Business

Another set of questions that an entrepreneur must address when organizing a business is whether to buy an existing business, start a new one, or seek a franchising agreement.

Buying an Existing Business   Buying an existing business offers a strong set of advantages. Because the entrepreneur can examine the business's historical records to determine the pattern of revenue and profit and the type of cash flow, much guesswork about what to expect is eliminated. The entrepreneur also acquires existing supplier, distributor, and customer networks. On the negative side, the entrepreneur inherits whatever problems the business may already have and may be forced to accept existing contractual agreements.

Starting a New Business   Starting a new business from scratch allows the owner to avoid the shortcomings of an existing business and to put his or her personal stamp on the enterprise. The entrepreneur also has the opportunity to choose suppliers, bankers, lawyers, and employees without worrying about existing agreements or contractual arrangements. More uncertainty is involved in starting a new business, however, than in taking over an existing one. The entrepreneur starts out with less information about projected revenues and cash flow, has to build a customer base from zero, and may be forced to accept unfavourable credit terms from suppliers. Because it is an unknown quantity, a new business may have difficulty borrowing money.

Franchising   An alternative to buying an existing business or starting one from scratch is entering into a **franchising agreement.** The entrepreneur pays a parent company (the **franchiser**) a flat fee or a share of the income from the business. In return, the entrepreneur (the **franchisee**) is allowed to use the company's trademarks, products, formulas, and business plan. Industries within which franchising is common include fast foods (e.g., McDonald's), specialty retail clothing stores (e.g., Benetton), personal computer stores (e.g., ComputerLand), and local automobile dealerships.[34] The *Managing in a Changing World* box highlights three highly successful franchise operations familiar to many students.

● **franchising agreement**
A contract between an entrepreneur (the **franchisee**) and a parent company (the **franchiser**); the entrepreneur pays the parent company for the use of the trademarks, products, formulas, and business plans

Franchising may reduce the entrepreneur's financial risk because many parent companies provide advice and assistance. They also provide proven production, sales, and marketing methods; training; financial support; and an established identity and image. Some franchisers also allow successful individual franchisees to grow by opening multiple outlets.

On the negative side, franchises may cost a lot of money. A McDonald's franchise costs several hundred thousand dollars. Also, the parent company often restricts the franchisee to certain types of products. A McDonald's franchisee cannot change the formula for milkshakes, alter the preparation of Big Macs, or purchase supplies from any other company. Some franchise agreements are difficult to terminate.[35]

Magicuts, Mr. Lube, and The Great Canadian Bagel

 Magicuts, Mr. Lube, and The Great Canadian Bagel are engaged in very different businesses, but they have something in common: they are all franchise operations.

Magicuts franchises cut and trim more heads than any other company in Canada. In its stand-alone outlets and those inside retailers like Zellers and Wal-Mart, the company charges as little as $8.00 per haircut. Magicuts' parent company, Premier Salons International of Markham, Ontario, operates 400 outlets in Canada and 650 in the United States.

Mr. Lube was founded in 1976 by Clifford Giese, who opened his first service centre in Edmonton, Alberta. He grew his company into a forty-five-store chain with service centres in major cities across Canada, and he initiated a franchise program in 1984. Esso Petroleum Canada bought the company in 1987. Today, Mr. Lube operates more than eighty stores across Canada, from coast to coast. Jim and Leslie Guenter, who operate two Mr. Lube outlets (one in Lethbridge and the other in Medicine Hat, Alberta), won the Mr. Lube Franchise of the Year Award in 1997. They attribute their success to their staff and strict adherence to the franchisor's formula for servicing automobiles.

Like Magicuts and Mr. Lube, the Great Canadian Bagel is a franchise operation. Its first two stores (opened in 1993, in Toronto) offered twenty-four varieties of baked bagels, twenty-one flavours of cream cheese spreads, and a selection of soups, salads, and made-to-order sandwiches. The company has steadily expanded since 1993 and today has more than 160 outlets, of which all but 11 are franchises.

References: "The History of Mr. Lube" (http://www.mrlube.com); "Franchise of the Year" (http://www.mrlube.com); "Great Canadian Bagel: Franchising" (http://www.greatcanadianbagel.com); and Richard Wright, "Our #1 Growth Company," *Profit: The Magazine for Canadian Entrepreneurs*, June 1996, pp. 34–35.

Despite the drawbacks, franchising is growing by leaps and bounds. Presently, 40 percent of Canadian retail sales go through franchises, and that figure is expected to climb.[36] Much of the attraction of franchising is that this approach to starting a new business involves limited risks. At the same time, however, also remember that no form of business is completely risk-free.

Sources of Management Help

The idea that small businesses benefit from management assistance has grown widely. Table 9.1 lists the many sources of management help now offered at little or no cost to entrepreneurs, both before and after they embark on a new business.

Table 9.1 covers not only federal help but also help from sources such as community colleges and universities and other organizations made up of small businesses. Heading the list is Canada Business Service Centres (CBSC). There are twelve CBSCs in Canada (one in each province, one in the Northwest Territories, and one in the Yukon) that provide information on government services, programs, and regulations. These centres are an initiative of the federal and provincial governments and, in some cases, the private sector. Currently, twenty-two federal business departments, together with other levels of government and nongovernmental organizations, participate in CBSCs. Each centre offers products and services geared to specific client bases. Services are offered by telephone, in person, by fax, and on the Web.[37]

TABLE 9.1 Sources of Help for Entrepreneurs

Federal, provincial, and local governments and agencies

Aboriginal Business Canada

Atlantic Canada Opportunities Agency

Business Development Bank of Canada

Canada Business Service Centres

Community Access Project

FedNor

Federal Office of Regional Development (Quebec)

Government Electronic Directory Services

Industry Canada Regional Offices

Ontario Business Connects

Western Economic Diversification Canada

Executive Guide to Year 2000 Computing Solutions

Services Offered

Financing

Accessing new markets

Tax requirements and services

Human resource issues

Management and skills development

Science, technology, and innovation

Business and legislation

Doing business via the information highway

Seminars and workshops

Counselling

Publications

Internet sites

Source: Adapted from Industry Canada Internet site (http://strategis.ic.gc.ca).

THE PERFORMANCE OF ENTREPRENEURIAL ORGANIZATIONS

The formulation and implementation of an effective strategy plays a major role in determining the overall performance of an entrepreneurial organization.[38] This section examines how entrepreneurial firms evolve over time and the attributes of these firms that enhance their chance for success.

The Life Cycle of Entrepreneurial Firms

The entrepreneurial life cycle is a series of predictable stages that small businesses pass through. A common pattern of evolution for entrepreneurial organizations is depicted in Figure 9.4.[39] This pattern is similar to the product life cycle discussed in Chapter 7, but it refers specifically to the challenges and changes in small entrepreneurial firms.

First comes the acceptance stage, in which the small business struggles to break even and survive. Entrepreneurial firms are usually small enough at this stage that they can spot obstacles to success and act quickly to remove them. Moreover, entrepreneurs usually have the skills needed to modify their products or services as required by customers during this stage. Such modifications are often necessary for small firms struggling to obtain enough cash from sales and other sources to continue operations. Many small organizations, despite the skill and effort of entrepreneurs, never emerge from the acceptance stage.

Next follows the breakthrough stage. In the preceding stage, the rate of growth is slow—so slow that it is often unnoticed. But in the breakthrough stage, growth is so fast and unpredictable that many entrepreneurs fail to keep pace with it. Caught unprepared, they blunder. Sales revenues spiral upward as problems begin to surface with cash flow, production, quality, and delivery. At the same time, competition may become more severe.

Many entrepreneurial firms struggle in their early years and never reach the breakthrough stage. Fortunately, there are several agencies able to provide information, financing, and support to small businesses as they grow.

FIGURE 9.4 Stages of Evolution for Entrepreneurial Firms

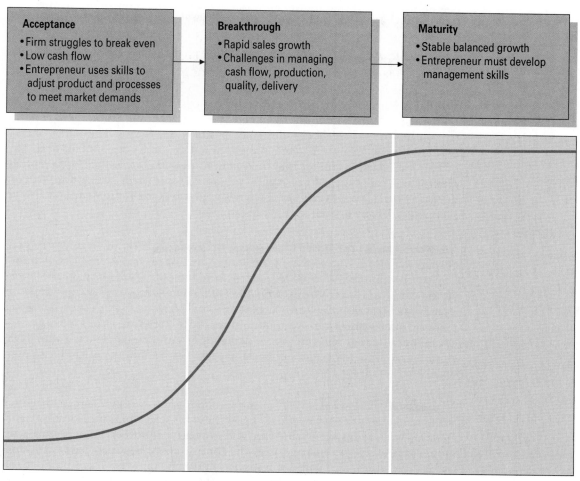

Acceptance
- Firm struggles to break even
- Low cash flow
- Entrepreneur uses skills to adjust product and processes to meet market demands

Breakthrough
- Rapid sales growth
- Challenges in managing cash flow, production, quality, delivery

Maturity
- Stable balanced growth
- Entrepreneur must develop management skills

Success

In the face of these pressures, entrepreneurs may apply hasty, ill-conceived solutions to problems. For example, if sales begin to level off or slip, they may hire specialists such as an accountant, a quality-control analyst, or a customer services representative to relieve the problem. As a result, costs go up, squeezing profits further.

The best way to become alerted to the problems presented by rapid growth is to continue updating the business plan. With a thorough, updated business plan in place, entrepreneurs are less likely to be surprised by breakthroughs.

In the mature stage, the lack of control of the breakthrough stage is replaced by a more stable, balanced period of steady growth. Organizations that survive to this stage can continue to grow for many years. In this last stage, however, entrepreneurs often face another challenge. Although they usually have the technical skills required during the acceptance stage, they often do not possess the managerial skills required during the mature stage. Entrepreneurs without these skills either have to develop them or turn the day-to-day operations of their organization over to professional managers and concentrate on new business opportunities or the creation of new organizations.[40]

Entrepreneurial firms often follow a pattern of evolution that resembles this curve. After an initial period of acceptance, during which the firm struggles and experiences low cash flow, the breakthrough stage is achieved. During this period, the firm experiences rapid sales growth and must focus on managing growth. When the maturity stage is reached, growth becomes more stable and the entrepreneur must begin to focus more attention on the actual management of the enterprise.

Reasons for Entrepreneurial Success

Many organizations successfully move through the stages listed in Figure 9.4 to become stable and mature organizations. Many factors contribute to this success, and six of the most common ones are described in the following sections.

Hard Work, Drive, and Dedication   An individual must have a strong desire to work independently and be willing to put in long hours to succeed as an entrepreneur. Successful entrepreneurs tend to be reasonable risk takers, self-confident, hard working, goal setters, and innovators.[41] In addition, small businesses generally benefit if the owner attends well to detail. Some entrepreneurs fail because they neglect the details of business operations. They may open a business for the glamour and excitement of it, but as the concomitant drudgery of entrepreneurship builds, they may ignore essential areas such as inventory control and collections. They may also ignore customer dissatisfaction, worker unrest, or financial difficulties, preferring to think that problems will solve themselves. Over time, though, they rarely do.

Market Demand for Products or Services Provided   For any business to succeed, demand must be sufficient for the product or service it provides. If a university community of 50,000 citizens and 15,000 students has one pizza parlour, demand for more is probably sufficient. If fifteen pizza parlours are already in operation, however, a new one will have to serve especially good pizza or offer something else unique if it is to succeed. Second Cup was successful because there was an unmet demand for good coffee; Tilley Endurables' clothing business was successful because there was an unmet demand for comfortable clothing for travel.

Managerial Competence   The entrepreneur must possess basic managerial competence. He or she needs to know how to select business locations and facilities, acquire financing, and hire and evaluate employees. The entrepreneur must also be able to manage growth, control costs, negotiate contracts, and make difficult choices and decisions. An entrepreneur who has a product for which there is tremendous demand might be able to survive for a while without managerial skills. Over time, and especially in the mature stage of the life cycle, however, the manager who lacks these skills is unlikely to succeed.

Luck   Some small businesses succeed purely because of luck. There was an element of luck in Alan McKim's success with Clean Harbors, an environmental "clean up" organization based in New England. McKim formed this business just as the federal government committed $1.6 billion (U.S.) to help clean up toxic waste. Although McKim might have succeeded anyway, the extra revenue generated by the government Superfund no doubt contributed to this success.[42]

Strong Control Systems   Small businesses, like all organizations, need strong control systems. Small businesses can be ruined by weak control. For example, too many slow-paying customers can reduce a small business's cash flow to a trickle. Excess inventory, employee theft, poor-quality products, plummeting sales, and insufficient profit margins can have equally disastrous effects. If the control system either does not alert the entrepreneur to these problems or alerts the entrepreneur too late, recovery may be difficult or impossible. (Control systems are discussed more fully in Part VI of the book.)

Sufficient Capitalization Small businesses need sufficient funds to survive start-up and growth. One rule of thumb is that an entrepreneur should have sufficient personal funds when starting out to be able to live with no business income for a year.[43] The entrepreneur needs to be able to maintain his or her personal life, cover all operating expenses, and still have an allowance for unexpected contingencies. An entrepreneur who is planning to pay next month's rent from a new business's profits may be courting disaster.

THE ROLE OF INTRAPRENEURSHIP IN LARGER ORGANIZATIONS

In recent years, many large businesses have realized that the entrepreneurial spirit that propelled their growth becomes stagnant after they transform themselves from a small but growing concern into a larger one. To help revitalize this spirit, some firms today encourage what they call intrapreneurship. **Intrapreneurs** are similar to entrepreneurs except that they develop a new business in the context of a large organization.

There are three intrapreneurial roles in large organizations.[44] To successfully use intrapreneurship to encourage creativity and innovation, the organization must find one or more individuals to perform these roles. The *inventor* is the person who actually conceives of and develops the new idea, product, or service by means of the creative process.

Because the inventor may lack the expertise or motivation to oversee the transformation of the product or service from an idea into a marketable entity, however, a second role comes into play. A *product champion* is usually a middle manager who learns about the project and becomes committed to it. He or she helps overcome organizational resistance and convinces others to take the innovation seriously. The product champion may have only limited understanding of the technological aspects of the innovation. Nevertheless, product champions are skilled at knowing how the organization works, whose support is needed to push the project forward, and where to go to secure the resources necessary for development.

A *sponsor* is a top-level manager who approves of and supports a project. This person may fight for the budget needed to develop an idea, overcome arguments against a project, and use organizational politics to ensure the project's survival. With a sponsor in place, the inventor's idea has a much better chance of being successfully developed.

Several firms have embraced intrapreneurship as a way to encourage creativity and innovation. Colgate-Palmolive has created a separate unit, Colgate Venture Company, staffed with intrapreneurs who develop new products. General Foods developed Culinova Group as a unit to which employees can take their ideas for possible development.

● **intrapreneur**
A person similar to an entrepreneur, except that he or she develops a new business in the context of a large organization

SUMMARY OF KEY POINTS

Entrepreneurship is the process of planning, organizing, operating, and assuming the risk of a business venture. An entrepreneur is someone who engages in entrepreneurship. In general, entrepreneurs start small businesses. Small businesses are an important source of innovation, create numerous jobs, and contribute to the success of large businesses.

In choosing strategies, entrepreneurs have to consider the characteristics of the industry in which they are going to conduct business. Entrepreneurs can use Porter's five forces framework to choose their industry. A small business must also emphasize its distinctive competencies. Small businesses generally have several distinctive competencies that they should exploit in choosing their strategy. Small businesses are usually skilled at identifying niches in established markets, identifying new markets, and acting quickly to obtain first-mover advantages. Small businesses are usually not skilled at exploiting economies of scale. Once an entrepreneur has chosen a strategy, the strategy is normally written down in a business plan. Writing a business plan forces an entrepreneur to plan thoroughly and to anticipate problems that might occur.

With a strategy and business plan in place, entrepreneurs must choose a structure to implement them. All of the structural issues summarized in the next five chapters of this book are relevant to the entrepreneur. In addition, the entrepreneur has some unique structural choices to make. In determining ownership and financial structure, the entrepreneur can choose between a sole proprietorship, a partnership, a corporation, and a few less common structures. In determining financial structure, an entrepreneur has to decide how much personal capital to invest in an organization, how much bank and government support to obtain, and whether to encourage venture capital firms to invest. Finally, entrepreneurs have to choose among the options of buying an existing business, starting a new business from scratch, or entering into a franchising agreement.

Most small businesses pass through a three-phase life cycle: acceptance, breakthrough, and maturity. There are several reasons why successful small businesses are able to move through all three of these stages of development: hard work, drive, and dedication; market demand for products or services provided; managerial competence; luck; strong control systems; and sufficient capitalization.

Some large organizations encourage a process they call intrapreneurship, a process similar to entrepreneurship but within the context of a large business. Inventor, product champion, and sponsor are three important intrapreneurial roles.

DISCUSSION QUESTIONS

Questions for Review

1. Why are entrepreneurs and small businesses important to society?
2. In which types of industries do small firms often excel? In which types of industries do small firms struggle?
3. List the ownership options available to entrepreneurs. What are the advantages and disadvantages of each?
4. What are the elements of success for small businesses?

Questions for Analysis

5. Entrepreneurs and small businesses play important roles in society. If these roles are so important, do you think that the government should do more to encourage the development of small business? Why or why not?
6. Franchising agreements seem to be particularly popular ways of starting a new business in industries in which retail outlets are geographically widely spread and where the quality of goods or services purchased can be evaluated only after the purchase has occurred. For example, a hamburger may look tasty, but you know for sure that it is well made only after you buy it and eat it. By going to a McDonald's, you know exactly the kind and quality of hamburger you will receive, even before you walk in the door. What is it about franchise arrangements that makes them so popular under these conditions?

7. What are the basic similarities and differences between entrepreneurship and intrapreneurship?

8. Develop a brief outline for starting a new business in a promising market niche.

Questions for Application

9. Interview the owner of a small business in your community. Evaluate how successful this small business has been. Using the criteria presented in this chapter, explain its success (or lack of success).

10. Using the information about managing a small business presented in this chapter, analyze whether you would like to work in a small business—either as an employee or as a founder. Given your personality, background, and experience, does working in or starting a new business appeal to you? What are the reasons for your opinion?

BUILDING EFFECTIVE COMMUNICATION SKILLS

Exercise Overview

Communication skills refer to the manager's abilities to both effectively convey ideas and information to others and to effectively receive ideas and information from others. Although communication skills are important to all organizations, some entrepreneurs argue that they are even more important in smaller organizations than they are in larger ones. This exercise will help you understand some of the complexities in communicating in smaller businesses.

Exercise Background

Assume that you are the owner/manager of a small retail chain. Your company sells moderate-priced apparel for professional men and women. You have ten stores located in Ontario and Quebec. Each store has a general manager responsible for the overall management of that specific store. Each store also has one assistant manager.

In addition, your corporate office is staffed by a human resource manager, an advertising specialist, and two buyers. In the past, each store was managed at the total discretion of its local manager. As a result, each store had a different layout, a different culture, and different policies and procedures.

You have decided that you want to begin opening more stores at a rapid pace. To expedite this process, however, you also want to standardize your stores. Unfortunately, however, you realize that this decision is bound to make many of your current managers unhappy. They will see it as a loss of authority and managerial discretion. Nevertheless, you believe that it is important to achieve standardization in all areas.

Your plans are to remodel all the stores to fit a standard layout. You also intend to develop a companywide policy and operations manual that each store must adhere to. This manual will specify exactly how each store will be managed. You plan to inform your managers of this plan first in a memo and then in a follow-up meeting to discuss questions and concerns.

Exercise Task

With the preceding background information as context, do the following:

1. Draft a memo that explains your intentions to the store managers.
2. Make a list of the primary objections you anticipate.
3. Outline an agenda for the meeting in which you plan to address the managers' questions and concerns.
4. Do you personally agree with this communication strategy? Why or why not?

Over the last five decades, Honest Ed's has grown from a small retail store to become one of Canada's most successful privately owned businesses. With 165,000 square feet of bargain shopping and 23,000 constantly flashing lights flickering outside, the store has become one of the most famous landmarks in downtown Toronto. Canada's first discount store continues to draw in over 10,000 customers daily.

The success behind Honest Ed's lies in the entrepreneurial spirit embodied in the company and its owner, Ed Mirvish. As a young boy growing up in Toronto, Ed Mirvish was not preoccupied with ball hockey like other kids his age. Instead, he spent his time bargaining with merchants and vendors, taking grocery orders from customers in the neighbourhood, and making deliveries by bicycle, with the hope of getting paid to support the family business. Today, in his eighties, he stands at the head of a business empire that has won him accolades from around the world. Described as a legendary entrepreneur, Ed Mirvish has become a local hero and national celebrity. In 1995, he was inducted into the Canadian Business Hall of Fame.

Ed Mirvish's small store was open for business almost sixty years ago, when he cashed his wife's $212 insurance policy. A high-school dropout at the age of 15 and short on cash, this entrepreneur set out to build a future based on hard work, dedication to his business, and honesty. Today, he is arguably one of Canada's most successful citizens, with more than two hundred awards and citations, including the Order of Canada and Commander of the British Empire—one rung below a British knighthood. Since establishing Honest Ed's at the current location in 1948, Ed Mirvish, like many entrepreneurs, has branched out into many other businesses. In 1962, he bought the Royal Alexandra Theatre, which was slated for demolition. As he later stated, it was an excellent business deal because of the price. His subsequent ventures into theatres included London's Old Vic Theatre and the Princess of Wales Theatre.

While building his theatrical business, Ed Mirvish also developed an appetite for the restaurant business. He now owns six restaurants in Toronto: Ed's Warehouse, Old Ed's, Ed's Italian, Ed's Most Honourable Chinese, Ed's Seafood, and Ed's Folly. Ed Mirvish also owns and runs Mirvish Village, which comprises artists' studios, shops, and a theatrical museum.

The success of Honest Ed's and the other businesses was achieved without the company establishing chain stores or going public—ideas that the entrepreneur rejects outright. Ed Mirvish states that his one store makes it unique in the world, and that even though he has a couple of thousand employees, he is still able to stay personally involved with almost all of them, every day. This business empire has also never had a partner from outside the family.

Ed Mirvish demands a lot from himself and those around him. While many people his age have retired, Mirvish is in his retail store by 8:00 a.m. for meetings. He heads to his restaurants for the lunch rush and spends the rest of the day at Mirvish Productions where he oversees some of Toronto's grandest theatres. He is rigid in his habits and meticulously tracks how he uses his time. Mirvish has also given back to his community and is legendary in the Toronto area. His annual birthday parties attract tens of thousands and his free Christmas turkey giveaways have people lining the streets before dawn.

While he has obviously worked very hard, Ed Mirvish attributes some of his success to luck and his drive to offer visitors to his discount store low-priced items at the expense of "frills" such as delivery, parking, refunds, and credit. This is in direct contrast to the strategies used by discount retail outlets such as Wal-Mart and Zellers. In an increasingly competitive retail environment, Honest Ed's will certainly face new challenges in the future. Whether or not the store will continue to thrive is anybody's guess.

Questions

1. What are some of the common characteristics of entrepreneurs? Does Ed Mirvish fit the "typical" entrepreneur mould?

2. In view of the increasing competition in the discount market, what challenges might Honest Ed's face in the future? Do you think the firm will survive? Why or why not?

3. Why do some entrepreneurs go public while others remain private? What are the advantages and disadvantages of each form of ownership and which is most likely to be used by entrepreneurial organizations?

References: "Two Tales of a City: Honest Ed and Sam the Record Man," *Financial Post*, December 2–4, 1995, pp. 22–23; "Ed Mirvish Tireless at 82," *Canadian Press Newswire*, June 10, 1997; "Ed Mirvish" (http://www.grey.net/MIRRORS/c2c/edmirvish.htm); Jack Batten, *Honest Ed's Story* (Toronto: Doubleday Canada Ltd., 1972); and "Honest Ed Honored by Hall of Fame Award," *The Toronto Star*, January 27, 1995, p. B3.

CHAPTER NOTES

1. "Engineered for Success," *Canadian Business*, December 1996, p. 112; "Jacques Wins Atlantic Entrepreneur of the Year Award," *The Chronicle-Herald* (Halifax), September 20, 1996, p. C3; and biography of Hector Jacques and company profile provided by Jacques Whitford. You can visit the Jacques Whitford Group Ltd. Web site (www.jacqueswhitford.com) or contact the company through its e-mail address (info@jacqueswhitford.com).

2. Murray B. Low and Ian C. MacMillan, "Entrepreneurship: Past Research and Future Challenges," *Journal of Management,* June 1988, pp. 139–159; and Barbara Bird, "Implementing Entrepreneurial Ideas: The Case for Intention," *Academy of Management Review,* July 1988, pp. 442–453.

3. Industry Canada, *Small Business in Canada: A Statistical Overview.* Ottawa: Industry Canada, 1996.

4. Bro Uttal, "Inside the Deal That Made Bill Gates $350,000,000," *Fortune,* July 21, 1986, pp. 23–33.

5. Low and MacMillan, "Entrepreneurship," and Arnold C. Cooper and William C. Dunkelberg, "Entrepreneurship and Paths to Business Ownership," *Strategic Management Journal,* January/February 1986, pp. 53–56.

6. "Canadian Bankers Association (CBA) *Financing a Small Business-Focus on Women Entrepreneurs* (Toronto: Canadian Bankers Association, 1996).

7. CBA, *Financing a Small Business—Focus on Women Entrepreneurs.*

8. William Nickels et al., *Understanding Canadian Business,* 2nd ed. (Toronto: Irwin, 1997) p. 194.

9. Industry Canada, *Small Business in Canada.*

10. See David L. Birch, *The Job Creation Process* (Cambridge, Mass.: MIT Program on Neighborhood and Regional Change, 1979); Nicholas C. Siropolis, *Small Business Management*, 5th ed. (Boston: Houghton Mifflin, 1994); and Stuart Gannes, "America's Fastest-Growing Companies," *Fortune,* May 23, 1988, pp. 28–40.

11. "Big vs. Small," *Time,* September 5, 1988, pp. 48–50; and J.A. Schumpeter, *Capitalism, Socialism, and Democracy,* 3rd ed. (New York: Harper & Row, 1950).

12. Nickels et al., *Understanding Canadian Business,* p. 210.

13. Industry Canada, *Small Business in Canada.*

14. Amar Bhide, "How Entrepreneurs Craft Strategies That Work," *Harvard Business Review,* March–April 1994, pp. 150–163.

15. Michael Porter, *Competitive Strategy* (New York: Free Press, 1980).

16. Uttal, "Inside the Deal That Made Bill Gates $350,000,000"; and Keith Hammonds, "Spreadsheet Wars: When Will Lotus Do Windows," *Business Week,* January 14, 1991, p. 42.

17. Erik Calonius, "Meet the King of Video," *Fortune,* June 4, 1990, p. 208.

18. See Faye Brookman, "Specialty Cosmetic Stores: A Hit with Frustrated Consumers," *Advertising Age,* March 4, 1991, p. 32; and Laurie Freeman, "Department Stores in Fight for Their Lives," *Advertising Age,* March 4, 1991, p. 29.

19. See Steve Zurier, "Distribution's Perfect Example," *Industrial Distribution,* April 1991, pp. 18–22; and Donald A. Duschesaneau and William B. Gartner, "A Profile of New Venture Success and Failure in an Emerging Industry," *Journal of Business Venturing,* September 1990, pp. 297–312.

20. F.M. Scherer, *Industrial Market Structure and Economic Performance,* 2nd ed. (Boston: Houghton Mifflin, 1980).

21. Thomas Rohan, "Maverick Remakes Old-Line Steel," *Industry Week,* January 21, 1991, pp. 26–30.

22. "Small Manufacturers Display Nimbleness the Times Require," *The Wall Street Journal,* December 29, 1993, pp. A1, A2.

23. See Kenneth Harling and Phoebe Quail, "Exploring a General Management Approach to Firm Management," *Agribusiness,* September 1990, pp. 425–441; and Charles Silear, "Where Did All the Pigs Go?" *Forbes,* March 19, 1990, pp. 152–156.

24. See Richard Pastore, "Small Is Big in PC Land," *Computerworld,* December 24, 1990, pp. 27, 29; and Pat Sweet, "The Evolution of the PC's," *Director,* March 1990, pp. 101–107.

25. The importance of discovering niches is emphasized in Charles Hill and Gareth Jones, *Strategic Management: An Integrative Approach,* 2nd ed. (Boston: Houghton Mifflin, 1992).

26. C. Roland Christensen, Norman A. Berg, and Malcolm Salter, "BIC Pen (A)," *Policy Formulation and Administration,* 8th ed. (Homewood, Ill.: Irwin, 1980), pp. 146–171.

27. See Siropolis, *Small Business Management,* and Richard M. Hodgetts and Donald F. Kuratko, *Effective Small Business Management,* 3rd ed. (Chicago: Harcourt Brace Jovanovich, 1989). The risks run at Boeing are described in "Running Ahead, but Running Scared," *Forbes,* May 13, 1991, pp. 38–40.

28. Siropolis, *Small Business Management.*

29. "Old-Fashioned Ways Still Work," *Forbes,* March 14, 1994, pp. 90–91.

30. See Thomas E. Copeland and J. Fred Weston, *Financial Theory and Corporate Policy,* 2nd ed. (Reading, Mass.: Addison-Wesley, 1983), for a discussion of the different kinds of claims that sources of capital can have on a firm. Eugene Fama and Michael Jensen discuss the advantages and disadvantages of various forms of corporate ownership in E. Fama and M. Jensen, "Agency Problems and Residual Claims," *Journal of Law and Economics,* June 1983,

pp. 327–349; and E. Fama and M. Jensen, "Separation of Ownership and Control," *Journal of Law and Economics,* June 1983, pp. 301–325. A more practical guide to choosing ownership structure is found in Hodgetts and Kuratko, *Effective Small Business Management.*

31. Jay Barney, Lowell Busenitz, James Fiet, and Doug Moesel, "The Structure of Venture Capital Governance," *Academy of Management Proceedings: "Best Papers 1989,"* Meeting of the Academy of Management, Washington, D.C., 1989, pp. 64–68.

32. "Persistence Pays in Search of Funds," *USA Today,* May 11, 1987, p. 3E.

33. Barney et al., "The Structure of Venture Capital Governance."

34. Faye Rice, "How to Succeed at Cloning a Small Business," *Fortune,* October 28, 1985, pp. 60–66; and "Franchising Tries to Divvy Up Risk," *USA Today,* May 11, 1987, p. 5E.

35. "Businesses Vie for More Control" *USA Today,* January 5, 1993, pp. 1B, 2B.

36. Nickels et al., *Understanding Canadian Business,* p. 177.

37. Information obtained from Industry Canada Internet site (http://strategis.ic.gc.ca).

38. Charles Burck, "The Real World of the Entrepreneur," *Fortune,* April 5, 1993, pp. 62–80.

39. Siropolis, *Small Business Management.*

40. Siropolis, *Small Business Management.*

41. Siropolis, *Small Business Management.*

42. See Jay Barney, "Strategic Factor Markets: Expectations, Luck, and Business Strategy," *Management Science,* October 1986, pp. 1231–1241.

43. Siropolis, *Small Business Management.*

44. See Gifford Pinchot III, *Intrapreneuring* (New York: Harper and Row, 1985).

Planning and Decision Making

NEWS ITEM:
Loblaws Launches Friendly Takeover of Provigo (1998, 2:00)

Loblaws, Canada's biggest grocery store chain, announces a friendly takeover of Provigo, Quebec's leading food retailer, creating Canada's largest food giant. Even Separatist Premier Lucien Bouchard applauds the deal, despite the fact that the deal strengthens economic links between Quebec and English Canada. Some concerns, however, are being expressed over what advantages, if any, will result for the consumer.

Questions:

1. What are the strategic advantages associated with this merger? What are the advantages of keeping each company's corporate identity?
2. What are the political implications of such a deal, particularly since a Quebec corporation is involved?

NEWS ITEM:
MacMillan Bloedel Announces an End to Clear-Cutting (1998, 2:00)

Well-known B.C. forest products giant MacMillan Bloedel, facing the reality of its tarnished public image—particularly in Europe—announces it will be ceasing its practice of clear-cutting forests. The announcement is met with guarded optimism by their long-standing foes in the environmentalist community.

Questions:

1. How will the decision to end clear-cutting help MacMillan Bloedel achieve its goals? Is this primarily an environmental issue or a market issue?
2. Do you think companies are becoming more concerned about environmental and social issues or are they simply reacting to maket forces?

NEWS ITEM:
Interview with Entrepreneurs **(1986, 12:15)**

Two entrepreneurs, including one of the men behind the extraordinary success of the Trivial Pursuit board game enterprise, discuss the path they took to success with their products.

Questions:

1. What were the similarities and differences in the strategies used by the creators of Trivial Pursuit and Balderdash?
2. What advice is offered to potential entrepreneurs who invent new games?

As international competition continues to escalate, businesses must constantly adjust their structure to ensure that it is promoting efficiency and effectiveness. Global companies like McDonald's and Philips, for example, must coordinate far-flung operations. At a local level, organizations focus on various training methods to keep everyone working together.

The Organizing Process

Basic Elements of Organizing

OBJECTIVES

After studying this chapter, you should be able to:

● *Identify the basic elements of organizations.*

● *Describe alternative approaches to designing jobs.*

● *Discuss the rationale and the most common bases for grouping jobs into departments.*

● *Describe the basic elements involved in establishing reporting relationships.*

● *Discuss how authority is distributed in organizations.*

● *Discuss the basic coordinating activities undertaken by organizations.*

● *Describe basic ways in which positions within an organization can be differentiated.*

Bell Canada Enterprises president and CEO Jean Monty announces that U.S. telephone company Ameritech Corporation will invest $5.1 billion to take 20 percent of Bell Canada. The deal was announced March 24, 1999.

At the end of 1997, with approximately 39,000 employees, Bell Canada was this country's sixteenth largest private-sector employer. Nevertheless, this was a drastic reduction from the 57,000 employees Bell had on its payroll in 1990, the 48,000 it had in 1995, or the 44,000 it had in 1996. Presumably the cuts were aimed at making Bell more competitive—something the company did not have to worry about when it had a virtual monopoly on the Canadian telephone business. The process of stripping Bell of its monopoly started in 1979 and was completed in 1992 when the Canadian Radio-television and Telecommunications Commission (CRTC) granted permission to other companies to offer long-distance service.

This move has forced Bell Canada to become more competitive, and downsizing seems to be a major part of this effort.

"The process of stripping Bell of its monopoly has forced [the company] to become more competitive."

Another part of Bell's strategy was to change its structure from one dictated by its status as a highly regulated local service and a competitive long-distance service. John McLennan, who became president and chief executive officer of Bell Canada in January 1994, shifted the structural focus from the regulatory regime to customers according to the size of their accounts—a shift to differentiation based on revenue gained from particular accounts. In light of this shift and of downsizing, Bell's employees must be aware that job security is highest for those in customer service and that those who are not working directly with customers are more vulnerable.

Working in an environment heavily influenced by downsizing has an impact on employee morale. While the company has offered severance packages and enhanced pension benefits for its early-departing employees, the stress of deciding whether to stay or go and the overall climate of insecurity must have an impact on employees. Of course, the decision of whether to leave or stay is not entirely up to the employee. In its announcement of layoffs made in mid-July 1997, the company targeted 2,200 employees—two-thirds from management ranks and one-third from administrative support.

The uncertainty at Bell was not limited to its employees: the July 1997 announcement of layoffs was greeted by heavy trading and a drop in the share price of Bell Canada Enterprises, Bell Canada's parent company.[1] ●

John McLennan undertook one of the biggest challenges facing a manager—to virtually reconstruct an entire organization. Bell Canada had a structure that no longer served its purpose. Thus that structure had to be changed and modified—in effect, rebuilt—to better fit the needs of the firm today. McLennan, who has since been replaced by Jean Monty as CEO of Bell Canada, began the process of dismantling and reconstructing various elements of the organization to better fit the company's competitive environment.

This chapter discusses many of the critical elements of organization structure that managers can control and is the first of five devoted to organizing, the second basic managerial function identified in Chapter 1. In Part III, we described managerial planning—deciding what to do. Organizing, the subject of Part IV, focuses on how to do it. We first elaborate on the meaning of organization structure. Subsequent sections explore the basic elements that managers use to create an organization.

THE ELEMENTS OF ORGANIZING

Imagine asking a child to build a castle with a set of building blocks. He selects a few small blocks and several larger ones. He uses some square ones, some round ones, and some triangular ones. When he finishes, he has his own castle, unlike any other. Another child, presented with the same task, constructs a different castle. The child's activities—choosing a certain combination of blocks and then putting them together in a unique way—are analogous to the manager's job of organizing.

Organizing is deciding how best to group organizational elements. Just as the child selects different kinds of building blocks, managers can choose a variety of structural possibilities. And just as the child can assemble the blocks in any number of ways, so too can managers put the organization together in many different ways. In this chapter, our focus is on the building blocks themselves—**organization structure**. In Chapter 11, we focus on how the blocks can be put together—organization design.

There are six basic building blocks that managers can use in constructing an organization: designing jobs, grouping jobs, establishing reporting relationships between jobs, distributing authority among jobs, coordinating activities between jobs, and differentiating between positions. The logical starting point is the first building block—designing jobs for people within the organization.[2]

DESIGNING JOBS

The very first building block of organization structure is job design. **Job design** is the determination of an individual's work-related responsibilities.[3] Despite the progress promised by the information age, many jobs are still dangerous and/or boring, as indicated in the *Environment of Management* box. For a machinist at Chrysler Canada, job design might specify what machines are to be operated, how they are to be operated, and what performance standards are expected. For a manager at Chrysler Canada, job design might involve defining areas of decision-making responsibility, identifying goals and expectations, and establishing appropriate indicators of success. The natural starting point for designing jobs is determining the level of desired specialization.

- **organizing**
Deciding how best to group organizational activities and resources

- **organization structure**
The set of elements that can be used to configure an organization

- **job design**
The determination of an individual's work-related responsibilities

Job Specialization

Job specialization is the degree to which the overall task of the organization is broken down and divided into smaller component parts. Job specialization evolved from the concept of *division of labour*. Adam Smith, an eighteenth-century economist, described how a pin factory used division of labour to improve productivity.[4] One person drew the wire, another straightened it, a third cut it, a fourth ground the point, and so on. Smith claimed that ten people working in this fashion were able to produce 48,000 pins in a day, whereas each person working alone could produce only 20 pins per day.

More recently, the best example of the impact of specialization is the automobile assembly line pioneered by Henry Ford and his contemporaries. Mass-production capabilities stemming from job specialization techniques have had a profound impact throughout the world. High levels of low-cost production transformed U.S. society during the first several decades of the twentieth century into one of the strongest economies in the history of the world.

Job specialization is a normal extension of organizational growth. For example, when Walt Disney started his company he did everything himself—wrote cartoons, drew them, and then marketed them to theatres. As the business grew, he eventually hired others to perform many of these same functions. As growth continued, so too did specialization. For example, as animation artists work on Disney movies today, they may specialize in drawing only a single character. And today, The Walt Disney Company has thousands of different specialized jobs. Clearly, no one person could perform them all.

> ● **job specialization**
> The degree to which the overall task of the organization is broken down and divided into smaller component parts

Benefits and Limitations of Specialization

Job specialization provides four benefits to organizations.[5] First, workers performing small, simple tasks will become very proficient at that task. Second, transfer time between tasks decreases. If employees perform several different tasks, some time is lost as they stop doing the first task and start doing the next. Third, the more narrowly defined a job is, the easier it is to develop specialized equipment to assist with that job. Fourth, when an employee who performs a highly specialized job is absent or resigns, the manager is able to train someone new at relatively low cost. Although specialization is generally thought of in terms of operating jobs, many organizations have extended the basic elements of specialization to managerial and professional levels as well.[6]

On the other hand, job specialization can have negative consequences. The foremost criticism is that workers who perform highly specialized jobs may become bored and dissatisfied. The job may be so specialized that it offers no challenge or stimulation. Boredom and monotony set in, absenteeism rises, and the quality of the work may suffer. Furthermore, the anticipated benefits of specialization do not always occur. For example, a study conducted at Maytag found that the time spent moving work-in-process from one worker to another was greater than the time needed for the same individual to change from job to job.[7] Thus, although some degree of specialization is necessary, it should not be carried to extremes because of the possible negative consequences. Managers must be sensitive to situations in which extreme specialization should be avoided. And indeed, several alternative approaches to designing jobs have been developed in recent years.

Deteriorating Jobs

 People die on the job: in Canada, 1,000 traumatic deaths occur on the job each year, compared with 8,000–11,000 in the United States. Additionally, in Canada, 800,000 workers suffer on-the-job injuries every year. This means that one out of fifteen workers in Canada can expect to be injured on the job. Most of the jobs involved in these deaths and injuries are those filled by unskilled, inexperienced, and/or part-time employees. High-school dropouts are far more likely to hold dangerous jobs than high-school graduates, especially as the skill level of better jobs continues to increase. In addition to deaths, however, are injuries and working conditions that bring to mind those described by Charles Dickens a century ago. What is frightening is that as industry fully enters the information age, more and more of these kinds of jobs are being created, and those who cannot handle these jobs increasingly are becoming part of the growing group of homeless people.

Workers at recycling plants are exposed to hazards from household trash, used hypodermic needles, dead animals, and chemicals. Building rehabilitation and demolition workers face dangerous and often disease-laden conditions. Shift workers experience difficulty in coping with changes in their biological clocks. Changes in shifts can lead to higher accident rates as well as an increase in alcohol and drug use.

Aside from actual danger, many jobs create extremely high levels of stress. Prison and nursing home employees, because the rate of growth in both areas is so great, frequently receive little training to prepare them for the stress they encounter on their jobs. In Canadian prisons, correctional officers not only have to cope with the stress of shift work in a potentially dangerous environment, but many are also exposed to the health hazards posed by secondhand smoke.

Other jobs, although they are not physically dangerous, are degrading psychologically to the personnel involved. Treated more like undisciplined children, these workers are frequently forbidden to talk or look around while at work, and their rest breaks are closely monitored. They are expected to meet extremely rigid standards under unpleasant, close supervision. For example, many telephone answering workers have their telephone calls timed with stopwatches, and in some financial services organizations form-processing personnel even have their individual keystrokes monitored.

Poultry workers, a group almost twice the size it was a decade ago, labour under severe conditions; even bathroom breaks are timed by managers with stopwatches. (In more extreme cases, people are denied access to bathroom breaks, a situation that can lead to medical problems. In Canada, the regulation of issues such as bathroom privileges is a provincial responsibility. In Ontario, for example, regulations require the availability of bathroom facilities, but they do not address the issue of giving employees time to use the facilities.) Injury and illness impact nearly 25 percent of poultry workers each year, making poultry processing the eleventh most dangerous industry in the United States. With its assembly-line process design, it is also third for cumulative trauma injuries such as carpal tunnel syndrome. Only the meatpacking and automobile body assembly industries, which also utilize assembly-line work designs, have higher injury rates. These work designs employ machine-pacing and have little worker control, which also contributes to high levels of stress on the job.

The poultry processing industry is also known for harsh work rules and motivation by fear, although companies usually claim that such charges are spread by unions in an effort to recruit more members. The U.S. Occupational Safety and Health Administration (OSHA), however, has frequently found "medical mismanagement" in the industry. Medical mismanagement includes failure to report injuries and having workers return to work before they are fully recovered—conditions that occur when workers are afraid of reporting accidents or missing too many days from work. Clearly, all jobs are not wonderful or even easy in the emerging world of high technology.

References: Tony Horwitz, "9 to Nowhere," *The Wall Street Journal*, December 1, 1994, pp. A1, A8, and A9; Aaron Bernstein, "The Young and the Jobless," *Business Week*, August 16, 1993, p. 107; Gordon Berlin and William McAllister, "Homelessness: Why Nothing Has Worked—And What Will," *Brookings Review*, Fall 1992, pp. 12–17; J.P. Leigh, "Employers Should Inform Prospective Employees of Job Hazards," *Occupational Hazards*, January 1991, pp. 45–46; Timothy H. Monk, "Shift Work and Safety," *Professional Safety*, April 1989, pp. 26–30; Wayne Cascio and Jim Thacker, *Managing Human Resources* (Toronto: McGraw-Hill Ryerson, 1994), p. 571; "Labour Minister Alfonso Gagliano Announces Canadian Occupational Safety and Health Week," Human Resources Development Canada press release, June 3, 1996; and Maggie Jackson, "On-the-Job Bathroom Breaks Become a Workplace Health Issue," *The Toronto Star*, March 23, 1998, p. D7.

Alternatives to Specialization

To counter the problems associated with specialization, managers have sought other approaches to job design that achieve a better balance between organizational demands for efficiency and productivity and individual needs for creativity and autonomy. Five alternative approaches are job rotation, job enlargement, job enrichment, the job characteristics approach, and work teams.[8]

Job Rotation   **Job rotation** involves systematically moving employees from one job to another. A worker in a warehouse might unload trucks on Monday, carry incoming inventory to storage on Tuesday, verify invoices on Wednesday, pull outgoing inventory from storage on Thursday, and load trucks on Friday. Thus the jobs do not change but, instead, workers move from job to job. Unfortunately, for this very reason, job rotation has not been very successful in enhancing employee motivation or satisfaction. Jobs that are amenable to rotation tend to be relatively standard and routine. Workers who are rotated to a "new" job may be more satisfied at first, but satisfaction soon wanes. Although companies such as CAMI have tried job rotation, it is most often used today as a training device to improve worker skills and flexibility.

Job Enlargement   On the assumption that doing the same basic task over and over is the primary cause of worker dissatisfaction, **job enlargement** was developed to increase the total number of tasks workers perform. As a result, all workers perform a wide variety of tasks, which presumably reduces the level of job dissatisfaction. Many organizations have used job enlargement, including IBM and Maytag. At Maytag, for example, the assembly line for producing washing-machine water pumps was systematically changed so that work that had originally been performed by six workers, who passed the work sequentially from one person to another, was performed by four workers, each of whom assembled a complete pump.[9] Unfortunately, although job enlargement does have some positive consequences, they are often offset by several disadvantages: (1) training costs usually rise, (2) unions have argued that pay should increase because the worker is doing more tasks, and (3) in many cases the work remains boring and routine even after job enlargement.

Job Enrichment   A more comprehensive approach, **job enrichment**, assumes that increasing the range and variety of tasks is not sufficient by itself to improve employee motivation.[10] Thus job enrichment attempts to increase both the number of tasks a worker does and the control the worker has over the job. To implement job enrichment managers remove some controls from the job, delegate more authority to employees, and structure the work in complete, natural units. These changes increase subordinates' sense of responsibility. Another part of job enrichment is to continually assign new and challenging tasks, thereby increasing employees' opportunity for growth and advancement.

AT&T was one of the first companies to try job enrichment. In one experiment, eight typists in a service unit prepared customer service orders. Faced with low output and high turnover, management determined that the typists felt little responsibility to clients and received little feedback. The unit was changed to create a typing team. Typists were matched with designated service representatives, the task was changed from ten specific steps to three more general steps, and job titles were upgraded. As a result, the frequency of order processing increased from 27 percent to 90 percent, the need for messenger service

Some firms today use job rotation to improve worker skills and to promote flexibility. For example, employees in this department store are trained to handle a number of different jobs. This employee is demonstrating an exercise bike to a prospective customer. He also works as a cashier and spends time in the store's warehouse stacking inventory and boxes.

● **job rotation**
An alternative to job specializatioin that involves systematically moving employees from one job to another

● **job enlargement**
An alternative to job specialization that involves giving the employee more tasks to perform

● **job enrichment**
An alternative to job specialization that involves increasing both the number of tasks the worker does and the control the worker has over the job

was eliminated, accuracy improved, and turnover became practically nil.[11] Other organizations that have tried job enrichment include Traveler's Insurance Company, IBM, and General Foods. This approach, however, also has disadvantages. For example, work systems should be analyzed before enrichment, but this seldom happens, and managers rarely ask for employee preferences when enriching jobs.

● **job characteristics approach**

An alternative to job specialization that suggests that jobs should be diagnosed and improved along five core dimensions, taking into account both the work system and employee preferences

Job Characteristics Approach   The **job characteristics approach** is an alternative to job specialization that does take into account the work system and employee preferences.[12] As illustrated in Figure 10.1, the job characteristics approach suggests that jobs should be diagnosed and improved along five core dimensions:

1. *Skill variety*: the number of things a person does in a job

2. *Task identity*: the extent to which the worker does a complete or identifiable portion of the total job

3. *Task significance*: the perceived importance of the task

4. *Autonomy*: the degree of control the worker has over how the work is performed

5. *Feedback*: the extent to which the worker knows how well the job is being performed

The higher a job rates on those dimensions, the more employees will experience various psychological states. Experiencing these states, in turn, presumably leads to high motivation, high-quality performance, high satisfaction, and low absenteeism and turnover. Finally, a variable called *growth-need strength* is presumed to affect how the model works for different people. People with a strong desire to grow, develop, and expand their capabilities (indicative of high growth-need strength) are expected to respond strongly to the presence or absence of the basic job characteristics; individuals with low growth-need strength are expected not to respond as strongly or consistently.

A large number of studies have been conducted to test the usefulness of the job characteristics approach. A division of Prudential Insurance, for example, used this approach in its claims department. Results included moderate declines in turnover and a small but measurable improvement in work quality. Other research findings have not supported this approach as strongly. Thus, although the job characteristics approach is one of the most promising alternatives to job specialization, it is probably not the final answer.[13]

● **work team**

An alternative to job specialization that allows an entire group to design the work system it will use to perform an interrelated set of tasks

Work Teams   Another alternative to job specialization is **work teams**. Under this arrangement, a group is given responsibility for designing the work system to be used in performing an interrelated set of jobs. In the typical assembly-line system, the work flows from one worker to the next, and each worker has a specified job to perform. In a work team, however, the group itself decides how jobs will be allocated. For example, the work team assigns specific tasks to members, monitors and controls its own performance, and has autonomy over work scheduling.[14] We discuss work teams more fully in Chapter 18.

The job characteristics approach to job design provides a viable alternative to job specialization. Five core job dimensions may lead to critical psychological states that, in turn, may enhance motivation, performance, satisfaction, absenteeism, and turnover.

Core job dimensions	Critical psychological states	Personal and work outcomes
• Skill variety • Task identity • Task significance	Experienced meaningfulness of the work	• High internal work motivation
• Autonomy	Experienced responsibility for outcomes of the work	• High-quality work performance
• Feedback	Knowledge of the actual results of work activities	• High satisfaction with the work • Low absenteeism and turnover

Employee growth-need strength

Source: J.R. Hackman and G.R. Oldham, "Motivation Through the Design of Work: Test of a Theory," *Organizational Behavior and Human Performance,* Vol. 16 (1976), pp. 250–279. Copyright © Academic Press, Inc. Reprinted by permission of Academic Press and the authors.

GROUPING JOBS: DEPARTMENTALIZATION

The second building block of organization structure is the grouping of jobs according to some logical arrangement. This process is called **departmentalization**. After establishing the basic rationale for departmentalization, we identify some common bases along which departments are created.

Rationale for Departmentalization

When organizations are small, the owner-manager can personally oversee everyone who works there. As an organization grows, however, personally supervising all the employees becomes more and more difficult for the owner-manager. Consequently, new managerial positions are created to supervise the work of others. Employees are not assigned to particular managers randomly. Rather, jobs are grouped according to some plan. The logic embodied in such a plan is the basis for all departmentalization.[15]

Most organizations group jobs into departments according to some underlying logic. Silicon Graphics, which created the special effects in *Jurassic Park,* groups its jobs by function. These employees are testing new computers and software to ensure that they can produce the desired effects.

● **departmentalization**
The process of grouping jobs according to some logical arrangement

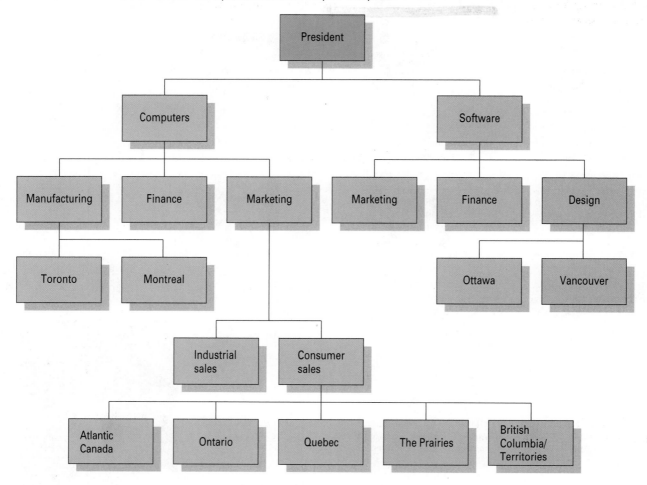

Organizations group jobs into departments. Apex—a hypothetical organization—uses all four of the primary bases of departmentalization—function, product, customer, and location. Like Apex, most large organizations use more than one type of departmentalization.

● **functional departmentalization**

Grouping jobs involving the same or similar activities

Common Bases for Departmentalization

Figure 10.2 presents a partial organizational chart for Apex Computers, a hypothetical firm that manufactures and sells computers and software. The chart shows that Apex uses each of the four most common bases for departmentalization: function, product, customer, and location.

Functional Departmentalization   The most common base for departmentalization, especially among smaller organizations, is by function.[16] **Functional departmentalization** groups together those jobs involving the same or similar activities. (The word *function* is used here to mean organizational functions such as finance and production, rather than the basic managerial functions such as planning or controlling.) The computer department at Apex has manufacturing, finance, and marketing departments.

This approach, most common in smaller organizations, has three advantages. First, each department can be staffed by experts in that functional area. Marketing experts can be hired to run the marketing function, for example. Second, supervision is also facilitated because an individual manager needs to be familiar with only a relatively narrow set of skills. And third, coordinating activities inside each department is easier.

On the other hand, as an organization begins to grow in size, several disadvantages of this approach may emerge. For one, decision making tends to become slower and more bureaucratic. Employees may also begin to concentrate too narrowly on their own units and lose sight of the total organizational system. Finally, accountability and performance become increasingly difficult to monitor. For example, determining whether a new product fails because of production deficiencies or a poor marketing campaign may not be possible.

Product Departmentalization **Product departmentalization**, a second common approach, involves grouping and arranging activities around products or product groups. Apex Computers has two product-based departments at the highest level of the firm. One is responsible for all activities associated with Apex's personal computer business, and the other handles the software business. Most larger businesses adopt this form of departmentalization for grouping activities at the business or corporate level.

- **product departmentalization**
Grouping activities around products or product groups

Product departmentalization has three major advantages. First, all activities associated with one product or product group can be easily integrated and coordinated. Second, the speed and effectiveness of decision making are enhanced. Third, the performance of individual products or product groups can be assessed more easily and objectively, thereby improving the accountability of departments for the results of their activities.

Product departmentalization also has two major disadvantages. For one, managers in each department may focus on their own product or product group to the exclusion of the rest of the organization. That is, a marketing manager may see her or his primary duty as helping the group rather than helping the overall organization. For another, administrative costs rise because each department must have its own functional specialists for things like marketing research and financial analysis.

Customer Departmentalization Under **customer departmentalization**, the organization structures its activities to respond to and interact with specific customers or customer groups. The lending activities in most banks, for example, are usually tailored to meet the needs of different kinds of customers (i.e., business, consumer, mortgage, and agricultural loans). Figure 10.2 shows that the marketing branch of Apex's computer business has two distinct departments—industrial sales and consumer sales. The industrial sales department handles marketing activities aimed at business customers, whereas the consumer sales department is responsible for wholesaling computers to retail stores catering to individual purchasers.

- **customer departmentalization**
Grouping activities to respond to and interact with specific customers or customer groups

The basic advantage of this approach is that the organization is able to use skilled specialists to deal with unique customers or customer groups. It takes one set of skills to evaluate a balance sheet and lend a business $70,000 for operating capital and a different set of skills to evaluate an individual's creditworthiness and lend $15,000 for a new car. However, a fairly large administrative staff is required to integrate the activities of the various departments. In banks, for example, coordination is necessary to make sure that the organization does not overcommit itself in any one area and to handle collections on delinquent accounts from a diverse set of customers.

Location Departmentalization **Location departmentalization** groups jobs on the basis of defined geographic sites or areas. The defined sites or areas

- **location departmentalization**
Grouping jobs on the basis of defined geographic sites or areas

may range in size from a hemisphere to only a few blocks of a large city. The manufacturing branch of Apex's computer business has two plants—one in Montreal and another in Toronto. Similarly, the design division of its software design unit has two labs—one in Ottawa and the other in Vancouver. Apex's consumer sales group has five sales territories corresponding to different regions of Canada. Transportation companies and police departments (divisions represent geographic areas of a city), use location departmentalization.

The primary advantage of location departmentalization is that it enables the organization to respond easily to unique customer and environmental characteristics in the various regions. On the negative side, a larger administrative staff may be required if the organization must keep track of units in scattered locations.

Other Forms of Departmentalization   Although most organizations are departmentalized by function, product, location, or customer, other forms are occasionally used. Some organizations group certain activities by time. Consider, for example, a company that operates on shifts. Each shift has a superintendent, who reports to the plant manager, as well as its own functional departments. Time is thus the framework for the company's organizational activities. Organizations that use time as a basis for grouping jobs include some hospitals and many airlines. In other situations, departmentalization by sequence is appropriate. Many university students, for instance, must register in sequence: last names starting with A through E register in line 1, F through L in line 2, and so on. Other areas that may be organized in sequence include credit departments (specific employees run credit checks according to customer name) and insurance claims divisions (by policy number).

Other Considerations   Two final points about job grouping remain to be made. First, departments are often called something entirely different—divisions, units, sections, and bureaus are all common synonyms. The higher we look in an organization, the more likely we are to find departments referred to as divisions. Nevertheless, the underlying logic behind all the labels is the same: they represent groups of jobs that have been yoked together according to some unifying principle. Second, almost any organization is likely to employ multiple bases of departmentalization, depending on level.[17] Although Apex Computers is a hypothetical firm we created to explain departmentalization, it is quite similar to many real organizations in that it uses a variety of bases of departmentalization for different levels and different sets of activities.

ESTABLISHING REPORTING RELATIONSHIPS

The third basic element of organizing is the establishment of reporting relationships among positions. Suppose, for example, that the owner-manager of a small business has just hired two new employees, one to handle marketing and one to handle production. Will the marketing manager report to the production manager, will the production manager report to the marketing manager, or will each report directly to the owner-manager? These questions reflect the basic issues involved in establishing reporting relationships: clarifying the chain of command and the span of management.

Chain of Command

Chain of command is an old concept, first popularized in the early years of this century. For example, early writers about the **chain of command** argued that clear and distinct lines of authority need to be established among all positions in the organization. The chain of command actually has two components. The first, called *unity of command*, suggests that each person within an organization must have a clear reporting relationship to one and only one boss (as we see in Chapter 11, newer models of organization design successfully violate this premise). The second, called the *scalar principle*, suggests that there must be a clear and unbroken line of authority that extends from the lowest to the highest position in the organization. The popular saying "The buck stops here" is derived from this idea—someone in the organization must ultimately be responsible for every decision.

● **chain of command**
A clear and distinct line of authority among the positions in an organization

Narrow versus Wide Spans

Another part of establishing reporting relationships is determining how many people will report to each manager. This defines the **span of management** (sometimes called the *span of control*). For years managers and researchers sought to determine the optimal span of management. For example, should it be relatively narrow (with few subordinates per manager) or relatively wide (with many subordinates)? One early writer, A. V. Graicunas, went so far as to quantify span of management issues.[18] Graicunas noted that a manager must deal with three kinds of interactions with and among subordinates: direct (the manager's one-to-one relationship with each subordinate), cross (among the subordinates themselves), and group (between groups of subordinates). The number of possible interactions of all types between a manager and subordinates can be determined by the following formula:

● **span of management**
The number of people who report to a particular manager

$$I = N \left(\frac{2^N}{2} + N - 1 \right)$$

where I is the total number of interactions with and among subordinates and N is the number of subordinates.

If a manager has only two subordinates, six potential interactions exist. If the number of subordinates increases to three, the possible interactions total eighteen. With five subordinates there are one hundred possible interactions. Although Graicunas offers no prescription for what N should be, his ideas demonstrate how complex the relationships become when more subordinates are added. The important point is that each additional subordinate adds more complexity than the previous one did. Going from nine to ten subordinates is very different from going from three to four.

Another early writer, Ralph C. Davis, described two kinds of spans: an operative span for lower-level managers and an executive span for middle and top managers. He argued that operative spans could approach thirty subordinates, whereas executive spans should be limited to between three and nine (depending on the nature of the managers' jobs, the growth rate of the company, and similar factors). Lyndall F. Urwick suggested that an executive span should never exceed six subordinates, and General Ian Hamilton reached the same conclusion.[19] Today we recognize that the span of management is a crucial factor in structuring organizations but that there are no universal, cut-and-dried prescriptions for an ideal or optimal span.[20] Later we summarize some important variables that influence the appropriate span of management in a particular situation. First, however, we describe how the span of management affects the overall structure of an organization.

Tall versus Flat Organizations

Imagine an organization with thirty-one managers and a narrow span of management. As shown in Figure 10.3, the result is a relatively tall organization with five layers of management. With a somewhat wider span of control, however, the flat organization shown in Figure 10.3 emerges. This configuration has only three layers of management.

What difference does it make whether the organization is tall or flat? One early study at Sears Roebuck and Co. found that a flat structure led to higher levels of employee morale and productivity.[21] Researchers have also argued that a tall structure is more expensive (because of the larger number of managers involved) and that it fosters more communication problems (because of the increased number of people through whom information must pass). On the other hand, a wide span of management in a flat organization may result in a manager's having more administrative responsibility (because there are fewer managers) and more supervisory responsibility (because there are more subordinates reporting to each manager). If these additional responsibilities become excessive, the flat organization may suffer.[22]

Wide spans of management result in flat organizations, which may lead to increased employee morale and productivity as well as increased managerial responsibility. Many organizations today, including IBM and Bell Canada, are moving toward flat structures to improve communication and flexibility.

F I G U R E   10.3   Tall versus Flat Organizations

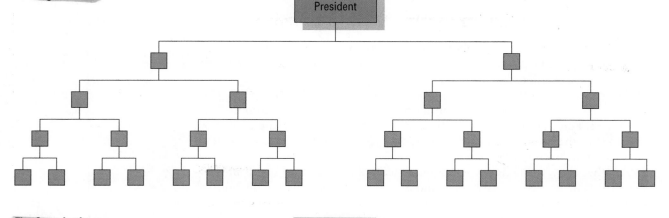

Tall Organization

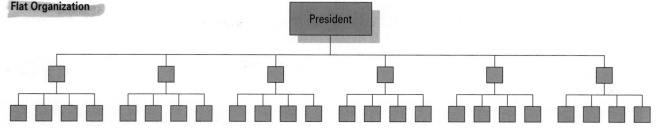

Flat Organization

Many experts agree that businesses can function effectively with fewer layers of organization than they currently have. IBM and Bell Canada, for example, have recently eliminated several layers of management. One reason for this trend is that improved organizational communication networks allow managers to stay in touch with a larger number of subordinates than was possible just a few years ago.[23]

Determining the Appropriate Span

Of course, the initial question remains: how do managers determine the appropriate span for their unique situations? Although no perfect formula exists, researchers have identified a set of factors that influence the span for a particular circumstance.[24] Some of these factors are listed in Table 10.1. For example, if the manager and subordinates are competent and well trained, a wide span may be effective. Physical dispersion is also important. The more widely subordinates are scattered, the narrower the span should be. On the other hand, if all the subordinates are in one location, the span can be somewhat wider. The amount of nonsupervisory work expected of the manager is also important. Some managers, especially at the lower levels of an organization, spend most or all of their time supervising subordinates. Other managers spend a lot of time doing paperwork, planning, and engaging in other managerial activities. Thus these managers may need a narrower span.

Some job situations also require a great deal of interaction between supervisor and subordinates. In general, the more interaction that is required, the narrower the span should be. Similarly, if there is a fairly comprehensive set of standard procedures, a relatively wide span is possible. If only a few standard procedures exist, however, the supervisor usually has to play a larger role in overseeing day-to-day activities and may find a narrower span more efficient.

T A B L E 10 . 1 Factors Influencing the Span of Management

1. Competence of supervisor and subordinates (the greater the competence, the wider the potential span)

2. Physical dispersion of subordinates (the greater the dispersion, the narrower the potential span)

3. Extent of nonsupervisory work in manager's job (the more nonsupervisory work, the narrower the potential span)

4. Degree of required interaction (the more required interaction, the narrower the potential span)

5. Extent of standardized procedures (the more procedures, the wider the potential span)

6. Similarity of tasks being supervised (the more similar the tasks, the wider the potential span)

7. Frequency of new problems (the higher the frequency, the narrower the potential span)

8. Preferences of supervisors and subordinates

Although researchers have found advantages to the flat organization (less expensive, fewer communication problems than a tall organization, for example), a number of factors may favour an organization's developing a tall organization.

Task similarity is also important. If most of the jobs being supervised are similar, a supervisor can handle a wider span. When each employee is performing a different task, more of the supervisor's time is spent on individual supervision. Likewise, if new problems that require supervisory assistance arise frequently, a narrower span may be called for. If new problems are relatively rare, though, a wider span can be established. Finally, the preferences of both supervisor and subordinates may affect the optimal span. Some managers prefer to spend less time actively supervising their employees, and many employees prefer to be more self-directed in their jobs. A wider span may be possible in these situations.[25]

In some organizational settings, other factors may influence the optimal span of management. The relative importance of each factor also varies in different settings. It is unlikely that all eight factors will suggest the same span; some may suggest a wider span, and others may indicate a need for a narrow span. Hence, managers must assess the relative weight of each factor or set of factors when deciding what the optimal span of management is for their unique situation.

DISTRIBUTING AUTHORITY

● **authority**
Power that has been legitimized by the organization

Another important building block in structuring organizations is the determination of how authority is to be distributed among positions. **Authority** is power that has been legitimized by the organization.[26] Distributing authority is another normal outgrowth of increasing organizational size. For example, when an owner-manager hires a sales representative to market his products, he needs to give the new employee appropriate authority to make decisions about delivery dates, discounts, and so forth. If every decision requires the approval of the owner-manager, he is no better off than he was before he hired the sales representative. The power given to the sales representative to make certain kinds of decisions, then, represents the establishment of a pattern of authority—the sales representative can make some decisions alone and others in consultation with co-workers; the sales representative must defer some decisions to the boss. Two specific issues that managers must address when distributing authority are delegation and decentralization.[27]

The Delegation Process

● **delegation**
The process by which a manager assigns a portion of his or her total work load to others

Delegation is the establishment of a pattern of authority between a superior and one or more subordinates. Specifically, **delegation** is the process by which managers assign a portion of their total workload to others.[28]

Reasons for Delegation   The primary reason for delegation is to enable the manager to get more work done. Subordinates help ease the manager's burden by doing major portions of the organization's work. In some instances, a subordinate may have more expertise in addressing a particular problem than the manager does. For example, the subordinate may have had special training in developing information systems or may be more familiar with a particular product line or geographic area. Delegation also helps develop subordinates. By participating in decision making and problem solving, subordinates learn about overall operations and improve their managerial skills.

Parts of the Delegation Process   In theory, as shown in Figure 10.4, the delegation process involves three steps. First, the manager assigns responsibility, or gives the subordinate a job to do. The assignment of responsibility might range from telling a subordinate to prepare a report to placing the person in charge of a task force. Along with the assignment, the individual is also given the authority to do the job. The manager may give the subordinate the power to requisition needed information from confidential files or to direct a group of other workers. Finally, the manager establishes the subordinate's accountability—that is, the subordinate accepts an obligation to carry out the task assigned by the manager.

These three steps do not occur mechanically, however. Indeed, when a manager and a subordinate have developed a good working relationship, the major parts of the process may be implied rather than stated. The manager may simply mention that a particular job must be done. A perceptive subordinate may realize that the manager is actually assigning the job to her. From past experience with the boss, she may also know, without being told, that she has the necessary authority to do the job and that she is accountable to the boss for finishing the job as "agreed."

Problems in Delegation   Unfortunately, problems often arise in the delegation process. For example, a manager may be reluctant to delegate. Some managers are so disorganized that they are unable to plan work in advance and, as a result, cannot delegate appropriately. Similarly, some managers may worry that subordinates will do too well and pose a threat to their own advancement. And finally, managers may not trust the subordinate to do the job well. Similarly, some subordinates are reluctant to accept delegation. They may be afraid that failure will result in a reprimand. They may also perceive that there are no rewards for accepting additional responsibility. Or they may simply prefer to avoid risk and, therefore, want their boss to take all responsibility.

There are no quick fixes for these problems. The basic issue is communication. Subordinates must understand their own responsibility, authority, and accountability, and the manager must come to recognize the value of effective delegation. With the passage of time, subordinates should develop to the point where they can make substantial contributions to the organization. At the same time, managers should recognize that a subordinate's satisfactory performance is not a threat to their own career but an accomplishment by both the subordinate who did the job and the manager who trained the subordinate and was astute enough to entrust the subordinate with the project. Ultimate responsibility for the outcome, however, continues to reside with the manager.

F I G U R E 10.4   Steps in the Delegation Process

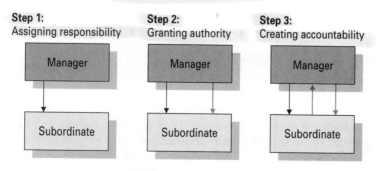

Step 1:
Assigning responsibility

Step 2:
Granting authority

Step 3:
Creating accountability

A manager must learn to successfully delegate responsibility to subordinates. Improving communication skills can help managers do this. A manager must not be reluctant to delegate, nor must he or she fear that the subordinate will do the job so well that the manager's advancement is threatened.

Decentralization and Centralization

● **decentralization**
The process of systematically delegating power and authority throughout the organization to middle and lower-level managers

Just as authority can be delegated from one individual to another, organizations also develop patterns of authority across a wide variety of positions and departments. **Decentralization** is the process of systematically delegating power and authority throughout the organization to middle and lower-level managers. It is important to remember that decentralization is actually one end of a continuum anchored at the other end by **centralization**, the process of systematically retaining power and authority in the hands of higher-level managers. Hence, a decentralized organization is one in which decision-making power and authority are delegated as far down the chain of command as possible. Conversely, in a centralized organization, decision-making power and authority are retained at the higher levels of management. No organization is ever completely decentralized or completely centralized: some firms position themselves toward one end of the continuum, and some lean the other way.[29] The *Managing in a Changing World* box discusses how Pepsi has recently adopted a more decentralized approach.

● **centralization**
The process of systematically retaining power and authority in the hands of higher-level managers

What factors determine an organization's position on the decentralization–centralization continuum? One common determinant is the organization's external environment. Usually, the greater the complexity and uncertainty of the environment, the greater is the tendency to decentralize. Another crucial factor is the history of the organization. Firms have a tendency to do what they have done in the past, so there is likely to be some relationship between what an organization did in its early history and what it chooses to do today in terms of centralization or decentralization. The nature of the decisions being made is also considered. The costlier and riskier the decision, the more pressure there is to centralize. Organizations also consider the abilities of lower-level managers. If lower-level managers do not have the ability to make high-quality decisions, there is likely to be a high level of centralization. If lower-level managers are well qualified, top management can take advantage of their talents by decentralizing; in fact, if top management doesn't, talented lower-level managers may leave the organization.[30]

A manager has no clear-cut guidelines to determine whether to centralize or decentralize. Many successful organizations such as General Electric are quite decentralized. Equally successful firms such as McDonald's have remained centralized. IBM has recently undergone a transformation from using a highly centralized approach to a much more decentralized approach to managing its operations. A great deal of decision-making authority was passed from the hands of a select group of top executives down to six product and marketing groups. The reason for the move was to speed the company's ability to make decisions, introduce new products, and respond to customers.[31] For years, most Japanese firms have been highly centralized. Recently, though, many leading Japanese firms have moved toward decentralization.[32]

COORDINATING ACTIVITIES

● **coordination**
The process of linking the activities of the various departments of the organization

A fifth major element of organizing is coordination. As we discuss earlier, job specialization and departmentalization involve breaking jobs down into small units and then combining those jobs into departments. Once this has been accomplished, the activities of the departments must be linked—systems must be put into place to keep the activities of each department focused on the attainment of organizational goals. This is accomplished by **coordination**—the process of linking the activities of the various departments of the organization.

PepsiCo Restructures

PepsiCo began restructuring—that is, changing its corporate organizational structure—in the early 1990s. It moved away from a structure that was based on highly decentralized, regional divisions to one with national divisions with limited local adaptation. Frito-Lay, for instance, had to cope with huge volumes in all of its products, coupling high levels of service to its distribution outlets with that volume. This meant trying simultaneously to be responsive to regional markets and maintain national brand standards of quality and service. To accomplish this, Frito-Lay developed an information system that integrated planning, operations, and executive decision making. Later PepsiCo incorporated that information system into the Restaurant Data Center linking PepsiCo Food Systems, Taco Bell Corp., and KFC. Subsequently, on January 23, 1997, PepsiCo announced that it intended to spin off its restaurant businesses.

Bringing together major brands at a national level would better enable PepsiCo to conduct marketing research, facilitate ethnic marketing, and coordinate media and entertainment activities. PepsiCo still needed to retain a local franchising system to ensure responsiveness at that level, but, at the same time, it needed a much more coordinated national organization to ensure the highest quality and service. The Restaurant Data Center was intended to be a client-server computer system designed to help PepsiCo accomplish those organizational goals.

PepsiCo flipped its pyramidal organization chart upside down to try to suggest the nature of these changes in structure. Calling this putting the "right side" up, PepsiCo suggested by the change that customers and workers were the more important parts of the organization in terms of achieving effectiveness and efficiency. Interestingly, other companies also redrew organization charts to try to suggest the nature of changes taking place. Eastman Kodak Company's became known as the pizza chart because the new chart looked like a pizza with pepperoni scattered on it.

Nevertheless, Pepsi was still working to cut costs and develop a strategy to compete in channels that are not necessarily all that well understood. PepsiCo's performance was strong but competition constantly kept it changing. PepsiCo had learned that financial tactics in the face of fundamental economic changes were not sufficient. Thus PepsiCo was not only changing its organizational structure, but it was also changing its organizational culture. That process was expected to take a long time, but PepsiCo was strong enough to be able to do it.

References: John McManus, "The Rightside Up Company Turns Itself Inside Out," *Brandweek*, July 18, 1994, p. 15; Nell Margolis, "Pepsico Firms Choose 'Insourcing,'" *Computerworld*, March 29, 1993, p. 1; "Congratulations. You're Moving to a New Pepperoni," *Business Week*, December 20, 1993, pp. 80–81; "We Have a Big Pond to Play In," *Forbes*, September 13, 1993, pp. 216–224; Patricia Winters, "Pepsi Refocuses with New Structure," *Advertising Age*, September 28, 1992, pp. 3, 47; and "PepsiCo Announces Plan to Spin Off Restaurants," press release, PepsiCo, January 23, 1997

The Need for Coordination

The primary reason for coordination is that departments and work groups are interdependent—they depend on each other for information and resources to perform their respective activities. The greater the interdependence between departments, the more coordination the organization requires if departments are to be able to perform effectively. There are three major forms of interdependence: pooled, sequential, and reciprocal.[33]

Pooled interdependence represents the lowest level of interdependence. Units with pooled interdependence operate with little interaction—the output of the units is pooled at the organizational level. The Gap clothing stores operate with pooled interdependence. Each store is considered a department by the parent corporation. Each has its own operating budget, staff, and so forth. The profits or losses from each store are "added together" at the organizational level. The stores are interdependent to the extent that the final success or failure of one store affects the others, but they do not generally interact on a day-to-day basis.

● **pooled independence**
When units operate with little interaction, their output is simply pooled

● **sequential**
interdependence
When the output of one unit
becomes the input of another
in sequential fashion

In **sequential interdependence**, the output of one unit becomes the input for another in a sequential fashion. This creates a moderate level of interdependence. At Nissan, for example, one plant assembles engines and then ships them to a final assembly site at another plant where the cars are completed. The plants are interdependent in that the final assembly plant must have the engines from engine assembly before it can perform its primary function of producing finished automobiles. But the level of interdependence is generally one-way—the engine plant is not necessarily dependent on the final assembly plant.

● **reciprocal**
interdependence
When activities flow both
ways between units

Reciprocal interdependence exists when activities flow both ways between units. This form is clearly the most complex. Within a Canadian Pacific Hotel, for example, the reservations department, front-desk check-in, and housekeeping are all reciprocally interdependent. Reservations has to provide front-desk employees with information about how many guests to expect each day, and housekeeping needs to know which rooms require priority cleaning. If any of the three units does not do its job properly, the others will all be affected.

Structural Coordination Techniques

Because of the obvious coordination requirements that characterize most organizations, many techniques for achieving coordination have been developed. Some of the most useful devices for maintaining coordination among interdependent units are the managerial hierarchy, rules and procedures, liaison roles, task forces, and integrating departments.[34]

The Managerial Hierarchy   Organizations that use the hierarchy to achieve coordination place one manager in charge of interdependent departments or units. In a distribution centre, major activities include receiving and unloading bulk shipments from railroad cars and loading other shipments onto trucks for distribution to retail outlets. The two groups (receiving and shipping) are interdependent in that they share the loading docks and some equipment. To ensure coordination and minimize conflict, one manager is usually in charge of the whole operation.

Rules and Procedures   Routine coordination activities can be handled via rules and standard procedures. In a distribution centre, an outgoing truck shipment has priority over an incoming rail shipment. Thus when trucks are to be loaded, the shipping unit has access to all the auxiliary forklifts. This priority is specifically stated in a rule. But, as useful as rules and procedures often are in routine situations, they are not particularly effective when coordination problems are complex or unusual.

Liaison Roles   We introduced the liaison role of management in Chapter 1. As a device for coordination, a manager in a liaison role coordinates interdependent units by acting as a common point of contact. This individual may not have any formal authority over the groups but instead simply facilitates the flow of information between units. Two engineering groups working on component systems for a large project might interact through a liaison. The liaison maintains familiarity with each group as well as with the overall project. She can answer questions and otherwise serve to integrate the activities of all the groups.

Task Forces   A task force may be created when the need for coordination is acute. When interdependence is complex and several units are involved, a single

Nike, the leader in professional athletic shoes, is an example of a flat organization. Many other large corporations are moving toward this structure (see Figure 10.3 on p. 280).

liaison person may not be sufficient. Instead, a task force might be assembled by drawing one representative from each group. The coordination function is thus spread across several individuals, each of whom has special information about one of the groups involved. When the project is completed, task force members return to their original positions. For example, a university overhauling its degree requirements might establish a task force made up of representatives from each department affected by the change. Each person retains her or his regular departmental affiliation and duties but also serves on the special task force. After the new requirements are agreed on, the task force is dissolved.

Integrating Departments Integrating departments are occasionally used for coordination. They are similar to task forces but are more permanent. An integrating department generally has some permanent members as well as members who are assigned temporarily from units that are in need of coordination. One study found that successful firms in the plastics industry, which is characterized by complex environments, used integrating departments to maintain internal integration and coordination.[35] An integrating department usually has more authority than a task force and may even be given some budgetary control by the organization.

In general, the greater the degree of interdependence, the more attention the organization must devote to coordination. When interdependence is pooled or simple sequential, the managerial hierarchy or rules and procedures are often sufficient. When more complex forms of sequential or simpler forms of reciprocal interdependence exist, liaisons or task forces may be more useful. When reciprocal interdependence is complex, task forces or integrating departments are needed. Of course, the manager must also rely on her or his own experience and insights when choosing coordination techniques for the organization.

DIFFERENTIATING BETWEEN POSITIONS

● **line position**
A position in the direct chain of command that is responsible for the achievement of an organization's goals

The last building block of organization structure is differentiating between line and staff positions in the organization. A **line position** is a position in the direct chain of command that is responsible for the achievement of an organization's goals. A **staff position** is intended to provide expertise, advice, and support for line positions.

Differences Between Line and Staff

● **staff position**
A position intended to provide expertise, advice, and support for line positions

The most obvious difference between line and staff is purpose—line managers work directly toward organizational goals, whereas staff managers advise and assist. But other distinctions exist as well. One important difference is authority. Line authority is generally thought of as the formal or legitimate authority created by the organizational hierarchy. Staff authority is less concrete and may take a variety of forms. One form is the authority to advise. In this instance, the line manager can choose whether to seek or to avoid input from the staff; even when advice is sought, the manager might still choose to ignore it.

Another form of staff authority is called compulsory advice. In this case, the line manager must listen to the advice but can choose to heed it or ignore it. For example, the Pope is expected to listen to the advice of the Sacred College, but he may follow his own beliefs when making decisions. Perhaps the most important form of staff authority is called functional authority—formal or legitimate authority over activities related to the staff member's specialty. For example, a human resource staff manager may have functional authority when there is a question of discrimination in hiring. Conferring functional authority is probably the most effective way to use staff positions because the organization is able to take advantage of specialized expertise while also maintaining a chain of command.

Administrative Intensity

● **administrative intensity**
The degree to which managerial positions are concentrated in staff positions

Organizations sometimes attempt to balance their emphasis on line versus staff positions in terms of administrative intensity. **Administrative intensity** is the degree to which managerial positions are concentrated in staff positions. An organization with a high administrative intensity is one with many staff positions relative to the number of line positions; low administrative intensity reflects relatively more line positions. Although staff positions are important in many different areas, they tend to proliferate unnecessarily. Organizations usually like to spend most of their human resource dollars on line managers because by definition they contribute to the organization's basic goals. A surplus of staff positions represents a drain on an organization's cash and an inefficient use of resources.

Many organizations have taken steps over the past few years to reduce their administrative intensity by eliminating staff positions. In the Bell Canada layoffs announced in July 1997, management accounted for two-thirds of the proposed cuts and administrative support for one-third. IBM has cut its corporate staff workforce from 7,000 to 2,300. Burlington Northern generates almost $7 billion (U.S.) in annual sales and manages a workforce of 43,000 with a corporate staff of only seventy-seven managers![36]

SUMMARY OF KEY POINTS

Organizations are made up of a series of elements. The most common of these involve designing jobs, grouping jobs, establishing reporting relationships, distributing authority, coordinating activities, and differentiating between positions.

Job design is the determination of an individual's work-related responsibilities. The most common form is job specialization. Because of various drawbacks to job specialization, managers have experimented with job rotation, job enlargement, job enrichment, the job characteristics approach, and work teams as alternatives.

After jobs are designed, they are grouped into departments. The most common bases for departmentalization are function, product, customer, and location. Each has its own unique advantages and disadvantages. Large organizations employ multiple bases of departmentalization at different levels.

Establishing reporting relationships starts with clarifying the chain of command. The span of management partially dictates whether the organization is relatively tall or flat. In recent years, there has been a trend toward flatter organizations. Several situational factors influence the ideal span.

Distributing authority starts with delegation. Delegation is the process by which the manager assigns a portion of his or her total workload to others. Systematic delegation throughout the organization is decentralization. Centralization involves keeping power and authority at the top of the organization. Several factors influence the appropriate degree of decentralization.

Coordination is the process of linking the activities of the various departments of the organization. Pooled, sequential, or reciprocal interdependence among departments is a primary reason for coordination. Managers can draw on several techniques to help achieve coordination.

A line position is a position in the direct chain of command that is responsible for the achievement of an organization's goals. In contrast, a staff position provides expertise, advice, and support for line positions. Administrative intensity is the degree to which managerial positions are concentrated in staff positions.

DISCUSSION QUESTIONS

Questions for Review

1. What is job specialization? What are the advantages and disadvantages of specialization?
2. What is meant by departmentalization? Why and how is departmentalization carried out?
3. In what general ways can organizations be shaped? What implications does each of these ways have with regard to the distribution of authority within the organization?

4. How are positions differentiated in organizations? What are the advantages and disadvantages of such differentiation?

Questions for Analysis

5. Seeing how specialization can be utilized in manufacturing organizations is easy. How can it be used by other types of organizations such as hospitals, churches, schools, and restaurants? Should those organizations use specialization? Why or why not?
6. Try to develop a different way to departmentalize your college or university, a local fast-food restaurant, a manufacturing firm, or some other organization. What might be the advantages of your form of organization?
7. Which type of position (line, staff, administrative) is most important to an organization? Why? Could an organization function without any of them? Why or why not?

Questions for Application

8. Go to the library and locate organization charts for ten different organizations. Look for similarities and differences among them and try to account for what you find.
9. Contact two very different local organizations (retailing firm, manufacturing firm, church, civic club, etc.) and interview top managers to develop organization charts for each organization. How do you account for the similarities and differences between them?
10. How many people does the head of your academic department supervise? The dean of your faculty? The president of your university or college? Why do different spans of management exist among these officials? How might you find out if the spans are appropriate in size?

BUILDING EFFECTIVE DIAGNOSTIC SKILLS

Exercise Overview

Diagnostic skills enable a manager to visualize the most appropriate response to a situation. This exercise will help you develop your diagnostic skills as they relate to issues of centralization and decentralization in an organization.

Exercise Background

Managers must often change the degree of centralization or decentralization in their organization. Begin this exercise by reflecting on two very different scenarios. In scenario A, assume that you are the top manager in a large organization. The organization has a long and well-known history of being very centralized. For valid reasons beyond the scope of this exercise, assume that you have decided to make the firm much more decentralized. For scenario B, assume the exact opposite situation. That is, you are the top manager of a firm that has always used decentralization but has now decided to become much more centralized.

Exercise Task

With the preceding background information as context, do the following:

1. Make a list of the major barriers you see to implementing decentralization in scenario A.

2. Make a list of the major barriers you see to implementing centralization in scenario B.

3. Which scenario do you think would be easiest to actually implement? That is, is it likely to be easier to move from centralization to decentralization or from decentralization to centralization? Why?

4. Given a choice of starting your own career in a firm that is either highly centralized or highly decentralized, which do you think you would prefer? Why?

Minnesota Mining and Manufacturing, better known as 3M, is among the most innovative and profitable companies in the world today. Among its best-known products are Post-It Notes, Scotch Magic tape, and Scotchguard Fabric Protection. But beyond these household phrases, 3M makes more than 60,000 individual products. The firm also has the ambitious goal of deriving 30 percent of its sales each year from products that are less than four years old.

One key to 3M's amazing success is its unusual structure. If asked, 3M executives can produce an organization chart that shows a neat and tidy arrangement for positions, departments, and reporting relationships that looks as traditional as any hierarchy in existence. Underneath the president, for example, are three major divisions: one for consumer products, one for industrial products, and one for the firm's international business activities. Within each division is the standard array of corporate functions, such as finance and marketing.

But 3M executives are also quick to add that although their firm can be drawn like a traditional and hierarchical pyramid, that's far from how things actually work at the company. Indeed, managers describe the firm's "real" structure as looking something like an upside-down table with hundreds of legs. The table top itself, again residing on the bottom, consists of thirty-three technology platforms—a technology from which the firm can develop multiple products for multiple markets.

The legs growing up from the platforms are actually businesses derived from one or more technologies. No one really knows how many legs—or businesses—exist at any given time, but top managers estimate the number at between five hundred and one thousand. Wrapped around the legs are three sets of overriding elements that tie together the entire company—its financial goals and disciplines, its human resource philosophies, and its corporate values.

Another interesting part of 3M's success is what it calls "bootleg time." Each manager and scientist at the company is expected to spend approximately 15 percent of her or his time just tinkering with products—trying to figure out new uses for them, ways

of making them faster, or ways of making them cheaper, for example.

A good example of how this approach has helped the company is the now legendary story of the invention of Post-It Notes. It seems that one research scientist was working on a new glue but couldn't get it to bond properly. He vented his frustrations to his colleagues and then put the project aside. A few weeks later another scientist was trying to figure out how he could attach written notes to the pages of his church hymnal without permanently damaging the pages. He borrowed some of the glue from the first scientist, brushed it on the back of his notes, and found that he could later remove them without damaging either the notes or his hymnal. And today, Post-It products account for almost $1 billion (U.S.) in annual revenues for the firm.

But the structure that pulls all this off is bewildering, sometimes even to 3M itself. As already noted, for example, top managers profess to not really know how many businesses exist within the corporation at any given time. Likewise, they claim to not know how many labs the firm has. What they do know, however, is that the firm has one huge central lab where scientists can test ideas and where the accumulated knowledge of the firm is stored. Satellite labs are testing grounds, meanwhile, where scientists first develop ideas. And when scientists can't get funding from their own business, they are encouraged to shop their ideas to other 3M businesses. Confusing? No doubt. But also enormously profitable.

Questions

1. Identify the key parts of 3M's organization structure.

2. Why doesn't 3M use a more conventional structure?

3. Why don't more firms use 3M's model for organization structure?

References: Thomas A. Stewart, "3M Fights Back," *Fortune*, February 5, 1996, pp. 94–99; and *Hoover's Handbook of American Business 1998* (Austin, Tex.: Hoover's Business Press, 1998), pp. 934–935.

CHAPTER NOTES

1. Lawrence Suitees, "Bell to Cut 2200 More Jobs," *The Globe and Mail*, July 18, 1997, pp. A1, A6; Philip Demont, "Bell Plans Internal Overhaul," *Financial Post*, May 28, 1996, p. 8; Peter Hadekel, "Turning the Corner on Cutbacks," *The Gazette* (Montreal), October 23, 1995, pp. C1, C4; John Lorinc, "Guerilla in Gray Flannel," *Canadian Business*, October 1994, pp. 95–109; and "Ranking by Profits," *Report on Business Magazine*, July 1998, p. 100.

2. "Rethinking Work," *Business Week*, October 17, 1994, pp. 74–86.

3. Ricky W. Griffin and Gary McMahan "Motivation Through Job Design," in Jerald Greenberg (Ed.) *Organizational Behavior—The State of the Science* (Hillsdale, N.J.: Lawrence Erlbaum Associates), pp. 23–44.

4. Adam Smith, *Wealth of Nations* (New York: Modern Library, 1937; originally published in 1776).

5. Ricky W. Griffin, *Task Design* (Glenview, Ill.: Scott, Foresman, 1982).

6. Anne S. Miner, "Idiosyncratic Jobs in Formal Organizations," *Administrative Science Quarterly*, September 1987, pp. 327–351.

7. M.D. Kilbridge, "Reduced Costs Through Job Enlargement: A Case," *Journal of Business*, Vol. 33, 1960, pp. 357–362.

8. Griffin and McMahan, "Motivation Through Job Design."

9. Kilbridge, "Reduced Costs Through Job Enrichment."

10. Frederick Herzberg, *Work and the Nature of Man* (Cleveland: World Press, 1966).

11. Robert Ford, "Job Enrichment Lessons from AT&T," *Harvard Business Review*, January–February 1973, pp. 96–106.

12. J. Richard Hackman and Greg R. Oldham, *Work Redesign* (Reading, Mass.: Addison-Wesley, 1980).

13. For recent analyses of job design issues, see Ricky W. Griffin, "A Long-Term Investigation of the Effects of Work Redesign on Employee Perceptions, Attitudes, and Behaviors," *Academy of Management Journal*, June 1991, pp. 425–435; and Michael A. Campion, "Interdisciplinary Approaches to Job Design: A Constructive Replication with Extensions," *Journal of Applied Psychology*, August 1988, pp. 467–481.

14. "Some Plants Tear Out Long Assembly Lines, Switch to Craft Work," *The Wall Street Journal*, October 24, 1994, pp. A1, A4.

15. Richard L. Daft, *Organization Theory and Design*, 5th ed. (St. Paul, Minn.: West, 1995).

16. Daniel Twomey, Frederick C. Scherr, and Walter S. Hunt, "Configuration of a Functional Department: A Study of Contextual and Structural Variables," *Journal of Organizational Behavior*, Vol. 9, 1988, pp. 61–75.

17. David Ketchen, James Thomas, and Charles Snow, "Organizational Configurations and Performance: A Comparison of Theoretical Approaches," *Academy of Management Journal*, 1993, Vol. 36, No. 6, pp. 1278–1313.

18. A.V. Graicunas, "Relationships in Organizations," *Bulletin of the International Management Institute*, March 7, 1933, pp. 39–42.

19. Ralph C. Davis, *Fundamentals of Top Management* (New York: Harper & Row, 1951); Lyndall F. Urwick, *Scientific Principles and Organization* (New York: American Management Association, 1938), p. 8; and Ian Hamilton, *The Soul and Body of an Army* (London: Edward Arnold, 1921), pp. 229–230.

20. David D. Van Fleet and Arthur G. Bedeian, "A History of the Span of Management," *Academy of Management Review*, 1977, pp. 356–372.

21. James C. Worthy, "Factors Influencing Employee Morale," *Harvard Business Review*, January 1950, pp. 61–73.

22. Dan R. Dalton, William D. Todor, Michael J. Spendolini, Gordon J. Fielding, and Lyman W. Porter, "Organization Structure and Performance: A Critical Review," *Academy of Management Review*, January 1980, pp. 49–64.

23. Brian Dumaine, "The Bureaucracy Busters," *Fortune*, June 17, 1991, pp. 36–50.

24. David Van Fleet, "Span of Management Research and Issues," *Academy of Management Journal*, September 1983, pp. 546–552.

25. See Edward E. Lawler III, "Substitutes for Hierarchy," *Organizational Dynamics*, Summer 1988, pp. 4–15, for a recent analysis of these and other factors that can influence the appropriate span of management.

26. See Daft, *Organization Theory and Design*.

27. William Kahn and Kathy Kram, "Authority at Work: Internal Models and Their Organizational Consequences," *Academy of Management Review*, 1994, Vol. 19, No. 1, pp. 17–50.

28. Carrie R. Leana, "Predictors and Consequences of Delegation," *Academy of Management Journal*, December 1986, pp. 754–774.

29. Daft, *Organization Theory and Design*. See also J. Meyer, W.R. Scott, and D. Strang, "Centralization, Fragmentation, and School District Complexity," *Administrative Science Quarterly*, June 1987, pp. 186–201.

30. "Toppling the Pyramids," *Canadian Business*, May 1993, pp. 61–65.

31. "IBM Unveils a Sweeping Restructuring in Bid to Decentralize Decision-Making," *The Wall Street Journal*, January 29, 1988, p. 3.

32. "Maverick Managers," *The Wall Street Journal*, November 14, 1988, p. R14.

33. James Thompson, *Organizations in Action* (New York: McGraw-Hill, 1967). For a recent discussion, see Bart Victor and Richard S. Blackburn, "Interdependence: An Alternative Conceptualization," *Academy of Management Review*, July 1987, pp. 486–498.

34. Jay R. Galbraith, *Designing Complex Organizations* (Reading, Mass.: Addison-Wesley, 1973); and Jay R. Galbraith, *Organizational Design* (Reading, Mass.: Addison-Wesley, 1977).

35. Paul R. Lawrence and Jay W. Lorsch, "Differentiation and Integration in Complex Organizations," *Administrative Science Quarterly*, March 1967, pp. 1–47.

36. "Vaunted IBM Culture Yields to New Values: Openness, Efficiency," *The Wall Street Journal*, Nov. 11, 1988, pp. A1, A4; Thomas Moore, "Goodbye, Corporate Staff," *Fortune*, December 21, 1987, pp. 65–76; and "CBS Frantically Woos Hollywood to Help It Win Back Viewers," *The Wall Street Journal*, Febuary 9, 1989, pp. A1, A12.

Managing Organization Design

OBJECTIVES

After studying this chapter, you should be able to:

- *Describe the basic nature of organization design.*

- *Identify and explain the two basic universal perspectives on organization design.*

- *Identify and explain several situational influences on organization design.*

- *Discuss how an organization's strategy and its design are interrelated.*

- *Describe the basic forms of organization design that characterize many organizations.*

- *Describe emerging issues in organization design.*

OUTLINE

The Nature of Organization Design
Universal Perspectives on Organization
  Design
    Bureaucratic Model
    Behavioural Model
Situational Influences on Organization Design
    Core Technology
    Environment
    Organizational Size
    Organizational Life Cycle
Strategy and Organization Design
    Corporate-Level Strategy
    Business-Level Strategy
    Organizational Functions
Basic Forms of Organization Design
    Functional (U-Form) Design
    Conglomerate (H-Form) Design
    Divisional (M-Form) Design
    Matrix Design
    Hybrid Designs
Emerging Issues in Organization Design
    The Team Organization
    The Virtual Organization
    The Learning Organization

Retail Management students receive a tour of a brand new Hudson's Bay Company Outfitters store.

The Hudson's Bay Company, established in 1670, is Canada's oldest corporation and its largest department store retailer. Hudson's Bay has two major operating divisions: the Bay and Zellers, which together account for approximately 40 percent of Canadian department store sales and almost 8 percent of all retail sales excluding food and automobiles.

With 101 stores across the country, the Bay claims to be Canada's fashion department store. Stores are located in urban and suburban sites. The company is structured such that merchandise selection, procurement, and sales promotion are centralized and much of its service functions are integrated on a corporate basis. In 1997, the Bay reported revenues of approximately $2.5 billion.

Zellers is a chain of discount department stores that targets the budget-minded customer. It is owned by Hudson's Bay Company and, with its 350 stores, is Canada's largest department store. Its 1997 revenues of approximately $3.8 billion represented almost 25 percent of all department store sales and 45 percent of the discount store market in Canada. At Zellers, merchandising and sales promotion are centralized.

> **"In a clear example of how organizational structure can affect a company's frontline operations, Hudson's Bay has admitted that the Bay and Zellers are two basically different businesses with different foci."**

The huge revenues generated by the Hudson's Bay Company did not translate into profits. Its 1996 profit of $36.1 million placed it 157th on the list of profitable Canadian corporations. In 1997, the company lost $90 million and continued to struggle in 1998. The company turned to cost cutting to boost its profits, with restructuring as part of the exercise. In the summer of 1996, Zellers headquarters was moved from Montreal and consolidated with the Hudson's Bay head office in Toronto. The move was expected to save $92 million over five years. Moreover, the Bay and Zellers intended to share expertise, particularly in the area of merchandise buying.

However, just one year after the consolidation of purchasing at Zellers and the Bay, the decision was reversed. In a clear example of how organizational structure can affect a company's frontline operations, Hudson's Bay has admitted that the Bay and Zellers are two basically different businesses with different foci: the Bay is a traditional department store like Sears while Zellers is a discount department store like Wal-Mart. Thus, while the consolidation of accounting and other operations should lead to improved efficiency, the consolidation of purchasing at the Bay and Zellers has been counterproductive.[1] ●

The Hudson's Bay Company's managers successfully created a large, national retail chain. The retailer was enormously successful for years, but it has recently stumbled and is now trying to regain its momentum. One of the major ingredients in managing any business is the creation of a structure to link the various elements that make up the organization. The Hudson's Bay's managers have chosen a divisional approach. This divisional design has both helped and hurt the organization in its quest for effectiveness. The divisional design, moreover, is but one of several different designs they could have chosen to structure the company.

In Chapter 10, we identified the basic elements that go into creating an organization. In this chapter, we explore how those elements can be combined to create an overall design for the organization. We first discuss the nature of organization design. We then describe early approaches aimed at identifying universal models of organization design. Situational factors, such as technology, environment, size, and life cycle, are then introduced. Next we discuss the relationship between an organization's strategy and its structure. Basic forms of organization design are described next. We conclude by presenting three related issues in organization design.

THE NATURE OF ORGANIZATION DESIGN

What is organization design? In Chapter 10, we noted that job specialization and span of management are among the common elements of organization structure. We also described how the appropriate degree of specialization can vary, as can the appropriate span of management. Not really addressed, however, were questions of how specialization and span might be related to one another. For example, should a high level of specialization be matched with a certain span? And will different combinations of each work best with different bases of departmentalization? These and related issues are associated with questions of organization design.[2]

● **organization design**
The overall set of structural elements and the relationships among those elements used to manage the total organization

Organization design is the overall set of structural elements and the relationships among those elements used to manage the total organization. Thus organization design is a means to implement strategies and plans to achieve organizational goals. As we discuss organization design, keep in mind two important points. First, organizations are not designed and then left intact. Most organizations change almost continuously as a result of factors such as situations and people. (The processes of organization change are discussed in Chapter 12.) Second, organization design for larger organizations is complex and has so many nuances and variations that descriptions of them must be simplified to be described in basic terms.

UNIVERSAL PERSPECTIVES ON ORGANIZATION DESIGN

In Chapter 2, we made the distinction between contingency and universal approaches to solving management problems. Recall, for example, that universal perspectives try to identify the "one best way" to manage organizations, and contingency perspectives suggest that appropriate managerial behaviour in a given situation depends on, or is contingent on, unique elements in that situation. The foundation of contemporary thinking about organization design can be traced back to two early universal perspectives: the bureaucratic model and the behavioural model.

Bureaucratic Model

We also noted in Chapter 2 that Max Weber, an influential German sociologist, was a pioneer of classical organization theory. At the core of Weber's writings was the bureaucratic model of organizations.[3] The Weberian perspective suggests that a **bureaucracy** is a model of organization design based on a legitimate and formal system of authority. Many people associate bureaucracy with "red tape," rigidity, and passing the buck. For example, how many times have you heard people refer disparagingly to "government bureaucracy"? And many managers believe that bureaucracy in the Japanese government is a major impediment to Canadian and American firms' ability to do business there.

● **bureaucracy**
A universal model of organization design based on a legitimate and formal system of authority

Weber viewed the bureaucratic form of organization as logical, rational, and efficient. He offered the model as a framework to which all organizations should aspire; the "one best way" of doing things. According to Weber, the ideal bureaucracy exhibits five basic characteristics:

1. The organization should adopt a distinct division of labour, and each position should be filled by an expert.

2. The organization should develop a consistent set of rules to ensure that task performance is uniform.

3. The organization should establish a hierarchy of positions or offices that creates a chain of command from the top of the organization to the bottom.

Some bureaucracies, such as Canada Post, are trying to portray themselves as less impersonal. Canada Post is becoming more service-oriented as it fights competition from Federal Express and UPS.

4. Managers should conduct business in an impersonal way and maintain an appropriate social distance between themselves and their subordinates.

5. Employment and advancement should be based on technical expertise, and employees should be protected from arbitrary dismissal.

Perhaps the best examples of bureaucracies today are government agencies and universities. Consider, for example, the steps you must go through and the forms you must fill out to apply for university admission, request housing, register each semester, change majors, submit a degree plan, substitute a course, and file for graduation. The reason these procedures are necessary is that universities deal with large numbers of people who must be treated equally and fairly. Hence rules, regulations, and standard operating procedures are needed. Some bureaucracies, such as Canada Post, are trying to portray themselves as less mechanistic and impersonal. The strategy of Canada Post, for example, is to become more service-oriented as a way to fight competitors like Federal Express and United Parcel Service.

A primary strength of the bureaucratic model is that several of its elements (such as reliance on rules and employment based on expertise) do, in fact, often improve efficiency. Bureaucracies also help prevent favouritism (because everyone must follow the rules) and make procedures and practices very clear to everyone. Unfortunately, however, this approach also has several disadvantages. One major disadvantage is that the bureaucratic model results in inflexibility and rigidity. Once rules are created and put into place, making exceptions or changing them is often difficult. In addition, the bureaucracy often results in the neglect of human and social processes within the organization.[4] The *Environment of Management* box details how and why Thermos dropped its bureaucratic systems to become more flexible.

Behavioural Model

● **behavioural model**
A universal model of organization design that paralleled the emergence of the human relations school of management thought; the model emphasized developing work groups and interpersonal processes

Another important universal model of organization design was the **behavioural model**, which paralleled the emergence of the human relations school of management thought. Rensis Likert, a management researcher, studied several large organizations to determine what made some more effective than others.[5] He found that the organizations in his sample that used the bureaucratic model of design tended to be less effective than those that used a more behaviourally oriented model consistent with the emerging human relations movement—in other words, organizations that paid more attention to developing work groups and were more concerned about interpersonal processes.

● **System 1 design**
A form of organization design based on legitimate and formal authority; developed as part of the behavioural model or organization design

Likert developed a framework that characterized organizations in terms of eight important processes: leadership, motivation, communication, interactions, decision making, goal-setting, control, and performance goals. Likert believed that all organizations could be placed on a set of dimensions describing each of these eight elements. He argued that the basic bureaucratic form of organization, which he called a **System 1 design**, anchored one end of each dimension. The characteristics of the System 1 organization in Likert's framework are summarized in Table 11.1.

● **System 4 design**
A form of organization design that uses a wide array of motivational processes and promotes open and extensive interaction processes; developed as part of the behavioural model of organization design

Also summarized in this table are characteristics of Likert's other extreme form of organization design, called **System 4 design**, which was based on the behavioural model. For example, a System 4 organization uses a wide array of motivational processes, and its interaction processes are open and extensive. Other distinctions between System 1 and System 4 organizations are equally obvious. In between the System 1 and System 4 extremes lie the System 2 and

Thermos Redesigns Itself

Two innovations from the Thermos Company expected to hit the market in 1999 are a soft-sided water jug and the Ice Chest Express, a wheeled cooler that was developed with insight gained from observing people at the beach. Back in 1994, Thermos introduced its "Super Lunch'R Eco-Logic Reusable Lunch Box System." Developed from research that included student sketches of what they wanted and discussions with both parents and children, these boxes were novel. Made of high-impact plastic, they have modular spaces for a sandwich, a Thermos vacuum bottle, and fruit. These boxes were expected to stir up the lunch box market in which Thermos is already the leader.

Just a year earlier, Thermos had won numerous design competitions for a revolutionary new approach to the home grill market. The product—the Thermal Electric Grill—was designed to appeal to people for whom gas is not an option and/or for those concerned about the pollution generated by charcoal grills. The new grill is clean, compact, stylish, and convenient.

The Thermos Company, now owned by the Japanese manufacturer Nippon Sanso, is not an organization previously known for high levels of innovation and design creativity. Indeed, the standard outdoor grill was usually an ugly black box. Lunch boxes hadn't changed much either. What led to the sudden burst of creativity that resulted in redesigned lunch boxes and outdoor grills? A redesigned organization is the answer.

Growth at the Thermos Company had slowed considerably by 1990 when Monte Peterson took over as CEO. To reinvigorate Thermos, he redesigned the whole organization. When Peterson took over, Thermos was structured into functional areas such as marketing, manufacturing, and engineering. Three years later he had replaced those with flexible, interdisciplinary teams.

Consider how the electric grill was developed. First, a product design team was created. Engineering, marketing, manufacturing, and finance were all represented on the team. The focus was the customer—what did people who wanted to cook out need? Outsiders from Fitch, an industrial design firm, also were included. The second step was to define the market. The team interviewed, watched, and listened to potential customers. They then had to define the product. This third step is where prototypes were developed and prices established. During all of this, Peterson made sure that all groups involved were working in parallel. While some were gathering marketing information, others were working on design. This meant that manufacturing was involved throughout the process to ensure that the final product could be easily manufactured.

References: Fara Warner, "Message in a Bottle: Thermos Updates Its Image," *Brandweek*, January 31, 1994, p. 32; Brian Dumaine, "Payoff from the New Management," *Fortune*, December 13, 1993, pp. 103–110; James Braham, "Winners by Design," *Machine Design*, July 9, 1993, pp. 24–32; "1993 Industrial Design Excellence Awards— The Cleaner Patio Sizzler," *Business Week*, June 7, 1993, pp. 60–61;

System 3 organizations. Likert argued that System 4 should be adopted by all organizations. He suggested that managers should emphasize supportive relationships, establish high performance goals, and practise group decision making to achieve a System 4 organization. Many organizations attempted to adopt the System 4 design during its period of peak popularity. In 1969, General Motors converted one of its plants from a System 2 to a System 4 organization. Over a period of three years, direct and indirect labour efficiency improved, as did tool-breakage rates, scrap costs, and quality.[6]

Like the bureaucratic model, the behavioural approach has both strengths and weaknesses. Its major strength is that it emphasizes human behaviour by stressing the value of an organization's employees. Likert and his associates thus paved the way for a more humanistic approach to designing organizations. Unfortunately, the behavioural approach also argues that there is one best way to design organizations—as a System 4. As we see, however, evidence is strong that there is no

TABLE 11.1 System 1 and System 4 Organizations

System 1 Organization	System 4 Organization
1. **Leadership process** includes no perceived confidence and trust. Subordinates do not feel free to discuss job problems with their superiors, who in turn do not solicit their ideas and opinions.	1. **Leadership process** includes perceived confidence and trust between superiors and subordinates in all matters. Subordinates feel free to discuss job problems with their superiors, who in turn solicit their ideas and opinions.
2. **Motivational process** taps only physical, security, and economic motives through the use of fear and sanctions. Unfavourable attitudes toward the organization prevail among employees.	2. **Motivational process** taps a full range of motives through participatory methods. Attitudes are favourable toward the organization and its goals.
3. **Communication process** is such that information flows downward and tends to be distorted, inaccurate, and viewed with suspicion by subordinates.	3. **Communication process** is such that information flows freely throughout the organizational—upward, downward, and laterally. The information is accurate and undistorted.
4. **Interaction process** is closed and restricted; subordinates have little effect on departmental goals, methods, and activities.	4. **Interaction process** is open and extensive; both superiors and subordinates are able to affect departmental goals, methods, and activities.
5. **Decision process** occurs only at the top of the organization; it is relatively centralized.	5. **Decision process** occurs at all levels through group processes; it is relatively decentralized.
6. **Goal-setting process** is located at the top of the organization; discourages group participation.	6. **Goal-setting process** encourages group participation in setting high, realistic objectives.
7. **Control process** is centralized and emphasizes fixing of blame for mistakes.	7. **Control process** is dispersed throughout the organization and emphasizes self-control and problem solving.
8. **Performance goals** are low and passively sought by managers who make no commitment to developing the human resources of the organization.	8. **Performance goals** are high and actively sought by superiors who recognize the necessity of making a full commitment to developing, through training, the human resources of the organization.

Source: From Rensis Likert, *The Human Organization*, pp. 197–211. Copyright © 1967 by McGraw-Hill, Inc. Adapted with permission from the publisher.

The behavioural model identifies two extreme types of organization design called System 1 and System 4. The two designs vary in terms of eight fundamental processes. The System 1 design is considered to be somewhat rigid and inflexible.

● **situational view of organization design**
Based on the assumption that the optimal design for any given organization depends on a set of relevant situational factors

one best approach to organization design.[7] What works for one organization may not work for another, and what works for one organization may change as that organization's situation changes. Hence universal models like bureaucracy and System 4 have been largely supplanted by newer models that take contingency factors into account. In the next section, we identify a number of factors that help determine the best organization design for a particular situation.

SITUATIONAL INFLUENCES ON ORGANIZATION DESIGN

The **situational view of organization design** is based on the assumption that the optimal design for any given organization depends on a set of relevant situational factors.[8] That is, situational factors play a role in determining the best organization design for any particular circumstance. Four such factors—technology, environment, size, and organizational life cycle—are discussed here. Another, strategy, is described in the next section.

Core Technology

Technology is the conversion processes used to transform inputs (such as materials or information) into outputs (such as products or services). Most organizations use multiple technologies, but an organization's most important one is called its *core technology*. Although most people visualize assembly lines and machinery when they think of technology, the term can also be applied to service organizations. For example, a brokerage firm like Midland Walwyn uses technology to transform investment dollars into income in much the same way that Nova Chemicals Corporation uses natural resources to manufacture chemical products.

The link between technology and organization design was first recognized by Joan Woodward.[9] Woodward studied one hundred manufacturing firms in southern England. She collected information about such things as the history of each organization, its manufacturing processes, its forms and procedures, and its financial performance. Woodward expected to find a relationship between the size of an organization and its design, but no such relationship emerged. As a result, she began to seek other explanations for differences. Close scrutiny of the firms in her sample led her to recognize a potential relationship between technology and organization design. This follow-up analysis led Woodward to first classify the organizations according to their technology. Three basic forms of technology were identified by Woodward:

1. *Unit or small-batch technology.* The product is custom-made to customer specifications or else it is produced in small quantities. Organizations using this form of technology include a tailor shop, a printing shop, and a photography studio.

Technology is an important situational determinant of organization design. This Indonesian factory is using an assembly-line type, or large-batch, operation to manufacture Barbie Dolls for Mattel. Because of its reliance on this technology, the firm is likely to be relatively bureaucratic.

2. *Large-batch or mass-production technology. The* product is manufactured in assembly-line fashion by combining component parts into another part or finished product. Examples include automobile manufacturers like Subaru, washing-machine companies like Whirlpool Corporation, and electronics firms like Philips.

3. *Continuous-process technology.* Raw materials are transformed to a finished product by a series of machine or process transformations. The composition of the materials themselves is changed. Examples include petroleum refineries like Chevron Canada and Shell and chemical companies like Dow Chemical and Potash Corporation of Saskatchewan.

These forms of technology are listed in order of their assumed levels of complexity. That is, unit or small-batch technology is presumed to be the least complex and continuous-process technology the most complex. Woodward found that different configurations of organization design were associated with each technology.

As technology became more complex in Woodward's sample, the number of levels of management increased (that is, the organization was taller). The executive span of management also increased, as did the relative size of its staff component. The supervisory span of management, however, first increased and then decreased as technology became more complex, primarily because much of the work in continuous-process technologies is automated. Fewer workers are needed, but the skills necessary to do the job increase. These findings are consistent with the discussion of the span of management in Chapter 10—the more complex the job, the narrower the span should be.

At a more general level of analysis, Woodward found that the two extremes (unit or small-batch and continuous-process) tended to be very similar to Likert's System 4 organization, whereas the middle-range organizations (large-batch or mass-production) were much more like bureaucracies or System 1. The large-batch and mass-production organizations also had a higher level of specialization.[10] Finally, she found that organizational success was related to the extent to which organizations followed the typical pattern. For example, successful continuous-process organizations tended to be more like System 4 organizations, whereas less-successful firms with the same technology were less like System 4 organizations.

Thus technology clearly appears to play an important role in determining organization design. As future technologies become even more diverse and complex, managers will have to be even more aware of technologies' impact on the design of organizations. For example, the increased use of robotics may necessitate alterations in organization design to better accommodate different assembly methods. Likewise, increased usage of new forms of information technology will almost certainly cause organizations to redefine the nature of work and the reporting relationships among individuals.[11]

Environment

In addition to the various relationships described in Chapter 3, environmental elements and organization design are specifically linked in a number of ways. The first widely recognized analysis of environment–organization design linkages was provided by Tom Burns and G.M. Stalker.[12] Like Woodward, Burns and Stalker worked in England. Their first step was identifying two extreme forms of organizational environment: stable (one that remains relatively constant over time) and unstable (subject to uncertainty and rapid change). Next they studied the designs of organizations in each type of environment. Not surprisingly, they found that organizations in stable environments tended to have a different kind of design from organizations in unstable environments. The two kinds of design that emerged, summarized in Table 11.2, were called mechanistic and organic organization.

A **mechanistic organization**, quite similar to the bureaucratic or System 1 model, was most frequently found in stable environments. Free from uncertainty, organizations structured their activities in rather predictable ways by means of rules, specialized jobs, and centralized authority. Mechanistic organizations are also quite similar in nature to bureaucracies. Although no environment is completely stable, Zellers and Harvey's use mechanistic designs. Each Harvey's restaurant, for example, has prescribed methods for restaurant design and food-ordering processes. No deviations are allowed from these methods.

● **mechanistic organization**
A rigid and bureaucratic form of design most appropriate for stable environments

TABLE 11.2 Mechanistic and Organic Organizations

Mechanistic	Organic
1. Tasks are highly fractionated and specialized; little regard is paid to clarifying relationship between tasks and organizational objectives.	1. Tasks are more interdependent; emphasis is on relevance of tasks and organizational objectives.
2. Tasks tend to remain rigidly defined unless altered formally by top management.	2. Tasks are continually adjusted and redefined through interaction of organization members.
3. Specific roles are defined (rights, obligations, and technical methods are prescribed for each member).	3. Generalized roles are defined (members accept general responsibility for task accomplishment beyond individual role definition).
4. Structure of control, authority, and communication is hierarchical; sanctions derive from employment contract between employee and organization.	4. Structure of control, authority, and communication is a network; sanctions derive more from community of interest than from contractual relationship.
5. Information relevant to situation and operations of the organization is formally assumed to rest with chief executive.	5. Leader is not assumed to be omniscient; knowledge centres are identified throughout organization.
6. Communication is primarily vertical between superior and subordinate.	6. Communication is both vertical and horizontal, depending on where needed information resides.
7. Communications primarily take form of instructions and decisions issued by superiors, of information and requests for decisions supplied by inferiors.	7. Communications primarily take form of information and advice.
8. Insistence on loyalty to organization and obedience to superiors is present.	8. Commitment to organization's tasks and goals is more highly valued than loyalty or obedience.
9. Importance and prestige are attached to identification with organization and its members.	9. Importance and prestige are attached to affiliations and expertise in external environment.

Source: Adapted from Tom Burns and G.M. Stalker, *The Management of Innovation* (London: Tavistock, 1961), pp. 119–122. Used with permission.

organic organization
A fluid and flexible design most appropriate for unstable and unpredictable environments

differentiation
The extent to which the organization is broken down into subunits

integration
The extent to which the subunits of an organization must work together in a coordinated fashion

organizational size
The number of full-time or full-time equivalent employees

An **organic organization**, on the other hand, was most often found in unstable and unpredictable environments, in which constant change and uncertainty usually dictate a much higher level of fluidity and flexibility. Motorola and 3M (facing rapid technological change) each use organic designs. A manager at Motorola, for example, has considerable discretion over how work is performed and how problems can be solved.

These ideas were extended by Paul R. Lawrence and Jay W. Lorsch.[13] They agreed that environmental factors influence organization design but believed that this influence varies between different units of the same organization. In fact, they predicted that each organizational unit has its own unique environment and responds by developing unique attributes. Lawrence and Lorsch suggested that organizations could be characterized along two primary dimensions.

One of these dimensions, **differentiation**, is the extent to which the organization is broken down into subunits. A firm with many subunits is highly differentiated; one with few subunits has a low level of differentiation. The second dimension, **integration**, is the degree to which the various subunits must work together in a coordinated fashion. For example, if each unit competes in a different market and has its own production facilities, they may need little integration. Lawrence and Lorsch reasoned that the degree of differentiation and integration needed by an organization depends on the stability of the environments that its subunits faced.[14]

Organizational Size

The size of an organization is yet another factor that affects its design. Although several definitions of size exist, we define **organizational size** as the total number of full-time or full-time–equivalent employees. A team of researchers at the University of Aston in Birmingham, England, believed that Woodward had failed to find a size-structure relationship (which was her original expectation) because almost all the organizations she studied were relatively small (three-fourths had fewer than five hundred employees).[15] Thus they decided to undertake a study of a wider array of organizations to determine how size and technology both individually and jointly affect an organization's design.

Their primary finding was that technology did in fact influence structural variables in small firms, probably because all their activities tended to be centred around their core technology. In large firms, however, the strong technology-design link broke down, most likely because technology is not as central to ongoing activities in large organizations. The Aston studies yielded a number of basic generalizations: when compared with small organizations, large organizations tend to be characterized by higher levels of job specialization, more standard operating procedures, more rules, more regulations, and a greater degree of decentralization.

Organizational Life Cycle

Of course, size is not constant. As we noted in Chapter 9, for example, some small businesses are formed but soon disappear. Others remain as small, independently operated enterprises as long as their owner-manager lives. A few, like Compaq Computer, Magna, and Reebok, skyrocket to become organizational giants. And occasionally large organizations reduce their size through layoffs or divestitures. For example, Navistar is today far smaller than was its previous incarnation as International Harvester Co. Although no clear pattern explains changes in size, many organizations progress through a four-stage **organizational life cycle**.[16]

The first stage is the *birth* of the organization. At Compaq Computer, this occurred in 1984 when a handful of Texas Instruments engineers resigned, raised some venture capital, and began to design and build portable computers. The second stage, *youth*, is characterized by growth and the expansion of all organizational resources. Compaq passed through the youth stage in 1985 and entered the third stage, *midlife*, around the beginning of 1986. Midlife is a period of gradual growth evolving eventually into stability. The company remains in midlife today, with sales in excess of $1 billion (U.S.) annually. Compaq has not yet reached the final stage of an organization's life cycle, *maturity*. Maturity is a period of stability, perhaps eventually evolving into decline. Eaton's is an example of a mature organization—it is experiencing little or no growth and appears to be falling behind the rest of the retailing industry today.

Managers must confront a number of organization design issues as the organization progresses through these stages. In general, as an organization passes from one stage to the next, it becomes bigger, more mechanistic, and more decentralized. It also becomes more specialized, devotes more attention to planning, and takes on an increasingly large staff component. Finally, coordination demands increase, formalization increases, organizational units become geographically more dispersed, and control systems become more extensive. Thus an organization's size and design are clearly linked, and this link is dynamic because of the organizational life cycle.[17]

● **organizational life cycle**
A natural sequence of stages most organizations pass through as they grow and mature

STRATEGY AND ORGANIZATION DESIGN

Another important determinant of an organization's design is the strategy adopted by its top managers.[18] In general, corporate and business strategies both affect organization design. Basic organizational functions such as finance and marketing can also affect organization design in some cases.

Corporate-Level Strategy

As we noted in Chapter 7, an organization can adopt a variety of corporate-level strategies. Its choice will partially determine what type of design will be most effective. For example, a firm that pursues a single-product strategy likely relies on functional departmentalization and can use a mechanistic design. If either unrelated or related diversification is used to spur growth, managers need to decide how to arrange the various units within the organizational umbrella. For example, if the firm is using related diversification, there needs to be a high level of coordination among the various units to capitalize on the presumed synergistic opportunities inherent in this strategy. On the other hand, firms using unrelated diversification more likely rely on a strong hierarchical reporting system so that corporate managers can better monitor the performance of individual units within the firm.[19]

An organization that adopts the portfolio approach to implement its corporate-level strategies must also ensure that its design fits its strategy. For example, each strategic business unit may remain a relatively autonomous unit within the organization. But managers at the corporate level need to decide how much decision-making latitude to give the heads of each unit (a question of decentralization), how many corporate-level executives are needed to oversee the operations of various units (a question of span of management), and how much information is shared among the units (a question of coordination).[20]

Business-Level Strategy

Business-level strategies affect the design of individual businesses within the organization as well as the overall organization itself. An organization pursuing a defender strategy, for example, is likely to be somewhat tall and centralized, have narrow spans of management, and perhaps take a functional approach to departmentalization. Thus it may generally follow the bureaucratic approach to organization design.

In contrast, a prospecting type of organization is more likely to be flatter and decentralized. With wider spans of management, it tries to be very flexible and adaptable in its approach to doing business. A business that uses an analyzer strategy is likely to have an organization design somewhere in between these two extremes (perhaps being a System 2 or 3 organization). Given that a reactor is essentially a strategic failure, its presumed strategy is probably not logically connected to its design.

Generic competitive strategies can also affect organization design. A firm using a differentiation strategy, for example, may structure departments around whatever it is using as a basis for differentiating its products (i.e., marketing in the case of image, manufacturing in the case of quality). A cost leadership strategy necessitates a strong commitment to efficiency and control. Thus such a firm is more centralized as it tries to control costs. A firm using a focus strategy may design itself around the direction of its focus (i.e., location departmentalization if its focus is geographic region, customer departmentalization if its focus is customer groups).

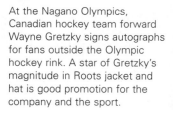

At the Nagano Olympics, Canadian hockey team forward Wayne Gretzky signs autographs for fans outside the Olympic hockey rink. A star of Gretzky's magnitude in Roots jacket and hat is good promotion for the company and the sport.

Organizational Functions

The relationship between an organization's functional strategies and its design is less obvious and may be subsumed under corporate- or business-level concerns. If the firm's marketing strategy calls for aggressive marketing and promotion, separate departments may be needed for advertising, direct sales, and promotion. If its financial strategy calls for low debt, it may need only a small finance department. If production strategy calls for manufacturing in diverse locations, organization design arrangements need to account for this geographic dispersion. Human resource strategy may call for greater or lesser degrees of decentralization as a way to develop skills of new managers at lower levels in the organization. And research and development strategy may dictate various designs for managing the R&D function itself. A heavy commitment to R&D, for example, may require a separate unit with a vice president in charge. A lesser commitment to R&D may be achieved with a director and a small staff.

BASIC FORMS OF ORGANIZATION DESIGN

Because technology, environment, size, life cycle, and strategy can all influence organization design, it should come as no surprise that organizations adopt many different kinds of designs. Most designs, however, fall into one of four basic categories. Others are hybrids based on two or more of the basic forms.

Functional (U-Form) Design

The **functional design** is an arrangement based on the functional approach to departmentalization as detailed in Chapter 10. This design has been termed the **U-form** (for unitary) by the noted economist Oliver E. Williamson.[21] Under the U-form arrangement, the members and units in the organization are grouped into functional departments such as marketing and production.

For the organization to operate efficiently in this design, there must be considerable coordination across departments. This integration and coordination are most commonly the responsibility of the CEO and members of senior management. Figure 11.1 shows the U-form design as applied to the corporate level of a small manufacturing company. In a U-form organization, none of the functional areas can survive without the others. Marketing, for example, needs products from operations to sell and funds from finance to pay for advertising. The WD-40 Company, which makes a popular lubricating oil, and McIlhenny Company, which makes Tabasco Sauce, are both examples of firms that use the U-form design.

In general, this approach shares the basic advantages and disadvantages of functional departmentalization. Thus it allows the organization to staff all important positions with functional experts and facilitates coordination and integration. On the other hand, it also promotes a functional, rather than an organizational, focus and tends to promote centralization. And as we noted in Chapter 10, functionally based designs are most commonly used in small organizations because an individual CEO can easily oversee and coordinate the entire organization. As an organization grows, the CEO finds staying on top of all functional areas increasingly difficult.

● **functional (U-form) design**
An organization design based on the functional approach to departmentalization

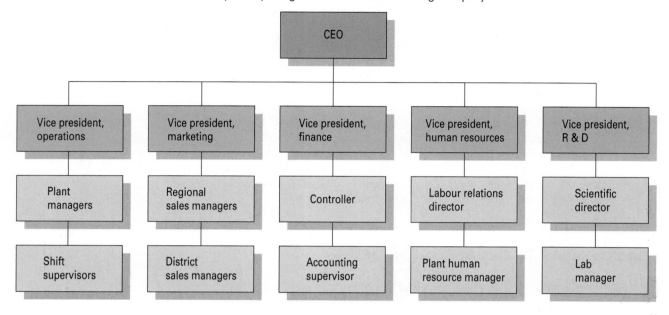

The U-form design is based on functional departmentalization. This small manufacturing firm uses managers at the vice-presidential level to coordinate activities within each functional area of the organization. Note that each functional area is dependent on the others.

● **conglomerate (H-form) design**

An organization design used by an organization comprising a set of unrelated businesses

Conglomerate (H-Form) Design

Another common form of organization design is the conglomerate, or **H-form**, approach.[22] The **conglomerate** design is used by an organization made up of a set of unrelated businesses. Thus the **H-form design** is essentially a holding company that results from unrelated diversification. (The "H" in this term stands for holding.)

This approach is based loosely on the product form of departmentalization (see Chapter 10). Each business or set of businesses is operated by a general manager who is responsible for its profits or losses, and each general manager functions independently of the others. Pearson PLC, a British firm, uses the H-form design. As illustrated in Figure 11.2, Pearson consists of four business groups. Although its periodicals and publishing operations are related to one another, its other businesses are clearly unrelated. Other firms that use the H-form design include General Electric (aircraft engines, appliances, broadcasting, financial services, lighting products, plastics, and other unrelated businesses) and Imasco (tobacco, drug stores, financial services, and other unrelated businesses).

In an H-form organization, a corporate staff usually evaluates the performance of each business, allocates corporate resources across companies, and shapes decisions about buying and selling businesses. The basic shortcoming of the H-form design is the complexity associated with holding diverse and unrelated businesses. Managers usually find comparing and integrating activities across a large number of diverse operations difficult. Research by Michael Porter suggests that many organizations following this approach achieve only average-to-weak financial performance.[23] Thus, although some North American firms are still using the H-form design, many have also abandoned it for other approaches.

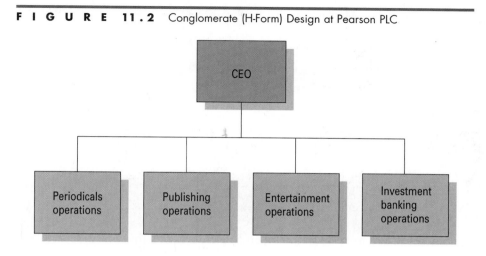

Pearson PLC, a British firm, uses the conglomerate form of organization design. This design, which results from a strategy of unrelated diversification, is a complex one to manage. Managers find that comparing and integrating activities among the dissimilar operations are difficult. Companies may abandon this design for another approach, such as the M-form design.

Divisional (M-Form) Design

In the divisional design, which is becoming increasingly popular, a product form of organization is also used; in contrast to the H-form, however, the divisions are related. Thus the **divisional design**, or **M-form** (for multidivisional), is based on multiple businesses in related areas operating within a larger organizational framework. This design results from a strategy of related diversification.

Some activities are extremely decentralized down to the divisional level; others are centralized at the corporate level.[24] For example, as shown in Figure 11.3 Dylex uses this approach. Each of its divisions is headed by a general manager and operates with reasonable autonomy, but the divisions also coordinate their activities as is appropriate. Other firms that use this approach are The Walt Disney Company (theme parks, movies, and merchandising units, all interrelated) and Hewlett-Packard (computers, printers, scanners, electronic medical equipment, and other electronic instrumentation), and, as discussed in our opening incident, the Hudson's Bay Co.

The opportunities for coordination and shared resources represent one of the biggest advantages of the M-form design. At The Limited, an American specialty apparel chain, marketing research and purchasing departments are centralized. Thus a buyer can inspect a manufacturer's entire product line, buy some designs for The Limited chain, others for The Limited Express, and still others for Lerner (divisions of The Limited). (However, as shown by the reversal of the decision to consolidate purchasing at the Bay and Zellers, this approach does not always work.) The M-form design's basic objective is to optimize internal competition and cooperation. Healthy competition among divisions for resources can enhance effectiveness, but cooperation should also be promoted. Research suggests that the M-form organization that can achieve and maintain this balance will outperform large U-form and all H-form organizations.[25]

● **divisional (M-form) design**
An organization design in which multiple businesses in related areas operate within a larger organizational framework; based on the product approach to departmentalization

Matrix Design

The **matrix design**, another common approach to organization design, is based on two overlapping bases of departmentalization.[26] The foundation of a matrix is a set of functional departments. A set of product groups, or temporary departments, is then superimposed across the functional departments.

● **matrix design**
An organization design wherein a product-based form of departmentalization is superimposed onto an existing functional arrangement

FIGURE 11.3 Multidivisional (M-Form) Design at Dylex Limited

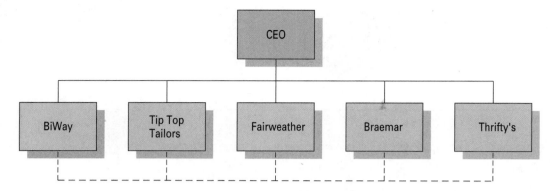

Dylex Limited uses the multidivisional approach to organization design. Although each of its units operates with relative autonomy, they all function in the same general market. This design resulted from a strategy of related diversification. Other firms that use M-form designs include PepsiCo and Woolworth Corporation.

● **project manager**
Head of a project group composed of representatives or workers from different functional departments

● **multiple-command structure**
A structure in which an individual reports to both a functional superior and one or more project managers simultaneously

Employees in a matrix are simultaneously members of a functional department (such as engineering) and of a project team.

Figure 11.4 shows a basic matrix design. At the top of the organization are functional units headed by vice presidents of engineering, production, finance, and marketing. Each of these managers has several subordinates. Along the side of the organization are a number of positions called **project manager**. Each project manager heads a project group composed of representatives or workers from the functional departments. Note from the figure that a matrix reflects a **multiple-command structure**—any given individual reports to both a functional superior and one or more project managers.

The project groups, or teams, are assigned to designated projects or programs. For example, the company might be developing a new product. Representatives are chosen from each functional area to work as a team on the new product. They also retain membership in the original functional group. At any given time, a person may be a member of several teams as well as a member of a functional group. Ford Motor Co. used this approach in creating its popular Taurus automobile. It formed a group called "Team Taurus" made up of designers, engineers, production specialists, marketing specialists, and other experts from different areas of the company. This group facilitated getting a very successful product to the market at least a year earlier than would have been possible using Ford's previous approaches. More recently, the firm used the same approach to create the newest version of the Mustang.

Many organizations have used the matrix design, including Xerox Canada, Monsanto Company, NCR, General Motors, and municipal, provincial, and federal government agencies. Some organizations, however, such as Citibank and the Dutch firm Philips, adopted and then dropped the matrix design. Thus it is important to recognize that a matrix design is not always appropriate.

The matrix form of organization design is most often used in one of three situations.[27] First, a matrix may work when there is strong pressure from the environment. For example, intense external competition may dictate the sort of strong marketing thrust that is best spearheaded by a functional department, but the diversity of a company's products may argue for product departments. Second, a matrix may be appropriate when large amounts of information need to be processed. For example, creating lateral relationships by means of a matrix is one effective way to increase the organization's capacity to process information. Third, the matrix design may work when there is pressure for shared

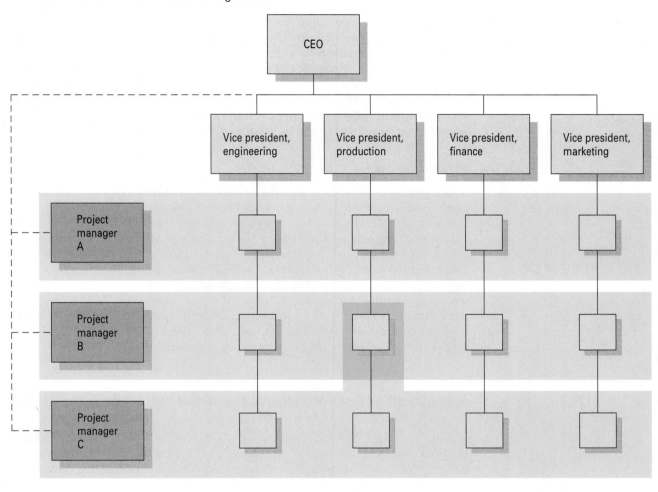

resources. For example, a company that has ten product departments may have resources for only three marketing specialists. A matrix design would allow all the departments to share the company's scarce marketing resource.

Both advantages and disadvantages are associated with the matrix design. Researchers have observed six primary advantages of matrix designs. First, it enhances flexibility because teams can be created, redefined, and dissolved as needed. Second, because they assume a major role in decision making, team members are likely to be highly motivated and committed to the organization. Third, employees in a matrix organization have considerable opportunity to learn new skills. A fourth advantage of a matrix design is that it provides an efficient way for the organization to take full advantage of its human resources. Fifth, team members retain membership in their functional unit so that they can serve as a bridge between the functional unit and the team, enhancing cooperation. Sixth, the matrix design gives top management a useful vehicle for decentralization. Once the day-to-day operations have been delegated, top management can devote more attention to areas such as long-range planning.

A matrix organization design is created by superimposing a product form of departmentalization onto an existing functional organization. Project managers coordinate teams of employees drawn from different functional departments. Thus a matrix relies on a multiple-command structure.

On the other hand, the matrix design also has some major disadvantages. Employees may be uncertain about reporting relationships, especially if they are simultaneously assigned to a functional manager and to several project managers. To complicate matters, some managers see the matrix as a form of anarchy in which they have unlimited freedom. Another set of problems is associated with the dynamics of group behaviour. Groups take longer than individuals to make decisions, may be dominated by one individual, and may compromise too much. They may also get bogged down in discussion and not focus on their primary objectives. Finally, in a matrix more time may also be required for coordinating task-related activities.[28]

Hybrid Designs

Some organizations use a design that represents a hybrid of two or more of the common forms of organization design. For example, an organization may have five related divisions and one unrelated division, making its design a cross between an M-form and an H-form. Indeed, few companies use a design in its pure form: most firms have one basic organization design as a foundation to managing the business but maintain sufficient flexibility so that temporary or permanent modifications can be made for strategic purposes. Ford, for example, used the matrix approach to design the Taurus and the Mustang, but the company is basically a U-form organization showing signs of moving to an M-form design. As we noted earlier, any combination of factors may dictate the appropriate form of design for any particular company.

EMERGING ISSUES IN ORGANIZATION DESIGN

Finally, in today's complex and ever-changing environment, managers must continue to learn about and experiment with new forms of organization design. Many organizations are creating designs for themselves that maximize their ability to adapt to changing circumstances and to a changing environment. They try to accomplish this goal by not becoming too compartmentalized or too rigid. As we noted earlier, bureaucratic organizations are slow, inflexible, and hard to change. To avoid these problems, then, organizations can try to be as different from bureaucracies as possible—operating with relatively few rules, general job descriptions, and so forth. This final section highlights some of the more important emerging issues.[29]

The Team Organization

● **team organization**
An approach to organization design that relies almost exclusively on project-type teams, with little or no underlying functional hierarchy

Some organizations today are using the **team organization**, an approach to organization design that relies almost exclusively on project-type teams, with little or no underlying functional hierarchy. Within such an organization people float from project to project, according to their skills and the demands of those projects. At Cypress Semiconductor, T.J. Rodgers refuses to allow the organization to grow so large that it can't function this way. Whenever a unit or group starts getting too large, he simply splits it into smaller units. Consequently, all units within the organization are small. This design allows them to change direction, explore new ideas, and try new methods without dealing with a rigid bureaucratic organizational context. Although few organizations have actually reached this level of adaptability, Hewlett-Packard and Xerox are among those moving toward it.[30] *The Managing in a Changing World* box examines some of the issues involved in teamwork.

The Virtual Organization

Closely related to the team organization is the virtual organization. A **virtual organization** has little or no formal structure. Such an organization typically has only a handful of permanent employees and a very small staff and administrative headquarters facility. As the needs of the organization change, its managers bring in temporary workers, lease facilities, and outsource basic support services to meet the demands. As the situation changes, the temporary workforce also changes, with some people leaving the organization and others entering. Facilities and the services subcontracted to others change as well. Thus, the organization exists only in response to its needs. For example, Global Research Consortium (GRC) is a virtual organization. GRC offers research and consulting services to firms doing business in Asia. As clients request various services GRC's staff of three permanent employees subcontract the work to an appropriate set of several dozen independent consultants and/or researchers with whom it has relationships. At any given time, therefore, GRC may have several projects underway and twenty or thirty people working on projects. As the projects change, so does the composition of the organization.

* **virtual organization**
An approach to organization design that has little or no formal structure

The Learning Organization

Another recent approach to organization design is the so-called learning organization. Organizations that adopt this approach work to integrate their own improvement with ongoing employee learning and development. Specifically, a **learning organization** is one that works to facilitate the lifelong learning and personal development of all of its employees while continually transforming itself to respond to changing demands and needs.[31]

Although managers might approach the concept of a learning organization from a variety of perspectives, improved quality, continuous improvement, and performance measurement are frequent goals. The basic premise is that the most consistent and logical strategy for achieving continuous improvement is by constantly upgrading employee talent, skill, and knowledge. For example, if each employee in an organization learns one new thing each day and can translate that knowledge into work-related practice, continuous improvement will logically follow. Indeed, organizations that wholeheartedly embrace this approach believe that the only way to achieve continuous improvement is to ensure constant learning by employees.

* **learning organization**
An approach to organization design that works to facilitate the lifelong learning and personal development of all of its employees while continually transforming itself to respond to changing demands and needs

In recent years, many organizations have implemented this approach. For example, the Shell Oil Company recently purchased an executive conference centre. The centre boasts state-of-the-art classrooms and instructional technology, lodging facilities, a restaurant, and recreational amenities such as a golf course, swimming pool, and tennis courts. Line managers at the firm rotate through the Shell Learning Center, as the facility has been renamed, and serve as teaching faculty. Such teaching assignments last from a few days to several months. All Shell employees routinely attend training programs, seminars, and related activities, all the while learning the latest information they need to contribute more effectively to the firm.

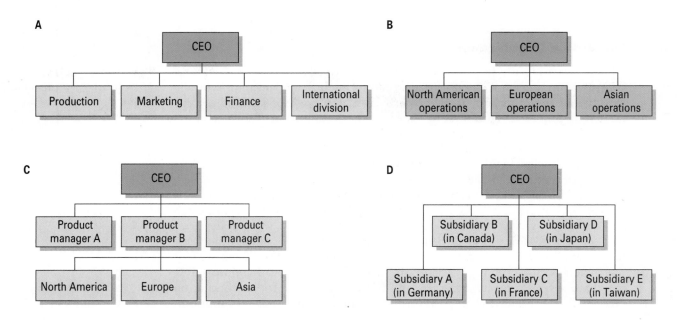

Companies that compete in international markets must create an organization design that fits their own unique circumstances. These four general designs are representative of what many international organizations use. Each is derived from one of the basic forms of organization design.

Issues in International Organization Design

Another emerging issue in organization design is the trend toward the internationalization of business. As we discussed in Chapter 5, most businesses today interact with suppliers, customers, or competitors (or all three) from other countries. The relevant issue for organization design is how to design the firm to deal most effectively with international forces and compete in global markets. For example, consider a moderate-size company that has just decided to "go international." Should it set up an international division, retain its current structure and establish an international operating group, or make its international operations an autonomous subunit?[32]

Figure 11.5 illustrates four of the most common approaches to organization design used for international purposes. Design A is the simplest, relying on a separate international division; Levi Strauss & Co. uses this approach. Design B, used by Ford Motor Co., is an extension of location departmentalization to international settings. An extension of product departmentalization, with each product manager being responsible for all product-related activities regardless of location, is shown in design C. Finally, design D, most typical of larger multinational corporations, is an extension of the multidivisional structure with branches located in various foreign markets; Nestlé and Unilever use design D.

The Individual or the Team?

Some managers today are facing a real dilemma. The cultural norms that have guided them during much of their careers have stressed individual achievement and accomplishment. People are supposed to work hard toward their own goals—both personal and professional—and organizations are supposed to recognize and reward the fruits of their labours. And indeed, most companies today still rely heavily on individually based systems for evaluating performance and providing rewards. In addition, many organizations are also stressing to their employees the importance of personal career management.

But this approach to doing business often runs counter to teamwork. Within the context of a team, individuals are supposed to subordinate their own work goals, for example, and do what's best for the team—regardless of how it affects them personally. Thus individual performance may be optimized to help the team, and an individual may have little to personally show for his or her special contributions. In addition, organizations have trouble assessing team performance and providing team-based rewards.

So managers may have to make tough decisions. Do I do what's best for me, in terms of personal rewards, recognition, and career development opportunities, even if it compromises my contributions to my team? Or do I selflessly do what's best for my team, even if it means that my own performance gets understated and my career development opportunities are constrained?

To make the team concept really work, an organization must alter the way it treats people. In particular, the organization that wants to use teams effectively has to find ways to allow individual team members to meet their own goals, to continue to learn new skills, and to maintain and improve their standing in the labour market.

References: Thomas A. Stewart, "The Great Conundrum—You vs. the Team," *Fortune*, November 25, 1996, pp. 165–166; and Mary Cianni and Donna Wnuck, "Individual Growth and Team Enhancement: Moving Toward a New Model of Career Development," *Academy of Management Executive*, February 1997, pp. 105–115.

SUMMARY OF KEY POINTS

Organization design is the overall set of structural elements and the relationships among those elements used to manage the total organization.

Two early universal models of organization design were the bureaucratic model and the behavioural model. These models attempted to prescribe how all organizations should be designed.

The situational view of organization design is based on the assumption that the optimal organization design is a function of situational factors. Four important situational factors are technology, environment, size, and organizational life cycle. Each of these factors plays a role in determining how an organization should be designed.

An organization's strategy also helps shape its design. In various ways, corporate- and business-level strategies both affect organization design. Basic organizational functions like marketing and finance also play a role in shaping design.

Many organizations today adopt one of four basic organization designs: functional (U-form), conglomerate (H-form), divisional (M-form), or matrix. Other organizations use a hybrid design derived from two or more of these basic designs.

Four emerging issues in organization design are the team organization, the virtual organization, the learning organization, and the design of international businesses.

DISCUSSION QUESTIONS

Questions for Review

1. Compare and contrast the bureaucratic and behavioural models of organization design. What are the advantages and disadvantages of each?
2. What are the basic situational factors that affect an organization's design?
3. How are an organization's strategy and its structure related?
4. Describe the basic forms of organization design. Outline the advantages and disadvantages of each.

Questions for Analysis

5. Can bureaucratic organizations avoid the problems usually associated with bureaucracies? If so, how? If not, why not? Do you think bureaucracies are still necessary? Why or why not? Is retaining the desirable aspects of bureaucracy and eliminating the undesirable ones possible? Why or why not?
6. The matrix organization design is complex and difficult to implement successfully. Why then do so many organizations use it?
7. Identify common and unique problems in organization design confronted by international businesses when compared with domestic businesses.

Questions for Application

8. What form of organization does your university or college use? What form does your municipal government use? What similarities and differences do you see? Why?
9. A question in Chapter 7 asked you to interview the manager of a local small business to determine how (or if) he or she formulates strategy. Interview that same manager again to obtain a description of his or her organization design. Can you identify any links between the manager's strategy and the structure of his or her organization? Share your findings with the class.
10. Interview members of a local organization (fast-food chain, department store, book store, bank, etc.) to ascertain how adaptable they perceive their organization to be.

BUILDING EFFECTIVE DECISION-MAKING SKILLS

Exercise Overview

Decision-making skills refer to the manager's ability to correctly recognize and define problems and opportunities and to then select an appropriate course of action to solve problems and capitalize on opportunities. The purpose of this exercise is to give you insights into how managers must make decisions within the context of creating an organization design.

Exercise Background

Assume that you have decided to open a casual sportswear business in your local community. Your products will be athletic caps, shirts, shorts, and sweats emblazoned with the logos of your university and local high schools. You are a talented designer and have developed some ideas that will make your products unique and very popular. You also have inherited enough money to get your business up and running and to cover about one year of living expenses (that is, you do not need to pay yourself a salary).

You intend to buy sportswear in various sizes and styles from other suppliers. Your firm will then use silk-screen processes and add the logos and other decorative touches to the products. Local clothing store owners have seen samples of your products and have indicated a keen interest in selling them. You know, however, that you will still need to service accounts and keep your customers happy.

You are now trying to determine how many people you need to get your business going and how to most effectively group them into an organization. You realize that you can start out quite small and then expand as sales warrant. However, you also worry that if you are continually adding people and re-arranging your organization, confusion and inefficiency will result.

Exercise Task

Step One: Under each of the following scenarios, decide how to best design your organization. Sketch a basic organization chart to show your thoughts.

Scenario 1—You will sell the products yourself, and you intend to start with a workforce of five people.

Scenario 2—You intend to oversee production yourself, and you intend to start with a workforce of nine people.

Scenario 3—You do not intend to handle any one function yourself, but you will oversee the entire operation; you intend to start with a workforce of fifteen people.

Step Two: Form small groups of four to five people each. Compare your various organization charts, focusing on similarities and differences.

Step Three: Working in the same group, assume that five years have passed and your business has been a big success. You have a large plant for making your products and are shipping them to six provinces. You employ almost five hundred people. Create an organization design that you think best fits this organization.

Follow-Up Questions

1. How clear or ambiguous were the decisions about organization design?
2. What are your thoughts about starting out too large so as to maintain stability, as opposed to starting small and then growing?
3. Which basic factors did you consider in choosing a design?

Federal Express Keeps Strategy and Structure Aligned with the Environment

Since its founding in 1973, Federal Express Corporation (FedEx) has grown from 389 employees servicing a few cities to a company that employs about 137,000 people servicing 212 countries. In fact, FedEx is now the world's largest express transportation company. In 1990, FedEx became the first company in the service sector to win the prestigious Malcolm Baldridge National Quality Award for quality in business (analysts see this award as the Nobel Prize of business awards). By 1998, annual revenues had climbed to $24 billion and the company commanded approximately 43 percent of the air express market.

In 1987, FedEx purchased its Canadian licensee, Cansica Inc., and began operations as Federal Express Canada Ltd. (FedEx Canada). Starting with a workforce of approximately 400, FedEx Canada now has more than 3,500 employees. In 1994, FedEx became the first global express transportation company to receive worldwide ISO 9001 quality certification throughout its entire system, including Canada.

The organization's philosophy, which drives its strategies and structure, is summed up in a maxim made popular by its CEO and founder, Frederick Smith: when people are placed first, they will provide the highest possible service and profits. The "people–service–profit" goals serve, either singularly or in some combination, as the foundation for almost all quality initiatives, organizational structuring, management guidelines, and strategies at FedEx. At the top of FedEx's list of corporate priorities is people. The company designs its strategies and systems to focus on the people aspect, ensuring that employees feel valued and empowered. Empowerment is achieved through open communication, training opportunities, quality improvement tools, and management leadership.

The corporate philosophy has a direct impact on the organizational structure. In keeping with the customer- and employee-oriented philosophy, the company maintains a flat organizational hierarchy, diagrammed as an inverted pyramid, with only five management layers separating customers and front-line employees (at the top of the inverted pyramid) and executive management. In addition to the cost savings a flat organizational hierarchy offers, the company emphasizes that the structure facilitates clear two-way communications. FedEx Canada is organized by functional departments and its service area is divided into four regions: Eastern, Western, Central Canada, and Metropolitan Toronto.

The express transportation sector is becoming increasingly competitive, with players such as United Parcel Service and Purolator keeping constant pressure on FedEx. In an industry that depends on the speed and efficiency of service, FedEx has had to adapt to, and sometimes lead, changes in its environment. In this regard, FedEx has developed several high-tech systems, including the following: the COSMOS (Customer Operations Service Master On-line System), a computerized tracking system designed to determine the exact location of a package at all times; the EXPRESSCLEARSM customs clearance system, which electronically transmits shipment information to customs so that processing can begin prior to the arrival of the actual packages; and a computerized digital dispatch system that communicates with couriers in their vans via computer screens. In March 1996, as the drive into cyberspace became a business necessity, FedEx Canada launched its highly rated Web site in both English and French. Some of the features include tracking packages, locating the nearest dropbox, e-mailing FedEx departments, and ordering supplies. In its attempts to improve customer service, the company offers a money-back guarantee on service commitment and a similar guarantee on the ability to track a package within thirty minutes.

In response to global competition, FedEx has implemented several restructuring initiatives. However, instead of undergoing a single large restructuring strategy, FedEx Canada is constantly reengineering and evolving by making small changes that increase customer efficiency. These changes are carried out without employee downsizing as the company maintains its "no-layoff" policy. The introduction of advanced information technologies has played a large role in the reengineering efforts and has allowed for further "flattening" and flexibility in the organizational structure.

Federal Express Keeps Strategy and Structure Aligned with the Environment (Continued)

Questions

1. Describe the organizational design of Federal Express Canada. How does it seem to fit its environment?

2. What are the advantages and disadvantages of a "flat" organizational structure? Which are more pertinent to FedEx Canada? Why?

3. In what ways does FedEx's organization seem to be adaptive?

References: Douglas Blackmon, "Parcel Pickup Explores High-Tech Frontier," *The Globe and Mail*, June 2, 1997, B4; AMA Management Briefing, *Blueprints for Service Quality: The Federal Express Approach* (New York: AMA, 1991); Naresh Agarwal and Parbudyal Singh, "Organizational Rewards for a Changing Workplace," *International Journal of Technology Management* (forthcoming); http://fedex.ca; interviews with senior management at FedEx Canada; and FedEx, Annual Report, 1998 (http://www.fdxcorp.com).

CHAPTER NOTES

1. Marina Strauss, "Bay, Zellers Drop Joint Buying Strategy," *The Globe and Mail,* July 1997, pp. B1, B4; Susan Gittens, "Two Steps Forward, One Back," *Canadian Business,* June 1996, pp. 126–127; Brian Hutchinson, "Is This Any Way to Run a Discount Store?" *Canadian Business,* September 1996, pp. 36–41; Hudson's Bay Co., Annual Report, 1995, p. 1; "Investor Relations" (http://www.hbc.com); and "The Top 1000," *Report on Business Magazine,* July 1998, p. 132.

2. See Richard L. Daft, *Organization Theory and Design,* 5th ed. (St. Paul, Minn.: West, 1995); and Gareth Jones, *Organization Theory* (Reading, Mass.: Addison-Wesley, 1995).

3. Max Weber, *Theory of Social and Economic Organizations,* trans. by T. Parsons (New York: Free Press, 1947).

4. For detailed discussions of the strengths and weaknesses of the bureaucratic model, see James L. Perry and Hal G. Rainey, "The Public-Private Distinction in Organization Theory: A Critique and Research Strategy," *Academy of Management Review,* April 1988, pp. 182–201; and Thomas A. Leitko and David Szczerbacki, "Why Traditional OD Strategies Fail in Professional Bureaucracies," *Organizational Dynamics,* Winter 1987, pp. 52–65.

5. Rensis Likert, *New Patterns in Management* (New York: McGraw-Hill, 1961); and Rensis Likert, *The Human Organization* (New York: McGraw-Hill, 1967).

6. William F. Dowling, "At General Motors: System 4 Builds Performance and Profits," *Organizational Dynamics,* Winter 1975, pp. 23–28.

7. Daft, *Organization Theory and Design.*

8. For descriptions of situational factors, see Robert K. Kazanjian and Robert Drazin, "Implementing Internal Diversification: Contingency Factors for Organization Design Choices," *Academy of Management Review,* April 1987, pp. 342–354; Allen Bluedorn, "Pilgrim's Progress: Trends and Convergence in Research on Organizational Size and Environments," *Journal of Management,* Summer 1993, pp. 163–191; and Jones, *Organization Theory.*

9. Joan Woodward, *Industrial Organization: Theory and Practice* (London: Oxford University Press, 1965).

10. Joan Woodward, *Management and Technology, Problems of Progress Industry,* No. 3 (London: Her Majesty's Stationery Office, 1958).

11. William Bridges, "The End of the Job," *Fortune,* September 19, 1994, pp. 62–74.

12. Tom Burns and G.M. Stalker, *The Management of Innovation* (London: Tavistock, 1961).

13. Paul R. Lawrence and Jay W. Lorsch, *Organization and Environment* (Homewood, Ill.: Irwin, 1967).

14. For detailed discussions of the environment–organization design relationship, see Masoud Yasai-Ardekani, "Structural Adaptations to Environments," *Academy of Management Review,* January 1986, pp. 9–21; Christine S. Koberg and Geraldo R. Ungson, "The Effects of Environmental Uncertainty and Dependence on Organizational Performance: A Comparative Study," *Journal of Management,* Winter 1987, pp. 725–737; and Barbara W. Keats and Michael A. Hitt, "A Causal Model of Linkages Among Environmental Dimensions, Macro Organizational Characteristics, and Performance," *Academy of Management Journal,* September 1988, pp. 570–598.

15. Derek S. Pugh and David J. Hickson, *Organization Structure in Its Context: The Aston Program I* (Lexington, Mass.: D.C. Heath, 1976).

16. Robert H. Miles and Associates, *The Organizational Life Cycle* (San Francisco: Jossey-Bass, 1980). See also "Is Your Company Too Big?" *Business Week,* March 27, 1989, pp. 84–94.

17. Douglas Baker and John Cullen, "Administrative Reorganization and Configurational Context: The Contingent Effects of Age, Size, and Change in Size," *Academy of Management Journal,* Vol. 36, No. 6, 1993, pp. 1251–1277.

18. See Charles W.L. Hill and Gareth Jones, *Strategic Management: An Analytic Approach,* 3rd ed. (Boston: Houghton Mifflin Co., 1995).

19. William Kahn and Kathy Kram, "Authority at Work: Internal Models and Their Organizational Consequences," *Academy of Management Review,* Vol. 19, No. 1, 1994, pp. 17–50.

20. Richard D'Aveni and David Ravenscroft, "Economies of Integration versus Bureaucrat Costs: Does Vertical Integration Improve Performance?" *Academy of Management Journal,* Vol. 37, No. 5, 1994, pp. 1167–1206.

21. Oliver E. Williamson, *Markets and Hierarchies* (New York: Free Press, 1975).

22. Williamson, *Markets and Hierarchies.*

23. Michael E. Porter, "From Competitive Advantage to Corporate Strategy," *Harvard Business Review,* May–June 1987, pp. 43–59.

24. Williamson, *Markets and Hierarchies.*

25. Jay B. Barney and William G. Ouchi (Eds.), *Organizational Economics* (San Francisco: Jossey-Bass, 1986), and Robert E. Hoskisson, "Multidivisional Structure and Performance: The Contingency of Diversification Strategy," *Academy of Management Journal,* December 1987, pp. 625–644. See also Bruce Lamont, Robert Williams, and James Hoffman, "Performance During 'M-Form' Reorganization and Recovery Time: The Effects of Prior Strategy and Implementation Speed," *Academy of Management Journal,* Vol. 37, No. 1, 1994, pp. 153–166.

26. Stanley M. Davis and Paul R. Lawrence, *Matrix* (Reading, Mass.: Addison-Wesley, 1977).

27. Davis and Lawrence, *Matrix.*

28. See Lawton Burns and Douglas Wholey, "Adoption and Abandonment of Matrix Management Programs: Effects

of Organizational Characteristics and Interorganizational Networks," *Academy of Management Journal*, Vol. 36, No. 1, pp. 106–138.

29. Raymond E. Miles, Charles C. Snow, John A. Matthews, Grant Miles, and Henry J. Coleman Jr., "Organizing in the Knowledge Age: Anticipating the Cellular Form," *Academy of Management Executive*, November 1997, pp. 7–24.

30. "The Horizontal Corporation," *Business Week*, December 20, 1993, pp. 76–81; and Shawn Tully, "The Modular Corporation," *Fortune*, February 8, 1993, pp. 106–114.

31. Peter Senge, *The Fifth Discipline* (New York: Free Press, 1993). See also Alessandro Lomi, Erik R. Larsen, and Ari Ginsberg, "Adaptive Learning to Organizations: A System Dynamics-Based Exploration," *Journal of Management*, Vol. 23, No. 4, 1997, pp. 561–582.

32. For a recent discussion of these issues, see William G. Egelhoff, "Strategy and Structure in Multinational Corporations: A Revision of the Stopford and Wells Model," *Strategic Management Journal*, Vol. 9, 1988, pp. 1–14. See also Ricky W. Griffin and Michael Pustay, *International Business—A Managerial Perspective*, 2nd ed. (Reading, Mass.: Addison Wesley, 1999).

Managing Organization Change and Innovation

12

OBJECTIVES

After studying this chapter, you should be able to:

● *Describe the nature of organization change, including forces for change and planned versus reactive change.*

● *Discuss the steps in organization change and how to manage resistance to change.*

● *Identify and describe major areas of organization change.*

● *Discuss the need for and approaches to organization reengineering.*

● *Discuss the assumptions, techniques, and effectiveness of organization development.*

● *Describe the innovation process, forms of innovation, the failure to innovate, and how organizations can promote innovation.*

OUTLINE

This 1999 M-Class 4x4 represents Mercedes' entry into the competitive sport utility vehicle market.

Daimler-Benz is Germany's largest industrial firm and one of its most important. The firm is best known for its line of luxury cars sold under the name Mercedes Benz. Mercedes also manufactures commercial vans, trucks, buses, and industrial diesel engines.

A few years ago, Daimler-Benz managers, concerned that the firm was too reliant on its Mercedes division, decided to diversify. Through an aggressive strategy based on acquiring new firms and growing other existing Daimler-Benz businesses, the company was transformed into a diversified conglomerate. One division consisted of aerospace businesses. A second was created for financial services. A third included industrial and manufacturing units dealing with automation and rail systems. Mercedes-Benz made up the fourth division.

Despite its major investments and managerial commitments, Daimler-Benz continued to struggle. Especially problematic were the aerospace and financial services units whose losses were so great in 1995 that the entire corporation lost money for the first time in decades.

> **"In such a situation, you either run away or fix it yourself."** (Jurgen Schrempp)

That same year, the board promoted Jurgen Schrempp to the position of CEO and gave him a mandate to turn things around—and quickly. One of his first major moves, in turn, also proved to be very controversial and ultimately cost the firm one of its most highly regarded executives. Up until Daimler's recent problems, the Mercedes unit operated with virtual autonomy. Mercedes-Benz, for example, had its own CEO, Helmut Werner. And indeed, many observers had been surprised that Daimler's board had tapped Schrempp over Werner to take the top spot.

To achieve his mandate, Schrempp decided Mercedes would need to be folded into Daimler's corporate structure. His arguments were (1) that the firm's other units needed more access to the managerial, technical, and operational expertise at Mercedes and (2) that costs could be lowered by consolidating administrative expenses. Not surprisingly, Werner opposed this move. Although he had several reasonable arguments for keeping Mercedes independent, it was also clear that Schrempp's proposal would undermine Werner's authority.

Schrempp eventually prevailed. Werner quickly left the firm and Schrempp forged ahead at full speed: Mercedes was incorporated into Daimler, and several underperforming businesses were closed or sold. Daimler's pending merger with Chrysler announced in mid-1998 reflected the firm's new commitment to growth. Schrempp also supported the building of the first Mercedes factory outside of Germany—in Alabama—and arranged for Daimler-Benz to become the first German firm to be listed on the New York Stock Exchange. Within two years, his managerial moves had begun to pay dividends. Profits began to surge once more, and new Mercedes products became the talk of the industry. But to make these dreams a reality, Schrempp had to basically dismantle and then reassemble his firm so that it more closely resembles one of its high-powered roadsters than one of its busses.[1] ●

Managers at Daimler-Benz have had to grapple with something all managers eventually confront: the need for change. They first perceived the need to make certain changes aimed at fostering diversification. Later, they realized that this strategy was not working and that other changes were necessary to get the firm back on track. Making these changes, however, required the CEO to overcome internal politics. The changes were costly in a variety of ways, but they seem to be paying off as the firm has regained its financial vitality.

Understanding when and how to implement change is a vital part of management. This chapter describes how organizations manage change. We first examine the nature of organization change and identify the basic issues of managing change. We then identify and describe major areas of change. Next we look at reengineering, a major change program undertaken by many firms recently. We then examine organization development and conclude by discussing a related area, organizational innovation.

THE NATURE OF ORGANIZATION CHANGE

● **organization change**
Any substantive modification to some part of the organization

Organization change is any substantive modification to some part of the organization.[2] Thus change can involve virtually any aspect of an organization: work schedules, bases for departmentalization, span of management, machinery, organization design, people themselves, and so on. It is important to keep in mind that any change in an organization may have effects extending beyond the actual area where the change is implemented. For example, when a company installs a new computerized production system, employees must be trained to operate new equipment, the compensation system must be adjusted to reflect new skill levels, the span of management of supervisors may be altered, jobs may be redesigned, and the selection criteria for new employees may also have to be changed to accommodate the new reality.[3]

Forces for Change

Why do organizations find change necessary? The basic reason is that something relevant to the organization either has changed or is going to change. The organization consequently has little choice but to change as well. Indeed, a primary reason for the problems that organizations often face is failure to anticipate or respond properly to changing circumstances. Forces for change may be external or internal to the organization.[4]

External Forces External forces for change derive from the organization's general and task environments. For example, two energy crises, a maturing Japanese automobile industry, floating currency exchange rates, and floating international interest rates—all manifestations of the international dimension of the general environment—have profoundly influenced North American automobile companies. New rules of production and competition have forced them to dramatically alter the way they do business. In the political area, new laws, court decisions, and regulations affect organizations. The technological dimension may yield new production techniques that the organization needs to explore. The economic dimension is affected by inflation, the cost of living, and money supplies. The sociocultural dimension, reflecting societal values, determines what kinds of products or services will be accepted in the market.

Because of its proximity to the organization, the task environment is an even more powerful force for change. Competitors influence an organization through their price structures and product lines. When Compaq lowers the prices it charges for computers, Dell and IBM often have little choice but to follow suit. Because customers determine what products can be sold at what prices, organizations must be concerned with consumer tastes and preferences. Suppliers affect organizations by raising or lowering prices or changing product lines. Regulators can have dramatic effects on an organization. For example, if the federal or a provincial occupational health and safety agency rules that a particular production process is dangerous to workers, it can force a firm to close a plant until it meets higher safety standards.

Internal Forces A variety of forces inside the organization may cause change. If top management revises the organization's strategy, organization change is likely to result. A decision by an electronics company to enter the home computer market or a decision to increase a ten-year product sales goal by 3 percent would occasion many organization changes. Unions can force change when they negotiate for higher wages or strike. Other internal forces for change may be reflections of external forces. As sociocultural values shift, for example, workers' attitudes toward their jobs may also shift—and workers may demand a change in working hours or working conditions. In such a case, even though the force is rooted in the external environment, the organization must respond directly to the internal pressure it generates.

Planned versus Reactive Change

planned change
Change that is designed and implemented in an orderly and timely fashion in anticipation of future events

reactive change
A piecemeal response to circumstances as they develop

Some change is planned well in advance; other change comes about as a reaction to unexpected events. **Planned change** is change that is designed and implemented in an orderly and timely fashion in anticipation of future events. **Reactive change** is a piecemeal response to events as they occur. Because reactive change may be hurried, the potential for poorly conceived and executed change is increased. Planned change is almost always preferable to reactive change.[5]

Software Kinetics Ltd., an Ottawa-based privately held company, provides an example of how planned change may benefit an organization. Software Kinetics had worked with the Transportation Safety Board of Canada (TSB) to create the world's first software system to produce video recreations of aircraft accidents. Although the TSB did not see this technology as a commercial venture, Software Kinetics obtained a licence for the technology from the TSB and plans to market a version of the system. Software Kinetics will thus have to transform itself from a narrowly focused high-tech company to one also concerned with marketing, finance, and new approaches to human resource management. By all indications, it is a challenge the company seems prepared to meet.[6] Caterpillar, on the other hand, is a firm guilty of reactive change. A few years ago it was caught flat-footed by a worldwide recession in the construction industry, suffered enormous losses and took several years to recover. Had managers at Caterpillar anticipated the need for change earlier, they might have been able to respond more quickly.

The importance of approaching change from a planned, as opposed to reactive, perspective is reinforced by the frequency of organization change. Most companies or divisions of large companies implement some form of moderate change at least every year and one or more major changes every four to five years.[7] Managers who sit back and respond only when they have to are likely to spend a lot of time hastily changing and rechanging things. A more effective approach is to anticipate forces urging change and plan ahead to deal with them.

MANAGING CHANGE IN ORGANIZATIONS

Organization change is a complex phenomenon. A manager cannot simply wave a wand and implement a planned change like magic. Instead, any change must be systematic and logical to have a realistic opportunity to succeed. To carry this off, the manager needs to understand the steps of effective change and how to counter employee resistance to change.

Models of the Change Process

Researchers have developed a number of models or frameworks outlining steps for change over the years. The Lewin model was one of the first, although a more comprehensive approach is usually more useful.

The Lewin Model Kurt Lewin, a noted organizational theorist, suggested that every change requires three steps.[8] The first step is *unfreezing*—individuals who will be affected by the impending change must be led to recognize why the change is necessary. Next the *change itself* is implemented. Finally, *refreezing* involves reinforcing and supporting the change so that it becomes a part of the system. For example, one of the changes Caterpillar faced in response to the recession involved a massive workforce reduction. The first step (unfreezing) was convincing the United Auto Workers to support the reduction because of its importance to long-term effectiveness. After this unfreezing was accomplished, 30,000 jobs were eliminated (implementation). Then Caterpillar worked to improve its damaged relationship with its workers (refreezing) by guaranteeing future pay hikes and promising no more cutbacks. As interesting as Lewin's model is, it unfortunately lacks operational specificity. Thus a more comprehensive perspective is often needed.

A Comprehensive Approach to Change   The comprehensive approach to change takes a systems view and delineates a series of specific steps that often lead to successful change. This expanded model is illustrated in Figure 12.1. The first step is recognizing the need for change. Reactive change might be triggered by employee complaints, declines in productivity or turnover, court injunctions, sales slumps, or labour strikes. Recognition may simply be managers' awareness that change in a certain area is inevitable. For example, managers may be aware of the general frequency of organizational change undertaken by most organizations and recognize that their organization should probably follow the same pattern. The immediate stimulus might be the result of a forecast indicating new market potential, the accumulation of cash surplus for possible investment, or an opportunity to achieve and capitalize on a major technological breakthrough. Managers might also initiate change today because indicators suggest that it will be necessary in the near future.

Managers must next set goals for the change. To increase market share, to enter new markets, to restore employee morale, to settle a strike, and to identify investment opportunities all might be goals for change. Third, managers must diagnose what brought on the need for change. Turnover, for example, might be caused by low pay, poor working conditions, poor supervisors, or employee dissatisfaction. Thus, although turnover may be the immediate stimulus for change, managers must understand its causes to make the right changes.

FIGURE 12.1   Steps in the Change Process

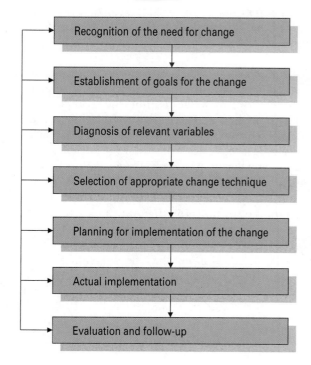

Managers must understand how and why to implement change. A manager who, when implementing change, follows a logical and orderly sequence such as the one shown here is more likely to succeed than is a manager whose change process is haphazard and poorly conceived.

The next step is to select a change technique that will accomplish the intended goals. If turnover is caused by low pay, a new reward system may be needed. If the cause is poor supervision, interpersonal skills training may be called for. (Various change techniques are summarized later in this chapter.) After the appropriate technique has been chosen, its implementation must be planned. Issues to consider include the costs of the change, its effects on other areas of the organization, and the degree of employee participation appropriate for the situation. If the change is implemented as planned, the results should then be evaluated. If the change was intended to reduce turnover, managers must check turnover after the change has been in effect for a while. If turnover is still too high, other changes may be necessary.[9]

Understanding Resistance to Change

Another element in the effective management of change is understanding the resistance that often greets change.[10] Managers need to know why people resist change and what can be done about their resistance. When Westinghouse replaced all its typewriters with computer terminals and personal computers, most people responded favourably. One manager, however, resisted the change to the point where he began leaving work every day at noon. It was some time before he began staying in the office all day again. Such resistance is common for a variety of reasons.

Uncertainty   Perhaps the biggest cause of employee resistance to change is uncertainty. In the face of impending change, employees may become anxious and nervous. They may worry about their ability to meet new job demands, they may think that their job security is threatened, or they may simply dislike ambiguity. RJR Nabisco was recently the target of an extended and confusing takeover battle, and during the entire time employees were nervous about the impending change. *The Wall Street Journal* described them this way: "Many are angry at their leaders and fearful for their jobs. They are swapping rumors and spinning scenarios for the ultimate outcome of the battle for the tobacco and food giant. Headquarters staffers in Atlanta know so little about what's happening in New York that some call their office 'the mushroom complex,' where they are kept in the dark."[11]

Threatened Self-Interests   Many impending changes threaten the self-interests of some managers within the organization. A change might potentially diminish their power or influence within the company, so they fight it. Managers at Sears, Roebuck and Co. recently developed a plan calling for a new type of store. The new stores would be somewhat smaller than typical Sears stores and would not be located in large shopping malls. Instead, they would be located in smaller strip centres. They would carry clothes and other "soft goods" but not hardware, appliances, furniture, or automotive products. When executives in charge of the excluded product lines heard about the plan, they raised such strong objections that the entire idea was delayed indefinitely.

Different Perceptions   A third reason that people resist change is due to different perceptions. A manager may make a decision and recommend a plan for change on the basis of her own assessment of a situation. Others in the organization may resist the change because they do not agree with the manager's assessment or perceive the situation differently. The 1994 baseball strike provides a good case-in-point. Baseball owners argued that a salary cap was necessary to control costs, while the players union believed that such a cap would only serve to lower salaries. As a result of these different perceptions, a lengthy strike occurred, which damaged the credibility of the game.

Feelings of Loss Many changes involve altering work arrangements in ways that disrupt existing social networks. Because social relationships are important, most people resist any change that might adversely affect those relationships. Other intangibles threatened by change include power, status, security, familiarity with existing procedures, and self-confidence. For example, Steven Jobs hired John Sculley to bring professional management to Apple. He later found that he did not like Sculley's changes and wanted things as they were before. His own status and self-confidence were being threatened. Jobs tried to oust Sculley, lost a power struggle with the board of directors, and then left himself. He later returned to the company he founded.

Managing Resistance to Change

Of course, a manager should not give up in the face of resistance to change. Although there are no sure-fire cures, there are several techniques that at least have the potential to overcome resistance.[12]

Participation Participation is often the most effective technique for overcoming resistance to change. Employees who participate in planning and implementing a change are better able to understand the reasons for the change. Uncertainty is reduced, and self-interests and social relationships are less threatened. Having had an opportunity to express their ideas and assume the perspectives of others, employees are more likely to accept the change gracefully. A classic study of participation monitored the introduction of a change in production methods among four groups in a Virginia pyjama factory.[13] The two groups that were allowed to fully participate in planning and implementing the change improved their productivity and satisfaction significantly, relative to the two groups that did not participate. In another example, 3M Company recently attributed $10 million (U.S.) in cost savings to employee participation in several organization change activities.[14]

Education and Communication Educating employees about the need for and the expected results of an impending change should reduce their resistance. If open communication is established and maintained during the change process, uncertainty can be minimized. Caterpillar used these methods during many of its cutbacks to reduce resistance. First, it educated union representatives about the need for and potential value of the planned changes. Then management told all employees what was happening, when it would happen, and how it would affect them individually.

Facilitation Several facilitation procedures are also advisable. For instance, making only necessary changes, announcing those changes well in advance, and allowing time for people to adjust to new ways of doing things can help reduce resistance to change. One manager at a Prudential regional office spent several months systematically planning a change in work procedures and job design. He then became too hurried, coming in over the weekend with a work crew and rearranging the office layout. When employees walked in on Monday

A force-field analysis can help a manager facilitate change. A manager able to identify forces acting both for and against a change can see where to focus efforts to remove barriers to change (such as offering training and relocation to displaced workers). By removing the forces against the change, resistance can be at least partially overcome.

FIGURE 12.2 Force-Field Analysis for Plant Closing at Chrysler Canada

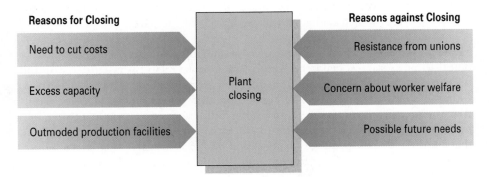

morning, they were hostile, anxious, and resentful. What was a promising change became a disaster, and the manager had to scrap the entire plan.

Force-Field Analysis   Although force-field analysis may sound like something out of a Star Trek movie, it can help overcome resistance to change. In almost any change situation, forces are acting for and against the change. To facilitate the change, managers start by listing each set of forces and then trying to tip the balance so that the forces facilitating the change outweigh those hindering the change. It is especially important to try to remove or at least minimize some of the forces acting against the change. Suppose, for example, that Chrysler Canada is considering a plant closing as part of a change. As shown in Figure 12.2, three factors are reinforcing the change: Chrysler Canada needs to cut costs, it has excess capacity, and the plant has outmoded production facilities. At the same time, there is resistance from the Canadian Auto Workers (CAW), concern for workers being put out of their jobs, and a feeling that the plant might be needed again in the future. Chrysler Canada might start by convincing the CAW that the closing is necessary by presenting profit and loss figures. It could then offer relocation and retraining to displaced workers. And it might shut down the plant and put it in "moth balls" so that it could be renovated later. The three major factors hindering the change are thus eliminated or reduced in importance.

AREAS OF ORGANIZATION CHANGE

We noted earlier that change can involve virtually any part of an organization. In general, however, most change interventions involve organization structure and design, technology and operations, or people. The most common areas of change within each of these broad categories are listed in Table 12.1.

Changing Structure and Design

Organization change might be focused on any of the basic components of organization structure or on the organization's overall design. Thus the organization might change the way it designs its jobs or its bases of departmentalization. Likewise, it might change reporting relationships or the distribution of authority. For example, we noted in Chapter 10 the trend toward flatter organizations. Coordination mechanisms and line and staff configurations are also subject to change. On a larger scale, the organization might change its overall design. For example, a growing business could decide to drop its functional design and adopt a divisional design. Or it might transform itself into a matrix. Finally, the organization might change any part of its human resource management system, such as its selection criteria, its performance appraisal methods, or its compensation package.[15]

Changing Technology and Operations

Technology is the conversion process used by an organization to transform inputs into outputs. Because of the rapid rate of all technological innovation, technological changes are becoming increasingly important to many organizations. Table 12.1 lists several areas where technological change is likely to be experienced. One important area of change involves equipment. To keep pace with competitors, firms periodically find that replacing existing machinery and equipment with newer models is necessary.

A change in work processes or work activities may be necessary if new equipment is introduced or new products are manufactured. In manufacturing industries, the major reason for changing a work process is to accommodate a change in the materials used to produce a finished product. Consider a firm that manufactures battery-operated flashlights. For many years flashlights were made of metal, but now most are made of plastic. A firm might decide to move from metal to plastic flashlights because of consumer preferences, raw materials costs, or other reasons. Whatever the reason, the technology necessary to make flashlights from plastic differs importantly from that used to make flashlights from metal. Work process changes may occur in service organizations as well as in manufacturing firms. As traditional barber shops and beauty parlours are replaced by hair salons catering to both sexes, for example, the hybrid organizations have to develop new methods for handling appointments and setting prices.

A change in work sequence may or may not accompany a change in equipment or a change in work processes. Making a change in work sequence means

TABLE 12.1 Areas of Organization Change		
Organization Structure and Design	**Technology and Operations**	**People**
Job design	Equipment	Abilities and skills
Departmentalization	Work processes	Performance
Reporting relationships	Work sequences	Perceptions
Authority distribution	Information systems	Expectations
Coordination mechanisms	Control systems	Attitudes
Line-staff structure		Values
Overall design		
Culture		
Human resource management		

Organization change can affect any part, area, or component of an organization. Most change, however, fits into one of three general areas: organization structure and design, technology and operations, and people.

Technology is a major area of change for many organizations. *Shift* magazine targets the workplace and lifestyle of those involved in the new media and the often seamless interchange between the two.

altering the order or sequence of the workstations involved in a particular manufacturing process. For example, a manufacturer might have two parallel assembly lines producing two similar sets of machine parts. The lines might converge at one central quality control unit where tolerances are verified by inspectors. The manager, however, might decide to change to periodic rather than final inspection. Under this arrangement, one or more inspections are established farther up the line. Work sequence changes can also be made in service organizations. The processing of insurance claims, for example, could be changed. The sequence of logging and verifying claims, requesting cheques, getting countersignatures, and mailing cheques could be altered in several ways, such as combining the first two steps or routing the claims through one person while another handles cheques.

One form of technological change that has been especially important in recent years is change in information systems. It is hard to find a major popular magazine that has not written about the computer invasion. Simultaneous advances in personal computers and network tie-in systems have created vast potential for change in most workplaces. The basic goal behind the adoption of computers in offices is to create an information-processing station for each employee. The person at each workstation can manipulate ideas and drafts that are still in preliminary form; create, store, and retrieve documents; and distribute final copies. Organizational control systems may also be targets of change.[16]

Changing People

A third area of organization change has to do with human resources. For example, an organization might decide to change the skill level of its workforce. This change might be prompted by changes in technology or by a general desire to upgrade the quality of the workforce. Thus training programs and new selection criteria might be needed. The organization might also decide to improve its workers' performance level. In this instance, a new incentive system or performance-based training might be in order.

Perceptions and expectations are also a common focus of organization change. Workers in an organization might believe that their wages and benefits are not as high as they should be. Management, however, might have evidence that shows the firm is paying a competitive wage and providing a superior benefit package. The change, then, would be centred on informing and educating the workforce about the comparative value of its compensation package. A common way to do this is to publish a statement that places an actual dollar value on each benefit provided and compares that amount to what other local organizations are providing their workers. Change might also be directed at employee attitudes and values. In many organizations today, managers are trying to eliminate adversarial relationships with workers and adopt a more collaborative relationship. In many ways, changing attitudes and values is perhaps the hardest thing for management to do.

End of Exam Questions.

REENGINEERING IN ORGANIZATIONS

Many organizations today are going through massive and comprehensive change programs involving all aspects of organization design, technology, and people. Although various terms are used, the term currently in vogue for these changes is *reengineering*. Specifically, **reengineering** is the radical redesign of all aspects of a business to achieve major gains in cost, service, or time.[17]

● **reengineering**
The radical redesign of all aspects of a business to achieve major gains in cost, service, or time

The Need for Reengineering

Why are so many organizations finding it necessary to reengineer themselves? We noted in Chapter 2 that all systems, including organizations, are subject to entropy—a normal process leading to system decline. An organization is behaving most typically when it maintains the status quo, doesn't change in sync with its environment, and starts consuming its own resources to survive. In a sense, that is what IBM and Bell Canada did. The firms' managers grew complacent and assumed that their historic prosperity would continue and that they need not worry about environmental shifts, foreign competition, and so forth—and entropy set in. The key is to recognize the beginning of the decline and to immediately move toward reengineering. Major problems occur when managers either don't recognize the onset of entropy until it is well advanced or else are complacent in taking steps to correct it.

Steps in the Reengineering Process

Figure 12.3 shows the general steps in reengineering. The first step is setting goals and developing a strategy for reengineering. The organization must know in advance what reengineering is supposed to accomplish and how those accomplishments will be achieved. The *Managing in a Changing World* box portrays how a poorly articulated reengineering effort can be less successful than anticipated. Next, top managers must begin and direct the reengineering effort. If a CEO simply announces that reengineering is to occur but does nothing else, the program is unlikely to be successful. But if the CEO is constantly involved in the process, underscoring its importance and taking the lead, reengineering stands a much better chance of success.

Most experts also agree that successful reengineering is usually accompanied by a sense of urgency. People in the organization must see the clear and present need for the changes being implemented and appreciate their importance.

Procter & Gamble Trails in Innovation

 Procter & Gamble Co. (P&G) has been regarded as a global packaged consumer goods leader for many years. Nevertheless, even leaders can have problems. P&G's problems began showing up in the late 1980s. Even though it was spending nearly $1 billion (U.S.) annually on research and development, P&G was not getting to the market first with some of the latest products in certain lines. Despite P&G's introducing more than two hundred different product and packaging improvements between 1990 and 1993, it lagged behind on some major innovative product changes. For instance, late in 1993 Kimberly-Clark introduced a premium disposable diaper with Velcro fasteners and a clothlike outer cover, and P&G was placed in the role of follower. As a result, P&G decided to undergo the most substantial reengineering the company had ever had in its more than 150 years.

By 1993 P&G announced a plan to close thirty plants and reduce employment by a total of about 30,000 jobs worldwide over a period of three to four years. In 1994 it announced that, in its North American operations, it would close four plants, eliminate production lines at six other plants, and reduce its workforce by nearly 2,000. Although some of the personnel reduction would come from early retirements and transfers, there were to be significant numbers of layoffs.

Most observers did not expect P&G to get rid of laundry detergents or, for that matter, any products that would cost it market share or shelf space in groceries. It was predicted that P&G would continue to differentiate its brands and introduce new products, reduce package sizes, and strengthen secondary brands in regional markets where they tend to sell best.

Indeed, no clear pattern emerged from the plant closings. Plants that were closed produced dishwashing detergents and glycerin, soap and fatty acids, Folgers coffee, and health and beauty care products. The closed production lines included incontinence products, health and beauty care, fabric softeners, laundry and household cleaning products, as well as others not disclosed. Given that P&G produces many of its products in different locations, the final impact of these closings on actual brand availability remained to be seen.

In addition to this massive restructuring, P&G adopted a value pricing strategy to lower the prices on its brands, hoping to keep customers (see the *Managing in a Changing World* box in Chapter 8). Indeed, the change in pricing was so abrupt that some grocers and distributors were upset and threatened to drop P&G's products.

Now, in an effort to boost its sales to $70 billion (U.S.) by the year 2005, P&G has launched "Organization 2005," an initiative aimed at reorganizing its businesses according to products rather than geography.

References: Bill Saporito, "Behind the Tumult at P&G," *Fortune*, March 7, 1994, pp. 74–82; "P&G Details Plans to Close Factories, Lay Off 12% of Work Force by 1995," *The Wall Street Journal*, January 14, 1994, p. B3; Jennifer Lawrence, "P&G Losing Ground in Product Innovation," *Advertising Age*, November 15, 1993, p. 44; Jennifer Lawrence, "Don't Look for P&G to Pare Detergents," *Advertising Age*, May 31, 1993, pp. 3, 42; Steve Weinstein, "Will Procter's Gamble Work?" *Progressive Grocer*, July 1992, pp. 36–40; and Kelley Holland and Peter Galuszka, "Procter's Latest Gamble," *Business Week*, September 14, 1998, p. 58.

In addition, most successful reengineering efforts start with a new, clean slate. That is, rather than assuming that the existing organization is a starting point and then trying to modify it, reengineering usually starts by asking questions such as how are customers best served and competitors best neutralized. New approaches and systems are then created and imposed in place of existing ones.

Finally, reengineering requires a careful blend of top-down and bottom–up involvement. On the one hand, strong leadership is necessary, but too much involvement by top management can make the changes seem autocratic. Similarly, employee participation is also important, but too little involvement by leaders can undermine the program's importance and create a sense that top managers don't care. Thus care must be taken to carefully balance these two countervailing forces.

FIGURE 12.3 The Reengineering Process

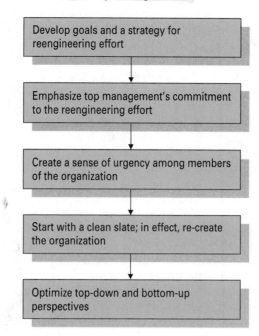

Develop goals and a strategy for reengineering effort

Emphasize top management's commitment to the reengineering effort

Create a sense of urgency among members of the organization

Start with a clean slate; in effect, re-create the organization

Optimize top-down and bottom-up perspectives

Reengineering is a major redesign of all areas of an organization. To be successful, reengineering requires a systematic and comprehensive assessment of the entire organization. Goals, top management support, and a sense of urgency help the organization re-create itself and blend both top-level and bottom-up perspectives.

ORGANIZATION DEVELOPMENT

We noted in several places the importance of people and change. A special area of interest that focuses almost exclusively on people is organization development.

OD Assumptions

Organization development is concerned with changing attitudes, perceptions, behaviours, and expectations. More precisely, **organization development** is "an effort (1) *planned*, (2) *organization wide*, and (3) *managed* from the *top* to (4) increase *organization effectiveness* and *health* through (5) *planned interventions* in the organization's 'process,' using *behavioural science* knowledge."[18] The theory and practice of OD are based on several very important assumptions. The first is that employees have a desire to grow and develop. Another is that employees have a strong need to be accepted by others within the organization. Still another critical assumption of OD is that the total organization and the way it is designed will influence the way individuals and groups within the organization behave. Thus some form of collaboration between managers and their employees is necessary to (1) take advantage of the skills and abilities of the employees and (2) eliminate aspects of the organization that retard employee growth, development, and group acceptance. Because of the intense personal nature of many OD activities, many large organizations rely on one or more OD consultants (either full-time employees assigned to this function or outside OD experts) to implement and manage their OD program.

● **organization development**
An effort that is planned, organization wide, and managed from the top; it is intended to increase organization effectiveness and health through planned interventions in the organization's process, using behavioural science knowledge

OD Techniques

Several kinds of interventions or activities are generally considered to be part of organization development.[19] Some OD programs may use only one or a few of these; other programs use several of them at once.

Diagnostic Activities   Just as a physician examines patients to diagnose their current condition, an OD diagnosis analyzes the current condition of an organization. To carry out this diagnosis, managers use questionnaires, opinion or attitude surveys, interviews, archival data, and meetings to assess various characteristics of the organization. The results from this diagnosis may generate profiles of the organization's activities, which can then be used to identify problem areas in need of correction.

Team Building   Team-building activities are intended to enhance the effectiveness and satisfaction of individuals who work in groups or teams and to promote overall group effectiveness. Project teams in a matrix organization are good candidates for these activities. An OD consultant might interview team members to determine how they feel about the group; then an off-site meeting could be held to discuss the issues that surfaced and to iron out any problem areas or member concerns. Caterpillar used team building as one method for changing the working relationships between workers and supervisors from confrontational to cooperative.[20]

Survey Feedback   In survey feedback, each employee responds to a questionnaire intended to measure perceptions and attitudes (for example, satisfaction and supervisory style). Everyone involved, including the supervisor, receives the results of the survey. The aim of this approach is usually to change the behaviour of supervisors by showing them how their subordinates view them. After the feedback has been provided, workshops may be conducted to evaluate results and suggest constructive changes.

Education   Educational activities focus on classroom training. Although such activities can be used for technical or skill-related purposes, an OD educational

Team building is an increasingly common organization development technique. These managers are participating in one popular method of team building. As they work together to scale this small cliff, the goal is for them to build trust and to learn how to more effectively work together.

activity typically focuses on "sensitivity skills"—that is, it teaches people to be more considerate and understanding of the people they work with. Participants often go through a series of experiential or role-playing exercises to learn better how others in the organization feel.

Intergroup Activities   The focus of intergroup activities is on improving the relationships between two or more groups. We noted in Chapter 10 that, as group interdependence increases, so do coordination difficulties. Intergroup OD activities are designed to promote cooperation or resolve conflicts that arose as a result of interdependence. Experiential or role-playing activities are often used to bring this about.

Third-Party Peacemaking   Another approach to OD is through third-party peacemaking, which is most often used when substantial conflict exists within the organization. Third-party peacemaking can be appropriate on the individual, group, or organization level. The third party, usually an OD consultant, uses a variety of mediation or negotiation techniques to resolve any problems or conflicts between individuals or groups.

Technostructural Activities   Technostructural activities are concerned with the design of the organization, the technology of the organization, and the interrelationship of design and technology with people on the job. A structural change such as an increase in decentralization, a job design change such as an increase in the use of automation, and a technological change involving a modification in workflow all qualify as technostructural OD activities if their objective is to improve group and interpersonal relationships within the organization.

Process Consultation   In process consultation, an OD consultant observes groups in the organization to develop an understanding of their communication patterns, decision-making and leadership processes, and methods of cooperation and conflict resolution. The consultant then provides feedback to the involved parties about the processes he or she has observed. The goal of this form of intervention is to improve the observed processes. A leader who is presented with feedback outlining deficiencies in his or her leadership style, for example, might be expected to change to overcome them.

Life and Career Planning   Life and career planning helps employees formulate their personal goals and evaluate strategies for integrating their goals with the goals of the organization. Such activities might include specification of training needs and plotting a career map. General Electric Co. has a reputation for doing an outstanding job in this area.

Coaching and Counselling   Coaching and counselling provide nonevaluative feedback to individuals. The purpose is to help people both develop a better sense of how others see them and learn behaviours that will assist others in achieving their work-related goals. The focus is not on how the individual is performing today; instead, it is on how the person can perform better in the future.

Planning and Goal Setting   More pragmatically oriented than many other interventions are activities designed to help managers improve their planning and goal setting. Emphasis still falls on the individual, however, because the intent is to help individuals and groups integrate themselves into the overall planning process. The OD consultant might use the same approach as in process consultation, but the focus is more technically oriented on the mechanics of planning and goal setting.

The Effectiveness of OD

Given the diversity of activities encompassed by organization development, it is not surprising that managers report mixed results from various OD interventions. Organizations that actively practise some form of OD include CAMI, Hewlett-Packard Canada, Procter & Gamble, ITT Corporation, Polaroid, and B.F. Goodrich. Goodrich, for example, has trained sixty persons in OD processes and techniques. These trained experts have subsequently become internal OD consultants to assist other managers in applying the techniques.[21] Many other managers, in contrast, report that they have tried OD but discarded it.[22]

OD will probably remain an important part of management theory and practice. Of course, there are no sure things when dealing with social systems such as organizations, and the effectiveness of many OD techniques is difficult to evaluate. Because all organizations are open systems interacting with their environments, an improvement after an OD intervention may be attributable to the intervention, but it may also be attributable to changes in economic conditions, luck, or other factors.[23]

ORGANIZATIONAL INNOVATION

● **innovation**
The managed effort of an organization to develop new products or services or new uses for existing products or services

A final element of organization change that we address is innovation. **Innovation** is the managed effort of an organization to develop new products or services or new uses for existing products or services. Innovation is clearly important because without new products or services, any organization will fall behind its competition. The *Environment of Management* box shows how innovation has played a major role at Nortel.

The Innovation Process

The organizational innovation process consists of developing, applying, launching, growing, and managing the maturity and decline of creative ideas.[24] This process is depicted in Figure 12.4.

Innovation Development Innovation development involves the evaluation, modification, and improvement of creative ideas. Innovation development can transform a product or service with only modest potential into a product or service with significant potential. Parker Brothers, for example, decided during innovation development not to market an indoor volleyball game but instead sell separately the appealing little foam ball designed for the game. The firm will never know how well the volleyball game would have sold, but the Nerf ball and numerous related products have generated millions of dollars in revenues for Parker Brothers.[25]

Innovation Application Innovation application is the stage in which an organization takes a developed idea and uses it in the design, manufacturing, or delivery of new products, services, or processes. At this point the innovation emerges from the laboratory and is transformed into tangible goods or services.

One example of innovation application is the use of radar-based focusing systems in Polaroid's instant cameras. The idea of using radio waves to discover the location, speed, and direction of moving objects was first applied extensively by Allied forces during World War II. As radar technology developed during the following years, the electrical components needed became smaller and more streamlined. Researchers at Polaroid applied this well-developed technology in a new way.[26]

Application Launch Application launch is the stage in which an organization introduces new products or services to the marketplace. The important question is not "Does the innovation work?" but "Will customers want to purchase the innovative product and service?" History is full of creative ideas that did not generate enough interest among customers to be successful. Some notable innovation failures include Sony's seat warmer, the Bricklin automobile (built in New Brunswick from 1974 to 1976), the movie *Heaven's Gate* (which lost almost US$100 million before it was pulled from theatres), and Polaroid's SX-70 instant camera (which cost US$3 billion to develop, but never sold more than 100,000 units in a year).[27] Thus despite development and application, new products and services can still possibly fail at the application launch phase.

Application Growth Once an innovation has been successfully launched, it then enters the stage of application growth. This is a period of high economic performance for an organization because demand for the product or service is often greater than supply. Organizations that fail to anticipate this stage may unintentionally limit their growth, as Gillette did by not anticipating demand for its Sensor razor blades. At the same time, overestimating demand for a new product can be just as detrimental to performance. Unsold products can sit in warehouses for years.

Innovation Maturity After a period of growing demand, an innovative product or service often enters a period of maturity. Innovation maturity is the stage in which most organizations in an industry have access to an innovation and are applying it in approximately the same way. The technological application of an innovation during this stage of the innovation process can be very

Organizations actively seek to manage the innovation process. These steps illustrate the general life cycle that characterizes most innovations today. Of course, as with creativity, the innovation process will suffer if it is approached too mechanically and rigidly.

FIGURE 12.4 The Innovation Process

Development
The organization evaluates, modifies, and improves on a creative idea.

Application
The organization uses the developed idea in design, manufacturing, or delivery of new products, services, or processes.

Launch
The organization introduces new products or services to the marketplace.

Decline
Demand for an innovation decreases, and substitute innovations are developed and applied.

Maturity
Most competing organizations have access to the idea.

Growth
Demand for new products or services grows.

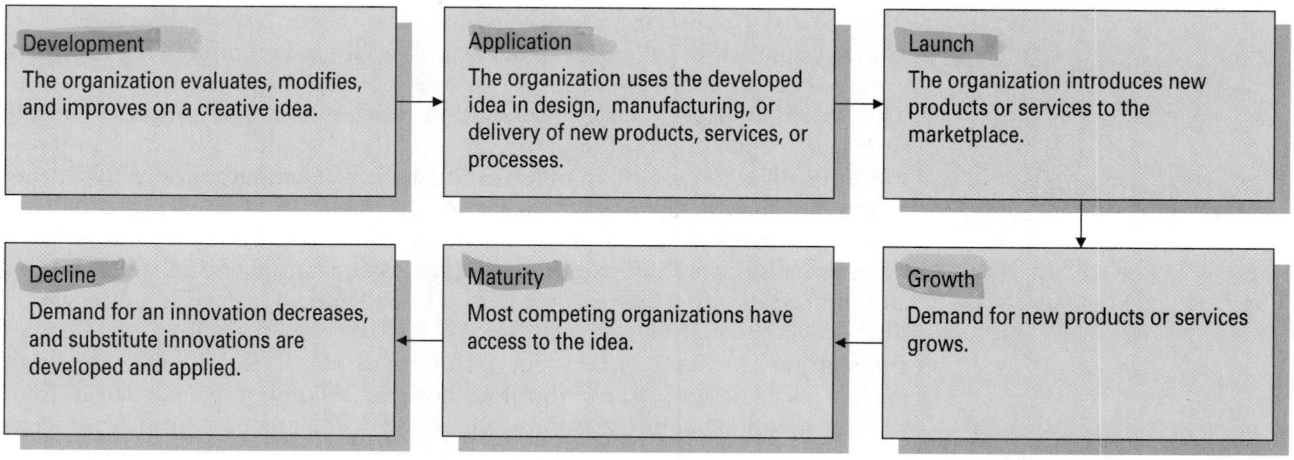

Nortel's Business Is Innovation

 The Smart Base Transceiver Station (BTS) is one of Nortel's many innovations: it offers 50 percent more coverage than conventional equipment. Another of Nortel's innovations is the Magellan Passport, the first ATM to transport voice as variable bit rate (VBR) traffic. The Northern Telecom Type 4BIFS protector module is yet another innovation: it protects networks from overvoltage and sneak current damage. The company is working on more new products, including new wireless technology that will handle faxes and a voice recognition system that will make it possible to operate a telephone without touching it. It seems only fitting that on October 1, 1997, John Roth, an engineer and research and development specialist, became Nortel's first CEO to be picked from the ranks in thirty years. His appointment should ensure that Nortel will maintain its reputation as Canada's leading high-tech corporation. In 1997, the company spent $3.1 billion (by far the highest expenditure by any company in Canada) or 15 percent of its revenue on research and development.

The nature of Nortel's business dictates that it continue to spend heavily on research and development: 50 percent of the products the company sells did not exist five years ago. Nortel designs, manufactures, and supplies a wide range of products for digital networks of all kinds. Its customers are local and long-distance telecommunications companies; cellular, mobile, radio, and personal communications service providers; businesses; universities; governments; cable television companies; competitive local access providers; and other network operators around the world. Of Nortel's 80,000 employees, 20,000 are engaged in research and development at forty-eight sites worldwide. In 1994, the company hired one of every three Canadians who graduated with master's or doctorates in electrical engineering and computer science. All of this underlines the fact that the business of Nortel is innovation.

Nortel, which prior to 1995 was known as Northern Telecom, was founded in 1895 as the manufacturing branch of Bell Telephone Company of Canada. It was incorporated as Northern Electric and Manufacturing Company Limited. After a series of mergers and acquisitions between 1895 and 1976, the company became known as Northern Telecom in 1976. As a result of a merger with Bay Networks, the company is now called Nortel Networks.

References: Bruce Livesey, "Tag Team," *Report on Business Magazine*, July 1997, pp. 39–48; Daniel Stoffman, "Mr. Clean," *Canadian Business*, June 1996, pp. 59–65; "Operations Overview and Company History," at Nortel's Web site (http://www.nortel.com); Jason Meyers, "Nortel's Smart BTS Moves to the Head of the Class," *Telephony*, March 25, 1996, p. 6; Kieran Taylor, "North Telecom's Magellan Passport," *Data Communications*, January 1996, pp. 42–44; Toni Rossi and Barry Slotnick, "Prescription for Electro-Xenophobia: Solid-State Overvoltage Protection," *Telephony*, February 6, 1995, p. 32; "50 Top R&D Companies," *Report on Business Magazine*, July 1998, p. 97; and "Corporate Facts" (http://www.nortelnetworks.com).

---

sophisticated. Because most firms have access to the innovation, however, either as a result of their developing the innovation on their own or copying the innovation of others, it does not provide competitive advantage to any one of them. The time that elapses between innovation development and innovation maturity varies depending on the particular product or service. Whenever an innovation involves the use of complex skills (such as a complicated manufacturing process or highly sophisticated teamwork), moving from the growth to the maturity phase will take longer. In addition, if the skills needed to implement these innovations are difficult to imitate, then strategic imitation may be delayed and the organization may enjoy a period of sustained competitive advantage.

Innovation Decline Every successful innovation bears its own seeds of decline. Because an organization does not gain a competitive advantage from an innovation at maturity, it must encourage its creative scientists, engineers, and managers to begin looking for new innovations. This continued search for competitive advantage usually leads new products and services to move from the creative process through innovation maturity, and finally to innovation decline. Innovation decline is the stage during which demand for an innovation decreases and substitute innovations are developed and applied.

Forms of Innovation

Each creative idea an organization develops poses a different challenge for the innovation process. Innovations can be radical or incremental, technical or managerial, and product or process.

Radical versus Incremental Innovations   **Radical innovations** are new products or technologies developed by an organization that completely replace the existing products or technologies in an industry. **Incremental innovations** are new products or processes that modify existing ones. Firms that implement radical innovations fundamentally shift the nature of competition and the interaction of firms within their environments. Firms that implement incremental innovations alter, but do not fundamentally change, competitive interaction in an industry.

Over the last several years, organizations have introduced many radical innovations. For example, compact disk technology has virtually replaced long-playing vinyl records in the recording industry, and high-definition television seems likely to replace regular television technology (both black-and-white and colour) in the near future. Whereas radical innovations like these tend to be very visible and public, incremental innovations actually are more numerous. One example is Ford's sports utility vehicle, Explorer. Although other companies had similar products, Ford more effectively combined the styling and engineering that resulted in increased demand for all sports utility vehicles.

Technical versus Managerial Innovations   **Technical innovations** are changes in the physical appearance or performance of a product or service, or the physical processes through which a product or service is manufactured. Many of the most important innovations over the last fifty years have been technical. For example, the serial replacement of the vacuum tube with the transistor, the transistor with the integrated circuit, and the integrated circuit with the microchip has greatly enhanced the power, ease of use, and speed of operation of a wide variety of electronic products. Not all innovations developed by organizations are technical, however. **Managerial innovations** are changes in the management process by which products and services are conceived, built, and delivered to customers. Managerial innovations do not necessarily affect the physical appearance or performance of products or services directly. In effect, reengineering, as we discuss earlier, represents a managerial innovation.

Product versus Process Innovations   Perhaps the two most important types of technical innovations are product innovations and process innovations. **Product innovations** are changes in the physical characteristics or performance of existing products or services or the creation of brand new products or services. **Process innovations** are changes in the way products or services are manufactured, created, or distributed. Whereas managerial innovations generally affect the broader context of development, process innovations directly affect manufacturing.

- **radical innovation**
A new product, service, or technology that completely replaces an existing one

- **incremental innovation**
A new product, service, or technology that modifies an existing one

- **technical innovation**
A change in appearance or performance of products or services or the physical processes through which a product or service passes

- **managerial innovation**
Change in the management process in an organization

- **product innovation**
A change in the physical characteristics of a product or service or the creation of a new one

- **process innovation**
A change in the way a product or service is manufactured, created, or distributed

The implementation of robotics, as we discuss earlier, is a process innovation. As Figure 12.5 shows, the effect of product and process innovations on economic return depends on the stage of the innovation process that a new product or service occupies. At first, during development, application, and launch, the physical attributes and capabilities of an innovation most affect organizational performance. Thus product innovations are particularly important during these beginning phases. Later, as an innovation enters the phases of growth, maturity, and decline, an organization's ability to develop process innovations such as fine-tuning manufacturing, increasing product quality, and improving product distribution becomes important to maintaining economic return.

Japanese organizations have often excelled at process innovation. The market for 35mm cameras was dominated by German and other European manufacturers when, in the early 1960s, Japanese organizations such as Canon and Nikon began making cameras. Although some of these early Japanese products were not very successful, these companies continued to invest in their process technology and eventually they were able to increase quality and decrease manufacturing costs. Now these Japanese organizations dominate the worldwide market for 35mm cameras, and the German companies, because they were not able to maintain the same pace of process innovation, are struggling to maintain market share and profitability.

The Failure to Innovate

To remain competitive in today's economy, organizations *must* be innovative. And yet many organizations that should be innovative are not successful at bringing out new products or services, or do so only after innovations created by others are very mature. Organizations may fail to innovate for at least three reasons.

Lack of Resources   Innovation is expensive in terms of dollars, time, and energy. If a firm does not have sufficient money to fund a program of innovation, or does not currently employ the kinds of employees it needs to be innovative, it may lag

As the innovation process moves from development to decline, the economic return from product innovations gradually declines. In contrast, the economic return from process innovations increases during this same process.

FIGURE 12.5   Effects of Product and Process Innovation on Economic Return

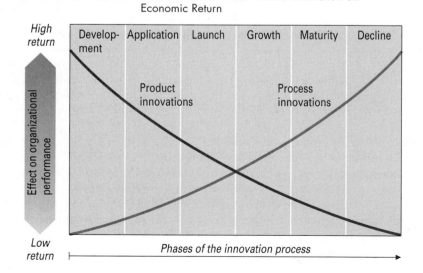

behind in innovation. Even highly innovative organizations cannot become involved in every new product or service its employees think up. For example, numerous other commitments in the electronic instruments and computer industry forestalled Hewlett-Packard from investing in Steve Jobs and Steve Wozniak's idea for a personal computer. With infinite resources of money, time, and technical and managerial expertise, HP might have entered this market early. Because the firm did not have this flexibility, however, it had to make some difficult choices about which innovations to invest in.

Failure to Recognize Opportunities Because firms cannot pursue all innovations, they need to develop the capability to carefully evaluate innovations and to select the ones that hold the greatest potential. To obtain a competitive advantage, an organization usually must make investment decisions before the innovation process reaches the mature stage. The earlier the investment, however, the greater the risk. If organizations are not skilled at recognizing and evaluating opportunities, they may be overly cautious and fail to invest in innovations that turn out later to be successful for other firms.

Resistance to Change As we discussed earlier, many organizations tend to resist change. Innovation means giving up old products and old ways of doing things in favour of new products and new ways of doing things. These kinds of changes can be personally difficult for managers and other members of an organization. Thus resistance to change can slow the innovation process.

Promoting Innovation in Organizations

A wide variety of ideas for promoting innovation in organizations has been developed over the years. One method, intrapreneurship, we discussed in Chapter 9. Two other specific ways for promoting innovation are through the reward system and through the organizational culture.

The Reward System A firm's reward system is the means by which it encourages and discourages certain behaviours by employees. Major components of the reward system include salaries, bonuses, and perquisites. Using the reward system to promote innovation is a fairly mechanical but nevertheless effective management technique. The idea is to provide financial and nonfinancial rewards to people and groups that develop innovative ideas. Once the members of an organization understand that they will be rewarded for such activities, they are more likely to work creatively. Ottawa-based Corel Corp., in addition to paying attractive salaries, offers annual stock options to its employees, usually right after launching new products.[28]

It is important for organizations to reward creative behaviour, but it is vital to avoid punishing creativity when it does not result in highly successful innovations. It is the nature of the creative and innovative processes that many new product ideas will simply not work out in the marketplace. Each process is fraught with too many uncertainties to generate positive results every time. An individual may have prepared herself to be creative, but an insight may not be forthcoming. Or managers may attempt to apply a developed innovation, only to recognize that it does not work. Indeed, some organizations operate according to the assumption that if all their innovative efforts succeed, then they are probably not taking enough risks in research and development. At 3M, nearly 60 percent of the creative ideas suggested each year do not succeed in the marketplace.

Managers need to be very careful in responding to innovative failure. If innovative failure is due to incompetence, systematic errors, or managerial sloppiness, then a firm should respond appropriately, for example, by withholding raises or reducing promotion opportunities. People who act in good faith to develop an innovation that simply does not work out, however, should not be punished for failure. If they are, they will probably not be creative in the future. A punitive reward system will discourage people from taking risks and therefore reduce the organization's ability to obtain competitive advantages.

Organizational Culture   As we discussed in Chapter 3, an organization's culture consists of the set of values, beliefs, and symbols that help guide behaviour. A strong, appropriately focused organizational culture can be used to support innovative activity. A well-managed culture can communicate a sense that innovation is valued and will be rewarded and also that occasional failure in the pursuit of new ideas is not only acceptable but even expected. In addition to reward systems and intrapreneurial activities, companies such as 3M, Corning, Monsanto, Procter & Gamble, Texas Instruments, Johnson & Johnson, and Merck are all known to have strong, innovation-oriented cultures that value individual creativity, risk taking, and inventiveness.[29] As described in the *Environment of Management* box, Nortel's business is innovation; the same can be said of Kanata, Ont.–based Newbridge Networks.

SUMMARY OF KEY POINTS

Organization change is any substantive modification to some part of the organization. Change may be prompted by forces internal or external to the organization. In general, planned change is preferable to reactive change.

Managing the change process is very important. The Lewin model provides a general perspective on the steps involved in change, although a comprehensive model is usually more effective. People tend to resist change because of uncertainty, threatened self-interests, different perceptions, and feelings of loss. Participation, education and communication, facilitation, and force-field analysis are methods for overcoming this resistance.

Many different change techniques or interventions are used. The most common ones involve changing organization structure and design, technology, and people. There are several specific areas of change within each of these broad categories.

Reengineering is the radical redesign of all aspects of a business to achieve major gains in cost, service, or time. It is occasionally needed to offset entropy. The basic steps are developing goals and strategies, conveying the involvement of top management, creating a sense of urgency, starting with a clean slate, and balancing top-down and bottom-up perspectives.

Organization development is concerned with changing attitudes, perceptions, behaviours, and expectations. Its effective use relies on an important set of assumptions. There are conflicting opinions about the effectiveness of several OD techniques.

The innovation process has six steps: development, application, launch, growth, maturity, and decline. Basic categories of innovation include radical, incremental, technical, managerial, product, and process innovations. Despite the importance of innovation, many organizations fail to innovate because they lack the required creative individuals or are committed to too many other creative activities, fail to recognize opportunities, or resist the change that innovation requires. Organizations can use a variety of tools to overcome these problems, including the reward system, intrapreneurship, and organizational culture.

DISCUSSION QUESTIONS

Questions for Review

1. What forces or kinds of events lead to organization change? Identify each force or event as planned or reactive change.
2. How is each step in the process of organization change implemented? Are some of the steps likely to meet with more resistance than others? Why or why not?
3. What are the various areas of organization change? In what ways are they similar and in what ways do they differ?
4. What are the steps in the innovation process?

Questions for Analysis

5. Could reactive change of the type identified in question 1 have been planned for ahead of time? Why or why not? Should all organization change be planned? Why or why not?
6. A company has recently purchased equipment that, when installed, will do the work of one hundred employees. The workforce of the company is very concerned and is threatening to take some kind of action. If you were the human resource manager, what would you try to do to satisfy all parties concerned? Why?
7. Think of several relatively new products or services that you use. What form of innovation was each?

Questions for Application

8. Some people resist change while others welcome change enthusiastically. To deal with the first group, one needs to overcome resistance to change; to deal with the second, one needs to overcome resistance to stability. What advice can you give a manager facing the latter situation?
9. Can a change made in one area of an organization—in technology, for instance—not lead to change in other areas? Why or why not?
10. Find out more about one of the techniques for organization development presented in this chapter. What are the advantages and disadvantages of that technique relative to other techniques?

BUILDING EFFECTIVE INTERPERSONAL SKILLS

Exercise Overview

A manager's interpersonal skills are her or his ability to understand and motivate individuals and groups. These abilities are especially important during a period of change. Thus, this exercise will help you understand how to apply your interpersonal skills to a change situation.

Exercise Background

Assume that you are the manager of a retail store in a local shopping mall. Your staff consists of seven full-time and ten part-time employees. The full-time employees have worked together as a team for three years. The part-timers are all local university students; a few of them have worked in the store for more than a year, but there tends to be a lot of turnover among this group.

Your boss, the regional manager, has just informed you that the national chain that owns your store is planning to open a second store in the same mall. She has also informed you that you must plan and implement the following changes:

1. You will serve as manager of both stores until the sales volume of the new store warrants its own full-time manager.
2. You are to designate one of the full-time employees in your present store as the assistant manager, since you will be in the store less often now.
3. To have experienced workers in the new store, you are to select three of your current full-time workers to move to the new store, one of whom should also be appointed as assistant manager of that store.
4. You can hire three new people to replace those transferred from your existing store and three new people to work at the new store.
5. You can decide for yourself how to deploy your part-timers, but you will need a total of ten in the existing store and eight at the new store.

You realize that many of your employees will be unhappy with these changes. They all know each other and work well together. However, the new store will be in a new section of the mall and will be a very nice place to work.

Exercise Task

With this background information in mind, do the following:
1. Determine the likely reasons for resistance to this change from your workers.
2. Determine how you will decide about promotions and transfers (make whatever assumptions you think are warranted).
3. Outline how you will inform your employees about the change.
4. An alternative strategy would involve keeping the existing staff intact and hiring new employees for the new store. Outline a persuasion strategy for trying to convince your boss that this option is better.

Levi Strauss Hikes Up Its Pants

 Levi Strauss & Co. and the ubiquitous denim blue jeans it sells around the world have been industry icons for years. The firm can trace its roots back to the mid-nineteenth century when its namesake immigrated to the United States from Bavaria. Shortly after arriving in San Francisco during the California gold rush, Levi Strauss decided that it was a safer bet to produce equipment for other miners than it was to set out with his own pick and shovel. Work pants crafted from heavy canvas proved to be his most successful product, and the rest, as they say, is history.

Strauss began colouring the pants with blue pigments and enlisted the aid of a friend to provide what would become the trademark rivets to key stress points. The firm grew slowly but surely for decades, always led by one of Strauss's direct descendants. But Levi's real growth started in the 1950s when its pants became an essential uniform for the youth of North America.

The momentum continued into the 1960s as denim took its place alongside incense, tie-died shirts, and long hair as symbols of a rebellious youth. And as the baby boomers, who were the youth of the 1950s and 1960s, grew into adulthood, Levi's jeans became their fashion mainstay. The name Levi's became almost synonymous with blue jeans. During the 1970s through the 1990s, Levi also expanded rapidly overseas, and today the brand is sold in more than seventy countries.

Under the leadership of Robert Hass (Levi Strauss's great-great-grandnephew), Levi also forged an innovative relationship with its employees. High levels of job security, an innovative reward structure, and an open and participative approach to management created a loyal and dedicated workforce that helped keep the organization at the top of its industry.

But as the 1990s grew to a close, Levi Strauss seemed to hit a wall. And as a result, the firm has had to reexamine every aspect of its business operations and simultaneously redefine its relationship with its workforce. The catalyst for change was an almost-sudden drop in market share. For example, in 1990 Levi held 30.9 percent of the jeans market in the United States. But by 1997 that figure had plummeted to just 18.7 percent. Similarly, the firm's market share among 15- to 19-year-old consumers

dropped from 33 percent in 1993 to 26 percent in 1997.

As a result of this alarming trend, company executives faced an intense and detailed period of introspection to find out what was happening to the company. Their conclusion was that Levi Strauss had been so successful with its core baby-boomer consumers that it had essentially neglected younger consumers. As a result, top-end designers such as Tommy Hilfiger and Ralph Lauren and discounted store brands sold at Sears and J.C. Penney took market share from Levi. Similarly, the jeans giant had also ignored emerging fashion trends like wide-legged and baggy jeans.

Once they saw their problem, executives took quick action on a number of fronts. Most painfully, the company announced that it was closing eleven of its plants in the United States and Canada and laying off one-third of its North American workforce. Needless to say, this step served to dramatically and unalterably change its relationship with its workforce. The company also acknowledged that it needed to alter the composition of its executive team to boost creativity and market knowledge. Too many company officials, it said, had come up through the ranks and knew only one way of doing things—the old tried-and-true Levi's way. Thus one goal now is to fill 30 percent of all new management jobs with outsiders. Experts agree that Levi will need some time to get its act together again, but they also acknowledge that the changes seem to fit the situation as well as a pair of the firm's jeans fit after a long day at the office.

Questions

1. What forces led to the need for change at Levi Strauss?

2. What kinds of changes can you identify at Levi?

3. One mistake a firm can make is failing to change when it needs to; another is changing too quickly. How can managers like those at Levi best position themselves to change when they need to—not too quickly, but not too late either?

References: "Levi's Is Hiking Up Its Pants," *Business Week*, December 1, 1997, pp. 70–75; "Its Share Shrinking, Levi Strauss Lays Off 6,395," *The Wall Street Journal*, November 4, 1997, pp. B1, B8; "Levi's Get the Blues," *Time*, November 17, 1997, p. 66; and Kelley Holland, Pat Wechsler, and Linda Himelstein, "Jean Therapy," *Business Week*, November 17, 1997, p. 52.

CHAPTER NOTES

1. Alex Taylor III, "Neutron Jurgen Ignites a Revolution at Daimler-Benz," *Fortune*, November 10, 1997, pp. 144–152; "A Tough Deadline," *Forbes*, April 22, 1996, pp. 165–173; and "Dustup at Daimler," *Business Week,* February 3, 1997, pp. 52–53.

2. For excellent reviews of this area, see Richard W. Woodman, "Organization Change and Development: New Arenas for Inquiry and Action," *Journal of Management*, June 1989, pp. 205–228; and William Pasmore and Mary Fagans, "Participation, Individual Development, and Organizational Change: A Review and Synthesis," *Journal of Management*, June 1992, pp. 375–397.

3. For additional insights into how technological change affects other parts of the organization, see P. Robert Duimering, Frank Safayeni, and Lyn Purdy, "Integrated Manufacturing: Redesign the Organization Before Implementing Flexible Technology," *Sloan Management Review*, Summer 1993, pp. 47–56.

4. Thomas A. Stewart, "How to Lead a Revolution," *Fortune*, November 28, 1994, pp. 48–61.

5. Peter Robertson, Darryl Roberts, and Jerry Porras, "Dynamics of Planned Organizational Change: Assessing Empirical Support for a Theoretical Model," *Academy of Management Journal*, Vol. 36, No. 3, 1993, pp. 619–634.

6. Ian Austen, "Videos from the Dead," *Canadian Business*, February 27, 1998, pp. 72–75.

7. John P. Kotter and Leonard A. Schlesinger, "Choosing Strategies for Change," *Harvard Business Review*, March–April 1979, p. 106. See also Anne Fisher, "Making Change Stick," *Fortune*, April 17, 1995, pp. 121–133.

8. Kurt Lewin, "Frontiers in Group Dynamics: Concept, Method, and Reality in Social Science," *Human Relations*, June 1947, pp. 5–41.

9. See Connie J.G. Gersick, "Revolutionary Change Theories: A Multilevel Exploration of the Punctuated Equilibrium Paradigm," *Academy of Management Review*, January 1991, pp. 10–36.

10. See Gerald Andrews, "Mistrust, the Hidden Obstacle to Empowerment," *HR Magazine*, November 1994, pp. 66–74, for a good illustration of how resistance emerges.

11. "RJR Employees Fight Distraction Amid Buy-out Talks," *The Wall Street Journal*, November 1, 1988, p. A8.

12. See Paul R. Lawrence, "How to Deal with Resistance to Change," *Harvard Business Review*, January–February 1969, pp. 4–12, 166–176, for a classic discussion.

13. Lester Coch and John R.P. French, Jr., "Overcoming Resistance to Change," *Human Relations*, August 1948, pp. 512–532.

14. Charles K. Day, Jr., "Management's Mindless Mistakes," *Industry Week*, May 29, 1987, p. 42. See also "Inspection from the Plant Floor," *Business Week*, April 10, 1989, pp. 60–61.

15. David A. Nadler, "The Effective Management of Organizational Change," in Jay W. Lorsch (Ed.), *Handbook of Organizational Behavior* (Englewood Cliffs, N.J.: Prentice-Hall, 1987), pp. 358–369.

16. Jeffrey A. Alexander, "Adaptive Change in Corporate Control Practices," *Academy of Management Journal*, March 1991, pp. 162–193.

17. Thomas A. Stewart, "Reengineering—The Hot New Managing Tool," *Fortune*, August 23, 1993, pp. 41–48.

18. Richard Beckhard, *Organization Development: Strategies and Models* (Reading, Mass.: Addison-Wesley, 1969), p. 9. Italics in original.

19. Wendell L. French and Cecil H. Bell, Jr., *Organization Development: Behavioral Science Interventions for Organization Improvement*, 2nd ed. (Englewood Cliffs, N.J.: Prentice-Hall, 1978).

20. William G. Dyer, *Team Building Issues and Alternatives* (Reading, Mass.: Addison-Wesley, 1980).

21. Roger J. Hower, Mark G. Mindell, and Donna L. Simmons, "Introducing Innovation Through OD," *Management Review*, February 1978, pp. 52–56.

22. "Is Organization Development Catching On? A Personnel Symposium," *Personnel*, November–December 1977, pp. 10–22.

23. For a recent discussion on the effectiveness of various OD techniques in different organizations, see John M. Nicholas, "The Comparative Impact of Organization Development Interventions on Hard Criteria Measures," *Academy of Management Review*, October 1982, pp. 531–542.

24. L.B. Mohr, "Determinants of Innovation in Organizations," *American Political Science Review*, 1969, pp. 111–126; G.A. Steiner, *The Creative Organization* (Chicago: University of Chicago Press, 1965); R. Duncan and A. Weiss, "Organizational Learning: Implications for Organizational Design," in B.M. Staw (Ed.), *Research in Organizational Behavior*, Vol. 1 (Greenwich, Conn.: JAI Press, 1979), pp. 75–123; and J.E. Ettlie, "Adequacy of Stage Models for Decisions on Adoption of Innovation," *Psychological Reports*, 1980, pp. 991–995.

25. Beth Wolfensberger, "Trouble in Toyland," *New England Business*, September 1990, pp. 28–36.

26. See Alan Patz, "Managing Innovation in High Technology Industries," *New Management*, September 1986, pp. 54–59.

27. "Flops," *Business Week*, August 16, 1993, pp. 76–82.

28. Tamsen Tillson, "Corel Inside Out," *Canadian Business Technology*, Spring 1997, pp. 58–62.

29. See Steven P. Feldman, "How Organizational Culture Can Affect Innovation," *Organizational Dynamics*, Summer 1988, pp. 57–68.

Managing Human Resources in Organizations

13

OBJECTIVES

After studying this chapter, you should be able to:

● *Describe the environmental context of human resource management, including its strategic importance and its relationship with legal and social factors.*

● *Discuss how organizations attract human resources, including human resource planning, recruiting, and selecting.*

● *Describe how organizations develop human resources, including training and development, performance appraisal, and performance feedback.*

● *Discuss how organizations maintain human resources, including the determination of compensation and benefits and career planning.*

● *Discuss labour relations, including how employees form unions and the mechanics of collective bargaining.*

Saturn relies heavily on its human resources to compete against other automakers.

Saturn has been hailed as the future of the North American automobile industry. General Motors Corp. first announced plans for its new subsidiary in the early 1980s, and the first automobile rolled out of the new Spring Hill, Tennessee, Saturn factory in 1990. The guiding premise behind Saturn was to model automobile production after successful methods used in Japan—for example, advanced technology, worker participation, and production based on work teams.

Because General Motors itself is unionized, the Saturn operation was launched with the full participation of its unions, especially the United Auto Workers (UAW). When the firm began hiring workers for Spring Hill, the agreement was that any current GM employee belonging to the UAW could apply for a transfer to Saturn. In the beginning, Saturn chose workers from that labour pool who were most attuned to the ideas of cooperation and participation. In addition, all new Saturn workers received up to 700 hours of training. This

> **"These folks are tougher to integrate into Saturn." (Timothy Epps, Saturn human resource manager)**

training included not only basic production techniques and methods, but also conflict management and interpersonal relations skills necessary for smoothly functioning work teams. These teams, comprising around fifteen workers each, handle virtually everything from hiring new employees to setting budgets to overseeing operations throughout the Saturn plant.

The Saturn automobile itself has been a big success. Indeed, it is so successful that the prevailing culture at Spring Hill is threatened. Demand for Saturn automobiles has forced the plant to add shifts and put many of its workers on fifty-hour workweeks. As a result, many of these workers have experienced increased stress, fatigue, and burnout. Management has also been charged by the UAW with exerting more control and pressure to meet new manufacturing projections.

In addition, a new labour contract between the UAW and GM signed in 1990 mandates that Saturn now hire only GM workers who have lost their jobs at other GM plants. As a result, the plant is taking on more and more new workers who are angry at losing their other job and are often prone to distrust management.

General Motors has also cut training programs for new hires. Instead of 700 hours of training, new employees get only 170 hours of training, mostly in job-related skills. Taken together, these changes are seen by some Saturn employees as a sign that traditional GM practices are creeping into the organization. Nevertheless, on September 4, 1998, the UAW and Saturn affirmed their unique contract, one that rewards productivity and offers employees a voice in how the company is managed.[1] ●

Human resources are clearly an integral part of Saturn's success. Saturn took a unique approach when it selected and trained its first employees. Moreover, it used the people hired and trained through that unique approach to launch one of the most successful automobiles in history. Today, however, the firm is subtly changing its way of dealing with human resources. It remains to be seen whether it will be able to maintain its success with its new approach.

This chapter is about how organizations manage the people who work for them. This set of processes is called human resource management, or HRM. We start by describing the environmental context of HRM. We then discuss how organizations attract human resources. Next we describe how organizations seek to further develop the capacities of their human resources. We also examine how high-quality human resources are maintained by organizations. We conclude by discussing labour relations.

THE ENVIRONMENTAL CONTEXT OF HUMAN RESOURCE MANAGEMENT

● **human resource management (HRM)**
The set of organizational activities directed at attracting, developing, and maintaining an effective workforce

Human resource management (HRM) is the set of organizational activities directed at attracting, developing, and maintaining an effective workforce.[2] Human resource management takes place within a complex and ever-changing environmental context. Three particularly vital components of this context are HRM's strategic importance and the legal and social environment of HRM.

The Strategic Importance of HRM

Human resources are critical for effective organizational functioning.[3] HRM (or personnel, as it is sometimes called) was once relegated to second-class status in many organizations, but its importance has grown dramatically in the last two decades. Its new importance stems from increased legal complexities, the recognition that human resources are a valuable means for improving productivity, and the awareness today of the costs associated with poor human resource management.[4] The *Environment of Management* box discusses how several organizations are placing increased emphasis on the quality of their human resources.

Indeed, managers now realize that the effectiveness of their HR function has a substantial impact on the bottom-line performance of the firm. Poor human resource planning can result in spurts of hiring followed by layoffs—costly in terms of unemployment compensation payments, training expenses, and morale. Haphazard compensation systems do not attract, keep, and motivate good employees, and outmoded recruitment practices can expose the firm to expensive and embarrassing discrimination lawsuits. Consequently, the chief human resource executive of most large businesses is a vice president directly accountable to the CEO, and many firms are developing strategic HR plans and are integrating those plans with other strategic planning activities.[5]

Even organizations with as few as two hundred employees usually have a human resource manager and a human resource department charged with overseeing these activities. Responsibility for HR activities, however, is shared between the HR department and line managers. The HR department may recruit and initially screen candidates, but the final selection is usually made by

Human Capital

Organizations have gradually begun to realize that improving technology and cutting costs improve performance only up to a point. To move beyond that point, the organization must focus on its employees, its most important resource. This realization has increased the importance of employee development and consequently the role of human resource managers has changed and their impact on organizations has increased. A variety of human resource practices are used to improve employee performance.

In 1987, management at *The Globe and Mail* developed a performance evaluation system for its nine hundred employees, six hundred of whom were unionized. Managers from the various departments of the newspaper supported the idea of a structured performance appraisal system, but they worried that it would become too routine and therefore meaningless in terms of providing feedback to employees. The managers decided to avoid this pitfall by focusing on employee development and performance improvement. The system they implemented—a process called personal development planning (PDP)—was well received by both employees and managers because the emphasis was on employee development rather than on performance appraisal.

Nortel, a leading provider of digital network solutions with 68,000 employees worldwide, and headquarters in Brampton, Ontario, recognized that in order to become a global corporation it would have to implement changes within the human resource area.

At the core of those changes is an appreciation of the importance of understanding the nature of, and reasons for, differences in people. Nortel's aspiration to become a global corporation means valuing differences in people and capitalizing on this appreciation in both organizational and business terms. For example, the company's reward programs vary according to cultural, societal, and business needs. In some countries, the focus is on cash while in others it is on benefits. In all cases, however, the mix reflects both intrinsic and extrinsic rewards and is linked to Nortel's overall business strategy.

CAMI is a joint venture between General Motors and Suzuki with operations in Ingersoll, Ontario. It began production in 1989 with a workforce of approximately 2,100, most of whom are members of the Canadian Auto Workers (CAW). One of the major forces influencing organizational practices at CAMI is an adherence to *kaizen,* the Japanese business philosophy of continuous incremental improvement of the production process. One *kaizen* activity involves the participation of workers through formal suggestions known as *teians.* Workers submit *teians* and their teams are rewarded on the basis of the savings realized from their implementation.

References: David Robertson et al., *The CAMI Report: Lean Production in a Unionized Auto Plant* (Willowdale, Ont.: CAW–Canada Research Development, 1993); "Designing a New Performance Appraisal System at The Globe & Mail," *Business Quarterly,* Autumn 1992, p. 676; and John Cartland, "Reward Policies in a Global Corporation," *Business Quarterly,* Autumn 1995, pp. 93–96.

managers in the department where the new employee will work. Similarly, although the HR department may establish performance appraisal policies and procedures, the actual evaluating and coaching of employees is done by their immediate superiors.

The Legal Environment of HRM

A number of laws regulate various aspects of employee–employer relations, especially in the areas of discrimination in employment, employment equity, compensation and benefits, labour relations, and occupational safety and health. While there are some federal laws that apply to these areas, many of them fall exclusively within provincial jurisdiction and therefore provincial legislation prevails. The major categories of legislation are summarized in Table 13.1.

In 1998, Nicole Tremel, then vice-president of the Public Service Alliance of Canada, celebrates after the Canadian Human Rights Commission ruled that thousands of female civil servants are entitled to equal pay for work of equal value. However, the pay equity ruling has yet to be passed into law.

The Charter of Rights and Freedoms   The Canadian Charter of Rights and Freedoms is an important part of the Canadian Constitution. It enshrines the right of every individual to equality in all matters within the power of the federal and provincial governments. Although it does not directly govern the conduct of the private sector, its impact has been felt in a number of areas related to employment treatment before and under the law. For instance, a Supreme Court decision on the equality provision of the Charter concluded that it was discriminatory to exclude pregnant employees from disability benefits available to other employees in the workplace.[6] Court decisions based on the Charter have also influenced the interpretation of human rights law affecting the workplace.

The Charter has made it possible for organizations to undertake endeavours to promote employment equity. Section 15(2) of the Charter allows for any law, program, or activity that intends to ameliorate conditions of disadvantaged individuals or groups, including those who are disadvantaged because of race, national or ethnic origin, colour, religion, sex, age, or mental or physical disability.

Human Rights Legislation   The right of every Canadian to equality of opportunity in the workplace and to freedom from discrimination in the workplace is enshrined in federal, provincial, and territorial human rights legislation. Federal legislation affecting the workplace applies to employees of organizations that are under the direct control of the federal government or are regulated by the federal government (for example, the banking industry). Provincial legislation affecting the workplace applies to everyone else.

While there are many similarities in the various human rights codes, there are some significant differences as well. For instance, until 1998 not all human rights acts in Canada specifically protected people from discrimination in employment on the basis of sexual orientation. Alberta, Prince Edward Island, and the Northwest Territories did not afford individuals protection on this ground. However, on April 2, 1998, the Supreme Court of Canada ordered that homosexuals be protected under Alberta human rights legislation. This 8–0 landmark

TABLE 13.1 The Legal Environment of HRM

Major Legislation

1. *Canadian Charter of Rights and Freedoms, Part 1 of the Constitution Act, 1982.* Guarantees every individual fundamental rights and freedoms. Section 15 provides for equality before and under the law and equal protection and benefit of the law.

2. *Canadian Human Rights Act, RSC 1985.* Along with corresponding provincial human rights legislation prohibits discrimination on the grounds of race, ancestry, place of origin, colour, ethnic origin, citizenship, creed, sex, disability, age, marital status, family status, and record of offences in all aspects of employment.

3. *Federal Employment Equity Act, RSC 1986* and *Federal Contractors Compliance Program.* Seek to ensure that those employed by the federal government both directly and indirectly through federal contracts aim to create and maintain a workforce that is representative of the population.

4. *Canadian Human Rights Act.* Along with provincial employment standards acts and pay equity acts seeks to achieve equal pay for equal work and equal pay for work of equal value.

5. *Canada Labour Code* and *Public Service Staff Relations Act, RSC 1967.* Regulate the labour relations of all federal Crown employees. All other employees are regulated by provincial labour codes. These laws establish procedures by which employees can establish labour unions and require organizations to collectively bargain in good faith with legally formed unions.

6. *Federal and provincial occupational health and safety legislation.* Seeks to provide safe working conditions by promoting vigilance and accountability.

> As much as any area of management, HRM is subject to wide-ranging laws and court decisions. These laws and decisions affect the human resource function in many different areas.

[handwritten note: Saskatchewan Tommy Douglas —had made a bill of rights.]

decision amended that province's legislation by reading into law new rights that elected politicians had refused to grant. The Supreme Court's ruling had a similar effect on legislation in Prince Edward Island and the Northwest Territories.

The Ontario Human Rights Code is illustrative of the type of protection afforded to persons in the workplace. It is built upon the principle that employment decisions should be based on merit and not on criteria that are unrelated to job performance. The code is intended to promote equal employment opportunity regardless of race, ancestry, place of origin, colour, ethnic origin, citizenship, creed, handicap, age, marital status, family status, ancestry, sex, sexual orientation, or record of offences.

The right to "equal treatment with respect to employment" prescribed in human rights legislation covers all aspects of employment, including recruitment, hiring, training, transfer, promotion, apprenticeship terms, dismissal, and layoffs. It also covers the terms and conditions of employment, hours of work, vacation benefits, shift work, discipline, and performance evaluation. For example, an employment advertisement that contains a requirement of "Canadian experience" will discourage qualified applicants who are recent immigrants to Canada. This type of advertising is prohibited by those codes that prohibit discrimination on the basis of "place of origin" (British Columbia, Alberta, Saskatchewan, Ontario, New Brunswick, and the Northwest Territories) unless "Canadian experience" is a genuine and reasonable job requirement. Prohibited grounds of discussion in employment are summarized in Table 13.2.

TABLE 13.2 Prohibited Grounds of Discrimination in Employment

Prohibited Grounds	Fed.	B.C.	Alta.	Sask.	Man.	Ont.	Que.	N.B.	P.E.I.	N.S.	Nfld.	N.W.T.	Y.T.
Race or colour	•	•	•	•	•	•	•	•	•	•	•	•	•
Religion or creed	•	•	•	•	•	•	•	•	•	•	•	•	•
Age	•	•	•	•	•	•	•	•	•	•	•	•	•
		(19–65)	(18+)	(18–64)		(18–65)					(19–65)		
Sex (includes pregnancy or childbirth)	•	•1	•	•	•2	•	•	•	•1	•	•1	•1	•
Marital status	•	•	•	•	•	•	•3	•	•	•	•	•	
Physical/Mental handicap or disability	•	•	•	•	•	•	•	•	•	•	•	•	•
Sexual orientation	•	•	•	•	•	•	•	•	•	•	•	•	
National or ethnic origin (includes linguistic background)	•			•4	•	•5	•	•	•	•	•	•4	•
Family status	•	•	•	•	•	•	•3	•	•			•	•
Dependence on alcohol or drug	•	•7	•1	•1	•1	•1	•8	•1,7	•1	•7	•		
Ancestry or place of origin		•	•	•	•	•		•				•	•
Political belief		•		•			•		•	•	•9		•
Based on association				•	•			•	•	•			•
Pardoned conviction	•	•				•	•					•	
Record of criminal conviction		•					•			•			•
Source of income			•	•10	•		•11		•	•			
Assignment, attachment, or seizure of pay											•		
Social condition/origin						•					•		
Language						•12	•						•

1. Complaints accepted based on policy.
2. Includes gender-determined characteristics.
3. Quebec uses the term "civil status."
4. Defined as nationality.
5. Ontario's Code includes citizenship and ethnic origin.
6. Saskatchewan defines a parent-child relationship.
7. Previous dependence only.
8. Included in "handicap ground."
9. Prohibition on basis of political opinion.
10. Defined as "receipt of public assistance."
11. Included under social condition.
12. Complaints accepted on grounds of ancestry, ethnic origins, place of origin, race.

Harassment on any of the prohibited grounds is considered a form of discrimination.

Source: *Prohibited Grounds of Discrimination in Canada,* December 1998. Reproduced with the permission of the Minister of Public Works and Government Services Canada.

Eight of the human rights acts in Canada specifically prohibit sexual harassment in the workplace: federal, Alberta, Manitoba, Ontario, Quebec, New Brunswick, Nova Scotia, and Newfoundland. In other jurisdictions, sexual harassment is prohibited as a form of sex discrimination. Some acts define harassment; the Newfoundland Human Rights Code, for example, states that to harass "means to engage in a course of vexatious comment or conduct that is known or ought reasonably to be known as unwelcome."

Human rights legislation applies to trade unions and self-governing professions as well as employers. In interpreting human rights law, Canadian courts have broadened the meaning of the term *discrimination* to include situations where the discrimination was not necessarily intentional. Where the result of actions or practices has discriminatory results, the fact that there was no intent to discriminate is irrelevant.

a Canadian Term.

Employment Equity Legislation   The 1986 federal Employment Equity Act requires all federally regulated employers (Bell Canada, Canada Post, and Canadian banks, for example) to take steps toward achieving employment equity for women, Aboriginal peoples, racial minorities, and people with disabilities. The purpose of this legislation is to achieve equality in the workplace so that no person shall be denied employment opportunities or benefits for reasons unrelated to ability and, in the fulfillment of that goal, to correct the conditions of disadvantage in employment experienced by persons in these groups. Federally regulated organizations employ approximately 10 percent of the Canadian workforce.

To broaden the reach of the federal government initiatives in this area, the government introduced the Federal Contractors Compliance Program. Provincially regulated employers (universities for example) who bid on federal government goods and services contracts worth at least $200,000 are required to demonstrate a commitment to employment equity by complying with specific employment equity criteria. Approximately 1,350 employers and over a million employees are covered by this program. Employers are required to achieve and maintain a representative workforce by taking certain specified steps, such as reviewing and changing human resource systems to remove barriers.[7]

Slightly over 70% of what a man earns.

Pay Equity Legislation   While employment equity and pay equity share a common goal—namely, the elimination of inequity in the workplace—the two are quite different. Employment equity covers all employment systems, from hiring to promotion and retention, whereas pay equity focuses on fair compensation for specific work being done. Two approaches have been used to bring about equality in compensation in the workplace. One seeks equal pay for equal work or equal pay for similar work, while the other seeks equal pay for work of equal value. All the provinces protect the concept of equal pay for equal work either in human rights legislation or in employment (or labour) standards acts. The International Labour Organization's Equal Remuneration Convention prompted the federal government to include the concept of equal pay for work of equal value in its Human Rights Act. Several provinces (Manitoba, Prince Edward Island, Nova Scotia, and Ontario) have enacted proactive pay equity legislation promoting this concept.

Equal pay for [scribble] work of equal value.

Labour Relations Legislation   Union activities and management's behaviour toward unions constitute another heavily regulated area. The Canada Labour Code, which covers federally regulated employees, outlines the rights of these employees in relation to certification and such issues as occupational safety and health. The 1967 Public Service Staff Relations Act gives the federal public sector certification rights. Other employees' rights in relation to certification and related matters are covered by provincial labour legislation. Generally, labour relations legislation gives workers the right to organize unions, provides for a certification process, outlines the provisions for collective bargaining in good faith, and provides for the resolution of various forms of disputes between employer and union.

Occupational Health and Safety Legislation Occupational health and safety law in the Canada Labour Code and in all the provinces is directed at providing safe working conditions. It imposes both general and specific duties on the workplace parties in order to protect health and safety. Generally, it gives workers the right to know about potential hazards, to participate in resolving health and safety concerns, and to refuse to work in unsafe conditions. In at least four provinces (Alberta, British Columbia, Newfoundland, and Nova Scotia), the legislation categorizes the issue in the form of a "duty" to refuse to work. All but two Canadian jurisdictions (Prince Edward Island and Nova Scotia) require a joint (management/employee) health and safety committee or a worker health and safety representative. There are provisions for penalties for contraventions of the legislation or for a failure to comply with orders of inspectors.

Emerging Legal Issues Several other areas of legal concern have emerged during the past few years. One is sexual harassment. Studies have found that sexual harassment is one of the most serious and widespread problems experienced by women in the workplace. Sexual harassment is specifically prohibited in eight of the human rights acts in Canada. In the other jurisdictions, it is prohibited as a form of sex discrimination. Employers are obliged to create a workplace free of harassment and discrimination. Human rights tribunals and the courts have held employers liable for sexual harassment when management was directly involved or failed to respond appropriately to complaints. Organizations that develop a policy for the workplace and ensure that all personnel are aware of the policy can minimize the potential for liability.[8]

Another emerging human resource management issue is alcohol and drug abuse. Both alcoholism and drug dependence are major problems today. Recent court rulings have tended to define alcoholics and drug addicts as disabled persons, thereby protecting them under the same laws that protect other disabled persons. AIDS has emerged as another important legal issue. Persons with AIDS are also protected under human rights laws that protect the disabled. The Canadian Human Rights Commission and other similar bodies have made sample AIDS policies available.[9]

Social Change and HRM

Beyond the objective legal context of HRM, various social changes are also affecting how organizations interact with their employees. First, many organizations are using more and more temporary workers today. This trend allows them to add workers as necessary without the risk that they may have to eliminate their jobs in the future. This also cuts labour costs because temporary workers earn no benefits and are often paid less than permanent workers. On the other hand, temporary workers also tend to be less loyal to an organization and may lack the job-specific skills to perform at a high level. Still, the number of temporary workers in Canada rose from 799,000 in 1992 to 970,000 in 1994.[10]

Second, dual-career families are much more common today than just a few years ago. Organizations are finding that they must make accommodations for employees who are dual-career partners. These accommodations may include delaying transfers, offering employment to the spouses of current employees to retain them, and providing more flexible work schedules and benefits packages. A related aspect of social change and HRM, workforce diversity, is covered more fully in Chapter 14.

Employment at will is also becoming an important issue. Although employment at will has legal implications, its emergence as an issue is socially driven. **Employment at will** is a traditional view of the workplace that says organizations can fire an employee for any reason. Increasingly, however, people are arguing that organizations should be able to fire only people who are poor performers or who violate rules and, conversely, not be able to fire people who report safety violations to federal and provincial occupational health and safety agencies or refuse to perform unethical activities. Several court cases in recent years have upheld this emerging view and have limited many organizations' ability to terminate employees to those cases where there is clear and just cause or as part of an organization-wide cutback.

● **employment at will**
A traditional view of the workplace that says organizations can fire their employees for whatever reason they want; recent court judgments are limiting employment at will

ATTRACTING HUMAN RESOURCES

With an understanding of the environmental context of human resource management as a foundation, we are now ready to address its first substantive concern—attracting qualified people who are interested in employment with the organization.

Human Resource Planning

The starting point in attracting qualified human resources is planning. HR planning, in turn, involves job analysis and forecasting the demand and supply of labour.

Job Analysis   **Job analysis** is a systematic analysis of jobs within an organization. A job analysis is made up of two parts. The *job description* lists the duties of a job, the job's working conditions, and the tools, materials, and equipment used to perform it. The *job specification* lists the skills, abilities, and other credentials needed to do the job. Job analysis information is used in many human resource activities. For instance, knowing about job content and job requirements is necessary to develop appropriate selection methods and job-relevant performance appraisal systems and to set equitable compensation rates.[11]

● **job analysis**
A systematized procedure for collecting and recording information about jobs

Forecasting Human Resource Demand and Supply   After managers fully understand the jobs to be performed within the organization, they can start planning for the organization's future human resource needs. Figure 13.1 summarizes the steps most often followed. The manager starts by assessing trends in past human resources usage, future organizational plans, and general economic trends. A good sales forecast is often the foundation, especially for smaller organizations. Historical ratios can then be used to predict demand for employees such as operating employees and sales representatives. Of course, large organizations use much more complicated models to predict their future human resource needs.

Forecasting the supply of labour is really two tasks: forecasting the internal supply (the number and type of employees who will be in the firm at some future date) and forecasting the external supply (the number and type of people who will be available for hiring in the labour market at large). The simplest approach merely adjusts present staffing levels for anticipated turnover and promotions. Again, though, large organizations use extremely sophisticated models to make these forecasts.

Union Oil Company, for example, has a complex forecasting system for keeping track of the present and future distributions of professionals and managers. The Union Oil system can spot areas where there will eventually be too many qualified professionals competing for too few promotions or, conversely, too few good people available to fill important positions. Similarly, the Ontario Ministry of Transportation and Communications has a computerized succession planning system for middle and senior management.[12]

At higher levels of the organization, managers plan for specific people and positions. The technique most commonly used is the **replacement chart**, which lists each important managerial position, who occupies it, how long he

● **replacement chart**
Lists each important managerial position in the organization, who occupies it, how long he or she will probably remain in the position, and who is or will be a qualified replacement

Attracting human resources cannot be left to chance if an organization expects to function at peak efficiency. Human resource planning involves assessing trends, forecasting the supply demand of labour, and then developing appropriate strategies for addressing any differences.

F I G U R E   13.1   Human Resource Planning

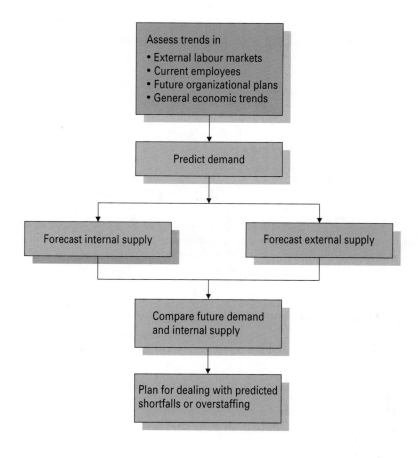

or she will probably stay in it before moving on, and who (by name) is now qualified or soon will be qualified to move into the position. This technique allows ample time to plan developmental experiences for persons identified as potential successors to critical managerial jobs. Charles Knight, CEO of Emerson Electric Co., has an entire room dedicated to posting the credentials of his top seven hundred executives.[13]

To facilitate both planning and identifying persons for current transfer or promotion, some organizations also have an **employee information system**, or **skills inventory**. Such systems are usually computerized and contain information on each employee's education, skills, work experience, and career aspirations. Such a system can quickly locate all the employees in the organization who are qualified to fill a position requiring, for instance, a degree in chemical engineering, three years of experience in an oil refinery, and fluency in French.

Forecasting the external supply of labour is a different problem altogether. How does a manager, for example, predict how many electrical engineers will be seeking work in Alberta three years from now? To get an idea of the future availability of labour, planners must rely on information from outside sources such as government reports and figures supplied by universities on the number of students in major fields.

Matching Human Resource Supply and Demand   After comparing future demand and internal supply, managers can make plans to manage predicted shortfalls or overstaffing. If a shortfall is predicted, new employees can be hired, present employees can be retrained and transferred into the understaffed area, individuals approaching retirement can be convinced to stay on, or labour-saving or productivity-enhancing systems can be installed.

If the organization needs to hire, the external labour supply forecast helps managers plan how to recruit, based on whether the type of person needed is readily available or scarce in the labour market. As we noted earlier, the trend in temporary workers also helps managers in staffing by affording them with extra flexibility. If overstaffing is expected to be a problem, the main options are transferring the extra employees, not replacing individuals who quit, encouraging early retirement, and laying people off.[14]

Recruiting Human Resources

Once an organization has an idea of its future human resource needs, the next phase is usually recruiting new employees. **Recruiting** is the process of attracting qualified persons to apply for the jobs that are open. Where do recruits come from? Some recruits are found internally; others come from outside of the organization.

Internal recruiting means considering present employees as candidates for openings. Promotion from within can help build morale and keep high-quality employees from leaving the firm. In unionized firms, the procedures for notifying employees of internal job change opportunities are usually spelled out in the union contract. For higher-level positions, a skills inventory system may be used to identify internal candidates, or managers may be asked to recommend individuals who should be considered. One disadvantage of internal recruiting is its "ripple effect." When an employee moves to a different job, a replacement must be found. In one organization, 454 job movements were necessary as a result of filling 195 initial openings![15]

● **employee information system (skills inventory)**
Contains information on each employee's education, skills, experience, and career aspirations; usually computerized

● **recruiting**
The process of attracting individuals to apply for jobs that are open

● **internal recruiting**
Considering current employees as applicants for higher-level jobs in the organization

- **external recruiting**
Getting people from outside the organization to apply for jobs

External recruiting involves attracting persons outside the organization to apply for jobs. External recruiting methods include advertising, campus interviews, employment agencies or executive search firms, referrals by present employees, and hiring "walk-ins" or "gate-hires" (people who show up without being solicited). Of course, a manager must select the most appropriate methods, using the government employment service to find maintenance workers but not a nuclear physicist, for example. Private employment agencies can be a good source of clerical and technical employees, and executive search firms specialize in locating top-management talent.

The organization must also keep in mind that recruiting decisions often go both ways—the organization is recruiting an employee, but the prospective employee is also selecting a job.[16] Thus the organization wants to put its best foot forward, treat all applicants with dignity, and strive for a good person-job fit. Hiring the "wrong" employee—one who flops and either quits or must be fired—generally costs the organization in lost productivity and training. These costs vary according to industry and position.

- **realistic job preview (RJP)**
Provides the applicant with a real picture of what performing the job the organization is trying to fill would be like

One generally successful method for facilitating a good person-job fit is through the so-called **realistic job preview** (RJP).[17] As the term suggests, the RJP involves providing the applicant with a real picture of what performing the job that the organization is trying to fill would be like.

Selecting Human Resources

Once the recruiting process has attracted a pool of applicants, the next step is to select whom to hire. The intent of the selection process is to gather from applicants information that will predict their job success and then to hire the candidates likely to be most successful. Of course, the organization can only gather information about factors that are predictive of future performance. The process of determining the predictive value of information is called **validation**.

- **validation**
Determining the extent to which a selection device is really predictive of future job performance

Two basic approaches to validation are predictive validation and content validation. *Predictive validation* involves collecting the scores of employees or applicants on the device to be validated and correlating their scores with actual job performance. A significant correlation means that the selection device is a valid predictor of job performance. *Content validation* uses logic and job analysis data to establish that the selection device measures the exact skills needed for successful job performance. The most critical part of content validation is a careful job analysis showing exactly what duties are to be performed. The test is then developed to measure the applicant's ability to perform those duties.

Application Blanks   The first step in selection is usually asking the candidate to fill out an application blank. Application blanks are an efficient method of gathering information about the applicant's previous work history, educational background, and other job-related demographic data. They should not contain questions about areas not related to the job such as gender, religion, or national origin. Application blank data are generally used informally to decide whether a candidate merits further evaluation, and interviewers use application blanks to familiarize themselves with candidates before interviewing them.

Tests   Tests of ability, skill, aptitude, or knowledge that is relevant to the particular job are usually the best predictors of job success, although tests of general intelligence or personality are occasionally useful as well. In addition to

Application Blank → Application Form

being validated, tests should be administered and scored consistently. All candidates should be given the same directions, should be allowed the same amount of time, and should experience the same testing environment (temperature, lighting, distractions).[18]

Interviews   Although a popular selection device, interviews are sometimes poor predictors of job success. For example, biases inherent in the way people perceive and judge others on first meeting affect subsequent evaluations by the interviewer. Interview validity can be improved by training interviewers to be aware of potential biases and by increasing the structure of the interview. In a structured interview, questions are written in advance and all interviewers follow the same question list with each candidate they interview. This procedure introduces consistency into the interview procedure and allows the organization to validate the content of the questions to be asked.[19]

For interviewing managerial or professional candidates, a somewhat less structured approach can be used. Question areas and information-gathering objectives are still planned in advance, but the specific questions vary with the candidates' backgrounds. Trammell Crow Real Estate Investors uses a novel approach in hiring managers. Each applicant is interviewed not only by two or three other managers but also by a secretary or young leasing agent. This provides information about how the prospective manager relates to nonmanagers.[20]

Assessment Centres   Assessment centres are a popular method used to select managers and are particularly good for selecting current employees for promotion. The assessment centre is a content-valid simulation of major parts of the managerial job. A typical assessment lasts two to three days, with groups of six to twelve persons participating in a variety of managerial exercises. Centres may also include interviews, public speaking, and standardized ability tests. Candidates are assessed by several trained observers—usually managers several levels above the job for which the candidates are being considered. Assessment centres are quite valid if properly designed and are fair to members of minority groups and women.[21] For some firms, the assessment centre is a permanent facility created for these activities. For other firms, the assessment activities are performed in a multipurpose location such as a conference room. AT&T pioneered the assessment centre concept. For years the firm has used assessment centres to make virtually all of its selection decisions for management positions.

Other Techniques   More and more organizations are requiring that applicants in whom they are interested take physical exams. Organizations are also increasingly using drug tests, especially in situations in which drug-related performance problems could create serious safety hazards.[22] For example, applicants for jobs in a nuclear power plant would likely be tested for drug use. And some organizations today even run credit checks on prospective employees.

DEVELOPING HUMAN RESOURCES

Regardless of how effective a selection system is, however, most employees need additional training if they are to grow and develop in their jobs. Evaluating their performance and providing feedback are also necessary.

Training and Development

● **training**
Teaching operational or technical employees how to do the job for which they were hired

● **development**
Teaching managers and professionals the skills needed for both present and future jobs

In HRM, **training** usually refers to teaching operational or technical employees how to do the job for which they were hired. **Development** refers to teaching managers and professionals the skills needed for both present and future jobs. Most organizations provide regular training and development programs for managers and employees.[23] For example, in 1996 IBM Canada spent $44 million on training for its 13,323 employees.[24] Moreover, corporations such as Bell Canada, the Canadian Imperial Bank of Commerce, the Bank of Montreal, and Ontario Hydro have their own training institutes. However, Canada as a whole ranks seventeenth in the world with respect to its commitment to corporate training, behind such countries as Ireland, Belgium, and Luxembourg.[25]

Assessing Training Needs   The first step in developing a training plan is to determine what needs exist. For example, if employees do not know how to operate the machinery necessary to do their jobs, a training program on how to operate the machinery is clearly needed. On the other hand, when a group of office workers is performing poorly, training may not be the answer. The problem could be motivation, aging equipment, poor supervision, inefficient work design, or a deficiency of skills and knowledge. Only the last could be remedied by training. As training programs are being developed, the manager should set specific and measurable goals specifying what participants are to learn. Managers should also plan to evaluate the training program after employees complete it. The training process from start to finish is diagrammed in Figure 13.2.

Common Training Methods   As shown in Table 13.3, many different training and development methods are available. Selection of methods depends on many considerations, but perhaps the most important is training content. When

Organizations today are increasingly aware of the importance of training their employees. Large companies often have their own training divisions, while smaller ones rely on outside training programs and facilitators.

the training content is factual material (such as company rules or explanations of how to fill out forms), assigned reading, programmed learning, and lecture methods work well. When the content is interpersonal relations or group decision making, however, firms must use a method that allows interpersonal contact such as role playing or case discussion groups. When employees must learn a physical skill, methods allowing practice and the actual use of tools and material are needed, as in on-the-job training or vestibule training. (Vestibule training enables participants to focus on safety, learning, and feedback rather than productivity.) Interactive video is also becoming popular. This approach, which relies on a computer-video hookup, is a promising method for combining several training methods. Xerox Corp., Massachusetts Mutual Life Insurance Co., and Ford Motor Co. have all reported tremendous success with this method.[26]

FIGURE 13.2 The Training Process

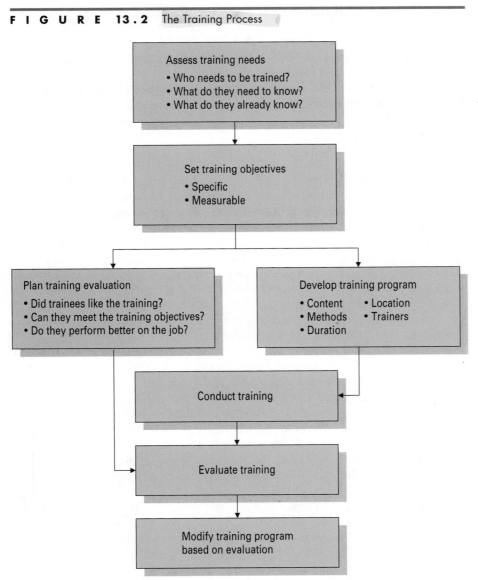

Managing the training process can go a long way toward enhancing its effectiveness. If training programs are well conceived and well executed, both the organization and its employees benefit. Following a comprehensive process helps managers ensure that the objectives of the training program are met.

Evaluation of Training   Training and development programs should always be evaluated. Typical evaluation approaches include measuring one or more relevant criteria (such as attitudes or performance) before and after the training and determining whether the criteria changed. Evaluation measures collected at the end of training are easy to get, but actual performance measures collected when the trainee is on the job are more important. Trainees may say that they enjoyed the training and learned a lot, but the true test is whether their job performance improves after their training.

Performance Appraisal

● **performance appraisal**
A formal assessment of how well an employee is doing his or her job

When employees are trained and settled into their jobs, one of management's next concerns is performance appraisal. **Performance appraisal** is a formal assessment of how well employees are performing their job. Employees' performance should be evaluated regularly for many reasons. One reason is that performance appraisal may be necessary for validating selection devices or assessing the impact of training programs. A second reason is administrative—to aid in making decisions about pay raises, promotions, and training. Still another reason is to provide feedback to employees to help them improve their present performance and plan future careers.

Because performance evaluations often help determine wages and promotions, they must be fair and nondiscriminatory. In the case of appraisals, content validation is used to show that the appraisal system accurately measures performance on important job elements and does not measure traits or behaviour that are irrelevant to job performance.[27]

Common Appraisal Methods   Two basic categories of appraisal methods commonly used in organizations are objective methods and judgmental methods. *Objective measures* of performance include actual output (that is, number of units produced), scrappage rate, dollar volume of sales, and number of claims processed. Objective performance measures may be contaminated by "opportunity bias" if some persons have a better chance to perform than others. For example, a sales representative selling snow blowers in Calgary has a greater opportunity than does a colleague selling the same product in Victoria. Fortunately, adjusting raw performance figures for the effect of opportunity bias and thereby arriving at figures that accurately represent each individual's performance is often possible.

Another type of objective measure, the special performance test, is a method in which each employee is assessed under standardized conditions. This kind of appraisal also eliminates opportunity bias. For example, GTE Southwest Inc. has a series of prerecorded calls that operators in a test booth answer. The operators are graded on speed, accuracy, and courtesy in handling the calls. Performance tests measure ability, but they do not measure the extent to which one is motivated to use that ability on a daily basis. (For example, a high-ability person may be a lazy performer except when being tested.) Special performance tests must therefore be supplemented by other appraisal methods to provide a complete picture of performance.

Judgmental methods, including ranking and rating techniques, are the most common way to measure performance. Ranking compares employees directly with each other and orders them from best to worst. Ranking has a number of

TABLE 13.3 Training and Development Methods

Method	Comments
Assigned readings	Readings may or may not be specially prepared for training purposes.
Behaviour modelling training	Use of a videotaped model displaying the correct behaviour, then trainee role playing and discussion of the correct behaviour. Used extensively for supervisor training in human relations.
Business simulation	Both paper simulations (such as in-basket exercises) and computer-based business "games" are used to teach management skills.
Case discussion	Real or fictitious cases or incidents are discussed in small groups.
Conference	Small-group discussion of selected topics, usually with the trainer as leader.
Lecture	Oral presentation of material by the trainer, with limited or no audience participation.
On the job	Includes no instruction; casual coaching by more experienced employees and carefully structured explanation, demonstration, and supervised practice by a qualified trainer.
Programmed instruction	Self-paced method using text or computer followed by questions and answers; expensive to develop.
Role playing	Trainees act out roles with other trainees, such as "boss giving performance appraisal" and "subordinate reacting to appraisal" to gain experience in human relations.
Sensitivity training	Also called T-group and laboratory training, this is an intensive experience in a small group, in which individuals give each other feedback and try out new behaviours. It is said to promote trust, open communication, and understanding of group dynamics.
Vestibule training	Supervised practice on manual tasks in a separate work area where the emphasis is on safety, learning, and feedback rather than productivity.
Interactive video	Newly emerging technique using computers and video technology.
CD-ROM	CD-ROM technology used to provide combinations of other methods, such as readings, lecture, and video.

Organizations that engage in training and development activities can select from a variety of different methods. Managers must carefully assess their training and development needs and select the most appropriate method. For example, assigned reading might be effective in teaching new employees about company policies, but on-the-job training might be more effective in teaching current employees how to operate new equipment.

drawbacks. Ranking is difficult for large groups because the persons in the middle of the distribution may be hard to distinguish from one another accurately. Comparisons of people in different work groups are also difficult. For example, an employee ranked third in a strong group may be more valuable than an employee ranked first in a weak group. Another criticism of ranking is that the manager must rank people on the basis of overall performance, although each person likely has both strengths and weaknesses. Furthermore, rankings do not provide useful information for feedback. To be told that one is ranked third is not nearly so helpful as to be told that the quality of one's work is outstanding, its quantity is satisfactory, one's punctuality could use improvement, and one's paperwork is seriously deficient.

Rating differs from ranking in that it compares each employee with a fixed standard rather than with other employees. A rating scale provides the standard. Figure 13.3 gives examples of three graphic rating scales for a bank teller. Each consists of a performance dimension to be rated (punctuality, congeniality, and accuracy) followed by a scale on which to make the rating. In constructing graphic rating scales, performance dimensions that are relevant to job performance must be selected. In particular, they should focus on job behaviours and results rather than on personality traits or attitudes.

The **Behaviourally Anchored Rating Scale (BARS)** is a sophisticated and useful rating method for evaluating performance. Supervisors construct rating scales with associated behavioural anchors. They first identify relevant performance dimensions and then generate anchors—specific, observable behaviours typical of each performance level. Figure 13.4 shows an example of a behaviourally anchored rating scale for the dimension "inventory control."

The other scales in this set, developed for the job of department manager in a chain of specialty stores, include "handling customer complaints," "planning special promotions," "following company procedures," "supervising sales personnel," and "diagnosing and solving special problems." BARS can be effective because it requires that management take proper care in constructing the scales and it provides useful anchors for supervisors to use in evaluating people. It is costly, however, because outside expertise is usually needed and because scales must be developed for each job within the organization. A recent variation on BARS is the behavioural observation scale, or BOS. Like BARS, a BOS uses behavioural anchors but also addresses frequencies with which those behaviours are observed.

Errors in Performance Appraisal Errors or biases can occur in any kind of rating or ranking system. One common problem is recency error—the tendency to base judgments on the subordinate's most recent performance because it is most easily recalled. Often a rating or ranking is intended to evaluate performance over an entire time period, such as six months or a year, so the recency error does introduce error into the judgment. Other errors include overuse of one part of the scale—being too lenient, being too severe, or giving everyone a rating of "average."

Halo error is allowing the assessment of an employee on one dimension to "spread" to ratings of that employee on other dimensions. For instance, if an employee is outstanding on quality of output, a rater might tend to give her or him higher marks than deserved on other dimensions. Errors can also occur because of race, sex, or age discrimination, intentionally or unintentionally. The best way to offset these errors is to ensure that a valid rating system is developed at the outset and then to train managers in how to use it.

● **Behaviourally Anchored Rating Scale (BARS)**
A sophisticated rating method in which supervisors construct a rating scale associated with behavioural anchors

FIGURE 13.3 Graphic Rating Scales for a Bank Teller

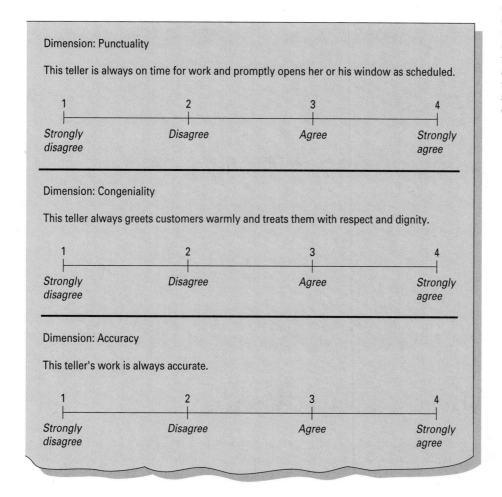

Performance Feedback

The last step in most performance appraisal systems is giving feedback to subordinates about their performance. This is usually done in a private meeting between the person being evaluated and his or her boss. The discussion should generally be focused on the facts—the assessed level of performance, how and why that assessment was made, and how it can be improved in the future. Feedback interviews are not easy to conduct. Many managers are uncomfortable with the task, especially if feedback is negative and subordinates are disappointed by what they hear. Properly training managers, however, can help them conduct more effective feedback interviews.[28]

A recent innovation in performance appraisal used in many organizations today is called "360 degree" feedback: managers are evaluated by everyone around them—their boss, their peers, and their subordinates. Such a complete and thorough approach provides people with a far richer array of information about their performance than does a conventional appraisal given just by the boss. Of course, such a system also takes considerable time and must be handled to not breed fear and mistrust in the workplace.[29]

F I G U R E 13.4 Behaviourally Anchored Rating Scale

Job: Specialty store manager
Dimension: Inventory control

7 Always orders in the right quantities and at the right time

6 Almost always orders at the right time but occasionally orders too much or too little of a particular item

5 Usually orders at the right time and almost always in the right quantities

4 Often orders in the right quantities and at the right time

3 Occasionally orders at the right time but usually not in the right quantities

2 Occasionally orders in the right quantities but usually not at the right time

1 Never orders in the right quantities or at the right time

MAINTAINING HUMAN RESOURCES

After organizations have attracted and developed an effective workforce, they must also make every effort to maintain that workforce. To do so requires effective compensation and benefits as well as career planning.

Determining Compensation

compensation
The financial remuneration given by the organization to its employees in exchange for their work

Compensation is the financial remuneration given by the organization to its employees in exchange for their work. There are three basic forms of compensation. Wages are the hourly compensation paid to operating employees. The minimum hourly wage paid in Canada varies by jurisdiction (federal, provincial, territorial), from $5.25 to $7.20 per hour. *Salary* refers to compensation paid for total contributions, as opposed to being based on hours worked. For example, managers earn an annual salary, usually paid monthly. They receive the salary regardless of the number of hours they work. Finally, *incentives* represent special compensation opportunities that are usually tied to performance. Sales commissions and bonuses are among the most common incentives.

Compensation is an important and complex part of the organization–employee relationship. Basic compensation is necessary to provide employees with the means to maintain a reasonable standard of living. Beyond this, however, compensation also provides a tangible measure of the value of the individual to the organization. If employees do not earn enough to meet their basic economic goals, they will seek employment elsewhere. Likewise, if they believe that their contributions are undervalued by the organization, they may leave or exhibit poor work habits, low morale, and little commitment to the organization. Thus designing an effective compensation system is clearly in the organization's best interests.[30]

A good compensation system can help attract qualified applicants, retain present employees, and stimulate high performance at a cost reasonable for one's industry and geographic area. To set up a successful system, management must make decisions about wage levels, the wage structure, and the individual wage determination system.

Wage-Level Decision   The wage-level decision is a management policy decision about whether the firm wants to pay above, at, or below the going rate for labour in the industry or the geographic area.[31] Most firms choose to pay near the average. Those that cannot afford more pay below average. Large, successful firms may like to cultivate the image of being "wage leaders" by intentionally paying more than average and thus attracting and keeping high-quality employees. IBM, for example, pays top dollar to get the new employees it wants. McDonald's, on the other hand, often pays close to the minimum wage. The level of unemployment in the labour force also affects wage levels. Pay declines when labour is plentiful and increases when labour is scarce.

Once managers make the wage-level decision, they need information to help set actual wage rates. Managers need to know what the maximum, minimum, and average wages are for particular jobs in the appropriate labour market. This information is collected by means of a wage survey. Area wage surveys can be conducted by individual firms or by local HR or business associations. Professional and industry associations often conduct surveys and make the results available to employers.

Wage-Structure Decision   Wage structures are usually set up through a procedure called **job evaluation**—an attempt to assess the worth of each job relative to other jobs.[32] At Ben & Jerry's Homemade Inc., company policy dictates that the highest-paid employee in the firm cannot make more than seven times what the lowest-paid employee earns. The simplest method for creating a wage structure is to rank jobs from those that should be paid the most (for example, the president) to those that should be paid the least (for example, a mail clerk or a janitor).

In a smaller firm with few jobs (like Ben & Jerry's, for example), this method is quick and practical, but larger firms with many job titles require more sophisticated methods. The next step is setting actual wage rates on the basis of a combination of survey data and the wage structure that results from job evaluation. Jobs of equal value are often grouped into wage grades for ease of administration.

Individual Wage Decisions   After wage-level and wage-structure decisions are made, the individual wage decision must be addressed. This decision concerns how much to pay each employee in a particular job. Although the easiest decision is to pay a single rate for each job, more typically a range of pay rates is associated with each job. For example, the pay range for an individual job might be $6.85 to $7.45 per hour, with different employees earning different rates within the range.

A system is then needed for setting individual rates. This may be done on the basis of seniority (enter the job at $6.85, for example, and increase 10 cents

● **job evaluation**
An attempt to assess the worth of each job relative to other jobs

per hour every six months on the job), initial qualifications (inexperienced people start at $6.85, more experienced start at a higher rate), or merit (raises above the entering rate are given for good performance). Combinations of these bases may also be used.

Determining Benefits

● **benefits**

Things of value other than compensation that an organization provides to its workers

Benefits are things of value other than compensation the organization provides to its workers. The average company spends an amount equal to more than one-third of its cash payroll on employee benefits. Thus an average employee who is paid $30,000 per year averages about $10,500 more per year in benefits.

Benefits come in several forms. Pay for time not worked includes sick leave, vacation, holidays, and unemployment compensation. Insurance benefits often include life and health insurance for employees and their dependents. Workers' compensation is a legally required insurance benefit that provides medical care and disability income for employees injured on the job. The Canada Pension Plan (in Quebec the Quebec Pension Plan) is a government pension plan to which both employers and employees contribute. Many employers also provide a private pension plan to which they and their employees contribute. Employee service benefits include such things as tuition reimbursement and recreational opportunities.

Some organizations have instituted "cafeteria benefit plans" whereby basic coverage is provided for all employees but employees are then allowed to choose which additional benefits they want (up to a cost limit based on salary). For example, an employee with five children might decide to choose medical and dental coverage for dependents, a single employee might prefer more vacation time, and an older employee might elect increased pension benefits. Flexible systems are expected to encourage people to stay in the organization and even help the company attract new employees.[33]

In recent years, companies have also started offering even more innovative benefits as a way of accommodating different needs. On-site childcare, mortgage assistance, and generous paid leave programs are becoming popular.[34] At the same time, however, companies such as Chrysler, Allied Signal, Genentech, and other companies have started eliminating some benefits because of the escalating cost of insurance.[35] Of course, eliminating benefits can create resentment among employees.

A good benefits plan may encourage people to join and stay with an organization, but it seldom stimulates high performance because benefits are tied more to membership in the organization than to performance. To manage their benefits programs effectively, companies should shop carefully, avoid redundant coverage, and provide only those benefits that employees want. Benefits programs should also be explained to employees in plain English so that they can use the benefits appropriately and appreciate what the company is providing.

Career Planning

A final aspect of maintaining human resources is career planning. Few people work in the same jobs their entire career. Some people change jobs within one organization, others change organizations, and many do both. When these movements are haphazard and poorly conceived, both the individual and the organization suffer. Thus planning career progressions in advance is in everyone's best interest.[36] Of course, planning a thirty-year career for a newcomer just joining the organization is difficult. But planning can help map out what areas the individual is most interested in and help the person see what opportunities are available within the organization.

MANAGING LABOUR RELATIONS

Labour relations is the process of dealing with employees who are represented by a union.[37] Managing labour relations is an important part of HRM. The *Managing in a Changing World* box underscores the importance of effective labour relations.

● **labour relations**
The process of dealing with employees when they are represented by a union

How Employees Form Unions

For employees to form a new local union, several things must occur. First, employees must become interested in having a union. Nonemployees who are professional organizers employed by a national union—such as the Canadian Auto Workers (CAW) or the Canadian Union of Public Employees (CUPE)—may generate interest by making speeches and distributing literature outside the workplace. Inside, employees who want a union try to convince other workers of the benefits of a union.

The second step is to collect employees' signatures on authorization cards. These cards state that the signer wishes to vote to determine if the union will represent him or her. The percentage of the employees in the potential bargaining unit that must sign these cards to show the federal or provincial labour relations board that interest is sufficient to justify holding a vote varies according to jurisdiction, from a low of 25 percent in Saskatchewan to 40–60 percent in New Brunswick.[38] Before an election can be held, however, the bargaining unit must be defined. The bargaining unit consists of all employees who will be eligible to vote in the election and to join and be represented by the union if one is formed.

The election is supervised by a labour relations board representative and is conducted by secret ballot. In some jurisdictions, if 50 percent of those voting vote for the union, then the union becomes certified as the official representative of the bargaining unit. In other jurisdictions, a 50 percent vote of all those eligible is required. The new union then organizes itself and elects officers; it will soon be ready to negotiate the first contract. The union-organizing process is diagrammed in Figure 13.5. If workers become disgruntled with their union, the labour relations board can arrange a decertification election. The results of such an election determine whether the union remains certified.

Organizations usually prefer that employees not be unionized because unions limit management's freedom in many areas. Management may thus wage its own campaign to convince employees to vote against the union. "Unfair labour practices" are often committed at this point. For instance, it is an unfair labour practice for management to promise to give employees a raise (or any other benefit) if the union is defeated. Experts agree that the best way to avoid unionization is to practise good employee relations all the time—not just when threatened by a union election. Providing absolutely fair treatment with clear standards in the areas of pay, promotion, layoff, and discipline; having a complaint or appeal system for persons who feel unfairly treated; and avoiding any kind of favouritism will help make employees feel that a union is unnecessary.

Labour–Management Relations at Canada Post

There are few services Canadians value more than the smooth, efficient delivery of the mail. This is perhaps why labour relations at Canada Post have attracted the attention of Canadians over the years. It would be fair to characterize labour relations at Canada Post as less than harmonious. Since 1967, when postal employees won the right to strike, there have been numerous work stoppages of various magnitude and duration. For example, from July 18 to August 8, 1968, 2,400 postal employees were on strike; from October 21, 1975, to December 3, 1975, almost 18,000 employees were on strike. A wildcat strike in 1978 was followed by other strikes in 1987, 1991, and 1997. The 1997 strike, which lasted from November 19 to December 4, involved 45,000 employees and was ended by government legislation.

Canada Post has a letter monopoly and competes in the courier business through its purchase of Purolator Courier in 1993. The Crown corporation is a $5 billion per year business that employs 64,000 employees, processes almost 12 billion letters and parcels annually, and uses twenty-two plants, 20,000 postal outlets, and more than six thousand vehicles. The corporation claims that labour accounts for 63 percent of its costs. This is clearly one of the reasons for Canada Post's contentious relations with its employees.

There is every indication that labour–management relations at Canada Post are still troubled. Another holiday season postal strike in the not too distant future is a very real possibility.

References: Terence Corcoran, "Did the Posties Win the Strike?" *The Globe and Mail*, December 6, 1997, p. B2; Mike Byfield, "The Strong Fatten While Consumers Pay Dearly," *British Columbia Report*, December 15, 1997, pp. 10–11; Mike Byfield, "Letter from the Publisher," *British Columbia Report*, December 15, 1997, p. 67; Jay Bryan, "It's Time to Clean Up the Mess at Canada Post," *The Gazette* (Montreal), November 22, 1997, p. C1; Shawn McCarthy, "Postal Standoff Chokes Mail," *The Globe and Mail*, November 18, 1997, pp. A1, A3; William Walker, "Postal Service Future at Stake," *The Toronto Star*, November 19, 1997, p. A2; Minister of Supplies and Services Canada, *Strikes and Lockouts in Canada* (Ottawa: Government of Canada, 1985); and David Stewart-Patterson, *Post Mortem—Why Canada's Mail Won't Move* (Toronto: Macmillan, 1987).

Collective Bargaining

● **collective bargaining**
The process of agreeing on a satisfactory labour contract between management and a union

The intent of **collective bargaining** is to agree on a labour contract between management and the union that is satisfactory to both parties. The contract contains agreements about conditions of employment such as wages, hours, promotion, layoff, discipline, benefits, methods of allocating overtime, vacations, rest periods, and the grievance procedure. The process of bargaining may go on for weeks, months, or longer, with representatives of management and the union meeting to make proposals and counterproposals. The resulting agreement must be ratified by the union membership. If it is not approved, the union may strike to put pressure on management, or it may choose not to strike and simply continue negotiating until a more acceptable agreement is reached.

● **grievance procedure**
The means by which a labour contract is enforced

The **grievance procedure** is the means by which the contract is enforced. Most of what is in a contract concerns how management will treat employees. When employees feel that they have not been treated fairly under the contract, they file a grievance to correct the problem. The first step in a grievance procedure is for the aggrieved employee to discuss the alleged contract violation with her immediate superior. Often the grievance is resolved at this stage. If the employee still believes that she is being mistreated, however, the grievance can be appealed to the next level. A union official can help an aggrieved employee present her case. If the manager's decision is also unsatisfactory to the employee, additional appeals to successively higher levels are made, until finally all in-company steps are exhausted. The final step is to submit the grievance to *binding arbitration*. An arbitrator is a labour relations expert who is paid jointly

F I G U R E   13.5 The Union-Organizing Process

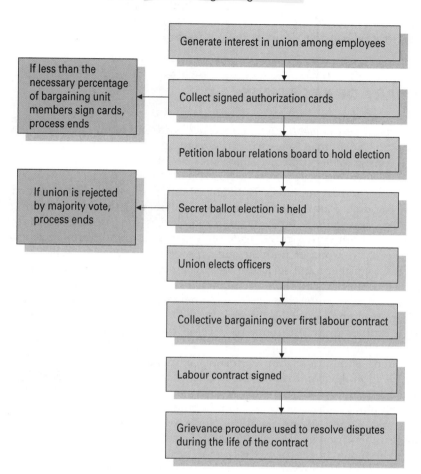

Generate interest in union among employees

If less than the necessary percentage of bargaining unit members sign cards, process ends

Collect signed authorization cards

Petition labour relations board to hold election

If union is rejected by majority vote, process ends

Secret ballot election is held

Union elects officers

Collective bargaining over first labour contract

Labour contract signed

Grievance procedure used to resolve disputes during the life of the contract

If employees of an organization want to form a union, the law prescribes a specific set of procedures that both employees and the organization must follow. Assuming that these procedures are followed and the union is approved, the organization must engage in collective bargaining with the new union.

Managing labour relations can be a critical concern to an organization. A strike by the United Food and Commercial Workers Union (UFCW) against Maple Leaf was called in November 1997. Hundreds of Maple Leaf employees walked the picket line in Edmonton.

by the union and management. The arbitrator studies the contract, hears both sides of the case, and renders a decision that both parties must obey. The grievance system for resolving disputes about contract enforcement prevents any need to strike during the term of the contract.[39]

SUMMARY OF KEY POINTS

Human resource management is concerned with attracting, developing, and maintaining the human resources an organization needs. Its environmental context consists of its strategic importance and the legal and social environments that affect human resource management.

Attracting human resources is an important part of the HRM function. Human resource planning starts with job analysis and then focuses on forecasting the organization's future need for employees, forecasting the availability of employees both within and outside the organization, and planning programs to ensure that the proper number and type of employees are available when needed. Recruitment and selection are the processes by which job applicants are attracted, assessed, and hired. Methods for selecting applicants include application blanks, tests, interviews, and assessment centres. Any method used for selection should be properly validated.

Organizations must also work to develop their human resources. Training and development enable employees to perform their present jobs effectively and to prepare for future jobs. Performance appraisals are important for validating selection devices, assessing the impact of training programs, deciding pay raises and promotions, determining training needs, and providing helpful feedback to employees. Both objective and judgmental methods of appraisal can be applied, and a good system usually includes several methods. The validity of appraisal information is always a concern because it is difficult to accurately evaluate the many aspects of a person's job performance.

Maintaining human resources is also important. Compensation rates must be fair compared with rates for other jobs within the organization and with rates for the same or similar jobs in other organizations in the labour market. Properly designed incentive or merit pay systems can encourage high performance, and a good benefits program can help attract and retain employees. Career planning is also a major aspect of human resource management.

If a majority of a company's nonmanagement employees so desire, they have the right to be represented by a union. Management must engage in collective bargaining with the union in an effort to agree on a contract. While the contract is in effect, the grievance system is used to settle disputes with management.

DISCUSSION QUESTIONS

Questions for Review

1. What is job analysis and how is it related to human resource planning?
2. Describe recruiting and selection. What are the major sources for recruits? What are the common selection methods?
3. What is the role of compensation and benefits in organizations? How should the amount of compensation and benefits be determined?
4. What are the basic steps that employees can follow if they wish to unionize?

Questions for Analysis

5. What are the advantages and disadvantages of internal and external recruiting? Which do you feel is best in the long term? Why? Be sure to think about this issue from the standpoint of both the organization and individuals (whether inside or outside of the organization) who might be considered for positions.

6. How do you know if a selection device is valid? What are the possible consequences of using invalid selection methods? How can an organization ensure that its selection methods are valid?

7. Are benefits more important than compensation to an organization? To an individual? Why?

Questions for Application

8. Write a description and specifications for a job that you have held (office worker, checkout clerk, salesperson, lifeguard). Then contact a company with such a job and obtain an actual description and specification from that firm. In what ways are your description and specification like theirs? In what ways are they different?

9. Contact a local organization to determine how that organization evaluates the performance of employees in complex jobs such as middle or higher-level manager, scientist, lawyer, or market researcher. What problems with performance appraisal can you note?

10. Interview someone who is or has been a member of a union to determine his or her reasons for joining. Would you join a union? Why or why not?

BUILDING EFFECTIVE TECHNICAL SKILLS

Exercise Overview

Technical skills refer to the manager's abilities to accomplish or understand work done in an organization. Many managers must have technical skills to hire appropriate people to work in the organization. This exercise will help you use technical skills as part of the selection process.

Exercise Background

Variation one: If you currently work full-time, or have worked full-time in the past, select two jobs with which you have some familiarity. Select one job that is relatively low in skill level, responsibility, required education, and pay and one job that is relatively high in skill level, responsibility, required education, and pay. The exercise will be more useful to you if you use real jobs that you can relate to at a personal level.

Variation two: If you have never worked full-time, or if you are not personally familiar with an array of jobs, assume that you are a manager for a small manufacturing facility. You need to hire individuals to fill two jobs. One job is for the position of plant custodian. This individual will sweep floors, clean bathrooms, empty trash cans, and so forth. The other person will be office manager. This individual will supervise a staff of three clerks and secretaries, administer the plant payroll, and coordinate the administrative operations of the plan.

Exercise Task

With the preceding information as background, do the following:

1. Identify the most basic skills that you think are necessary for someone to perform each job effectively.
2. Identify the general indicators or predictors of whether or not a given individual can perform each job.
3. Develop a brief set of interview questions that you might use to determine whether or not an applicant has the qualifications to perform each job.
4. How important is it that a manager hiring employees to perform a job have the technical skills to do that job him- or herself?

 **W**hen Paul Galvin began making car radios in Chicago in 1929, he brought in Daniel Noble, a university professor, to help him with mobile design, and gradually they built and installed the first commercially manufactured car radio. It was named Motorola for *motor* and *victrola*.

In the 1950s, Motorola turned to solid-state electronic devices and semiconductors. Later it began manufacturing integrated circuits and microprocessors. By the early 1990s, Motorola was either first or second in chips for personal computers and other devices, two-way radios, cellular phones, pagers, and automotive semiconductors. Motorola was the first large company to earn the Malcolm Baldridge National Quality Award. It is also frequently referred to as the best managed company in the United States.

One of its keys to success is training. In 1980, Motorola established an education service department with two goals—expand participative management and improve product quality. From 1985 to 1987, Motorola's top executives spent seventeen days each in the classroom, after which the training was moved to lower levels of the organization. During this process, Motorola discovered that some of its employees could not read; others could not comprehend basic quality control statistics and computations. Motorola established training to increase literacy and mathematics comprehension levels and changed hiring practices to reduce their occurrences in the future.

Motorola had been spending 4 percent of its payroll for training, but in 1994 the company announced plans to increase that amount dramatically. Every person was expected to undergo forty hours of training each year, and Motorola hoped to quadruple that by the year 2000. Even though promotions are frequently tied to the new skills obtainable through this training, some employees resist it; to get them to go, they are actually threatened with termination. Those who don't seem to learn what is taught may be demoted to jobs requiring fewer new skills.

This level of focus on training is characteristic of what have come to be known as learning organizations. A learning organization facilitates the lifelong learning and personal development of all of its employees while continually transforming itself to respond to changing demands and needs. Learning organizations typically use networking and individual/group recognition (positive contingent reinforcement in technical terms), have a customer orientation, and develop people skills. Management styles in those organizations are characterized by openness, communication, self-determination, leadership, and a focus on the organization's strengths.

Motorola's training is highly business specific. It might set a goal to cut costs in a particular area and then develop a course on how to do that. In addition, the corporate culture is instilled in personnel during the training. That culture is regimented, efficient, and driven.

Sixty-hour workweeks are common, and the pressure to "do it right the first time" can be intense. Motorola suggests that while it allows people to make a mistake and learn from it, it also does not allow them to repeat such mistakes. Developing training to enable its personnel to cope with the stress that arises from such a high-performance environment may be Motorola's next big training challenge.

Questions

1. What are the advantages and disadvantages to a learning organization?

2. Should Motorola change its training to make it more general and less geared to specific company problems? Why or why not?

3. There seem to be many contradictions in this description of Motorola—it is described as regimented, efficient, and driven but uses participative management and teams. Are these, in fact, contradictions? Why or why not?

References: Ronald Henkoff, "Keeping Motorola on a Roll," *Fortune*, April 18, 1994, pp. 67–78; "Motorola: Training for the Millennium," *Business Week*, March 28, 1994, pp. 158–162; and William Wiggenhorn, "Motorola U: When Training Becomes an Education," *Harvard Business Review*, July/August 1990, pp. 71–83.

CHAPTER NOTES

1. "Saturn: Labor's Love Lost?" *Business Week*, February 8, 1993, pp. 122–124; Gary Hoover, Alta Campbell, and Patrick J. Spain (Eds.), *Hoover's Handbook of American Business 1995* (Austin, Tex.: The Reference Press, 1994), pp. 548–549; "A Shocker at GM," *Business Week*, January 23, 1995, p. 47; and Karla Miller, "Saturn and Union Agree to Keep Unique Contract," *The Detroit News* (online edition), September 5, 1998.

2. For a complete review of human resource management, see Cynthia D. Fisher, Lyle F. Schoenfeldt, and James B. Shaw, *Human Resource Management*, 2nd ed. (Boston: Houghton Mifflin, 1993).

3. David Terpstra and Elizabeth Rozell, "The Relationship of Staffing Practices to Organizational Level Measures of Performance," *Personnel Psychology*, Spring 1993, pp. 27–38.

4. Patrick Wright and Gary McMahan, "Strategic Human Resources Management: A Review of the Literature," *Journal of Management*, June 1992, pp. 280–319.

5. Augustine Lado and Mary Wilson, "Human Resource Systems and Sustained Competitive Advantage: A Competency-Based Perspective," *Academy of Management Review*, Vol. 19, No. 4, 1994, pp. 699–727.

6. *Brooks v. Canada Safeway* (1989), 59 D.L.R. (4th) 321.

7. Caroline Agocs, Catherine Burr, and Felicity Somerset, *Employment Equity: Cooperative Strategies for Organizational Change* (Scarborough, Ont.: Prentice-Hall Canada, 1992), p. 5.

8. Phebe-Jane Poole, *Diversity: A Business Advantage* (Ajax, Ont.: Poole Publishing Company, 1997), p. 153.

9. Lori McDowell, *Human Rights in the Workplace: A Practical Guide* (Scarborough, Ont.: Carswell, 1997), pp. 7–58.

10. "Businesses Show 21 Percent Increase in Temporary Jobs," *The Chronicle-Herald* (Halifax), March 4, 1996, p. A7.

11. David Bowen, Gerald Ledford, and Barry Nathan, "Hiring for the Organization, Not the Job," *The Academy of Management Executive*, November 1991, pp. 35–45.

12. L.J. Reypert, "Succession Planning in the Ministry of Transportation and Communications Province of Ontario," *Human Resource Planning*, Vol. 4, 1992, pp. 151–156.

13. "Shades of Geneen at Emerson Electric," *Fortune*, May 22, 1989, p. 39.

14. Leonard Greenhalgh, Anne T. Lawrence, and Robert I. Sutton, "Determinants of Work Force Reduction Strategies in Declining Organizations," *Academy of Management Review*, April 1988, pp. 241–254.

15. Michael R. Carrell and Frank E. Kuzmits, *Personnel: Human Resource Management*, 3rd ed. (New York: Merrill, 1989).

16. Robert Gatewood, Mary Gowan, and Gary Lautenschlager, "Corporate Image, Recruitment Image, and Initial Job Choice Decisions," *Academy of Management Journal*, Vol. 36, No. 2, 1993, pp. 414–427.

17. Mary K. Suszko and James A. Breaugh, "The Effects of Realistic Job Previews on Applicant Self-Selection and Employee Turnover, Satisfaction, and Coping Ability," *Journal of Management*, Fall 1986, pp. 513–523.

18. Frank L. Schmidt and John E. Hunter, "Employment Testing: Old Theories and New Research Findings," *American Psychologist*, October 1981, pp. 1128–1137; see also "New Test Quantifies the Way We Work," *The Wall Street Journal*, February 7, 1990, p. B1.

19. Robert Liden, Christopher Martin, and Charles Parsons, "Interviewer and Applicant Behaviors in Employment Interviews," *Academy of Management Journal*, Vol. 36, No. 2, 1993, pp. 372–386.

20. Brian Dumaine, "The New Art of Hiring Smart," *Fortune*, August 17, 1987, pp. 78–81.

21. Paul R. Sackett, "Assessment Centers and Content Validity: Some Neglected Issues," *Personnel Psychology*, Vol. 40, 1987, pp. 13–25.

22. Abby Brown, "To Test or Not to Test," *Personnel Administrator*, March 1987, pp. 67–70.

23. See Bernard Keys and Joseph Wolfe, "Management Education and Development: Current Issues and Emerging Trends," *Journal of Management*, June 1988, pp. 205–229, for a recent review.

24. IBM Canada Web site (http://www.can.IBM.com).

25. *Sector Competitiveness Framework Series: Education and Training Services* (Ottawa: Industry Canada, 1998).

26. "Videos Are Starring in More and More Training Programs," *Business Week*, September 7, 1987, pp. 108–110.

27. For recent discussions of why performance appraisal is important, see Walter Kiechel III, "How to Appraise Performance," *Fortune*, October 12, 1987, pp. 239–240; and Donald J. Campbell and Cynthia Lee, "Self-Appraisal in Performance Evaluation: Development Versus Evaluation," *Academy of Management Review*, April 1988, pp. 302–314.

28. Barry R. Nathan, Allan Mohrman, and John Milliman, "Interpersonal Relations as a Context for the Effects of Appraisal Interviews on Performance and Satisfaction: A Longitudinal Study," *Academy of Management Journal*, June 1991, pp. 352–369.

29. Brian O'Reilly, "360 Feedback Can Change Your Life," *Fortune*, October 17, 1994, pp. 93–100.

30. Jaclyn Fierman, "The Perilous New World of Fair Pay," *Fortune*, June 13, 1994, pp. 57–64.

31. Caroline L. Weber and Sara L. Rynes, "Effects of Compensation Strategy on Job Pay Decisions," *Academy of Management Journal*, March 1991, pp. 86–109.

32. Peter Cappelli and Wayne F. Cascio, "Why Some Jobs Command Wage Premiums: A Test of Career Tournament and Internal Labor Market Hypotheses," *Academy of Management Journal*, December 1991, pp. 848–868.

33. "To Each According to His Needs: Flexible Benefits Plans Gain Favor," *The Wall Street Journal*, September 16, 1986, p. 29.

34. "The Future Look of Employee Benefits," *The Wall Street Journal*, September 7, 1988, p. 21.

35. "Firms Forced to Cut Back on Benefits," *USA Today*, November 29, 1988, pp. 1B, 2B.

36. Robert Waterman, Judith Waterman, and Betsy Collard, "Toward a Career-Resilient Workforce," *Harvard Business Review*, July–August 1994, pp. 87–95.

37. Barbara Presley Nobel, "Reinventing Labor," *Harvard Business Review*, July–August 1993, pp. 115–125.

38. A. Craig and N. Solomon, *The System of Industrial Relations in Canada,* 4th ed. (Scarborough, Ont.: Prentice-Hall Canada, 1993).

39. For recent research on collective bargaining, see Wallace N. Davidson III, Dan L. Worrell, and Sharon H. Garrison, "Effect of Strike Activity on Firm Value," *Academy of Management Journal*, June 1988, pp. 387–394; John M. Magenau, James E. Martin, and Melanie M. Peterson, "Dual and Unilateral Commitment Among Stewards and Rank-and-File Union Members," *Academy of Management Journal*, June 1988, pp. 359–376; and Brian E. Becker, "Concession Bargaining: The Meaning of Union Gains," *Academy of Management Journal*, June 1988, pp. 377–387.

Managing Workforce Diversity in Organizations

14

OBJECTIVES

After studying this chapter, you should be able to:

● *Discuss the nature of workforce diversity, including its meaning and reasons for its increase.*

● *Identify and describe the major dimensions of diversity in organizations.*

● *Describe diversity in different contexts.*

● *Discuss the primary impact of diversity on organizations.*

● *Describe individual and organizational strategies and approaches to coping with diversity.*

● *Discuss the six characteristics of the fully multicultural organization.*

OUTLINE

The Royal Bank of Canada has done an exemplary job of managing diversity. Tailoring its services to the needs of specific customer groups is just one example of its successful management of diversity.

More and more organizations are recognizing the importance of diversity issues. The Royal Bank of Canada, the nations's largest financial institution, is an example of an organization that has addressed diversity with a multipronged approach: in the workforce, in the marketplace, and in the organization's structures. In its newsletter, the Royal Bank has stated that "there is a world of opportunity to be gained from tapping people's differences and pooling their insights and experiences. Organizations that leverage diversity are in a much better position to benefit from well-rounded, creative thinking internally and reach more segments of an increasingly diverse marketplace."

The Royal Bank recognized that understanding and valuing differences within the workforce could lead to increased productivity on the part of employees and, consequently, to increased revenues for the bank. The bank cites several examples of successful management of diversity that led to bottom-line benefits: older or retired employees helping the organization provide

> **"There is a world of opportunity to be gained from tapping people's differences and pooling their insights and experiences."**

appropriate services to the seniors market; partnerships with Aboriginal peoples that resulted in increased opportunities to provide services to the Aboriginal community; and the addition of women to a product development team, which provided male team members with a new perspective on the reaction of female customers to new products.

With respect to the marketplace, the Royal Bank has tailored its services to meet the needs of specific customer groups. For example, in Toronto's Chinese community, where four out of every five clients are of Chinese origin, the bank staff are predominantly of Chinese origin and conduct business primarily in Mandarin or Cantonese. Product brochures, advertisements, and marketing materials are translated into Mandarin and Cantonese—a clear indication of the bank's belief that providing culture-sensitive services is financially rewarding.

Internally, the bank has launched a number of initiatives to promote dialogue and understanding of diversity issues. Diversity conferences have been attended by managers across the country. To achieve longer-term results, a Diversity Business Council made up of senior management has been given the task of establishing clear priorities for leveraging diversity. The highly successful Work and Family program, which enables employees to utilize flexible work arrangements, has received widespread approval within the bank and appears to have had a positive impact on employee performance and attitudes.

The Royal Bank believes that managing diversity is a sound approach to business. As expressed in the bank's newsletter, "Diversity management takes into account the diversity of the customers we serve in order to provide quality service. It's also about fostering a workplace that taps the potential of all employees by respecting their differences as well as their similarities."[1] ●

ike most other organizations in the world today, the Royal Bank has seen tremendous changes in the composition of its workforce during the last several decades. Once dominated by white male managers, the bank now employs people at a variety of organizational levels from a diverse set of backgrounds. And like other organizations today, the Royal Bank has encountered more than a few challenges along the way as it has sought to address the variety of issues, opportunities, and problems that its increasingly diverse workforce has created.

This chapter is about workforce diversity in organizations. We begin by exploring the meaning of diversity and the management of diversity. We then identify the reasons for its increase and discuss common dimensions of diversity and diversity in different contexts. The impact of diversity on the organization is then explored. We next address individual strategies and organizational approaches for managing diversity. Finally, we characterize and describe the fully multicultural organization.

THE NATURE OF WORKFORCE DIVERSITY

Workforce diversity has become a very important issue in many organizations, both in Canada and abroad. A logical starting point, then, is to establish the meaning of diversity and the management of diversity.

The Meaning of Diversity

● **diversity**
Exists in a group or organization when its members differ from one another along one or more important dimensions such as age, gender, or ethnicity

Diversity exists in a group or organization when its members differ from one another along one or more important dimensions.[2] Thus diversity is not an absolute phenomenon wherein a group or organization is or is not diverse. Instead, diversity can be conceptualized as a continuum. If everyone in the group or organization is exactly like everyone else, there is no diversity whatsoever. If everyone is different along every imaginable dimension, total diversity exists. In reality, of course, these extremes are more hypothetical than real. Most settings are characterized by a level of diversity somewhere between these extremes. Therefore, diversity should be thought of in terms of degree or level of diversity along relevant dimensions.

The dimensions of diversity might include gender, age, ethnic origin, or any of several others. Some differences such as education, sexual orientation, or socioeconomic class are not visible. In the context of the workplace, diversity refers to differences that have an impact on the employees, the organization, and the marketplace or clientele that the organization serves. The Conference Board of Canada defines managing diversity as "an organizational culture that values differences and maximizes the potential of all employees."[3] The broader the definition of diversity, the easier it is for all employees to accept the notion that diversity is beneficial to all within the organization.

Reasons for Increasing Diversity

As we noted earlier, organizations today are becoming increasingly diverse along many different dimensions. Although several different factors account for these trends and changes, four of the more important ones are illustrated in Figure 14.1.

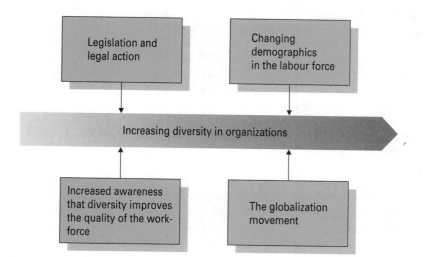

Cultural diversity is increasing in most organizations today for four basic reasons. These reasons promise to make diversity even greater in the future.

One factor contributing to increased diversity is changing demographics in the labour force. As more women and minorities enter the labour force, for example, the available pool of talent from which organizations hire employees is changing in both size and composition. If talent within each segment of the labour pool is evenly distributed (for example, if the number of very talented men in the workforce as a percentage of all men in the workforce is the same as the number of very talented women in the labour force as a percentage of all

Louis Garneau, who started the successful Quebec cycling equipment firm Louis Garneau Sport in 1983, is an example of how francophones have steadily been replacing the once-dominant Anglo presence in Quebec business.

women in the workforce), it follows logically that, over time, proportionately more women and proportionately fewer men will be hired by an organization.[4]

A related factor contributing to diversity is the increased awareness by organizations that they can improve the overall quality of their workforce by hiring and promoting the most talented people available. By casting a broader net in recruiting and looking beyond traditional sources for new employees, organizations are finding more broadly qualified and better qualified employees from many different segments of society. Thus these organizations are finding that diversity can be a source of competitive advantage.[5]

Another reason for the increase in diversity is that legislation and legal actions have forced organizations to hire more broadly. In earlier times, organizations in Canada were essentially free to discriminate against women and visible minorities. Thus most organizations were dominated by white males. But over the last thirty years or so, various laws have outlawed discrimination against these and other groups. As we detailed in Chapter 13, organizations are expected to hire and promote people today solely on the basis of their qualifications.

A final factor contributing to increased diversity in organizations is the globalization movement. Organizations that have opened offices and related facilities in other countries have had to learn to deal with different customs, social norms, and mores. Strategic alliances and foreign ownership also contribute, as managers today are more likely to have job assignments in other countries and/or to work with foreign managers within their own countries. As employees and managers move from assignment to assignment across national boundaries, organizations and their subsidiaries within each country thus become more diverse.

DIMENSIONS OF DIVERSITY

As we indicated earlier, many different dimensions of diversity can characterize an organization. In this section, we discuss age, gender, ethnicity, language, and other dimensions of diversity.

Age Distribution

One important dimension of diversity in any organization is the age distribution of its workforce. The average age of the Canadian workforce is gradually increasing and will continue to do so for the next several years. In 1994, almost one-third of working-age people were between 45 and 64 years of age. It is anticipated that by 2016, this population will increase to 44 percent of working-age people.[6] Figure 14.2 presents age distributions for Canadian workers in 1971, 1991, and 1996.

Several factors are contributing to this pattern. For one, the baby-boom generation (a term used to describe the unusually large number of people who were born in the twenty-year period after World War II) continues to age. Declining birth rates among the post–baby-boom generations simultaneously account for smaller percentages of new entrants into the labour force. Another factor that contributes to the aging workforce is improved health and medical care. As a result of these improvements, people are able to remain productive and active for longer periods of time. Combined with higher legal limits for mandatory retirement, more and more people are working beyond the age at which they might have retired just a few years ago.[7] (Nevertheless, as a result of government cutbacks and corporate downsizing, the average age of retirement in Canada fell from 64.9 in 1982 to 62.3 in 1997.)

How does this trend affect organizations? Older workers tend to have more experience, to be more stable, and to make greater contributions to productivity than younger workers. On the other hand, despite improvements in health and medical care, an aging worker population is likely to mean more people with work disabilities. Statistics Canada estimates that by 2015, 60 percent of people with disabilities will be between 45 and 64 years of age compared with 46 percent in 1993.[8] There is increasing pressure on older workers to update their skills and keep up with the technological changes that are an inevitable part of the information age. Finally, the stability in the workforce brought about by the baby-boomers means that younger workers, although fewer in number, may have difficulty establishing themselves in certain careers.

Gender

As more and more women have entered the workforce, organizations have subsequently experienced changes in the relative proportions of male and female employees. If the current entry rate of women into the labour force continues, it is estimated that they will constitute 50 percent of the labour force by the year 2000.[9] Statistics Canada data indicate that the labour force activity of married women with children has grown rapidly. In 1993, 70 percent of women with children under 16 were in the labour force, as compared with 55 percent in 1981. Studies of women in the workforce have also revealed that the average pay of women working full-time is approximately 70 percent of that of their male counterparts; that 60 percent of female workers hold clerical, sales, and service jobs; and that women are much more likely than men to be working part-time.

FIGURE 14.2 The Aging of Canada's Working-Age Population

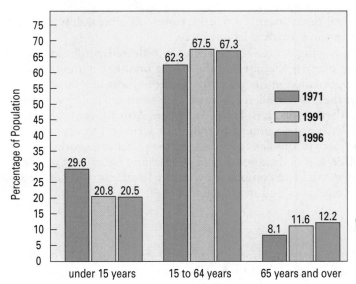

Canada's working-age population is getting older. The percentage of people under 15 is declining. Among working-age people (15 to 64), baby-boomers (those aged 30 to 49) have gone from 38 percent of that group in 1971 to almost 50 percent in 1996.

[handwritten notes:] www.statcan.ca
31,413,990 → population
40-44 → baby boomers
almost evenly distributed → male/female
increasingly aging → affected by baby boomers

Adapted with permission from Statistics Canada, *The Daily*, Cat. no. 11-001, July 29, 1997.

A major gender-related problem that many organizations face today is the so-called glass ceiling. The **glass ceiling** describes a barrier that keeps women from advancing to top management positions in many organizations.[10] This ceiling is a real barrier that is difficult to break, but it is also often so subtle as to not be visible. Although women occupy more than 10 percent of managerial and administrative positions, very few women are permitted to move up to the executive level. A survey of Canada's top companies indicates that less than 1 percent of the top management jobs (chair, president, or CEO) are held by women, while only 1.6 percent of the jobs of corporate vice president and above are held by women.[11]

Why does the glass ceiling exist? One reason is that some male managers are still reluctant to promote female managers.[12] As a result, many talented women choose to leave their jobs in large organizations and start their own businesses. Recall from Chapter 9, for example, that most new Canadian businesses today are started by women. In spite of their increasing numbers in the workplace, women in Canada have less access than men to positions of authority, less involvement in decision-making activities, and fewer of the economic rewards associated with such measures of workplace power.[13]

Ethnicity

A third major dimension of cultural diversity in organizations is **ethnicity** and colour. Changing immigration patterns have led to major changes in the ethnocultural composition of Canadians. Between 1986 and 1991, the proportion of the Canadian population reporting ethnic origins other than British, French, or Canadian increased by 20 percent. Among major Canadian cities, the increase was 26 percent in Toronto, 29 percent in Vancouver, and 30 percent in Montreal. Changes in relation to the visible minority population are particularly significant. Between 1986 and 1991, the total estimated visible minority population in Canada increased by 58 percent to approximately 2.5 million, or 9 percent of Canada's total population. By 2006, it is estimated that the total population of visible minorities will be 5.6 million, or 18 percent of Canada's total population.[14] Table 14.1 presents a breakdown of immigrant participation in the Canadian labour force.

In Canada, varying degrees of diversity are reflected within individual organizations. Like women, members of the visible minority communities are generally underrepresented in the executive ranks of most organizations. It should be noted that there is considerable variation within each of these communities (Asian, Arab, Pacific Islanders, Latin American, African, etc.). Unlike women, these groups have not organized to lobby for change. Organizations that recognize the impact of the changing face of the Canadian workforce as well as the marketplace will be in a position to harness the benefits of diversity. At the same time, they will be in compliance with the letter and spirit of the Canadian human rights law described in Chapter 13.

Language

While Canada has become home to a highly diverse mix of linguistic groups in recent decades, Canada is an officially bilingual country. Approximately one in four Canadians is francophone. In addition to Quebec, there are also large francophone populations in New Brunswick and Ontario. For companies

TABLE 14.1 Immigrants in the Canadian Labour Force

	Experienced Labour Force		
	Total[1]	Immigrants	Recent immigrants[2]
All Occupations	100.0	100.0	100.0
Management	9.0	10.0	7.2
Business, finance, and administrative	19.0	17.7	14.2
Natural and applied sciences	5.0	6.5	6.8
Health	5.0	5.3	3.7
Social science, education, government service, and religion	6.8	6.0	4.3
Art, culture, recreation and sport	2.7	2.5	2.3
Sales and service	26.0	25.6	33.7
Trades, transport, and equipment operators	14.1	12.5	9.8
Occupations unique to primary industry	4.8	2.6	2.5
Occupations unique to processing, manufacturing, and utilities	7.6	11.4	15.5

1. Includes immigrants, nonimmigrants, and nonpermanent residents.
2. Includes persons who immigrated to Canada between 1991 and 1996 (first four months only of 1996.)

Adapted with permission from Statistics Canada, *The Daily,* Cat. no. 11-001, March 17, 1998.

Notwithstanding certain ethnic stereotypes, immigrants to Canada are very often highly skilled. In some sectors, immigrants often fill employment needs that are not being met by the indigenous workforce.

doing business in Canada, the large number of francophones is an important factor not only in terms of their marketing, packaging, and corporate identity, but also in terms of how they utilize and manage their workforces.

In recent decades, Quebec has seen the rise of a new class of francophone businesspersons who have begun to change the face of the province's once Anglo-dominated business elite. Members of this new generation of managers and entrepreneurs are for the most part completely bilingual and thus able not only to conduct business and understand the majority of francophone culture in their native province, but also to help move their businesses—and the Quebec economy as a whole—into new markets both in Canada and abroad. (See the Chapter Closing Case in Chapter 1 for a profile of Laurent Beaudoin, former CEO of one of Quebec's largest home-grown companies, Bombardier.)

The province of New Brunswick has persuaded businesses to locate there by aggressively promoting one of its chief assets: a bilingual workforce. The desirability of such a workforce has been most evident in the case of corporate telephone call centres, many of which need to be able to provide service in French or English to their customers across the country. Some of the major companies that have moved their call centre operations to New Brunswick in recent years include the Royal Bank, Federal Express, and Purolator. Along with the provincial government, these companies have been able to attract personnel not only by offering positions that utilize their linguistic skills, but also by emphasizing the lower costs of living in Moncton or Saint John, as opposed to larger Canadian cities.

Linguistic diversity beyond French and English can be especially important for global organizations. For instance, a Spanish speaker in the decision-making loop could have saved General Motors the expense of trying to market the Chevy Nova in Mexico. "Nova" in Spanish means "it doesn't go."

Founded by Diane Dupuy, Famous People Players is more than just a theatre company. The company is dedicated to the integration of people who are developmentally handicapped. Through its life skills program, performers are given the motivation and skills to develop their creative abilities. Trained by Humber College's School of Hospitality and Restaurant Management in preparing and serving food, Famous People Players nourishes both stomach and soul.

Other Dimensions of Diversity

In addition to age, gender, ethnicity, and language, organizations are also confronting other dimensions of diversity. People with disabilities are accounting for an increasing percentage of the workforce. Statistics Canada estimates that by 2016, people with disabilities that affect them at work will account for 8 percent of the population aged 15 to 64. The majority will reside in Ontario (42 percent), British Columbia (16 percent), and Quebec (15 percent). This trend will significantly affect workplace accommodations for employees.

Single parents, dual-career couples, gays and lesbians, people with special dietary preferences, and people with different political ideologies and viewpoints also represent major dimensions of diversity in today's organizations. The particular needs of the "sandwich generation" (those between 45 and 55) will also have some impact upon organizations as people in this group find themselves responsible not only for the care of their children, but also for the care of parents or other elderly relatives. As the *Managing in a Changing World* box shows, white men also constitute an important diversity group that organizations must acknowledge as well.

DIVERSITY IN DIFFERENT CONTEXTS

If managers are to truly understand and appreciate diversity, they must also recognize its role in different contexts. Two of the more important different diversity contexts relevant to managers are diversity in other countries and diversity as a force for social change.

Diversity in Other Countries

We have already noted the increasing presence of diversity in Canadian organizations. But how does this compare with diversity in other countries? In the paragraphs that follow we first examine diversity in the United States, next in European countries, then in Japan, and finally in other parts of the world.

Diversity in the United States As in Canada, and for similar reasons, the average age of the U.S. workforce is gradually increasing and will continue to do so for the next several years. The percentage of male employees to female employers is also changing. By the year 2000, it is expected that the percentage of male employees will have shrunk to 53 percent from the 1988 figure of 55 percent.[15] In spite of the gains achieved through Title VII of the Civil Rights Act (as amended by the Equal Employment Opportunity Act of 1972), women continue to experience barriers to advancement within many organizations. Whereas women constitute almost 45 percent of all managers, there are only two female CEOs among the one thousand largest businesses in the United States.

Most organizations within the United States reflect varying degrees of ethnicity comprising whites, African-Americans, Hispanics, and Asians. Projections for the year 2000 indicate that the biggest changes will involve whites and Hispanics. The percentage of whites in the workforce is expected to drop from 79 percent to 74 percent, while the percentage of Hispanics is expected to climb from 7 percent to 19 percent. The percentage of African-Americans and Asians is expected to climb only about 1 percent each.

U.S. organizations have for some time recognized the importance of workforce diversity. According to Department of Labor projections, only 15 percent of new entrants to the U.S. workforce will be white males; 85 percent will consist of women, minorities, and immigrants. Major corporations such as Avon and Xerox Corp. have developed strategies to create and maintain a diverse workforce.

Diversity in Europe European organizations face the same aging workforce as their Canadian counterparts. But they tend to have less diversity in terms of gender. For example, most European firms have even fewer women executives than do Canadian firms. Because equal employment and the feminist movement each came to Europe later than to Canada, large numbers of women in Europe did not begin to pursue professional careers until just a few years ago. Although this pattern has lately changed, the relative percentage of women in managerial positions in Europe is somewhat less than is found in Canadian organizations.

In contrast to Canadian organizations, however, European firms are considerably more diverse in terms of national origin. This is because Europe comprises many relatively small nations. Companies in Europe have long been accustomed to doing business in a variety of countries. And for decades, managers have moved from country to country, either for promotions within their firm or for jobs in new firms. As a result, many European companies have a rich tradition of diversity.

Diversity in Japan Japanese organizations also have their own unique diversity profiles. In some ways, these diversity profiles resemble those found in European organizations. For example, the Japanese also have a workforce that is becoming ever older and that comprises relatively few women, especially in managerial positions. The traditional career path in Japan has been for women who finished school to work a few years in clerical positions and then to "drop out" to start a family. Until recently, few ever returned to the workforce.

North American firms in Japan have been a major reason for shifts in career opportunities for women in that country. Fighting an acute labour shortage in

White Men Are a Diversity Group, Too

Managing diversity means more than meeting legal requirements of employment and pay equity. It is more than assuaging guilt feelings over injustices of the past. Managing diversity means recognizing that all types of people can contribute to accomplishing the organization's objectives; it is a strategic weapon in highly competitive marketplaces. *All types of people* embodies all minorities, including the emerging minority of white men. Indeed, in the workforce as a whole, white men became a minority in the late 1980s.

Despite the importance of managing diversity to organizational effectiveness, in 1991 less than a third of companies surveyed indicated that they had any form of training in how to manage diversity. Perhaps in part because of the lack of such programs, some white men are increasingly becoming frustrated, resentful, and afraid. Without such training programs, higher-level managers are prone to exclude white men from being part of the company's diversity program as well as to inadvertently engage in reverse discrimination. The rules are changing quickly, and organizations need active, ongoing diversity management programs tied to their objectives to avoid both current and future problems.

Unfortunately, some diversity training programs exacerbate the problem rather than alleviate it. In some instances, discussion groups have become encounter groups. Members of these groups seem determined to lash out against all white men and the organization itself rather than recognize the contributions others have made and focus on how best to change for the future. This can happen, in particular, if the top executives do not truly understand diversity or if they are not truly committed to doing something about it. One way of ensuring such top-level commitment, of course, is to see that the board of directors reflects the diversity likely to be experienced within the company.

Managing diversity is difficult in a group or organization where there are several women or minorities but not enough for everyone to regard diversity as normal and routine. Virtually all organizations will be in that situation as different departments and divisions respond to the marketplace and employ more women and minorities. The presence of little or no training or, worse yet, the wrong kind of training is especially unfortunate.

References: "White, Male, and Worried," *Business Week*, January 31, 1994, pp. 50–55; Rosabeth Moss Kanter, "Men and Women: Equal Partners?" *Executive Excellence*, November 1993, pp. 8–9; R. Roosevelt Thomas, Jr., *Beyond Race and Gender* (New York: AMACOM, 1991); and Patricia A. Galagan, "Tapping the Power of a Diverse Workforce," *Training and Development Journal*, March 1991, pp. 38–44.

Japan, firms like IBM and Motorola started offering women who were leaving to have children a guaranteed job later if they wished to return to work. To the surprise of many traditional Japanese managers, large numbers of women have indeed chosen to return to work after a few years. Now many Japanese organizations have begun to make similar offers.

Whereas the number of female managers in Japan lags behind Canada and the United States and mirrors the situation in Europe, Japanese organizations have little diversity of other forms and varieties. For example, because Japan's borders were long closed to immigrants, Japanese firms have little diversity in terms of ethnicity and national origin. Most Japanese managers tend to be Japanese nationals. The Japanese are also only just now beginning to provide accommodations for their physically challenged employees and similar groups.

Diversity in Other Parts of the World Although North America, Japan, and Europe are the major economic centres in the world today, diversity patterns in selected other parts of the world are also worth mentioning. Increasingly important areas of Pacific Asia include South Korea, Taiwan, Hong Kong, and neighbouring countries. In general, diversity in these countries mirrors that of Japan—little ethnic diversity because of restrictive immigration laws, relatively few women because of social norms, and an aging workforce. But in Australia, which has had more open immigration policies, ethnic diversity in the workforce is perhaps as great as in any other single country in the world today. Mexico has relatively little diversity. Few accessible statistics exist for assessing diversity in most other countries.

The message of these diversity patterns for managers in international businesses is both simple and complex. The simple message is that such managers must be prepared to confront a variety of diversity issues when they are conducting business in other countries. Although some of the dimensions—age and gender, for instance—are the same, they also must be considered within the cultural context of the particular country. The complex message is that while understanding and addressing diversity issues within a single country is difficult enough, coping with such issues across many different countries greatly magnifies the role of diversity in the organization.

Diversity as a Force for Social Change

Diversity can have a notable impact on organizations as a force for social change. This generally occurs as the composition of an organization's workforce gradually comes to fully mirror the composition of its surrounding labour market. For example, if a manager in an organization learns to effectively interact with a diverse set of people at work, it follows logically that she or he will be better equipped to deal with a diverse set of people in other settings. And conversely, an individual who is comfortable interacting with diverse settings should have little problem when encountering diversity at work. Thus diversity in organizations both facilitates and is facilitated by social change in the environment.

Another way that organizations affect social change is through the images they use to promote themselves and their products. An organization that runs print ads showing only white male executives in its workplace conveys a certain image of itself. In contrast, an organization that uses diverse groups as representatives conveys a different image. As described in the Chapter Closing Case, CITY-TV reflects Toronto's diversity.

THE IMPACT OF DIVERSITY ON ORGANIZATIONS

There is no question that organizations are becoming ever more diverse. But what is the impact of this diversity on organizations? As we see, diversity provides both opportunities and challenges for organizations. Diversity also plays a number of important roles in organizations today.

Diversity as Competitive Advantage

Many organizations are also finding that diversity can be a source of competitive advantage in the marketplace. In general, six arguments have been proposed for how diversity contributes to competitiveness.[16] These are illustrated in Figure 14.3.

The *cost argument* suggests that organizations that learn to cope with diversity generally have higher levels of productivity and lower levels of turnover and absenteeism. Those organizations that do a poor job of managing diversity, on the other hand, suffer from problems of lower productivity and higher levels of turnover and absenteeism. Because each of these factors has a direct impact on costs, the former organization remains more competitive than the latter. When Deloitte & Touche became aware of the high turnover of women in the company, it devoted time and resources to remedy the situation. As a result of its Initiative for the Retention and Advancement of Women, launched in 1993, turnover decreased at all levels, more women advanced through the ranks, and more women and men were attracted to a company they regarded as progressive.[17]

The *resource acquisition argument* for diversity suggests that organizations that manage diversity effectively become known among women and minorities as good places to work. These organizations are thus better able to attract qualified employees from among these groups. Given the increased importance of these groups in the overall labour force, organizations that can attract talented employees from all segments of society are likely to be more competitive.

The *marketing argument* suggests that organizations with diverse workforces are better able to understand different market segments than are less diverse organizations. For example, a cosmetics firm like Avon that wants to sell its products to women and blacks can better understand how to create such products and effectively market them if women and black managers are available to provide inputs into product development, design, packaging, advertising, and so forth.[18]

The *creativity argument* for diversity suggests that organizations with diverse workforces are generally more creative and innovative than are less diverse organizations. If an organization is dominated by one population segment, it follows that its members generally adhere to norms and ways of thinking that reflect that segment. Moreover, they have little insight or stimulus for new ideas that might be derived from different perspectives. The diverse organization, in contrast, is characterized by multiple perspectives and ways of thinking and is therefore more likely to generate new ideas and ways of doing things.

Related to the creativity argument is the *problem-solving argument*. Diversity carries with it an increased pool of information. In virtually any organization,

Many organizations today are finding that diversity can be a source of competitive advantage. A variety of arguments have been developed to support this viewpoint. For example, a black sales representative for Revlon helped that firm improve its packaging and promotion for its line of darker skin tone cosmetics.

F I G U R E 14.3 How Diversity Promotes Competitive Advantage

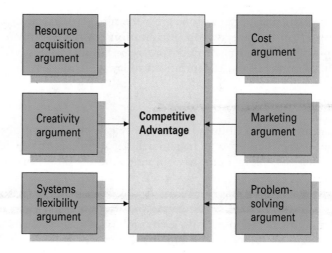

there is some information that everyone has and other information that is unique to each individual. In an organization with little diversity, the larger pool of information is common and the smaller pool is unique. But in a more diverse organization, the unique information is larger. Thus, because more information can be brought to bear on a problem, there is a higher probability that better solutions can be identified.[19]

Finally, the *systems flexibility argument* for diversity suggests that organizations must become more flexible as a way of managing a diverse workforce. As a direct consequence, the overall organizational system also becomes more flexible. As we discussed in Chapters 3 and 11, organizational flexibility enables the organization to better respond to changes in its environment. Thus, by effectively managing diversity within its workforce, an organization simultaneously becomes better equipped to address its environment.[20]

Diversity as a Source of Conflict

Unfortunately, diversity in an organization can also become a major source of conflict. This conflict can arise for a variety of reasons. One potential avenue for conflict is when an individual thinks that someone has been hired, promoted, or fired because of her or his diversity status.[21] For example, suppose that a male executive loses a promotion to a female executive. If he believes that she was promoted because the organization simply wanted to have more female managers rather than because she was the better candidate for the job, he will likely feel resentful toward both her and the organization itself.

Another source of conflict stemming from diversity is through misunderstood, misinterpreted, or inappropriate interactions between people of different groups. For example, suppose that a male executive tells a sexually explicit joke to a new female executive. He may intentionally be trying to embarrass her, he may be clumsily trying to show her that he treats everyone the same, or he may think he is making her feel like part of the team. Regardless of his intent, however, if she finds the joke offensive she will justifiably feel anger and hostility. These feelings may be directed at only the offending individual or more generally toward the entire organization if she believes that its culture facilitates such behaviours. And of course, sexual harassment itself is both unethical and illegal.

Conflict can also arise as a result of other elements of diversity. For example, when a Canadian manager publicly praises a Japanese employee for his outstanding work, the action stems from the dominant cultural belief in North America that such recognition is important and rewarding. But because the Japanese culture places a much higher premium on group loyalty and identity than on individual accomplishment, the employee will likely feel ashamed and embarrassed. Thus a well-intentioned action may backfire and result in unhappiness.

Conflict may also arise as a result of fear, distrust, or individual prejudice. Members of the dominant group in an organization may worry that newcomers from other groups pose a personal threat to their own position in the organization. For example, when U.S. firms have been taken over by Japanese firms, U.S. managers have sometimes been resentful or hostile to Japanese managers assigned to work with them. People may also be unwilling to accept people who are different from themselves. And personal bias and prejudices are still very real among some people today and can lead to potentially harmful conflict.[22]

MANAGING DIVERSITY IN ORGANIZATIONS

Because of the tremendous potential that diversity holds for competitive advantage, as well as the possible consequences of diversity-related conflict, much attention has been focused in recent years on how individuals and organizations can better manage diversity.[23] In the sections that follow, we first discuss individual strategies for dealing with diversity and then summarize organizational approaches to managing diversity.

Individual Strategies for Dealing with Diversity

One important element of managing diversity in an organization consists of things that individuals themselves can do. The four basic attitudes that individuals can strive for are understanding, empathy, tolerance, and willingness to communicate.[24]

Understanding   The first of these is understanding the nature and meaning of diversity. Some managers have taken the basic concepts of employment equity to an unnecessary extreme. They know that, by law, they cannot discriminate against people on the basis of sex, race, and so forth. Thus in following this mandate they come to believe that they must treat everyone the same.

But this belief can cause problems when translated into workplace behaviours among people after they have been hired because people are not the same. Although people need to be treated fairly and equitably, managers must understand that differences among people do, in fact, exist. Thus any effort to treat everyone the same, without regard to their fundamental human differences, will only lead to problems. Managers *must* understand that cultural factors cause people to behave in different ways and that these differences should be accepted.

Empathy   Related to understanding is empathy. People in an organization should try to understand the perspective of others. For example, suppose a woman joins a group that has traditionally comprised men. Each man may be a little self-conscious as to how to act toward the new member and may be interested in making her feel comfortable and welcome. But they may be able to do this even more effectively by empathizing with how she may feel. For example, she may feel disappointed or elated about her new assignment, she may be confident or nervous about her position in the group, and she may be experienced or inexperienced in working with male colleagues. By learning more about her feelings the group members can further facilitate their ability to work together effectively.

Tolerance   A third related individual approach to dealing with diversity is tolerance. Even though managers learn to understand diversity, and even though they may try to empathize with others, the fact remains that they may still not accept or enjoy some aspect of others' behaviour. For example, one organization recently reported that it was experiencing considerable conflict among its U.S. and Israeli employees. The Israeli employees always seemed to want to argue about every issue that arose. The U.S. managers preferred to conduct business more harmoniously and became uncomfortable with the conflict. Finally, after considerable discussion it was learned that many Israeli employees simply enjoy arguing and just see it as part of getting work done.

RCMP Constable Baltej Singh Dhillon, here shown training in Regina, was part of a controversy in the early 1990s. He and other Sikh mounties won the right to wear turbans and beards on the force.

The firm's U.S. employees still do not enjoy the arguing, but they are more willing to tolerate it as a fundamental cultural difference between themselves and their colleagues from Israel.[25]

Willingness to Communicate A final individual approach to dealing with diversity is communication. Problems often get magnified over diversity issues because people are afraid or otherwise unwilling to openly discuss issues that relate to diversity. For example, suppose that a young employee has a habit of making jokes about the age of an older colleague. Perhaps the young colleague means no harm and is just engaging in what she sees as good-natured kidding. But the older employee may find the jokes offensive. If the two do not communicate, the jokes will continue and the resentment will grow. Eventually, what started as a minor problem may erupt into a much bigger one.

For communication to work, it must be two way. If a person wonders if a certain behaviour is offensive to someone else, the curious individual should just ask. Similarly, if someone is offended by the behaviour of another person, he or she should explain to the offending individual how the behaviour is perceived and request that it be stopped. As long as such exchanges are friendly, low key, and nonthreatening, they will generally have a positive outcome. Of course, if the same message is presented in an overly combative manner or if a person continues to engage in offensive behaviour after having been asked to stop, problems will only escalate. At this point, third parties within the organization may have to intervene. And in fact, most organizations today have one or more systems in place to address questions and problems that arise as a result of diversity. We now turn our attention to various ways that organizations can indeed better manage diversity.

Organizational Approaches to Managing Diversity

Whereas individuals are important in managing diversity, the organization itself must play a fundamental role.[26] Through its various policies and practices, people in the organization come to understand what behaviours are and are not appropriate. Diversity training is an even more direct method for managing diversity. The organization's culture is the ultimate context from which diversity must be addressed. The *Environment of Management* box discusses how Warner Lambert, Union Gas, and Oracle are managing diversity.

Organizational Policies   The starting point in managing diversity is the policies that an organization adopts that directly or indirectly affect how people are treated. Obviously, for instance, the extent to which an organization embraces the premise of employment equity will to a large extent determine the potential diversity within an organization. But the organization that follows the law to the letter differs from the organization that actively seeks a diverse and varied workforce.

Another aspect of organizational policies that affects diversity is how the organization addresses and responds to problems that arise from diversity. Consider the example of a manager charged with sexual harassment. If the organization's policies put an excessive burden of proof on the individual being harassed and invoke only minor sanctions against the guilty party, it is sending a clear signal as to the importance of such matters. But the organization that has a balanced set of policies for addressing questions like sexual harassment sends its employees a message that diversity and individual rights and privileges are important.

Indeed, perhaps the major policy through which an organization can reflect its stance on diversity is its mission statement. If the organization's mission statement articulates a clear and direct commitment to diversity, it follows that everyone who comes into contact with that mission statement will grow to understand and accept the importance of diversity, at least to that particular organization.

Organizational Practices   Organizations can also help manage diversity through a variety of ongoing practices and procedures. Avon's creation of networks for various groups represents one example of an organizational practice that fosters diversity. In general, the idea is that because diversity is characterized by differences among people, organizations can more effectively manage that diversity by following practices and procedures that are based on flexibility rather than rigidity.

Benefits packages, for example, can be structured to better accommodate individual situations. An employee who is part of a dual-career couple and who has no children may require relatively little insurance (perhaps because his spouse's employer provides more complete coverage) and would like to be able to schedule vacations to coincide with those of his spouse. An employee who is a single parent may need a wide variety of insurance coverage and prefer to schedule his vacation time to coincide with school holidays.

Flexible working hours are also a useful organizational practice to accommodate diversity. Differences in family arrangements, religious holidays, cultural events, and so forth may each dictate that employees have some degree of flexibility in when they work. For example, a single parent may need to leave the office every day at 4:30 to pick up the children from their daycare centre. An organization that truly values diversity will make every reasonable attempt to accommodate such a need.

Organizations can also facilitate diversity by making sure that its important committees and executive teams are diverse. Even if diversity exists within the broader organizational context, an organization that does not reflect diversity

Managing Diversity at Warner Lambert, Union Gas, and Oracle

 Canada has been called a nation of immigrants and, more recently, a nation of immigrants from all parts of the globe. One could argue that based on its long-standing multicultural policies, Canada has led the world in recognizing the value of diversity in the workplace and in society as a whole. Warner Lambert, Union Gas, and Oracle are among the growing number of Canadian corporations that have implemented diversity programs.

At Warner Lambert Canada Inc., diversity is a key component of the corporation's business strategy. Valuing diversity and managing a diverse workforce are regarded more than human resource issues. As the company puts it, "The more our organization reflects the consumer population, the more it will be in sync with what customers want, need and are looking for." In pursuit of its diversity objective, Warner Lambert established a Diversity Task Force whose mission it is to ensure that the culture at the company supports its commitment in the area of diversity. The company reports that although its diversity program is still in its infancy, it has already realized some of the benefits of managing diversity (for example, employee retention).

Union Gas Limited is based in Chatham, Ontario. With 700,000 customers and 2,600 employees across Ontario, the company is aware that its diverse consumer base and workforce is key to its business success. Union Gas has been working on developing an equitable work environment for some time now, and its efforts seem to be having an impact on employee commitment and satisfaction. According to one survey, 88 percent of its employees believe that Union Gas is one of the best workplaces.

Oracle Corporation Canada Inc. strives for full integration of all its employees, including those with disabilities. The corporation's equal opportunity program is committed to fairness in hiring, recruiting, and accommodating potential employees. Oracle Canada regularly participates in career fairs and has established a technical internship program that places special emphasis on diverse groups.

Warner Lambert, Union Gas, and Oracle have joined other Canadian corporations in recognizing the diversity advantage.

References: "Diversity at Work: Sharing the Experience" (http://www.equalopportunity.on.ca); Jeffrey Gandz, "A Business Case for Diversity" (http://www.equalopportunity.on.ca); and Phebe-Jane Poole, *Diversity: A Business Advantage* (Ajax, Ont.: Poole Publishing Company, 1997).

in groups like committees and teams implies that diversity is not a fully ingrained element of its culture. In contrast, if all major groups and related work assignments reflect diversity, the message is a quite different one.

Diversity Training   Many organizations are finding that diversity training is an effective means for managing diversity and minimizing its associated conflict. **Diversity training** is training that is specifically designed to better enable members of an organization to function in a diverse workplace. This training can take a variety of forms. For example, many organizations find it useful to help people learn more about their similarities to and differences from others. Men and women can be taught to work together more effectively and can gain insights into how their own behaviours affect and are interpreted by others. In one organization, a diversity training program helped male managers gain insights into how various remarks they made to one another could be interpreted by others as being sexist. In the same organization, female managers learned how to point out their discomfort with those remarks without appearing overly hostile.[27]

Similarly, white and black managers may need training to better understand each other. Managers at Mobil Corporation noticed that four black colleagues

● **diversity training**
Training that is specifically designed to better enable members of an organization to function in a diverse workplace

never seemed to eat lunch together. After a diversity training program, they came to realize that the black managers felt that if they ate together, their white colleagues would be overly curious about what they might be talking about. Thus they avoided close associations with one another because they feared calling attention to themselves.[28]

Some organizations even go so far as to provide language training for their employees as a vehicle for managing diversity. Motorola, for example, provides English language training for its foreign employees on assignment in the United States.

Organizational Culture The ultimate test of an organization's commitment to managing diversity is its culture.[29] Regardless of what managers say or put in writing, unless there is a basic and fundamental belief that diversity is valued, it cannot ever become truly an integral part of an organization. An organization that really wants to promote diversity must shape its culture so that it clearly underscores top management commitment to and support of diversity in all of its forms throughout every part of the organization. With top management support, however, and reinforced with a clear and consistent set of organizational policies and practices, diversity can become a basic and fundamental part of an organization. At Oracle Corporation Canada Inc., all managers attend a workplace diversity information session, and the company's president and CEO regularly reminds hiring managers of Oracle's commitment to a barrier-free and inclusive workplace.[30]

TOWARD THE MULTICULTURAL ORGANIZATION

multicultural organization
An organization that has achieved high levels of diversity, is able to fully capitalize on the advantages of diversity, and has few diversity-related problems

Many organizations today are grappling with cultural diversity. We noted back in Chapter 5 that whereas many organizations are becoming increasingly global, no truly global organization exists. In similar fashion, although organizations are becoming ever more diverse, few are truly multicultural. The **multicultural organization** has achieved high levels of diversity, is able to fully capitalize on the advantages of the diversity, and has few diversity-related problems.[31] One recent article described the six basic characteristics of such an organization.[32] These characteristics are illustrated in Figure 14.4.

First, the multicultural organization is characterized by *pluralism*. This means that every group represented in an organization works to better understand every other group. Thus employees of one cultural group try to understand employees of another cultural group and vice versa. In addition, every group represented within an organization has the potential to influence the organization's culture and its fundamental norms.

Second, the multicultural organization achieves *full structural integration*. Full structural integration suggests that the diversity within an organization is a complete and accurate reflection of the organization's external labour market. If around half of the labour market is female, then about half of the organization's employees are female. Moreover, this same proportion is reflected at all levels of the organization. There are no glass ceilings or other subtle forms of discrimination.

Third, the multicultural organization achieves *full integration of the informal network*. This characteristic suggests that there are no barriers to entry and participation in any organizational activity. For example, people enter and exit

FIGURE 14.4 The Multicultural Organization

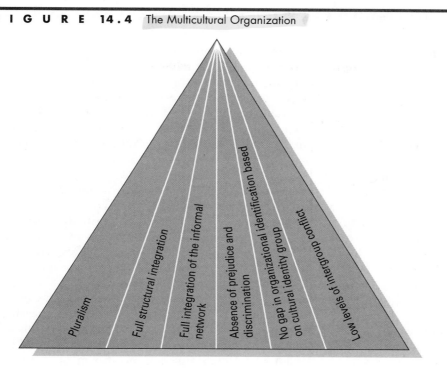

Based on Taylor H. Cox, "The Multicultural Organization," in *The Academy of Management Executive*, May 1991, pp. 34–47. Republished with permission of Academy of Management, Briar Cliff Manor, NY, via Copyright Clearance Centre, Inc.

Few, if any, organizations have become truly multicultural. At the same time, more and more organizations are moving in this direction. When an organization becomes multicultural, it reflects the six basic characteristics shown here.

lunch groups, social networks, communication grapevines, and other informal aspects of organizational activity without regard to age, gender, ethnicity, or other dimension of diversity.

Fourth, the multicultural organization is characterized by an *absence of prejudice and discrimination*. No traces of bias exist, and prejudice is eliminated. Discrimination is not practised in any shape, form, or fashion. And discrimination is nonexistent not because it is illegal but because of the lack of prejudice and bias. People are valued, accepted, and rewarded purely on the basis of their skills and what they contribute to the organization.

Fifth, in the multicultural organization there is *no gap in organizational identification based on cultural identity group*. In many organizations today, people tend to make assumptions about organizational roles based on group identity. For example, many people walking into an office and seeing a man and woman conversing tend to assume that the woman is the secretary and the man is the manager. No such tendencies exist in the multicultural organization. People recognize that men and women are equally likely to be managers and secretaries.

Finally, there are *low levels of intergroup conflict* in the multicultural organization. We noted earlier that conflict is a likely outcome of increased diversity. The multicultural organization has evolved beyond this point to a state of virtually no conflict among people who differ. People within the organization fully understand, empathize with, have tolerance for, and openly communicate with everyone else. Values, premises, motives, attitudes, and perceptions are so well understood by everyone that any conflict that does arise is over meaningful and work-related issues as opposed to differences in age, gender, ethnicity, or other dimensions of diversity.

SUMMARY OF KEY POINTS

Diversity exists in a group or organization when its members differ from one another along one or more important dimensions. Diversity is increasing in organizations today because of changing demographics, the desire by organizations to improve their workforce, legal pressures, and increased globalization.

There are several important dimensions of diversity. Three of the more important ones are age, gender, and ethnicity. The overall age of the workforce is increasing. More women are also entering the workplace, although there is still a glass ceiling in many settings. In Canada, ethnic diversity in the workplace is increasing.

Diversity can impact an organization in a number of different ways. For example, it can be a source of competitive advantage (i.e., cost, resource acquisition, marketing, creativity, problem solving, and systems flexibility arguments). On the other hand, diversity can also be a source of conflict in an organization.

Managing diversity in organizations can be done by both individuals and the organization itself. Individual approaches to dealing with diversity include understanding, empathy, tolerance, and willingness to communicate. Major organizational approaches are through policies, practices, diversity training, and culture.

Few, if any, organizations have become truly multicultural. The major dimensions that characterize organizations as they eventually achieve this state are pluralism, full structural integration, full integration of the informal network, an absence of prejudice and discrimination, no gap in organizational identification based on cultural identity group, and low levels of intergroup conflict attributable to diversity.

DISCUSSION QUESTIONS

Questions for Review

1. Why is diversity increasing in many organizations today?
2. Identify the major dimensions of diversity and discuss recent trends for each.
3. Summarize the basic impact of diversity on organizations.
4. Discuss the four basic individual approaches and the four basic organizational approaches to managing diversity.

Questions for Analysis

5. The text outlines many different advantages of diversity in organizations. Can you think of any disadvantages?
6. What are the basic dimensions of diversity that most affect you personally?
7. When you finish school and begin your career, what should you be prepared to do to succeed in a diverse workforce?

Questions for Application

8. Visit the registrar's office or office of admissions at your college or university. Using their enrollment statistics, determine the relative diversity on your campus. Is the student population more or less diverse than the faculty?

9. Assume that you are starting a new organization that is likely to grow rapidly. Develop a diversity plan for becoming a multicultural organization.

10. Assume that you work for a large multinational organization. You have just learned that you are being transferred to India. You also know that you will be the first person of your ethnicity to work there. What steps might you take before you go to minimize diversity-related problems that your presence might cause?

BUILDING EFFECTIVE DIAGNOSTIC SKILLS

Exercise Overview

Diagnostic skills enable a manager to visualize the most appropriate response to a situation. This exercise gives you an opportunity to practise using diagnostic skills as they relate to organizational culture and multicultural issues and challenges.

Exercise Background

Your firm has recently undergone a significant increase in its workforce. Many of the new workers you have hired are immigrants from Eastern Europe and Asia. Several do not speak English very well, but all are diligent workers who appear to be trying very hard to be successful and to fit in with their co-workers.

Recently, however, some problems have come to your attention. For one thing, several of your female workers have begun to complain about an increase in sexual harassment. For another, your supervisors have noticed an increase in tardiness and absenteeism among all of your workers.

You know that you need to take some kind of action. However, you are unsure how to proceed. Consequently, you have decided to spend a few days thinking about what to do.

Exercise Task

With the preceding background information as context, do the following:

1. Think of as many causes as you can for each of the two problems you are facing.
2. Determine how you might address each problem, given the potential array of factors that might have contributed to them.
3. What role might organizational culture be playing in this situation, apart from issues of multiculturalism?
4. What role might multiculturalism be playing in this situation, apart from issues of organizational culture?

CITY–TV Reflects Toronto's Diversity

 In 1972, CITY–TV was seen as radical when it went on the air in Toronto with an ethnically diverse mix of on-air employees. At that time, even though Toronto was already one of the world's most ethnically diverse cities, the on-air image of its TV stations was virtually all white. It was an era when many TV journalists were asked to change their names if they sounded "too ethnic" and accents were discouraged. CITY–TV was one of the first TV stations in the city to seek out journalists who reflected the city's demographic makeup. Among the top personalities at CITY–TV today are Harold Hosein, Lorne Honickman, Jojo Chintoh, Wilson Lee, George Lagogianes, Anne Mroczkowski, Gord Martineau, and Dominic Sciullo.

Not all the TV stations in Toronto have followed CITY-TV's lead in employing staff as diverse as the city they serve. Not surprisingly, some of the greatest advances have been made at the multilingual station, CFMT. CITY-TV's initiative on this issue can be traced to the leadership of its founder and president, Moses Znaimer. From the outset, Znaimer sought out reporters and other on-air staff of diverse origins, including Italian, West Indian, Korean, Ukrainian, and East Indian. He believed that television should be "democratized" and thus recruited many employees from nontraditional backgrounds. In some cases, he turned waiters and secretaries into TV personalities. Some members of his ethnic talent pool have since gone on to jobs with other stations in Toronto and elsewhere.

Taking the initiative on a socially charged issue requires strong leadership. In its early days, CITY–TV attracted opposition and sometimes open hostility. The latter was evident when the station hired a black man with "an unusual name and accent" to cover crime. Fortunately, attitudes have changed considerably since those early days.

As many analysts note, while CITY's approach may be based on its president's vision of democratizing television, it also makes good business sense. It does so because the station's core audience of younger, urban viewers is more ethnically diverse than that of other stations. Moreover, the demographic base of the city as a whole is also becoming increasingly diverse. Studies show that more than half of Toronto's population is already classified as "ethnic" (that is, not of British or French origin). In fact, it is projected that nonwhites will make up 45 percent of the city's population by 2001. Thus, CITY's strategy seems to be future-oriented as well.

Like CITY-TV, many business organizations are beginning to realize the economic gains of a diversified workforce. A recent Conference Board of Canada study reported that Canadian companies that have embraced diversity management programs in their workplaces are significantly enhancing their ability to understand and compete in new markets within Canada and internationally. The globalization of world trade and the increasing ethnocultural diversity of markets inside Canada underpin the business case for managing diversity.

Some observers feel that company-driven diversity management programs are more sustainable than legislation-driven programs. Others argue that nonsupport by governments, coupled with organizational downsizing, may hinder the realization of a diverse workforce. For now, CITY–TV appears to be staying the course.

Questions

1. What definition of diversity does CITY–TV seem to be following? Why?

2. What general guidance does CITY–TV's experience with diversity suggest to other organizations that wish to develop a more diverse workforce?

3. Do you think that CITY–TV will continue to have a diverse on-air staff in the future? Why or why not?

References: "TV Nations: Why Ethnic Broadcasters Are Booming *Financial Post*, November 17, 1995, p. 7; Christine Taylor, "Building a Business Case for Diversity," *The Canadian Business Review*, Spring 1995, pp. 12–15; Jim McElgunn, "Mixing It Up at CITY-TV: The On-Air Staff at Moses Znaimer's Toronto TV Station Reflects the City's Ethnic Diversity," *Marketing*, July 19, 1993, pp. 13–14; Leonard Kubas, "Marketers Can Profit as Ethnic Changes Continue," *Marketing*, July 13/20, 1992, p. 28; and "Tapping into Cultural Diversity Can Open Doors," *Financial Post*, August 19/21, 1995, p. 27.

CHAPTER NOTES

1. "Ranking by Profits," *Report on Business Magazine*, July 1998, p. 100; "United by Diversity," Royal Bank of Canada Web site (http://www.royalbank.com); "Making the Differences Work," *Royal Bank Newsletter*, October 1996; and Phebe-Jane Poole, *Diversity: A Business Advantage* (Ajax, Ont.: Poole Publishing Company, 1997).

2. Marlene G. Fine, Fern L. Johnson, and M. Sallyanne Ryan, "Cultural Diversity in the Workplace," *Public Personnel Management*, Fall 1990, pp. 305–319.

3. Phebe-Jane Poole, *Diversity: A Business Advantage* (Ajax, Ont.: Poole Publishing Company, 1997), p. 7.

4. Badi G. Foster, Gerald Jackson, William E. Cross, Bailey Jackson, and Rita Hardiman, "Workforce Diversity and Business," *Training and Development Journal*, April 1988, pp. 38–42.

5. Sam Cole, "Cultural Diversity and Sustainable Futures," *Futures*, December 1990, pp. 1044–1058.

6. Tina Chui, "Canada's Population Charting into the 21st Century," *Canadian Social Trends*, Autumn 1996, pp. 3–7.

7. Janet Bagnall, "Regretting Retirement," *The Windsor Star*, August 23, 1997, p. G12.

8. Chui, "Canada's Population Charting into the 21st Century," p. 5.

9. Trevor Wilson, *Diversity at Work: The Business Case for Equity* (Toronto: John Wiley & Sons, 1996).

10. Gary Powell and D. Anthony Butterfield, "Investigating the 'Glass Ceiling' Phenomenon: An Empirical Study of Actual Promotions to Top Management," *Academy of Management Journal*, Vol. 37, No. 1, 1994, pp. 68–86.

11. "The Boys' Club," *The Financial Post Magazine*, September 1993, pp. 16–23.

12. Jaclyn Fierman, "Why Women Still Don't Hit the Top," *Fortune*, July 30, 1990, pp. 40–62.

13. Elaine Carey, "Glass Still Keeps Women from Top Jobs," *The Sunday Star*, August 10, 1997 p. A1.

14. Christine Taylor, "Building a Business Case for Valuing Ethnocultural Diversity" (Ottawa: Conference Board of Canada, 1995).

15. *Occupational Outlook Handbook* (Washington, D.C.: U.S. Bureau of Labor Statistics, 1990–1991).

16. Based on Taylor H. Cox and Stacy Blake, "Managing Cultural Diversity: Implications for Organizational Competitiveness," *The Academy of Management Executive*, August 1991, pp. 45–56.

17. Gillian Flynn, "Deloitte & Touche Changes Women's Minds: Cultural Audit Boosts Retention," *Personnel Journal*, April 1996, pp. 56–68.

18. For an example, see "Get to Know the Ethnic Market," *Marketing*, June 17, 1991, p. 32.

19. C. Marlene Fiol, "Consensus, Diversity, and Learning in Organizations," *Organization Science*, August 1994, pp. 403–415.

20. Douglas Hall and Victoria Parker, "The Role of Workplace Flexibility in Managing Diversity," *Organizational Dynamics*, Summer 1993, pp. 5–14.

21. "As Population Ages, Older Workers Clash with Younger Bosses," *The Wall Street Journal*, June 13, 1994, pp. A1, A8.

22. Patti Watts, "Bias Busting: Diversity Training in the Workforce," *Management Review*, December 1987, pp. 51–54.

23. See Stephenie Overman, "Managing the Diverse Work Force," *HRMagazine*, April 1991, pp. 32–36.

24. Lennie Copeland, "Making the Most of Cultural Differences at the Workplace," *Personnel*, June 1988, pp. 52–60.

25. "Firms Address Workers' Cultural Variety," *The Wall Street Journal*, February 10, 1989, p. B1.

26. Sara Rynes and Benson Rosen, "What Makes Diversity Programs Work?" *HRMagazine*, October 1994, pp. 67–75.

27. "Learning to Accept Cultural Diversity," *The Wall Street Journal*, September 12, 1990, pp. B1, B9.

28. "Firms Address Workers' Cultural Variety."

29. Anthony Carnevale and Susan Stone, "Diversity—Beyond the Golden Rule," *Training and Development*, October 1994, pp. 22–27.

30. Ontario Ministry of Citizenship, Culture and Recreation, "Diversity at Work: Sharing the Experience" (http://www.equalopportunity.on.ca).

31. Dinesh D'Souza, "Multiculturalism 101," *Policy Review*, Spring 1991, pp. 22–30.

32. This discussion derives heavily from Taylor H. Cox, "The Multicultural Organization," *The Academy of Management Executive*, May 1991, pp. 34–47.

CTV   The Organizing Process

NEWS ITEM:
Postal Workers React to End of Strike (1997, 2:00)

Across the country, Canadian postal workers react with anger, resentment, and some resignation as they learn that they have been forced back to work. Complicating the situation is that the Christmas season, the busiest time of the year for the post office, has already begun.

Questions:

1. Had the postal workers not been forced back to work, what sort of damage could have been done to their public image if they had caused the mail to stop completely during the Christmas season?
2. What issues will managers have to face as employees return to work against their will?

NEWS ITEM:
Women Protest Against Pay Equity Appeal (1998, 1:45)

Canadian women are up in arms over the announcement that the Canadian government has decided to appeal a ruling on pay equity that would have seen them receive compensation for years of inequitable pay. It is expected that the total value of the back wages payable would reach several billion dollars.

Questions:

1. Is the Canadian government acting in the public interest?
2. Do you think that it is the public sector or the private sector that treats women more equitably?

NEWS ITEM:
Trading Stocks Using Computers (1998, 2:00)

A Toronto man is using the latest in computer technology to buy and sell stocks. More and more, trading is leaving the chaotic world of the stock exchange floor and is being conducted online. Now average people can get their hands on the tools, resources, and information they need to buy and sell on their own, but there are potential dangers in this brave new world of lightning-fast financial transactions.

Questions:

1. How will this revolution change the structure of the investment industry?
2. Is there a greater chance for people to be bilked by fraudulent investment schemes, such as the Bre-X fiasco seen in the video case in Part II?

Managers today must constantly strive to understand individual behaviour and motivate people in an increasingly diverse context. Overseeing a large workforce on a construction project and dealing with individual employees on a one-to-one basis both require leadership skills.

The Leading Process

Basic Elements of Individual Behaviour in Organizations

OBJECTIVES

After studying this chapter, you should be able to:

● *Explain the nature of the individual–organization relationship.*

● *Define personality and describe personality attributes that affect behaviour in organizations.*

● *Discuss individual attitudes in organizations and how they affect behaviour.*

● *Describe basic perceptual processes and the role of attributions in organizations.*

● *Discuss the causes and consequences of stress and describe how it can be managed.*

● *Explain how workplace behaviours can directly or indirectly influence organizational effectiveness.*

OUTLINE

Understanding Individuals in Organizations
    The Psychological Contract
    The Person–Job Fit
    The Nature of Individual Differences
Personality and Individual Behaviour
    Personality Formation
    Personality Attributes in Organizations
Attitudes and Individual Behaviour
    Attitude Formation and Change
    Work-Related Attitudes
Perception and Individual Behaviour
    Basic Perceptual Processes
    Perception and Attribution
Stress and Individual Behaviour
    Causes of Stress
    Consequences of Stress
    Managing Stress
Types of Workplace Behaviour
    Performance Behaviours
    Withdrawal Behaviours
    Organizational Citizenship

Team members at CAMI Automotive inspect the quality of economy cars built on the plant's assembly lines.

CAMI Automotive is a 50-50 joint venture between General Motors of Canada Ltd. and Suzuki Motor Co. Ltd. The company began production in April 1989, making Geo Metro, Chevrolet Sprint, Pontiac Firefly, and Suzuki Swift subcompacts as well as GM Tracker and Suzuki Sidekick four-wheel drive sports vehicles. Running at full capacity, with a workforce of about 2,400, CAMI's plant in Ingersoll, Ontario, can produce 200,000 vehicles per year. Most employees at CAMI are represented by the Canadian Auto Workers (CAW).

While the joint venture between GM and Suzuki is a business partnership, the Japanese approach to production emphasizes another partnership: one between management and employees. The partnership is driven by *kaizen,* or the process of continuous improvement whereby teams of employees make decisions about such matters as meeting production goals, quality circles (small teams of

> **"The 'understanding' between CAMI and its employees has changed dramatically."**

employees) monitor and make suggestions for improving product quality, and a concerted effort is made to improve quality of work life by increasing employee participation in the production process.

The business partnership and the labour–management partnership approach combine to make CAMI a very interesting workplace, one shaped by a Canadian union, Japanese and American owners, and a Japanese production system. An obvious concern for management and employees in such an organization would be the establishment of a psychological contract, which refers to the basic assumptions employees have about their relationships within their organization. Management sets the stage for a healthy psychological contract by providing prospective employees with documents that spell out the company's values and expectations. In formulating their assumptions about their relationships with CAMI, employees should be influenced by the company's initial statement of its values and expectations.

Is the hybrid (Japanese–North American) approach to employer–employee relations working? A CAW research group tracked employee attitudes at CAMI between March 1990 and November 1991. On four different occasions during this period, a random sample of workers was surveyed. The responses to four questions are somewhat surprising. In the first round, 43.4 percent of respondents had a positive view of CAMI's status as a different kind of place to work; by the fourth round, this figure had fallen to 11.5 percent. In the first round, 42.6 percent of respondents saw CAMI's egalitarian approach to dress codes, parking, and cafeterias as a good thing; only 6.3 percent felt this way by the fourth round. In the first round, 56 percent of respondents viewed CAMI as being democratic; by the fourth round, this figure had fallen to 25.9 percent. In the first round, 56.98 percent of respondents saw CAMI as a cooperative and helpful organization; only 16.7 percent did so by the fourth round. These figures clearly indicate that the "understanding" between CAMI and its employees has changed dramatically. [1] ●

CAMI and its employees have certainly redefined their relationship with one another. To do so, they each assessed how well their respective needs and capabilities matched the other's. A variety of different and unique characteristics that reside in each and every employee affects how they feel about these changes, how they will alter their future attitudes about the firm, and how they perform their jobs. These characteristics reflect the basic elements of individual behaviour in organizations.

This chapter describes several of these basic elements and is the first of several chapters designed to develop a more complete perspective on the leading function of management. In the next section, we investigate the psychological nature of individuals in organizations. The next section introduces the concept of personality and discusses several important personality attributes that can influence behaviour in organizations. We then examine individual attitudes and perception and their role in organizations. The role of stress in the workplace is then discussed. Finally, we describe a number of basic individual behaviours that are important to organizations.

UNDERSTANDING INDIVIDUALS IN ORGANIZATIONS

As a starting point in understanding human behaviour in the workplace we must consider the basic nature of the relationship between individuals and organizations. We must also gain an appreciation of the nature of individual differences.

The Psychological Contract

Most people have a basic understanding of a contract. When we buy a car or sell a house, for example, both buyer and seller sign a contract that specifies the terms of the agreement. A psychological contract is similar in some ways to a standard legal contract, but it is less formal and well-defined. In particular, a **psychological contract** is the overall set of expectations held by an individual with respect to what he or she will contribute to the organization and what the organization, in return, will provide to the individual.[2] Thus a psychological contract is not written on paper nor are all of its terms explicitly negotiated.

The essential nature of a psychological contract is illustrated in Figure 15.1. The individual makes a variety of contributions to the organization—things such as effort, skills, ability, time, and loyalty, for example. These contributions presumably satisfy the organization's various needs and requirements. That is, because the organization may have hired the person because of her skills, the organization can reasonably expect that she will subsequently display those skills in the performance of her job.

In return for these contributions, the organization provides inducements to the individual. Some inducements, like pay and career opportunities, are tangible rewards. Others, like job security and status, are more intangible. Just as the contributions available from the individual must satisfy the organization's needs, the inducements offered by the organization must serve the individual's needs. That is, if a person accepts employment with an organization because he thinks he will earn an attractive salary and have an opportunity to advance, he will subsequently expect that those rewards will actually be forthcoming.

- **psychological contract**
The overall set of expectations held by an individual with respect to what he or she will contribute to the organization and what the organization will provide to the individual

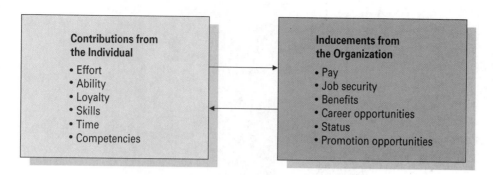

Contributions from the Individual
- Effort
- Ability
- Loyalty
- Skills
- Time
- Competencies

Inducements from the Organization
- Pay
- Job security
- Benefits
- Career opportunities
- Status
- Promotion opportunities

Psychological contracts are the basic assumptions that individuals have about their relationships with their organization. Such contracts are defined in terms of contributions by the individual relative to inducements from the organization.

If both the individual and organization perceive that the psychological contract is fair and equitable, they will be satisfied with the relationship and will likely continue it. On the other hand, if either party sees an imbalance or inequity in the contract it may initiate a change. For example, the individual may request a pay raise or promotion, decrease her contributed effort, or look for a better job elsewhere. The organization can also initiate change by requesting that the individual improve his skills through training, transferring the person to another job, or terminating the person's employment altogether.

A basic challenge faced by the organization, then, is to manage psychological contracts. The organization must ensure that it is getting value from its employees. At the same time, it must also be sure that it is providing employees with appropriate inducements. If the organization is underpaying its employees for their contributions, for example, they may perform poorly or leave for better jobs elsewhere. On the other hand, if they are being overpaid relative to their contributions, the organization is incurring unnecessary costs.

The Person–Job Fit

One specific aspect of managing psychological contracts is managing the person–job fit. **Person–job fit** is the extent to which the contributions made by the individual match the inducements offered by the organization. In theory, each employee has a specific set of needs that he wants fulfilled and a set of job-related behaviours and abilities to contribute. Thus if the organization can take perfect advantage of those behaviours and abilities and exactly fulfill his needs, it will have achieved a perfect person–job fit.[3]

Of course, such a precise level of person–job fit is seldom achieved. There are several reasons for this. One reason is that organizational selection procedures are imperfect. Organizations can make approximations of employee skill levels when making hiring decisions and can improve them through training. But even simple performance dimensions are hard to measure objectively and validly.

Another reason for imprecise person–job fits is that both people and organizations change. An individual who finds a new job stimulating and exciting may find the same job boring and monotonous after a few years. And when the organization adopts new technology, it has changed the skills it needs from its employees. Still another reason for imprecision in the person–job fit is that each individual is unique. Measuring skills and performance is difficult enough; assessing needs, attitudes, and personality is far more complex. Each of these

● **person–job fit**
The extent to which the contributions made by the individual match the inducements offered by the organization

Achieving a good person–job fit is an important goal in any organization. These tree planters combine good fitness and capacity for hard physical work with their love of the outdoors. Typically, these people would not be happy behind a desk every day.

individual differences serves to make matching individuals with jobs a difficult and complex process.

The Nature of Individual Differences

- **individual differences**

Personal attributes that vary from one person to another

Individual differences are personal attributes that vary from one person to another. Individual differences may be physical, psychological, and emotional. Taken together, all of the individual differences that characterize any specific person serve to make that individual unique from everyone else. Much of the remainder of this chapter is devoted to individual differences. Before proceeding, however, we must also note the importance of the situation in assessing the behaviour of individuals.

Are specific differences that characterize a given individual good or bad? Do they contribute to or detract from performance? The answer, of course, is that it depends on the circumstances. One person may be very dissatisfied, withdrawn, and negative in one job setting but very satisfied, outgoing, and positive in another. Working conditions, co-workers, and leadership are all important ingredients. The *Managing in a Changing World* box describes how the organizational context provided by Husky affects and is affected by the behaviour of the people within it.

Thus whenever an organization attempts to assess or account for individual differences among its employees, it must also be sure to consider the situation in which behaviour occurs. Individuals who are satisfied or productive workers in one context may prove to be dissatisfied or unproductive workers in another context. Attempting to consider both individual differences and contributions in relation to inducements and contexts, then, is a major challenge for organizations as they attempt to establish effective psychological contracts with their employees and achieve optimal fits between people and jobs.

PERSONALITY AND INDIVIDUAL BEHAVIOUR

- **personality**

The relatively permanent set of psychological and behavioural attributes that distinguish one person from another

Personality traits represent some of the most fundamental sets of individual differences in organizations today. **Personality** is the relatively stable set of psychological and behavioural attributes that distinguish one person from

Husky Injection Molding Systems Ltd.

Husky Injection Molding Systems Ltd. of Bolton, Ontario, is an international supplier of injection moulding systems that are used to make such products as pop bottles, food containers, medical products, and car bumpers. In 1998, the company, which has customers in seventy countries, reported sales of $762 million (U.S.), and a net income of $45.9 million (U.S.). By the year 2000, Husky is expected to be one of the five dominant companies in the injection moulding machinery business, with annual sales of $1 billion (U.S.). Husky has come a long way since 1953, when founder and president, Robert Schad, started operations in a Toronto garage by designing a snowmobile. Today the company employs approximately 2,300 people worldwide.

While Husky's growth and financial performance are impressive, the company is also attracting attention for its enlightened approach to human resource management. It is an approach that has led one best-selling author and management consultant to describe Husky as one of the ten greatest firms he has ever encountered. Fundamental to the company's approach to human resource management is respect for its employees. Workers at Husky's Bolton headquarters are able, through a rotating employee council, to bring their concerns directly to Robert Schad.

Among the benefits employees asked for and received is an on-site fitness centre. This centre is only part of the company's wellness program, which includes an on-site naturopath, massage therapist, chiropractor, and medical doctor—all in one building called Copper House, which is also home to Husky's child-care facility. The company's approach to employees' wellness is also reflected in its cafeteria menu: meat entrées are sold at full price while vegetarian entrées are subsidized.

Husky's wellness program is only part of its generous employee benefits. It also pays for tuition and books for employees who attend college or university. Moreover, the company offers profit-sharing and employee share-purchasing plans, together with salaries that are considered high in the industry.

It would appear that Husky's healthy respect for its employees is paying off. The company's financial well-being is partly due to a committed workforce. Absenteeism at Husky is 2.4 days per year in an industry where the average is nine. Workers' compensation claims are so low that the company receives a rebate from the compensation board.

References: Bruce Livesey, "Provide and Conquer," *Report on Business Magazine*, March 1997, pp. 34–42; "What Do You Mean There Are No More Donuts," *The Financial Post Magazine*, December 1996, p. 10; Husky, Annual Report, 1998 (http://www.husky.on.ca); Greg Keenan, "Husky and Healthy," *The Globe and Mail*, August 1, 1995, p. B8; Susan Noakes, "A Company That Exercises Together Stays Together," *Financial Post*, March 24, 1995, p. 16; Angela Downey, "Fit to Work," *Business Quarterly*, Winter 1996, pp. 69–74; and "Performance 2000," *Canadian Business*, June 26/July 10, 1998, p. 150.

another.[4] Understanding basic personality attributes is important because they affect people's behaviour in organizational situations and people's perceptions of and attitudes toward the organization. They also play a role in how people handle stress at work.

Personality Formation

The basic personality of a manager or employee is formed before she or he ever becomes a member of an organization. Indeed, personality formation starts at birth and continues throughout adolescence. Hereditary characteristics (e.g., body shape and height) and the social (e.g., family and friends) and cultural (e.g., religion and values) context in which people grow up all interact to shape their basic personalities. As people grow into adulthood, their personalities become very clearly defined and stable.

But a person's personality can still be changed as a result of organizational experiences. For example, a manager subjected to prolonged periods of stress or conflict at work may become increasingly withdrawn, anxious, and irritable. Although removing the stressful circumstances may eventually temper these characteristics, the individual's personality may also reflect permanent changes. From a more positive perspective, continued success, accomplishment, and advancement may cause an individual to become increasingly self-confident and outgoing. And situational influences can also affect personality in unexpected ways. For example, an honest employee experiencing severe financial pressures may be tempted to steal money from the organization.

These types of extreme examples aside, managers should recognize that they can do little to change the basic personalities of their subordinates. Instead, they should work to understand the basic nature of their subordinates' personalities and how attributes of those personalities affect the subordinates' work behaviour.

Personality Attributes in Organizations

Over the past few decades, a considerable amount of research has been conducted to identify and further our understanding of personality attributes that are relevant to managers. Several of the more important attributes that have been identified and studied are listed and defined in Table 15.1.

Locus of control refers to the degree to which an individual believes that behaviour has a direct impact on the consequences of that behaviour.[5] Some people, for example, believe that if they work hard they are certain to succeed.

• **locus of control**
The degree to which an individual believes that behaviour has a direct impact on the consequences of that behaviour

---

A number of personality traits are especially relevant in the workplace. Among these personality traits are locus of control, self-efficacy, authoritarianism, dogmatism, self-esteem, self-monitoring, and risk propensity.

TABLE 15.1   Major Personality Attributes

Personality Attribute	Description
Locus of control	The extent to which an individual believes that his or her behaviour has a direct impact on the consequences of that behaviour
Self-efficacy	A person's beliefs about his or her capabilities to perform a task
Authoritarianism	The extent to which an individual believes that power and status differences are appropriate within hierarchical social systems like organizations
Dogmatism	Reflects the rigidity of a person's beliefs and his or her openness to other viewpoints
Self-monitoring	The extent to which a person pays close attention to and subsequently emulates the behaviour of others
Self-esteem	The extent to which a person believes that he or she is a worthwhile and deserving individual
Risk propensity	The degree to which an individual is willing to take chances and make risky decisions

They also may believe that people who fail do so simply because they lack ability or motivation. Because these people believe that each person is in control of his or her life, they are said to have an *internal locus of control*. On the other hand, some people think that what happens to them is a result of fate, chance, luck, or the behaviour of other people. For example, an employee who fails to get a promotion may attribute that failure to a politically motivated boss or just bad luck, rather than to her own lack of skills or poor performance record. Because these people think that forces beyond their control dictate what happens to them, they are said to have an *external locus of control*.

As a personality attribute, locus of control has clear implications for organizations. For example, individuals with an internal locus of control may have a relatively strong desire to participate in the governance of their organizations and have a voice in how they do their jobs. Thus they may prefer a decentralized organization and a leader who gives them freedom and autonomy. They may also be more likely to resist control. And they may be most comfortable under a reward system that recognizes individual performance and contributions. People with an external locus of control, on the other hand, are more likely to prefer a more centralized organization where decisions are taken out of their hands. They may also gravitate to structured jobs where standard procedures are defined for them. Similarly, they may also prefer a leader who makes most of the decisions and could prefer a reward system that puts a premium on seniority.

A related but subtly different personality trait is that of self-efficacy. **Self-efficacy** is an individual's beliefs about her or his capabilities to perform a task.[6] Individuals with high self-efficacy believe that they can perform well on a given task or job. They consequently exhibit high self-confidence and seek out tasks that will challenge them and their abilities. On the other hand, people with low self-efficacy are more prone to doubt their capabilities, will exhibit low self-confidence, and may seek out tasks or jobs that are relatively easy and present little challenge.

Authoritarianism is the extent to which an individual believes that power and status differences are appropriate within hierarchical social systems like organizations.[7] For example, a person who is highly authoritarian may accept directives or orders from someone with more authority purely because the other person is "the boss." A person who is not highly authoritarian may still carry out appropriate and reasonable directives from the boss, but he or she is also more likely to question things, express disagreement with the boss, and even to refuse to carry out

● **self-efficacy**
An individual's beliefs about her or his capabilities to perform a task

● **authoritarianism**
The extent to which an individual believes that power and status differences are appropriate within hierarchical social systems like organizations

Former Montreal Canadiens goaltender Ken Dryden clearly has an internal locus of control. He has been successful in many areas—as an award-winning hockey player and member of the Hockey Hall of Fame and as a lawyer. His coolness under pressure was extraordinary. He will always be remembered for his stance in the crease when the whistle stopped play, resting on his stick with his arms folded. Today he is president and general manager of the Toronto Maple Leafs.

orders if they are for some reason objectionable. A manager who is highly authoritarian may be relatively autocratic and demanding, and subordinates who are highly authoritarian are more likely to accept this behaviour from their leader. On the other hand, a manager who is less authoritarian may allow subordinates a bigger role in making decisions, and less authoritarian subordinates respond positively to this behaviour.[8]

Dogmatism is the rigidity of a person's beliefs and his or her openness to other viewpoints.[9] The popular terms for dogmatism are *close-minded* and *open-minded*. For example, suppose a manager has such strong beliefs about how certain procedures should be carried out that he is unwilling to even listen to a new idea for doing it more efficiently. We might say this person is close-minded, or highly dogmatic. A manager in the same circumstances who is very receptive to listening to and trying new ideas can be seen as more open-minded, or less dogmatic. Dogmatism can be either beneficial or detrimental to organizations. Given the changing nature of organizations and their environments, individuals who are not dogmatic are more likely to be useful and productive organizational members.

Self-monitoring is the extent to which a person pays close attention to and subsequently emulates the behaviour of others.[10] A highly self-monitoring person pays very close attention to the behaviour of others for cues on how to act in different situations. For example, this person may tend to dress like others and imitate their work behaviours. Thus he or she tends to be somewhat of a conformist and is not likely to initiate change. A less self-monitoring person, in contrast, is more independent and freely chooses different forms of behaviour. This person pays less attention to how others dress and their work behaviours. Such an individual is also more likely to be an initiator of change.

Self-esteem is the extent to which a person believes that he or she is a worthwhile and deserving individual.[11] A person with high self-esteem is likely to seek high-status jobs, have confidence in his or her ability to achieve higher levels of performance, and derive great intrinsic satisfaction from his or her accomplishments. In contrast, a person with less self-esteem may be content to remain in a lower-level job, be less confident of his or her ability, and focus on extrinsic rewards.

Risk propensity is the degree to which an individual is willing to take chances and make risky decisions. A manager with a high risk propensity, for example, might be willing to experiment with new ideas and gamble on new products. She might also lead the organization in new and different directions. This manager might also be a catalyst for innovation. But the same individual might also jeopardize the continued well-being of the organization if the risky decisions prove to be bad ones. A manager with low risk propensity might lead to a stagnant and overly conservative organization or help the organization successfully weather turbulent and unpredictable times by maintaining stability and calm. Thus the potential consequences of risk propensity to an organization are heavily dependent on that organization's environment.

ATTITUDES AND INDIVIDUAL BEHAVIOUR

Another important element of individual behaviour in organizations is attitudes. **Attitudes** are complexes of beliefs and feelings that people have about specific ideas, situations, or other people. Attitudes are important because they

- **dogmatism**
The rigidity of a person's beliefs and his or her openness to other viewpoints

- **self-monitoring**
The extent to which a person pays close attention to and subsequently emulates the behaviour of others

- **self-esteem**
The extent to which a person believes that he or she is a worthwhile and deserving individual

- **risk propensity**
The degree to which an individual is willing to take chances and make risky decisions

- **attitude**
A complex of beliefs and feelings that people have about specific ideas, situations, or other people

are the mechanism through which most people express their feelings. An employee's statement that he feels underpaid by the organization reflects his feelings about his pay. Similarly, when a manager says that she likes the new advertising campaign, she is expressing her feelings about the organization's marketing efforts.

Attitudes have three components, as Figure 15.2 shows. The *affective component* of an attitude reflects an individual's feelings and emotions about a situation. The *cognitive component* of an attitude is derived from an individual's knowledge about a situation. It is important to note that cognition is subject to individual perceptions (something we discuss more fully later). Thus one person might "know" that a certain political candidate is better than another, and someone else may "know" just the opposite. Finally, the *intentional component* of an attitude reflects how an individual expects to behave in the situation.

To illustrate these three components, consider the case of a manager who places an order for some supplies for his organization from a new office supply firm. Suppose many of the items he orders are out of stock, others are overpriced, and still others arrive damaged. When he calls someone at the supply firm for assistance, he is treated rudely and gets disconnected before his claim is resolved. When asked how he feels about the new office supply firm, he might respond, "I don't like that company (affective component). They are the worst office supply firm I've ever dealt with (cognitive component). I'll never do business with them again (intentional component)."

People try to maintain consistency among the three components of their attitudes as well as among all their attitudes. However, circumstances sometimes arise that lead to conflicts. The conflict individuals may experience among their own attitudes is called **cognitive dissonance**.[12] For example, an individual has vowed never to work for a big, impersonal corporation and intends instead to open her own business and be her own boss. Unfortunately, a series of financial setbacks leads her to have no choice but to take a job with a large company and work for someone else. Thus cognitive dissonance occurs: the affective and cognitive components of the individual's attitude conflict with

● **cognitive dissonance**
The conflict an individual may experience among his or her attitudes

FIGURE 15.2 Components of Individual Attitudes

Individual attitudes can generally be broken down into three separate components. These are the affective, cognitive, and intentional components.

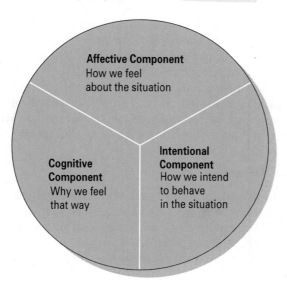

Affective Component
How we feel
about the situation

**Cognitive
Component**
Why we feel
that way

**Intentional
Component**
How we intend
to behave
in the situation

intended behaviour. To reduce cognitive dissonance, which is usually an uncomfortable experience for most people, the individual just described might tell herself the situation is only temporary and that she can go back out on her own in the near future. Or she might revise her cognitions and decide that working for a large company is more pleasant than she had ever expected.

Attitude Formation and Change

Individual attitudes form over time as a result of repeated personal experiences with ideas, situations, or people. The situational view of attitude formation suggests that strong attitudes evolve from the socially constructed realities in which people live, such as educational, family, or work situations.[13] Students who attend a university class, for instance, receive situational information from fellow students and the professor about what is expected of them and what will happen in the class. This information helps shape their attitudes about the class, the professor, and the other students. Because the situational information differs in every class, the attitudes in each specific class may also vary.

Looking closely at attitudes that are situationally specific and learned is one very important way to understand individual behaviour in organizations. For example, suppose that an organization is considering moving its headquarters to a new location. If the manager knows that employees have a positive attitude toward the current facility because they live nearby and because they find it to be warm and comfortable, he might realize that they will resist the move and that many may quit. On the other hand, if employees have a negative attitude toward the current facility because it is in an unsafe neighbourhood and they find it cramped and uncomfortable, they are likely to welcome a move.

As noted earlier, attitudes are not as stable as personality attributes. For example, attitudes may change as a result of new information. A manager may have a negative attitude about a new colleague because of his lack of job-related experience. After working with the new person for a while, however, the manager may come to realize that he is actually very talented and will subsequently develop a more positive attitude. Attitudes can also change as a result of changes in the object of the attitude. For example, if employees have a negative attitude about their pay because they feel underpaid, a big salary increase may result in more positive attitudes about their pay.

Attitude change can also occur when the object of the attitude becomes less important or less relevant to the person. For example, an employee has a negative attitude about his company's health insurance. When his spouse gets a new job with an organization that has outstanding health insurance benefits, his attitude toward his own insurance may become more moderate simply because he no longer has to worry about it. Finally, as noted earlier, individuals may change their attitudes as a way of reducing cognitive dissonance. However, deeply rooted attitudes that have a long history are very difficult to change.

Work-Related Attitudes

People in organizations form attitudes about many different things. For example, employees are likely to have attitudes about their salary, promotion possibilities, their boss, employee benefits, the food in the company cafeteria, and the colour of the company softball team uniforms. Of course, some of these attitudes are more important than others. Especially important attitudes are job satisfaction or dissatisfaction, organizational commitment, and job involvement.

Job Satisfaction or Dissatisfaction **Job satisfaction** or **dissatisfaction** is an attitude that reflects the extent to which an individual is gratified by or fulfilled in his or her work. Extensive research conducted on job satisfaction has indicated that personal factors such as an individual's needs and aspirations determine this attitude, along with group and organizational factors such as relationships with co-workers, supervisors and working conditions, work policies, and compensation.[14] In a survey of one thousand Canadian workers conducted in the summer of 1997, 90 percent of the respondents reported being satisfied with their jobs, with two-thirds claiming to be "very satisfied."[15]

A satisfied employee tends to be absent less often, to make positive contributions, and to stay with the organization. In contrast, a dissatisfied employee may be absent more often, may experience stress that disrupts co-workers, and may be continually looking for another job. Contrary to what a lot of managers believe, however, high levels of job satisfaction do not necessarily lead to higher levels of performance.

Organizational Commitment and Job Involvement Two other important work-related attitudes are organizational commitment and job involvement. **Organizational commitment** is an attitude that reflects an individual's identification with and attachment to the organization itself.[16] A person with a high level of commitment is likely to see herself as a true member of the organization (for example, referring to the organization in personal terms like "we make high-quality products"), to overlook minor sources of dissatisfaction with the organization, and to see herself remaining a member of the organization. In contrast, a person with less organizational commitment is likely to see himself as an outsider (for example, referring to the organization in less personal terms like "they don't pay their employees very well"), to express dissatisfaction about things, and to not see himself as a long-term member of the organization.

Job involvement results in an individual's tendency to exceed the normal expectations associated with his or her job. An employee with little job involvement sees a job as just something to do to earn a living. Thus all of her motivation is extrinsic and she has little or no interest in learning how to perform the job better. On the other hand, a person with a lot of job involvement will derive intrinsic satisfaction from the job itself and will want to learn more and more about how to perform the job more effectively.

Richard Steers demonstrated that these two attitudes strengthen with an individual's age, years with the organization, sense of job security, and participation in decision making.[17] Employees who feel committed to an organization and involved with their jobs have highly reliable habits, plan a long tenure with the organization, and muster more effort in performance. Although there are not many definitive things that organizations can do to create and promote these attitudes, a few specific guidelines are available. First, if the organization treats its employees fairly and provides reasonable rewards and job security, those employees are more likely to be satisfied and committed. Second, allowing employees to have a say in how things are done can also promote all three attitudes. And designing jobs so that they are interesting and stimulating can enhance job involvement in particular.

● **job satisfaction or dissatisfaction**
An attitude that reflects the extent to which an individual is gratified by or fulfilled in his or her work

● **organizational commitment**
An attitude that reflects an individual's identification with and attachment to the organization itself

● **job involvement**
Results in an individual's tendency to exceed the normal expectations associated with his or her job

PERCEPTION AND INDIVIDUAL BEHAVIOUR

As noted earlier, an important element of an attitude is the individual's perception of the object about which the attitude is formed. Because perception plays a role in a variety of other workplace behaviours, managers need to have a general understanding of basic perceptual processes.[18] The role of attributions is also important.

Basic Perceptual Processes

Perception is the set of processes by which an individual becomes aware of and interprets information about the environment. As shown in Figure 15.3, basic perceptual processes that are particularly relevant to organizations are selective perception and stereotyping.

Selective Perception   **Selective perception** is the process of screening out information with which we are uncomfortable or that contradicts our beliefs. For example, suppose that a manager is exceptionally fond of a particular worker. The manager has a very positive attitude about the worker and thinks that he is a top performer. One day the manager notices that the worker seems to be goofing off. Selective perception may cause the manager to quickly forget what he observed. Similarly, suppose that a manager has formed a very negative image of a particular worker. She thinks that this worker is a poor performer and never does a good job. When she happens to observe an example of high performance from the worker, she, too, may not remember it for very long. In one sense, selective perception is beneficial because it allows us to disregard minor bits of information. Of course, this only holds true if our basic perception is accurate. If selective perception causes us to ignore important information, however, it can become quite detrimental.

Stereotyping   **Stereotyping** is the process of categorizing or labelling people on the basis of a single attribute. Common attributes from which people often

FIGURE 15.3 Perceptual Processes

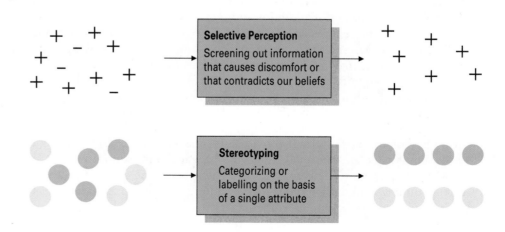

stereotype are race and gender. Of course, stereotypes along these lines are inaccurate and can be harmful. For example, suppose that a manager forms the stereotype that women can perform only certain tasks and that men are best suited for other tasks. To the extent that this affects the manager's hiring practices, the manager is (1) costing the organization valuable talent for both sets of jobs, (2) violating federal law, and (3) behaving unethically. On the other hand, certain forms of stereotyping can be useful and efficient. Suppose, for example, that a manager believes that communication skills are important for a particular job and that speech communication majors tend to have exceptionally good communication skills. As a result, whenever he interviews candidates for jobs he pays especially close attention to speech communication majors. To the extent that communication skills truly predict job performance and that majoring in speech communication does indeed provide those skills, this form of stereotyping can be beneficial.

Perception and Attribution

Perception is also closely linked with another process called attribution. **Attribution** is a mechanism through which we observe behaviour and then attribute causes to it.[19] The behaviour that is observed may be our own or that of others. For example, suppose someone realizes one day that she is working fewer hours than before, that she talks less about her work, and that she calls in sick more frequently. She might conclude from this that she must have become disenchanted with her job and subsequently decide to quit. Thus she observed her own behaviour, attributed a cause to it, and developed what she thought was a consistent response.

> **attribution**
> A mechanism through which people observe behaviour and attribute causes to it

More common is attributing cause to the behaviour of others. For example, if the manager of the individual just described has observed the same behaviour, he might form exactly the same attribution. On the other hand, he might instead decide that she has a serious illness, that he is driving her too hard, that she is experiencing too much stress, that she has a drug problem, or that she is having family problems.

The basic framework around which we form attributions is *consensus* (the extent to which other people in the same situation behave the same way), *consistency* (the extent to which the same person behaves in the same way at different times), and *distinctiveness* (the extent to which the same person behaves in the same way in other situations). For example, a manager who observes that an employee is late for a meeting might further realize that the employee is the only one who is late (low consensus), recall that he is often late for other meetings (high consistency), and subsequently realize that the same employee is sometimes late for work and when returning from lunch (low distinctiveness). This pattern of attributions might cause the manager to decide that the individual's behaviour should be changed. As a result, the manager might meet with the subordinate and establish some punitive consequences for future tardiness.

STRESS AND INDIVIDUAL BEHAVIOUR

Another important element of behaviour in organizations is stress. **Stress** is an individual's response to a strong stimulus called a stressor.[20] Stress generally follows a cycle referred to as the **General Adaptation Syndrome**, or **GAS**,[21]

> **stress**
> An individual's response to a strong stimulus called a stressor

> **General Adaptation Syndrome (GAS)**
> A cycle that stress generally follows

shown in Figure 15.4. According to this view, when an individual first encounters a stressor, the GAS is initiated and the first stage, alarm, is activated. He may feel panic, may wonder how to cope, and may feel helpless. For example, a manager who is told to prepare a detailed evaluation of his firm's plan to buy a competitor might first react by thinking, "How will I ever get this done by tomorrow?"

If the stressor is too intense, the individual may feel unable to cope and never really try to respond to its demands. In most cases, however, after a short period of alarm, the individual gathers some strength and starts to resist the negative effects of the stressor. For example, the manager with the evaluation to write may calm down, call home to say he's working late, roll up his sleeves, order out for coffee, and get to work. Thus at stage 2 of the GAS, the person is resisting the effects of the stressor.

In many cases, the resistance phase may end the GAS. If the manager is able to complete the evaluation earlier than expected, he may drop it in his briefcase, smile to himself, and head home tired but satisfied. On the other hand, prolonged exposure to a stressor without resolution may bring on stage 3 of the GAS—exhaustion. At this stage, the individual literally gives up and can no longer resist the stressor. The manager, for example, might fall asleep at his desk at 3 a.m. and never finish the evaluation.

We should note that stress is not all bad.[22] In the absence of stress, we may experience lethargy and stagnation. An optimal level of stress, on the other hand, can result in motivation and excitement. Too much stress, however, can have negative consequences. It is also important to understand that stress can be caused by "good" as well as "bad" things. Excessive pressure, unreasonable demands on our time, and bad news can all cause stress. But receiving a bonus and then deciding what to do with the money can also be stressful. So, too, can receiving a promotion, gaining recognition, and similar "good" things.

One important line of thinking about stress focuses on **Type A** and **Type B personalities**.[23] Type A individuals are extremely competitive, very devoted to work, and have a strong sense of time urgency. They are likely to be aggressive, impatient, and very work-oriented. They have a lot of drive and want to accomplish as much as possible as quickly as possible. Type B individuals are less competitive, less devoted to work, and have a weaker sense of time urgency. Such individuals are less likely to experience conflict with other people and

● **Type A personality**
A personality type in which individuals are extremely competitive, very devoted to work, and have a strong sense of time urgency

● **Type B personality**
A personality type in which individuals are less competitive, less devoted to work, and have a weaker sense of time urgency than persons with Type A personality

The General Adaptation Syndrome represents the normal process by which we react to stressful events. At stage 1—alarm—we feel panic and alarm and our level of resistance to stress drops. Stage 2—resistance— represents our efforts to confront and control the stressful circumstance. If we fail, we may eventually reach step 3—exhaustion—and just give up or quit.

FIGURE 15.4 The General Adaptation Syndrome

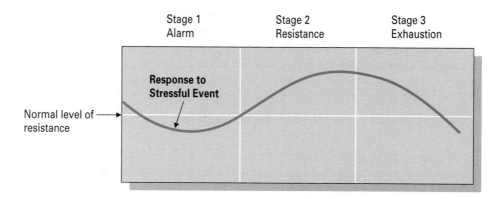

more likely to have a balanced, relaxed approach to life. They are able to work at a constant pace without time urgency. Type B people are not necessarily more or less successful than are Type A people, but they are less likely to experience stress.

Causes of Stress

Stress is obviously not a simple phenomenon. As illustrated in Figure 15.5, several different things can cause stress. Note that this list only includes work-related conditions. We should keep in mind that stress can be the result of personal circumstances as well.[24]

Work-related stressors fall into one of four categories—task, physical, role, and interpersonal demands. *Task demands* are associated with the task itself. Some occupations are inherently more stressful than others. Having to make fast decisions, decisions with less than complete information, or decisions that have relatively serious consequences are some of the things that can make jobs stressful. The jobs of surgeon, airline pilot, and stockbroker are relatively more stressful than the jobs of general practitioner, airplane baggage loader, and office receptionist. Although a general practitioner makes important decisions, he or she is also likely to have time to make a considered diagnosis and fully explore a number of different treatments. But during surgery, the surgeon must make decisions quickly while realizing that the wrong one may endanger the patient's life.

Physical demands are stressors associated with the job setting. Working outdoors in extremely hot or cold temperatures, or even in an improperly heated or cooled office, can lead to stress. A poorly designed office, which makes privacy or social interaction difficult, can result in stress, as can poor lighting and inadequate work surfaces. Even more severe are actual threats to health. Examples include jobs like coal mining, poultry processing, and toxic waste handling.

Role demands can also cause stress. (Roles are discussed more fully in Chapter 19.) A role is a set of expected behaviours associated with a position in a group or organization. Stress can result from either role ambiguity or role conflict that people can experience in groups. For example, an employee who is feeling pressure from her boss to work longer hours while also being asked by her family for more time at home will almost certainly experience stress. Similarly, a new employee experiencing role ambiguity because of the organization's poor orientation and training practices will also suffer from stress.

Interpersonal demands are stressors associated with relationships that confront people in organizations. For example, group pressures regarding restriction of output and norm conformity can lead to stress. Leadership style may also cause stress. An employee who feels a strong need to participate in decision making may feel stress if his boss refuses to allow participation. And individuals with conflicting personalities may experience stress if required to work too closely together. A person with an internal locus of control might be frustrated when working with someone who prefers to wait and just let things happen.

Consequences of Stress

As we noted earlier, the results of stress may be positive or negative. The negative consequences may be behavioural, psychological, or medical. Behaviourally stress may lead to detrimental or harmful actions such as

F I G U R E   15.5   Causes of Work Stress

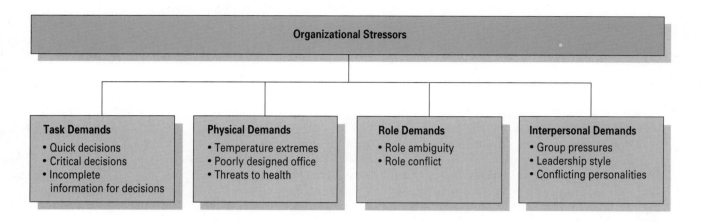

There are several different causes of work stress in organizations. Four general sets of organizational stressors are task demands, physical demands, role demands, and interpersonal demands.

● **burnout**
A feeling of exhaustion that can develop when someone experiences too much stress for an extended period of time

smoking, alcoholism, overeating, and drug abuse. Other stress-induced behaviours are accident proneness, violence toward self or others, and appetite disorders. The *Environment of Management* box discusses recent increases in workplace violence, a behaviour that is thought to be largely stress-induced.

Psychological consequences of stress interfere with an individual's mental health and well-being. These outcomes include sleep disturbances, depression, family problems, and sexual dysfunction. Managers are especially prone to sleep disturbances when they experience stress at work.[25] Medical consequences of stress affect an individual's physiological well-being. Heart disease and stroke have been linked to stress, as have headaches, backaches, ulcers and related disorders, and skin conditions such as acne and hives.

Individual stress also has direct consequences for businesses. For an operating employee, stress may translate into poor-quality work and lower productivity. For a manager, stress can cause faulty decision making and disrupt working relationships. Withdrawal behaviours can also result from stress. People who are experiencing job stress are more likely to call in sick or to leave the organization than employees who are not. More subtle forms of withdrawal may also occur. A manager may start missing deadlines, for example, or taking longer lunch breaks. Employees may also withdraw by developing feelings of indifference. The irritation displayed by people under great stress can make getting along with them difficult. Job satisfaction, morale, and commitment can all suffer as a result of excessive levels of stress. So, too, can motivation to perform.

Another consequence of stress is **burnout**—a feeling of exhaustion that can develop when someone experiences too much stress for an extended period of time. Burnout results in constant fatigue, frustration, and helplessness. Increased rigidity follows, as does a loss of self-confidence and psychological withdrawal. The individual dreads going to work, often puts in longer hours but gets less accomplished than before, and exhibits mental and physical exhaustion. Because of the damaging effects of burnout, some firms are taking steps to help avoid it. For example, British Airways provides all of its employees with training designed to help them recognize the symptoms of burnout and develop strategies for avoiding it.

Violence at Work

In 1999, Pierre Lebrun, a former garage stores clerk with Ottawa Carleton Transport, killed four employees of that company before turning his gun on himself. In 1992, Valery Fabrikant, an engineering professor, killed four of his colleagues at Montreal's Concordia University. In 1989, Marc Lepine murdered fourteen female students at the University of Montreal's École Polytechnique. Experts refer to crimes such as these as indirect violence, which can be defined as violence in workplaces where violence is not a recognized hazard. Violence against workers in occupations such as law enforcement where violence is a recognized hazard is referred to as direct violence. Whether direct or indirect, violence in the workplace should be of concern to employers. While Canadian figures are not available, workplace violence in the United States is on the rise and has become commonplace.

Managers must take reasonable steps to ensure that employees, customers, and business associates are protected. Managers must take steps to prevent violence at their businesses, especially by their employees. Managers must examine safety and security programs to make sure that they can adequately protect their assets. Labour disputes, particularly if they are acrimonious, may incite some striking workers to sabotage or vandalize property. To avoid violence, managers should use a consistent, sympathetic approach when informing individuals that they are being terminated. The most important step managers can take is to institute policies designed to defuse volatile situations before they reach the point of violence. Threats and intimidation should be prohibited. Reports of potential violence should be promptly investigated. Outlets should be provided for personnel to vent their feelings and frustrations. An emergency plan to deal with violence, should it arise, needs to be developed, including ways in which to secure the premises.

The organization's human resource (HR) professionals are most qualified to develop programs for assisting laid-off individuals. HR personnel can help develop outplacement and counselling services, retraining programs, and other forms of assistance that can greatly reduce the risk of workplace violence. Unfortunately, many organizations cut their human resource departments as one of the first steps in cost reduction, downsizing, or other restructuring programs.

References: Paul Luke, "Fight Against Violence Arrives at Workplace," *Calgary Herald*, September 28, 1996, p. H3; Gay Abbate, "On-the-Job Violence New Threat, Police Say," *The Globe and Mail*, July 19, 1991, p. A6; Christine Woolsey, "Workplace Security Plans Worth Employing," *Business Insurance*, June 6, 1994, pp. 14–15; Roberta Maynard, "Avoiding Worker Violence Over Terminations," *Nation's Business*, May 1994, p. 13; Daniel Weisberg, "Preparing for the Unthinkable," *Management Review*, March 1994, pp. 58–61; Jenny C. McCune, "The Age of Rage," *Small Business Reports*, March 1994, pp. 35–41; and James Alan Fox and Jack Levin, "Termination Can Be Murder," *Boston Globe*, May 2, 1993.

Managing Stress

Given the potential consequences of stress, it follows that both people and organizations should be concerned about how to limit its more damaging effects. Numerous ideas and approaches have been developed to help manage stress. Some are strategies for individuals, and others are strategies for organizations.[26]

One way that people manage stress is through exercise. People who exercise regularly feel less tension and stress, are more self-confident, and are more optimistic. Their better physical condition also makes them less susceptible to many common illnesses. People who don't exercise regularly, on the other hand, tend to feel more stress and are more likely to be depressed. They are also more likely to have heart attacks. And because of their physical condition they are more likely to contract illnesses.

Another method people use to manage stress is relaxation. Relaxation allows individuals to adapt to, and therefore better deal with, their stress. Relaxation comes in many forms, such as taking regular vacations. A recent study found that people's attitudes toward a variety of workplace characteristics improved significantly after a vacation. People can also learn to relax while on their jobs. For example, some experts recommend that people take regular rest breaks during their normal workday.

People can also use time management to control stress. The idea behind time management is that many daily pressures can be reduced or eliminated if individuals do a better job of managing time. One approach to time management is to make a list every morning of the things to be done that day. The items on the list are then grouped into three categories: critical activities that must be performed, important activities that should be performed, and optional things that can be delegated or postponed. The individual performs the items on the list in their order of importance.

Finally, people can manage stress through support groups. A support group can be as simple as a group of family members or friends to enjoy leisure time with. Going out after work with a couple of co-workers to a hockey game or a movie, for example, can help relieve stress that builds up during the day. Family and friends can help people cope with stress on an ongoing basis and during times of crisis. For example, an employee who has just learned that she did not get the promotion she has been working toward for months may find it helpful to have a good friend to lean on. People also may make use of more elaborate and formal support groups. Community centres or churches, for example, may sponsor support groups for people who have recently gone through a divorce, the death of a loved one, or some other tragedy.

Organizations are also beginning to realize that they should be involved in helping employees cope with stress. One argument for this is that because the business is at least partially responsible for stress, it should also help relieve it. Another is that stress-related insurance claims by employees can cost the organization considerable sums of money. Still another is that workers experiencing lower levels of detrimental stress are able to function more effectively. AT&T has initiated a series of seminars and workshops to help its employees cope with the stress they face in their jobs. The firm was prompted to develop these seminars for all three of the reasons just noted.

A wellness stress program is a special part of the organization specifically created to help employees manage stress. Organizations have adopted stress management programs, health promotion programs, and other kinds of programs for this purpose. The AT&T seminar program noted earlier is similar to this idea, but true wellness programs are ongoing activities that have a number of different components. They commonly include exercise-related activities as well as classroom instruction and counselling programs dealing with smoking cessation, weight reduction, and general stress management.

Some companies are developing their own programs or using existing programs of this type. Husky Injection Molding Systems, for example, has a fitness centre at its corporate headquarters in Bolton, Ontario. Other firms negotiate discounted health club membership rates with local establishments. For the instructional part of the program the organization can again either sponsor its own training or perhaps jointly sponsor seminars with a local YMCA, civic organization, or church. Organization-based fitness programs facilitate employee exercise, a positive outcome, but such programs can be quite costly. Still, more and more companies are developing fitness programs for employees.

Both individuals and organizations can contribute to the effective management of stress on the part of employees. Health spas are an increasingly popular method for stress reduction. Individuals can spend a few days or weeks at such spas, learning how to better control their emotions, keep stress in check, and live a healthier and more balanced life. These spa participants are wearing mud masks as part of their therapy.

TYPES OF WORKPLACE BEHAVIOUR

Now that we have looked closely at how individual differences can influence behaviour in organizations, let's turn our attention to what we mean by workplace behaviour. **Workplace behaviour** is a pattern of action by the members of an organization that directly or indirectly influences organizational effectiveness. Important workplace behaviours include performance and productivity, absenteeism and turnover, and organizational citizenship.

● **workplace behaviour**
A pattern of action by the members of an organization that directly or indirectly influences organizational

Performance Behaviours

Performance behaviours are the total set of work-related behaviours that the organization expects the individual to display. Thus they derive from the psychological contract. For some jobs, performance behaviours can be narrowly defined and easily measured. For example, an assembly-line worker who sits by a moving conveyor and attaches parts to a product as it passes by has relatively few performance behaviours. He or she is expected to remain at the workstation and correctly attach the parts. Performance can often be assessed quantitatively by counting the percentage of parts correctly attached.

● **performance behaviours**
The total set of work-related behaviours that the organization expects the individual to display

For many other jobs, however, performance behaviours are more diverse and much more difficult to assess. For example, consider the case of a research and development scientist. The scientist works in a lab trying to find new scientific breakthroughs that have commercial potential. The scientist must apply knowledge learned in graduate school with experience gained from previous research. Intuition and creativity are also important elements. And accomplishing the desired breakthrough may take months or even years. As we discussed in Chapter 13, organizations rely on a number of different methods for evaluating performance. The key is to match the evaluation mechanism with the job being performed.

Withdrawal Behaviours

Another important type of work-related behaviour is behaviour that results in withdrawal—absenteeism and turnover. **Absenteeism** occurs when an individual does not show up for work. The cause may be legitimate (illness, jury duty, death in the family, etc.) or feigned (reported as legitimate but actually just an excuse to stay home). When an employee is absent, her or his work does not get done at all or a substitute must be hired to do it. In either case, the quantity or quality of actual output is likely to suffer. Obviously, some absenteeism is expected. The important concern of organizations is to minimize feigned absenteeism and reduce legitimate absences as much as possible. High absenteeism may be a symptom of other problems as well, such as job dissatisfaction and low morale.

● **absenteeism**
An individual's not showing up for work

Turnover occurs when people quit their jobs. An organization usually incurs costs in replacing individuals who have quit, but if turnover involves especially productive people, it is even more costly. Turnover seems to result from a number of factors including aspects of the job, the organization, the individual, the labour market, and family influences. In general, a poor person–job fit is also a likely cause of turnover.

● **turnover**
Employees' quitting their jobs

Efforts to directly manage turnover are frequently fraught with difficulty, even in organizations that concentrate on rewarding good performers. Of course, some turnover is inevitable and in some cases it may even be desirable. For example, if the organization is trying to cut costs by reducing its staff, having people voluntarily choose to leave is preferable to having to terminate them. And if the people who choose to leave are low performers or express high levels of job dissatisfaction, the organization may also benefit from turnover.

Organizational Citizenship

● organizational citizenship
The behaviour of individuals that makes a positive overall contribution to the

Organizational citizenship refers to the behaviour of individuals that makes a positive overall contribution to the organization.[27] Consider, for example, an employee who does work that is acceptable in terms of both quantity and quality. However, she refuses to work overtime, she won't help newcomers learn the ropes, and she is generally unwilling to make any contribution to the organization beyond the strict performance of her job. Although this person may be seen as a good performer, she is not likely to be seen as a good organizational citizen.

Another employee may exhibit a comparable level of performance. In addition, however, he will always work late when the boss asks him to, he takes time to help newcomers learn their way around, and he is perceived as being helpful and committed to the organization's success. Whereas his level of performance may be seen as equal to that of the first worker, he is also likely to be seen as a better organizational citizen.

The determinant of organizational citizenship behaviours is likely to be a complex mosaic of individual, social, and organizational variables. For example, the personality, attitudes, and needs of the individual must be consistent with citizenship behaviours. Similarly, the social context or work group in which the individual works must facilitate and promote such behaviours (we discuss group dynamics in Chapter 19). The organization itself, especially its culture, must be able to promote, recognize, and reward these types of behaviours if they are to be maintained. Although the study of organizational citizenship is still in its infancy, preliminary research suggests that it may play a powerful role in organizational effectiveness.[28]

SUMMARY OF KEY POINTS

Understanding individuals in organizations is an important consideration for all managers. A basic framework for facilitating this understanding is the psychological contract—the set of expectations held by people with respect to what they will contribute to the organization and what they expect in return. Organizations strive to achieve an optimal person–job fit, but this process is complicated by the existence of individual differences.

Personality is the relatively stable set of psychological and behavioural attributes that distinguish one person from another. Managers can do little to alter personality. Instead, they should strive to understand the effects of important personality attributes such as locus of control, self-efficacy, authoritarianism, dogmatism, self-monitoring, self-esteem, and risk propensity.

The three components of attitudes are the affective component, the cognitive component, and the intentional component. Whereas personality is relatively stable, some attitudes can be formed and changed easily. Others are more constant. Job satisfaction or dissatisfaction, organizational commitment, and job involvement are important work-related attitudes.

Perception is the set of processes by which an individual becomes aware of and interprets information about the environment. Basic perceptual processes include selective perception and stereotyping. Perception and attribution are also closely related.

Stress is an individual's response to a strong stimulus. The General Adaptation Syndrome outlines the basic stress process. Stress can be caused by task, physical, role, and interpersonal demands. Consequences of stress include organizational and individual outcomes as well as burnout. Stress can be managed in several ways.

Workplace behaviour is a pattern of action by the members of an organization that directly or indirectly influences organizational effectiveness. Performance behaviours are the set of work-related behaviours the organization expects the individual to display in fulfilling the psychological contract. Basic withdrawal behaviours are absenteeism and turnover. Organizational citizenship refers to behaviour of individuals that makes a positive overall contribution to the organization.

DISCUSSION QUESTIONS

Questions for Review

1. What is a psychological contract? Why is it important?
2. Identify and describe five basic personality attributes.
3. What are the components of an individual's attitude?
4. Identify and describe several important workplace behaviours.

Questions for Analysis

5. An individual was heard to describe someone else as having "no personality." What is wrong with this statement? What did the individual actually mean?
6. Describe a circumstance in which you formed a new attitude about something.
7. As a manager, how would you go about trying to make someone a better organizational citizen?

Questions for Application

8. Write the psychological contract you have in this class. That is, what do you contribute, and what inducements are available? Compare your contract with those of some of your classmates. In what ways are they similar, and in what ways is yours unique?
9. Assume that you are going to hire three new employees for the department store you manage. One will sell shoes, one will manage the toy department, and one will work in the stockroom. Identify the basic characteristics you want in each of the people to achieve a good person–job fit.
10. Make a list of the things that cause stress for the typical university student. Now make a list of how university students manage stress. Compare your lists with those of three of your classmates.

BUILDING EFFECTIVE DIAGNOSTIC & CONCEPTUAL SKILLS

Exercise Overview

Conceptual skills refer to a manager's ability to think in the abstract, whereas diagnostic skills focus on responses to situations. These skills must frequently be used together to better understand the behaviour of others in the organization, as illustrated by this exercise.

Exercise Background

Human behaviour is a complex phenomenon in any setting, but especially so in organizations. Understanding how and why people choose particular behaviours can be difficult and frustrating, but quite important. Consider, for example, the following scenario.

Sandra Buckley has worked in your department for several years. Until recently, she has been a "model" employee. She was always on time, or early, for work and stayed late whenever necessary to get her work done. She was upbeat, cheerful, and worked very hard. She frequently said that the company was the best place she had ever worked and that you were the perfect boss.

About six months ago, however, you began to see changes in Sandra's behaviour. She occasionally comes in late, and you cannot remember the last time she agreed to work past 5:00. She also complains a lot. Other workers have started to avoid her, because she is so negative all the time. You also suspect that she may be looking for a new job.

Exercise Task

Using the preceding scenario as background, do the following:

1. Assume that you have done some background work to find out what has happened. Write a brief scenario with more information that might explain why Sandra's behaviour has changed (for example, your case might include the fact that you recently promoted someone else when Sandra might have expected to get the job). Make your scenario as descriptive as possible.
2. Relate elements of your case to the various behavioural concepts discussed in this chapter.
3. Decide whether or not you might be able to resolve things with Sandra to overcome whatever issues have arisen. That is, do you think you can correct the situation?
4. Which behavioural process or concept discussed in this chapter is easiest to change? Which is the most difficult to change?

Flextime

Once a relatively rare phenomenon in the corporate world, flexible work arrangements have become more commonplace. Such arrangements are especially evident in the banking industry. Under the Royal Bank of Canada's flexible work program, employees can work off-site provided it is to the mutual advantage of the bank and the employee. The Royal Bank's program is called Work and Family. The Bank of Montreal has a similar program called Flexing Your Options, while the Canadian Imperial Bank of Commerce has established a Work and Lifestyle program. The other major Canadian banks have similar programs.

In addition to flexible schedules, these programs encompass such arrangements as compressed workweeks, telecommuting, job sharing, and permanent part-time work arrangements. In 1996, 1,200 Royal Bank employees had nontraditional work arrangements, with job sharing and flexible hours being the most prevalent; an independent study found a 30 percent increase in productivity among these employees. Of course, flexible work arrangements are not limited to the banking industry. The Great-West Life Assurance Company, based in Winnipeg, is one of a growing number of Canadian companies to offer a job-sharing program and other flexible work arrangements.

With compressed workweeks, individuals can work longer hours but with fewer days. This creates larger blocks of time that they can use for family purposes. Two-income and dual-career couples can arrange such schedules so that one or the other is available for parenting for longer periods at a time. Flextime permits individuals to arrive at and leave from work at different times. Thus workers can better fit schedules to traffic flows and parenting duties such as taking children to hockey games or figure skating classes. Flexplace or telecommuting permits individuals to work from their homes or other locations rather than having to come to a central office. Part-time arrangements usually involve job sharing in which two individuals, each working half-time, per-

form a job normally held by a single person. Almost all of these approaches make managing family responsibilities along with job responsibilities easier.

Although flexible work arrangements can lead to improved productivity, morale, and retention rates, they may make little difference unless the organization's culture is also flexible. The managerial mindset of "face-time" must change. Face-time refers to the strongly held and deeply ingrained view that if people are present at work for forty hours a week, at their desks shuffling papers, then they must be accomplishing their work no matter how little output they actually produce. If managers won't give up the notion of face-time, flexible policies are not likely to have much of an impact. Further, communication is critical. Co-workers, subordinates, superiors, and customers all must clearly understand how the arrangement works including responsibilities and day-to-day schedules of availability for those using the system.

Questions

1. What different sorts of flexible work arrangements exist? What are the advantages and disadvantages of each of them?

2. What basic individual characteristics seem to be served by flexible work arrangements? Might they also be served by other organizational arrangements? If so, what; if not, why not?

3. What are the assumptions underlying "face-time"? If you owned a company, would you be willing to give up face-time for flexible time? Why or why not?

References: William Nickels et al., *Understanding Canadian Business*, 2nd ed. (Toronto: Irwin, 1997), pp. 383–386; Richard Wright, "Making the Job Fit the Banker," *Canadian Banker*, November/December, 1993, pp. 16–19; "More Companies Experiment with Workers' Schedules," The *Wall Street Journal*, January 13, 1994, pp. B1, B6; Catherine Romano, "What's Your Flexibility Factor?" *Management Review*, January 1994, p. 9; Julie Cohen Mason, "Flexing More Than Muscle: Employees Want Time on Their Side," *Management Review*, March 1992, pp. 6–9; and Christine Scordato and Julie Harris, "Workplace Flexibility," *HRMagazine*, January 1990, pp. 75–78.

CHAPTER NOTES

1. David Robertson et al., *The CAMI Report: Lean Production in a Unionized Auto Plant* (Willowdale, Ont.:CAW-Canada Research Department, 1993); Jeb Blount, "Behind the Lines," *Canadian Business*, January 1990, pp. 62–67; David Morrison, "Psychological Contracts and Change," *Human Resource Management,* Fall 1994, pp. 353–372; and "About CAMI" (http://cami.ca).

2. Lynn McGarlane Shore and Lois Tetrick, "The Psychological Contract as an Explanatory Framework in the Employment Relationship," in C.L. Cooper and D.M. Rousseau (Eds.), *Trends in Organizational Behavior* (London: John Wiley & Sons Ltd., 1994), pp. 58–70.

3. Sandra Robinson, Matthew Kraatz, and Denise Rousseau, "Changing Obligations and the Psychological Contract: A Longitudinal Study," *Academy of Management Journal,* Vol. 37, No. 1, 1994, pp. 137–152; and Jennifer A. Chatman, "Improving Interactional Organizational Research: A Model of Person–Organization Fit," *Academy of Management Review,* July 1989, pp. 333–349.

4. Lawrence Pervin, "Personality," in Mark Rosenzweig and Lyman Porter (Eds.), *Annual Review of Psychology,* Vol. 36 (Palo Alto, Calif.: Annual Reviews, 1985), pp. 83–114; S.R. Maddi, *Personality Theories: A Comparative Analysis*, 4th ed. (Homewood, Ill.: Dorsey, 1980).

5. J.B. Rotter, "Generalized Expectancies for Internal vs. External Control of Reinforcement," *Psychological Monographs,* Vol. 80, 1966, pp. 1–28.

6. Cynthia Lee and Philip Bobko, "Self-Efficacy Beliefs: Comparison of Five Measures," *Journal of Applied Psychology,* Vol. 79, No. 3, 1994, pp. 364–369.

7. T.W. Adorno, E. Frenkel-Brunswick, D.J. Levinson, and R.N. Sanford, *The Authoritarian Personality* (New York: Harper & Row, 1950).

8. "Who Becomes an Authoritarian?" *Psychology Today,* March 1989, pp. 66–70.

9. Edward Necka and Malgorzata Kubiak, "The Influence of Training in Metaphorical Thinking on Creativity and Level of Dogmatism," *Polish Psychological Bulletin,* Vol. 20, 1989, pp. 69–78; and A.F. Kostin, "The Truth of History and Stereotypes of Dogmatism," *Soviet Studies in History,* Vol. 27, 1988, pp. 85–96.

10. "Thinking About Ourselves and Others: Self-Monitoring and Social Knowledge," *Journal of Personality and Social Psychology,* Vol. 39, 1980, pp. 222–234.

11. Barbara Foley Meeker, "Cooperation, Competition, and Self-Esteem: Aspects of Winning and Losing," *Human Relations,* Vol. 43, 1990, pp. 205–220; and Jon L. Pierce, Donald G. Gardner, and Larry L. Cummings, "Organization-Based Self-Esteem: Construct Definition, Measurement, and Validation," *Academy of Management Journal,* 1989, Vol. 32, pp. 622–648.

12. Leon Festinger, *A Theory of Cognitive Dissonance* (Palo Alto, Calif.: Stanford University Press, 1957).

13. Gerald Salancik and Jeffrey Pfeffer, "An Examination of Need-Satisfaction Models of Job Attitudes," *Administrative Science Quarterly,* Vol. 22, 1977, pp. 427–456; and Gerald Salancik and Jeffrey Pfeffer, "A Social Information Processing Approach to Job Attitudes and Task Design," *Administrative Science Quarterly,* Vol. 23, 1978, pp. 224–253.

14. Patricia C. Smith, L.M. Kendall, and Charles Hulin, *The Measurement of Satisfaction in Work and Behavior* (Chicago: Rand-McNally, 1969).

15. Eric Beauchesne, "Job Survivors Well Prepared," *The Windsor Star*, October 8, 1997, p. D9.

16. Randall Dunham, Jean Grube, and Maria Castaneda, "Organizational Commitment: The Utility of an Integrative Definition," *Journal of Applied Psychology,* Vol. 79, No. 3, 1994, pp. 370–380.

17. Richard M. Steers, "Antecedents and Outcomes of Organizational Commitment," *Administrative Science Quarterly,* Vol. 22, 1977, pp. 46–56.

18. Kathleen Sutcliffe, "What Executives Notice: Accurate Perceptions in Top Management Teams," *Academy of Management Journal,* Vol. 37, No. 5, 1994, pp. 1360–1378.

19. See H.H. Kelley, *Attribution in Social Interaction* (Morristown, N.J.: General Learning Press, 1971), for a classic treatment of attribution.

20. For a recent overview of the stress literature, see Frank Landy, James Campbell Quick, and Stanislav Kasl, "Work, Stress, and Well-Being," *International Journal of Stress Management,* Vol. 1, No. 1, 1994, pp. 33–73.

21. Hans Selye, *The Stress of Life* (New York: McGraw-Hill, 1976).

22. Selye, *The Stress of Life.*

23. M. Friedman and R.H. Rosenman, *Type A Behaviour and Your Heart* (New York: Alfred A. Knopf, 1974).

24. "Work and Family," *Business Week*, June 28, 1993, pp. 80–88.

25. Anne Fisher, "Welcome to the Age of Overwork," *Fortune*, November 30, 1992, pp. 64–71.

26. Alan Farnham, "Who Beats Stress—And How," *Fortune*, October 7, 1991, pp. 71–86.

27. See Dennis W. Organ, "Personality and Organizational Citizenship Behavior," *Journal of Management,* Vol. 20, No. 2, 1994, pp. 465–478, for recent findings regarding this behaviour.

28. Mary Konovsky and S. Douglas Pugh, "Citizenship Behavior and Social Exchange," *Academy of Management Journal,* Vol. 37, No. 3, 1994, pp. 656–669.

Motivating Employee Performance

16

OBJECTIVES

After studying this chapter, you should be able to:

- *Characterize the nature of motivation, including its importance and basic historical perspectives.*

- *Identify and describe the major content perspectives on motivation.*

- *Identify and describe the major process perspectives on motivation.*

- *Describe reinforcement perspectives on motivation.*

- *Identify and describe other perspectives on motivation as well as popular motivational strategies.*

- *Describe the role of organizational reward systems in motivation.*

OUTLINE

A recent survey found that most Canadians are satisfied with their jobs and that training goes a long way toward maintaining a high level of satisfaction.

An international survey released in February 1999 found that 69 percent of Canadians are satisfied with their jobs, placing Canada tenth among a list of thirty-five countries headed by Switzerland. An international study of workers in thirteen countries released in September 1996 by the research firm Walker Information found that Canadian workers are the most committed to their employers. One month later, a national poll sponsored by the Royal Bank of Canada and conducted by the Angus Reid Group found that 45 percent of Canadian workers are very satisfied with their jobs and a further 45 percent are satisfied with their jobs. Further analysis revealed that those employees who were most satisfied held jobs for which they had been trained and also possessed the skills necessary to advance in their jobs.

The findings of these three surveys may not be telling the whole story. In their struggle to survive in a highly competitive business environment, some companies have turned to unconventional methods in order to motivate their employees. For example, some employees of TransAlta Utilities, Alberta's largest utility company, resigned after being subjected to cultlike methods aimed at improving morale and productivity. Seminars that cost Sasktel $2 million reportedly turned the company's offices into a "pressure cooker" and led to calls (by a member of the Saskatchewan legislature) for an independent inquiry. While some companies have used cultlike methods to motivate employees, others have allegedly been more directly influenced by nonmainstream religious organizations or cults. Allstate Insurance managers were subjected to training sessions based on the doctrines of the Church of Scientology, while Hydro-Québec has faced allegations that it hired Luc Jouret, a former leader of the Solar Temple cult, as a consultant and motivational speaker.

Of course, many companies still use conventional methods to motivate employees. Sears, the American retail giant with stores in Canada, is using participatory management and a new pay system to motivate its employees. Starting in 1996, every employee's compensation includes a customer service factor. Research also supports the more conventional strategies for motivating employees. For example, a recent Ernst and Young survey found that one of the most effective and least expensive ways to motivate employees is to demonstrate to them how their jobs help the company make money.[1] ●

> **"Sears … is using participatory management and a new pay system to motivate its employees."**

Understanding how the new pay system at Sears works is fairly easy. More difficult, however, is understanding why it works. The answer is rooted in employee motivation. Virtually any organization is capable of having a motivated workforce. The trick is figuring out how to create a system in which employees can receive rewards that they genuinely want by performing in ways that fit the organization's goals and objectives.

In most settings, people can choose how hard they work and how much effort they expend. Thus managers need to understand how and why employees make different choices regarding their own performance. The major ingredient behind this choice is motivation, the subject of this chapter. We first examine the nature of employee motivation and then explore the major perspectives on motivation. Newly emerging approaches are then discussed. We conclude with a description of rewards and their role in motivation.

THE NATURE OF MOTIVATION

● **motivation**
The set of forces that cause people to behave in certain ways

Motivation is the set of forces that cause people to behave in certain ways.[2] On any given day, an employee may choose to work as hard as possible at a job, to work just hard enough to avoid a reprimand, or to do as little as possible. The goal for the manager is to maximize the occurrence of the first incident and minimize the occurrence of the last one. This goal becomes all the more important when we understand how important motivation is in the workplace.[3]

The Importance of Employee Motivation

Individual performance is generally determined by three things: motivation (the desire to do the job), ability (the capability to do the job), and the work environment (the tools, materials, and information needed to do the job). If an employee lacks ability, the manager can provide training or replace the worker.

The Canadian women's hockey team is jubilant after winning the final game against the United States in the Women's World Championship in Helsinki on March 14, 1999. Because the U.S. won the Olympic gold medal against them in 1998, the Canadian team was highly motivated to win the next major tournament.

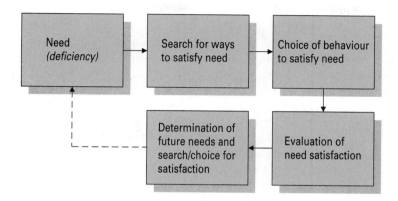

The motivation process progresses through a series of discrete steps. Content, process, and reinforcement perspectives on motivation address different parts of this process.

If there is an environmental problem, the manager can also usually make adjustments to promote higher performance. But if motivation is the problem, the task for the manager is more challenging. Individual behaviour is a complex phenomenon, and the manager may be hard-pressed to figure out the precise nature of the problem and how to solve it. Thus motivation is important because of its significance as a determinant of performance and because of its intangible character.[4]

The motivation framework in Figure 16.1 is a good starting point for understanding how motivated behaviour occurs. The motivation process begins with needs, or a deficiency. For example, because a worker feels that she is underpaid, she experiences a deficiency and a need for more income. In response to this need, the worker searches for ways to satisfy it, such as working harder to try to earn a raise or seeking a new job. Next, she chooses an option to pursue. After carrying out the chosen option—working harder and putting in more hours for a reasonable period of time, for example—she then evaluates her success. If her hard work resulted in a pay raise, she probably feels good about things and will continue to work hard. If no raise has been provided, she is likely to try another option.

Historical Perspectives on Motivation

Reviewing earlier approaches helps us appreciate what we know about employee motivation. In general, motivation theory has evolved through three different eras: the traditional approach, the human relations approach, and the human resource approach.

The Traditional Approach   The traditional approach to employee motivation is best represented by the work of Frederick W. Taylor.[5] As we noted in Chapter 2, Taylor suggested the use of an incentive pay system. He believed that management knew more about the jobs being performed than the workers did, and he assumed that economic gain was everyone's primary motivation. Other assumptions of the traditional approach were that work is inherently unpleasant for most people and that the money employees earn is more important than the nature of the job they are performing. Hence, people could be expected to perform any kind of job if they were paid enough. Although the role of money as a motivating factor cannot be dismissed, proponents of the traditional approach took too narrow a view of the role of monetary compensation and also failed to consider other motivational factors.

The Human Relations Approach   The human relations approach (also summarized in Chapter 2) grew out of the work at Western Electric of Elton Mayo and his associates.[6] The human relationists emphasized the role of social processes in the workplace. Their basic assumptions were that employees want to feel useful and important, that employees have strong social needs, and that these needs are more important than money in motivating employees. Advocates of the human relations approach advised managers to make workers feel important and allow them a modicum of self-direction and self-control in carrying out routine activities. The illusion of involvement and importance was expected to satisfy workers' basic social needs and result in higher motivation to perform. For example, a manager might allow a work group to participate in making a decision, even though he or she had already determined what the decision would be. The symbolic gesture of seeming to allow participation was expected to enhance motivation, even though no real participation took place.

The Human Resource Approach   The human resource approach to motivation carries the concepts of needs and motivation one step further. Whereas the human relationists believed that the illusion of contribution and participation enhanced motivation, the human resource view assumes that the contributions themselves are valuable to both individuals and organizations. It assumes that people want to contribute and are able to make genuine contributions. Management's task, then, is to encourage participation and to create a work environment that makes full use of the human resources available. This philosophy guides most contemporary thinking about employee motivation.[7] At Ford, CAMI, 3M, Algoma Steel (Canada's third largest steel producer), and Hewlett-Packard, for example, management is calling on work teams to solve a variety of problems and to make substantive contributions to the organization. Sears is clearly trying to capitalize on the strength of its human resources through its new pay system.

CONTENT PERSPECTIVES ON MOTIVATION

● **content perspectives**
Approaches to motivation that try to answer the question, "What factor or factors motivate people?"

Content perspectives on motivation focus on the first part of the motivation process—needs and need deficiencies. More specifically, **content perspectives** address the question, "What factors in the workplace motivate people?" Labour leaders often argue that workers can be motivated by more pay, shorter working hours, and improved working conditions. Meanwhile, some experts suggest that motivation can be enhanced by providing employees with more autonomy and greater responsibility. Both of these views represent content views of motivation. The former asserts that motivation is a function of pay, working hours, and working conditions; the latter suggests that autonomy and responsibility are motivating factors. Two widely known content perspectives on motivation are the need hierarchy and the two-factor theory.

The Need Hierarchy Approach

The need hierarchy approach has been advanced by many theorists. Need hierarchies assume that people have different needs that can be arranged in a hierarchy of importance. The two best known are Maslow's hierarchy of needs and the ERG theory.

Maslow's Hierarchy of Needs   Abraham Maslow, a human relationist, argued that people are motivated to satisfy five need levels.[8] **Maslow's hierarchy of needs** is shown in Figure 16.2. At the bottom of the hierarchy are the *physiological needs*—things like food, sex, and air that represent basic issues of survival and biological function. In organizations, these needs are generally satisfied by adequate wages and the work environment itself, which provides restrooms, adequate lighting, comfortable temperatures, and ventilation.

Next are the *security needs* for a secure physical and emotional environment. Examples include the desire for housing and clothing and the need to be free from worry about money and job security. These needs can be satisfied in the workplace by job continuity (no layoffs), a grievance system (to protect against arbitrary supervisory actions), and an adequate insurance and retirement benefits package (for security against illness and provision of income in later life). Even today, however, depressed industries and economic decline can put people out of work and restore the primacy of security needs.

Belongingness needs relate to social processes. They include the need for love and affection and the need to be accepted by one's peers. These needs are satisfied for most people by family and community relationships outside of work and friendships on the job. A manager can help satisfy these needs by allowing social interaction and by making employees feel like part of a team or work group.

● **Maslow's hierarchy of needs**
A theory of motivation that suggests that people must satisfy five groups of needs in order—physiological, security, belongingness, esteem, and self-actualization

---

F I G U R E   16.2   Maslow's Hierarchy of Needs

Source: Adapted from Abraham H. Maslow, "A Theory of Human Motivation," *Psychological Review*, vol. 50, 1943, pp. 370–396.

Maslow's hierarchy suggests that human needs can be classified into five categories and that these categories can be arranged in a hierarchy of importance. A manager should understand that an employee may not be satisfied with only a salary and benefits; he or she may also need challenging job opportunities to experience self-growth and satisfaction.

Esteem needs actually comprise two different sets of needs: the need for a positive self-image and self-respect and the need for recognition and respect from others. A manager can help address these needs by providing a variety of extrinsic symbols of accomplishment such as job titles, nice offices, and similar rewards as appropriate. At a more intrinsic level, the manager can provide challenging job assignments and opportunities for the employee to feel a sense of accomplishment.

At the top of the hierarchy are the *self-actualization needs*. These involve realizing one's potential for continued growth and individual development. The self-actualization needs are perhaps the most difficult for a manager to address. In fact, it can be argued that these needs must be met entirely from within the individual. But a manager can help by promoting a culture wherein self-actualization is possible. For instance, a manager could give employees a chance to participate in making decisions about their work and the opportunity to learn new things about their jobs and the organization.

Maslow suggests that the five need categories constitute a hierarchy. An individual is motivated first and foremost to satisfy physiological needs. As long as they remain unsatisfied, the individual is motivated only to fulfill them. When satisfaction of physiological needs is achieved they cease to act as primary motivational factors and the individual moves "up" the hierarchy and becomes concerned with security needs. This process continues until the individual reaches the self-actualization level. Maslow's concept of the need hierarchy has a certain intuitive logic and has been accepted by many managers. But research has revealed certain shortcomings and defects in the theory. Some research has found that five levels of need are not always present and that the order of the

For many people, such as former reinsurance underwriter Lisa Hannaford-Glass of Wolfville, N.S., meeting various needs may involve leaving high-stress, big-city jobs, as she did. A major challenge for managers today is to ensure that employees can enjoy individual growth within their careers.

levels is not always the same as postulated by Maslow.[9] In addition, people from different cultures are likely to have different need categories and hierarchies.

ERG Theory In response to these and similar criticisms, Clayton Alderfer has proposed an alternative hierarchy of needs called the **ERG theory of motivation**.[10] The letters *E*, *R*, and *G* stand for existence, relatedness, and growth. This theory collapses the need hierarchy developed by Maslow into three levels. *Existence needs* correspond to the physiological and security needs. *Relatedness needs* focus on how people relate to their social environment. In Maslow's hierarchy, they would encompass both the need to belong and the need to earn the esteem of others. *Growth needs*, the highest level in Alderfer's schema, include the needs for self-esteem and self-actualization.

Although the ERG theory assumes that motivated behaviour follows a hierarchy in somewhat the same fashion as suggested by Maslow, there are two important differences. First, the ERG theory suggests that more than one level of need can cause motivation at the same time. For example, it suggests that people can be motivated by a desire for money (existence), friendship (relatedness), and the opportunity to learn new skills (growth) all at once.

Second, the ERG theory has what has been called a *frustration-regression* element that is missing from Maslow's need hierarchy. Maslow maintained that an individual will remain at one level of needs until achieving satisfaction. In contrast, ERG theory suggests that if needs remain unsatisfied the individual becomes frustrated, regresses to a lower level, and begins to pursue those things again. For example, a worker previously motivated by money (existence needs) may have just been awarded a pay raise sufficient to satisfy those needs. Suppose that he then attempts to establish more friendships to satisfy relatedness needs. If for some reason he finds that becoming better friends with others in the workplace is impossible, he eventually gets frustrated and regresses to being motivated to earn even more money.

The ERG theory is relatively new compared with Maslow's need hierarchy, but research suggests that it may be a more valid account of motivation in organizations.[11] Managers should not, of course, rely too heavily on any one perspective to guide their thinking about employee motivation. The important insights to be gleaned from the need hierarchy view are that some needs may be more important than others and that people may change their behaviour after any particular set of needs has been satisfied.

The Two-Factor Theory

Another popular content perspective on motivation is the **two-factor theory**.[12] Frederick Herzberg developed his theory by asking two hundred accountants and engineers to recall occasions when they had been satisfied with their work and highly motivated and occasions when they had been dissatisfied and unmotivated. Surprisingly, he found that different sets of factors were associated with satisfaction and with dissatisfaction—that is, a person might identify "low pay" as causing dissatisfaction but would not necessarily mention "high pay" as a cause of satisfaction. Instead, different factors—such as recognition or accomplishment—were cited as causing satisfaction.

This finding led Herzberg to conclude that the traditional view of job satisfaction was incomplete. That view assumed that satisfaction and dissatisfaction are at opposite ends of a single continuum. People might be satisfied, dissatisfied,

● **ERG theory of motivation**
A theory of motivation that suggests that people's needs are grouped into three possibly overlapping categories—existence, relatedness, and growth

● **two-factor theory of motivation**
A theory of motivation that suggests that people's satisfaction and dissatisfaction are influenced by two independent sets of factors—motivation factors and hygiene factors

or somewhere in between. But Herzberg's interviews had identified two different dimensions altogether: one ranging from satisfaction to no satisfaction and the other ranging from dissatisfaction to no dissatisfaction.

This perspective, along with several examples of factors that affect each continuum, is shown in Figure 16.3. Note that the factors influencing the satisfaction continuum—called motivation factors—are related specifically to the work content. The factors presumed to cause dissatisfaction—called hygiene factors—are related to the work environment.

Based on these findings, Herzberg argues that there are two stages in the process of motivating employees. First, managers must ensure that the hygiene factors are not deficient. Pay and security must be appropriate, working conditions must be safe, technical supervision must be acceptable, and so on. By providing hygiene factors at an appropriate level, managers do not stimulate motivation but merely ensure that employees are "not dissatisfied." Employees whom managers attempt to "satisfy" through hygiene factors alone will usually do just enough to get by. Thus managers should proceed to stage two—giving employees the opportunity to experience motivation factors such as achievement and recognition. The result is predicted to be a high level of satisfaction and motivation. Herzberg also goes a step further than most theorists and describes exactly how to use the two-factor theory in the workplace. Specifically, he recommends job enrichment, as discussed in Chapter 10. He argues that jobs should be redesigned to provide higher levels of the motivation factors.

The two-factor theory suggests that job satisfaction has two different dimensions. A manager who tries to motivate an employee using only hygiene factors such as pay and good working conditions will likely not succeed. To motivate employees and produce a high level of satisfaction, managers must also offer factors such as responsibility and the opportunity for advancement (motivation factors).

FIGURE 16.3   The Two-Factor Theory of Motivation

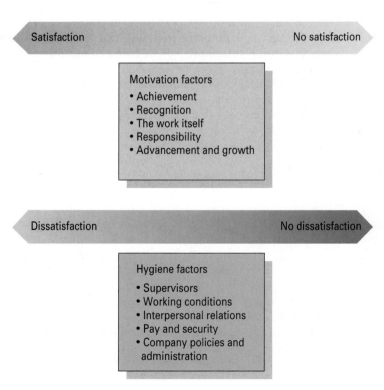

Although widely accepted by many managers, Herzberg's two-factor theory is not without its critics. One criticism is that the findings in Herzberg's initial interviews are subject to different explanations. Another charge is that his sample was not representative of the general population and that subsequent research often failed to uphold the theory.[13] At the present time, Herzberg's theory is not held in high esteem by researchers in the field. The theory has had a major impact on managers, however, and has played an important role in increasing their awareness of motivation and its importance in the workplace.

Individual Human Needs

In addition to these theories, research has also focused on specific individual human needs that are important in organizations. The three most important individual needs are achievement, affiliation, and power.[14]

The **need for achievement**, the best known of the three, is the desire to accomplish a goal or task more effectively than in the past. People with a high need for achievement have a desire to assume personal responsibility, a tendency to set moderately difficult goals, a desire for specific and immediate feedback, and a preoccupation with their task. David C. McClelland, the psychologist who first identified this need, argues that only about 10 percent of the U.S. population has a high need for achievement. In contrast, almost 25 percent of the workers in Japan have a high need for achievement. The *Environment of Management* box describes how Terry Matthews has caused Newbridge Networks Corp. to be permeated by a high need for achievement.

The **need for affiliation** is less well understood. Like Maslow's belongingness need, the need for affiliation is a desire for human companionship and acceptance. People with a strong need for affiliation are likely to prefer (and perform better in) a job that entails a lot of social interaction and offers opportunities to make friends.

The need for power has also received considerable attention as an important ingredient in managerial success.[15] The **need for power** is the desire to be influential in a group and to control one's environment. Research has shown that people with a strong need for power are likely to be superior performers, have good attendance records, and occupy supervisory positions. One study found that managers as a group tend to have a stronger power motive than the general population and that successful managers have stronger power motives than less successful managers.[16]

In summary, the major content perspectives on motivation focus on individual needs. Maslow's need hierarchy, the ERG theory, the two-factor theory, and the needs for achievement, affiliation, and power all provide useful insights into factors that cause motivation. What they do not do is shed much light on the process of motivation. They do not explain why people might be motivated by one factor rather than by another at a given level or how people might go about trying to satisfy the different needs. These questions involve behaviours or actions, goals, and feelings of satisfaction—concepts that are addressed by various process perspectives on motivation.

● **need for achievement**
The desire to accomplish a goal or task more effectively than in the past

● **need for affiliation**
The desire for human companionship and acceptance

● **need for power**
The desire to be influential in a group and to control one's environment

Matthews Is Motivated

 At a recent annual meeting, Newbridge Networks Corp.'s chairman, Terry Matthews, announced a major agreement the company had secured to provide the British telecommunications giant BT PLC with equipment for its new broadband multiservice network. The deal, worth more than half a billion dollars, led to an almost 10 percent rise in Newbridge shares on the day of the announcement. However, institutional investors did not approve of the plan to increase employee stock options from 22 million to 25 million shares. This move, while diluting the value of institutional investors' stock, is seen as being critical to maintaining a highly motivated workforce at Newbridge—a factor recognized by Matthews as the main ingredient of the company's recipe for success in the world marketplace.

Newbridge Networks Corp.'s fortunes have fluctuated since Matthews founded it in 1986, but the company now appears to be on solid ground. Newbridge's estimated revenue for the third quarter of its 1999 fiscal year is $450 million, a 25 percent increase from the third quarter of fiscal 1998. Newbridge is a leading multinational corporation that specializes in designing, manufacturing, and servicing networking products and systems used in multimedia communications. Newbridge's asynchronous mode transfer (ATM) technology is a major part of its business. Its customers include the world's largest telecommunications service providers, more than 10,000 corporate

customers, and government organizations. The company has approximately six thousand employees working in facilities in Canada, the United States, Latin America, Europe, the Middle East, Africa, Asia, and Australia.

Newbridge's stunning growth since its founding in 1986 is in large part due to Terry Matthews and his highly motivated workforce. Matthews started working in the telecommunications field at age 16, when he joined British Telecom in his native Wales. He moved to Canada in 1969 and prior to founding Newbridge was involved in establishing a consulting company and Mitel Corporation. As suggested by the recent move to increase Newbridge's employee stock option plan from 22 million to 25 million shares, Matthews regards a highly motivated workforce as a key element in a corporation's success. His strategy for motivating employees thus involves not only offering financial rewards associated with stock options but also recognizing employees as the cornerstone of corporate success. In keeping with this philosophy, Matthews provides his employees with both relevant feedback and quarterly reports on Newbridge's progress.

References: Jean Pascal Souque and Jacek Warda, "A Winning Formula," *Canadian Business Review,* Summer 1996, pp. 7–13; Shawn McCarthy, "Newbridge Sees Deal Putting It in Majors," *The Globe and Mail,* September, 5, 1997, p. B1; "Estimates of Financial Results for Third Quarter Fiscal 1999" http://www.newbridge.com), February 4, 1999; and "The Top 1000," *Report on Business Magazine,* July 1998, p. 102.

PROCESS PERSPECTIVES ON MOTIVATION

● **process perspectives**
Approaches to motivation that focus on why people choose certain behavioural options to satisfy their needs and how they evaluate their satisfaction after they have attained these goals

Process perspectives are concerned with how motivation occurs. Rather than attempting to identify or list motivational stimuli, **process perspectives** focus on why people choose certain behavioural options to satisfy their needs and how they evaluate their satisfaction after they have attained these goals. Two popular process perspectives on motivation are expectancy theory and equity theory.

Expectancy Theory

● **expectancy theory**
A theory of motivation that suggests that motivation depends on two things—how much we want something and how likely we think we are to get it

The expectancy theory of motivation has many different forms and labels; we describe its most basic form. Essentially, **expectancy theory** suggests that motivation depends on two things—how much we want something and how likely we think we are to get it. Assume that you are approaching graduation and looking for a job. You see in the want ads that the Royal Bank of Canada is seeking a new vice president with a starting salary of $350,000 per year. Even though you might want the job, you will not apply because you realize that you have little chance of getting it. The next ad that you see is for someone to scrape bubble gum from underneath theatre seats for a starting salary of $7 an hour. Even though you could probably get this job, you do not apply because you do not want it. Then you see an ad for a management trainee for a big company with a starting salary of $40,000. You will probably apply for this job because you want it and because you think that you have a reasonable chance of getting it.[17]

The formal expectancy framework was developed by Victor Vroom.[18] Expectancy theory rests on four basic assumptions. First, it assumes that behaviour is determined by a combination of forces in the individual and in the environment. Second, it assumes that people make decisions about their own behaviour in organizations. Third, it assumes that different people have different types of needs, desires, and goals. Fourth, it assumes that people make choices from among alternative plans of behaviour based on their perceptions of the extent to which a given behaviour will lead to desired outcomes.[19]

Figure 16.4 summarizes the basic expectancy model. The model suggests that motivation leads to effort and that effort, combined with employee ability and environmental factors, results in performance. Performance, in turn, leads to various outcomes, each of which has an associated value called its valence. The most important parts of the expectancy model cannot be shown in the figure, however. These are the individual's expectation that effort will lead to high performance, that performance will lead to outcomes, and that each outcome will have some kind of value.

Effort-to-Performance Expectancy The **effort-to-performance expectancy** is the individual's perception of the probability that effort will lead to high performance. When the individual believes that effort will lead directly to high performance, expectancy is quite strong (close to 1.00). When

● **effort-to-performance expectancy**
The individual's perception of the probability that his or her effort will lead to high performance

▬▬▬

The expectancy theory of motivation is a complex but relatively accurate portrayal of how motivation occurs. According to this model, a manager must understand what employees want (such as pay, promotions, or status) to begin to motivate them.

F I G U R E   16.4   The Expectancy Model of Motivation

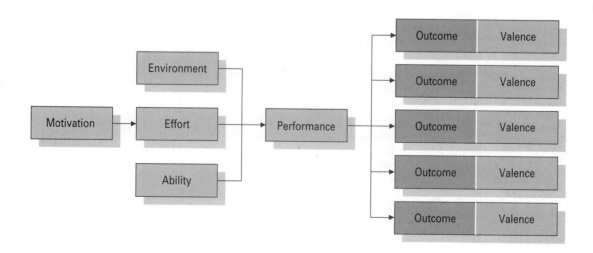

the individual believes that effort and performance are unrelated, the effort-to-performance expectancy is very weak (close to 0). The belief that effort is somewhat but not strongly related to performance carries with it a moderate expectancy (somewhere between 0 and 1).

performance-to-outcome expectancy
The individual's perception that her or his performance will lead to a specific outcome

Performance-to-Outcome Expectancy   The **performance-to-outcome expectancy** is the individual's perception that performance will lead to a specific outcome. For example, if the individual believes that high performance will result in a pay raise, the performance-to-outcome expectancy is high (approaching 1.00). The individual who believes that high performance may lead to a pay raise has a moderate expectancy (between 1.00 and 0). The individual who believes that performance has no relationship with rewards has a low performance-to-outcome expectancy (close to 0).

outcome
A consequence of behaviour in an organizational setting; usually a reward such as a pay raise or fast promotion

valence
An index of how much an individual desires a particular outcome; it is the attractiveness of the outcome to the

Outcomes and Valences   Expectancy theory recognizes that an individual's behaviour results in a variety of **outcomes**, or consequences, in an organizational setting. A high performer, for example, may get bigger pay raises, faster promotions, and more praise from the boss. On the other hand, she may also be subject to more stress and incur resentment from co-workers. Each of these outcomes also has an associated value, or **valence**—an index of how much an individual values a particular outcome. If the individual wants the outcome, its valence is positive; if the individual does not want the outcome, its valence is negative; and if the individual is indifferent to the outcome, its valence is zero.

It is this part of expectancy theory that goes beyond the content perspectives on motivation. Different people have different needs, and they try to satisfy these needs in different ways. For an employee who has a high need for achievement and a low need for affiliation, the pay raise and promotions just cited as outcomes of high performance might have positive valences, the praise and resentment zero valences, and the stress a negative valence. For an employee with a low need for achievement and a high need for affiliation, the pay raise, promotions, and praise might all have positive valences, whereas both resentment and stress could have negative valences.

For motivated behaviour to occur, three conditions must be met. First, the effort-to-performance expectancy must be greater than zero (the individual must believe that if effort is expended, high performance will result). The performance-to-outcome expectancy must also be greater than zero (the individual must believe that high performance will lead to certain outcomes). And the sum of the valences for the outcomes must be greater than zero. (One or more outcomes may have negative valences if they are more than offset by the positive valences of other outcomes. For example, the attractiveness of a pay raise, a promotion, and praise from the boss may outweigh the unattractiveness of more stress and resentment from co-workers.) Expectancy theory suggests that when these conditions are met, the individual is motivated to expend effort.

The Porter-Lawler Extension   An interesting extension of expectancy theory has been proposed by Porter and Lawler.[20] Recall from Chapter 2 that the human relationists assumed that employee satisfaction causes good performance. We also noted that research has not supported such a relationship. Porter and Lawler suggest that there may indeed be a relationship between satisfaction and performance but that it goes in the opposite direction—that is, high performance may lead to high satisfaction. Figure 16.5 summarizes Porter and Lawler's logic. Performance results in rewards for an individual. Some of these are extrinsic (such as pay and promotions); others are intrinsic (such as self-esteem and accomplishment). The individual evaluates the equity, or fairness, of the rewards relative to the effort expended and the level of performance attained. If the rewards are perceived to be equitable, the individual is satisfied.

Implications for Managers   Expectancy theory can be useful for managers who are trying to improve the motivation of their subordinates, and managers can follow a series of steps to implement the basic ideas of the theory. First, figure out the outcomes each employee is likely to want. Second, decide what kinds and levels of performance are needed to meet organizational goals. Then make sure that the desired levels of performance are attainable. Also make sure that desired outcomes and desired performance are linked. Next, analyze the complete situation for conflicting expectancies, and ensure that the rewards are large enough. Finally, make sure that the total system is equitable (fair to all).[21] These issues are explored in more detail later in this chapter when we discuss organizational reward systems.

Of course, expectancy theory has its limitations. Although the theory makes sense and has been generally supported by empirical research, it is quite difficult to apply.[22] To really use the complete theory in the workplace, for example, managers must identify all the potential outcomes for each employee, determine all relevant expectancies, and then balance everything somehow to maximize employee motivation. Nevertheless, it is not difficult to identify human resource management practices that are consistent with expectancy theory. For example, the recognition program of Ressorts Liberté Inc., which is based on the number of hours worked by employee and control of costs over which employees have influence, allows employees to receive cash when they need it most (Christmas, July, and September), rewards employees who work the most hours, and obliges the company to open its books to its employees.[23]

F I G U R E   16.5   The Porter-Lawler Extension of Expectancy Theory

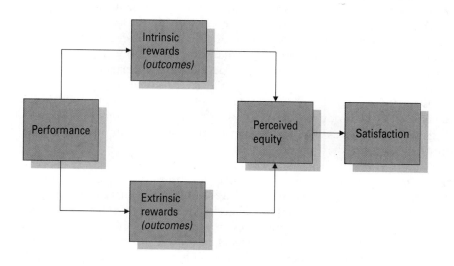

The Porter-Lawler extension of expectancy theory suggests that if performance results in equitable rewards, people will be more satisfied. Thus performance can lead to satisfaction. Managers must therefore be sure that any system of motivation includes rewards that are fair, or equitable, for all.

Source: Edward E. Lawler, III, and Lyman W. Porter, "The Effect of Performance on Job Satisfaction," *Industrial Relations*, October 1967, p. 23. Used with permission of the University of California.

Equity Theory

● **equity theory**
Suggests that people are
motivated to seek social equity
in the rewards they receive for
performance

After needs have stimulated the motivation process and the individual has chosen an action that is expected to satisfy those needs, the individual assesses the fairness, or equity, of the resultant outcome. Much of our current thinking on equity has been shaped by the **equity theory** of motivation developed by J. Stacy Adams. Adams contends that people are motivated to seek social equity in the rewards they receive for performance.[24] Equity is an individual's belief that the treatment he or she is receiving is fair relative to the treatment received by others.

The Equity Comparison Process According to equity theory, outcomes from a job include pay, recognition, promotions, social relationships, and intrinsic rewards. To get these rewards, the individual makes inputs to the job, such as time, experience, effort, education, and loyalty. The theory suggests that people view their outcomes and inputs as a ratio and then compare it to the ratio of someone else. This other "person" may be someone in the work group or some sort of group average or composite. The process of comparison looks like this:

$$\frac{\text{Outcomes (self)}}{\text{Inputs (self)}} \quad \frac{?}{=} \quad \frac{\text{Outcomes (other)}}{\text{Inputs (other)}}$$

Both the formulation of the ratios and comparisons between them are very subjective and are based on individual perceptions. As a result of comparisons, three conditions may result: the individual may feel equitably rewarded, underrewarded, or overrewarded. A feeling of equity will result when the two ratios are equal. This may occur even though the other person's outcomes are greater than the individual's own outcomes—provided that the other's inputs are also proportionately greater. Suppose that Mark has a high-school education and earns only $30,000. He may still feel equitably treated relative to Susan, who earns $40,000, because she has a university degree.

People who feel underrewarded try to reduce the inequity. Such an individual might decrease her inputs by exerting less effort, increase her outcomes by asking for a raise, distort the original ratios by rationalizing, try to get the other person to change her or his outcomes or inputs, leave the situation, or change the object of comparison. An individual may also feel overrewarded relative to another person. This is not likely to be terribly disturbing to most people, but research suggests that some people who experience inequity under these conditions are somewhat motivated to reduce it.[25] Under such a circumstance, the person might increase his inputs by exerting more effort, reduce his outcomes by producing fewer units (if paid on a per unit basis), distort the original ratios by rationalizing, or attempt to reduce the inputs or increase the outcomes of the other person.

Implications for Managers The single most important idea for managers to remember from equity theory is that if rewards are to motivate employees, they must be perceived as being equitable and fair. If a person achieves rewards as a result of performance and regards these rewards as equitable, satisfaction results. A second implication is that managers need to consider the nature of the "other" to whom the employee is comparing herself or himself. In recent years, for example, the number of dual-career couples has increased dramatically, and husband-and-wife equity comparisons have ruined both marriages and careers.[26] On balance, the research support for equity theory is mixed.[27] The concepts of equity and social comparisons are certainly important for the manager to consider, but it is also apparent that managers should not rely only on this framework in attempting to manage employee motivation.

REINFORCEMENT PERSPECTIVES ON MOTIVATION

A third element of the motivational process addresses why some behaviours are maintained over time and why other behaviours change. As we have seen, content perspectives focus on needs, and process perspectives explain why people choose various behaviours to satisfy needs and how they evaluate the equity of the rewards they get for those behaviours. Reinforcement perspectives explain the role of those rewards as they cause behaviour to change or remain the same over time. Specifically, **reinforcement theory** argues that behaviour that results in rewarding consequences is likely to be repeated, whereas behaviour that results in punishing consequences is less likely to be repeated. This approach to explaining behaviour was originally tested on animals, but B.F. Skinner and others have been instrumental in demonstrating how reinforcement theory also applies to human behaviour.[28]

Kinds of Reinforcement in Organizations

In organizational settings, four basic kinds of reinforcement can result from behaviour—positive reinforcement, avoidance, punishment, and extinction.[29] These are summarized in Table 16.1. Two kinds of reinforcement strengthen or maintain behaviour, whereas the other two weaken or decrease behaviour. **Positive reinforcement**, a method of strengthening behaviour, is a reward or a positive outcome after a desired behaviour is performed. When a manager observes an employee doing an especially good job and offers praise, the praise serves to positively reinforce the behaviour of good work. Other positive reinforcers in organizations include pay raises, promotions, and awards. "Employee of the month" recognition awards, common in the retail and service industries, are another example of a positive reinforcer, as is the $27.4 million received by Power Financial's CEO, Robert Gratton, in 1997.[30] The other method of strengthening desired behaviour is through **avoidance**. An employee may come to work on time to avoid a reprimand. In this instance, the employee is motivated to perform the behaviour of punctuality to avoid an unpleasant consequence that is likely to follow tardiness.

Punishment is used by some managers to weaken undesired behaviours. When an employee is loafing, coming to work late, doing poor work, or interfering with the work of others, the manager might resort to reprimands, discipline, or fines. The logic is that the unpleasant consequence will reduce the likelihood that the employee will choose that particular behaviour again. Given the counterproductive side effects of punishment (such as resentment and hostility), using the other kinds of reinforcement if at all possible is often advisable. **Extinction** can also be used to weaken behaviour, especially behaviour that has previously been rewarded. When an employee tells an off-colour joke and the boss laughs, the laughter reinforces the behaviour and the employee may continue to tell off-colour jokes. By simply ignoring this behaviour and not reinforcing it, the boss can cause the behaviour to subside and eventually become "extinct."

Positive reinforcement is a powerful way to strengthen good behaviours. After IBM donated computers to a grade school, students wrote these thank you notes. The notes represent positive reinforcement for the managers at IBM, who are now more likely to make new contributions in the future.

● **reinforcement theory**
An approach to motivation that explains the role of rewards as they cause behaviour to change or remain the same over time

● **positive reinforcement**
A method of strengthening behaviour with rewards or positive outcomes after a desired behaviour is performed

● **avoidance**
Used to strengthen behaviour by avoiding unpleasant consequences that would result if the behaviour were not performed

● **punishment**
Used to weaken undesired behaviours by using negative outcomes or unpleasant consequences when the behaviour is performed

● **extinction**
Used to weaken undesired behaviours by simply ignoring or not reinforcing that behaviour

Providing Reinforcement in Organizations

Not only is the kind of reinforcement important, but so is when or how often it occurs. Various strategies are possible for providing reinforcement, which are also listed in Table 16.1. The **fixed-interval schedule** provides reinforcement at fixed intervals of time, regardless of behaviour. A good example of this schedule is the weekly or monthly paycheque. This method provides the least incentive for good work because employees know that they will be paid regularly regardless of their effort. A **variable-interval schedule** also uses time as the basis for reinforcement, but the time interval varies from one reinforcement to the next. This schedule is appropriate for praise or other rewards based on visits or inspections. When employees do not know when the boss is going to drop by, they tend to maintain a reasonably high level of effort all the time.

A **fixed-ratio schedule** gives reinforcement after a fixed number of behaviours, regardless of the time that elapses between behaviours. This results in an even higher level of effort. Piece-rate pay is an example of a fixed-ratio schedule. The **variable-ratio schedule**, the most powerful schedule in terms of maintaining desired behaviours, varies the number of behaviours needed for each reinforcement. A supervisor who praises an employee for her second order, the seventh order after that, the ninth after that, then the fifth, and then the third is using a variable-ratio schedule. The employee is motivated to increase the frequency of the desired behaviour because each performance increases the probability of receiving a reward. Of course, a variable-ratio schedule is difficult (if not impossible) to use for formal rewards such as pay because keeping track of who was rewarded when would be too complicated.

EMERGING PERSPECTIVES ON MOTIVATION

In addition to the established models and theories of motivation, two promising emerging perspectives are goal-setting theory and the Japanese approach.

Goal-Setting Theory

Goal-setting theory suggests that managers and subordinates should set goals for the individual on a regular basis.[31] These goals should be moderately difficult and very specific. Moreover, they should be of a type that the employee will accept and commit to accomplishing. Rewards should also be tied directly to reaching the goals. Goal-setting theory helps the manager tailor rewards to individual needs, clarify expectancies, maintain equity, and provide systematic reinforcement. Thus it provides a comprehensive framework for integrating the other approaches. As illustrated in Figure 16.6, the goal-setting theory of motivation bears close resemblance to both the basic expectancy theory and the Porter-Lawler extension of expectancy discussed earlier.[32]

The Japanese Approach

Another approach to motivation that has earned increasing popularity is the so-called Japanese approach. This is not really a theory or model but a philosophy of management. In many ways, it extends from the human resource per-

TABLE 16.1 Elements of Reinforcement Theory

Arrangement of the Reinforcement Contingencies

1. **Positive reinforcement.** Strengthens behaviour by providing a desirable consequence.

2. **Avoidance.** Strengthens behaviour by allowing escape from an undesirable consequence.

3. **Punishment.** Weakens behaviour by providing an undesirable consequence.

4. **Extinction.** Weakens behaviour by not providing a desirable consequence.

Schedules for Applying Reinforcement

1. **Fixed interval.** Reinforcement applied at fixed time intervals, regardless of behaviour.

2. **Variable interval.** Reinforcement applied at variable time intervals, regardless of behaviour.

3. **Fixed ratio.** Reinforcement applied after a fixed number of behaviours, regardless of time.

4. **Variable ratio.** Reinforcement applied after a variable number of behaviours, regardless of time.

A manager who wants the best chance of reinforcing a behaviour would likely offer the employee a positive reinforcement after a variable number of behaviours (variable ratio reinforcement). For example, the manager could praise the employee after the third, fourth, sixth, ninth, and so on credit card applications received.

spective. The basic idea underlying the Japanese approach is to bring management and workers together as partners. Historically, in North America the management–worker relationship has ranged from antagonistic to merely indifferent. In Japan, however, managers and workers see themselves as one group, and the result is that everyone is highly committed and motivated. A good example of an organization using the Japanese approach in North America is Domino's Pizza. No one at Domino's is called an employee; instead, employees are said to be team members, team leaders, or coaches. A large percentage of the company's profits is distributed back to workers, all employees own stock, and all employees work together toward Domino's best interests.[33]

Popular Motivational Strategies

Managers trying to enhance the motivation of their employees can adopt specific motivational strategies derived from one or more theories discussed in the previous sections. **Behaviour modification**, or **OB Mod** (for organizational behaviour modification), is a technique for applying the concepts of reinforcement theory in organizational settings.[34] An OB Mod program starts by specifying behaviours that are to be increased (such as producing more units) or decreased (such as coming to work late). These target behaviours are then tied to specific forms or kinds of reinforcement. Although many organizations (such as Procter & Gamble, Warner-Lambert, and Ford Motor Co.) have used OB Mod, the best-known application has been at Emery Air Freight. Management believed that the containers used to consolidate small shipments into fewer, larger shipments were not being packed efficiently. Through a system of self-monitored feedback and rewards, Emery increased container usage from 45 percent to 95 percent and saved more than $3 million (U.S.) during the first three years of the program.[35]

● **behaviour modification (OB Mod**; organizational behaviour modification) A technique for applying the concepts of reinforcement theory in organizational settings

modified workweek
A strategy for increasing motivation by helping individuals satisfy higher-order needs through the use of alternative work schedules

One of the most important emerging theories of motivation is goal-setting theory. This theory suggests that goal difficulty, specificity, acceptance, and commitment combine to determine an individual's goal-directed effort. This effort, when complemented by appropriate organizational support and individual abilities and traits, results in performance. Finally, performance is seen as leading to intrinsic and extrinsic rewards, which, in turn, result in employee satisfaction.

Many organizations also use a **modified workweek** for employees as a strategy for increasing motivation. The modified workweek helps individuals satisfy higher-level needs and provides an opportunity to fulfill several needs simultaneously. One alternative is the *compressed workweek*, whereby people work forty hours in less than the traditional five full workdays. The most common plan has people work ten hours a day for four days. Another popular plan is the *flexible work schedule*. In this approach, employees are required to work during a certain period called core time and can choose what other hours to work. Thus an individual can come in early and leave early, come in late and leave late, or come in early, take a long lunch, and leave late. Allowing employees to work at home or to share jobs with others is also becoming popular. Working at home is especially useful for writers and others using computers. Job sharing allows two persons to work part-time while the organization still gets the benefit of a full-time "worker."[36] Many companies and organizations, including the Royal Bank of Canada, segments of the federal civil service, 3M Canada, the Canadian Imperial Bank of Commerce, and IBM Canada have experimented successfully with one or more of these modifications. By allowing employees some independence in terms of when they come to work and when they leave, managers acknowledge and show "esteem" for the employees' ability to exercise self-control.

Changing the nature of the task-related activities of work is also being used more and more as a motivational technique. The idea is that managers can use any of the alternatives to job specialization described in Chapter 10 as a motivational tool. More precisely, job rotation, job enlargement, job enrichment, the job characteristics approach, and autonomous work groups can all be used as part of a motivational program. A number of studies have shown that improvements in the design of work do often result in higher levels of motivation. One study at Texas Instruments, for example, found that job design resulted in decreased turnover and improved employee motivation.[37]

F I G U R E   16.6   The Expanded Goal-Setting Theory of Motivation

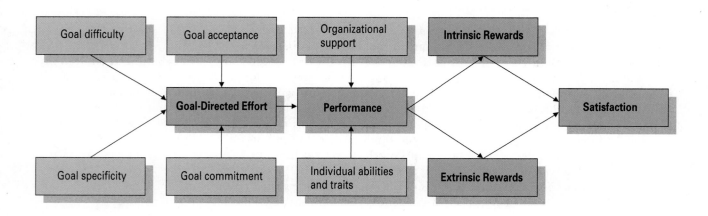

Finally, many organizations today are using empowerment and participation to boost motivation. The basic idea is that by giving workers more power and allowing them to participate more fully, they are able to pursue various needs that are important to them as individuals. Likewise, the actual activities themselves also facilitate the process of motivation. And achieving valued rewards as a result of contributing to the organization provides positive reinforcement. The *Managing in a Changing World* box discusses empowerment as a motivational innovation.

USING REWARD SYSTEMS TO MOTIVATE PERFORMANCE

Aside from these types of strategies, an organization's reward system is its most basic tool for managing employee motivation. An organizational **reward system** is the formal and informal mechanisms by which employee performance is defined, evaluated, and rewarded.

● **reward system**
The formal and informal mechanisms by which employee performance is defined, evaluated, and rewarded

Effects of Organizational Rewards

Organizational rewards can affect attitudes, behaviours, and motivation. Thus managers must clearly understand and appreciate their importance.

Effect of Rewards on Attitudes   Although employee attitudes such as satisfaction are not a major determinant of job performance, they are nonetheless important. They contribute to (or discourage) absenteeism and affect turnover,

---

M A N A G I N G   I N   A   C H A N G I N G   W O R L D

To Empower or Not to Empower—That Is the Question

Empowerment is a major motivational innovation being used by many organizations today. Its proponents argue that effective empowerment can result in a workforce that is more highly motivated and does higher-quality work than less empowered workers. And advocates urge all companies—big or small—to embrace empowerment and what it represents. Some advocates even suggest that empowerment is the only motivational strategy that makes sense in today's business world.

However, as it turns out, empowerment isn't for everyone. Indeed, a significant number of employees seem to prefer to put in their eight hours a day, have someone else make all the decisions, and simply draw their paycheque and go home. Some of these individuals don't want to work in the group or team context that almost always accompanies empowerment. Others don't want the accountability that usually goes with empowerment. And still others simply value other things more highly than having a voice in how they work.

Hence, in reality managers need to carefully assess the nature of their organization and the nature of their workforce. Empowerment can indeed work wonders—in the right settings. But trying to force empowerment into organizations where it doesn't fit or onto workers who don't want it can backfire. And backfiring empowerment can badly burn an unsuspecting organization!

References: "Not All Workers Find Empowerment as Neat as It Sounds," *The Wall Street Journal*, September 8, 1997, pp. A1, A13; and Robert E. Quinn and Gretchen M. Spreitzer, "The Road to Empowerment: Seven Questions Every Leader Should Consider," *Organizational Dynamics*, Autumn 1997, pp. 37–46.

and they help establish the culture of the organization. We can draw four major generalizations about employee attitudes and rewards.[38] First, employee satisfaction is influenced by how much is received and how much the individual thinks should be received. Second, employee satisfaction is affected by comparisons with what happens to others. Third, employees often misperceive the rewards of others. When an employee believes that someone else is making more money than that person really makes, the potential for dissatisfaction increases. Fourth, overall job satisfaction is affected by how satisfied employees are with both the extrinsic and intrinsic rewards they derive from their jobs. Drawing from the content theories and expectancy theory, this conclusion suggests that a variety of needs may cause behaviour and that behaviour may be channelled toward a variety of goals.

Effect of Rewards on Behaviours   An organization's primary purpose in giving rewards is to influence employee behaviour. Extrinsic rewards affect employee satisfaction, which, in turn, plays a major role in determining whether an employee remains on the job or seeks a new job. Reward systems also influence patterns of attendance and absenteeism; if rewards are based on actual performance, employees tend to work harder to earn those rewards.

Effect of Rewards on Motivation   Reward systems are clearly related to the expectancy theory of motivation. The effort-to-performance expectancy is strongly influenced by the performance appraisal that is often a part of the reward system. An employee is likely to put forth extra effort if he or she knows that performance will be measured, evaluated, and rewarded. The performance-to-outcome expectancy is affected by the extent to which the employee believes that performance will be followed by rewards. Finally, as expectancy theory predicts, each reward or potential reward has a somewhat different value for each individual. One person may want a promotion more than benefits; someone else may want just the opposite.

Designing Effective Reward Systems

What are the elements of an effective reward system? Experts agree that they have four major characteristics.[39] First, the reward system must meet the needs of the individual for basic necessities. These needs include the physiological and security needs identified by Maslow and Alderfer and the hygiene factors identified by Herzberg. Next, the rewards should compare favourably with those offered by other organizations. Unfavourable comparisons with people in other settings could result in feelings of inequity. Third, the distribution of rewards within the organization must be equitable. When some employees feel underpaid compared with others in the organization, the probable results are low morale and poor performance. (People are more likely to compare their situation with that of others in their own organization than with that of outsiders.) Fourth, the reward system must recognize that different people have different needs and choose different paths to satisfy those needs. Both content theories and expectancy theory contribute to this conclusion. Insofar as possible, a variety of rewards and a variety of methods for achieving them should be made available to employees.

New Approaches to Rewarding Employees

Organizational reward systems have traditionally been one of two kinds: a fixed hourly or monthly rate or an incentive system. Fixed-rate systems are familiar to most people. Hourly employees are paid a specific wage (based on job demands, experience, or other factors) for each hour they work. Salaried employees receive a fixed sum of money weekly or monthly. Although some reductions may be made for absences, the amount is usually the same regardless of whether the individual works less than or more than a normal amount of time.[40]

From a motivational perspective, such rewards can be tied more directly to performance through merit pay raises. A **merit system** is a reward system in which people get different pay raises at the end of the year, depending on their overall job performance.[41] When the organization's performance appraisal system is appropriately designed, merit pay is a good system for maintaining long-term performance. Increasingly, however, organizations are experimenting with various kinds of incentive systems. **Incentive systems** attempt to reward employees in proportion to what they do. A piece-rate pay plan is a good example of an incentive system. In a factory manufacturing luggage, for example, each worker may be paid 75 cents for each handle and set of locks installed on a piece of luggage. Hence, there is incentive for the employee to work hard: the more units produced, the higher the pay. Four increasingly popular incentive systems are profit sharing, gain sharing, lump-sum bonuses, and pay for knowledge.[42]

Profit sharing provides a varying annual bonus to employees based on corporate profits. This system unites workers and management toward the same goal—higher profits. Deciding how to allocate the profits, however, can result in equity problems. Ford, MacMillan Bloedel, and Dofasco all have had profit-sharing plans. Gain sharing is a group-based incentive system in which group members all get bonuses when predetermined performance levels are exceeded. Although this system can facilitate teamwork and trust, it may focus workers too narrowly on attaining the specific goals needed for the bonus while neglecting other parts of their jobs.

Another innovative method for rewarding employees is the lump-sum bonus. This method gives each employee a one-time cash bonus, rather than a base salary increase. The organization can control its fixed costs by not increasing base salaries; however, employees sometimes feel resentful that future bonuses are contingent on future performance. Lake Ontario Steel, Pillsbury Canada, and Boeing have successfully used this approach. Finally, pay-for-knowledge systems focus on paying the individual rather than the job. Under a traditional arrangement, two workers doing the same job are paid the same rate regardless of their skills. Under the new arrangement, people advance in pay grade for each new skill or set of skills they learn. This approach increases training costs but also results in a more highly skilled workforce. Schoolteachers in Canada often receive higher pay for increased training.

- **merit system**
  A reward system in which people get different pay raises at the end of the year depending on their overall job performance

- **incentive system**
  A reward system whereby people get different pay amounts at each pay period in proportion to what they do

SUMMARY OF KEY POINTS

Motivation is the set of forces that cause people to behave in certain ways. Motivation is an important consideration of managers because it, along with ability and environmental factors, determines individual performance. Thinking about motivation has evolved from the traditional view through the human relations approach to the human resource view.

Content perspectives on motivation are concerned with what factor or factors cause motivation. Popular content theories include Maslow's need hierarchy, the ERG theory, and Herzberg's two-factor theory. Other important needs are the needs for achievement, affiliation, and power.

Process perspectives on motivation deal with how motivation occurs. Expectancy theory suggests that people are motivated to perform if they believe that their effort will result in high performance, that this performance will lead to rewards, and that the positive aspects of the outcomes outweigh the negative aspects. Equity theory is based on the premise that people are motivated to achieve and maintain social equity.

The reinforcement perspective focuses on how motivation is maintained. Its basic assumption is that behaviour that results in rewarding consequences is likely to be repeated, whereas behaviour resulting in negative consequences is less likely to be repeated. Reinforcement contingencies can be arranged in the form of positive reinforcement, avoidance, punishment, and extinction, and they can be provided on fixed-interval, variable-interval, fixed-ratio, or variable-ratio schedules.

Two newly emerging approaches to employee motivation are goal-setting theory and the Japanese approach. Managers often adopt behaviour modification, modified workweeks, work redesign, and participation programs to enhance motivation.

Organizational reward systems are the primary mechanisms managers have for managing motivation. Properly designed systems can improve attitudes, behaviours, and motivation. Effective reward systems must provide sufficient rewards on an equitable basis at the individual level. Contemporary reward systems include merit systems and various kinds of incentive systems.

DISCUSSION QUESTIONS

Questions for Review

1. What are the basic historical perspectives on motivation?
2. Compare and contrast content, process, and reinforcement perspectives on motivation.
3. In what ways are the emerging perspectives on motivation like the content, process, and reinforcement perspectives? In what ways are they different?
4. What are the similarities and differences among the motivational strategies described in this chapter?

Questions for Analysis

5. Compare and contrast the different content theories. Can you think of any ways in which the theories are contradictory?
6. Expectancy theory seems to make a great deal of sense, but it is complicated. Some people argue that its complexity reduces its value to practising managers. Do you agree or disagree?
7. Offer examples other than those from this chapter to illustrate positive reinforcement, avoidance, punishment, and extinction.

Questions for Application

8. Think about the worst job you have held. What approach to motivation was used in that organization? Now think about the best job you have held.

What approach to motivation was used there? Can you base any conclusions on this limited information? If so, what?

9. Interview both managers and workers (or administrators and faculty) from a local organization. What views of or approaches to motivation seem to be in use in that organization?

10. Can you locate any local organizations that have implemented or are implementing any of the motivational strategies discussed in this chapter? If so, interview a manager and a worker to obtain their views on the program.

BUILDING EFFECTIVE INTERPERSONAL SKILLS

Exercise Overview

Interpersonal skills—the ability to understand and motivate individuals and groups—are especially critical when managers attempt to deal with issues associated with equity and justice in the workplace. This exercise will provide you with insights into how these skills may be used.

Exercise Background

You are the manager of a group of professional employees in the electronics industry. One of your employees, David Brown, has asked to meet with you. You think you know what David wants to discuss, and you are unsure how to proceed.

You hired David about ten years ago. During his time in your group he has been a solid, but not outstanding, employee. His performance, for example, has been satisfactory in every respect, but seldom outstanding. As a result, he has consistently received average performance evaluations, pay increases, and so forth. Indeed, he actually makes somewhat less today than do a couple of people with less tenure in the group but with stronger performance records.

The company has just announced an opening for a team leader position in your group, and you know that David wants the job. He feels that he has earned the opportunity to have the job on the basis of his consistent efforts. Unfortunately, you see things a bit differently. You really want to appoint another individual, Becky Thomas, to the job. Becky has worked for the firm for only six years but is your top performer. You want to reward her performance and think that she will do an excellent job. On the other hand, you do not want to lose David because he is a solid member of the group.

Exercise Task

Using the information above, respond to the following:

1. Using equity theory as a framework, how are David and Becky likely to see the situation?

2. Outline a conversation with David in which you tell him that you are offering the job to Becky.

3. What advice might you offer Becky, in her new job, about interacting with David?

4. What other rewards might you offer David to keep him motivated?

Motivational Challenges in Saudi Arabia

Changing the work-related needs, motives, and values of an individual in an organization is, on its own merits, a daunting challenge. Consider, then, the difficulties inherent in trying to change the needs, motives, and values of an entire population. This is exactly the task being confronted by businesses in Saudi Arabia. For decades Saudi Arabia relied heavily on so-called guest workers to perform most of its menial and service-oriented jobs. People from Pakistan, Egypt, and the Philippines, for example, could easily enter Saudi Arabia and find steady work performing jobs that were unattractive to locals. And companies in Saudi Arabia took advantage of this situation by routinely hiring these guest workers for less attractive jobs and paying them relatively low wages. Most guest workers found jobs in restaurants, as security guards, as custodians and maintenance people, and as package couriers.

Recently, however, the government of Saudi Arabia has changed its liberal guest-worker policy. For one thing, a huge baby boom of Saudis is now reaching employment age and there aren't enough jobs to go around. For another, the government, a large employer itself, is in the midst of downsizing and has fewer jobs to offer citizens. Officials are now taking a much harder stance regarding guest workers. For example, few new guest workers are being admitted. And as current workers' visas expire, they are not being renewed, forcing those workers to leave the country. One new law bans foreign workers from owning cars. In some cities in Saudi Arabia, authorities can automatically close down a retail store if someone other than a Saudi national is working behind the counter. And the government has ordered all companies to increase their native workforce by 5 percent each year.

A problem, however, arises from the prevailing work ethic reflected by the following quotation from a Saudi worker fired for coming to work late: "If I'm supposed to be here at 8 and I come in at 9, why can't I stay until 3:30 instead of 2:30?" Because most

Saudi workers have grown up in a privileged setting and have had autonomy over where and when they worked, they have trouble adjusting to more regimented and routine work situations. While progress is being made in some companies, others still face major motivational challenges. For example, McDonald's is having a difficult time attracting enough qualified Saudis to hold management positions in its restaurants. Most Saudis consider restaurant work demeaning, regardless of the actual position held.

And even though many workers are trying, they still have trouble adjusting to a traditional work environment. For example, when beginning higher-level business dealings in Saudi Arabia, managers typically spend a considerable amount of time exchanging information and asking questions about one another's families. Many young Saudis who are working in lower-level positions now still adhere to this practice; they may trade as many as a dozen pleasantries before getting down to business. And they are also prone to showing unfailing hospitality to visitors. Although this approach is desirable in some situations, in others it can be counterproductive. For example, Saudi workers have been known to walk off their job at a busy airline counter to have tea with a friend who has strolled up—Saudis consider it rude to not be sociable with visitors, regardless of the circumstances.

Questions

1. What motivational theories and techniques would you apply in the Saudi situation?

2. Would you consider taking a job in Saudi Arabia after graduation? Why or why not?

3. What needs and values of Saudi workers are illustrated in this case?

References: "Certain Work Is Foreign to Saudis, but That's Changing," *The Wall Street Journal*, September 12, 1996, pp. A1, A4; and Ricky W. Griffin and Michael W. Pustay, *International Business: A Managerial Perspective*, 2nd ed., Chapter 14 (Reading, Mass.: Addison–Wesley), 1999.

CHAPTER NOTES

1. Janet McFarland, "Canadian Workers Rank High in Happiness," *The Globe and Mail*, September 5, 1996, p. B13; Margot Gibb-Clark, "Canadian Workers Satisfied but Anxious," *The Globe and Mail,* October 8, 1996, p. B13; Darcy Henton, "When Motivation Crosses the Cult Line," *The Toronto Star*, June 14, 1996, p. A23; Judith Dobrzynski, "Sears Goes to the Circus to Motivate Employees," *The Globe and Mail,* January 10, 1996, p. B16; and Catherine Romano, "Innovation for Motivation," *Management Review*, March 1996, p. 6.

2. Richard M. Steers and Lyman W. Porter, *Motivation and Work Behavior*, 5th ed. (New York: McGraw-Hill, 1991).

3. Roland Kidwell and Nathan Bennett, "Employee Propensity to Withhold Effort: A Conceptual Model to Intersect Three Avenues of Research," *Academy of Management Review*, Vol. 18, No. 3, 1993, pp. 429–456.

4. Jeremiah J. Sullivan, "Three Roles of Language in Motivation Theory," *Academy of Management Review*, January 1988, pp. 104–115.

5. Frederick W. Taylor, *Principles of Scientific Management* (New York: Harper and Brothers, 1911).

6. Elton Mayo, *The Social Problems of an Industrial Civilization* (Boston: Harvard University Press, 1945); and Fritz J. Rothlisberger and W.J. Dickson, *Management and the Worker* (Boston: Harvard University Press, 1939).

7. See John Miner, Donald Crane, and Robert Vandenberg, "Congruence and Fit in Professional Role Motivation Theory," *Organization Science*, February 1994, pp. 86–98, for an example.

8. Abraham H. Maslow, "A Theory of Human Motivation," *Psychological Review*, Vol. 50, 1943, pp. 370–396; and Abraham H. Maslow, *Motivation and Personality* (New York: Harper & Row, 1954).

9. For a review, see Craig Pinder, *Work Motivation* (Glenview, Ill.: Scott, Foresman, 1984). See also Steers and Porter, *Motivation and Work Behavior*.

10. Clayton P. Alderfer, *Existence, Relatedness, and Growth* (New York: Free Press, 1972).

11. For an example, see Clayton P. Alderfer, "An Empirical Test of a New Theory of Human Needs," *Organizational Behavior and Human Performance*, April 1969, pp. 142–175. See also Pinder, *Work Motivation*.

12. Frederick Herzberg, Bernard Mausner, and Barbara Snyderman, *The Motivation to Work* (New York: Wiley, 1959); and Frederick Herzberg, "One More Time: How Do You Motivate Employees?" *Harvard Business Review*, January–February 1987, pp. 109–120.

13. Robert J. House and Lawrence A. Wigdor, "Herzberg's Dual-Factor Theory of Job Satisfaction and Motivation: A Review of the Evidence and a Criticism," *Personnel Psychology*, Winter 1967, pp. 369–389; and Victor H. Vroom, *Work and Motivation* (New York: Wiley, 1964). See also Pinder, *Work Motivation*.

14. David C. McClelland, *The Achieving Society* (Princeton, N.J.: Van Nostrand, 1961); and David C. McClelland, *Power: The Inner Experience* (New York: Irvington, 1975).

15. E. Cornelius and F. Lane, "The Power Motive and Managerial Success in a Professionally Oriented Service Company," *Journal of Applied Psychology*, January 1984, pp. 32–40.

16. David McClelland and David H. Burnham, "Power Is the Great Motivator," *Harvard Business Review*, March–April 1976, pp. 100–110.

17. See Michael Woika, "Pay Plan Based on Performance Motivates Employees," *HRMagazine*, December 1993, pp. 75–82, for an illustration.

18. Victor H. Vroom, *Work and Motivation* (New York: Wiley, 1964).

19. David A. Nadler and Edward E. Lawler III, "Motivation: A Diagnostic Approach," in J. Richard Hackman, Edward E. Lawler, and Lyman W. Porter (Eds.), *Perspectives on Behavior in Organizations*, 2nd ed. (New York: McGraw-Hill, 1983), pp. 67–78.

20. Lyman W. Porter and Edward E. Lawler III, *Managerial Attitudes and Performance* (Homewood, Ill.: Dorsey Press, 1968).

21. Nadler and Lawler, "Motivation: A Diagnostic Approach."

22. Terrence Mitchell, "Expectancy Models of Job Satisfaction, Occupation Preference, and Effort: A Theoretical, Methodological, and Empirical Appraisal," *Psychological Bulletin*, December 1974, pp. 1053–1077; and John P. Wanous, Thomas L. Keon, and Jania C. Latack, "Expectancy Theory and Occupational/Organizational Choices: A Review and Test," *Organizational Behavior and Human Performance*, August 1983, pp. 66–86. For recent findings, see also Lynn E. Miller and Joseph E. Grush, "Improving Predictions in Expectancy Theory Research: Effects of Personality, Expectancies, and Norms," *Academy of Management Journal*, March 1988, pp. 107–122.

23. *Motivating Personnel: A Condition Essential to Business Growth* (Montreal: Federal Office of Regional Development, December 1995).

24. J. Stacy Adams, "Towards an Understanding of Inequity," *Journal of Abnormal and Social Psychology*, November 1963, pp. 422–436; and Richard T. Mowday, "Equity Theory Predictions of Behavior in Organizations," in Steers and Porter, *Motivation and Work Behavior*, pp. 91–113.

25. For a review, see Paul S. Goodman and Abraham Fiedman, "An Examination of Adam's Theory of Inequity," *Administrative Science Quarterly*, September 1971, pp. 271–288.

26. "Pay Problems: How Couples React When Wives Out-Earn Husbands," *The Wall Street Journal*, June 19, 1987, p. 19.

27. Richard A. Cosier and Dan R. Dalton, "Equity Theory and Time: A Reformulation," *Academy of Management Review*, April 1983, pp. 311–319; and Richard C.

Huseman, John D. Hatfield, and Edward W. Miles, "A New Perspective on Equity Theory: The Equity Sensitivity Construct," *Academy of Management Review*, April 1987, pp. 222–234.

28. B.F. Skinner, *Beyond Freedom and Dignity* (New York: Knopf, 1971).

29. Fred Luthans and Robert Kreitner, *Organizational Behavior Modification and Beyond: An Operant and Social Learning Approach* (Glenview, Ill.: Scott, Foresman, 1985).

30. "50 Best-Paid CEOs," *Report on Business Magazine*, July 1998, p. 87.

31. Edwin Locke, "Toward a Theory of Task Performance and Incentives," *Organizational Behavior and Human Performance*, Vol. 3, 1968, pp. 157–189.

32. For recent developments, see Mark E. Tubbs and Steven E. Ekeberg, "The Role of Intentions in Work Motivation: Implications for Goal-Setting Theory and Research," *Academy of Management Review*, January 1991, pp. 180–199.

33. "When Are Employees Not Employees? When They're Associates, Stakeholders …," *The Wall Street Journal*, November 9, 1988, p. B1.

34. Luthans and Kreitner, *Organizational Behaviour Modification and Beyond*; and W. Clay Hamner and Ellen P. Hamner,

"Behavior Modification on the Bottom Line," *Organizational Dynamics*, Spring 1976, pp. 2–21.

35. "At Emery Air Freight: Positive Reinforcement Boosts Performance," *Organizational Dynamics*, Winter 1973, pp. 41–50.

36. Allan R. Cohen and Herman Gadon, *Alternative Work Schedules: Integrating Individual and Organizational Needs* (Reading, Mass.: Addison-Wesley, 1978).

37. Earl D. Weed, "Job Environment 'Cleans Up' at Texas Instruments," in J.R. Maher (Ed.), *New Perspectives in Job Enrichment* (New York: Van Nostrand, 1971), pp. 55–77.

38. Edward E. Lawler III, *Pay and Organizational Development* (Reading, Mass.: Addison-Wesley, 1981). See also Edward E. Lawler III, *Pay and Organizational Effectiveness: A Psychological View* (New York: McGraw-Hill, 1971).

39. Lawler, *Pay and Organizational Development*.

40. Bill Leonard, "New Ways to Pay Employees," *HRMagazine*, February 1994, pp. 61–69.

41. "Grading 'Merit Pay,'" *Newsweek*, November 14, 1988, pp. 45–46; and Frederick S. Hills, K. Dow Scott, Steven E. Markham, and Michael J. Vest, "Merit Pay: Just or Unjust Desserts," *Personnel Administrator*, September 1987, pp. 53–59.

42. Nancy J. Perry, "Here Come Richer, Riskier Pay Plans," *Fortune*, December 19, 1988, pp. 50–58.

Leadership and Influence Processes

17

OBJECTIVES

After studying this chapter, you should be able to:

● *Describe the nature of leadership and distinguish leadership from management.*

● *Discuss and evaluate the trait approach to leadership.*

● *Discuss and evaluate models of leadership focusing on behaviours.*

● *Identify and describe the major situational approaches to leadership.*

● *Identify and describe three related perspectives on leadership.*

● *Discuss political behaviour in organizations and how it can be managed.*

OUTLINE

ATCO CEO Ron Southern has used his strong leadership skills to turn around the company's fortunes.

The history of ATCO Ltd. reveals strong, determined, and positive leadership. With assets of over $4.4 billion and annual revenues of approximately $2 billion, ATCO is one of Canada's largest companies. Based in Calgary, the company ships mobile housing units to seventy-five countries; sells natural gas, electricity, and water through subsidiary Canadian Utilities Ltd.; and markets management and technical services with its third major arm, Frontec Corp.

ATCO was built from scratch after Ron Southern, the company's CEO and chairman, and his father, Donald, a Calgary fireman, bought some rental trailers for $2,000 in 1947. For a while, they rented out vacation trailers pur-chased in California, but by the 1950s they were building units to suit Canada's climate and tough conditions in work camps. They have since pio-neered the manufacture of camps for the Arctic and Antarctic, the deserts of the Middle East and

> **"The History of ATCO Ltd. reveals strong, determined, and positive leadershop."**

Asia, and, more recently, the war zone in Bosnia. As the company's core relocatable housing business grew, ATCO expanded into other businesses, including electric power, natural gas, and management services.

After earning a B.Sc. from the University of Alberta, Ron Southern rejoined the business, Alberta Trailer Hire Ltd. He became president in the 1950s and has since developed a reputation as a charismatic and determined leader. The negotiations sur-rounding one of ATCO's international ventures, a $1.4 billion power plant in London, England, illustrates Ron Southern's gritty character. After agreeing to sell ATCO nat-ural gas at 16 pence per British thermal unit, British Gas PLC unexpectedly raised the price to 24 pence. As the deal began to turn sour, Southern flew to London to meet with the chair of British Gas. With no appointment, he arrived in the lobby of the British Gas building at 6:00 A.M., only to find out that the executive was miles away. Southern rented a helicopter and camped out in the lobby of the chair's hotel until after midnight when the meeting finally took place. Two weeks later, British Gas said it would honour the original contract.

Many company officials and analysts cite Southern's ability to get people to work, his ability to see opportunities, and his resolve to see a plan through as some of his more outstanding leadership attributes. These characteristics were highlighted in 1984, when the company recorded its first loss.

Setting a profit goal of $5 million for the following year, he demanded that each manager review operations line by line and come up with a plan. He decreed that management meetings would be held every month, with all managers having monthly goals and reporting their progress. This exercise, which went on for thirty-three months, seems to have fulfilled its purpose. When ATCO reported its results in 1985, earnings came in at $11 million, more than double the goal set by Southern. Today, ATCO remains a profitable company. In recognition of his achievements, the Financial Post named Ron Southern its 1996 CEO of the year.[1] ●

Ron Southern has a relatively rare combination of skills that sets him apart from many others: he is both an astute leader and a fine manager, and he recognizes many of the challenges necessary to play both roles. He knows when to make tough decisions, when to lead and encourage his employees, and when to stand back and let them do their jobs. And thus far, ATCO is reaping big payoffs from his efforts.

This chapter examines people like Southern in detail by focusing on leadership and its role in management. We characterize the nature of leadership and trace through the three major approaches to studying leadership—traits, behaviours, and situations. After examining other perspectives on leadership, we conclude by describing another approach to influencing others—political behaviour in organizations.

THE NATURE OF LEADERSHIP

In Chapter 16, we described various models and perspectives on employee motivation. From the manager's standpoint, trying to motivate people is an attempt to influence their behaviour. In many ways, leadership too is an attempt to influence the behaviour of others. In this section, we first define leadership, then differentiate it from management, and conclude by relating it to power.

The Meaning of Leadership

- **leadership**
As a process, the use of noncoercive influence to shape the group's or organization's goals, motivate behaviour toward the achievement of those goals, and help define group or organization culture; as a property, the set of characteristics attributed to individuals who are perceived to be leaders

Leadership is both a process and a property.[2] As a process—what leaders actually do—leadership is the use of noncoercive influence to shape the group's or organization's goals, motivate behaviour toward the achievement of those goals, and help define group or organization culture.[3] As a property, leadership is the set of characteristics attributed to individuals who are perceived to be leaders. Thus **leaders** are people who can influence the behaviours of others without having to rely on force; leaders are people whom others accept as leaders.[4]

- **leader**
A person who can influence the behaviours of others without having to rely on force; a person accepted by others as a leader

Leadership versus Management

From these definitions, we can see that leadership and management are clearly related, but they are not the same. A person can be a manager, a leader, both, or neither.[5] Some of the basic distinctions between the two are summarized in Table 17.1. At the left side of the table are four elements that differentiate leadership from management. The two columns show how each element differs when considered from a management and a leadership point of view. For example, when executing plans, managers focus on monitoring results, comparing them with goals, and correcting deviations. In contrast, the leader focuses on energizing people to overcome bureaucratic hurdles to help reach goals. Thus when Ron Southern monitors the performance of his employees he is playing the role of manager. But when he inspires them to work harder at achieving their goals, he is a leader.

Organizations need both management and leadership if they are to be effective. Leadership is necessary to create change, and management is necessary to achieve orderly results. Management in conjunction with leadership can produce orderly change, and leadership in conjunction with management can keep the organization properly aligned with its environment. The *Environment of*

TABLE 17.1 Distinctions Between Management and Leadership

Activity	Management	Leadership
Creating an agenda	**Planning and budgeting.** Establishing detailed steps and timetables for achieving needed results; allocating the resources necessary to make those needed results happen	**Establishing direction.** Developing a vision of the future, often the distant future, and strategies for producing the changes needed to achieve that vision
Developing a human network for achieving the agenda	**Organizing and staffing.** Establishing some structure for accomplishing plan requirements, staffing that structure with individuals, delegating responsibility and authority for carrying out the plan, providing policies and procedures to help guide people, and creating methods or systems to monitor implementation	**Aligning people.** Communicating the direction by words and deeds to all those whose cooperation may be needed to influence the creation of teams and coalitions that understand the vision and strategies and accept their validity
Executing plans	**Controlling and problem solving.** Monitoring results vs. plan in some detail, identifying deviations, and then planning and organizing to solve these problems	**Motivating and inspiring.** Energizing people to overcome major political, bureaucratic, and resource barriers to change by satisfying very basic, but often unfulfilled, human needs
Outcomes	Produces a degree of predictability and order and has the potential to consistently produce major results expected by various stakeholders (e.g., for customers, always being on time; for shareholders, being on budget)	Produces change, often to a dramatic degree, and has the potential to produce extremely useful change (e.g., new products that customers want, new approaches to labour relations that help make a firm more competitive)

Management box describes some of the self-awareness issues that leaders can use to better understand their own approaches to management and to leadership.

Power and Leadership

To fully understand leadership, it is necessary to understand power. **Power** is the ability to affect the behaviour of others. One can have power without actually using it.[6] For example, a football coach has the power to bench a player who is not performing up to par. The coach seldom has to use this power because players recognize that the power exists and work hard to keep their starting positions. In organizational settings, there are usually five kinds of power: legitimate, reward, coercive, referent, and expert power.[7]

Legitimate Power　**Legitimate power** is power granted through the organizational hierarchy; it is the power accorded people occupying a particular position as defined by the organization. A manager can assign a subordinate tasks, and a subordinate who refuses to do them can be reprimanded or even fired. Such outcomes stem from the manager's legitimate power as defined and

Although management and leadership are related, they are also distinct constructs. Managers and leaders differ in how they go about creating an agenda, developing a rationale for achieving the agenda, executing plans, and in the types of outcomes they achieve.

● **power**
The ability to affect the behaviour of others

● **legitimate power**
Power granted through the organizational hierarchy; it is the power defined by the organization that is to be accorded people occupying particular positions

Learning About Yourself

Family businesses in particular seem to have problems developing leaders. In those businesses, a great deal of attention typically is paid to who will succeed to top positions without necessarily ensuring that those who will succeed have the proper leadership skills. Successors need to be self-confident; they need to be able to integrate individual goals into a larger group mission; and they must understand how to overcome resistance to change. In addition, being sensitive to others and their responses and developing self-awareness through introspection have been identified as two very important skills for successors to top positions in such family businesses. Those latter skills, however, are also emerging as leadership skills useful in any and all situations.

Many business schools are stressing the development of self-awareness. Corporations are including aspects of training in these skills in their executive education programs. In most instances, introspection, reflection, and meditation are being used as the devices or approaches for acquiring self-awareness and sensitivity to others. Self-awareness and sensitivity to others are especially critical skills in highly turbulent times when organizations are frequently changing and individuals are moved around in or even laid off from those organizations. Leaders who become self-reflective realize that they do not have all the solutions, which makes it easier for them to empower others to help the organization realize its objectives.

In trying to become self-aware, strive to be objective. Listen to the views of everyone around you and do not assume that they are biased or "out to get you." Next, try to learn from what you hear and how you respond to it. Learn to avoid the wrong way of doing things and interacting with people. Use that learning then to build your self-confidence so that you do more things right and fewer things wrong. As you become more self-confident, you should find accepting personal responsibility for your actions and their consequences easier. You should also become more tolerant of the uncertainty and ambiguity that go with change in turbulent, competitive environments. This, then, will enable you to find taking action and getting things done easier.

Introspective leaders seem to have a better balance in their lives—a balance between work and family and between self and job that enables them to handle the competing stresses associated with high-performance organizations in a competitive world.

References: Stratford Sherman, "Leaders Learn to Heed the Voice Within," *Fortune*, August 22, 1994, pp. 92–100; Clay Carr, "Empowered Organizations, Empowering Leaders," *Training and Development*, March 1994, pp. 39–44; John L. Ward and Craig E. Aronoff, "Preparing Successors to Be Leaders," *Nation's Business*, April 1994, pp. 54–55; and James F. Bolt, "Achieving the CEO's Agenda: Education for Executives," *Management Review*, May 1993, pp. 44–48.

vested in her or him by the organization. Legitimate power then is authority. All managers have legitimate power over their subordinates. The mere possession of legitimate power, however, does not by itself make someone a leader. Some subordinates only follow orders that are strictly within the letter of organizational rules and policies. If asked to do something not in their job description, they refuse or do a poor job. The manager of such employees is exercising authority but not leadership.[8]

● **reward power**
The power to give or withhold rewards, such as salary increases, bonuses, promotions, praise, recognition, and interesting job assignments

Reward Power **Reward power** is the power to give or withhold rewards. Rewards that a manager may control include salary increases, bonuses, promotion recommendations, praise, recognition, and interesting job assignments. In general, the greater the number of rewards a manager controls and the more important the rewards are to subordinates, the greater is the manager's reward power. If the subordinate sees as valuable only the formal organizational rewards provided by the manager, then the manager is not a leader. If the subordinate

Power plays a fundamental role in leadership. Conrad Black is chair of Hollinger Inc., an international newspaper and publishing company. He is shown here speaking at an annual shareholders meeting in 1998.

also wants and appreciates the manager's informal rewards like praise, gratitude, and recognition, however, then the manager is also exercising leadership.

Coercive Power   **Coercive power** is the power to force compliance by means of psychological, emotional, or physical threat. In the past, physical coercion in organizations was relatively common. In most organizations today, however, coercion is limited to verbal reprimands, written reprimands, disciplinary layoffs, fines, demotion, and termination. Some managers occasionally go so far as to use verbal abuse, humiliation, and psychological coercion in an attempt to manipulate subordinates. (Of course, most people would agree that these are not appropriate managerial behaviours.) The more punitive the elements under a manager's control and the more important they are to subordinates, the more coercive power the manager possesses. On the other hand, the more a manager uses coercive power, the more likely he is to provoke resentment and hostility and the less likely he is to be seen as a leader.[9]

Referent Power   Compared with legitimate, reward, and coercive power, which are relatively concrete and grounded in objective facets of organizational life, **referent power** is abstract. It is based on identification, imitation, loyalty, or charisma. Followers may react favourably because they identify in some way with a leader, who may be like them in personality, background, or attitudes. In other situations, followers might choose to imitate a leader with referent power by wearing the same kinds of clothes, working the same hours, or espousing the same management philosophy. Referent power may also take the form of charisma, an intangible attribute of the leader that inspires loyalty and enthusiasm. Thus a manager might have referent power, but it is more likely to be associated with leadership.

Expert Power   **Expert power** is derived from information or expertise. A manager who knows how to interact with an eccentric but important customer, a scientist who is capable of achieving an important technical break-

● **coercive power**
The power to force compliance by means of psychological, emotional, or physical threat

● **referent power**
The personal power that accrues to someone based on identification, imitation, loyalty, or charisma

● **expert power**
The personal power that accrues to someone based on his or her information or expertise

through that no other company has dreamed of, and a secretary who knows how to unravel bureaucratic red tape all have expert power over anyone who needs that information. The more important the information and the fewer the people who have access to it, the greater is the degree of expert power possessed by any one individual. In general, people who are both leaders and managers tend to have a lot of expert power.

Using Power How does a manager or leader use power? Several methods have been identified. One method is the *legitimate request,* which is based on legitimate power. The manager requests that the subordinate comply because the subordinate recognizes that the organization has given the manager the right to make the request. Most day-to-day interactions between manager and subordinate are of this type. Another use of power is *instrumental compliance,* which is based on the reinforcement theory of motivation. In this form of exchange, a subordinate complies to get the reward the manager controls. Suppose that a manager asks a subordinate to do something outside the range of the subordinate's normal duties, such as working extra hours on the weekend, terminating a relationship with a longstanding buyer, or delivering bad news. The subordinate complies and, as a direct result, reaps praise and a bonus from the manager. The next time the subordinate is asked to perform a similar activity, that subordinate recognizes that compliance is instrumental in her getting more rewards. Hence the basis of instrumental compliance is clarifying important performance–reward contingencies.

A manager is using *coercion* when she suggests or implies that the subordinate will be punished, fired, or reprimanded if he does not do something. *Rational persuasion* occurs when the manager can convince the subordinate that compliance is in the subordinate's best interest. For example, a manager might argue that the subordinate should accept a transfer because it would be good for the subordinate's career. In some ways, rational persuasion is like reward power except that the manager does not really control the reward.

Still another way that a manager can use power is through *personal identification.* A manager who recognizes that she has referent power over a subordinate can shape that subordinate's behaviour by engaging in the desired behaviours: the manager consciously becomes a model for the subordinate and exploits personal identification. Sometimes a manager can induce a subordinate to do something consistent with a set of higher ideals or values through an *inspirational appeal* such as a plea for loyalty. Referent power plays a role in determining the extent to which an inspirational appeal is successful because its effectiveness depends at least in part on the persuasive abilities of the leader.

A dubious method of using power is through *information distortion.* The manager withholds or distorts information to influence subordinates' behaviour. For example, if a manager has agreed to allow everyone to participate in choosing a new group member but subsequently finds one individual whom she really prefers, she might withhold some of the credentials of other qualified applicants so that the desired member is selected. The use of power in this manner is dangerous. It may be unethical, and if subordinates find out that the manager has deliberately misled them, they will lose their confidence and trust in that manager's leadership.[10]

THE SEARCH FOR LEADERSHIP TRAITS

The first organized approach to studying leadership analyzed the personal, psychological, and physical traits of strong leaders. The trait approach assumed that some basic trait or set of traits existed that differentiated leaders from non-leaders. If those traits could be defined, potential leaders could be identified. Researchers thought that leadership traits might include intelligence, assertiveness, above-average height, good vocabulary, attractiveness, self-confidence, and similar attributes.[11]

During the first several decades of this century, researchers conducted hundreds of studies in an attempt to identify important leadership traits. For the most part, the results of the studies were disappointing. For every set of leaders who possessed a common trait, researchers also found a long list of exceptions, and the list of suggested traits soon grew so long that it had little practical value. Alternative explanations usually existed even for relations between traits and leadership that initially appeared valid. For example, researchers observed that many leaders have good communication skills and are assertive. Rather than those traits being the cause of leadership, however, successful leaders may begin to display those traits after they have achieved leadership positions.

Although most researchers gave up trying to identify traits as predictors of leadership ability, many people still explicitly or implicitly adopt a trait orientation.[12] For example, politicians are all too often elected on the basis of personal appearance, speaking ability, or an aura of self-confidence.[13]

LEADERSHIP BEHAVIOURS

Spurred on by their lack of success in identifying useful leadership traits, researchers soon began to investigate other variables, especially the behaviours or actions of leaders. The new hypothesis was that effective leaders somehow behaved differently than less-effective leaders. Thus the goal was to develop a fuller understanding of leadership behaviours.

Michigan Studies

Researchers at the University of Michigan, led by Rensis Likert, began studying leadership in the late 1940s.[14] Based on extensive interviews with both leaders (managers) and followers (subordinates), this research identified two basic forms of leader behaviour: job-centred and employee-centred. Managers using **job-centred leader behaviour** pay close attention to subordinates' work, explain work procedures, and are keenly interested in performance. Managers using **employee-centred leader behaviour** are interested in developing a cohesive work group and ensuring that employees are satisfied with their jobs. Their primary concern is the welfare of subordinates.

The two styles of leader behaviour were presumed to be at the ends of a single continuum. Although this suggests that leaders may be extremely job-centred, extremely employee-centred, or somewhere in between, Likert studied only the two extremes for contrast. He argued that employee-centred leader behaviour tended to be more effective. We should also note the similarities between Likert's leadership research and his Systems 1 through 4 organization

● **job-centred leader behaviour**
The behaviour of leaders who pay close attention to the job and work procedures involved with that job

● **employee-centred leader behaviour**
The behaviour of leaders who develop cohesive work groups and ensure employee satisfaction

design (discussed in Chapter 11). Job-centred leader behaviour is consistent with the System 1 design (rigid and bureaucratic), whereas employee-centred leader behaviour is consistent with the System 4 design (organic and flexible). When Likert advocates moving organizations from System 1 to System 4, he is also advocating a transition from job-centred to employee-centred leader behaviour.

Ohio State Studies

At about the same time that Likert was beginning his leadership studies at the University of Michigan, a group of researchers at Ohio State University also began studying leadership.[15] The extensive questionnaire surveys conducted during the Ohio State studies also suggested that there are two basic leader behaviours or styles: initiating-structure behaviour and consideration behaviour. When using **initiating-structure behaviour**, the leader clearly defines the leader–subordinate role so that everyone knows what is expected, establishes formal lines of communication, and determines how tasks will be performed. Leaders using **consideration behaviour** show concern for subordinates and attempt to establish a friendly and supportive climate.

Although behaviours identified at Ohio State are similar to those described at the University of Michigan, they differ in important ways. One major difference is that the Ohio State researchers did not interpret leader behaviour as being one-dimensional: each behaviour was assumed to be independent of the other. Presumably, then, a leader could exhibit varying levels of initiating structure and at the same time varying levels of consideration.

At first, the Ohio State researchers thought that leaders who exhibit high levels of both behaviours would tend to be more effective than other leaders. A study at International Harvester Co. (now Navistar International Corp.), however, suggested a more complicated pattern.[16] The researchers found that employees of supervisors who ranked high on initiating structure were high performers but expressed low levels of satisfaction and had a higher absence rate. Conversely, employees of supervisors who ranked high on consideration had low performance ratings but high levels of satisfaction and few absences from work. Later research isolated other variables that make consistent prediction difficult and determined that situational influences also occurred. (This body of research is discussed in the section on situational approaches to leadership.)

Leadership Grid

Yet another behavioural approach to leadership is the Leadership Grid.[17] The Leadership Grid provides a means for evaluating leadership styles and then training managers to move toward an ideal style of behaviour. The Leadership Grid is shown in Figure 17.1. The horizontal axis represents **concern for production** (similar to job-centred and initiating-structure behaviours), and the vertical axis represents **concern for people** (similar to employee-centred and consideration behaviour). Note the five extremes of managerial behaviour: the 1,1 manager (impoverished management) who exhibits minimal concern for both production and people; the 9,1 manager (authority-compliance) who is highly concerned about production but exhibits little concern for people; the 1,9 manager (country club management) who has the exact opposite concerns from the 9,1 manager; the 5,5 manager (middle of the road management) who maintains

● **initiating-structure behaviour**
The behaviour of leaders who define the leader–subordinate role so that everyone knows what is expected, establish formal lines of communication, and determine how tasks will be performed

● **consideration behaviour**
The behaviour of leaders who show concern for subordinates and attempt to establish a warm, friendly, and supportive climate

● **concern for production**
That part of the Leadership Grid that deals with the job and task aspects of leader behaviour

● **concern for people**
That part of the Leadership Grid that deals with the human aspects of leader behaviour

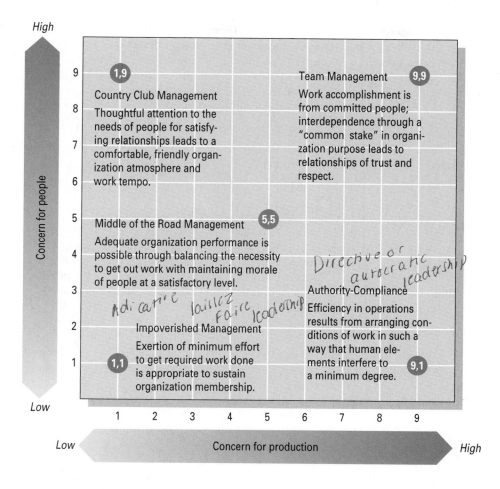

The Leadership Grid is a method of evaluating leadership styles. The overall objective of an organization using the Grid ® is to train its managers using organization development techniques so that they are more concerned for both people and production simultaneously (9,9 style on the grid).

Source: The Leadership Grid ® Figure from *Leadership Dilemmas–Grid Solutions*, by Robert R. Blake and Anne Adams McCanse. Houston: Gulf Publishing Company, p. 29. Copyright © 1991, by Scientific Methods, Inc. Reproduced by permission of the owners.

adequate concern for both people and production; and the 9,9 manager (team management) who exhibits maximum concern for both people and production.

According to this approach, the ideal style of managerial behaviour is 9,9, and there is a six-phase program to assist managers in achieving this style of behaviour. Although some companies have used the Leadership Grid with reasonable success, little published scientific evidence regarding its true effectiveness exists.

The leader-behaviour theories have played an important role in the development of contemporary thinking about leadership. In particular, they urge us not to be preoccupied with what leaders are (the trait approach) but to concentrate on what leaders do (their behaviours). Unfortunately, these theories also make universal prescriptions about what constitutes effective leadership. When we are dealing with complex social systems composed of complex individuals, few if any relationships are consistently predictable, and certainly no formulas for success are infallible. Yet the behaviour theorists tried to identify consistent relationships between leader behaviours and employee responses in the hope of finding a dependable prescription for effective leadership. As we might expect, they often failed. Other approaches to understanding leadership were therefore needed. The catalyst for these new approaches was the realization that, although interpersonal and task-oriented dimensions might be useful to describe the behaviour of leaders, they were not useful for predicting or prescribing it. The next step in the evolution of leadership theory was the creation of situational models.[18]

SITUATIONAL APPROACHES TO LEADERSHIP

Situational models assume that appropriate leader behaviour varies from one situation to another. The goal of a situational theory, then, is to identify important situational factors and to specify how they interact to determine appropriate leader behaviour. Before discussing the three major situational theories, we should first discuss an important early model that laid the foundation for subsequent developments. In a 1958 study of the decision-making process, Robert Tannenbaum and Warren H. Schmidt proposed a continuum of leadership behaviour. Their model is much like the original Michigan framework.[19] Besides purely job-centred behaviour (or "boss-centred" behaviour, as they termed it) and employee-centred ("subordinate-centred") behaviour, however, they identified several intermediate behaviours that a manager might consider. These are shown on the leadership continuum in Figure 17.2.

This continuum of behaviour moves from the one extreme of having the manager make the decision alone to the other extreme of having the employees make the decision with minimal guidance. Each point on the continuum is influenced by characteristics of the manager, subordinates, and the situation. Managerial characteristics include the manager's value system, confidence in subordinates, personal inclinations, and feelings of security. Subordinate characteristics include the subordinates' need for independence, readiness to assume responsibility, tolerance for ambiguity, interest in the

The degree to which leadership can be taught and learned has long been debated. Many organizations, such as the Canadian Armed Forces, have officers take part in leadership training exercises.

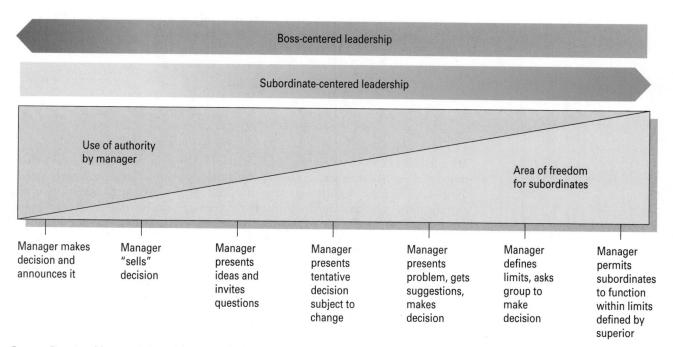

problem, understanding of goals, knowledge, experience, and expectations. Situational characteristics that affect decision making include the type of organization, group effectiveness, the problem itself, and time pressures. Although this framework pointed out the importance of situational factors, it was only speculative. It remained for others to develop more comprehensive and integrated theories. In the following sections, we describe the three most important and most widely accepted situational theories of leadership: the LPC theory, the path-goal theory, and the Vroom–Yetton–Jago model.

The Tannenbaum and Schmidt leadership continuum was an important precursor to modern situational approaches to leadership. The continuum identifies seven levels of leadership that range between the extremes of boss-centred and subordinate-centred leadership.

LPC Theory

The **LPC theory**, developed by Fred Fiedler, was the first true situational theory of leadership.[20] As we discuss later, LPC stands for least preferred co-worker. Beginning with a combined trait and behaviour approach, Fiedler identified two styles of leadership: task-oriented (analogous to job-centred and initiating-structure behaviour) and relationship-oriented (similar to employee-centred and consideration behaviour). He went beyond the earlier behavioural approaches by arguing that the style of behaviour is a reflection of the leader's personality, and that most personalities fall into one of his two categories, task-oriented or relationship-oriented by nature. Fiedler measures leader style by means of a controversial questionnaire called the **least preferred co-worker** (**LPC**) measure. To use the measure, a manager or leader is asked to describe the specific person with whom he or she is able to work least well—the LPC—

● **LPC theory**
A theory of leadership that suggests that the appropriate style of leadership varies with situational favourableness

● **least preferred co-worker (LPC)**
The measuring scale that asks leaders to describe the person with whom he or she is able to work least well

by filling in a set of sixteen scales anchored at each end by a positive or negative adjective. For example, three of the sixteen scales are:

Helpful — — — — — — — — Frustrating
      8 7 6 5 4 3 2 1

Tense — — — — — — — — Relaxed
      8 7 6 5 4 3 2 1

Boring — — — — — — — — Interesting
      8 7 6 5 4 3 2 1

The leader's LPC score is then calculated by adding up the numbers below the line checked on each scale. Note in these three examples that the higher numbers are associated with the positive qualities (helpful, relaxed, and interesting), whereas the negative qualities (frustrating, tense, and boring) have low point values. A high total score is assumed to reflect a relationship orientation and a low score a task orientation on the part of the leader. The LPC measure is controversial because researchers disagree about its validity. Some question exactly what an LPC measure reflects and whether the score is an index of behaviour, personality, or some other factor.[21] Nevertheless, the basic elements of the theory remain interesting on their own merits. Favourableness of the situation, favourableness and leader style, and flexibility of leader style each warrant special note.

Favourableness of the Situation   The underlying assumption of situational models of leadership is that appropriate leader behaviour varies from one situation to another. According to Fiedler, the key situational factor is the favourableness of the situation from the leader's point of view. This factor is determined by leader–member relations, task structure, and position power. *Leader–member relations* refer to the nature of the relationship between the leader and the work group. If the leader and the group have a high degree of mutual trust, respect, and confidence, and if they like one another, relations are assumed to be good. If there is little trust, respect, or confidence and if they do not like each other, relations are poor. Naturally, good relations are more favourable.

Task structure is the degree to which the group's task is well defined. The task is structured when it is routine, easily understood, and unambiguous and when the group has standard procedures and precedents to rely on. An unstructured task is nonroutine, ambiguous, and complex and has no standard procedures or precedents. You can see that high structure is more favourable for the leader, whereas low structure is less favourable. For example, if the task is unstructured, the group will not know what to do and the leader will have to play a major role in guiding and directing its activities. If the task is structured, the leader will not have to get so involved and can devote time to nonsupervisory activities. *Position power* is the power vested in the leader's position. If the leader has the power to assign work and to reward and punish employees, position power is assumed to be strong. But if the leader must get job assignments approved by someone else and does not administer rewards and punishment, position power is weak and accomplishing goals is more difficult. From the leader's point of view, strong position power is clearly preferable to weak position power. However, position power is not as important as task structure and leader–member relations.

FIGURE 17.3 The Least-Preferred Co-worker Theory of Leadership

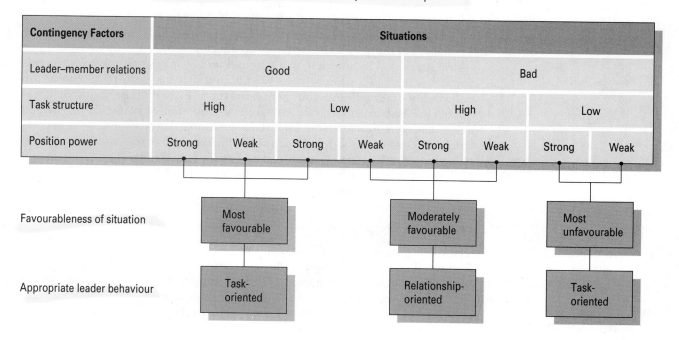

Contingency Factors	Situations							
Leader–member relations	Good				Bad			
Task structure	High		Low		High		Low	
Position power	Strong	Weak	Strong	Weak	Strong	Weak	Strong	Weak

Favourableness of situation: Most favourable — Moderately favourable — Most unfavourable

Appropriate leader behaviour: Task-oriented — Relationship-oriented — Task-oriented

Favourableness and Leader Style Fiedler and his associates conducted numerous studies linking the favourableness of various situations to leader style and the effectiveness of the group.[22] The results of these studies—and the overall framework of the theory—are shown in Figure 17.3. To interpret the model, look first at the situational factors at the top of the figure: good or bad leader–member relations, high or low task structure, and strong or weak leader-position power can be combined to yield eight unique situations. For example, good leader–member relations, high task structure, and strong leader-position power (at the far left) are presumed to define the most favourable situation; bad leader–member relations, low task structure, and weak leader-power (at the far right) are the least favourable. The other combinations reflect intermediate levels of favourableness.

Below each set of situations is shown the degree of favourableness and the form of leader behaviour found to be most strongly associated with effective group performance for those situations. When the situation is most and least favourable Fiedler has found that a task-oriented leader is most effective. When the situation is only moderately favourable, however, a relationship-oriented leader is predicted to be most effective.

Flexibility of Leader Style Fiedler argued that, for any given individual, leader style is essentially fixed and cannot be changed: leaders cannot change their behaviour to fit a particular situation because it is linked to their particular personality traits. Thus when a leader's style and the situation do not match, Fiedler argued that the situation should be changed to fit the leader's style. When leader–member relations are good, task structure low, and position power weak, the leader style most likely to be effective is relationship-oriented.

Fiedler's LPC theory of leadership suggests that appropriate leader behaviour varies as a function of the favourableness of the situation. Favourableness, in turn, is defined by task structure, leader–member relations, and the leader's position power. According to LPC theory, the most and least favourable situations call for task-oriented leadership, while moderately favourable situations suggest the need for relationship-oriented leadership.

If the leader is task-oriented, a mismatch exists. According to Fiedler, the leader can make the elements of the situation more congruent by structuring the task (by developing guidelines and procedures, for instance) and increasing power (by requesting additional authority or by other means).

Fiedler's contingency theory has been attacked on the grounds that it is not always supported by research, that his findings are subject to other interpretations, that the LPC measure lacks validity, and that his assumptions about the inflexibility of leader behaviour are unrealistic.[23] Fiedler's theory, however, was one of the first to adopt a situational perspective on leadership. It has helped many managers recognize the important situational factors that they must contend with, and it has fostered additional thinking about the situational nature of leadership. Moreover, in recent years Fiedler has attempted to address some of the concerns about his theory by revising it and adding such additional elements as cognitive resources.[24]

Path-Goal Theory

The path-goal theory of leadership—associated most closely with Martin Evans and Robert House—is a direct extension of the expectancy theory of motivation discussed in Chapter 16.[25] Recall that the primary components of expectancy theory included the likelihood of attaining various outcomes and the value associated with those outcomes. The **path-goal theory** of leadership suggests that the primary functions of a leader are to make valued or desired rewards available in the workplace and to clarify for the subordinate the kinds of behaviour that will lead to goal accomplishment and valued rewards—that is, the leader should clarify the paths to goal attainment.

● path-goal theory
A theory of leadership suggesting that the primary functions of a leader are to make valued or desired rewards available in the workplace and to clarify for the subordinate the kinds of behaviour that will lead to those rewards

Leader Behaviour   The most fully developed version of path-goal theory identifies four kinds of leader behaviour. *Directive leader behaviour* is letting subordinates know what is expected of them, giving guidance and direction, and scheduling work. *Supportive leader behaviour* is being friendly and approachable, showing concern for subordinate welfare, and treating members as equals. *Participative leader behaviour* is consulting subordinates, soliciting suggestions, and allowing participation in decision making. *Achievement-oriented leader behaviour* is setting challenging goals, expecting subordinates to perform at high levels, encouraging subordinates, and showing confidence in subordinates' abilities.

In contrast to Fiedler's theory, path-goal theory assumes that leaders can change their style or behaviour to meet the demands of a particular situation. For example, when encountering a new group of subordinates and a new project, the leader may be directive in establishing work procedures and in outlining what needs to be done. Next the leader may adopt supportive behaviour to foster group cohesiveness and a positive climate. As the group becomes familiar with the task and encounters new problems, the leader may exhibit participative behaviour to enhance group members' motivation. Finally, achievement-oriented behaviour may be used to encourage continued high performance.

Situational Factors   Like other situational theories of leadership, path-goal theory suggests that appropriate leader style depends on situational factors. Path-goal theory focuses on the situational factors of the personal characteristics of subordinates and environmental characteristics of the workplace.

Important personal characteristics include the subordinates' perception of their own ability and their locus of control. If people perceive that they are lacking in ability, they may prefer directive leadership to help them understand path-goal relationships better. If they perceive themselves to have a lot of ability, however, employees may resent directive leadership. Locus of control is a personality trait. People who have an internal locus of control believe that what happens to them is a function of their own efforts and behaviour. Those who have an external locus of control assume that fate, luck, or "the system" determines what happens to them. A person with an internal locus of control may prefer participative leadership, whereas a person with an external locus of control may prefer directive leadership. Managers can do little or nothing to influence the personal characteristics of subordinates, but they can shape the environment to take advantage of these personal characteristics by providing rewards and structuring tasks, for example.

Environmental characteristics include factors outside the subordinate's control. Task structure is one such factor. When task structure is high, directive leadership is less effective than when task structure is low. Subordinates do not usually need their boss to continually tell them how to do an extremely routine job. The formal authority system is another important environmental characteristic. Again, the higher the degree of formality, the less directive is the leader behaviour that will be accepted by subordinates.

The nature of the work group also affects appropriate leader behaviour. When the work group provides the employee with social support and satisfaction, supportive leader behaviour is less critical. When social support and satisfaction cannot be derived from the group, the worker may look to the leader for this support.

The basic path-goal framework as illustrated in Figure 17.4 shows that different leader behaviours affect subordinates' motivation to perform. Personal and environmental characteristics are seen as defining which behaviours lead to which outcomes. The path-goal theory of leadership is a dynamic and incomplete model. The original intent was to state the theory in general terms so that future research could explore a variety of interrelationships and modify the theory. Research that has been done suggests that the path-goal theory is a reasonably good description of the leadership process and that future investigations along these lines should enable us to discover more about the link between leadership and motivation.[26]

The path-goal theory of leadership suggests that managers can use four types of leader behaviour to clarify subordinates' paths to goal attainment. Personal characteristics of the subordinate and environmental characteristics within the organization both must be taken into account when determining which style of leadership will work best for a particular situation.

FIGURE 17.4 The Path-Goal Framework

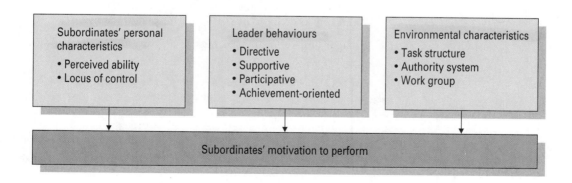

Vroom-Yetton-Jago Model

● **Vroom–Yetton–Jago (VYJ) model**
Predicts what kinds of situations call for what degrees of group participation

The **Vroom-Yetton-Jago (VYJ) model** predicts what kinds of situations call for what degrees of group participation. The VYJ model, then, sets norms or standards for including subordinates in decision making. The model was first proposed by Victor Vroom and Philip Yetton in 1973 and was revised and expanded in 1988 by Vroom and Arthur G. Jago.[27] The VYJ model is somewhat narrower than the other situational theories in that it focuses on only one part of the leadership process—how much decision-making participation to allow subordinates.

Basic Premises   The VYJ model argues that decision effectiveness is best gauged by the quality of the decision and by employee acceptance of the decision. Decision quality is the objective effect of the decision on performance. Decision acceptance is the extent to which employees accept and are committed to the decision. To maximize decision effectiveness, the VYJ model suggests that, depending on the situation, managers adopt one of five decision-making styles. As summarized in Table 17.2, there are two autocratic styles (AI and AII), two consultative styles (CI and CII), and one group style (GII).

The situation that is presumed to dictate an appropriate decision-making style is defined by a series of questions about the characteristics or attributes of the problem under consideration. To address the questions, the manager uses one of four decision trees. Two of the trees are used when the problem affects the entire group, and the other two are appropriate when the problem relates to an individual. One of each is to be used when the time necessary to reach a decision is important, and the others are to be used when time is less important but the manager wants to develop subordinates' decision-making abilities.

The difference between these is the degree of participation each provides for subordinates. The extreme forms are purely autocratic (AI) and total participation (GII). The other three styles fall between these extremes.

TABLE 17.2   Decision Styles in the Vroom-Yetton-Jago Model

Decision Style	Definition
AI	Manager makes the decision alone.
AII	Manager asks for information from subordinates but makes the decision alone. Subordinates may or may not be informed about what the situation is.
CI	Manager shares the situation with individual subordinates and asks for information and evaluation. Subordinates do not meet as a group, and the manager alone makes the decision.
CII	Manager and subordinates meet as a group to discuss the situation, but the manager makes the decision.
GII	Manager and subordinates meet as a group to discuss the situation, and the group makes the decision.

A = autocratic; C = consultative; G = group

Source: Reprinted from *Leadership and Decision-Making* by Victor H. Vroom and Philip W. Yetton, by permission of the University of Pittsburgh Press. Copyright © 1973 by the University of Pittsburgh Press.

Figure 17.5 shows the tree for time-driven group problems. The problem attributes defining the situation are arranged along the top of the tree and are expressed as questions. To use the tree, the manager starts at the left side of it and asks the first question. Thus the manager first decides whether the problem involves a quality requirement—that is, whether there are quality differences in the alternatives and if they matter. The answer determines the path to the second node, where the manager asks another question. The manager continues in this fashion until a terminal node is reached and an appropriate decision style is indicated. Each prescribed decision style is designed to protect the original goals

To use this decision tree, the manager asks a series of questions about the problem situation. The answers to each question lead the manager through the tree. At each endpoint is a recommended decision style (see Table 17.2) that is predicted to enhance decision quality and acceptance.

F I G U R E   17.5   Time-Driven Group Problem Decision Tree for VYJ Model

QR   Quality requirement: How important is the technical quality of this decision?

CR   Commitment requirement: How important is subordinate commitment to the decision?

LI   Leader's information: Do you have sufficient information to make a high-quality decision?

ST   Problem structure: Is the problem well structured?

CP   Commitment probability: If you were to make the decision by yourself, is it reasonably certain
       that your subordinate(s) would be committed to the decision?

GC   Goal congruence: Do subordinates share the organizational goals to be attained in solving this problem?

CO   Subordinate conflict: Is conflict among subordinates over preferred solutions likely?

SI   Subordinate information: Do subordinates have sufficient information to make a high-quality decision?

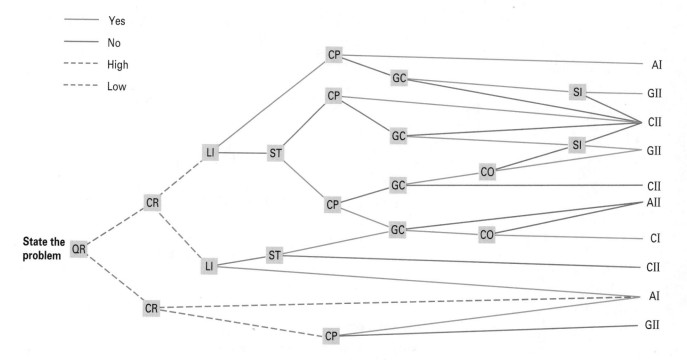

of the process (decision quality and subordinate acceptance) within the context of the group versus individual and time versus development framework.

Evaluation   The original version of the VYJ model has been widely tested. Indeed, one recent review concluded that it had received more scientific support than any other leadership theory.[28] The inherent complexity of the model presents a problem for many managers, however. Even the original version was criticized because of its complexity, and the revised VYJ model is far more complex than the original. To aid managers, computer software has been developed to facilitate managers' ability to define their situation, answer the questions about problem attributes, and develop a strategy for decision-making participation.[29]

Other Situational Approaches

In addition to the major theories, researchers have developed other situational models in recent years. We discuss the leader–member exchange model and the life cycle model.

• **leader–member exchange (LMX) model**
Stresses that leaders have different kinds of relationships with different subordinates

The Leader–Member Exchange Model   The **leader–member exchange (LMX) model** stresses that leaders have different kinds of relationships with different subordinates.[30] Each manager–subordinate relationship represents one vertical dyad. The model suggests that leaders establish special working relationships with a handful of subordinates called the in-group. Other subordinates remain in the out-group. Those in the in-group receive more of the manager's time and attention and also tend to be better performers. Early research on this model is quite promising.[31]

• **life cycle theory**
A model suggesting that appropriate leader behaviour depends on the maturity of the follower

Life Cycle Theory   Another well-known situational theory is the **life cycle theory**, which suggests that appropriate leader behaviour depends on the maturity of the followers.[32] In this context, maturity includes motivation, competence, and experience. The theory suggests that as followers become more mature, the leader needs to gradually move from a high level of task orientation to a low level. Simultaneously, employee-oriented behaviour should start low, increase at a moderate rate, and then decline again. This theory is well known among practising managers, but it has received little scientific support from researchers.[33]

RELATED PERSPECTIVES ON LEADERSHIP

Because of its importance to organizational effectiveness, leadership continues to be the focus of a great deal of research and theory building. New approaches that have attracted much attention are the concepts of substitutes for leadership, charismatic leadership, and transformational leadership.

Substitutes for Leadership

• **substitutes for leadership**
A concept that identifies situations in which leader behaviours are neutralized or replaced by characteristics of subordinates, the task, and the organization

The concept of **substitutes for leadership** was developed because existing leadership models and theories do not account for situations in which leadership is not needed.[34] They simply try to specify what kind of leader behaviour is appropriate. The substitute concepts, however, identify situations in which leader behaviours are neutralized or replaced by characteristics of the subordinate, the task, and the organization. For example, when a patient is delivered to a hospital emergency room, the professionals on duty do not wait to be told what to do by a leader. Nurses, doctors, and attendants all go into action without waiting for directive or supportive leader behaviour from the emergency-room supervisor.

Characteristics of the subordinate that may serve to neutralize leader behaviour include ability, experience, need for independence, professional orientation, and indifference toward organizational rewards. For example, employees with a high level of ability and experience may not need to be told what to do. Similarly, a subordinate's strong need for independence may render leader behaviour ineffective. Task characteristics that may substitute for leadership include routineness, the availability of feedback, and intrinsic satisfaction. When the job is routine and simple, the subordinate may not need direction. When the task is challenging and intrinsically satisfying, the subordinate may not need or want social support from a leader.

Organizational characteristics that may substitute for leadership include formalization, group cohesion, inflexibility, and a rigid reward structure. Leadership may not be necessary when policies and practices are formal and inflexible, for example. Similarly, a rigid reward system may rob the leader of reward power and thereby decrease the importance of the role. Preliminary research has provided support for the concept of substitutes for leadership.[35]

Charismatic Leadership

The concept of **charismatic leadership**, like trait theories, assumes that charisma is an individual characteristic of the leader. **Charisma** is a form of interpersonal attraction that inspires support and acceptance. All else equal, then, someone with charisma is more likely to be able to influence others than is someone without charisma. For example, a highly charismatic supervisor will be more successful in influencing subordinate behaviour than a supervisor who lacks charisma. Thus influence is again a fundamental element of this perspective.

● **charismatic leadership**
Assumes that charisma is an individual characteristic of the leader

● **charisma**
A form of interpersonal attraction that inspires support and acceptance

▬▬▬

Frank Stronach, founder and chairman of Magna International Inc., is a very charismatic man who is widely regarded as one of Canada's great entrepreneurs.

Robert House proposed a theory of charismatic leadership in 1977 based on research findings from a variety of social science disciplines.[36] His theory suggests that charismatic leaders are likely to have a lot of self-confidence, a firm conviction in their beliefs and ideals, and a strong need to influence people. They also tend to communicate high expectations about follower performance and express confidence in followers. Frank Stronach, the founder and chair of Magna International, is a charismatic leader. Even though Stronach has made his share of mistakes, this larger-than-life figure is regarded as one of Canada's great entrepreneurs.[37]

Today most experts acknowledge three elements of charismatic leadership in organizations.[38] First, the leader needs to be able to envision the future, to set high expectations, and to model behaviours consistent with meeting those expectations. Next, the charismatic leader must be able to energize others through a demonstration of personal excitement, personal confidence, and patterns of success. And finally, the charismatic leader enables others by supporting them, by empathizing with them, and by expressing confidence in them.[39]

Charismatic leadership ideas are quite popular among managers today and are the subject of numerous books and articles. Unfortunately, few studies have specifically attempted to test the meaning and impact of charismatic leadership. There are also lingering ethical issues about charismatic leadership that trouble some people. For example, charismatic leaders such as Adolf Hitler and Jim Jones are clear examples of the damage that charismatic leadership can create when misused.

Transformational Leadership

● **transformational leadership**
Leadership that goes beyond ordinary expectations by transmitting a sense of mission, stimulating learning experiences, and inspiring new ways of thinking

Another new perspective on leadership has been called by a number of labels: charismatic leadership, inspirational leadership, symbolic leadership, and transformational leadership. We use the term **transformational leadership** and define it as leadership that goes beyond ordinary expectations by transmitting a sense of mission, stimulating learning experiences, and inspiring new ways of thinking.[40] Because of rapid change and turbulent environments, transformational leaders are increasingly being seen as vital to the success of business.

A recent popular-press article identified seven keys to successful leadership: trusting one's subordinates, developing a vision, keeping cool, encouraging risk, being an expert, inviting dissent, and simplifying things.[41] Although this list was the result of a simplistic survey of the leadership literature, it is nevertheless consistent with the premises underlying transformational leadership. So too are recent examples cited as effective leadership. Take, for example, the case of MacMillan Bloedel Ltd., the Vancouver-based forest products conglomerate. When Tom Stephens became CEO, he faced the challenge of turning around a company that had not generated free cash flow in a decade and whose stock performance had been below the industry average for two decades. Stephens, who joined MacMillan Bloedel after rescuing Manville Corp., wasted no time in repositioning MacMillan Bloedel to be more efficient and profitable. Not only did he focus the company on its solid wood line, but he also seems to have inspired MacMillan Bloedel's employees by involving the union in the affairs of the company.[42] Stephens's transformational leadership turned around Manville Corp. and likely will do the same for MacMillan Bloedel. Other transformational leaders are Stephen Bachand of Canadian Tire and Matthew Barrett, former CEO of the Bank of Montreal. The *Managing in a Changing World* box describes yet another transformational leader. Given both its theo-

Japan's Greatest Leader?

Although it is not exactly a household name, Konosuke Matsushita may have been the greatest business leader in the history of Japan. Many consumers today know Matsushita as the company that makes such well-known brand-name products as Panasonic, Quasar, JVC, and Technics. And Matsushita is the world's largest consumer products maker.

Matsushita got his start in 1917. At that time, he worked for Osaka Light, an electric utility. But he quit his job when his boss refused to listen to his ideas about a new type of electric socket. He subsequently invested 200 yen (about US.$50—his entire life savings—to start a small electric business. His first workers contributed their time for free because he could not afford to pay them. After a shaky start, his company began to introduce one or two new products a month. His first "indulgences" were to pay his workers and to start hiring new employees.

In 1922, he got his big break. At that time, bicycle lights were powered either by candles or large, bulky batteries. Matsushita developed a new battery that was smaller, lighter, and much longer lasting than conventional ones. With this new product, Matsushita Electric took off. But the cornerstone of his business remained the loyal and dedicated employees who believed in his ability and integrity.

Even during the Great Depression of 1929, Matsushita refused to lay off workers. And when the world economy recovered, his firm again took off on its path to multinational status. Even though Matsushita died in 1989, the firm that bears his name remains firmly entrenched atop its industry. And its concerns for its workers has remained a central and enduring part of the firm's corporate culture.

References: John P. Kotter, "Matsushita: The World's Greatest Entrepreneur?" *Fortune*, March 31, 1997, pp. 105–111; John P. Kotter, *Matsushita Leadership* (New York: Free Press, 1997); and *Hoover's Handbook of World Business 1998* (Austin, Tex.: Hoover's Business Press, 1998), pp. 334–335.

retical appeal and its practical importance, the notion of transformational leadership is destined to become even more popular.

POLITICAL BEHAVIOUR IN ORGANIZATIONS

Another common influence on behaviour is politics. **Political behaviour** describes activities carried out for the specific purpose of acquiring, developing, and using power and other resources to obtain one's preferred outcomes.[43] Political behaviour may be undertaken by managers dealing with their subordinates, subordinates dealing with their managers, and managers and subordinates dealing with others at the same level. In other words, it may be directed upward, downward, or laterally. Decisions ranging from where to locate a manufacturing plant to where to put the company coffeepot are subject to political action. In any situation, individuals may engage in political behaviour to further their own ends, to protect themselves from others, to further goals they believe to be in the organization's best interest, or to simply acquire and exercise power. Power may be sought by individuals, by groups of individuals, or by groups of groups.[44]

Although political behaviour is difficult to study because of its sensitive nature, one survey found that many managers believe that politics influence salary and hiring decisions in their firms. Many also believe that the incidence of political behaviour is greater at the upper levels of their organizations and

● **political behaviour**
The activities carried out for the specific purpose of acquiring, developing, and using power and other resources to obtain one's preferred outcomes

less at the lower levels. More than one-half of the respondents believe that organizational politics is bad, unfair, unhealthy, and irrational but most suggest that successful executives have to be good politicians and be political to "get ahead."[45]

Common Political Behaviours

Research has identified four basic forms of political behaviour widely practised in organizations.[46] One form is *inducement*, which occurs when a manager offers to give something to someone else in return for that individual's support. For example, a product manager might suggest to another product manager that she will put in a good word with his boss if he supports a new marketing plan that she has developed. A second tactic is *persuasion*, which relies on both emotion and logic. An operations manager wanting to construct a new plant on a certain site might persuade others to support his goal on grounds that are objective and logical (land is less expensive, taxes are lower) as well as subjective and personal.

A third political behaviour involves the *creation of an obligation*. For example, one manager might support a recommendation made by another manager for a new advertising campaign. Although he may really have no opinion on the new campaign, he may think that by going along he is incurring a debt from the other manager and will be able to "call in" that debt when he wants to get something done and needs additional support. Finally, *coercion* is the use of force to get one's way. An example of coercion is a manager's threatening to withhold support, rewards, or other resources as a way to influence someone else.

Managing Political Behaviour

By its very nature, political behaviour is tricky to approach rationally and systematically. But managers can handle political behaviour so that it does not cause excessive damage. First, managers should be aware that even if their actions are not politically motivated, others may assume that they are. Second, by providing subordinates with autonomy, responsibility, challenge, and feedback, managers reduce the likelihood of subordinates' political behaviour. Third, managers should avoid using power if they want to avoid charges of political motivation. Fourth, managers should get disagreements out in the open so that subordinates will have less opportunity for political behaviour, using conflict for their own purposes. Finally, managers should avoid covert activities. Behind-the-scene activities give the impression of political intent even if none really exists.[47] Other guidelines include clearly communicating the bases and processes for performance evaluation, tying rewards directly to performance, and minimizing competition among managers for resources.[48]

Of course, those guidelines are a lot easier to list than they are to implement. The well-informed manager should not assume that political behaviour does not exist or, worse yet, attempt to eliminate it by issuing orders or commands. Instead, the manager must recognize that political behaviour exists in virtually all organizations and that it cannot be ignored or stamped out. It can, however, be managed in such a way that it will seldom inflict serious damage on the organization. It may even play a useful role in some situations.[49] For example, a manager may be able to take advantage of his or her political influence to stimulate a greater sense of social responsibility or to heighten awareness of the ethical implications of a decision.

SUMMARY OF KEY POINTS

As a process, leadership is the use of noncoercive influence to shape the group's or organization's goals, motivate behaviour toward the achievement of those goals, and help define group or organization culture. As a property, leadership is the set of characteristics attributed to individuals who are perceived to be leaders. Leadership and management are often related but are also different. Managers and leaders use legitimate, reward, coercive, referent, and expert power.

The trait approach to leadership assumed that some basic trait or set of traits differentiated leaders from nonleaders.

The leadership-behaviour approach to leadership assumed that the behaviour of effective leaders was somehow different from the behaviour of non-leaders. Research at the University of Michigan and Ohio State identified two basic forms of leadership behaviour—one concentrating on work and performance and the other concentrating on employee welfare and support. The Leadership Grid attempts to train managers to exhibit high levels of both forms of behaviour.

Situational approaches to leadership recognize that appropriate forms of leadership behaviour are not universally applicable and attempt to specify situations in which various behaviours are appropriate. The LPC theory suggests that a leader's behaviours should be either task-oriented or relationship-oriented depending on the favourableness of the situation. The path-goal theory suggests that directive, supportive, participative, or achievement-oriented leader behaviours may be appropriate, depending on the personal characteristics of subordinates and the environment. The Vroom-Yetton-Jago model maintains that leaders should vary the extent to which they allow subordinates to participate in making decisions as a function of problem attributes. The leader–member exchange model and the life cycle theory are two new situational theories.

Related leadership perspectives are the concept of substitutes for leadership, charismatic leadership, and the role of transformational leadership in organizations.

Political behaviour is another influence process frequently used in organizations. Managers can take steps to limit the effects of political behaviour.

DISCUSSION QUESTIONS

Questions for Review

1. Could someone be a manager but not a leader? A leader but not a manager? Both a leader and a manager? Explain.
2. What were the major findings of the Michigan and Ohio State studies of leadership behaviours? Briefly describe each group of studies and compare and contrast their findings.
3. What are the situational approaches to leadership? Briefly describe each and compare and contrast their findings.
4. Describe charismatic and transformation perspectives on leadership. How can they be integrated with existing approaches to leadership?

Questions for Analysis

5. How is it possible for a leader to be both task-oriented and relationship-oriented at the same time? Can you think of other forms of leader behaviour that are important to a manager? If so, share your thoughts with your class.
6. When all or most of the leadership substitutes are present, does the follower no longer need a leader? Why or why not?
7. Why should members of an organization be aware that political behaviour may be going on within the organization? What might occur if they were not aware?

Questions for Application

8. What traits seem best to describe student leaders? Military leaders? Business leaders? Political leaders? Religious leaders? What might account for the similarities and differences in your lists of traits?
9. Think about a decision that would affect you as a student. Use the Vroom-Yetton-Jago model to decide whether the administrator making that decision should involve students in the decision. Which parts of the model seem most important in making that decision? Why?
10. How do you know if transformational leadership is present in a group or organization? Could transformational leadership ever lead to dysfunctional outcomes for individuals or organizations? If so, why? If not, why not?

BUILDING EFFECTIVE DECISION-MAKING SKILLS

Exercise Overview

The Vroom-Yetton-Jago (VYJ) model of leadership is an effective method for determining how much participation a manager might allow his or her subordinates in making a decision. This exercise will enable you to refine your decision-making skills by applying the VYJ model to a hypothetical situation.

Exercise Background

Assume that you are the branch manager of the West Coast for an international manufacturing and sales company. The company is making a major effort to control costs and boost efficiency. As part of this effort, the firm recently installed a networked computer system linking sales representatives, customer service employees, and other sales support staff. The goal of this network was to increase sales while cutting sales expenses.

Unfortunately, just the opposite has resulted—sales are down slightly, while expenses are increasing. You have looked into this problem, and believe that the computer hardware people are using is fine. You also believe, however, that the software used to run the system is flawed. You believe it to be too hard to use and that it provides incomplete information.

Your employees disagree with your assessment, however. They believe that the entire system is fine. They attribute the problems to poor training in how to use the system and a lack of incentive for using it to solve many problems that they already know how to handle using other methods. Some of them also think that their colleagues are just resisting change.

Your boss has just called and instructed you to "solve the problem." She indicated that she has complete faith in your ability to do so, expects you to decide how to proceed, and wants a report suggesting a course of action in five days.

Exercise Task

Using the preceding background information, do the following:

1. Using your own personal preferences and intuition, describe how you would proceed.
2. Now use the VYJ model to determine a course of action.
3. Compare and contrast your initial approach and the approach suggested by the VYJ model.

Even though Compaq Computer was formed less than two decades ago, the firm seems to have already had two distinct lives. The first started when Rod Canion and two other former Texas Instruments engineers launched the firm in 1982. Their first product design was sketched on a paper place mat in a restaurant where they agreed to go into business together. Led by Canion's rational and deliberate decision-making style, Compaq did all the right things and in 1988 became the youngest firm to ever enter the *Fortune* 500.

It appears for a while that the firm's management could do no wrong. But, unfortunately, things have a way of changing in the computer business. Canion's strategy for Compaq was to sell primarily to big businesses and to act in a relatively slow and deliberate fashion so as to avoid mistakes. When Compaq began to falter in 1991, Canion was at a loss as to how to proceed and was eventually forced out by the firm's board of directors.

To get the firm back on track, the board tapped Eckhard Pfeiffer, a German marketing specialist who had previously headed Compaq's very successful European operations. Pfeiffer wasted little time in revamping the way that the firm did business. In short order he mandated that the firm develop and launch dozens of new products, that manufacturing become more efficient so that costs could be lowered, and that the dealer network selling Compaq computers be enlarged. He also announced new initiatives directed at selling computers to individual consumers and to schools, domains previously controlled by Dell and Apple, respectively.

Even the wildest optimist could not have predicted how successful Pfeiffer's approach would turn out to be. Under his watch, for example, Compaq more than tripled its share of the PC market, moving from 3.8 percent to 12 percent. Moreover, its profits in 1996 exceeded those of IBM and Apple combined. But Pfeiffer does not believe in standing still. Indeed, his ideas and strategies kept the firm in a constant state of flux. He continued to push for ever lower costs, ever greater productivity, and constant increases in market share, sales, and profits.

Pfeiffer took Compaq into new markets and encouraged managers to constantly be on the alert for new market opportunities. Indeed, under Pfeiffer's watch, in every business where it competed, Compaq grew at a faster pace than the market itself, and Pfeiffer announced a goal of transforming Compaq into a $40 billion (U.S.) Goliath by the turn of the century. With its acquisition of Digital Equipment Corporation in 1998, a record profit of $758 million (U.S.) in the fourth quarter of that year, and steady increases in sales, the firm is well positioned to achieve that goal.

How did he do it? His colleagues believe that Pfeiffer has two qualities that allowed him to first turn things around and then set forth in bold new directions at Compaq. The first is that he was able to clearly communicate his vision for the company to each of its managers and employees. The second is that he is able to impart a sense of urgency—a feeling that things have to be done *now*.

This latter characteristic has facilitated the ongoing sense of change that he believes must drive Compaq in the years to come. And he sees plenty of changes on the horizon—lower prices, more powerful machines, and technology unheard of today are all right around the corner. And many experts felt that Pfeiffer would have led Compaq around that corner first. However, as it did in 1991 with Rod Canion, Compaq's board of directors dismissed Pfeiffer on April 18, 1999, and the firm appears to be starting its third distinct life.

Questions

1. How would you describe Eckhard Pfeiffer as a leader? Would you want to work for him? Why or why not?

2. Discuss aspects of leadership presented in this chapter that are illustrated in this case.

3. What leadership challenges might Pfeiffer's successor face?

References: "Growth at Greater than Three Times the Market, Digital Market Accretive," (http://www.compaq.com), January 27, 1999; "Compaq: There's No End to Its Drive," *Business Week*, February 17, 1997, pp. 72–73; Stephanie Losee, "How Compaq Keeps the Magic Going," *Fortune*, February 21, 1994, pp. 90–92; and *Hoover's Handbook of American Business* 1997 (Austin, Tex.: Hoover's Business Press, 1997), pp. 390–391; and "Compaq Board of Directors Forms Office of Chief Executive Under Leadership of Benjamin Rosen: Eckhard Pfeiffer and Earl Mason Resign as CEO and CFO" (http://www.compaq.com), April 18, 1999.

CHAPTER NOTES

1. "Corporate Success, Southern Style: ATCO's Human Dynamo Plots His Multi-Billion-Dollar Conglomerate's Next Moves," *Western Report*, January 9, 1995, pp. 14–17; "The Master Builder: An All-Consuming Lesson in What It Takes to Build a Premier Corporation," *The Financial Post Magazine*, November 1996, pp. 14–25; "Southern Named Outstanding CEO," *Calgary Herald*, November 16, 1996, p. E10; "True Grit: CEO of the Year Ron Southern," *Financial Post*, June 29/July 1, 1996, p. 11; "Financial Post Names Southern CEO of the Year," *Canadian Press Newswire*, June 30, 1996; "ATCO Ltd.," *Financial Post Historical Reports* (Financial Post Data Group, 1996); and "The Top 1000," *Report on Business Magazine*, July 1998, p. 102.

2. Arthur G. Jago, "Leadership: Perspectives in Theory and Research," *Management Science*, March 1982, pp. 315–336.

3. Gary A. Yukl, *Leadership in Organizations*, 3rd ed. (Englewood Cliffs, N.J.: Prentice-Hall, 1995), p. 5.

4. Manfred F.R. Kets de Vries, "The Leadership Mystique," *The Academy of Management Executive*, August 1994, pp. 73–89.

5. See John P. Kotter, "What Leaders Really Do," *Harvard Business Review*, May–June 1990, pp. 103–111.

6. Daniel Brass and Marlene Burkhardt, "Potential Power and Power Use: An Investigation of Structure and Behavior," *Academy of Management Journal*, Vol. 36, No. 3, 1993, pp. 441–470.

7. John R.P. French and Bertram Raven, "The Bases of Social Power," in Dorwin Cartwright (Ed.), *Studies in Social Power* (Ann Arbor, Mich.: University of Michigan Press, 1959), pp. 150–167.

8. William Kahn and Kathy Kram, "Authority at Work: Internal Models and Their Organizational Consequences," *Academy of Management Review*, Vol. 19, No. 1, 1994, pp. 17–50.

9. John Voyer, "Coercive Organizational Politics and Organizational Outcomes: An Interpretive Study," *Organization Science*, February 1994, pp. 72–81.

10. For more information on the bases and uses of power, see Philip M. Podsakoff and Chester A. Schriesheim, "Field Studies of French and Raven's Bases of Power: Critique, Reanalysis, and Suggestions for Future Research," *Psychological Bulletin*, Vol. 97, 1985, pp. 387–411; Robert C. Benfari, Harry E. Wilkinson, and Charles D. Orth, "The Effective Use of Power," *Business Horizons*, May–June 1986, pp. 12–16; and Yukl, *Leadership in Organizations*.

11. Bernard M. Bass, *Bass and Stogdill's Handbook of Leadership*, 3rd ed. (Riverside, N.J.: Free Press, 1990).

12. Shelley A. Kirkpatrick and Edwin A. Locke, "Leadership: Do Traits Matter?" *The Academy of Management Executive*, May 1991, pp. 48–60.

13. Robert G. Lord, Christy L. De Vader, and George M. Alliger, "A Meta-Analysis of the Relation Between Personality Traits and Leadership Perceptions: An Application of Validity Generalization Procedures," *Journal of Applied Psychology*, August 1986, pp. 402–410.

14. Rensis Likert, *New Patterns of Management* (New York: McGraw-Hill, 1961); and Rensis Likert, *The Human Organization* (New York: McGraw-Hill, 1967).

15. The Ohio State studies stimulated many articles, monographs, and books. A good overall reference is Ralph M. Stogdill and A. E. Coons (Eds.), *Leader Behavior: Its Description and Measurement* (Columbus, Ohio: Bureau of Business Research, Ohio State University, 1957).

16. Edwin A. Fleishman, E.F. Harris, and H.E. Burt, *Leadership and Supervision in Industry* (Columbus, Ohio: Bureau of Business Research, Ohio State University, 1955).

17. Robert R. Blake and Jane S. Mouton, *The Managerial Grid* (Houston: Gulf Publishing, 1964); Robert R. Blake and Jane S. Mouton, *The New Managerial Grid* (Houston: Gulf Publishing, 1978); and Robert R. Blake and Jane S. Mouton, *The Versatile Manager: A Grid Profile* (Homewood, Ill.: Dow Jones–Irwin, 1981).

18. See Jan P. Muczyk and Bernard C. Reimann, "The Case for Directive Leadership," *The Academy of Management Executive*, November 1987, pp. 301–309, for a recent update.

19. Robert Tannenbaum and Warren H. Schmidt, "How to Choose a Leadership Pattern," *Harvard Business Review*, March–April 1958, pp. 95–101.

20. Fred E. Fiedler, *A Theory of Leadership Effectiveness* (New York: McGraw-Hill, 1967).

21. Chester A. Schriesheim, Bennett J. Tepper, and Linda A. Tetrault, "Least Preferred Co-Worker Score, Situational Control, and Leadership Effectiveness: A Meta-Analysis of Contingency Model Performance Predictions," *Journal of Applied Psychology*, Vol. 79, No. 4, 1994, pp. 561–573.

22. Fiedler, *A Theory of Leadership Effectiveness*; and Fred E. Fiedler and M.M. Chemers, *Leadership and Effective Management* (Glenview, Ill.: Scott, Foresman, 1974).

23. For recent reviews and updates, see Lawrence H. Peters, Darrell D. Hartke, and John T. Pohlmann, "Fiedler's Contingency Theory of Leadership: An Application of the Meta-Analysis Procedures of Schmidt and Hunter," *Psychological Bulletin*, Vol. 97, pp. 274–285; and Fred E. Fiedler, "When to Lead, When to Stand Back," *Psychology Today*, September 1987, pp. 26–27.

24. Fred E. Fiedler, M. M. Chemers, and L. Mahar, *Improving Leadership Effectiveness: The Leader Match Concept* (New York: Wiley, 1976).

25. Martin G. Evans, "The Effects of Supervisory Behavior on the Path-Goal Relationship," *Organizational Behavior and Human Performance*, May 1970, pp. 277–298; and Robert J. House and Terence R. Mitchell, "Path-Goal Theory of Leadership," *Journal of Contemporary Business*, Autumn 1974, pp. 81–98. See also Yukl, *Leadership in Organizations*.

26. For a recent review, see J.C. Wofford and Laurie Z. Liska, "Path-Goal Theories of Leadership: A Meta-Analysis," *Journal of Management*, Vol. 19, No. 4, 1993, pp. 857–876.

27. Victor H. Vroom and Philip H. Yetton, *Leadership and Decision-Making* (Pittsburgh: University of Pittsburgh Press, 1973); and Victor H. Vroom and Arthur G. Jago, *The*

New Leadership (Englewood Cliffs, N.J.: Prentice-Hall, 1988).

28. Yukl, *Leadership in Organizations.*

29. Vroom and Jago, *The New Leadership.*

30. Fred Dansereau, George Graen, and W.J. Haga, "A Vertical-Dyad Linkage Approach to Leadership Within Formal Organizations: A Longitudinal Investigation of the Role-Make Process," *Organizational Behavior and Human Performance,* Vol. 15, 1975, pp. 46–78; and Richard M. Dienesch and Robert C. Liden, "Leader–Member Exchange Model of Leadership: A Critique and Further Development," *Academy of Management Review,* July 1986, pp. 618–634.

31. Antoinette Phillips and Arthur Bedeian, "Leader-Follower Exchange Quality: The Role of Personal and Interpersonal Attributes," *Academy of Management Journal,* Vol. 37, No. 4, 1994, pp. 990–1001.

32. Paul Hersey and Kenneth H. Blanchard, *Management of Organizational Behavior,* 3rd ed. (Englewood Cliffs, N.J.: Prentice-Hall, 1977).

33. Yukl, *Leadership in Organizations.*

34. Steven Kerr and John M. Jermier, "Substitutes for Leadership: Their Meaning and Measurement," *Organizational Behavior and Human Performance,* December 1978, pp. 375–403.

35. See Charles C. Manz and Henry P. Sims, Jr., "Leading Workers to Lead Themselves: The External Leadership of Self-managing Work Teams," *Administrative Science Quarterly,* March 1987, pp. 106–129.

36. See Robert J. House, "A 1976 Theory of Charismatic Leadership," in J.G. Hunt and L.L. Larson (Eds.), *Leadership: The Cutting Edge* (Carbondale, Ill.: Southern Illinois University Press, 1977), pp. 189–207. See also Jay A. Conger and Rabindra N. Kanungo, "Toward a Behavioral Theory of Charismatic Leadership in Organizational Settings," *Academy of Management Review,* October 1987, pp. 637–647.

37. David Berman, "Which Part Doesn't Fit?" *Canadian Business,* February 26, 1999, pp. 21–25.

38. David A. Nadler and Michael L. Tushman, "Beyond the Charismatic Leader: Leadership and Organizational Change," *California Management Review,* Winter 1990, pp. 77–97.

39. See Boas Shamir, Robert House, and Michael Arthur, "The Motivational Effects of Charismatic Leadership: A Self-Concept Based Theory," *Organization Science,* November 1993, pp. 577–589; and Jay Conger and Rabindra Kanungo, "Charismatic Leadership in Organizations: Perceived Behavioral Attributes and Their Measurement," *Journal of Organizational Behavior,* Vol. 15, 1994, pp. 439–452.

40. James MacGregor Burns, *Leadership* (New York: Harper & Row, 1978). See also John J. Hater and Bernard M. Bass, "Superiors' Evaluations and Subordinates' Perceptions of Transformational and Transactional Leadership," *Journal of Applied Psychology,* November 1988, pp. 695–702; and Karl W. Kuhnert and Philip Lewis, "Transactional and Transformational Leadership: A Constructive/ Developmental Analysis," *Academy of Management Review,* October 1987, pp. 648–657.

41. Labich, "The Seven Keys to Business Leadership."

42. Peter Waal, "With a Vengeance," *Canadian Business,* April 10, 1998, pp. 34–42.

43. Jeffrey Pfeffer, *Power in Organizations* (Marshfield, Mass.: Pitman Publishing, 1981), p. 7.

44. Timothy Judge and Robert Bretz, "Political Influence Behavior and Career Success," *Journal of Management,* Vol. 20, No. 1, 1994, pp. 43–65.

45. Victor Murray and Jeffrey Gandz, "Games Executives Play: Politics at Work," *Business Horizons,* December 1980, pp. 11–23; and Jeffrey Gandz and Victor Murray, "The Experience of Workplace Politics," *Academy of Management Journal,* June 1980, pp. 237–251.

46. Don R. Beeman and Thomas W. Sharkey, "The Use and Abuse of Corporate Power," *Business Horizons,* March–April 1987, pp. 26–30.

47. Murray and Gandz, "Games Executives Play."

48. Beeman and Sharkey, "The Use and Abuse of Corporate Power."

49. Stefanie Ann Lenway and Kathleen Rehbein, "Leaders, Followers, and Free Riders: An Empirical Test of Variation in Corporate Political Involvement," *Academy of Management Journal,* December 1991, pp. 893–905.

Managing Interpersonal Relations and Communication

OBJECTIVES

After studying this chapter, you should be able to:

● *Describe the interpersonal nature of organizations.*

● *Describe the role and importance of communication in the manager's job.*

● *Identify the basic forms of interpersonal communication and cite advantages and disadvantages of each.*

● *Identify forms of organizational communication and cite characteristics of each.*

● *Discuss informal communication, including its various forms and types.*

● *Describe how the communication process can be managed to recognize and overcome barriers.*

Kodak is one of the world's most successful companies. But even successful companies can be derailed by bad news that is leaked to the press.

It's no secret that the recent performance of Eastman Kodak Company is a mixed bag. Its core businesses (film, paper, etc.) have mature markets with little growth opportunity, and the firm's latest ventures into new areas (such as pharmaceuticals) have generally been disappointing. To counter its problems, the firm implemented a major cost-cutting program and hired a new CEO, George Fisher.

Kodak's chief operating officer at the beginning of Fisher's tenure was Leo Thomas. Thomas had a long-standing reputation in the company as having a tough-minded and bold approach to problems. He stated his mind clearly—sometimes bluntly—and paid little attention to what others thought about him or the way he handled himself. In general, most executives at the firm gave him high marks for his executive skills, but a few expressed concern about his interpersonal style and worried that his bluntness would backfire.

In 1994, just such a thing happened. As the fourth quarter of the year approached, the company's financial managers realized that Kodak was not going to meet its profit goals. Thomas responded by writing a blistering memo in which he mandated severe cost cuts. For example, he ordered that travel and entertainment budgets be cut in half, banned personal computer purchases, and cut research and development spending budgets.

> **"People have told [Thomas] that these things are bound to leak, but he doesn't seem to care."**

Unfortunately for Kodak, someone leaked the memo to the press. The news caused a near-panic among analysts and investors who were holding Kodak stock. Fearing that bad financial news was looming, large numbers of shareholders sold their shares. The net result was that the market capitalization of Kodak (i.e., the total value of its stock) dropped $1.1 billion (U.S.) in two days.

After the carnage, analysts' opinions as to what it all meant differed. Many insiders believed that the market had overreacted. They reasoned that Thomas often wrote such memos, frequently sending them to hundreds of managers. But others criticized him for having written the memo to begin with. They argued that it had only been a matter of time before one of his memos was leaked to the outside.

Of equal interest to some people was why Thomas had written the memo to begin with. One theory was that he was feeling heat from Fisher, his new boss. Fisher was known to be pressuring managers to meet their profit goals, and Thomas may have simply been trying to show Fisher that he was doing his best to keep things on track. Regardless of the reasons, however, one thing was clear: the memo wreaked havoc— at least temporarily—with the financial community's opinion of Kodak.[1] ●

Source of Quotation: Former Kodak executive, referring to Leo Thomas, Kodak chief operating officer, quoted in *Business Week*, October 31, 1994, p. 52

The managers at Kodak have experienced one of an organization's biggest nightmares—a critical but potentially explosive internal document was released to the external environment. Its original, intended purpose and the actual results it created were two fundamentally different things. This sort of communication represents a major concern for organizations today. Indeed, managers around the world agree that communication is one of their most important tasks. It is important for them to communicate with others to convey their vision and goals for the organization. And it is important for others to communicate with them so that they will better understand what's going on in their environment and how they and their organizations can become more effective.

This chapter is the first of two that focus on interpersonal processes in organizations. We first establish the interpersonal nature of organizations and then discuss communication, one of the most basic forms of interaction among people. We begin by examining communication in the context of the manager's job. We then identify and discuss forms of interpersonal and organizational communication. After discussing informal communication, we describe how organizational communication can be effectively managed. In our next chapter, we discuss other elements of interpersonal relations, group and team processes, and conflict.

THE INTERPERSONAL NATURE OF ORGANIZATIONS

In Chapter 1, we noted how much of a manager's job involves scheduled and unscheduled meetings, telephone calls, and related activities. Indeed, a great deal of what all managers do involves interacting with other people, both inside and outside the organization. The schedule that follows is a typical day for a branch manager of a major corporation. He kept a log of his activities for several different days so that you could better appreciate the nature of managerial work.

8:00–8:15 A.M.	Arrive at work, review mail sorted by secretary.
8:15–8:30 A.M.	Read a financial newspaper.
8:30–9:15 A.M.	Meet with labour officials and plant manager to resolve minor labour disputes.
9:15–9:30 A.M	Review internal report and dictate correspondence for secretary to type.
9:30–10:00 A.M.	Meet with two marketing executives to reviewa advertising campaign.
10:00–noon	Meet with company executive committee to discuss strategy, budgetary issues, and competition (this committee meets weekly).
12:00–1:15 P.M.	Lunch with the financial vice president and two executives from another subsidiary of the parent corporation; primary topic of discussion is sports.
1:15–2:00 P.M.	Meet with human resource director and assistant about a recent Occupational Health and Safety inspection; establish a task force to investigate the problems identified and to suggest solutions.
2:00–2:30 P.M.	Conference call with four other company presidents.

2:30–3:00 P.M.	Meet with financial vice president about a confidential issue that came up at lunch (unscheduled).
3:00–3:30 P.M.	Work alone in office.
3:30–4:15 P.M.	Meet with a group of sales representatives and the company purchasing agent.
4:15–5:30 P.M.	Work alone in office.
5:30–7:00 P.M.	Play racquetball at nearby athletic club with marketing vice president.

How did this manager spend his time? He spent most of it working, communicating, and interacting with other people. And this compressed daily schedule does not include several brief telephone calls, conversations with his secretary, and conversations with other managers. Clearly, interpersonal relations, communication, and group processes are a pervasive part of all organizations and a vital part of all managerial activities.[2]

Interpersonal Dynamics

The nature of interpersonal relations in an organization is as varied as the individual members themselves. At one extreme, interpersonal relations can be personal and positive. This occurs when the two parties know each other, have mutual respect and affection, and enjoy interacting with one another. Two managers who have known each other for years, play golf together on weekends, and are close personal friends will likely interact positively at work. At the other extreme, interpersonal dynamics can be personal but negative. This is most likely when the parties dislike one another, do not have mutual respect, and do not enjoy interacting with one another. Suppose that a manager has fought openly for years to block the promotion of another manager within the organization. Over the objections of the first manager, however, the other man-

ExporCanada is a company jointly owned by Canada and Cuba in Havana. ExporCanada provides supplies to Cuba's hotel industry. Canada is Cuba's biggest trading partner but is challenged by the controversial Helms-Burton bill, a U.S. initiative that attempts to deter foreign investment in Cuba by any country.

ager eventually gets promoted to the same rank. When the two of them must interact, it will most likely be negatively.

Most interactions fall between these extremes, as members of the organization interact in a professional way focused primarily on goal accomplishment. The interaction deals with the job at hand, is relatively formal and structured, and is task-directed. Two managers may respect each other's work and recognize the professional competence that each brings to the job. However, they may also have few common interests and little to talk about besides the job they are doing. These different types of interaction may occur between individuals, between groups, or between individuals and groups and they can change over time. The two managers in the second scenario, for example, might decide to bury the hatchet and adopt a detached, professional manner. The two managers in the third example could find more common ground than they anticipated and evolve to a personal and positive interaction.

Outcomes of Interpersonal Behaviours

A variety of things can happen as a result of interpersonal behaviours. Recall from Chapter 16, for example, that numerous perspectives on motivation suggest that people have social needs. Interpersonal relations in organizations can be a primary source of need satisfaction for many people. For people with a strong need for affiliation, high-quality interpersonal relations can be an important positive element in the workplace. When this same person is confronted with poor-quality working relationships, however, the effect can be just as great in the other direction.

Interpersonal relations also serve as a solid basis for social support. Suppose that an employee receives a poor performance evaluation or is denied a promotion. Others in the organization can lend support because they share a common frame of reference—an understanding of the causes and consequences of what happened.[3] Good interpersonal relations throughout an organization can also be a source of synergy. People who support one another and who work well together can accomplish much more than people who do not support one another and who do not work well together. Another outcome, implied earlier, is conflict—people may leave an interpersonal exchange feeling angry or hostile. But a common thread weaves throughout all of these outcomes—communication between the people in the organization.

COMMUNICATION AND THE MANAGER'S JOB

As evidenced by the daily log presented earlier, a typical day for a manager includes doing desk work, attending scheduled meetings, placing and receiving telephone calls, reading correspondence, answering correspondence, attending unscheduled meetings, and tours.[4] Most of these activities involve communication. In fact, managers usually spend more than half of their time communicating in some way. Communication always involves two or more persons, so other behavioural processes such as motivation, leadership, and group and team processes all come into play. Top executives must handle communication effectively if they are to be true leaders. The *Environment of Management* box describes how the restaurant chain Olive Garden failed to live up to its stated commitment to open and honest communication.

Olive Garden Wilts

In the mid-1970s, General Mills Restaurants Inc. was seeking new market segments. Its forecast pointed to the full-service Italian segment as having strong potential, so it began a search for an existing concept with the intention of purchasing and expanding it in the United States and Canada. Unsuccessful in its attempt to find a full-service Italian restaurant concept, General Mills set out to develop its own using what it describes as a consumer-driven approach. The result of this exercise was the Olive Garden. A pilot restaurant was opened in Orlando, Florida, in 1982. In 1985, a second restaurant was opened and thereafter the pace of expansion quickened; by 1995, there were 460 units in the United States and 16 in Canada. In 1995, General Mills spun off the restaurant chain to Darden Restaurants Inc., a public company that is listed on the New York Stock Exchange and that also owns the Red Lobster chain.

Olive Garden seems to take great pride in a set of ideals that it calls "The Olive Garden Principles." The company, in an attempt to demonstrate that it is employee-oriented, claims that these principles were written by the employees themselves. The Olive Garden Principles consist of seven statements, the first of which reads, "We are committed to open and honest communication, mutual respect, and strong teamwork."

Olive Garden seems to have violated its first principle on September 13th, 1997, when it announced that, as of that day, it was closing eleven of its sixteen restaurants in Canada. Employees of the affected units were informed of the decision on the morning of the day the restaurants closed. Later that day customers discovered that the restaurants had ceased operations. News reports indicate that the employees were shocked and that surprised customers were peering in the doors of the closed restaurants.

References: Gary Rennie, "Local Olive Garden Among 26 Closed Restaurants," *The Windsor Star,* September 15, 1997, p. 3; Nicholas van Rijn, "1600 Out of Work at Olive Garden, Red Lobster," *The Toronto Star,* September 14, 1997, p. A3; Olive Bertin, "Darden Closes 26 Restaurants in Canada," *The Globe and Mail,* September 15, 1997, p. B3; and "The Olive Garden Principles" and "A History: How the Olive Garden Started" (http://www.olivegarden.com.)

A Definition of Communication

Imagine three managers working in an office building. The first is all alone but is nevertheless yelling for a subordinate to come help. No one appears, but he continues to yell. The second manager is talking on the telephone to a subordinate, but static on the line causes the subordinate to misunderstand some important numbers being provided by the manager. As a result, the subordinate sends 1,500 crates of eggs to 150 Fifth Street, when he should have sent 150 crates of eggs to 1500 Fifteenth Street. The third manager is talking in her office with a subordinate who clearly hears and understands what she is saying. Each of these managers is attempting to communicate but with different results.

Communication is the process of transmitting information from one person to another.[5] Did any of our three managers communicate? The last did and the first did not. How about the second? In fact, she did communicate. She transmitted information, and information was received. The problem was that the message transmitted and the message received were not the same. The words spoken by the manager were distorted by static and noise. **Effective communication**, then, is the process of sending a message in such a way that the message received is as close in meaning as possible to the message intended. Although the second manager engaged in communication, it was not effective.

Our definition of effective communication is based on the ideas of meaning and consistency of meaning. Meaning is the idea that the individual who ini-

● **communication**
The process of transmitting information from one person to another

● **effective communication**
The process of sending a message in such a way that the message received is as close in meaning as possible to the message intended

tiates the communication exchange wishes to convey. In effective communication, the meaning is transmitted in such a way that the receiving person understands it. For example, consider these messages:

1. The high today will be only 5 degrees.
2. It will be cold today.
3. Ceteris paribus.
4. Xn1gp bo5cz4ik ab19.

You probably understand the meaning of the first statement. The second statement may seem clear at first, but it is somewhat less clear than the first statement because cold is a relative condition and the word means different things to different people. Fewer still understand the third statement because it is written in Latin. None of you understands the last statement because it is written in a secret code that one of your authors developed as a child.

The Role of Communication in Management

We noted earlier the variety of activities that fill a manager's day. Meetings, telephone calls, and correspondence (including, increasingly, electronic messages) are all a necessary part of every manager's job—and all clearly involve communication. On a typical Monday, Nolan Archibald, CEO of Black & Decker, attended five scheduled meetings and two unscheduled meetings; had fifteen telephone conversations; received twenty-nine letters, memos, and reports; and dictated ten letters.[6] And Kodak's experiences clearly underscore the role of communication in management.

To better understand the linkages between communication and management, recall the variety of roles that managers must fill. Each of the ten basic managerial roles we discussed in Chapter 1 (see Table 1.2) would be impossible to fill without communication.[7] Interpersonal roles involve interacting with supervisors, subordinates, peers, and others outside the organization. Decisional roles require managers to seek out information to use in making decisions and then communicate those decisions to others. Informational roles focus specifically on acquiring and disseminating information.

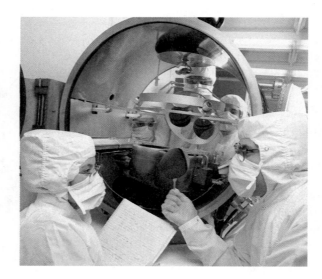

Communication is a vital part of any manager's job. Messages must be appropriately crafted, effectively transmitted, and properly received. Responses to messages from others are also critical. These managers are studying ways to manufacture microscopic electronic chips. They must communicate with one another effectively if their efforts are to pay off.

Communication also relates directly to the basic management functions of planning, organizing, leading, and controlling. Environmental scanning, integrating planning-time horizons, and decision making, for example, all necessitate communication. Delegation, coordination, and organization change and development also entail communication. Developing reward systems and interacting with subordinates as a part of the leading function would be impossible without some form of communication. And communication is essential to establishing standards, monitoring performance, and taking corrective actions as a part of control. Clearly, then, communication is a pervasive part of virtually all managerial activities.

The Communication Process

Figure 18.1 illustrates how communication generally takes place between people. The process of communication begins when one person (the sender) wants to transmit a fact, idea, opinion, or other information to someone else (the receiver). This fact, idea, or opinion has meaning to the sender, whether it be simple and concrete or complex and abstract. For example, if a marketing representative of a company lands a new account and wants to tell her boss about it, this fact and her motivation to tell her boss represent meaning.

The next step is to encode the meaning into a form appropriate to the situation. The encoding might take the form of words, facial expressions, gestures, or even artistic expressions and physical actions. For example, the marketing rep-

FIGURE 18.1 The Communication Process

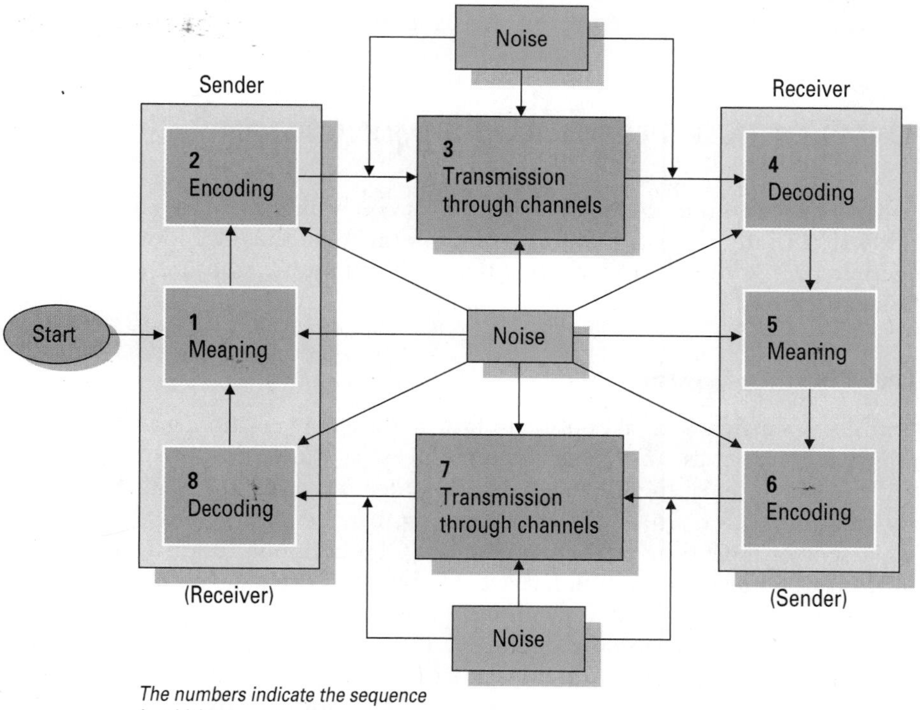

The numbers indicate the sequence
in which steps take place.

As the figure shows, noise can disrupt the communication process at any step. Managers must therefore understand that a conversation in the next office, a fax machine out of paper, and the receiver's worries may all thwart the manager's best attempts to communicate.

resentative might have said, "I just landed the Acme account," "We just got some good news from Acme," "Acme just made the right decision," or any number of other things. Clearly, the encoding process is influenced by the content of the message, the familiarity of sender and receiver, and other situational factors.

After the message has been encoded, it is transmitted through the appropriate channel or medium. The channel by which the present encoded message is being transmitted to you is the printed page. Common channels in organizations include meetings, memos, letters, reports, e-mail, and telephone calls. The marketing representative might have written her boss a note, called him on the telephone, or dropped by his office to convey the news. Because both she and her boss were out of the office when she got the news, she called and left a message for him on voice mail.

After the message is received, it is decoded back into a form that has meaning for the receiver. As we noted earlier, the consistency of this meaning can vary dramatically. On hearing about the Acme deal, the marketing representative's boss might have thought, "This'll mean a big promotion for both of us," "This is great news for the company," or "She's blowing her own horn too much again." In many cases, the meaning prompts a response, and the cycle is continued when a new message is sent by the same steps back to the original sender. The marketing representative's boss might have called her to offer congratulations, written her a personal note of praise, or sent a formal letter of acknowledgment.

"Noise" may disrupt communication anywhere along the way. Noise can be the sound of someone coughing, a truck driving by, or two people talking close at hand. It can also include disruptions such as a letter being lost in the mail (either traditional or electronic), a telephone line going dead, or one of the participants in a conversation being called away before the communication process is completed. If a congratulatory note written by the marketing representative's boss had gotten lost in the e-mail system, she might have felt unappreciated.

FORMS OF INTERPERSONAL COMMUNICATION

Managers need to understand several kinds of communication. Two forms, oral and written, are primarily interpersonal in nature; thus we discuss them together here. Other forms of organizational communication are covered in the next section.

Oral Communication

● **oral communication**
Face-to-face conversation, group discussions, telephone calls, and other circumstances in which the spoken word is used to transmit meaning

Oral communication takes place in face-to-face conversation, group discussions, telephone calls, and other circumstances in which the spoken word is used to express meaning. Henry Mintzberg demonstrated the importance of oral communication when he found that most managers spend between 50 and 90 percent of their time talking to people.[8] Oral communication is so prevalent for several reasons. As summarized in Table 18.1, the primary advantage of oral communication is that it promotes prompt feedback and interchange in the form of verbal questions or agreement, facial expressions, and gestures. Oral communication is also easy (all the sender needs to do is talk), and it can be done with little preparation (though careful preparation is advisable in certain situations). The sender does not need pencil and paper, computer, or other equipment. In one survey, 55 percent of the executives sampled felt that their own written communication skills were fair or poor so they chose oral communication to avoid embarrassment![9]

Nevertheless, oral communication also has drawbacks. It may suffer from problems of inaccuracy if the speaker chooses the wrong words to convey meaning or leaves out pertinent details, if noise disrupts the process, or if the receiver forgets part or all of the message. In a two-way discussion, there is seldom time for a thoughtful, considered response or for introducing many new facts, and there is no permanent record of what has been said. In addition, although most managers are comfortable talking to people individually or in small groups, fewer enjoy speaking to larger audiences.[10]

Written Communication

"Putting it in writing" can solve many of the problems inherent in oral communication. Nevertheless, and perhaps surprisingly, **written communication** is not as common as one might imagine, nor is it a mode of communication much respected by managers. One sample of managers indicated that only 13 percent of the mail they received was of immediate use to them.[11] More than 80 percent of the managers who responded to another survey indicated that the written communication they received was of fair or poor quality.[12]

● **written communication**
Memos, letters, reports, notes, and other circumstances in which the written word is used to transmit meaning

The biggest single drawback of written communication is that it inhibits feedback and interchange (see Table 18.1). When one manager sends another manager a letter, it must be written or dictated, typed, mailed, received, routed, opened, and read. Misunderstandings may take several days to be recognized, let alone rectified. A phone call could settle the whole matter in just a few minutes. Thus written communication often inhibits feedback and interchange and is usually more difficult and time consuming than oral communication. The opening incident reflects another drawback to written communication.

Of course, written communication offers some advantages. It is often quite accurate and provides a permanent record of the exchange. The sender can take the time to collect and assimilate the information and can draft and revise it before it is transmitted. The receiver can take the time to read it carefully and can refer to it repeatedly, as needed. For these reasons, written communication

T A B L E 18.1 Interpersonal Communication		
Form	**Advantages**	**Disadvantages**
Oral	1. Promotes feedback and interchange 2. Is easy to use	1. May suffer from inaccuracies 2. Leaves no permanent record 3. Seldom time for thoughtful response
Written	1. Tends to be more accurate 2. Provides a record of the communication	1. Inhibits feedback and interchange 2. Is more difficult and time consuming

The two basic forms of interpersonal communication are oral and written communication. Each has its own unique advantages and disadvantages. Managers should consider using oral communication when the message is impersonal, routine, and long.

is generally preferable when important details are involved. At times it is important to one or both parties to have a written record available as evidence of exactly what took place.

Choosing the Right Form

Which form of interpersonal communication should the manager use? The situation determines the best medium. Oral communication is often preferred when the message is personal, nonroutine, and brief. Written communication is usually best when the message is more impersonal, routine, and longer.[13] The manager can also combine media to capitalize on the advantages of each. For example, a quick telephone call to set up a meeting is easy and gets an immediate response. Following up the call with a reminder note helps ensure that the recipient will remember the meeting, and it provides a record of the meeting having been called. Recent breakthroughs in electronic communication have facilitated just such actions. As we discuss more fully later, mobile telephones, facsimile machines, and computer networks blur the differences between oral and written communication and help each be more effective.[14]

FORMS OF ORGANIZATIONAL COMMUNICATION

In addition to the two pure forms of interpersonal communication just described, other varieties of organizational communication are of concern to managers. Each of these involves oral or written communication, but each also extends to broad patterns of communication across the organization.[15] As shown in Figure 18.2, two of these forms of communication follow vertical and horizontal linkages in the organization.

Vertical Communication

● **vertical communication**
Communication that flows up and down the organization, usually along formal reporting lines; it takes place between managers and their subordinates and may involve several different levels of the organization

Vertical communication is communication that flows both up and down the organization, usually along formal reporting lines—that is, it is the communication that takes place between managers and their superiors and subordinates. Vertical communication may involve only two persons, or it may flow through several different organizational levels.

Upward Communication Upward communication consists of messages from subordinates to superiors. This flow is usually from subordinates to their direct superior, then to that person's direct superior, and so on up the hierarchy. Occasionally, a message might bypass a particular superior. The typical content of upward communication is requests, information that the lower-level manager thinks is important to the higher-level manager, responses to requests from the higher-level manager, suggestions, complaints, and financial information. Research has shown that upward communication is more subject to distortion than is downward communication. Subordinates are likely to withhold or distort information that makes them look bad. The greater the degree of difference in status between superior and subordinate and the greater the degree of distrust, the more likely the subordinate is to suppress or distort information.[16] For example, when Harold Geneen was CEO of ITT Corporation, subordinates routinely withheld information about problems from him if they thought that the news would make him angry and if they thought that they could solve the problem themselves without his ever knowing about it.[17]

Downward Communication   Downward communication occurs when information flows down the hierarchy from superiors to subordinates. The typical content of these messages is directives on how something is to be done, the assignment of new responsibilities, performance feedback, and general information that the higher-level manager thinks will be of value to the lower-level manager. Leo Thomas's memo at Kodak to other managers regarding cost cutting was downward communication. Vertical communication can, and usually should, be two way. That is, give-and-take communication with active feedback is generally likely to be more effective than one-way communication.[18]

Horizontal Communication

Whereas vertical communication involves a superior and a subordinate, **horizontal communication** involves colleagues and peers at the same level of the organization. For example, an operations manager might communicate to a marketing manager that inventory levels are running low and that projected delivery dates should be extended by two weeks. Horizontal communication probably occurs more among managers than among nonmanagers.

Horizontal communication serves a number of purposes. It facilitates coordination among interdependent units. For example, while researching the strategies of Japanese semiconductor firms in Europe, a manager at Motorola found a great deal of information that was relevant to his assignment. He also uncovered some additional information that was potentially important to

● **horizontal communication**
Communication that flows laterally within the organization; it involves colleagues and peers at the same level of the organization and may involve individuals from several different organizational units

Formal communication in organizations follows official reporting relationships and/or prescribed channels. For example, vertical communication, shown here with dashed lines, flows between levels in the organization and involves subordinates and their managers. Horizontal communication flows between people at the same level and is usually used to facilitate coordination.

F I G U R E   18.2   Formal Communication in Organizations

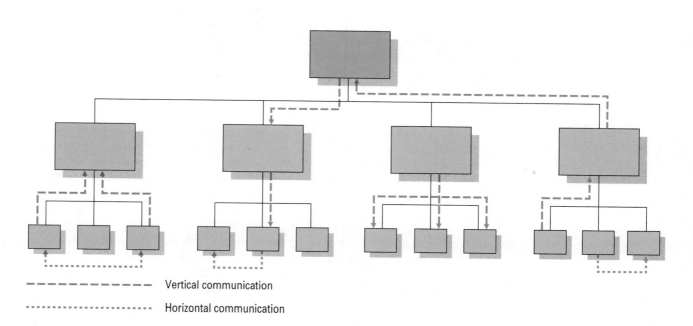

------- Vertical communication

·········· Horizontal communication

another department, so he passed it along to a colleague in that department, who used it to improve his own operations.[19] Horizontal communication can also be used for joint problem solving, as when two plant managers at a company get together to work out a new method to improve productivity. Finally, horizontal communication plays a major role in work teams with members drawn from several departments.

Formal Information Systems

Another increasingly important method of organizational communication is information systems, accomplished by either a managerial approach or an operational approach. The managerial approach involves the creation of a position usually called the chief information officer, or CIO.[20] The Royal Bank of Canada, TransCanada Pipe Lines, and Starbucks Coffee Co. all have such a position. The CIO is responsible for determining the information-processing needs and requirements of the organization and then putting in place systems that facilitate smooth and efficient organizational communication.

The operational approach, often a part of the CIO's efforts, involves the creation of one or more formal information systems linking all relevant managers, departments, and facilities in the organization. In the absence of such a system, a marketing manager, for example, may need to call a warehouse manager to find out how much of a particular product is in stock before promising shipping dates to a customer. An effective formal information system allows the marketing manager to get the information more quickly, and probably more accurately, by plugging directly into a computerized information system. Because of the increased emphasis and importance of these kinds of information systems, we cover them in detail in Chapter 22.

Electronic Communication

In recent years, the nature of organizational communication has changed dramatically, mainly because of breakthroughs in electronic communication capabilities, and the future promises even more change. Electronic typewriters and photocopying machines were early breakthroughs. The photocopier, for example, enabled a manager to distribute a typed report to large numbers of other people in an extremely short time. Computers have accelerated the process even more.

Managers are now able to have teleconferences in which they stay at their own locations (such as offices in different cities) but are seen on television monitors as they "meet."[21] A manager in Toronto can type a letter or memorandum into a computer, click icons with a mouse, and have it delivered to Vancouver. Highly detailed information can be retrieved with ease from large electronic databanks. This has given rise to a new version of an old work arrangement—*telecommuting* is the label given to a new electronic cottage industry. In a cottage industry, people work at home and periodically bring the product of their labour in to the company. In telecommuting, people work at home on their computers and transmit their work to the company by means of telephone modems. Among Canadian companies that have telecommuting arrangements are the Royal Bank of Canada, Bell Canada, and IBM Canada. Canada has been slower to embrace the trend to telecommuting than the United States, where it is estimated that as many as 35 million workers telecommute.[22] Estimates suggest that by the year 2001, the number of employees in Canada who do at least part of their work from home will reach 1.5 million.[23]

Cellular telephones, facsimile machines, and e-mail networks have made managers' communicating with one another even easier. Many now use cellular phones to make and receive calls while commuting to and from work and at lunch. Facsimile machines enable people using written communication media to get rapid feedback. The *Managing in a Changing World* box discusses how electronic communication is being used in universities—and some of the responses to it.

Psychologists, however, are beginning to associate some problems with these communication advances. For one thing, managers who are seldom in their "real" offices are likely to fall behind in their fields and to be victimized by organizational politics because they are not present to keep in touch with what's going on and to protect themselves. They drop out of the organizational grapevine and miss out on much of the informal communication that takes place. Moreover, the use of electronic communication at the expense of face-to-face meetings and conversations makes it hard to build a strong culture, develop solid working relationships, and create a mutually supportive atmosphere of trust and cooperativeness.[24]

INFORMAL COMMUNICATION IN ORGANIZATIONS

The aforementioned forms of organizational communication all represent planned, formal communication mechanisms. However, in many cases much of the communication that takes place in an organization transcends these formal channels and instead follows any of several informal methods. Figure 18.3 illustrates numerous examples of informal communication. Common forms of

Teleconferencing is an increasingly popular form of organizational communication. New technology is rapidly redefining how modern organizations communicate.

informal communication in organizations include communication networks, the grapevine, management by wandering around, and nonverbal communication.

Communication Networks

A **communication network** is the pattern through which the members of a group communicate. Researchers studying group dynamics have discovered several typical networks in groups consisting of three, four, and five members. Representative networks among members of five-member groups are shown in Figure 18.4.[25] In the wheel pattern, all communication flows through one central person who is probably the group's leader. In a sense the wheel is the most centralized network because one person receives and disseminates all information. The Y pattern is slightly less centralized—two persons are closer to the centre of the network. The chain offers a more even flow of information among members, although two persons (the ones at each end) interact with only one other person. This path is closed in the circle pattern. Finally, the all-channel network, the most decentralized, allows a free flow of information among all group members. Everyone participates equally, and the group's leader, if there is one, is not likely to have excessive power.

There are likely to be some interesting connections between the type of network that emerges in a group and that group's performance. For example, when the group's task is relatively simple and routine, centralized networks tend to perform with greatest efficiency and accuracy. The dominant leader facilitates performance by coordinating the flow of information. When a group of accounting clerks is logging incoming invoices and distributing them for payment, for example, one centralized leader can coordinate things efficiently. When the task is complex and nonroutine, such as making a major decision

F I G U R E   18.3   Informal Communication in Organizations

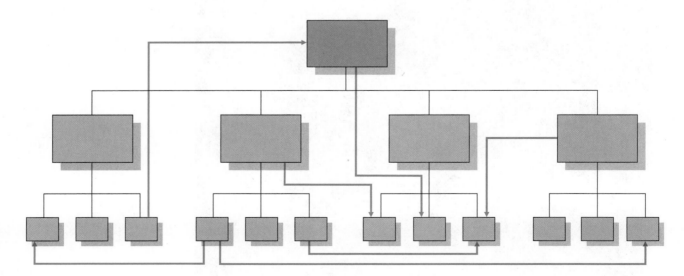

Electronic Communication

Communication is central to the process of teaching and learning. The rapidly changing nature of communication in institutions of higher learning is not without controversy. While some view the revolution in telecommunications as something positive, others see it as threatening the very concept of the university.

One technological change that is largely viewed as positive is electronic publishing. University libraries, faced with dwindling financial resources and rising costs for print materials, have turned to electronic journals. There are currently some 1,000 English-language journals online. While there is some debate about the extent of savings from electronic publishing, there is no doubt that the potential for timely dissemination of information is greatly enhanced by the electronic medium.

One controversial development spawned by modern telecommunications technology is the virtual classroom. Computer applications like Net Professor Suite combine videoconferencing, Intranet technology, and a Web-enabled database to make the virtual classroom a reality. Net Professor Suite, a product of Halifax-based Quagga Web Services Ltd., is being installed at Acadia University and will enable the uni-

versity to offer Internet distance education courses; all interaction between professors and students will be conducted electronically.

The advent of the virtual classroom has provoked dissent on campus. At York University, instructional technology was a major issue in the 1997 strike. As part of the settlement of that dispute, York professors won the right not to be forced to use instructional technology or deliver courses over the Internet. The Canadian Association of University Teachers has developed model clauses on the issue for its affiliates who are engaged in negotiating collective agreements. Professors argue that they are not modern-day Luddites (English workers who destroyed labour-saving machinery in the early nineteenth century), but they object to the commercialization of higher education and to the ability of universities to profit from what they see as their intellectual property. Moreover, they see the new ways of communicating with students as inferior pedagogy.

References: Kenneth Weiss, "A Wary Academia on Edge of Cyberspace," *The Los Angeles Times,* March 31, 1998, p. A1; Tom Mason, "A Win for the Aged," *Canadian Business,* April 10, 1998, p. 109; and Cristina Brandao, "Rewiring the Ivory Tower," *Canadian Business Technology,* Winter 1996, pp. 61–64.

about organizational strategy, decentralized networks tend to be most effective because open channels of communication permit more interaction and a more efficient sharing of relevant information. Managers should recognize the effects of communication networks on group and organizational performance and try to structure networks appropriately.

The Grapevine

The **grapevine** is an informal communication network that can permeate an entire organization. Grapevines are found in all organizations except the very smallest, but they do not always follow the same patterns as, nor do they necessarily coincide with, formal channels of authority and communication. Research has identified several kinds of grapevines.[26] The two most common are illustrated in Figure 18.5. The gossip chain occurs when one person spreads the message to many other people. Each one, in turn, may either keep the information confidential or pass it on to others. The gossip chain is likely to carry personal information. The other common grapevine is the cluster chain, in which one person passes the information to a selected few individuals. Some of the receivers pass the information to a few other individuals; the rest keep it to themselves.

● **grapevine**
An informal communication network among people in an organization

There is some disagreement about the accuracy of the information carried by the grapevine, but research is increasingly finding it to be fairly accurate, especially when the information is based on fact rather than speculation. One study found that the grapevine may be between 75 percent and 95 percent accurate.[27] That same study also found that informal communication is increasing in many organizations for two basic reasons. One contributing factor is the recent increase in merger, acquisition, and takeover activity. Because such activity can greatly affect the people within an organization, it follows that they may spend more time talking about it.[28] The second contributing factor is that as corporations move facilities from inner cities to suburbs, employees tend to talk less and less to others outside the organization and more and more to each other.

Attempts to eliminate the grapevine are fruitless, but fortunately the manager does have some control over it. By maintaining open channels of communication and responding vigorously to inaccurate information, the manager can minimize the damage the grapevine can do. The grapevine can actually be an asset. By learning who the important people in the grapevine are, for example, the manager can partially control the information they receive and use the grapevine to sound out employee reactions to new ideas such as a change in human resource policies or benefits packages. The manager can also get valuable information from the grapevine and use it to improve decision making.

Management by Wandering Around

Another increasingly popular form of informal communication is called **management by wandering around**.[29] The basic idea is that some managers keep in touch with what's going on by wandering around and talking with people—immediate subordinates, subordinates far down the organizational hierarchy, delivery people, customers, or anyone else who is involved with the company in some way. Bill Marriott, for example, frequently visits the kitchens, loading docks, and custodial work areas whenever he tours a Marriott hotel. He claims that by talking with employees throughout the hotel, he gets new ideas and has a better feel for the entire company.

A related form of organizational communication that really has no specific term is the informal interchange that takes place outside the normal work setting. Employees attending the company picnic, playing on the company softball team, or taking fishing trips together will almost always spend part of their time talking about work.

> ● **management by wandering around**
> An approach to communication that involves the manager literally wandering around and having spontaneous conversations with others

> Research on communication networks has identified five basic networks for five-person groups. These vary in terms of information flow, position of the leader, and effectiveness for different types of tasks. Managers might strive to create centralized networks when group tasks are simple and routine. Alternatively, managers can foster decentralized groups when group tasks are complex and nonroutine.

F I G U R E   18.4   Types of Communication Networks

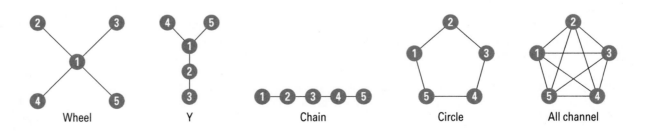

Nonverbal Communication

Nonverbal communication is a communication exchange that does not use words or that uses words to carry more meaning than the strict definition of the words themselves. Nonverbal communication is a powerful but little-understood form of communication in organizations. It often relies on facial expressions, body movements, physical contact, gestures, and inflection and tone. One study found that as much as 55 percent of a message's content is transmitted by facial expression and body posture; another 38 percent derives from inflection and tone. Words themselves account for only 7 percent of the content of the message.[30]

Research has identified three kinds of nonverbal communication practised by managers—images, settings, and body language.[31] In this context, images are the kinds of words people elect to use. "Damn the torpedoes, full speed ahead" and "Even though there are some potential hazards, we should proceed with this course of action" may convey the same meaning. Yet the person who uses the first expression may be perceived as a maverick, a courageous hero, an individualist, or a reckless and foolhardy adventurer. The person who uses the second might be described as aggressive, forceful, diligent, or narrow-minded and resistant to change. In short, our choice of words conveys much more than just the strict meaning of the words themselves.

The setting for communication also plays a major role in nonverbal communication. Boundaries, familiarity, the home turf, and other elements of the setting are all important. Much has been written about the symbols of power in organizations. The size and location of an office, the kinds of furniture in the office, and the accessibility of the person in the office all communicate useful information. For example, a manager may position her desk so that it is always between her and a visitor. This keeps her in charge. When she wants a less-formal dialogue, she moves around to the front of the desk and sits beside her visitor. Another manager may have his desk facing a side window so that when he turns around to greet a visitor there is never anything between them.

F I G U R E   18.5   Common Grapevine Chains Found in Organizations

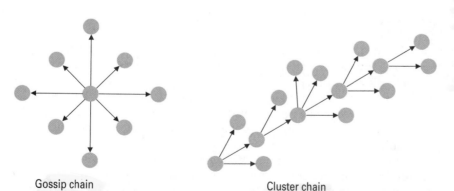

Gossip chain
(One person tells many)

Cluster chain
(Many people tell a few)

The two most common grapevine chains in organizations are the gossip chain (in which one person communicates messages to many others) and the cluster chain (in which many people pass messages to a few others).

Source: Based on Keith Davis and John W. Newstrom, *Human Behavior at Work: Organizational Behavior*, 8th ed. (New York: McGraw-Hill, 1989). Reproduced with permission.

A third form of nonverbal communication is body language.[32] The distance we stand from someone as we speak has meaning. In North America, standing very close to someone you are talking to generally signals either familiarity or aggression. The English and Germans stand farther apart than Canadians when talking, whereas the Arabs, Japanese, and Mexicans stand closer together.[33] Eye contact is another effective means of nonverbal communication. For example, prolonged eye contact might suggest either hostility or romantic interest. Other kinds of body language include body and arm movement, pauses in speech, and mode of dress.

The manager should be aware of the importance of nonverbal communication and recognize its potential impact. Giving an employee good news about a reward with the wrong nonverbal cues can destroy the reinforcement value of the reward. Likewise, reprimanding an employee but providing inconsistent nonverbal cues can limit the effectiveness of the sanctions. The tone of the message, where and how the message is delivered, facial expressions, and gestures can all amplify or weaken the message or change the message altogether.

MANAGING ORGANIZATIONAL COMMUNICATION

In view of the importance and persuasiveness of communication in organizations, it is vital for managers to understand how to manage the communication process.[34] Managers should understand how to maximize the potential benefits of communication and minimize the potential problems. We begin our discussion of communication management by considering the factors that might disrupt effective communication and how to deal with them.

Barriers to Communication

Several factors may disrupt the communication process or serve as barriers to effective communication.[35] As shown in Table 18.2, these may be divided into two classes: individual barriers and organizational barriers.

Individual Barriers   Several individual barriers may disrupt effective communication. One common problem is conflicting or inconsistent signals. Another is lack of credibility. A manager is sending conflicting signals when she says on Monday that things should be done one way but then prescribes an entirely different procedure on Wednesday. Inconsistent signals are being sent by a manager who says that he has an "open door" policy and wants his subordinates to drop by but keeps his door closed and becomes irritated whenever someone stops in. Credibility problems arise when the sender is not considered a reliable source of information. He may not be trusted or may not be perceived as knowledgeable about the subject at hand. When a politician is caught withholding information or when a manager makes a series of bad decisions, the extent to which they will be listened to and believed thereafter diminishes. In extreme cases, people may talk about something they obviously know little or nothing about. Some people are simply reluctant to initiate a communication exchange. This reluctance may occur for a variety of reasons. A manager may be reluctant to tell subordinates about an impending budget cut because he knows they will be unhappy about it. Likewise, a subordinate may be reluctant to transmit information upward for fear of reprisal or because she feels that such an effort would be futile.

Two other individual barriers to effective communication are poor listening skills and predispositions about the subject at hand. Some people are poor listeners. When someone is talking to them, they may be daydreaming, reading, or listening to another conversation. Because they are not concentrating on what is being said, they may not comprehend part or all of the message. They may even think that they really are paying attention, only to realize later that they cannot remember parts of the conversation. Receivers may also bring certain predispositions to the communication process. They may already have their minds made up. For example, a manager may have heard that his new boss is unpleasant and hard to work with. When she calls him in for an introductory meeting, he may be predisposed to dislike her and discount what she has to say.

Organizational Barriers Other barriers to effective communication involve the organizational context in which the communication occurs. Semantics problems arise when words have different meanings for different people. Words and phrases such as *profit, increased output,* and *return on investment* may have positive meanings for managers but less positive meanings for labour. Communication problems may arise when people of different power or status try to communicate with each other. The company president may discount a suggestion from an operating employee, thinking, "How can someone at that level help me run my business?" Or when the president goes out to inspect a new plant, workers may be reluctant to offer suggestions because of their lower status. The marketing vice president may have more power than the human resource vice president and consequently may not pay much attention to a staffing report submitted by the human resource department. If people perceive a situation differently, they may have difficulty communicating with one another. When two managers observe that a third manager has not spent much time in her office lately, one manager may believe that she has been to several important meetings whereas the other may think that she is "hiding out." If they need to talk about her in some official capacity, problems may arise because one has a positive impression and the other a negative impression.

Environmental factors may also disrupt effective communication. As mentioned earlier, noise may affect communication in many ways. Similarly, overload may be a problem when the receiver is sent more information than he or

TABLE 18.2 Barriers to Effective Communication	
Individual Barriers	**Organizational Barriers**
Conflicting or inconsistent cues	Semantics
Credibility about the subject	Status or power differences
Reluctance to communicate	Different perceptions
Poor listening skills	Noise
Predispositions about the subject	Overload

Numerous barriers can disrupt effective communication. Some of these barriers involve individual characteristics and processes. Others are a function of the organizational context in which communication is taking place.

she can effectively handle. When the manager gives a subordinate many jobs on which to work and at the same time the subordinate is told by family and friends to do other things, overload may result and communication effectiveness may diminish.

Improving Communication Effectiveness

Although many factors can disrupt communication, managers fortunately can resort to several techniques for improving communication effectiveness.[36] As shown in Table 18.3, these techniques include both individual and organizational skills.

Individual Skills   The single most important individual skill for improving communication effectiveness is being a good listener. Being a good listener requires that the individual be prepared to listen, not interrupt the speaker, concentrate on both the words and the meaning being conveyed, be patient, and ask questions as appropriate.[37] So important are good listening skills that some companies conduct programs to train their managers to be better listeners. Figure 18.6 illustrates the characteristics of poor listeners versus good listeners.

In addition to being a good listener, several other individual skills can also promote effective communication. Feedback, one of the most important, is facilitated by two-way communication. Two-way communication allows the receiver to ask questions, request clarification, and express opinions that let the sender know whether he or she has been understood. In general, the more complicated the message, the more useful two-way communication is. In addition, the sender should be aware of the meanings that different receivers might attach to various words. For example, when addressing shareholders, a manager might use the word *profits* often. When addressing labour leaders, however, she may choose to use *profits* less often.

Furthermore, the sender should try to maintain credibility. This can be accomplished by not pretending to be an expert, by "doing one's homework" and checking facts, and by otherwise being as accurate and honest as possible. The sender should also try to be sensitive to the receiver's perspective. A manager who must tell a subordinate that she has not been recommended for a promotion should recognize that the subordinate will be frustrated and unhappy. The content of the message and its method of delivery should be chosen accordingly. The manager should be primed to accept a reasonable

TABLE 18.3 Overcoming Barriers to Communication	
Individual Skills	**Organizational Skills**
Develop good listening skills	Follow up
Encourage two-way communication	Regulate information flows
Be aware of language and meaning	Understand the richness of media
Maintain credibility	
Be sensitive to receiver's perspective	
Be sensitive to sender's perspective	

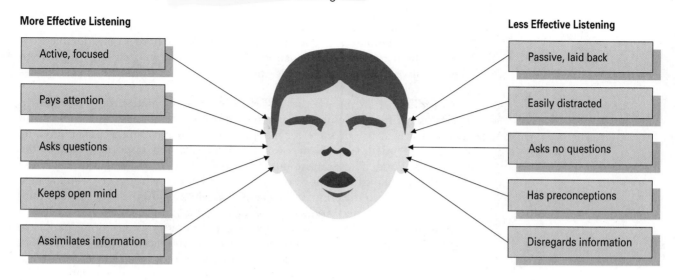

More Effective Listening

Active, focused

Pays attention

Asks questions

Keeps open mind

Assimilates information

Less Effective Listening

Passive, laid back

Easily distracted

Asks no questions

Has preconceptions

Disregards information

degree of hostility and bitterness without getting angry in return.[38] Finally, the receiver should also try to be sensitive to the sender's point of view. Suppose that a manager has just received some bad news—for example, that his position is being eliminated next year. Others should understand that he may be disappointed, angry, or even depressed for a while. Thus they might make a special effort not to take too much offence if he snaps at them, and they might look for signals that he needs someone to talk to.

Organizational Skills   Three useful organizational skills can also enhance communication effectiveness for both the sender and the receiver—following up, regulating information flow, and understanding the richness of different media. Following up simply involves checking at a later time to be sure that a message has been received and understood. After a manager mails a report to a colleague, she might call a few days later to make sure that the report has arrived. If it has, the manager might ask whether the colleague has any questions about it. Regulating information flow means that the sender or receiver takes steps to ensure that overload does not occur. For the sender, this could mean not passing too much information through the system at one time. For the receiver, it might mean notifying people that he is being asked to do too many things at once. Many managers limit the influx of information by periodically weeding out the list of journals and routine reports they receive, or they train a secretary to screen phone calls and visitors. Both parties should also understand the richness associated with different media. When a manager is going to lay off a subordinate temporarily, the message should be delivered in person. A face-to-face channel of communication gives the manager an opportunity to explain the situation and answer questions. When the purpose of the message is to grant a pay increase, written communication may be appropriate because it can be more objective and precise. The manager could then follow up the written notice with personal congratulations.

Effective listening skills are a vital part of communication in organizations. There are several things that can contribute to poor listening skills by individuals in organizations. Fortunately, there are also several things people can do to improve their listening skills.

SUMMARY OF KEY POINTS

Most of the activities that take place in an organization involve interpersonal dynamics—interactions between and among people. There is considerable variation in the nature of these dynamics, and they can range from very positive to very negative. Likewise, numerous outcomes can result from interpersonal relations as well.

Communication is the process of transmitting information from one person to another. Effective communication is the process of sending a message in such a way that the message received is as close in meaning as possible to the message intended. Communication is a pervasive and important part of the manager's world. The communication process consists of a sender encoding meaning and transmitting it to one or more receivers, who receive the message and decode it into meaning. In two-way communication the process continues with the roles reversed. Noise can disrupt any part of the overall process.

Interpersonal communication focuses on communication among people at work. Two important forms of interpersonal communication, oral and written, both offer unique advantages and disadvantages. Thus the manager should weigh the pros and cons of each when choosing a medium for communication.

There are a variety of forms of organizational communication. Vertical communication between superiors and subordinates may flow upward or downward. Horizontal communication involves peers and colleagues at the same level in the organization. Organizations also use information systems to manage communication. Electronic communication is likely to have a profound effect on managerial and organizational communication in the years to come.

A great deal of informal communication also occurs in organizations. Communication networks are recurring patterns of communication among members of a group. The grapevine is the informal communication network among people in an organization. Management by wandering around is also a popular informal method of communication. Nonverbal communication includes facial expressions, body movements, physical contact, gestures, and inflection and tone.

Managing the communication process necessitates recognizing the barriers to effective communication and understanding how to overcome them. Barriers can be identified at both the individual and organizational level. Likewise, both individual and organizational skills can be developed to overcome these barriers.

DISCUSSION QUESTIONS

Questions for Review

1. Define communication. What are the components of the communication process?
2. Which form of interpersonal communication is best for long-term retention? Why? Which form is best for getting across subtle nuances of meaning? Why?
3. Describe three different communication networks. Which type of network seems to most accurately describe the grapevine? Why?

4. What are the informal methods of communication? Identify five examples of nonverbal communication that you have recently observed.

Questions for Analysis

5. Can an organization function without communication? Why or why not?
6. At what points in the communication process can problems occur? Give examples of communication problems and indicate how they might be prevented or alleviated.
7. In terms of the barriers most likely to be encountered, what are the differences between horizontal and vertical communication in an organization? How might a formal information system be designed to reduce such barriers?

Questions for Application

8. What forms of communication have you experienced today? What form of communication is involved in a face-to-face conversation with a friend? A telephone call from a customer? A traffic light or crossing signal? A picture of a cigarette in a circle with a slash across it?
9. Interview a local manager to determine what forms of communication are used in his or her organization. Arrange to observe that manager for a couple of hours. What forms of communication did you observe?
10. How are electronic communication devices likely to affect the communication process in the future? Why? Interview someone from a local organization who uses electronic communication to see if she or he feels as you do.

BUILDING EFFECTIVE TECHNICAL SKILLS

Exercise Overview

Technical skills are the skills necessary to perform the work of the organization. This exercise will help you develop and apply technical skills involving the Internet and its potential for gathering information relevant to making important decisions.

Exercise Background

Assume that you are a manager for a large national retailer. You have been assigned the responsibility for identifying potential locations for the construction of a warehouse and distribution centre. The idea behind such a centre is that the firm can use its enormous purchasing power to buy many products in large, bulk quantities at relatively low prices. Individual stores can then order specific quantities they need from the warehouse.

The location will need an abundance of land. The warehouse itself, for example, will cover more than 1.5 hectares. In addition, it needs to be close to railroads and major highways because shipments will be arriving by both rail and trucks, although outbound shipments will be exclusively by truck. Other important considerations are that land prices and the cost of living should be relatively low and that weather conditions should be mild (so as to minimize disruptions to shipments).

The firm's general experience is that small to midsize communities work best. Moreover, warehouses are already in place in Western and Eastern Canada, so this new one will most likely be in Central Canada. Your boss has asked you to identify three or four possible sites.

Exercise Task

With the preceding information as a framework, do the following:
1. Use the Internet to identify as many as ten possible locations.
2. Use additional information from the Internet to narrow the set of possible locations to three or four.
3. Use the Internet to find out as much as possible about the potential locations.

Exxon's Communication Failure

Exxon Corporation is one of the world's best known businesses, tracing its roots to 1863 when John D. Rockefeller opened an oil refinery that would eventually become Standard Oil Company. The U.S. Department of Justice broke up Standard Oil under antitrust legislation in 1911. One surviving piece eventually became Exxon, which is now the largest U.S. oil company and one of the largest industrial companies in the world. But just because it is large and successful does not mean that it handles crisis communication well.

In 1989 an Exxon oil tanker, the *Exxon Valdez*, ran aground in Prince William Sound, Alaska, spilling nearly eleven million barrels of oil and causing tremendous environmental damage. Exxon's poor handling of the crisis sent a message to corporations worldwide that they needed to have better and more effective crisis-communication plans.

After the *Valdez* incident, Exxon was attacked for being too slow to respond, too slow to accept its responsibility, and for providing inadequate cleanup efforts. In a crisis situation such as the *Valdez* disaster, the primary task of management is to inform the public—through the media—about what has happened. Exxon's then-CEO, Lawrence Rawl, however, made no comment for nearly a week after the incident and instead relied on his staff to handle early communications. When he finally did make a public appearance, he seemed uninformed and unsure of the details of what was happening, which further fuelled negative reactions.

For example, Exxon claimed that the damage was minimal, but newscasts were clearly showing pictures of oil-covered beaches and rocks covered with thousands of dead birds and fish. The media essentially suggested that Exxon was not being completely honest and candid in its statements and public relations releases. Differences between accounts provided by Exxon and as covered by the media led to a negative public reaction and distrust of Exxon.

Delays, errors, and contradictions seemed to demonstrate that Exxon was arrogant, uncaring, and unaware of the environment in which it operated. The public quickly became outraged. Customers threatened a boycott and thousands of them even returned their credit cards (the actual impact of these actions, however, was virtually negligible). Nevertheless, in a full page newspaper advertisement ten days after the crisis, Rawl claimed that the company had acted swiftly and competently.

Unfortunately, Exxon's crisis-communications problems were confounded by internal problems of its own making. As it was still dealing with its environmental disaster, Exxon laid off more than 75,000 workers and reduced training for those that remained. Employees were asked to take early retirement or to relocate when Exxon moved to Texas from New York. Consequently, many Exxon employees were unhappy or worried about their own future. As a result, they were not particularly motivated or excited about helping the company overcome its problems.

Thus, although the press coverage of the *Valdez* crisis emphasized Rawl's difficulties in responding to the public outcry over the oil spill, morale and attitude problems among its employees also played a role. Exxon seemed to have image problems both within and without the company and was having communication problems of varying kinds.

Has Exxon ever learned its lesson? It does appear to finally be getting the message. For example, its crisis-communication plan now involves having video and telecommunications resources, senior executives trained in dealing with a hostile media, contacts with print and broadcast media, and a clear spokesperson, the new CEO, Lee Raymond, in place and prepared to deal with any situation imaginable. In the event of another disaster, the crisis team will meet every hour after a disaster occurs until it is resolved. The plan has also been tested in mock disaster drills and simulations. Had Exxon had such a plan ten years ago, most of its problems from the *Valdez* crisis could have been averted.

Questions

1. In what ways did Exxon not handle the communication process very well in the *Valdez* crisis?

2. What barriers to communication seemed to be involved in Exxon's response? Why or in what way?

Exxon's Communication Failure

3. What unintended messages did Exxon send as a result of the way it handled the *Valdez* crisis? How might it prevent any negative communication problems from such crises in the future?

References: *Hoover's Handbook of American Business 1998*, (Austin, Tex.: Hoover's Business Press, 1998), pp. 558–559; Daniel G. Johnson, "Crisis Management: Forewarned Is Forearmed," *Journal of Business Strategy*, March–April 1993, pp. 58–64; "Exxon Stops the Flow," *Time*, March 25, 1991, p. 51; Peter Nulty, "Exxon's Problem: Not What You Think," *Fortune*, April 23, 1990, pp. 202–204; and Sue Stephenson, "The Media and You," *HRMagazine*, June 1997, pp. 146–155.

CHAPTER NOTES

1. "Loose Lips Sink Stock Prices," *Business Week*, October 31, 1994, p. 52; Gary Hoover, Alta Campbell, and Patrick J. Spain (Eds.), *Hoover's Handbook of American Business 1995* (Austin, Tex.: The Reference Press, 1994), pp. 460–461; "Kodak's New Focus," *Business Week*, January 30, 1995, pp. 62–67; and Subrata Chakravarty, "Vindication," *Forbes*, September 7, 1998, pp. 62–65.

2. See John J. Gabarro, "The Development of Working Relationships," in Jay W. Lorsch (Ed.), *Handbook of Organizational Behavior* (Englewood Cliffs, N.J.: Prentice-Hall, 1987), pp. 172–189.

3. See Marcelline R. Fisilier, Daniel C. Ganster, and Bronston T. Mayes, "Effects of Social Support, Role Stress, and Locus of Control on Health," *Journal of Management*, Fall 1987, pp. 517–528.

4. Henry Mintzberg, *The Nature of Managerial Work* (New York: Harper & Row, 1973).

5. See Karl E. Weick and Larry D. Browning, "Argument and Narration in Organizational Communication," *Journal of Management*, Summer 1986, pp. 243–259.

6. John Huey, "The New Power in Black & Decker," *Fortune*, January 2, 1989, pp. 89–94.

7. Mintzberg, *The Nature of Managerial Work*.

8. Mintzberg, *The Nature of Managerial Work*.

9. "Unaccustomed as I am . . . ," *Forbes*, January 16, 1995, p. 100.

10. "Executives Who Dread Public Speaking Learn to Keep Their Cool in the Spotlight," *The Wall Street Journal*, May 4, 1990, pp. B1, B6.

11. Mintzberg, *The Nature of Managerial Work*.

12. Kiechel, "The Big Presentation."

13. Robert H. Lengel and Richard L. Daft, "The Selection of Communication Media as an Executive Skill," *The Academy of Management Executive*, August 1988, pp. 225–232.

14. Janet Fulk, "Social Construction of Communication Technology," *Academy of Management Journal*, Vol. 36, No. 5, 1993, pp. 921–950.

15. Nelson Phillips and John Brown, "Analyzing Communications In and Around Organizations: A Critical Hermeneutic Approach," *Academy of Management Journal*, Vol. 36, No. 6, 1993, pp. 1547–1576.

16. Walter Kiechel III, "Breaking Bad News to the Boss," *Fortune*, April 9, 1990, pp. 111–112.

17. Myron Magnet, "Is ITT Fighting Shadows—Or Raiders?" *Fortune*, November 11, 1985, pp. 25–28.

18. Mary Young and James Post, "How Leading Companies Communicate with Employees," *Organizational Dynamics*, Summer 1993, pp. 31–43.

19. Brian Dumaine, "Corporate Spies Snoop to Conquer," *Fortune*, November 7, 1988, pp. 68–76.

20. John J. Donovan, "Beyond Chief Information Officer to Network Manager," *Harvard Business Review*, September–October 1988, pp. 134–140.

21. "Software's New World Order," *Business Week*, February 27, 1995, pp. 78–79; and Stratford Sherman, "PC Products That Can Change Your Life," *Fortune*, March 6, 1995, pp. 183–192.

22. "These Top Executives Work Where They Play," *Business Week*, October 27, 1986, pp. 132–134; and "Escape from the Office," *Newsweek*, April 24, 1989, pp. 58–60.

23. "Teleworking Just Isn't There Yet," *Computing Canada*, December 14, 1998, p. 10.

24. Walter Kiechel III, "Hold for the Communicaholic Manager," *Fortune*, January 2, 1989, pp. 107–108.

25. A. Vavelas, "Communication Patterns in Task-Oriented Groups," *Journal of the Accoustical Society of America*, Vol. 22, 1950, pp. 725–730; and Jerry Wofford, Edwin Gerloff, and Robert Cummins, *Organizational Communication* (New York: McGraw-Hill, 1977).

26. Keith Davis, "Management Communication and the Grapevine," *Harvard Business Review*, September–October 1953, pp. 43–49.

27. "Spread the Word: Gossip Is Good," *The Wall Street Journal*, October 4, 1988, p. B1.

28. See David M. Schweiger and Angelo S. DeNisi, "Communication with Employees Following a Merger: A Longitudinal Field Experiment," *Academy of Management Journal*, March 1991, pp. 110–135.

29. See Tom Peters and Nancy Austin, *A Passion for Excellence* (New York: Random House, 1985).

30. Albert Mehrabian, *Non-Verbal Communication* (Chicago: Aldine, 1972).

31. Michael B. McCaskey, "The Hidden Messages Managers Send," *Harvard Business Review*, November–December 1979, pp. 135–148.

32. David Givens, "What Body Language Can Tell You That Words Cannot," *U.S. News & World Report*, November 19, 1984, p. 100.

33. Edward J. Hall, *The Hidden Dimension* (New York: Doubleday, 1966).

34. See Courtland L. Bove and John V. Thill, *Business Communication Today*, 3rd ed. (New York: McGraw-Hill, 1992).

35. See Otis W. Baskin and Craig E. Aronoff, *Interpersonal Communication in Organizations* (Glenview, Ill.: Scott, Foresman, 1980).

36. Joseph Allen and Bennett P. Lientz, *Effective Business Communication* (Santa Monica, Calif.: Goodyear, 1979).

37. Walter Kiechel III, "Learn How to Listen," *Fortune*, August 17, 1987, pp. 107–108.

38. For a recent discussion of these and related issues, see Eric M. Eisenberg and Marsha G. Witten, "Reconsidering Openness in Organizational Communication," *Academy of Management Review*, July 1987, pp. 418–426.

Managing Group and Team Processes

OBJECTIVES

After studying this chapter, you should be able to:

● *Define and identify types of groups and teams in organizations, discuss reasons people join groups and teams, and the stages of group and team development.*

● *Identify and discuss four essential characteristics of teams.*

● *Discuss interpersonal and intergroup conflict in organizations.*

● *Describe how organizations manage conflict.*

OUTLINE

3M's business is innovation, and teamwork is at the heart of the company's success.

Are teams and teamwork, currently popular management terms, just another management fad? The answer seems to be no according to noted management expert Peter Drucker and a 1995 survey of human resource executives, in which 44 percent of respondents called for more teamwork as a means of boosting organizational effectiveness. Used in this context, "team" refers to a mature group (i.e., a group that has reached the performing stage). According to a recent survey of four hundred team members in Canada and the United States, most groups comprise between eight and ten members.

The proliferation of teams in the workplace seems to be a worldwide phenomenon. The concept has found expression at a wide variety of organizations including Algoma Steel, Siemens, Motorola, and Fiat. Teams are an integral part of organizational structure at Campbell Soup Canada and 3M Canada as well. In the 1980s, Campbell's parent company expanded rapidly, but costs soared and by the early 1990s the company had to scale back drastically. The company's Canadian operations were heavily hit. Between 1980 and 1990, Campbell sold or closed seven of its eleven plants. In 1991, David Clark, president of Campbell Canada, decided to turn things around by transforming the way in which Campbell's workers viewed their jobs and company. He divided his top managers into nine teams and charged them with the task of adding $100,000 to the bottom line in three months. The teams came close to achieving their target—a feat made possible by the fact that employees at all levels were involved in the cost-cutting process.

> **"Teams are an integral part of organizational structure at Campbell Soup Canada and 3M Canada."**

3M Canada's human resources practices set the standard for its parent company. Foremost among these practices is teamwork. The company's plant in Brockville, Ontario, is considered a model for 3M plants around the world. At the Brockville factory, employees work in teams of six to eight, and the team orientation also guides the recruitment process in that all job applicants are placed in groups to assess their potential for teamwork. 3M's business is innovation, and teamwork is at the heart of the company's success.[1] ●

Managers at Campbell Soup Canada and 3M Canada recognized and took advantage of what many experts are increasingly seeing as a tremendous resource for all organizations—the power of groups and teams. Rather than operate as individual performers reporting to a supervisor, employees at Campbell Soup Canada and 3M Canada functioned as members of a team as they sought to design new products and new ways of doing business.

This chapter is about processes that lead to and follow from activities like those at Campbell Soup Canada and 3M Canada. In our last chapter, we established the interpersonal nature of organizations. We extend that discussion here by first introducing basic concepts of group and team dynamics. Subsequent sections explain the characteristics of groups and teams in organizations. We then describe interpersonal and intergroup conflict. We conclude with a discussion of how conflict can be managed.

GROUPS AND TEAMS IN ORGANIZATIONS

● **group**
Two or more persons who interact regularly to accomplish a common purpose or goal

Groups are a ubiquitous part of organizational life. They are the basis for much of the work that gets done, and they evolve both inside and outside the normal structural boundaries of the organization. We define a **group** as two or more persons who interact regularly to accomplish a common purpose or goal.[2] The purpose of a group or team may include preparing a new advertising campaign, informally sharing information, making important decisions, and fulfilling social needs.[3]

Types of Groups and Teams

In general, three basic kinds of groups are found in organizations—functional groups, task groups and teams, and informal or interest groups.[4] These are illustrated in Figure 19.1.

● **functional group**
A group created by the organization to accomplish a number of organizational purposes with an indefinite time horizon

Functional Groups   A **functional group** is a permanent group created by the organization to accomplish a number of organizational purposes with an unspecified time horizon. The marketing department of The Bay, the management department of the University of Waterloo, and the nursing staff of Toronto General Hospital are examples of functional groups. The marketing department at The Bay, for instance, seeks to plan effective advertising campaigns, increase sales, run in-store promotions, and develop a unique identity for the company. The functional group remains in existence after it attains its current objectives—those objectives are replaced by new ones.

● **task group**
A group created by the organization to accomplish a relatively narrow range of purposes within a stated or implied time horizon

Task Groups and Teams   A **task group** is a group created by the organization to accomplish a relatively narrow range of purposes within a stated or implied time horizon. Most committees and task forces are task groups. The organization specifies group membership and assigns a relatively narrow set of goals, such as developing a new product or evaluating a proposed grievance procedure. The time horizon for accomplishing these purposes is either specified (a committee may be asked to make a recommendation within sixty days) or implied (the project team will disband when the new product is developed). For example, Ford Motor Co. used a task force to design its first Taurus automobile. When the design was completed, the task force was dissolved.

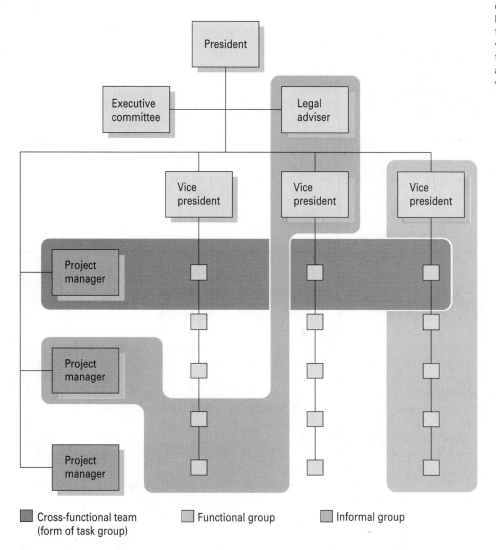

Cross-functional team (form of task group)   **Functional group**   **Informal group**

Every organization has many different types of groups. In this hypothetical organization, a functional group is shown within the orange area, a cross-functional group within the blue area, and an informal group within the green area.

Teams are a special form of task group that have become increasingly popular. In the sense used here, a **team** is a group of workers that functions as a unit, often with little or no supervision, to carry out organizational functions. Table 19.1 lists and defines some of the various types of teams that are being used today. Earlier forms of teams included autonomous work groups and quality circles. Today, teams are also sometimes called *self-managed teams*, *cross-functional teams*, or *high-performance teams*. Many firms today are routinely using teams to carry out most of their daily operations.[5]

Organizations create teams for a variety of reasons. For one, teams give more responsibility for task performance to the workers who are actually performing the tasks. They also empower workers by giving them greater authority and decision-making freedom. In addition, teams allow the organization to capitalize

● **team**
A group of workers that functions as a unit, often with little or no supervision, to carry out organizational functions

TABLE 19.1 Types of Teams	

Problem-solving team   Most popular type of team; comprises knowledge workers who gather to solve a specific problem and then disband

Management team   Consists mainly of managers from various functions like sales and production; coordinates work among other teams

Work team   An increasingly popular type of team, work teams are responsible for the daily work of the organization; when empowered, they are self-managed teams

Virtual team   A new type of work team that interacts by computer; members enter and leave the network as needed and may take turns serving as leader

Quality circle   Declining in popularity, quality circles, comprising workers and supervisors, meet intermittently to discuss workplace problems

Source: "Types of Teams" adapted from Brian Dumaine, "The Trouble With Teams," *Fortune*, September 5, 1994. Copyright © 1994 Time Inc. All rights reserved.

on the knowledge and motivation of their workers. Finally, they enable the organization to shed its bureaucracy and to promote flexibility and responsiveness.[6] The *Managing in a Changing World* box discusses how the use of work teams is leading to changes in offices and office space.

When an organization decides to use teams, it is essentially implementing a major form of organization change, as discussed in Chapter 12. Thus an organization must follow a logical and systematic approach to planning and implementing teams into its existing organization design. Recognizing that resistance may be encountered is also important. This resistance is most likely from first-line managers who will be giving up much of their authority to the team. Many organizations find that they must change the whole management philosophy of such managers away from being a supervisor to being a coach or facilitator.[7]

After teams are in place, managers should continue to monitor their contributions and how effectively they are functioning. In the best circumstance, teams become very cohesive groups with high performance norms. To achieve this state, the manager can use any or all of the techniques described later in this chapter for enhancing cohesiveness. If implemented properly, and with the support of the workers themselves, performance norms will likely be relatively high. That is, if the change is properly implemented, the team participants will understand the value and potential of teams and the rewards they may expect to get as a result of their contributions. On the other hand, poorly designed and implemented teams will do a less-effective job and may detract from organizational effectiveness.[8]

● **informal group, interest group**
A group created by its members for purposes that may or may not be relevant to the organization's goals

Informal or Interest Groups   An **informal** or **interest group** is created by its own members for purposes that may or may not be relevant to organizational goals. It also has an unspecified time horizon. A group of employees who lunch together every day may be discussing how to improve productivity, how to embezzle money, or local politics and sports. As long as the group members enjoy eating together, they will probably continue to do so. When lunches cease to be pleasant, they will seek other company or a different activity.

Redefining the Office

The recent trend toward the heavy use of work teams in organizations has produced an interesting byproduct: corresponding changes in offices and office space. Offices were traditionally laid out in geometric and symmetrical fashion. Specialists were grouped together, for example, with marketing managers in one location, finance managers in another, and so forth. Individual managers also had their own offices. Meetings were held in conference rooms scattered around the building.

But this physical arrangement often creates problems for teams. A marketing manager, for example, is likely to interact more with team members from design, manufacturing, and quality control than with other marketing managers. And meetings are so commonplace that teams may have to struggle to find an available meeting space.

To make a work space that is more conducive to teams, some organizations are building new facilities or remodelling older ones. These new work spaces have fewer interior walls but a lot more open space. In many businesses like Hewlett-Packard and Nortel Networks, large open spaces dominate buildings and other facilities; employees cluster around work tables and sit in comfortable chairs as they work together on projects. Their individual offices tend to be much smaller and become more of a place to store materials and make private telephone calls.

In some organizations, the "office" environment has changed even more. For example, at Chiat/Day, an advertising agency with locations in Montreal, Toronto, and Vancouver, workers do not have offices or even assigned workspaces. Mobile computer workstations are scattered throughout the facility. Employees simply take any empty seat, log on, and go to work. As they finish, they move to a lounge area or other open space. They can sit at an individual work table and work alone or around a table and work with others. These new office topographies are becoming increasingly popular as more and more businesses seek to capitalize fully on the power of work teams and social interaction at work.

References: Ronald Lieber, "Cool Offices," *Fortune*, December 9, 1996, pp. 204–210; and "Team Efforts, Technology Add New Reasons to Meet," *USA Today*, December 8, 1997, pp. 1A, 2A.

Informal groups can be a powerful force that managers cannot ignore. One writer described how a group of employees at a furniture factory subverted their boss's efforts to increase production. They tacitly agreed to produce a reasonable amount of work but not to work too hard. One man kept a stockpile of completed work hidden as a backup in case he got too far behind. In another example, auto workers described how they left out gaskets and seals and put soft-drink bottles inside doors.[9] Of course, informal groups can also be a positive force, as demonstrated several years ago when Delta's employees worked together to buy a new plane for the company to show their support.

Why People Join Groups and Teams

People join groups and teams for a variety of reasons. They join functional groups simply by virtue of joining organizations. People accept employment to earn money or to practise their chosen profession. Once inside the organization, they are assigned to jobs and roles and thus become members of functional groups. People in existing functional groups are told, are asked, or volunteer to serve on committees, task forces, and teams. People join informal or interest groups for a variety of reasons, most of them quite complex.[10]

Interpersonal Attraction   One reason that people form informal or interest groups is that they are attracted to each other. Many different factors contribute to interpersonal attraction.[11] When people see a lot of each other, pure proximity increases the likelihood that interpersonal attraction will develop. Attraction is increased when people have similar attitudes, personality, or economic standing.

Group Activities   Individuals may also be motivated to join a group because the activities of the group appeal to them. Jogging, playing bridge, bowling, discussing poetry, playing war games, and flying model airplanes are all activities that some people enjoy. Many of them are more enjoyable to participate in as a member of a group, and most require more than one person. Many large firms like Chrysler Canada and the Royal Bank of Canada have a football, softball, or bowling team. A person may join a bowling team not because of any noticeable attraction to other group members but simply because being a member of the group allows that person to participate in a pleasant activity. Of course, if the level of interpersonal attraction of the group is very low, a person may choose to forgo the activity rather than join the group.

Group Goals   The goals of a group may also motivate people to join. Greenpeace, which is dedicated to environmental conservation, is a good example of this kind of interest group. Various fundraising groups are another illustration. Members may or may not be personally attracted to the other fundraisers, and they probably do not enjoy the activity of knocking on doors asking for money, but they join the group because they subscribe to its goal.

Need Satisfaction   Still another reason for joining a group is to satisfy the need for affiliation. New residents in a community may join a neighbourhood group partially as a way to meet new people and partially just to be around other people. Likewise, newly divorced individuals often join support groups as a way to have companionship.

Instrumental Benefits   A final reason people join groups is that membership is sometimes seen as instrumental in providing other benefits to the individual. For example, it is fairly common for university students entering their final year to join several professional clubs or associations because listing such memberships on a résumé is thought to enhance the chances of getting a good job. Similarly, a manager might join a certain golf club not because she is attracted

Many people find great satisfaction in being part of a team working toward a goal. These volunteers are helping to clean up the Don River in Toronto.

to its members (although she might be) and not because of the opportunity to play golf (although she may enjoy it). The club's goals are not relevant and her affiliation needs may be satisfied in other ways. She may believe that being a member of this club will lead to important and useful business contacts, however, and the golf club membership is instrumental in establishing those contacts. Membership in civic groups such as Kiwanis and Rotary may be solicited for similar reasons.

Stages of Group and Team Development

Imagine the differences between a collection of five persons who have just been brought together to form a group or team and a group or team that has functioned like a well-oiled machine for years. Members of a new group or team are unfamiliar with how they will function together and are tentative in their interactions. In a group or team with considerable experience, members are familiar with one another's strengths and weaknesses and are therefore more secure in their role in the group. The former group or team is generally considered to be immature; the latter, mature. To progress from the immature phase to the mature phase, a group or team must go through certain stages of development, as shown in Figure 19.2.[12]

The first stage of development is called *forming*. The members of the group or team get acquainted and begin to test which interpersonal behaviours are acceptable and which are unacceptable to the other members. The members are very dependent on others at this point to provide cues about what is acceptable. The basic ground rules for the group or team are established and a tentative group structure may emerge. At Reebok International, for example, a merchandising team was created to handle its new sportswear business. The team leader and his members were barely acquainted and had to spend a few weeks getting to know one another.

The second stage of development, often slow to emerge, is *storming*. During this stage, there may be a lack of unity and uneven interaction patterns. At the same time, some members of the group or team may begin to exert themselves to become recognized as the group leader or at least to play a major role in shaping the group's agenda. In Reebok's team, some members advocated a rapid expansion into the marketplace; others argued for a slower entry. The first faction won, with disastrous results. Because of the rush, product quality was poor and deliveries were late. As a result, the team leader was fired and a new manager placed in charge.

The third stage of development, called *norming*, usually begins with a burst of activity. During this stage, each person begins to recognize and accept her or his role and to understand the roles of others. Members also begin to accept one another and to develop a sense of unity. There may also be temporary regressions to the previous stage. For example, the group or team might begin to accept one particular member as the leader. If this person later violates important norms and otherwise jeopardizes his or her claim to leadership, conflict might re-emerge as the group rejects this leader and searches for another. Reebok's new leader transferred several people away from the team and set up a new system and structure for managing things. The remaining employees accepted his new approach and settled into doing their jobs.

Performing, the final stage of group or team development, is again slow to emerge. The team really begins to focus on the problem at hand. The members enact the roles they have accepted, interaction occurs, and the efforts of the

As groups mature, they tend to evolve through four distinct stages of development. Managers must understand that group members need time to become acquainted, accept each other, develop a group structure, and become comfortable with their roles in the group before they can begin to work directly to accomplish goals.

F I G U R E 19.2 Stages of Group Development

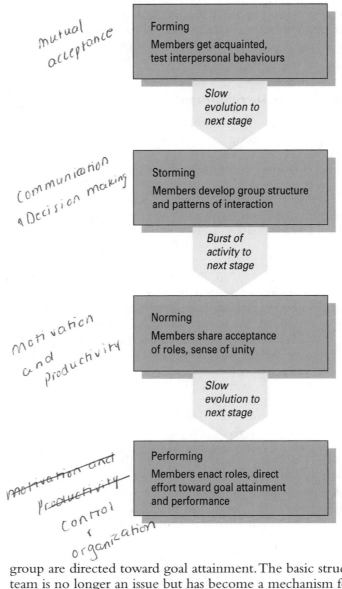

group are directed toward goal attainment. The basic structure of the group or team is no longer an issue but has become a mechanism for accomplishing the purpose of the group. Reebok's sportswear business is now growing consistently and has successfully avoided the problems that plagued it at first.[13]

CHARACTERISTICS OF TEAMS

As groups and teams mature and pass through the four basic stages of development, they begin to take on four important characteristics—a role structure, norms, cohesiveness, and informal leadership.[14]

Role Structures → cause stress

Each individual in a team has a part—or **role**—to play, in helping the group reach its goals. Some people are leaders, some do the work, some interface with other teams, and so on. Indeed, a person may take on a *task-specialist role* (concentrating on getting the group's task accomplished) or a *socioemotional role* (providing social and emotional support to others on the team). A few people, usually the leaders, perform both roles; a few others may do neither. The group's **role structure** is the set of defined roles and interrelationships among those roles that the group or team members define and accept. Each of us belongs to many groups—work groups, classes, families, and social organizations—and plays multiple roles.[15]

Role structures emerge as a result of role episodes, as shown in Figure 19.3. The process begins with the expected role—what other members of the team expect the individual to do. The expected role is translated into the sent role—the messages and cues that team members use to communicate the expected role to the individual. The perceived role is what the individual perceives the sent role to mean. Finally, the enacted role is what the individual actually does in the role. The enacted role, in turn, influences future expectations of the team. Of course, role episodes seldom unfold this easily. When major disruptions occur, individuals may experience role ambiguity, conflict, or overload.

Role Ambiguity **Role ambiguity** arises when the sent role is unclear. If your instructor tells you to write a term paper but refuses to provide more information, you will probably experience role ambiguity. You do not know what the topic is, how long the paper should be, what format to use, or when the paper is due. In work settings, role ambiguity can stem from poor job descriptions, vague instructions from a supervisor, or unclear cues from co-workers. The result is likely to be a subordinate who does not know what to do. Role ambiguity can be a major problem for both the individual who must contend with it and the organization that expects the employee to perform.

Role Conflict **Role conflict** occurs when the messages and cues composing the sent role are clear but contradictory or mutually exclusive.[16] One common form is *interrole conflict,* or conflict between roles. For example, if a person's boss says that to get ahead one must work overtime and on weekends, and the same person's spouse says that more time is needed at home with the family, conflict may result.[17] In a matrix organization, interrole conflict often arises between the roles one plays in different teams as well as between team roles and one's permanent role in a functional group.

● **role**
The part an individual plays in a group to help the group reach its goals

● **role structure**
The set of defined roles and interrelationships among those roles that the group or team members define and accept

● **role ambiguity**
Arises when the sent role is unclear and the individual does not know what is expected of him or her

● **role conflict**
Occurs when the messages and cues composing the sent role are clear but contradictory or mutually exclusive

Ex. basketball suppose to shoot the ball or pass it

F I G U R E 19.3 The Development of a Role

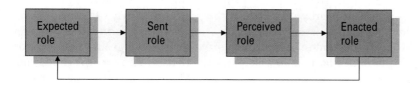

Roles and role structures within a group generally evolve through a series of role episodes. The first two stages of role development are group processes as the group members let individuals know what is expected of them. The other two parts are individual processes as the new group members perceive and enact their roles.

Intrarole conflict may occur when the person gets conflicting demands from different sources within the context of the same role. A manager's boss may tell her that she needs to put more pressure on subordinates to follow new work rules. At the same time, her subordinates may indicate that they expect her to get the rules changed. Thus the cues are in conflict, and the manager may be unsure about which course to follow. *Intrasender conflict* occurs when a single source sends clear but contradictory messages, such as when the boss says one morning that there can be no more overtime for the next month but after lunch tells someone to work late that same evening. *Person–role conflict* results from a discrepancy between the role requirements and the individual's personal values, attitudes, and needs. If a person is told to do something unethical or illegal, or if the work is distasteful (for example, firing a close friend), person–role conflict is likely.

Role conflict of all varieties is of particular concern to managers. Research shows that conflict may occur in a variety of situations and lead to a variety of adverse consequences, including stress, poor performance, and rapid turnover.[18]

● **role overload**
Occurs when expectations for the role exceed the individual's capabilities to perform

Role Overload   A final consequence of role structure disruptions is **role overload**, which occurs when expectations for the role exceed the individual's capabilities. Role overload can occur when a manager gives an employee several major assignments at once while increasing the person's regular workload. Role overload may also result when an individual takes on too many roles at one time. For example, a person trying to work extra-hard at his job, run for election to the school board, serve on a church committee, coach minor hockey, maintain an active exercise program, and be a contributing member to his family will probably encounter role overload.

Implications   In a functional group or team, the manager can take steps to avoid role ambiguity, conflict, and overload. Having clear and reasonable expectations and sending clear and straightforward cues go a long way toward eliminating role ambiguity. Consistent expectations that take into account the employee's other roles and personal value system may minimize role conflict. Role overload can be avoided simply by recognizing the individual's capabilities and limits. In friendship and interest groups, role structures are likely to be less formal; hence, the possibility of role ambiguity, conflict, or overload may not be so great. If one or more of these problems do occur, however, they may be difficult to handle. Because roles in friendship and interest groups are less likely to be partially defined by a formal authority structure or written job descriptions, the individual cannot turn to these sources to clarify a role.

Behavioural Norms

● **norm**
A standard of behaviour that the group accepts and expects of its members

Norms are standards of behaviour that the group or team accepts for its members. Most committees, for example, develop norms governing their discussions. A person who talks too much is perceived as doing so to make a good impression or to get his or her own way. Other members may not talk much to this person, may not sit nearby, may glare at the person, and may otherwise "punish" the individual for violating the norm. Norms, then, define the boundaries between acceptable and unacceptable behaviour.[19] Some groups develop norms that limit the upper bounds of behaviour to "make life easier" for the group. In general, these norms are counterproductive—don't make more than two comments in a committee discussion or don't produce any more than you have to.

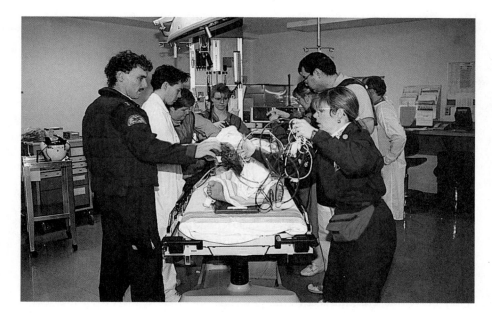

Roles structures are important in all groups, including hospital emergency teams. In the highly charged atmosphere of emergency medicine, such as this ER at Bow Valley Hospital in Calgary, it is imperative that all participants support one another and take direction from whoever is in charge.

Other groups may develop norms that limit the lower bounds of behaviour. These norms tend to reflect motivation, commitment, and high performance—don't come to meetings unless you've read the reports to be discussed or produce as much as you can. Managers can sometimes use norms for the betterment of the organization. For example, Eastman Kodak Company has successfully used group norms to reduce injuries in some of its plants.[20]

Norm Generalization   The norms of one group cannot always be generalized to another group. Some academic departments, for example, have a norm that suggests that faculty members dress up on teaching days. People who fail to observe this norm are "punished" by sarcastic remarks or even formal reprimands. In other departments, the norm may be casual clothes, and the person unfortunate enough to wear dress clothes may be punished just as vehemently. Even within the same work area, similar groups or teams can develop different norms. One team may strive always to produce above its assigned quota; another may maintain productivity just below its quota. The norm of one team may be to be friendly and cordial to its supervisor; that of another team may be to remain aloof and distant. Some differences are due primarily to the composition of the teams.

Norm Variation   In some cases, there can also be norm variation within a group or team. A common norm is that the least senior member of a group is expected to perform unpleasant or trivial tasks for the rest of the group. These tasks might be to wait on customers who are known to be small tippers (in a restaurant), to deal with complaining customers (in a department store), or to handle the low-commission line of merchandise (in a sales department). Another example is when certain individuals, especially informal leaders, violate some norms. If the team is meeting at 8 o'clock, anyone arriving late will be chastised for holding things up. Occasionally, however, the informal leader arrives a few minutes late. As long as this does not happen too often, the group will probably do nothing.

Norm Conformity Four sets of factors contribute to norm conformity. First, factors associated with the group are important. For example, some groups or teams may exert more pressure for conformity than others. Second, the initial stimulus that prompts behaviour can affect conformity. The more ambiguous the stimulus (for example, news that the team is going to be transferred to a new unit), the more pressure there is to conform. Third, individual traits determine the individual's propensity to conform (for example, more intelligent people are often less susceptible to pressure to conform).

Finally, situational factors such as team size and unanimity influence conformity. An individual learning the group's norms can do several different things. The most obvious is to adopt the norms. For example, the new male professor who notices that all the other men in the department dress up to teach can also start wearing a suit. A variation is to try to obey the "spirit" of the norm while retaining individuality. The professor may recognize that the norm is actually to wear a tie; thus he might succeed by wearing a tie with his sport shirt, jeans, and running shoes. The individual may also ignore the norm. When a person does not conform, several things can happen. At first the group may increase its communication with the deviant individual to try to bring her back in line. If this does not work, communication may decline. Over time, the group may begin to exclude the individual from its activities and, in effect, ostracize the person.

Finally, we need to briefly consider another aspect of norm conformity—socialization. **Socialization** is generalized norm conformity that occurs as a person makes the transition from being an outsider to being an insider. A newcomer to an organization, for example, gradually begins to learn the norms about such things as dress, working hours, and interpersonal relations. As the newcomer adopts these norms, she is being socialized into the organizational culture. Some organizations work to actively manage the socialization process; others leave it to happenstance.[21]

Cohesiveness

A third important team characteristic is cohesiveness. **Cohesiveness** is the extent to which members are loyal and committed to the group. In a highly cohesive team, the members work well together, support and trust one another, and are generally effective at achieving their chosen goal. In contrast, a team that lacks cohesiveness is not very coordinated and its members do not necessarily support one another fully; it may have a difficult time reaching goals. Of particular interest are the factors that increase and reduce cohesiveness; these are listed in Table 19.2. Also of interest are the consequences of team cohesiveness.

Factors That Increase Cohesiveness Five factors can increase the level of cohesiveness in a group or team. One of the strongest is intergroup competition. When two or more groups are in direct competition (for example, three sales groups competing for top sales honours or two hockey teams competing for a league championship), each group is likely to become more cohesive. Second, just as personal attraction plays a role in causing a group to form, so too does attraction enhance cohesiveness. Third, favourable evaluation of the entire group by outsiders can increase cohesiveness.[22] Thus a winning sales contest or a league title or receiving recognition and praise from a superior tends to increase cohesiveness.

● **socialization**
Generalized norm conformity that occurs as a person makes the transition from being an outsider to being an insider in the organization

● **cohesiveness**
The extent to which members are loyal and committed to the group; the degree of mutual attractiveness within the group

Similarly, if all the members of the group or team agree on their goals, cohesiveness increases.[23] And the more frequently members of the group interact with each other, the more likely the group is to become cohesive. A manager who wants to foster a high level of cohesiveness in a team might do well to establish some form of intergroup competition, assign members to the group who are likely to be attracted to one another, provide opportunities for success, establish goals that all members are likely to accept, and allow ample opportunity for interaction.

Factors That Reduce Cohesiveness Five factors are also known to reduce team cohesiveness. First, cohesiveness declines as a group increases in size. Second, when members of a team disagree on what the goals of the group should be, cohesiveness decreases. For example, when some members believe the group should maximize output and others think output should be restricted, cohesiveness declines. Third, intragroup competition reduces cohesiveness. When members are competing among themselves, they focus more on their own actions and behaviours than on those of the group.

Fourth, domination by one or more persons in the group or team causes overall cohesiveness to decline. Other members may feel that they are not being given an opportunity to interact and contribute, and they may become less attracted to the group as a consequence. Finally, unpleasant experiences that result from group membership reduce cohesiveness. A sales group that comes in last in a sales contest, an athletic team that sustains a long losing streak, and a work group reprimanded for poor-quality work may all become less cohesive as a result of their unpleasant experience. The *Environment of Management* box describes how organizations are helping survivors of layoffs maintain some semblance of cohesiveness.

Consequences of Cohesiveness In general, as teams become more cohesive their members tend to interact more frequently, conform more to norms, and become more satisfied with the team. Although cohesiveness may influence

Team cohesiveness is a major contributing factor to the performance and success of any team. These workers are part of a Habitat for Humanity team that constructs homes in countries around the world. They share the same goals and recognize the value of working together.

Several different factors can potentially influence the cohesiveness of a group. For example, a manager can establish intergroup competition, assign compatible members to the group, create opportunities for success, establish acceptable goals, and foster interaction to increase cohesiveness. Other factors can be used to decrease cohesiveness.

TABLE 19.2 Factors That Influence Group Cohesiveness

Factors That Increase Cohesiveness	Factors That Reduce Cohesiveness
Intergroup competition	Group size
Personal attraction	Disagreement on goals
Favourable evaluation	Intragroup competition
Agreement on goals	Domination
Interaction	Unpleasant experiences

team performance, performance is also influenced by the team's performance norms. Figure 19.4 shows how cohesiveness and performance norms interact to help shape team performance.

When both cohesiveness and performance norms are high, high performance results because the team wants to perform at a high level (norms) and its members are working together toward that end (cohesiveness). When norms are high and cohesiveness is low, performance is moderate. Although the team wants to perform at a high level, its members are not necessarily working well together. When norms are low, performance is low, regardless of whether group cohesiveness is high or low. The least-desirable situation occurs when low performance norms are combined with high cohesiveness. In this case, all team members embrace the standard of restricting performance (owing to the low performance norm), and the group is united in its efforts to maintain that standard (owing to the high cohesiveness). If cohesiveness is low, the manager might be able to raise performance norms by establishing high goals and rewarding goal attainment or by bringing in new group members who are high performers. But a highly cohesive group is likely to resist these interventions.[24]

Informal Leadership

Most functional groups and teams have a formal leader—that is, one appointed by the organization or chosen or elected by the members of the group. Because friendship and interest groups are formed by the members themselves, however, any formal leader must be elected or designated by the members. Although some groups do designate such a leader (a softball team may elect a captain, for example), many do not. Moreover, even when a formal leader is designated, the group or team may also look to others for leadership. An **informal leader** is a person who engages in leadership activities but whose right to do so has not been formally recognized. The formal and the informal leader in any group or team may be the same person, or they may be different people. We noted earlier the distinction between the task-specialist and socioemotional roles within groups. An informal leader is likely to be a person capable of carrying out both roles effectively. If the formal leader can fulfill one role but not the other, an informal leader often emerges to supplement the formal leader's functions. If the formal leader cannot fill either role, one or more informal leaders may emerge to carry out both sets of functions.[25]

● **informal leader**
A person who engages in leadership activities but whose right to do so has not been formally recognized by the organization or group

Survivors Need Help, Too

During the 1980s and 1990s, downsizing led to numerous layoffs among business organizations. Although human resource departments frequently tried to reduce the human costs of that restructuring, they tended to concentrate their efforts on providing assistance to those who were losing their jobs. Rarely did companies worry about the survivors; after all, they still had their jobs.

Survivors, however, frequently have considerable difficulties. AT&T found that nearly half of one group of managerial survivors had some sort of problem. Insomnia, high blood pressure, panic attacks, grinding teeth during sleep, marital strain, nail biting, ulcers, and other stress-related illnesses and disorders are experienced by most survivors as they live in constant fear that their jobs will be next. Survivors rarely have the same sense of loyalty to their employers as before the layoffs. They seldom take risks, and productivity can go down if the stress is great. Those who are afraid of being laid off in the future may become angry and perceive the whole restructuring effort as unfair. Further, to make up the workload for those who were laid off, survivors may be expected to work longer hours. Even if they are not expected to work harder, most of them do so in an effort to make themselves more valuable to their employers so that they will not be laid off in the future.

Not all survivors have problems. Some believe that they have greater job security and perceive the down-sizing as fair. To help those who do have problems, however, companies need to have a widespread acknowledgment of the existence of a new employment contract for employees to set survivors at ease. Information centres to prevent rumours from spreading and causing damage may be necessary. Extensive counselling programs are always beneficial to allay fears and reduce uncertainty. Jostens Learning Corporation even set up a hotline to let people anonymously vent their feelings to managers. Jostens found deep negative feelings among survivors, many of whom were actively in the job market.

Increasingly companies are learning that survivors need help. Companies like Scott Paper, Honeywell, Philip Morris, and Kraft, have held seminars for survivors to help them adapt to the inevitable change taking place around them. With this increase in attention the survivors of future restructurings will have an easier time than did their counterparts of just a few years ago.

References: A.J. Vogl, "Inhuman Resources," *Across the Board*, July/August 1994, pp. 25–30; Daniel C. Feldman and Carrie R. Leana, "Better Practices in Managing Layoffs," *Human Resource Management*, Summer 1994, pp. 239–260; David M. Noer, "Healing the Wounds," *Small Business Reports*, April 1994, pp. 58–60; and "Survivors of Layoffs Battle Angst, Anger, Hurting Productivity," *The Wall Street Journal*, December 6, 1993, pp. A1, A8

Is informal leadership desirable? In many cases, informal leaders are quite powerful because they draw from referent or expert power. When they are working in the best interest of the organization, they can be a tremendous asset. Notable athletes such as Wayne Gretzky and Mario Lemieux are classic examples of informal leaders. When informal leaders work counter to the goals of the organization, however, they can cause major difficulties. Such leaders may lower performance norms, instigate walkouts or wildcat strikes, or otherwise disrupt the organization.

INTERPERSONAL AND INTERGROUP CONFLICT

Of course, people do not always work smoothly together in an organization. Indeed, conflict is an inevitable element of interpersonal relationships in organizations. In this section we look at how conflict affects overall performance.

Group cohesiveness and performance norms interact to determine group performance. From the manager's perspective, high cohesiveness combined with high performance norms is the best situation, and high cohesiveness with low performance norms is the worst situation. Managers who can influence the level of cohesiveness and performance norms can greatly improve the effectiveness of a work group.

FIGURE 19.4 The Interaction Between Cohesiveness and Performance Norms

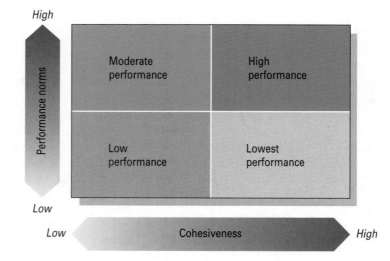

We also explore the causes of conflict between individuals, between groups, and between an organization and its environment.

The Nature of Conflict

● **conflict**
A disagreement between two or more individuals, groups, or organizations

Conflict is a disagreement among two or more individuals, groups, or organizations. This disagreement may be relatively superficial or very strong. It may be short-lived or exist for months or even years, and it may be work-related or personal. Conflict may manifest itself in a variety of ways. People may compete with one another, glare at one another, shout, or withdraw. Groups may band together to protect popular members or oust unpopular members. Organizations may seek legal remedy.

Most people assume that conflict must be avoided because it connotes antagonism, hostility, unpleasantness, and dissension. Indeed, managers and management theorists have traditionally viewed conflict as a problem to be avoided.[26] In recent years, however, we have come to recognize that although conflict can be a major problem, certain kinds of conflict may also be beneficial.[27] For example, when two members of a site selection committee disagree over the best location for a new plant, each may be forced to more thoroughly study and defend his or her preferred alternative. As a result of more systematic analysis and discussion, the committee may make a better decision and be better prepared to justify it to others than if everyone had agreed from the outset and accepted an alternative that was perhaps less well analyzed.

As long as conflict is handled cordially and constructively, it is probably serving a useful purpose in the organization. On the other hand, when working relationships are disrupted and the conflict has reached destructive levels it has likely become dysfunctional and needs to be addressed.[28] We discuss ways of dealing with such conflict later in this chapter.

F I G U R E   19.5 The Nature of Organizational Conflict

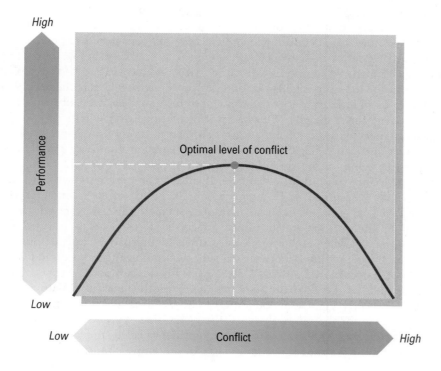

Optimal level of conflict

High / Low — Performance (vertical axis)

Low — Conflict — High (horizontal axis)

Either too much or too little conflict can be dysfunctional for an organization. In either case, performance may be low. However, an optimal level of conflict that sparks motivation, creativity, innovation, and initiative can result in higher levels of performance.

Figure 19.5 depicts the general relationship between conflict and performance for a group or organization. If there is absolutely no conflict in the group or organization, its members may become complacent and apathetic. As a result, group or organizational performance and innovation may subsequently begin to suffer. A moderate level of conflict among group or organizational members, on the other hand, can spark motivation, creativity, innovation, and initiative and raise performance. Too much conflict, though, can produce undesirable results such as hostility and lack of cooperation, which lower performance. Managers must find and maintain the optimal amount of conflict that fosters performance. Of course, what constitutes optimal conflict varies with both the situation and the people involved.[29]

Causes of Conflict

Conflict may arise in both interpersonal and intergroup relationships. Occasionally conflict between individuals and groups may be caused by particular organizational strategies and practices. A third arena for conflict is between an organization and its environment.

Interpersonal Conflict   Conflict between two or more individuals is almost certain to occur in any organization, given the great variety in perceptions, goals, attitudes, and so forth among its members. William Gates, founder and CEO of Microsoft Corp., and Kazuhiko Nishi, a former business associate from Japan, ended a long-term business relationship because of interpersonal conflict. Nishi accused Gates of becoming too political, and Gates charged that Nishi's behaviour became too unpredictable and erratic.[30]

A frequent source of interpersonal conflict in organizations is what many people call a personality clash—that is, when two people distrust each others' motives, dislike one another, or for some other reason simply can't get along. Conflict also may arise between people who have different beliefs or perceptions about some aspect of their work or their organization. For example, one manager may want the organization to require that all employees use IBM personal computers to promote standardization. Another manager may believe that employees should use a variety of equipment to recognize individuality. Similarly, a male manager may disagree with his female colleague over whether the organization is guilty of discriminating against women in promotion decisions.

Conflict also can result from excessive competitiveness among individuals. Two persons vying for the same job, for example, may resort to political behaviour in an effort to gain an advantage. If either competitor sees the other's behaviour as inappropriate, accusations are likely to result. Even after the "winner" of the job has been determined, such conflict may continue to undermine interpersonal relationships, especially if the reasons offered for selecting one candidate are ambiguous or open to alternative explanation.

One of the most bitter feuds in Canadian corporate history centred on a conflict over succession. In 1994, Wallace McCain was removed as co-CEO of McCain Foods by the chair of the company, his brother Harrison, with whom he had spent thirty-eight years building the frozen-food and juice empire. The apparent reason for the removal was Wallace McCain's appointment of his son, Michael, as CEO of McCain USA; the appointment placed Michael McCain in a good position to eventually become head of the entire company.[31]

Intergroup Conflict Conflict between two or more organizational groups is also quite common. For example, the members of a firm's marketing group may disagree with the production group over product quality and delivery schedules. Two sales groups may disagree over how to meet sales goals, and two groups of managers may have different ideas about how best to allocate organizational resources.

Many intergroup conflicts arise more from organizational causes than interpersonal causes. In Chapter 10, we described three forms of group interdependence—pooled, sequential, and reciprocal. Just as increased interdependence makes coordination more difficult, it also increases the potential for conflict. For example, recall that in sequential interdependence work is passed from one unit to another. Intergroup conflict may arise if the first group turns out too much work (the second group falls behind), too little work (the second group does not meet its own goals), or poor-quality work.

In Chapter 10, we discussed the differences between line managers and staff managers. Conflict may arise between these two types of managers when bounds of authority are called into question. Conflict may arise, for example, between marketing and computer systems personnel in firms that create customer databases.[32] In a department store, conflict can arise between stockroom employees and sales associates. The stockroom associates may be seen by sales associates as being slow in delivering merchandise to the sales floor so that it can be priced and shelved. The stockroom employees, in turn, may see the sales associates as not giving them enough lead time to get the merchandise delivered and failing to understand that they have additional duties besides carrying merchandise to the sales floor.

Just like people, different departments often have different goals. Further, these goals may often be incompatible. A marketing goal of maximizing sales, achieved partially by offering many products in a wide variety of sizes, shapes, colours, and models, probably conflicts with a production goal of minimizing costs, achieved partially by long production runs of a few items. Earlier in this chapter we noted that Reebok confronted this very situation. One group of managers wanted to introduce a new sportswear line as quickly as possible, whereas other managers wanted to expand more deliberately and cautiously. Because the two groups were not able to reconcile their differences effectively, conflict between the two factions led to quality problems and delivery delays that plagued the firm for months.

Competition for scarce resources can also lead to intergroup conflict. Most organizations—especially universities, hospitals, government agencies, and businesses in depressed industries—have limited resources. The Oldsmobile, Pontiac, and Chevrolet divisions of General Motors fought over the rights to manufacture the firm's new futuristic minivan.

Conflict Between Organization and Environment Conflict that arises between one organization and another is called interorganizational conflict. A moderate amount of interorganizational conflict resulting from business competition is, of course, expected, but sometimes conflict becomes more extreme. For example, the owners of Jordache Enterprises Inc. and Guess? Inc. have been battling in court for years over ownership of the Guess label, allegations of design theft, and several other issues.[33]

Conflict can also arise between an organization and other elements of its environment. For example, an organization may conflict with a consumer group over claims it makes about its products. McDonald's Corp. faced this problem a few years ago when it published nutritional information about its products that omitted details about fat content. A corporation may conflict with the government. For example, Pope and Talbot recently filed a lawsuit against the Canadian government alleging that Canada's softwood lumber agreement with the United States discriminates against the company, which operates in British Columbia, one of four provinces subject to export quotas on softwood lumber.[34] Or a firm might conflict with a supplier over the quality of raw materials. The firm may think the supplier is providing inferior materials, while the supplier thinks the materials are adequate. Finally, individual managers may obviously have disagreements with groups of workers. For example, a manager may think that her workers are doing poor-quality work and that they are unmotivated. The workers, on the other hand, may believe that they are doing a good job and that the manager is doing a poor job of leading them.

MANAGING CONFLICT IN ORGANIZATIONS

How do managers cope with all this potential conflict? Fortunately, as Table 19.3 shows, conflict can be stimulated for constructive ends, controlled before it gets out of hand, and resolved if it does. In the following sections, we look at ways of managing conflict.

TABLE 19.3 Methods for Managing Conflict

Stimulating conflict

Increase competition among individuals and teams.

Hire outsiders to shape things up.

Change established procedures.

Controlling conflict

Expand resource base.

Enhance coordination of interdependence.

Set supraordinate goals.

Match personalities and work habits of employees.

Resolving and eliminating conflict

Avoid conflict.

Convince conflicting parties to compromise.

Bring conflicting parties together to confront and negotiate conflict.

Stimulating Conflict

In some situations, an organization may stimulate conflict by placing individual employees or groups in competitive situations. Managers can establish sales contests, incentive plans, bonuses, or other competitive stimuli to spark competition. As long as the ground rules are equitable and all participants perceive the contest as fair, the conflict created by the competition is likely to be constructive because each participant will work hard to win (thereby enhancing some aspect of organizational performance).

Another useful method for stimulating conflict is to bring in one or more outsiders who will shake things up and present a new perspective on organizational practices. Outsiders may be new employees, current employees assigned to an existing work group, or consultants or advisers hired on a temporary basis. Of course, this action can also provoke resentment from insiders who believe that they were qualified for the position. The Beecham Group, a British company, hired an American for its CEO position expressly to change how the company did business.[35] His arrival brought with it new ways of doing things and a new enthusiasm for competitiveness. Unfortunately, some valued employees also chose to leave Beecham because they resented some of the changes.

Changing established procedures, especially procedures that have outlived their usefulness, can also stimulate conflict. Such actions cause people to reassess how they perform their jobs and whether they perform them correctly. For example, one university president announced that all vacant staff positions could be filled only after written justification had received his approval. Conflict arose between the president and the department heads who felt they had to do more paperwork than was necessary. Most requests were okayed, but because department heads now had to think through their staffing needs, a few unnecessary positions were appropriately eliminated.

Controlling Conflict

One method of controlling conflict is to expand the resource base. Suppose that a top manager receives two budget requests for $100,000 each. If she has only $180,000 to distribute, the stage is set for conflict because each group believes that its proposal is worth funding and will be unhappy if it is not fully funded. If both proposals are indeed worthwhile, she may be able to come up with the extra $20,000 from some other source and thereby avoid difficulty.

As noted earlier, pooled, sequential, and reciprocal interdependence can all result in conflict. If managers use an appropriate technique for enhancing coordination they can reduce the probability that conflict will arise. Techniques for coordination (described in Chapter 10) include making use of the managerial hierarchy, relying on rules and procedures, enlisting liaison persons, forming task forces, and integrating departments. In the department store example described earlier, conflict could be addressed by providing salespeople with clearer forms on which to specify the merchandise they need and in what sequence. If one coordination technique does not have the desired effect, a manager might shift to another one.

Competing goals can also be a potential source of conflict among individuals and groups. Managers can sometimes focus employee attention on higher-level, or superordinate, goals as a way of eliminating lower-level conflict. When the Canadian Auto Workers made wage concessions to ensure the survival of Canadian Airlines a few years ago, they were responding to a superordinate goal. Their immediate goal may have been higher wages for members, but they realized that without the airline, many of their members would not even have jobs.

Finally, managers should try to match the personalities and work habits of employees to avoid conflict between individuals. For instance, two valuable subordinates, one an extreme extrovert and the other an extreme introvert, should probably not be required to work together in an enclosed space. If conflict does arise between incompatible individuals, a manager might seek an equitable transfer for one or both of them to other units.

Resolving and Eliminating Conflict

Despite everyone's best intentions, conflict sometimes flares up. If it is disrupting the workplace, creating too much hostility and tension, or otherwise harming the organization, attempts must be made to resolve it. Some managers who are uncomfortable dealing with conflict choose to avoid the conflict and hope that it will go away. Avoidance may sometimes be effective in the short run for some kinds of interpersonal disagreements, but it does little to resolve long-run or chronic conflict. Even more unadvisable, though, is "smoothing"—minimizing the conflict and telling everyone that things will "get better." Often the conflict will only worsen as people continue to brood over it.

Compromise is striking a middle-range position between two extremes. This approach can work if it is used with care, but in most compromise situations someone wins and someone loses. Budget problems are one of the few areas amenable to compromise because of their objective nature. Assume, for example, that additional resources are not available to the manager mentioned earlier. She has $180,000 to divide, and each of two groups has submitted budget requests of $100,000. If the manager believes that both projects warrant funding, she can allocate $90,000 to each. The two groups having at least been treated equally may minimize the potential conflict.[36]

The confrontation approach to conflict resolution—also called interpersonal problem solving—consists of bringing the parties together to confront the conflict. The parties discuss the nature of their conflict and attempt to reach an agreement or a solution. Confrontation requires a reasonable degree of maturity on the part of the participants, and the manager must structure the situation carefully. If handled well, this approach can be an effective means of resolving conflict.[37]

Regardless of the approach, organizations and their managers must realize that conflict must be addressed if it is to serve constructive purposes and be prevented from bringing about destructive consequences. Conflict is inevitable in organizations, but its effects can be constrained with proper attention. At the Saskatchewan Research Council workplace mediation is used to resolve disputes. The organization has reported some success with this form of conflict resolution.[38]

SUMMARY OF KEY POINTS

A group is two or more persons who interact regularly to accomplish a common purpose or goal. General kinds of groups and teams in organizations are functional groups, task groups and teams, and informal or interest groups. A team is a group of workers that functions as a unit, often with little or no supervision, to carry out organizational functions.

People join functional groups and teams to pursue a career. Their reasons for joining informal or interest groups include interpersonal attraction, desire to participate in group activities, attraction to group goals, need satisfaction, and potential instrumental benefits. The stages of group and team development include testing and dependence (forming), intragroup conflict and hostility (storming), development of group cohesion (norming), and focusing on the problem at hand (performing).

Four important characteristics of teams are role structures, behavioural norms, cohesiveness, and informal leadership. Role structures define task and socioemotional specialists and may be victimized by role ambiguity, role conflict, or role overload. Norms are standards of behaviour for group or team members. Cohesiveness is the extent to which members are loyal and committed to the group or team. Several factors can increase or reduce group and team cohesiveness. The relationship between performance norms and cohesiveness is especially important. Informal leaders are those leaders whom the group members themselves choose to follow.

Conflict is a disagreement between two or more persons, groups, or organizations. Too little or too much conflict may hurt performance, but an optimal level of conflict may improve performance. Interpersonal and intergroup conflict in organizations may be caused by personality differences or by particular organizational strategies and practices. Organizations may encounter conflict with one another and with various elements of the environment.

Three methods of managing conflict are to stimulate it, control it, or resolve and eliminate it.

DISCUSSION QUESTIONS

Questions for Review

1. What is a group? Describe the several different types of groups and teams and indicate the similarities and differences between them.
2. Why do people join groups? Do all teams develop through all of the stages discussed in this chapter? Why or why not?
3. Describe the characteristics of teams. How might the management of a mature team differ from the management of a team that is not yet mature?
4. Describe the nature and causes of conflict in organizations. Is conflict always bad? Why or why not?

Questions for Analysis

5. Can a group possibly be of more than one type at the same time? If so, under what circumstances? If not, why not?
6. Think of several groups of which you have been a member. Why did you join each? Did each group progress through the stages of development discussed in this chapter? If not, why not?
7. Do you think teams are a valuable new management technique that will endure, or are they just a fad that will be replaced with something else in the near future?

Questions for Application

8. See if you can locate local organizations that regularly use groups in their operations. What kinds of groups do they use? How are they being used? Is that use effective? Why or why not?
9. Try to find out if a local business is using teams. If so, talk to a manager or team participant at the company and learn about their experiences.
10. Would a manager ever want to stimulate conflict in his or her organization? Why or why not? Interview several managers of local business organizations to obtain their views on the use of conflict and compare them to your answer to this question.

BUILDING EFFECTIVE TIME-MANAGEMENT SKILLS

Exercise Overview

Time-management skills refer to the manager's ability to prioritize work, to work efficiently, and to delegate appropriately. This exercise will enable you to develop time-management skills as they relate to running team meetings.

Exercise Background

Although teams and team meetings are becoming more and more common, some managers worry that they waste too much time. Here are ten suggestions for making meetings more efficient:

1. Have an agenda.
2. Only meet when there is a reason.
3. Set a clear starting and ending time.
4. Put a clock in front of everyone.
5. Take away all the chairs and make people stand.
6. Lock the door at starting time to "punish" latecomers.

7. Give everyone a role in the meeting.
8. Use visual aids.
9. Have a recording secretary to document what transpires.
10. Have a one-day-a-week meeting "holiday"—a day on which no one can schedule a meeting.

Exercise Task

With the preceding information as context, do the following:
1. Evaluate the likely effectiveness of each suggestion.
2. Rank the suggestions in terms of their likely value.
3. Add at least three other suggestions for improving the efficiency of a team meeting.

Teamwork and Worker Participation at Algoma

Algoma Steel, Canada's third largest steel producer, is based in Sault Ste. Marie, a community of about 80,000 located 700 kilometres north of Toronto. Almost five thousand people work at the Algoma mill, and another 23,000 jobs in the community are indirectly supported by the company. Today the company, which is largely owned by its employees, has an enviable track record with respect to worker participation, teamwork, and the settlement of worker–management conflict. However, the road to success has been bumpy to say the least.

Algoma Steel has operated in Sault Ste. Marie since 1901. While the company experienced many problems in its evolution, in the 1980s it was enveloped by a near-fatal crisis. Demand for all four of Algoma's main products—sheet, plate, seamless tube, and structural steel—declined due to the recession in North America. As a result of high interest rates, the high value of the Canadian dollar, high transportation costs, and the globalization of steel supply, Algoma incurred financial losses in most of the 1980s. It was against this backdrop that Dofasco, one of Canada's largest steel producers, acquired majority ownership of Algoma Steel in 1988. At that time, however, Dofasco was suffering from some of the same problems that plagued Algoma Steel.

These problems were compounded by a labour dispute in 1990 that resulted in a four-month strike by members of the United Steelworkers of America (USWA). Strikes at Algoma were nothing new. The company has a long history of adversarial worker–management relations. In fact, as early as 1903 the province had to dispatch four hundred militiamen from Toronto to deal with an angry mob of workers who had not been paid their wages by the fledgling company.

In 1991, Dofasco announced that it would completely write off its $700 million investment in Algoma and provide it with no further financial support. This move threatened the very existence of both the company (which was labouring under an $816.9 million debt) and the Sault Ste. Marie community. Algoma immediately announced that it would request federal and provincial financial help to keep it afloat; in addition, it would ask unionized workers for

concessions as it applied to the courts for protection against its creditors.

In its restructuring plan presented to the task force set up by the NDP government, Algoma Steel indicated that it would have to close half of its operations, lay off three thousand employees, impose a 20 percent pay cut, and eliminate several benefits. Employees would be granted 14 percent ownership. In a move that stunned the business community, the union (USWA) proposed a plan of its own. It called for majority employee ownership, major capital investment, workforce reductions without layoffs, and government assistance for employee training. Workers agreed to several concessions (including cuts in wages and benefits), while the provincial and federal governments offered financial assistance and worker training. The proposal was accepted.

Since the proposal's implementation, worker participation has taken on new meaning at Algoma. The new thirteen-member board of directors includes four nominees of the union and seven union-approved independents. The other two board members are the CEO (or his or her nominee) and one member from the salaried employees. Workers thus have a hands-on involvement in the strategic management of the company.

Changes have been implemented at the shop-floor level as well. By 1995, the company had 105 employee participation units and 49 self-directed work teams. The work teams are empowered to do everything from determining their own vacation schedules to redesigning their workplace for maximum efficiency. In the event of downsizing, surplus workers are reassigned, retrained, or given jobs that might once have been contracted out. Algoma reported that, in 1993, employees came forward with 437 suggestions, which resulted in savings of almost $1 million.

As a result of all the changes and an improvement in market conditions, Algoma made a profit of $127 million in 1994. Although the company has fallen on hard times recently (losing $59 million in 1998, as compared with a profit of $52 million in 1997), its employees now share the corporate dream and all its turbulence.

Questions

1. Describe Algoma's corporate culture as it relates to the use of teams and participation.

2. Can Algoma's return to profitability be sustained? Why or why not?

3. Using the Algoma case as an example, discuss how conflict is managed in employee-owned companies.

References: Morley Gunderson et al., "Employee Buyouts in Canada," *British Journal of Industrial Relations*, Vol. 33, 1995, pp. 417–442; Clyde Farnsworth, "Experiment in Worker Ownership Shows a Profit," *The New York Times,* August 14, 1993, p. 33; "Steel Resolve: A Unique Corporate Turnaround Has Pulled Algoma Steel Back from Near Oblivion," *The Financial Post Magazine,* April 1995, pp. 20–24; "A Good Working Relationship Between Management, Union: Algoma Sees Results from Cooperation," *Financial Post,* June 29/July 1, 1996, p. 20; "Pulling One Out of the Fire," *Plant,* Vol. 55, No. 16, 1996, pp.14–15; and Janet McFarland, "Algoma to Close Mills, Cut 800 Jobs," *The Globe and Mail,* February 3, 1999, p. B1.

CHAPTER NOTES

1. Jerry Zeidenberg, "HR and the Innovative Company," *Human Resources Professional*, June 1996, pp. 12–15; Wendy Trueman, "Alternate Visions," *Canadian Business*, March 1991, pp. 29–33; Robert Kreitner and Angelo Kinicki, *Organizational Behavior*, 4th ed. (Boston: Irwin McGraw-Hill, 1998), pp. 391–414; and Gladys Terichow, "Modern Plant Expansion Built on Work Ethic," *Winnipeg Free Press*, March 31, 1992, p. B20.

2. See Gregory Moorhead and Ricky W. Griffin, *Organizational Behavior*, 4th ed. (Boston: Houghton Mifflin, 1995), for a review of definitions of groups.

3. Marilyn E. Gist, Edwin A. Locke, and M. Susan Taylor, "Organizational Behavior: Group Structure, Process, and Effectiveness," *Journal of Management*, Summer 1987, pp. 237–257.

4. Dorwin Cartwright and Alvin Zander (Eds.), *Group Dynamics: Research and Theory*, 3rd ed. (New York: Harper & Row, 1968).

5. Brian Dumaine, "Payoff from the New Management," *Fortune*, December 13, 1993, pp. 103–110.

6. Glenn Parker, "Cross-Functional Collaboration," *Training and Development*, October 1994, pp. 49–58.

7. Michael Stevens and Michael Campion, "The Knowledge, Skill, and Ability Requirements for Teamwork: Implications for Human Resource Management," *Journal of Management*, Vol. 20, No. 2, 1994, pp. 503–530.

8. Brian Dumaine, "The Trouble with Teams," *Fortune*, September 5, 1994, pp. 86–92.

9. Robert Schrank, *Ten Thousand Working Days* (Cambridge, Mass.: MIT Press, 1978); and Bill Watson, "Counter Planning on the Shop Floor," in Peter Frost, Vance Mitchell, and Walter Nord (Eds.), *Organizational Reality*, 2nd ed. (Glenview, Ill.: Scott, Foresman, 1982), pp. 286–294.

10. Marvin E. Shaw, *Group Dynamics—The Psychology of Small Group Behavior*, 4th ed. (New York: McGraw-Hill, 1985).

11. Rupert Brown and Jennifer Williams, "Group Identification: The Same Thing to All People?" *Human Relations*, July 1984, pp. 547–560.

12. See Connie Gersick, "Marking Time: Predictable Transitions in Task Groups," *Academy of Management Journal*, June 1989, pp. 274–309.

13. Stuart Gannes, "America's Fastest-Growing Companies," *Fortune*, May 23, 1988, pp. 28–40.

14. See Michael Campion, Gina Medsker, and A. Catherine Higgs, "Relations Between Work Group Characteristics and Effectiveness: Implications for Designing Effective Work Groups," *Personnel Psychology*, Winter 1993, pp. 823–850, for a review of other team characteristics.

15. David Katz and Robert L. Kahn, *The Social Psychology of Organizations*, 2nd ed. (New York: Wiley, 1978), pp. 187–221.

16. Robert L. Kahn, D.M. Wolfe, R.P. Quinn, J.D. Snoek, and R.A. Rosenthal, *Organizational Stress: Studies in Role Conflict and Role Ambiguity* (New York: Wiley, 1964).

17. For recent research in this area, see Donna L. Wiley, "The Relationship Between Work/Nonwork Role Conflict and Job-related Outcomes: Some Unanticipated Findings," *Journal of Management*, Winter 1987, pp. 467–472; and Arthur G. Bedeian, Beverly G. Burke, and Richard G. Moffett, "Outcomes of Work–Family Conflict Among Married Male and Female Professionals," *Journal of Management*, September 1988, pp. 475–485.

18. See Donna M. Randall, "Multiple Roles and Organizational Commitment," *Journal of Organizational Behavior*, Vol. 9, 1988, pp. 309–317.

19. Daniel C. Feldman, "The Development and Enforcement of Group Norms," *Academy of Management Review*, January 1984, pp. 47–53. See also Monika Henderson and Michael Argyle, "The Informal Rules of Working Relationships," *Journal of Organizational Behavior*, Vol. 7, 1986, pp. 259–275.

20. "Companies Turn to Peer Pressure to Cut Injuries as Psychologists Join the Battle," *The Wall Street Journal*, March 29, 1991, pp. B1, B3.

21. Walter Kiechel III, "Love, Don't Lose, the Newly Hired," *Fortune*, June 6, 1988, pp. 271–274.

22. Matt Riggs and Patrick Knight, "The Impact of Perceived Group Success-Failure on Motivational Beliefs and Attitudes: A Causal Model," *Journal of Applied Psychology*, Vol. 79, No. 5, 1994, pp. 755–766.

23. Anne O'Leary-Kelly, Joseph Martocchio, and Dwight Frink, "A Review of the Influence of Group Goals on Group Performance," *Academy of Management Journal*, Vol. 37, No. 5, 1994, pp. 1285–1301.

24. For an example of how to increase cohesiveness, see Paul F. Buller and Cecil H. Bell, Jr., "Effects of Team Building and Goal Setting on Productivity: A Field Experiment," *Academy of Management Journal*, June 1986, pp. 305–328.

25. Nicole Steckler and Nanette Fondas, "Building Team Leader Effectiveness: A Diagnostic Tool," *Organizational Dynamics*, Winter 1995, pp. 20-35; and Susan Caminiti, "What Team Leaders Need to Know," *Fortune*, February 20, 1995, pp. 93–101.

26. Clayton P. Alderfer, "An Intergroup Perspective on Group Dynamics," in Jay W. Lorsch (Ed.), *Handbook of Organizational Behavior* (Englewood Cliffs, N.J.: Prentice-Hall, 1987), pp. 190–222. See also Eugene Owens and E. Leroy Plumlee, "Intraorganizational Competition and Interorganizational Conflict: More Than a Matter of Semantics," *Business Review*, Winter 1988, pp. 28–32.

27. Catherine Alter, "An Exploratory Study of Conflict and Coordination in Interorganizational Service Delivery Systems," *Academy of Management Journal*, September 1990, pp. 478–502.

28. Thomas Bergmann and Roger Volkema, "Issues, Behavioral Responses and Consequences in Interpersonal Conflicts," *Journal of Organizational Behavior*, Vol. 15, 1994, pp. 467–471.

29. Robin Pinkley and Gregory Northcraft, "Conflict Frames of Reference: Implications for Dispute Processes and Outcomes," *Academy of Management Journal*, Vol. 37, No. 1, 1994, pp. 193–205.

30. "How 2 Computer Nuts Transformed Industry Before Messy Breakup," *The Wall Street Journal*, August 27, 1986, pp. 1, 10.

31. Merle MacIsaac, "Picking Up the Pieces," *Canadian Business*, March 1995, pp. 28–33.

32. Lisa Petrison and Paul Wong, "Relationship Issues in Creating the Customer Database: The Potential for Interdepartmental Conflict Between Marketing and MIS," *Journal of Direct Marketing*, Autumn 1993, pp. 54–62.

33. "A 'Blood War' in the Jeans Trade," *Business Week*, November 13, 1989, pp. 74–81.

34. "Suing over Softwood, *Maclean's*, March 1, 1999, p. 43.

35. "Beecham's Chief Imports His American Ways," *The Wall Street Journal*, October 27, 1988, p. B9.

36. Todd Carver and Albert Vondra, "Alternative Dispute Resolution: Why It Doesn't Work and Why It Does," *Harvard Business Review*, May–June 1994, pp. 120–131.

37. "Battling Executives Seek Out Therapists," *The Wall Street Journal*, November 7, 1988, p. B1.

38. Tamsen Tillson, "War in the Work Zone," *Canadian Business*, September 1995, pp. 40–42.

The Leading Process

NEWS ITEM:
Companies Offering Lavish Incentives to Employees (1999, 1:30)

Increasingly, employers are realizing that in an era of low unemployment, an important factor in attracting and keeping employees is the benefit package they can offer. In many cases, benefits or perks are the deciding factor for a person considering taking a position. These can range from stock options to pool tables, from flexible hours to a dry cleaning service.

Questions:

1. This video segment suggests that benefits are becoming more important than salaries for some workers. What needs are being satisfied by these benefits?
2. Would you rather have higher wages or better benefits? Explain your answer.

NEWS ITEM:
Work-Related Stress (1997, 9:00)

In the modern world of work, stress is taking its toll on employees and their families. Researchers are now finding that it's not just upper-level managers who are at risk, but average employees as well. In Japan, It is estimated that as many as 10,000 people die every year as a direct result of being over-worked. All in all, it's a far cry from expectations of the future that people had back in the 1950s.

The Leading Process (Continued)

Questions:

1. What are the reasons for people needing to work harder?
2. What measures can employers and managers take to alleviate the types of stress seen in this video?
3. Author Bruce O'Hara proposes a 4-day, 32-hour workweek. What would be the benefits of such a workweek for companies? What problems might it create?

Control and total quality management are important considerations for managers in large or small enterprises. The concerns of this woman producing hand-painted tiles using a centuries-old process are much the same as those of the quality control team in a modern, high-tech textile factory.

VI

The Controlling Process

Basic Elements of Control

Canadian Tire Corporation is made up of three businesses: Canadian Tire Retail, Canadian Tire Financial Services, and Canadian Tire Petroleum. Canadian Tire Retail and its 426 associate stores are Canada's leading hard-goods retailer, with a stock of some 55,000 units of automotive parts and accessories and sports, leisure, and home products. Canadian Tire Financial Services finances and manages credit accounts arising from sales at associate stores and Canadian Tire Petroleum's 196 gasoline outlets. The latter's sales by volume make Canadian Tire Petroleum the largest independent retailer of gasoline in Canada. Associate dealers own the fixtures, equipment, and inventory of the stores they operate but must run

While many department-store chains fights a price war, Stephen Bachand, CEO of Canadian Tire, and his crew just keep on making money. The corporation is among the country's largest retailers.

their businesses in accordance with the corporation's overall strategy—a strategy they help develop.

Notwithstanding the input of associate dealers, controlling the operations of Canadian

> **"Controlling the operations of Canadian Tire is a formidable task."**

Tire is a formidable task. But Stephen Bachand, who assumed the position of chief executive officer in March 1993, appears to be up to the challenge. The associate dealers and the corporation had drifted far apart prior to Bachand's appointment, and the new CEO set out to mend the rift. He seems to have achieved that and more. Today, Canadian Tire is highly profitable and is regarded as the first of the large Canadian retailers to resist the Wal-Mart "invasion." For fiscal year 1998, Canadian Tire reported net earnings per share of $2.09, up 17.7 percent from 1997. The corporation closed the year with gross operating revenue of $4.3 billion (up 6.3 percent from 1997) and earnings before taxes of $249.7 million (up 19.2 percent from 1997). Bachand credits the efforts of Canadian Tire's 28,000 employees and 426 associate dealers with the improved performance. All have adhered to a corporate strategy that makes maximum use of the fact that 85 percent of Canadians live within a fifteen-minute drive of a Canadian Tire store.

Total control over operations is difficult to achieve. From time to time, an associate dealer will disregard the directives of the corporation. For example, an associate dealer in London, Ontario, might sell sports clothing or enter the windshield-replacement business, actions that are contrary to directives from head office. However, Canadian Tire's overall success is a testament to its commitment to improving both its services and its bottom line.[1] ●

tephen Bachand has relied on one of the four fundamental functions of management to revitalize Canadian Tire—control. He decided where he wanted the business to go, pointed it in that direction, and created systems to keep it on track. Any business can enhance its financial health by taking the same steps, although each organization must work with its own particular configuration of revenues and costs. The general framework for achieving and maintaining financial health is control.

As we discussed in Chapter 1, control is one of the four basic managerial functions that provide the organizing framework for this book. This is the first of three chapters devoted to this important area. In the first section of this chapter, we explain the purpose of control. We then look at types of control and the steps in the control process. The rest of the chapter examines the four levels of control most organizations must employ to remain effective: operations, financial, structural, and strategic control. We conclude by discussing the characteristics of effective control, noting why some people resist control, and describing what organizations can do to overcome this resistance. The remaining two chapters in this part focus on managing for total quality and managing information.

THE NATURE OF CONTROL IN ORGANIZATIONS

● **control**
The regulation of organizational activities so that some targeted element of performance remains within acceptable limits

Control is the regulation of organizational activities so that some targeted element of performance remains within acceptable limits.[2] Without this regulation, organizations have no indication of how well they perform in relation to their goals. Control, like a ship's rudder, keeps the organization moving in the proper direction. At any point in time, it compares where the organization is in terms of performance (financial, productive, or otherwise) to where it is supposed to be. Like a rudder, control provides an organization with a mechanism for adjusting its course if performance falls outside of acceptable boundaries. For example, FedEx has a performance goal of delivering 99 percent of its packages on time. If on-time deliveries fall to 97 percent, control systems signal the problem to managers so they can make necessary adjustments in operations to regain the target level of performance. An organization without effective control procedures is not likely to reach its goals—or, if it does reach them, to know that it has!

The Purpose of Control

As Figure 20.1 illustrates, control provides an organization with ways to adapt to environmental change, to limit the accumulation of error, to cope with organizational complexity, and to minimize costs. These four functions of control are worth a closer look.

Adapting to Environmental Change   In today's complex and turbulent business environment, all organizations must contend with change.[3] If managers could establish goals and achieve them instantaneously, control would not be needed. But between the time a goal is established and the time it is reached, many things can happen in the organization and its environment to disrupt movement toward the goal—or even to change the goal itself. A properly designed control system can help managers anticipate, monitor, and respond to changing circumstances.[4] In contrast, an improperly designed system can result

F I G U R E 20.1 The Purpose of Control

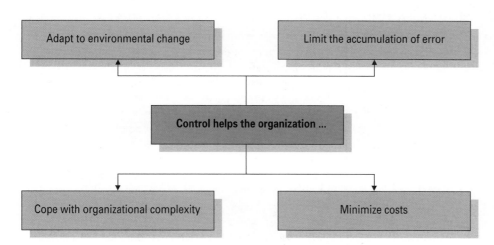

Control is one of the four basic management functions in organizations. The control function, in turn, has four basic purposes. Properly designed control systems are able to fulfill each of these purposes.

in organizational performance that falls far below acceptable levels. The *Environment of Management* box shows what can happen in this case.

Metalloy, a family-run metal casting company, signed a contract to make engine-seal castings for NOK, a big Japanese auto parts maker. Metalloy was satisfied when its first 5,000-unit production run yielded 4,985 acceptable castings and only 15 defective ones. NOK, however, was quite unhappy with this performance and insisted that Metalloy raise its standards. In short, global quality standards had shifted so dramatically that managers at Metalloy had lost touch with how high their own standards had to be in order to remain competitive.[5] A properly designed control system would have kept Metalloy's managers better attuned to rising standards.

Limiting the Accumulation of Error   Small mistakes and errors do not often seriously damage an organization's financial health. Over time, however, small errors may accumulate and eventually become very serious. For example, Whistler Corp., a large radar detector manufacturer, was once faced with such rapidly escalating demand that it essentially stopped worrying about quality. The defect rate rose from 4 percent to 9 percent to 15 percent and eventually reached 25 percent. One day, a manager realized that 100 of the firm's 250 employees were spending all of their time repairing defective units and that $2 million (U.S.) worth of inventory was waiting to be repaired. Had the company adequately controlled quality as it responded to increased demand, the problem would have never reached such proportions.[6]

Coping with Organizational Complexity   When a firm purchases only one raw material, produces one product, has a simple organization design, and enjoys constant demand for its product, its managers can maintain control with a very basic and simple system. But a business that produces many products from myriad raw materials and has a large market area, a complicated organization design, and many competitors needs a sophisticated system to maintain adequate control. Emery Air Freight was quite profitable until it bought Purolator Courier Corporation. The new Emery that resulted from the

Greyhound Out of Control?

Trouble is nothing new to Greyhound Lines. The bus company that began serving Minnesota miners in the early 1900s, carried draftees to training centres during World War II, and served as the set on which Clark Gable courted Claudette Colbert in the 1934 film *It Happened One Night* had to be bailed out by General Motors during the Great Depression at a cost of $1 million (U.S.). Deregulation caused Greyhound problems during the 1980s; when it cut wages to reduce its losses, a massive seven-week strike ensued. Sold by its parent company, now known as the Dial Corp., in 1987, Greyhound filed for reorganization under Bankruptcy Protection in 1990 as yet another strike crippled the company.

In 1991, Greyhound emerged from bankruptcy with new management. Frank J. Schmieder, an investment banker, was named CEO. In an effort to gain control over operations, Schmieder cut costs, upgraded buses and facilities, and reached an agreement with its drivers who were again on strike. Despite seeming to get control over costs, however, ridership did not increase and Greyhound was still limping along.

By early 1994, Schmieder was losing what little control he had established. Ridership fell by about 10 percent despite discounted fares on many routes. Indeed, many believed that the discounted fares were not controlled well: some fares were discounted far more than they needed to be in some markets. On-time performance fell from a high of 81 percent to a low of 59 percent. Passengers frequently got busy signals when they called for fare and schedule information. Those same passengers were frequently upset to discover that when Greyhound cut its fleet size to reduce costs, it also reduced service on some of its most popular routes. A touted national computer reservation system turned out to be a dud. Advertising campaigns were flip-flopped.

Investors began to exercise their own control. Connor, Clark & Company, a Toronto-based investment management firm that owned more than 18 percent of Greyhound, called for the removal of Schmieder. Four days after that, following a special meeting of the board of directors, Schmieder resigned. A spokesperson for the board stated that the board had been discussing for several months who should be part of the management team needed to implement a major overhaul of the organization. Following Schmieder's resignation, a temporary CEO was named. In October 1997, Greyhound was purchased by Laidlaw Inc.

References: "Greyhound Is Limping Badly," *Business Week*, August 22, 1994, p. 32; Gregory E. David, "Greyhound Lines: Goodbye, Dog Days?" *Financial World*, July 5, 1994, p. 16; "Another Dogfight at Greyhound?" *Business Week*, September 2, 1991, p. 43; "Labor May Still Have Greyhound Collared," *Business Week*, November 26, 1990, p. 60; and Laidlaw, Annual Report, 1998 (http://www.laidlaw.com).

---

acquisition was much bigger and more complex, but it added no new controls to operations. Consequently, Emery began to lose money and market share, costs increased, and service deteriorated until the company was on the verge of bankruptcy. Some analysts still question whether Emery will ever regain its former levels of performance.

Minimizing Costs   When practised effectively, control can also help reduce costs and boost output. For example, by switching to a new method of mining and ensuring compliance with the new technique, Sifto Canada's Goderich mine reduced production costs by 25 percent and enhanced worker safety at the same time.[7] As the company discovered, effective control systems can eliminate waste, lower labour costs, and improve output per unit of input.

Control is one of an organization's most fundamental functions. The Red River floodway is capable of diverting 60,000 cubic feet per second of water around the city of Winnipeg. Gates to the city's south allow some of the water to take its natural course through the city. The remainder is diverted into the floodway, which was responsible for preventing massive disaster to the city in the spring of 1997.

Types of Control

The examples of control used thus far have illustrated the regulation of several organizational activities, from producing quality products to coordinating complex organizations. Organizations practise control in a number of different areas and at different levels, and the responsibility for managing control is widespread.

Areas of Control   Control can focus on any area of an organization. Most organizations define areas of control in terms of the four basic types of resources they use: physical, human, information, and financial resources. Control of physical resources includes inventory management (stocking neither too few nor too many units in inventory), quality control (maintaining appropriate levels of output quality), and equipment control (supplying the necessary facilities and machinery). Control of human resources includes selection and placement, training and development, performance appraisal, and compensation. Control of information resources includes sales and marketing forecasting, environmental analysis, public relations, production scheduling, and economic forecasting. Financial control involves managing the organization's debt so that it does not become excessive, ensuring that the firm always has enough cash on hand to meet its obligations but that it does not have excess cash in a chequing account, and that receivables are collected and bills paid on a timely basis.

In many ways, the control of financial resources is the most important area because financial resources are related to the control of all the other resources in an organization: too much inventory leads to storage costs, poor selection of human resources leads to termination and rehiring expenses, and inaccurate sales forecasts lead to disruptions in cash flows and other financial effects. Financial issues tend to pervade most control-related activities. Indeed, financial issues are the basic problem faced by Emery Air Freight. Various inefficiencies and operating blunders put the company in a position where it lacked the money to service its debt (make interest payments on loans), had little working capital (cash to cover daily operating expenses), and was too heavily leveraged (excessive debt) to borrow more money.

Levels of Control   Just as control can be broken down by area, as Figure 20.2 shows it can also be broken down by level within the organizational system. Operations control focuses on the processes the organization uses to transform resources into products or services (quality control is one type of operations control).[8] Financial control is concerned with the organization's financial resources. (Monitoring receivables to make sure that customers are paying their bills on time is an example of financial control.) Structural control is concerned with how the elements of the organization's structure are serving their intended purposes. (Monitoring the administrative ratio to make sure that staff expenses do not become excessive is an example of structural control.) Finally, strategic control focuses on how effectively the organization's corporate, business, and functional strategies are succeeding in helping the organization meet its goals and objectives.[9] (For example, if a corporation has been unsuccessful in implementing its strategy of related diversification, its managers need to identify the reasons and either change the strategy or renew their efforts to implement it.) We discuss these four levels of control more fully later in this chapter.

Responsibilities for Control   Traditionally, managers have been responsible for overseeing the wide array of control systems and concerns in organizations. They decide which types of control the organization will use, and they implement control systems and take actions based on the information provided by control systems. Thus ultimate responsibility for control rests with all managers throughout an organization.

Most larger organizations also have one or more specialized managerial positions called controller. A **controller** is responsible for helping line managers with their control activities, for coordinating the organization's overall control system, and for gathering and assimilating relevant information. Many businesses that use an H-form or M-form organization design (see Chapter 11) have several controllers: one for the corporation and one for each division. The job of controller is especially important in organizations where control systems are complex.[10]

In addition, many organizations are also beginning to use operating employees to help maintain effective control. Indeed, employee participation is often used as a vehicle for allowing operating employees an opportunity to help facilitate organizational effectiveness. For example, Whistler Corporation increased employee participation in an effort to turn its quality problems around. As a starting point, Whistler eliminated the quality control unit, formerly responsible for checking product quality at the end of the assembly process. Next, it encouraged all operating employees to check their own work and told them that they would be responsible for correcting their own errors. As a result, Whistler has eliminated its quality problems and is now highly profitable once again.

Steps in the Control Process

Regardless of the type or levels of control systems an organization needs, any control process has four fundamental steps.[11] These are illustrated in Figure 20.3.

Establish Standards   The first step in the control process is establishing standards. A **control standard** is a target against which subsequent performance will be compared. Employees at Taco Bell fast-food restaurant, for example, work toward the following service standards:

● **controller**
A position in organizations that helps line managers with their control activities

● **control standard**
A target against which subsequent performance is to be compared

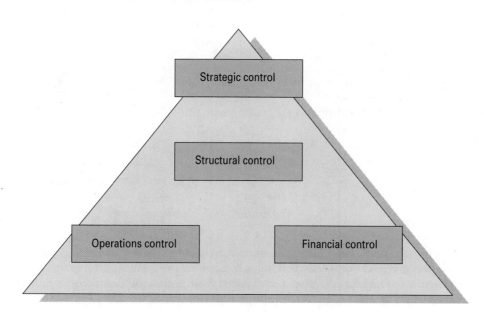

1. A minimum of 95 percent of all customers will be greeted within three minutes of their arrival.

2. Preheated tortilla chips will not sit in the warmer more than thirty minutes before they are served to customers.

3. Empty tables will be cleaned within five minutes after being vacated.

Standards established for control purposes should be expressed in measurable terms. Note that standard 1 has a time limit of three minutes and an objective target of 95 percent of all customers. In standard 3, the objective target is implied: "all" empty tables.

Control standards should also be consistent with the organization's goals. Taco Bell has organizational goals involving customer service, food quality, and restaurant cleanliness. A control standard for a retailer like the Home Depot should be consistent with its goal of increasing its annual sales volume by 25 percent within five years. A hospital trying to shorten a patient's average hospital stay will have control standards that reflect current averages. Control standards can be as narrow or as broad as the level of activity to which they apply and must follow logically from organizational goals and objectives.

A final aspect of establishing standards is to identify performance indicators. Performance indicators are measures of performance that provide information that is directly relevant to what is being controlled. For example, suppose that an organization is following a tight schedule in building a new plant. Relevant performance indicators could be buying a site, selecting a building contractor, and ordering equipment. Monthly sales increases are not, however, directly relevant. On the other hand, if control is focused on revenue, monthly sales increases are relevant, whereas buying land for a new plant is less relevant.

Measure Performance   The second step in the control process is measuring performance. Performance measurement is a constant, ongoing activity for

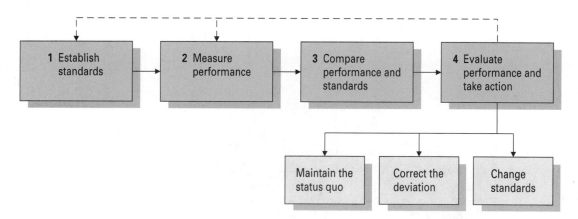

Having an effective control system can help ensure that an organization achieves its goals. Implementing a control system, however, is a systematic process that generally proceeds through four interrelated steps.

most organizations. For control to be effective, performance measures must be valid. Daily, weekly, and monthly sales figures measure sales performance, and production performance may be expressed in terms of unit cost, product quality, or volume produced. Employee performance is often measured in terms of quality or quantity of output, but for many jobs measuring performance is not so straightforward.

A research and development scientist at Connaught Laboratories, for example, may spend years working on a single project before achieving a breakthrough. A manager who takes over a business on the brink of failure may need months or even years to turn things around. Valid performance measurement, however difficult to obtain, is nevertheless vital in maintaining effective control, and performance indicators usually can be developed. The scientist's progress, for example, may be partially assessed by peer review, and the manager's success may be evaluated by her ability to convince creditors that she will eventually be able to restore profitability.

Compare Performance Against Standards   The third step in the control process is comparing measured performance against established standards. Performance may be higher than, lower than, or identical to the standard. In

These research scientists may spend years working on a project before achieving a breakthrough. Performance measurement, although still necessary, may become more unorthodox.

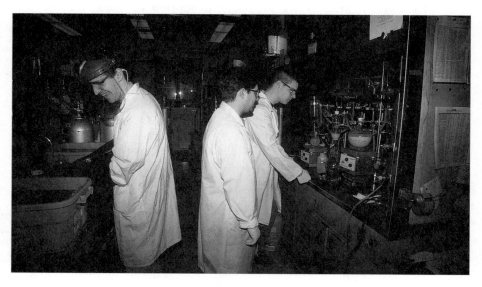

some cases, comparison is easy. The goal of each product manager at General Electric is to make the product either number-one or number-two (on the basis of total sales) in its market. Because this standard is clear and total sales are easy to calculate, determining whether this standard has been met is relatively simple. Sometimes, however, comparisons are less clear-cut. If performance is lower than expected, management must decide how much deviation from standards to allow before taking remedial action. For example, is increasing sales by 7.9 percent when the standard is 8 percent close enough?

The timetable for comparing performance to standards depends on a variety of factors, including the importance and complexity of what is being controlled. For longer-run and higher-level standards, annual comparisons may be appropriate. In other circumstances, more frequent comparisons are necessary. For example, a business with a cash shortage may need to monitor its on-hand cash reserves daily. We noted earlier the cash-flow problems Emery Air Freight faced after it purchased Purolator Courier. As part of their efforts to improve the firm's control, Emery's managers eventually started monitoring their cash reserves weekly.

Consider Corrective Action   The final step in the control process is determining the need for corrective action. Decisions regarding corrective actions draw heavily on a manager's analytic and diagnostic skills. After comparing performance against control standards, one of three actions is appropriate: maintain the status quo (do nothing), correct the deviation, or change the standard. Maintaining the status quo is preferable when performance essentially matches the standard, but more likely some action is needed to correct a deviation from the standard.

Sometimes performance that is higher than expected may also cause problems for organizations. For example, when Ford Motor Co. introduced its new Contour in 1994, demand was so strong that there were waiting lists and many customers were willing to pay more than the suggested retail price to obtain a car. The company was reluctant to increase production, primarily because it feared demand would eventually drop. At the same time, however, it didn't want to alienate potential customers. Consequently, Ford decided to simply reduce its advertising. This somewhat curtailed demand and limited customer frustration.

Changing an established standard usually is necessary if it was set too high or too low at the outset. This is apparent if most employees routinely beat the standard by a wide margin or if no employees ever meet the standard. Also, standards that seemed appropriate when they were established may need to be adjusted because circumstances have changed.

OPERATIONS CONTROL

One of the four levels of control practised by most organizations, **operations control,** is concerned with the processes the organization uses to transform resources into products or services. As Figure 20.4 shows, the three forms of operations control—preliminary, screening, and post-action—occur at different points in relation to the transformation processes used by the organization.

● **operations control**
Focuses on the processes the organization uses to transform resources into products or services

Preliminary Control

preliminary control
Attempts to monitor the quality or quantity of financial, material, human, and information resources before they actually become part of the system

Preliminary control concentrates on the resources—financial, material, human, and information—that the organization brings in from the environment. Preliminary control attempts to monitor the quality or quantity of these resources before they enter the organization. Firms like PepsiCo and General Mills hire only college graduates for their management training program, and even then only after applicants satisfy several interviewers and selection criteria. In this way, they control the quality of the human resources entering the organization. When Marks&Spencer orders merchandise to be manufactured under its own brand name, it specifies rigid standards of quality, thereby controlling physical inputs. Organizations also control financial and information resources. For example, some privately held companies limit the extent to which outsiders can buy their stock, and television networks verify the accuracy of news stories before they are broadcast.

Screening Control

screening control
Focuses on meeting standards for products or service quality or quantity during the actual transformation process; relies heavily on feedback processes during the transformation process

Screening control focuses on meeting standards for product and/or service quality or quantity during the actual transformation process itself. Screening control relies heavily on feedback processes. For example, in a Compaq Computer factory computer system components are checked periodically as each unit is being assembled. This is done to ensure that all the components that have been assembled up to that point are working properly. The periodic quality checks provide feedback to workers so they know what, if any, corrective actions to take. Because they are useful in identifying the cause of problems, screening controls tend to be used more often than other forms of control.

More and more companies are adopting screening controls because they effectively promote employee participation and catch problems early in the overall transformation process. For example, Corning recently adopted screening controls for use in manufacturing television glass. In the past, finished television screens

Most organizations develop multiple control systems that incorporate all three basic forms of control. For example, the publishing company that produced this book screens inputs by hiring only qualified persons, typesetters, and printers (preliminary control). In addition, quality is checked during the transformation process such as after the manuscript is typeset (screening control), and the outputs—printed and bound books—are checked before they are shipped from the bindery (post-action control).

F I G U R E   20.4   Forms of Operations Control

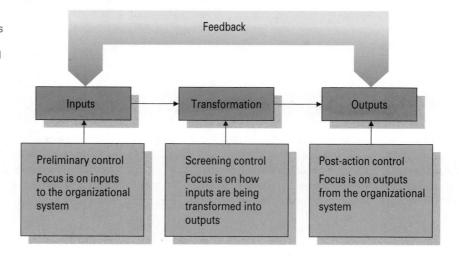

were inspected only after they were finished. Unfortunately, more than 4 percent of them were later returned by customers because of defects. Now the glass screens are inspected at each step in the production process rather than at the end, and the return rate from customers has dropped to .03 percent.[12]

Post-Action Control

Post-action control focuses on the outputs of the organization after the transformation process is complete. Corning's old system was post-action control—final inspection after the product is completed. Although Corning abandoned its post-action control system, this still may be an effective method of control, primarily if a product can be manufactured in only one or two steps or if the service is fairly simple and routine. Although post-action control alone may not be as effective as preliminary or screening control, it can provide management with information for future planning. For example, if a quality check of finished goods indicates an unacceptably high defect rate, the production manager knows that he or she must identify the causes and take steps to eliminate them. Post-action control also provides a basis for rewarding employees. Recognizing that an employee has exceeded personal sales goals by a wide margin, for example, may alert the manager that a bonus or promotion is in order.[13]

Most organizations use more than one form of operations control. For example, Honda's preliminary control includes hiring only qualified employees and specifying strict quality standards when ordering parts from other manufacturers. Honda uses numerous screening controls in checking the quality of components during assembly of cars. A final inspection and test drive as each car rolls off the assembly line is part of the company's post-action control. Organizations employ a wide variety of techniques to facilitate operations control.

- **post-action control**
Monitors the outputs or results of the organization after the transformation process is complete

FINANCIAL CONTROL

Financial control is the control of financial resources as they flow into the organization (i.e., revenues, shareholder investments), are held by the organization (i.e., working capital, retained earnings), and flow out of the organization (i.e., pay expenses). Businesses must manage their finances so that revenues are sufficient to cover costs and still return a profit to the firm's owners. The *Managing in a Changing World* box vividly illustrates the damage that can result from weak financial controls. Not-for-profit organizations such as universities have the same concerns: their revenues (from tax dollars or tuition) must cover operating expenses and overhead. A complete discussion of financial management is beyond the scope of this book, but we examine the control provided by budgets and other financial control tools.

- **financial control**
Concerned with the organization's financial resources

Budgetary Control

A **budget** is a plan expressed in numerical terms.[14] Organizations establish budgets for work groups, departments, divisions, and the whole organization. The usual time period for a budget is one year, although breakdowns of budgets by the quarter or month are also common. Budgets are generally expressed in financial terms, but they may occasionally be expressed in units of output, time, or other quantifiable factors.

- **budget**
A plan expressed in numerical terms

Because of their quantitative nature, budgets provide yardsticks for measuring performance and facilitate comparisons across departments, between levels in the organization, and from one time period to another. Budgets serve four primary purposes. They help managers coordinate resources and projects (because they use a common denominator, usually dollars), help define the established standards for control, and provide guidelines about the organization's resources and expectations. Finally, budgets enable the organization to evaluate the performance of managers and organizational units.

Types of Budgets Most organizations develop and make use of three different kinds of budgets—financial, operating, and nonmonetary. Table 20.1 summarizes the characteristics of each of these.

A financial budget indicates where the organization expects to get its cash for the coming time period and how it plans to use it. Because financial resources are critically important, the organization needs to know where those resources will be coming from and how they are to be used. The financial budget provides answers to both of these questions. Usual sources of cash include sales revenue, short- and long-term loans, the sale of assets, and the issuance of new stock.

An operating budget is concerned with planned operations within the organization. It outlines what quantities of products and/or services the organization intends to create and what resources will be used to create them. IBM creates an operating budget that specifies how many of each model of its personal computer will be produced each quarter.

A nonmonetary budget is simply a budget expressed in nonfinancial terms, such as units of output, hours of direct labour, machine hours, or square-foot/metre allocations. Nonmonetary budgets are most commonly used by managers at the lower levels of an organization. For example, a plant manager can schedule work more effectively knowing that he or she has eight thousand labour hours to allocate in a week, rather than trying to determine how to best spend $76,451 in wages in a week.

Developing Budgets Traditionally, top management and the controller developed budgets and then imposed them on lower-level managers. Although some organizations still follow this pattern, many contemporary organizations now allow all managers to participate in the budget process. As a starting point, top management generally issues a call for budget requests, accompanied by an indication of overall patterns the budgets may take. For example, if sales are expected to drop in the next year, managers may be told up front to prepare for cuts in operating budgets.

As Figure 20.5 shows, the heads of each operating unit typically submit budget requests to the head of their division. An operating unit head might be a department manager in a manufacturing or wholesaling firm or a program director in a social service agency. Division heads might include plant managers, regional sales managers, or faculty deans. The division head integrates and consolidates the budget requests from operating unit heads into one overall division budget request. A great deal of interaction among managers usually takes place at this stage, as the division head coordinates the budgetary needs of the various departments.

Division budget requests are then forwarded to a budget committee. The budget committee is usually composed of top managers. The committee reviews budget requests from several divisions and, once again, duplications and

Pitfalls in International Strategic Control

In today's changing world, many international businesses are grappling with the question of how to control far-flung global operations. Some prefer a centralized approach, with decisions made by senior executives at headquarters. Others lean more toward decentralized control for foreign operations, with decisions made by local managers close to the action. Managers must remember, however, that decentralized control is not the same thing as no control.

The financial disaster at Baring Brothers in 1995 provides an all too clear illustration of what can happen when this distinction is ignored. Baring Brothers is one of the oldest and most respected banks in England. During its fabled history—spanning 233 years—this venerable institution financed the Napoleonic Wars for Great Britain, financed the Louisiana Purchase for the United States, and was banker to the House of Windsor. Baring was always conservatively managed and until recently was one of England's most trusted banking operations. International expansion with too little control, however, brought the firm to its knees.

Like many major banks today, Baring Brothers opened offices in many major cities around the world. One of the bank's subsidiaries was Baring Futures PLC, an investment firm specializing in complex futures trading markets. In 1992, Baring Futures sent a young broker named Nick Leeson to work in its Singapore office. Leeson performed admirably for the firm, earning vast sums of money with his impressive understanding of Asian financial markets. He received accolades from his superiors for his ability to run a tight operation with little outside control.

Disaster struck in early 1995, however. As investigators would soon discover, Leeson had made a number of questionable investments in 1994, investments which had undermined the financial strength of the firm and which would eventually force it into bankruptcy. The basic mistake Leeson made was to place complex futures orders based on what he expected the Tokyo stock market to do. Had his expectations been met, Baring would have made a fortune. The earthquake that struck Kobe, Japan, in 1994, however, disrupted the Nikkei index so much that Leeson's highly leveraged deals fell apart and Baring was driven to its knees.

Leeson was able to inflict so much damage single-handedly because Baring trusted him to the point that it had no controls over his actions. In most investment houses, one person or group and another person or group serves as overseer. This latter function is for strategic control—to ensure that the traders are not taking unnecessary risks and that they have financial backing to cover any losses they might incur.

Unfortunately, Baring allowed Leeson to perform both functions with no external oversight. He made trades, confirmed them himself, and then authorized the funds to cover them. As his deals went sour following the Kobe disaster, the lack of control kept managers in England from recognizing the problems he had created. Indeed, with no one overseeing his actions, he desperately made riskier investments in an attempt to recoup his losses. Without anyone checking his work, he eventually drove the firm's debts to $1.4 billion (U.S.).

Eventually, Baring learned that it had incurred huge losses with no financial backing. It launched an investigation. After the disaster was discovered, Leeson fled the country but was soon apprehended in Germany. Baring, meanwhile, could find no investors to cover its losses and was taken over by the Bank of England. It was eventually sold to a Dutch finance group, Internationale Nederlanden Groep, when that firm agreed to inject $1.3 billion (U.S.) into the bank to return it to solvency.

References: "Busted!" *Newsweek*, March 13, 1995, pp. 36–47; "The Lesson from Barings" Straits,'" *Business Week*, March 13, 1995, pp. 30–32; "Barings' Debacle: High-Finance Thriller Laced with Greek Tragedy," *Associated Press News Story*, March 5, 1995; and "Barings Is Back in Business," *USA Today*, March 7, 1995, p. 2B.

inconsistencies are corrected. Finally, the budget committee, the controller, and the CEO review and agree on the overall budget for the organization as well as specific budgets for each operating unit. These decisions are then communicated back to each manager.

Organizations use a variety of types of budgets to help manage their control function. The three major categories of budgets are financial, operating, and nonmonetary budgets. There are several different types of budgets in each category. Each budget must be carefully matched with the specific function being controlled in order to be most effective.

TABLE 20.1 Types of Budgets

Type of Budget	What Budget Shows
Financial budget	**Sources and uses of cash**
Cash-flow or cash budget	All sources of cash income and cash expenditures in monthly, weekly, or daily periods
Capital expenditures budget	Costs of major assets such as a new plant, machinery, or land
Balance sheet budget	Forecast of the organization's assets and liabilities in the event all other budgets are met
Operating budget	**Planned operations in financial terms**
Sales or revenue budget	Income the organization expects to receive from normal operations
Expense budget	Anticipated expenses for the organization during the coming time period
Profit budget	Anticipated differences between sales or revenues and expenses
Nonmonetary budget	**Planned operations in nonfinancial terms**
Labour budget	Hours of direct labour available for use
Space budget	Square feet or metres of space available for various functions
Production budget	Number of units to be produced during the coming time period

Strengths and Weaknesses of Budgeting   Budgets offer a number of advantages, but they also have weaknesses as well. On the plus side, budgets facilitate effective control. Placing dollar values on operations enables managers to monitor operations better and pinpoint problem areas. Budgets also facilitate coordination and communication between departments because they express diverse activities in a common denominator (dollars). Budgets help maintain records of organizational performance and are a logical complement to planning. That is, as managers develop plans they should consider control measures to accompany them. Organizations can use budgets to link plans and control by first developing budgets as part of the plan and then using those budgets as a part of control.

A weakness of budgets is that some managers apply budgets too rigidly. Budgets are intended to serve as frameworks, but managers sometimes fail to recognize that changing circumstances may warrant budget adjustments. The process of developing budgets can also be very time consuming. Finally, budgets may limit innovation and change. When all available funds are allocated to

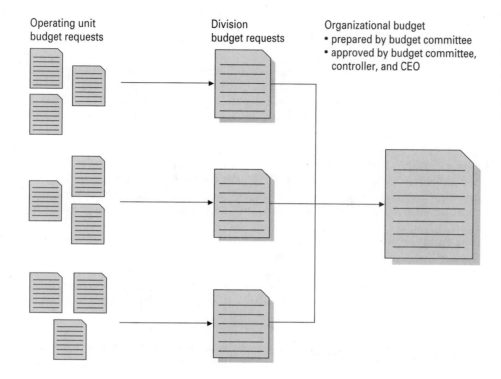

Operating unit
budget requests

Division
budget requests

Organizational budget
• prepared by budget committee
• approved by budget committee,
controller, and CEO

Most organizations use the same basic process to develop budgets. Operating units are requested to submit their budget requests to divisions. These divisions, in turn, compile unit budgets and submit their own budgets to the organization. An organizational budget is then compiled for approval by the budget committee, controller, and CEO.

specific operating budgets, procuring additional funds to take advantage of an unexpected opportunity may be impossible.[15]

Indeed, for these very reasons, some organizations are working to scale back their budgeting system. Although most organizations will continue to use budgets, the goal is to make them less confining and rigid. For example, Xerox and 3M have both cut back on their budgeting systems by reducing the number of budgets they generate and by injecting more flexibility into the budgeting process.[16]

Other Tools of Financial Control

Although budgets are the most common means of financial control, other useful tools are financial statements, ratio analysis, and financial audits.

Financial Statements   A **financial statement** is a profile of some aspect of an organization's financial circumstances. Financial statements are prepared and presented in commonly accepted and required ways.[17] The two most basic financial statements prepared and used by virtually all organizations are a balance sheet and an income statement.

The **balance sheet** lists the organization's assets and liabilities at a specific point in time, usually the last day of an organization's fiscal year. For example, the balance sheet may summarize the financial condition of an organization on December 31, 1999. Most balance sheets are divided into current assets (assets

● **financial statement**
A profile of some aspect of an organization's financial circumstances

● **balance sheet**
List of an organization's assets and liabilities at a specific point in time

that are relatively liquid, or easily convertible into cash), fixed assets (assets that are longer-term in nature and less liquid), current liabilities (debts and other obligations that must be paid in the near future), long-term liabilities (payable over an extended period of time), and shareholders' equity (the owners' claim against the assets).

● **income statement**
A summary of financial performance over a period of time

Whereas the balance sheet reflects a snapshot profile of an organization's financial position at a single point in time, the **income statement** summarizes financial performance over a period of time, usually one year. For example, the income statement might be for the period January 1, 1999, through December 31, 1999. The income statement adds up all income to the organization and then subtracts all expenses, debts, and liabilities. The "bottom line" of the statement represents net income, or profit. Information from the balance sheet and income statement is used to compute important financial ratios.

Ratio Analysis Financial ratios compare different elements of a balance sheet and income statement to one another. **Ratio analysis** is the calculation of one or more financial ratios to assess some aspect of the financial health of an organization. Organizations use a variety of different financial ratios as part of financial control. For example, *liquidity ratios* indicate how liquid (easily converted into cash) an organization's assets are. *Debt ratios* reflect ability to meet long-term financial obligations. *Return ratios* show managers and investors how much return the organization is generating relative to its assets. *Coverage ratios* help estimate the organization's ability to cover interest expenses on borrowed capital. *Operating ratios* indicate the effectiveness of specific functional areas rather than on the total organization.

● **ratio analysis**
The calculation of one or more financial ratios to assess some aspect of the organization's financial health

Financial Audits **Audits** are independent appraisals of an organization's accounting, financial, and operational systems. The two major types of financial audit are the external audit and the internal audit.

● **audit**
An independent appraisal of an organization's accounting, financial, and operational systems

External audits are financial appraisals conducted by experts who are not employees of the organization.[18] External audits are typically concerned with determining that the organization's accounting procedures and financial statements are compiled in an objective and verifiable fashion. The organization contracts with chartered accountants (CAs) for this service. The CA's main objective is to verify for shareholders, Revenue Canada, and other interested parties that the methods by which the organization's financial managers and accountants prepare documents and reports are legal and proper. External audits are so important that publicly held corporations are required by law to have external audits regularly, as assurance to investors that the financial reports are reliable.

Some organizations are also starting to employ external auditors to review other aspects of their financial operations. For example, there are now auditing firms that specialize in checking corporate legal bills. An auditor for the Fireman's Fund Insurance Corporation uncovered several thousands of dollars in legal fee errors. Other auditors are beginning to specialize in real estate, employee benefits, and pension plan investments.[19]

Whereas external audits are conducted by external accountants, an *internal audit* is handled by employees of the organization. Its objective is the same as that of an external audit—to verify the accuracy of financial and accounting procedures used by the organization. Internal audits also examine the efficiency and appropriateness of financial and accounting procedures. Because the staff members who conduct them are a permanent part of the organization, internal audits tend to be more expensive than external audits. But employees, who are more familiar with the organization's practices, may also point out significant aspects of the accounting system besides its technical correctness. Large organizations such as the Canadian Imperial Bank of Commerce and Ford have internal auditing staffs that spend all their time conducting audits of different divisions and functional areas of the organizations. Smaller organizations may assign accountants to an internal audit group on a temporary or rotating basis.

STRUCTURAL CONTROL

Structural control is concerned with how the elements of the organization's structure are serving their intended purposes. Organizations can create designs for themselves that result in very different approaches to control. Two major forms of structural control, bureaucratic control and clan control, represent opposite ends of a continuum, as shown in Figure 20.6.[20] The six dimensions shown in the figure represent perspectives adopted by the two extreme types of structural control. That is, they have different goals, degrees of formality, performance focus, organization designs, reward systems, and levels of participation. Although a few organizations fall precisely at one extreme or the other, most tend toward one end but may have specific characteristics of either.

● **structural control**
Concerned with how the elements of the organization's structure are serving their intended purpose

Bureaucratic Control

Bureaucratic control is an approach to organization design characterized by formal and mechanistic structural arrangements. As the term suggests, it follows the bureaucratic model. The goal of bureaucratic control is employee compliance. Organizations that use it rely on strict rules and a rigid hierarchy, insist that employees meet minimally acceptable levels of performance, and often have a tall structure. They focus their rewards on individual performance and allow only limited and formal employee participation.

A typical Canadian university applies structural controls that reflect many elements of bureaucracy. The organization relies on numerous rules to regulate employee travel, expense accounts, and other expenses. There is a push for new performance appraisal systems that precisely specify minimally acceptable levels of performance for everyone. The organization's structure is becoming increasingly taller and rewards are increasingly based on individual contributions. Perhaps most importantly, many employees at Canadian universities are arguing that they have too small a voice in how their organizations are managed.

● **bureaucratic control**
A form of organizational control characterized by formal and mechanistic structural arrangements

Clan Control

Clan control, in contrast, is an approach to organizational design characterized by informal and organic structural arrangements. As Figure 20.6 shows, its goal is employee commitment to the organization. Accordingly, it relies heavily on group norms and a strong corporate culture, and it gives employees the responsibility for controlling themselves. Employees are encouraged to perform beyond minimally acceptable levels. Organizations using this approach are usually relatively flat. They direct reward at group performance and favour widespread employee participation.

● **clan control**
An approach to organizational control based on informal and organic structural arrangements

Organizational control
generally falls somewhere
between the two extremes
of bureaucratic and clan
control. A typical Canadian
university uses bureaucratic
control, whereas Levi
Strauss uses clan control.

F I G U R E   20.6 Organizational Control

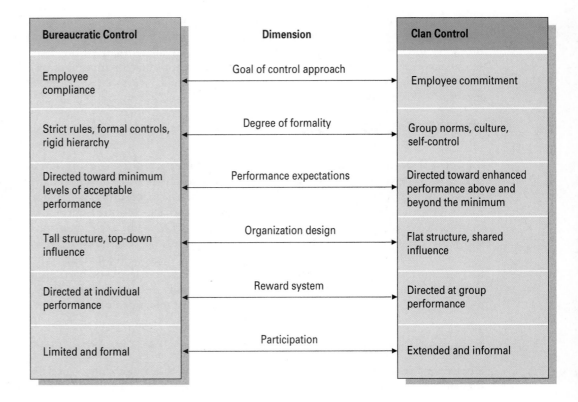

Levi Strauss practises clan control. The firm's managers use groups as the basis for work and have created a culture wherein group norms help facilitate high performance. Rewards are subsequently provided to the higher-performing groups and teams. The company's culture also reinforces contributions to the overall team effort, and employees have a strong sense of loyalty to the organization. Levi's has a flat structure, and power is widely shared. Employee participation is encouraged in all areas of operation.

STRATEGIC CONTROL

Given the obvious importance of an organization's strategy, the organization must also assess how effective that strategy is in helping the organization meet its goals.[21] To do this requires that the organization integrate its strategy and control systems. This is especially true for the global organization.

Integrating Strategy and Control

Strategic control generally focuses on five aspects of organizations—structure, leadership, technology, human resources, and information and operational control systems. For example, an organization should periodically examine its structure to determine whether it is facilitating the attainment of its strategic goals. Suppose that a firm using a functional (U-form) design has an established goal of achieving a 20 percent sales growth rate per year, but performance indicators show that it is currently growing at a rate of only 10 percent per year. Detailed analysis might reveal that the current structure is inhibiting growth in some way (for example, by slowing decision making and inhibiting innovation) and that a divisional (M-form) design is more likely to bring about the desired growth (by speeding decision making and promoting innovation).

In this way, **strategic control** focuses on the extent to which implemented strategy achieves the organization's strategic goals. If, as just outlined, one or more avenues of implementation are inhibiting the attainment of goals, that avenue should be changed. Consequently, the firm might need to alter its structure, replace essential leaders, adopt new technology, modify its human resources, or change its information and operational control systems.

● **Strategic control**
Focuses on how effectively the organization's strategies are succeeding in helping the organization meet its goals

International Strategic Control

Because of both their relatively large size and the increased complexity associated with international business, global organizations must take an especially

With a view to long-term use, Calgary is using the site of the former Winter Olympics to lure new business. A member of the national Nordic combined ski team, Chris Holland flies through the air during summer jumping at Canada Olympic Park in Calgary. The jump in the background is the 90-metre jump built for the 1988 Olympics.

pronounced strategic view of their control systems. One very basic question that must be addressed is whether to manage control from a centralized or decentralized perspective.[22] Under a centralized system, each organizational unit around the world is responsible for frequently reporting the results of its performance to headquarters. Managers from the home office often visit foreign branches to observe first-hand how the units are functioning.

British Petroleum, Unilever, Procter & Gamble, and Sony each use this approach. They believe that centralized control is effective because it allows the head office to keep better informed of the performance of foreign units and to maintain more control over how decisions are made. For example, British Petroleum discovered that its Australian subsidiary was not billing its customers for charges as quickly as were its competitors. By shortening the billing cycle, BP now receives customer payments five days faster than before. Managers believe that they discovered this oversight only because of a centralized financial control system.

Organizations that use a decentralized control system require foreign branches to report performance information less frequently and in less detail. For example, each unit may submit summary performance statements quarterly and provide full statements only once a year. Similarly, visits from the head office are less frequent and less concerned with monitoring and assessing performance. IBM, Ford, and Royal Dutch/Shell Group all use this approach. Because Ford practises decentralized control of its design function, European designers have developed several innovative automobile design features. Managers believe that if they had been more centralized, designers would not have had the freedom to develop their new ideas.

MANAGING CONTROL IN ORGANIZATIONS

Effective control, whether at the operations, financial, structural, or strategic level, successfully regulates and monitors organizational activities. To use the control process, managers must recognize the characteristics of effective control and understand how to identify and overcome occasional resistance to control.[23]

Characteristics of Effective Control

Control systems tend to be most effective when they are integrated with planning and when they are flexible, accurate, timely, and objective.

Integration with Planning   Control should be linked with planning. The more explicit and precise this linkage, the more effective the control system. The best way to integrate planning and control is to account for control as plans develop. In other words, as goals are set during the planning process, attention should be paid to developing standards that will reflect how well the plan is realized. Managers at Champion Spark Plug Company decided to broaden their product line to include a full range of automotive accessories— a total of twenty-one new products. As a part of this plan, managers decided in advance what level of sales they wanted to realize from each product for each of the next five years. They established these sales goals as standards against which actual sales would be compared. Thus by accounting for their control system as they developed their plan, managers at Champion did an excellent job of integrating planning and control.

Flexibility   The control system itself must be flexible enough to accommodate change. Consider, for example, an organization whose diverse product line requires seventy-five different raw materials. The company's inventory control system must be able to manage and monitor current levels of inventory for all seventy-five materials. When a change in product line changes the number of raw materials needed, or when the required quantities of the existing materials change, the control system should be flexible enough to handle the revised requirements. The alternative—designing and implementing a new control system—is an avoidable expense. Champion's control system includes a mechanism that automatically shipped products to major customers to keep their inventory at predetermined levels. The firm had to adjust this system when one of its biggest customers decided not to stock the full line of Champion products. Because its control system was flexible, modifying it was relatively simple.

Accuracy   Managers make a surprisingly large number of decisions based on inaccurate information. Field representatives may hedge their sales estimates to make themselves look better. Production managers may hide costs to meet their targets. Human resource managers may overestimate their female recruiting prospects to meet employment equity goals. In each case, the information other managers receive is inaccurate, and the results of inaccurate information may be quite dramatic. If sales projections are inflated, a manager might cut advertising (thinking it is no longer needed) or increase advertising (to further build momentum). Similarly, a production manager unaware of hidden costs may quote a sales price much lower than desirable. Or a human resource manager may speak out publicly on the effectiveness of the company's recruiting of women, only to find out later that these prospects have been overestimated. In each case, the result of inaccurate information is inappropriate managerial action.

Timeliness   Timeliness does not necessarily mean quickness; it rather describes a control system that provides information as often as is necessary. Because Champion has a wealth of historical data on its sparkplug sales, it does not need information on sparkplugs as frequently as it needs sales feedback for its newer products. Retail organizations usually need sales results daily so that they can manage cash flow and adjust advertising and promotion. In contrast, they may require information about physical inventory only quarterly or annually. In general, the more uncertain and unstable the circumstances, the more frequently measurement is needed.

Objectivity   The control system should provide information that is as objective as possible. To appreciate this, imagine the task of a manager responsible for control of his organization's human resources. He asks two plant managers to submit reports. One manager notes that morale at his plant is "okay," that grievances are "about where they should be," and that turnover is "under control." The other reports that absenteeism at her plant is running at 4 percent, that sixteen grievances have been filed this year (compared with twenty-four last year), and that turnover is 12 percent. The second report will almost always be more useful than the first. Of course, managers also need to look beyond the numbers when assessing performance. For example, a plant manager may be boosting productivity and profit margins by putting too much pressure on workers and using poor-quality materials. As a result, impressive short-run gains may be overshadowed by longer-run increases in employee turnover and customer complaints.

Resistance to Control

Managers sometimes make the mistake of assuming that the value of an effective control system is self-evident to employees. This is not always so, however. Many employees resist control, especially if they feel overcontrolled, if they think that control is inappropriately focused or rewards inefficiency, or if they are uncomfortable with accountability.

Overcontrol   Occasionally, organizations try to control too many things. This becomes especially problematic when the control directly affects employee behaviour. An organization that instructs its employees when to come to work, where to park, when to have morning coffee, and when to leave for the day exerts considerable control over people's daily activities. Yet many organizations attempt to control not only these but other aspects of work behaviour as well. Troubles arise when employees perceive these attempts to limit their behaviour as being unreasonable. A company that tells its employees how to dress, how to arrange their desks, and how to wear their hair may meet with resistance. Employees at Chrysler used to complain because if they drove a non-Chrysler vehicle they were forced to park in a distant parking lot. People felt that these efforts to control their personal behaviour (i.e., what kind of car to drive) were excessive. Managers eventually removed these controls and now allow open parking.

Inappropriate Focus   The control system may be too narrow or it may focus too much on quantifiable variables and leave no room for analysis or interpretation. A sales standard that encourages high-pressure tactics to maximize short-run sales may do so at the expense of goodwill from long-term customers. Such a standard is too narrow. A university reward system that encourages faculty members to publish large numbers of articles but fails to consider the quality of the work is also inappropriately focused. Employees resist the intent of the control system by focusing their efforts at only the performance indicators being used.

Rewards for Inefficiency   Imagine two operating departments that are approaching the end of the fiscal year. Department 1 expects to have $5,000 of its budget left over; department 2 is already $3,000 in the red. As a result, department 1 is likely to have its budget cut for the next year ("They had money left, so they obviously got too much to begin with"), and department 2 is likely to get a budget increase ("They obviously haven't been getting enough money"). Thus department 1 is punished for being efficient and department 2 is rewarded for being inefficient. (No wonder departments commonly hasten to deplete their budgets as the end of the year approaches!) As with inappropriate focus, people resist the intent of this control and behave in ways that run counter to the organization's intent.

Too Much Accountability   Effective controls allow managers to determine whether employees successfully discharge their responsibilities. If standards are properly set and performance accurately measured, managers know when problems arise and which departments and individuals are responsible. People who do not want to be answerable for their mistakes or who do not want to work as hard as their boss might therefore resist control. For example, American Express has a system that provides daily information on how many calls each of its operators handles. If one operator has typically worked at a slower pace and handled fewer calls than other operators, that individual's deficient performance can now be easily pinpointed.

Overcoming Resistance to Control

Perhaps the best way to overcome resistance to control is to create effective control to begin with. If control systems are properly integrated with organizational planning and if the controls are flexible, accurate, timely, and objective, the organization is less likely to overcontrol, to focus on inappropriate standards, or to reward inefficiency. Two other ways to overcome resistance are encouraging participation and developing verification procedures.

Encourage Employee Participation   As noted in Chapter 12, participation can help overcome resistance to change. By the same token, when employees are involved with planning and implementing the control system, they are less likely to resist it. For instance, employee participation in planning, decision making, and quality control at the Listowel, Ontario–based operations of Campbell Soup resulted in improved customer relations and substantial savings.[24]

Develop Verification Procedures   Multiple standards and information systems provide checks and balances in control and allow the organization to verify the accuracy of performance indicators. Suppose a production manager argues that she failed to meet a certain cost standard because of increased prices of raw materials. A properly designed inventory control system either supports or contradicts her explanation. Suppose that an employee who was fired for excessive absences argues that he was not absent "for a long time." An effective human resource control system should have records that support the termination. Resistance to control declines because these verification procedures protect both employees and management. If the production manager's claim about the rising cost of raw materials is supported by the inventory control records, she will not be held solely accountable for failing to meet the cost standard, and some action may be taken to lower the cost of raw materials.

SUMMARY OF KEY POINTS

Control is the regulation of organizational activities so that some targeted element of performance remains within acceptable limits. Control provides ways to adapt to environmental change, to limit the accumulation of errors, to cope with organizational complexity, and to minimize costs. Control can focus on physical, human, information, and financial resources and includes operations, financial, structural, and strategic levels. Control is the function of managers, the controller, and, increasingly, of operating employees.

Steps in the control process are (1) establish standards of expected performance, (2) measure actual performance, (3) compare performance against standards, and (4) evaluate the comparison and take appropriate action.

Operations control focuses on the processes the organization uses to transform resources into products or services. Preliminary control is concerned with the resources that serve as inputs to the system. Screening control is concerned with the transformation processes used by the organization. Post-action control is concerned with the outputs of the organization. Most organizations need multiple control systems because no one system alone can provide adequate control.

Financial control focuses on controlling the organization's financial resources. The foundation of financial control is the budget, or a plan expressed in numerical terms. Most organizations rely on financial, operating, and non-monetary budgets. Financial statements, various kinds of ratios, and external and internal audits are also important tools organizations use as part of financial control.

Structural control addresses how well an organization's structural elements serve their intended purpose. Two basic forms of structural control are bureaucratic and clan control. Bureaucratic control is relatively formal and mechanistic, whereas clan control is informal and organic. Most organizations use a form of organizational control somewhere in between these two extremes.

Strategic control focuses on how effectively the organization's strategies are succeeding in helping the organization meet its goals. The integration of strategy and control is generally achieved through organization structure, leadership, technology, human resources, and information and operational control systems. International strategic control is also important for multinational organizations. A basic question that global organizations must address is whether to practise centralized or decentralized control.

One way to increase the effectiveness of control is to fully integrate planning and control. The control system should also be flexible, accurate, timely, and as objective as possible. Employees may resist organizational controls if they feel overcontrolled, if they think that control is inappropriately focused, if they are being rewarded for inefficiency, or if they desire to avoid accountability. Managers can overcome this resistance by improving the effectiveness of controls and by allowing employee participation and developing verification procedures.

DISCUSSION QUESTIONS

Questions for Review

1. What is the purpose of organizational control? Why is it important?
2. What are the steps in the control process? Which step is likely to be the most difficult to perform? Why?
3. What are the similarities and differences among the various forms of operations control? What are the costs and benefits of each form?
4. How can a manager understand and overcome resistance and make control effective?

Questions for Analysis

5. How is the controlling process related to the functions of planning, organizing, and leading?
6. Are the differences in bureaucratic control and clan control related to differences in organization structure? If so, how? If not, why not? (Note that the terms sound similar to those used to discuss the organizing process.)

7. Do you use a budget for your personal finances? Relate your experiences with budgeting to the discussion in the chapter.

Questions for Application

8. Does your college or university have a controller? If so, find out how the position fits into the organization's design. If not, why do you think such a position has not been created?
9. Interview several local managers to determine which form of operations control—preliminary, screening, post-action, or multiple—is most frequently used by them. How might you account for what you found?
10. Ask managers from different parts of the same organization or from different organizations what makes controls effective. How do their views compare with those presented in this chapter? Why might differences exist?

BUILDING EFFECTIVE DECISION-MAKING SKILLS

Exercise Overview

Decision-making skills refer to the manager's ability to correctly recognize and define problems and opportunities and to then select an appropriate course of action to solve problems and capitalize on opportunities. This exercise will enable you to practise your decision-making skills in relation to organizational control.

Exercise Background

Assume that you are the top manager of a medium-size, family-owned manufacturing company. Several family members work in various managerial positions, but you have just been hired to run the company. The company has a longstanding tradition of avoiding debt and owns several smaller businesses in related industries.

Over the last few years, the company has lagged in productivity and efficiency and now finds itself in desperate straits. Profits have just about disappeared, and one of your bigger competitors may be planning an attempt to take over the business. You have asked a consulting firm to help you identify alternatives for turning things around. The primary options are as follows:

1. Issue a public stock offering (IPO) to raise funds.
2. Borrow money from a bank to finance a turnaround.
3. Sell several of the smaller operations to fund a turnaround.
4. Seek a buyer for the entire firm.

Exercise Task

With the preceding background information as context, do the following:
1. Evaluate each option from a strategic standpoint.
2. Explain how each option relates to control.
3. Select the option that you like the best.
4. Describe the barriers you will probably encounter with the option you have chosen.

When the Town of York was incorporated as the City of Toronto in 1834, it was a compact community of about 10,000 residents. Most journeys within the city were short and carried out on foot or on horseback. Most thoroughfares, such as Yonge Street and Lakeshore Boulevard, offered suburban and long-distance stagecoach services. The arrival of steam railways in the 1850s further revolutionized intercity travel.

Established in 1849, Toronto's first scheduled urban transportation service, the Williams Omnibus Bus Line, carried passengers in horse-drawn stagecoaches along Yonge Street. By 1920, several other services were in operation, each with its own fares and streetcars. This confusing situation led to the provincial legislation that created the Toronto Transportation Commission in 1920. In 1921, the Commission took over the existing nine transit systems. In 1954, the Commission, renamed the Toronto Transit Commission (TTC), came under the jurisdiction of the Municipality of Metropolitan Toronto and became the sole provider of public transportation in Metro Toronto.

The TTC grew rapidly in the middle of the twentieth century. In 1954, the Union Station–Eglinton section of the Yonge Street subway—Canada's first—was opened. Today, the TTC has an extensive transportation system that operates under one fare structure and is linked by subway cars, buses, streetcars, Wheel-Trans community buses for physically challenged riders, and the Scarborough Rapid Transit cars. Over time, the TTC, through a complex control system, has carved a reputation as North America's safest and most reliable transit system. The TTC has been a frequent winner of the American Public Transit Association's annual safety award.

One reason for the TTC's reliability is a highly computerized system that enables customers to call a number to find out when a bus will arrive at a particular stop; usually, the bus arrives on time. A new system will enable riders to call a central phone number for a wide range of information, such as which combination of buses to take to get to a specific location.

In 1995, the TTC's Wheel Transit information system was a finalist in the Computerworld Smithsonian Awards (CWSA). CWSA honours corporations, organizations, and individuals who use technology to create positive change in society. The TTC Wheel Transit information system is a central system that schedules five thousand trips per day for disabled citizens, optimizing the routes of over 130 buses and coordinating the use of twelve taxi companies for ambulatory passengers.

Many aspects of the TTC's control system came under public scrutiny following a 1995 subway crash (the worst in TTC history) in which three passengers were killed and scores injured. Lulled by a sense of complacency and restricted by budgetary constraints, the TTC had allowed essential operational and administrative controls to deteriorate. The inquest into the accident revealed that basic elements of control were not in place. The major problems—inadequate maintenance of equipment and signals, poor communications with transit control, and insufficient personnel training—had been compounded not only by cuts to the TTC's budget but by declining revenues from passenger fares (largely the result of a drop in ridership).

Since the accident, the TTC has been reorganized so that surface and subway operations are clearly divided and there are more transparent lines of responsibility. Greater emphasis is being placed on the technical side of the business. In addition to managers with more technical savvy, there is a requirement for better-trained drivers and other personnel. As well, trains and tunnels are being outfitted with improved communications equipment, and there are plans for a new, high-tech computerized control centre.

Questions

1. What forms of control are evident at the TTC? Give examples of each.

2. What specific measures could the TTC have implemented to avoid the 1995 accident?

3. Do you think the TTC will be able to maintain its reputation as North America's safest transit system in the future? Why or why not?

References: Mike Filey, *The TTC Story: The First Seventy-Five Years* (Toronto: Dundurn Press, 1996); http://www.metrotor.on.ca/services/abc/ttc.html; "Canadians Nominated for CWSA," *Computer Dealer News*, May 31, 1995, p. 2; "Bringing Two Worlds Together: Computer Telephony Integration," *Computing Canada*, August 2, 1995, pp. 35–41; Jack Lee Anne, "Tunnel Vision: Did the Toronto Transit Commission's Reputation as the Continent's Safest System Blind it to the Gradual Deterioration of Its Safety Culture?" *Occupational Health and Safety*, January/February, 1997, pp. 32–37; and Samuelian Christine, "Transit Commission Shows Improvement in Operations," *Canadian Press Newswire*, April 10, 1997.

CHAPTER NOTES

1. Stephen Bachand, "There's a Lot More to Canadian Tire," *Business Quarterly*, Spring 1995, pp. 31–39; John Lorinc, "Road Warrior," *Canadian Business*, October 1995, pp. 26–43; "Stephen Bachand's New Attitude at Canadian Tire," *Financial Post*, February 17, 1996, p. 7; "Canadian Tire Corporation Limited First Quarter Earnings Per Share Up 12.4 Percent," *Canada NewsWire*, May 9, 1997; "Business Overview at a Glance" (http://cantire2.canadiantire.ca); and "Canadian Tire 1998 Earnings Per Share Up 17.1%" (http://www.canadiantire.ca), February 4, 1999.

2. Anne Tsui and Susan Ashford, "Adaptive Self-Regulation: A Process View of Managerial Effectiveness," *Journal of Management*, Vol. 20, No. 1, 1994, pp. 93–121.

3. Thomas A. Stewart, "Welcome to the Revolution," *Fortune*, December 13, 1993, pp. 66–77.

4. William Taylor, "Control in an Age of Chaos," *Harvard Business Review*, November–December 1994, pp. 64–70.

5. Joel Dreyfuss, "Victories in the Quality Crusade," *Fortune*, October 10, 1988, pp. 80–88.

6. Dreyfuss, "Victories in the Quality Crusade."

7. Mark Sproule, "It's Working in a Salt Mine, Everyday," *Canadian Mining Journal*, April 1998, pp. 23–26.

8. Sim Sitkin, Kathleen Sutcliffe, and Roger Schroeder, "Distinguishing Control from Learning in Total Quality Management: A Contingency Perspective," *Academy of Management Review*, Vol. 19, No. 3, 1994, pp. 537–564.

9. James P. Walsh and James K. Seward, "On the Efficiency of Internal and External Corporate Control Mechanisms," *Academy of Management Review*, July 1990, pp. 421–458.

10. Robert Lusch and Michael Harvey, "The Case for an Off-Balance-Sheet Controller," *Sloan Management Review*, Winter 1994, pp. 101–110.

11. Edward E. Lawler III and John G. Rhode, *Information and Control in Organizations* (Pacific Palisades, Calif.: Goodyear, 1976); and Robert N. Anthony, *The Management Control Function* (Boston, Mass.: The Harvard Business School Press, 1988).

12. Dreyfuss, "Victories in the Quality Crusade."

13. Anthony, *The Management Control Function*.

14. See Belverd E. Needles, Jr., Henry R. Anderson, and James C. Caldwell, *Principles of Accounting*, 5th ed. (Boston: Houghton Mifflin, 1993.)

15. Christopher K. Bart, "Budgeting Gamesmanship," *The Academy of Management Executive*, November 1988, pp. 285–294.

16. Thomas A. Stewart, "Why Budgets Are Bad for Business," *Fortune*, June 4, 1990, pp. 179–190.

17. Needles, Anderson, and Caldwell, *Principles of Accounting*.

18. Needles, Anderson, and Caldwell, *Principles of Accounting*.

19. "Auditors of Corporate Legal Bills Thrive," *The Wall Street Journal*, February 13, 1991, p. B1.

20. William G. Ouchi, "The Transmission of Control Through Organizational Hierarchy," *Academy of Management Journal*, June 1978, pp. 173–192; and Richard E. Walton, "From Control to Commitment in the Workplace," *Harvard Business Review*, March–April 1985, pp. 76–84.

21. Peter Lorange, Michael F. Scott Morton, and Sumantra Ghoshal, *Strategic Control* (St. Paul, Minn.: West, 1986).

22. Christopher Holland, Geoff Lockett, Jean-Michel Richard, and Ian Blackman, "The Evolution of a Global Cash Management System," *Sloan Management Review*, Fall 1994, pp. 37–46.

23. See Diana Robertson and Erin Anderson, "Control System and Task Environment Effects on Ethical Judgment: An Exploratory Study of Industrial Salespeople," *Organization Science*, November 1993, pp. 617–629, for a recent study of effective control.

24. Wendy Trueman, "Alternate Visions," *Canadian Business*, March 1991, pp. 29–33.

Managing for Total Quality in Organizations

OBJECTIVES

After studying this chapter, you should be able to:

● *Explain the meaning of quality and the importance of managing total quality.*

● *Explain the meaning and importance of managing productivity, productivity trends, and ways to improve productivity.*

● *Explain the nature of operations management and its role in managing quality.*

● *Identify and discuss the components involved in designing operations systems for quality.*

● *Discuss technology and its role in operations management.*

● *Identify and discuss the components involved in using operations systems for quality.*

OUTLINE

Robert Eaton has made quality improvement one of Chrysler's most important goals. And his efforts are paying off—many of the firm's newer products such as the Neon and Cirrus have indeed been recognized for their high quality.

The merger of Chrysler and Daimler Benz in May 1998 created the world's third largest automobile manufacturer—a marriage that would not have happened had Chrysler not changed its ways. As the 1970s drew to a close, Chrysler Corp., the number-three automobile company in North America, teetered on the brink of bankruptcy. Supported by government-backed loans and the pure strength of will shown by CEO Lee Iacocca, Chrysler gradually righted itself and returned to profitability. New products like the K-cars and the minivan and the acquisition of American Motors (and its popular Jeep) provided new avenues for growth and profitability.

Iacocca resigned in 1992 and was replaced by Robert Eaton, previously head of Chrysler's European operations and now co-chair of Daimler Chrysler. One of the first things Eaton recognized was that even though Chrysler was profitable, Chrysler automobiles were still near the bottom of most lists of high-quality automobiles. Eaton pinned the firm's hopes on several new products such as the Chrysler Cirrus and the Dodge Neon.

> **"We've talked about quality for ten years. The difference this time is, we're actually doing it." (Chrysler engineer, John Fernandez)**

Eaton's first step was to change how Chrysler made cars. He implemented a team approach throughout the organization and continually stressed the importance of quality. He also stretched the time the firm would devote to development to avoid hurrying and to provide more time to correct defects. Eaton also created a new executive position called Vice President for Customer Satisfaction and Vehicle Quality. In addition, he changed the way that defects were counted to provide more useful information to everyone in the company.

The Neon was the first of the three new products Chrysler launched, appearing in mid-1994. During development of the Neon, Chrysler paid more attention to quality than ever before in its history. Every supplier, for example, was forced to explain in writing how it would ensure delivery of flawless parts. Unfortunately, when the Neon was first launched, a few things had been overlooked. For example, after the production of ten thousand cars Chrysler discovered a leaky seal that could cause a loss of braking power. In addition, it found that plastic radiator supports had to be replaced with metal ones. Although the Neon proved to be better than other Chrysler products, it was not nearly as good as the firm had hoped.

Next came the Cirrus. Eaton himself took a very personal interest in this new model. For example, when the first prototype was assembled in early 1994, he spent two days driving it. He was so disappointed in the car that he delayed its launch six months so that numerous defects and shortcomings could be corrected. Fortunately, the extra time was worthwhile: in 1994, the car was named Motor Trend's "Car of the Year." Since then Chrysler has won this award two more times: in 1996 for the Dodge Caravan, and in 1999 for the Chrysler 300M, assembled in Bramalea, Ontario.[1] ●

Managers at Chrysler have learned two valuable lessons. First, quality is critically important in today's competitive business environment. Quality and productivity have become major determinants of business success or failure today. And second, achieving higher levels of quality is not easy. Simply ordering that quality be improved is about as effective as waving a magic wand.[2]

In this chapter, we explore quality and its role in business today. We first discuss managing for total quality. We then discuss productivity, which is closely related to quality. Next we introduce operations management and its role in improving quality. The remaining three sections of the chapter discuss designing operations systems, technology and quality, and using operations systems for quality.

MANAGING TOTAL QUALITY

As just noted, quality has become a central issue in managing organizations today.[3] The catalyst for its emergence as a mainstream management concern was foreign business, especially Japanese. And nowhere was it more visible than in the auto industry. During the energy crisis in the late 1970s, many people bought Toyotas, Hondas, and Nissans because they were more fuel-efficient than North American cars. Consumers soon found, however, that not only were the Japanese cars more fuel-efficient, they were also of higher quality than North American cars. Parts fit together better, the trim work was neater, and the cars were more reliable. Thus after the energy crisis subsided, Japanese cars remained formidable competitors because of their reputations for quality.

The Meaning of Quality

● **quality**
The totality of features and characteristics of a product or service that bear on its ability to satisfy stated or implied needs

Quality may be defined as the totality of features and characteristics of a product or service that bear on its ability to satisfy stated or implied needs.[4] Quality has several different attributes. Table 21.1 lists eight basic dimensions that determine the quality of a particular product or service. For example, a product that is durable and reliable is of higher quality than a product that is less durable and reliable.

Quality is also relative. For example, a Lincoln Continental is a higher-grade car than a Ford Taurus, which, in turn, is a higher-grade car than a Ford Escort. The difference in quality stems from differences in design and other features. The Escort, however, is considered a high-quality car relative to its engineering specifications and price. Likewise, the Taurus and Continental may also be high-quality cars, given their standards and prices. Thus quality is both an absolute (as compared to some standard) and a relative (compared to price and competing products/services) concept.

Quality is relevant for both products and services. Although its importance for products like cars and computers was perhaps recognized first, service firms such as airlines and restaurants have also come to see that quality is a vitally important determinant of their success or failure. Service quality, as we discuss later in this chapter, has thus also become a major competitive issue in Canadian industry today.

TABLE 21.1 Eight Dimensions of Quality

1. **Performance.** A product's primary operating characteristic. Examples are automobile acceleration and a television set's picture clarity.
2. **Features.** Supplements to a product's basic functioning characteristics, such as power windows on a car.
3. **Reliability.** A probability of not malfunctioning during a specified period.
4. **Conformance.** The degree to which a product's design and operating characteristics meet established standards.
5. **Durability.** A measure of product life.
6. **Serviceability.** The speed and ease of repair.
7. **Aesthetics.** How a product looks, feels, tastes, and smells.
8. **Perceived quality.** As seen by a customer.

Source: From David A. Garvin, "Competing on the Eight Dimensions of Quality," *Harvard Business Review,* November/December 1987.

These eight dimensions generally capture the meaning of quality, which is a critically important ingredient to organizational success today. Understanding the basic meaning of quality is a good first step to more effectively managing it.

The Importance of Quality

To help underscore the importance of quality, the National Quality Institute, established in 1992 with seed money from Industry Canada and the private sector, recognizes outstanding Canadian organizations through its Canada Awards for Excellence program. These countrywide awards, inaugurated in 1983, are given to organizations in the business, government, education, and health-care sectors. In 1998, Canada Awards for Excellence recipients included Amex Canada Inc.; Flemington Public School in North York, Ontario; John Deere Limited; and Telus Mobility Inc. The 1997 recipients included BC Tel Education in Burnaby, British Columbia; the Orillia Soldiers Memorial Hospital in Orillia, Ontario; Brock Telecom in Brockville, Ontario; and Glen Park Public School in North York, Ontario. Among the 1996 winners was the IBM customer service department.

In the United States, the federal government created the **Malcolm Baldrige Award**, named after the former Secretary of Commerce who championed quality in U.S. industry. The award, administered by an agency of the Commerce Department, is given annually to firms that achieve major improvements in the quality of their products or services. That is, the award is based on changes in quality, as opposed to absolute quality. Recent winners of the Baldrige Award include Motorola, the Cadillac Division of General Motors, and divisions of Texas Instruments, AT&T, Xerox, and Westinghouse.

Unfortunately, as discussed more fully in the *Managing in a Changing World* box, there is also a dark side to the quality movement. Quality is also an important concern for individual managers and organizations for three very specific reasons: competition, productivity, and costs.[6]

Competition Quality has become one of the most competitive points in business today. Ford, Chrysler, and General Motors each argue, for example, that its cars are higher in quality than the cars of the others. IBM, Apple Computer, and Compaq Computer stress the quality of their products as well. And Air Canada and Canadian Airlines each argues that it provides the best and most reliable service. In adopting quality as a major point of competition, a

● **Malcolm Baldridge Award**
Prestigious award given to firms that achieve major quality improvements

Harry Truderung, president of Telus Mobility, with his 1998 Canada Awards for Excellence trophy.

business tries to prevent itself from falling behind not only foreign competition but also other firms in its own country.[7]

Productivity   Managers have also come to recognize that quality and productivity are related. In the past, many managers thought that they could increase output (productivity) only by decreasing quality. Managers today have learned the hard way that such an assumption is almost always wrong. If a firm installs a meaningful quality enhancement program, three things are likely to result. First, the number of defects is likely to decrease, causing fewer returns from customers. Second, because the number of defects goes down, resources (materials and people) dedicated to reworking flawed output are decreased. Third, because making employees responsible for quality reduces the need for quality inspectors, the organization is able to produce more units with fewer resources.

Costs   Improved quality also lowers costs. Poor quality results in higher returns from customers, high warranty costs, and lawsuits from customers injured by faulty products. Future sales are lost because of disgruntled customers. An organization with quality problems often has to increase inspection expenses just to catch defective products. We noted in an earlier chapter, for example, how Whistler Corp. was using 100 of its 250 employees just to fix poorly assembled radar detectors.[8]

Total Quality Management

● **total quality management (TQM)**
A strategic commitment by top management to change its whole approach to business to make quality a guiding factor in everything it does

Once an organization makes a decision to enhance the quality of its products and services, it must then decide how to implement this decision. The most pervasive approach to managing quality has been called **total quality management**, or **TQM**—a real and meaningful effort by an organization to change its whole approach to business to make quality a guiding factor in everything the organization does.[9] Figure 21.1 highlights the major ingredients in TQM.

Limits to Quality

 The quality movement has had many failures. A survey of five hundred companies in the United States by Arthur D. Little indicated that only one-third believed that their quality programs were having a significant impact on their competitiveness. Another study by McKinsey and Company indicated that nearly two-thirds of quality programs that had been in place for two or more years had failed because of poor results. Research evidence suggested that those that seemed to succeed were relatively short-lived, perhaps only three to five years.

Wallace Company, manufacturer of oil equipment, won the Malcolm Baldrige National Quality Award in 1990 and filed for bankruptcy protection in 1992. Johnson & Johnson set up quality teams that travelled around the country to benchmark its products against those of its competitors, and its costs increased dramatically. Varian Associates, a maker of scientific equipment, trained its personnel in quality and was able to boost on-time delivery from 42 percent to 92 percent, but its sales growth became sluggish and its profits turned into losses. Nissan's engine technology is viewed as the best in the industry, as are some of its manufacturing plants, but in 1999 the company found itself facing serious financial problems. As these and other reports became public, the interest in the quality movement in general waned. Indeed, the number of applicants for the Baldrige award fell from an all-time high of more than one hundred in 1991 to just more than seventy by 1994.

Numerous explanations have been proffered for these failures. One is that attempting to obtain results in a short period is less effective than the incremental, slow, and gradual approach. Inexperience with quality management and particularly with setting the correct quality objectives has been identified as yet another cause of failure. Improper training—not training at all, not training in statistical quality control, not training the right people, or trying to train everyone at once—has been suggested as another problem. Failure of the CEO or president to assume and retain complete charge of the quality effort is also very frequently mentioned as a reason for failure of the programs.

For a quality management program to have a good chance for success, process, inventory, and other basic control approaches must first be in place. Then the company must make careful cost measurements to establish current costs as well as to establish targets for the quality program. Customers must be surveyed and interviewed to determine just what the major factors are that bring them back and drive them away. Those factors, then, become the focus of the quality management program and are tested on a limited basis to ensure that they will work before they are adopted by the whole organization. Finally, the whole program must be monitored and revamped as necessary to keep it working over time, especially as competitors match the organization's offerings.

References: "Quality: How to Make It Pay," *Business Week*, August 8, 1994, pp. 54–59; R. Ray Gehani, "The Tortoise vs. the Hare," *Quality Progress*, May 1994, pp. 99–103; Kevin Doyle, "Who's Killing Total Quality?" *Incentive*, August 1992, pp. 12–19; "The Cracks in Quality," *Economist*, April 18, 1992, pp. 67–68; Ricky W. Griffin, "Consequences of Quality Circles in an Industrial Setting: A Longitudinal Assessment," *Academy of Management Journal*, June 1988, pp. 338–358; and Frank Gibney, Jr., "Nissan Calls for a Tow," *Time*, March 1, 1999, pp. 38–40.

Strategic Commitment The starting point for TQM is a strategic commitment by top management. Such commitment is important for several reasons. First, the organizational culture must change to recognize that quality is not just an ideal but is instead an objective goal that must be pursued.[10] Robert Eaton's taking two days out of his schedule to test drive the Chrysler Cirrus helped alter the firm's culture regarding quality. Second, a decision to pursue the goal of quality carries with it some real costs—for expenditures such as new equipment and facilities. Again, Eaton's decision to delay the Cirrus cost the firm money, at least in the short run. Thus without a commitment from top management, quality improvement will prove to be just a slogan or gimmick, with little or no real change.

F I G U R E 21.1 Total Quality Management

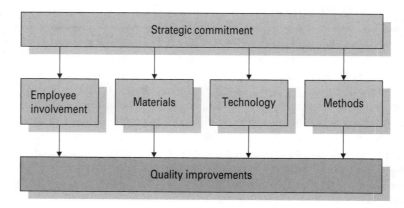

Employee Involvement   Employee involvement is another critical ingredient in TQM. Virtually all successful quality enhancement programs involve making the person responsible for doing the job responsible for making sure it is done right.[11] By definition, then, employee involvement is a critical component in improving quality. Work teams, discussed in Chapter 19, are common vehicles for increasing employee involvement.

Materials   Another important part of TQM is improving the quality of the materials that organizations use. Suppose that a company that assembles stereos buys chips and circuits from another company. If the chips have a high failure rate, consumers will return defective stereos to the company whose nameplate appears on them, not to the company that made the chips. The stereo firm then loses in two ways: it must refund money back to customers and it has a damaged reputation. As a result, many firms have increased the quality requirements they impose on their suppliers as a way of improving the quality of their own products. Recall from our opening incident that Chrysler has raised its expectations regarding the quality of parts and materials it will buy from others.

Technology   New forms of technology are also useful in TQM programs. Automation and robots, for example, can often make products with higher precision and better consistency than can people. Investing in higher-grade machines capable of doing jobs more precisely and reliably often improves quality. For example, AT&T has achieved notable improvements in product quality by replacing many of its machines with new equipment. Similarly, most Canadian auto and electronics firms have all made significant investments in technology to help boost quality.

Methods   Improved methods can improve product and service quality. Methods are operating systems used by the organization during the actual transformation process. American Express Company, for example, has found ways to cut its approval time for new credit cards from twenty-two to only eleven days. This results in improved service quality.[12]

TQM Tools and Techniques

Beyond the strategic context of quality, managers can also rely on several specific tools and techniques for improving quality. Among the most popular today are benchmarking, outsourcing, speed, ISO 9000, and statistical quality control.

Benchmarking   **Benchmarking** is the process of learning how other firms do exceptionally high-quality things. Some approaches to benchmarking are simple and straightforward. For example, Xerox Corp. routinely buys copiers made by other firms and takes them apart to see how they work. This enables the firm to stay abreast of its competitors' improvements and changes. When Ford was planning the Taurus, it identified the four hundred features customers identified as being most important to them. It then found the competing cars that did the best job on each feature. Ford's goal was to equal or surpass each of its competitors on those four hundred features. Other benchmarking strategies are more indirect. For example, many firms study how L.L. Bean manages its mail order business and how Federal Express tracks packages for applications that they can employ in their own businesses.[13]

Outsourcing   Another innovation for improving quality is outsourcing. **Outsourcing** is the process of subcontracting services and operations to other firms that can do them cheaper or better (or both). If a business performs each and every one of its own administrative and business services and operations, it is almost certain to be doing at least some of them in an inefficient and/or low quality manner. If those areas can be identified and outsourced, the firm will save money and realize a higher-quality service or operation. For example, until recently Eastman Kodak Company handled all of its own computing operations. Those operations were subcontracted to IBM, which now handles all of Kodak's computing. The result is higher-quality computing systems and operations at Kodak for less money than it was spending before.[14] However, outsourcing is often a cause of labour–management tension.

Speed   A third popular TQM technique is speed. **Speed** is the time needed by the organization to get something accomplished, and it can be emphasized in any area, including developing, making, and distributing products or services.[15] One recent survey identified speed as the number-one strategic issue confronting managers in the 1990s.[16] A good illustration of the power of speed comes from General Electric. At one point the firm needed six plants and three weeks to produce and deliver custom-made industrial circuit-breaker boxes. By making speed a priority, the same product can now be delivered in three days, and only a single plant is involved. Table 21.2 identifies a number of basic suggestions that have helped companies increase the speed of their operations. For example, GE found it better to start from scratch with a remodelled plant, rather than trying to use the existing facilities. GE also wiped out the need for approvals by eliminating most managerial positions and set up teams as a basis for organizing work. Stressing the importance of the schedule helped Motorola build a new plant and start production of a new product in only eighteen months.

ISO 9000   Still another useful technique for improving quality is ISO 9000. **ISO 9000** refers to a set of quality standards created by the International Organization for Standardization. There are five sets of standards covering areas such as product testing, employee training, record keeping, supplier relations,

TABLE 21.2 Guidelines for Increasing the Speed of Operations

1. Start from scratch (it's usually easier than trying to do what the organization does now faster).
2. Minimize the number of approvals needed to do something (the fewer people who have to approve something, the faster it will get done).
3. Use work teams as a basis for organization (teamwork and cooperation work better than individual effort and conflict).
4. Develop and adhere to a schedule (a properly designed schedule can greatly increase speed).
5. Don't ignore distribution (making something faster is only part of the battle).
6. Integrate speed into the organization's culture (if everyone understands the importance of speed, things will naturally get done quicker).

Source: Adapted from Brian Dumaine, "How Managers Can Succeed Through Speed," *Fortune*, February 13, 1989, pp. 54–59. Time Inc. All rights reserved.

and repair policies and procedures. Firms that want to meet these standards apply for certification and are audited by a firm chosen by the organization's domestic affiliate (in Canada, this is the Standards Council of Canada). These auditors review every aspect of the firm's business operations in relation to the standards. Many firms report that merely preparing for an ISO 9000 audit has been helpful. Many firms today, including General Electric, Du Pont, Eastman Kodak, British Telecom, and Philips Electronics, are urging—or in some cases requiring—that their suppliers achieve ISO 9000 certification.[17]

● **statistical quality control (SQC)**
A set of specific statistical techniques that can be used to monitor quality; includes acceptance sampling and in-process sampling

Statistical Quality Control   A final quality control technique is **statistical quality control (SQC)**. As the term suggests, SQC is primarily concerned with managing quality. Moreover, it is a set of specific statistical techniques that can be used to monitor quality. *Acceptance sampling* involves sampling finished goods to ensure that quality standards have been met. Acceptance sampling is effective only when the correct percentage of products that should be tested (for example, 2, 5, or 25 percent) is determined. This decision is especially important when the test renders the product useless. Flash cubes, wine, and collapsible steering wheels, for example, are consumed or destroyed during testing. Another SQC method is *in-process sampling*. In-process sampling involves evaluating products during production so that needed changes can be made. The painting department of a furniture company might periodically check the tint of the paint it is using. The company can then adjust the colour as necessary to conform to customer standards. The advantage of in-process sampling is that it allows problems to be detected before they accumulate.

MANAGING PRODUCTIVITY

Although the current focus on quality by Canadian companies is a relatively recent phenomenon, managers have been aware of the importance of productivity for several years. The stimulus for this attention was a recognition that productivity growth in many other G-8 countries (the United States, Japan, France,

Russia, Germany, Italy, and the United Kingdom) has exceeded that in Canada since the mid-1970s.[18] In this section, we describe the meaning of productivity and underscore its importance. After summarizing recent productivity trends, we suggest ways in which organizations can increase their productivity.

The Meaning of Productivity

In a general sense, **productivity** is an economic measure of efficiency that summarizes the value of outputs relative to the value of the inputs used to create them.[19] Productivity can be and often is assessed at different levels of analysis and in different forms.

● **productivity**
An economic measure of efficiency that summarizes what is produced relative to the inputs used to produce them

Levels of Productivity　By level of productivity we mean the units of analysis used to calculate or define productivity. For example, aggregate productivity is the total level of productivity achieved by a country. Industry productivity is the total productivity achieved by all the firms in a particular industry. Company productivity, just as the term suggests, is the level of productivity achieved by an individual company. Unit and individual productivity refer to the productivity achieved by a unit or department within an organization and the level of productivity attained by a single person.

Forms of Productivity　Productivity has many different forms. Total factor productivity is defined by the following formula:

$$\text{Productivity} = \frac{\text{Outputs}}{\text{Inputs}}$$

Total factor productivity is an overall indicator of how well an organization uses all of its resources, such as labour, capital, materials, and energy, to create all of its products and services. The biggest problem with total factor productivity is that all the ingredients must be expressed in the same terms—dollars (adding hours of labour to number of units of a raw material in a meaningful way is difficult). Total factor productivity also gives little insight into how things can be changed to improve productivity. Consequently, most organizations find calculating a partial productivity ratio more useful. Such a ratio uses only one category of resource. For example, labour productivity could be calculated by this simple formula:

$$\text{Labour productivity} \quad = \quad \frac{\text{Outputs}}{\text{Direct labour}}$$

This method has two advantages. First, transforming the units of input into some other unit is not necessary. Second, this method provides managers with specific insights into how changing different resource inputs affects productivity. Suppose that an organization can manufacture one hundred units of a particular product with twenty hours of direct labour. The organization's labour productivity index is 5 (or 5 units per labour hour). Now suppose that worker efficiency is increased (through one of the ways we discuss later in this chapter) so that the same twenty hours of labour results in the manufacture of 120 units of the product. The labour productivity index increases to 6 (6 units per labour hour), and the firm can see the direct results of a specific managerial action.

The Importance of Productivity

Managers consider it important that their firms maintain high levels of productivity for a variety of reasons. Firm productivity is a primary determinant of an organization's level of profitability and, ultimately, its ability to survive. If one organization is more productive than another, it will have more products to sell at lower prices and have more profits to reinvest in other areas. Productivity also partially determines people's standards of living within a particular country. At an economic level, businesses consume resources and produce goods and services. The goods and services created within a country can be used by that country's own citizens or exported for sale in other countries. The more goods and services the businesses within a country can produce, the more goods and services the country's citizens will have. Even goods that are exported result in financial resources flowing back into the home country. Thus the citizens of a highly productive country are likely to have notably higher standards of living than are the citizens of a country with low productivity.

Productivity Trends

The United States has one of the highest levels of productivity in the world. For example, Japanese workers produce only about 76 percent as much as U.S. workers, and German workers produce about 84 percent as much.[20] Canadian workers produce about 87 percent as much as U.S. workers.[21] An interesting trend began in the 1960s, however, and continued into the 1980s. During this time, the productivity growth rate in the United States slowed, especially in comparison to the rates in other industrialized countries. That is, although U.S. workers continued to be the most productive workers in the world, their counterparts in Japan, Germany, and similar countries began to close the gap. Productivity in Canada rose steadily from 77 percent of that in the United States in 1950 to 87 percent in 1992.[22]

This trend was a primary factor in the decisions made by U.S. businesses to retrench, retool, and become more competitive in the world marketplace. As a result, productivity trends have now levelled out and U.S. workers are generally maintaining their lead in most industries. While productivity in Canadian manufacturing has fallen behind such productivity in the United States since 1986, Canada has outperformed the United States in the services sector and in industries such as construction and mining.[23] Nevertheless, U.S. manufacturers are now considered to be 50 percent more productive than their Canadian counterparts.[24]

Figure 21.2 illustrates recent trends in productivity growth for the total Canadian economy. As shown, by 1996 productivity had regained some of the ground lost in the 1990–92 recession. The *Environment of Management* box discusses workforce changes in relation to productivity.

Improving Productivity

How does a business or industry improve its productivity? Numerous specific suggestions made by experts generally fall into two broad categories: improving operations and increasing employee involvement.

Improving Operations One way that firms can improve operations is by spending more on research and development. R&D spending helps identify new products, new uses for existing products, and new methods for making products. Each of these contributes to productivity. For example, Bausch & Lomb almost missed the boat on extended-wear contact lenses because the company had neglected R&D. When Bausch & Lomb became aware that its major competitors were almost a year ahead in developing the new lenses, management made R&D a top-priority concern. As a result, the company made several scientific breakthroughs, shortened the time needed to introduce new products, and greatly enhanced both total sales and profits—and all with a smaller workforce than the company used to employ.

Another way firms can boost productivity through operations is by reassessing and revamping their transformation facilities. We noted earlier how one of GE's modernized plants does a better job than six antiquated ones. Just building a new factory is no guarantee of success, but IBM, Ford, and many other businesses have achieved dramatic productivity gains by revamping their production facilities. Facilities refinements are not limited to manufacturers. In

F I G U R E   21.2 Canadian Productivity Trends, 1981–1996

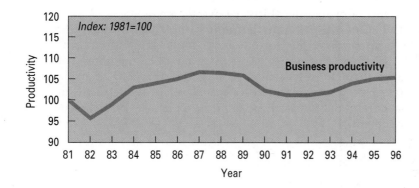

Adapted with permission from Statistics Canada, *The Daily,* Cat. no. 11-001, June 5, 1997, p. 4.

recent years, many fast-food restaurants have added drive-through windows, and many are moving soft-drink dispensers out to the restaurant floor so that customers can get their own drinks. Each of these moves is an attempt to increase the speed with which customers can be served and thus to increase productivity.

Increasing Employee Involvement   The other major thrust in productivity enhancement has been toward employee involvement. We noted earlier that participation can enhance quality. So, too, can it boost productivity. Examples of this involvement are an individual worker being given a bigger voice in how she does her job, a formal agreement of cooperation between management and labour, and total involvement throughout the organization.[25] GE eliminated most of the supervisors at one new circuit-breaker plant and put control in the hands of workers.

Another popular method is increasing the flexibility of an organization's workforce by training employees to perform a number of different jobs. Such cross-training allows the firm to function with fewer workers because workers can be transferred easily to areas where they are most needed. For example, Ingersoll, Ont.–based CAMI encourages workers to learn numerous jobs within the plant. At a Motorola plant, 397 of 400 employees have learned at least two skills under a similar program.

Rewards are essential to making employee involvement work. Firms must reward people for learning new skills and using them proficiently. At Motorola, for example, workers who master a new skill are assigned for five days to a job requiring them to use that skill. If they perform with no defects, they are moved to a higher pay grade, and then they move back and forth between jobs as they are needed. If there is a performance problem, they receive more training and practice. This approach is fairly new, but preliminary indicators suggest that it can increase productivity notably. Many unions resist such programs because they threaten job security and reduce a person's identification with one skill or craft.

MANAGING QUALITY THROUGH OPERATIONS MANAGEMENT

● **operations management**
The total set of managerial activities used by an organization to transform resource inputs into products, services, or both

We noted earlier that both quality and productivity can be enhanced through various elements of operations. But what exactly are operations? And how are they managed? **Operations management** is the set of managerial activities used by an organization to transform resource inputs into products, services, or both. When IBM buys electronic components, assembles them into computers, and then ships them to customers, it is relying on operations management. When a Pizza Hut employee orders food and paper products and then combines dough, cheese, and tomato paste to create a pizza, he or she is using operations management.

The Importance of Operations

Operations is an important functional concern for organizations because efficient and effective management of operations goes a long way toward ensuring quality and productivity. Inefficient or ineffective operations management, on

Workforce Changes

 Everyone knows that the workforce is changing, but not everyone knows that it is getting smaller as a percentage of the total population. The participation rate for women, or women employed or seeking employment as a percentage of the total number of women in the population, had been rising for years. In thirty years, it went from below 40 percent to nearly 58 percent by 1996. Indeed, that rise was strong enough to offset a declining participation rate for men. The male participation rate is approaching 70 percent after having been almost 80 percent in the early 1960s. The female rate seems to have stabilized, however, so that the overall rate is lower than it had been in the past, which means that workers are not as plentiful as they once had been.

A slower return to the workforce after childbirth and women staying in school longer than in the past partially account for the levelling off of the female participation rate, but no one seems to know why the male participation rate has fallen. Nevertheless, if the economy were to enter a period of strong growth and the workforce participation rate for women stayed low, sizable labour shortages could result. Normally such shortages would lead to strong inflationary pressures on both wages and salaries, which would be bad economic news. However, that does not seem to be happening in the 1990s.

In an effort to boost productivity, organizations are investing in new technology. In 1997, North American companies spent $1.2 trillion on information technology alone, a figure that is expected to rise to $2.1 trillion by the year 2002. But much of that new technology requires a more skilled workforce as well as a greater use of autonomous work teams, which also require more skilled people. That emphasis on more skill is one reason that women along with men are staying in school longer. In addition, companies will also have to invest more heavily in training, especially in task- or job-relevant skills, as opposed to the more general education provided by schools, colleges, and universities.

If that training also includes quality improvement training and education, additional benefits may accrue to the company providing it. Performance measures in many companies indicate that quality improvement programs have a positive impact on workforce productivity, particularly in the short term.

References: Dean Elmuti and Yunus Kathawala, "A Preliminary Analysis of Deming's Quality Improvement Program: Some Insights," *Production and Inventory Management Journal*, Second Quarter 1994, pp. 52–57; "Workers May Get Scarce but Nobody's Scared," *Business Week*, July 11, 1994, pp. 95–96; "Companies Worried About Workforce Performance," *Industrial Engineering*, June 1994, p. 6; and Anthony Patrick Carnevale, "Put Quality to Work: Train America's Workforce," *Training and Development Journal*, November 1990, pp. 31–49. Loren Falkenberg, Thomas Stone, and Noah Metz, *Human Resource Management in Canada*, 4th ed. (Toronto: Harcourt Brace and Company Canada, 1999), p. 19; Statistics Canada, "Labour Force, Employed and Unemployed, Numbers and Rates, 1996" (http://statcan.ca); and Geoffrey Rowan, "Fewer Benefits Emerge from Dubious IT Spending," *The Globe and Mail*, April 15, 1998, p. B25.

the other hand, almost inevitably leads to lower levels of both quality and productivity. In an economic sense, operations management provides utility, or value, of one type or another, depending on the nature of the firm's products or services. If the product is a physical good, such as a Yamaha motorcycle, operations provides form utility by combining many dissimilar inputs (sheet metal, rubber, paint, combustion engines, and human craftsmanship) to produce the desired output. The inputs are converted from their incoming forms into a new physical form. This conversion is typical of manufacturing operations and essentially reflects the organization's technology.

In contrast, the operations activities of Air Canada provide time and place utility through its services. The airline transports passengers and freight according to agreed-on departure and arrival places and times. Other service operations, such as The Beer Store or Club Monaco, provide place and possession utility by bringing the customer and products made by others together.

Club Monaco's flagship store, in the heart of Toronto's most fashionable retail district, provides place and possession utility by bringing customers and products together in this historic building that was once the food science building at University of Toronto.

Although the organizations in these examples produce different kinds of products or services, their operations processes share many important features.[26]

Manufacturing and Production

● **manufacturing**
A form of business that combines and transforms resource inputs into tangilble outcomes.

Because manufacturing once dominated industry, the entire area of operations management used to be called production management. **Manufacturing** is a form of business that combines and transforms resources into tangible outcomes that are then sold to others. The Goodyear Tire & Rubber Company is a manufacturer because it combines rubber and chemical compounds and uses blending equipment and moulding machines to create tires. Gibbard is a manufacturer because it buys wood and metal components, pads, and fabric and then combines them into furniture.

As Canadian manufacturers seek to improve productivity in the context of falling productivity growth rates and a widening gap between U.S. and Canadian manufacturing productivity, it is useful to examine the experience of American manufacturers. During the 1970s, manufacturing entered a long period of decline in the United States, primarily because of foreign competition. U.S. firms had grown lax and sluggish, and new foreign competitors came onto the scene with new equipment and much higher levels of efficiency. For example, steel companies in the Far East were able to produce high-quality steel for much lower prices than were U.S. companies like Bethlehem Steel and U.S. Steel (now USX Corporation) and Canadian companies like Stelco and Dofasco. Faced with a battle for survival, many companies underwent a long and difficult period of change by eliminating waste and transforming themselves into leaner and more efficient and responsive entities. They reduced their workforces dramatically, closed antiquated or unnecessary plants, and modernized their remaining plants. In recent years, their efforts have started to pay dividends as U.S. business has regained its competitive position in many different industries. Although manufacturers from other parts of the world are still formidable competitors and U.S. firms may never again be competitive in some markets, the overall picture is much better than it was just a few years ago.

Service Operations

From 1986 to 1996, the contribution of manufacturing to the Canadian gross domestic product declined from 29.5 to 25.7 percent while that of the service sector increased from 67.6 to 72.1 percent.[27] A **service organization** is one that transforms resources into intangible outputs and creates time or place utility for its customers. For example, ScotiaMcLeod Inc. makes stock transactions for its customers, Budget leases cars to its customers, and your local hairdresser cuts your hair. Managers have come to see that many of the tools, techniques, and methods that are used in a factory are also useful to a service firm. For example, managers of automobile plants and hair salons each have to decide how to design their facility, identify the best location for it, determine optimal capacity, make decisions about inventory storage, set procedures for purchasing raw materials, and set standards for productivity and quality.

● **service organization**
An organization that transforms resources into intangible outputs and creates time or place utility for its customers

The Role of Operations in Organizational Strategy

By this point you should clearly realize that operations management is very important to organizations. Beyond its direct impact on quality and productivity, it also directly influences the organization's overall level of effectiveness. For example, the deceptively simple strategic decision whether to stress high quality regardless of cost, lowest possible cost regardless of quality, or some combination of the two, has numerous important implications. A highest-possible quality strategy dictates state-of-the-art technology and rigorous control of product design and materials specifications. A combination strategy might call for lower-grade technology and less concern about product design and materials specifications. Just as strategy affects operations management, so too does operations management affect strategy. Suppose that a firm decides to upgrade the quality of its products or services. The organization's ability to implement the decision is dependent in part on current production capabilities and other resources. If existing technology does not permit higher-quality work and if the organization lacks the resources to replace its technology, increasing quality to the desired new standards will be difficult.

DESIGNING OPERATIONS SYSTEMS FOR QUALITY

The problems faced by operations managers as they attempt to improve quality revolve around the acquisition and utilization of resources for conversion. Their goals include both efficiency and effectiveness. Organizations must address a number of issues and decisions as operations systems are designed. The most basic ones are product-service mix, capacity, and facilities.

Product-Service Mix

A natural starting point in designing operations systems to enhance quality and productivity is determining the **product-service mix**. This decision flows from corporate, business, and marketing strategies. Managers have to make a number of decisions about their products and services, starting with how many and what kinds to offer. The Procter & Gamble Co., for example, makes regular, tartar-control, and gel formulas of Crest toothpaste and packages them in

● **product-service mix**
How many and what kinds of products or services (or both) to offer

several different sizes of tubes and pumps. The organization also has to make decisions regarding the level of quality desired, the optimal cost of each product or service, and exactly how each is to be designed. GE, for example, reduced the number of parts in its industrial circuit breakers from 28,000 to 1,275. The whole process involved product design.

Capacity

● **capacity**
The amount of products, services, or both that can be produced by an organization

The **capacity** decision involves choosing the amount of products, services, or both that can be produced by the organization. Determining whether to build a factory capable of making five thousand or eight thousand units per day is a capacity decision. So, too, is deciding whether to build a restaurant with 100 or 150 seats or a bank with five or ten teller stations. The capacity decision is truly a high-risk one because of the uncertainties of future product demand and the large monetary stakes involved. An organization that builds capacity exceeding its needs may commit resources (capital investment) that it can never recover. Many firms made this mistake during the 1960s and 1970s. Alternatively, an organization can build a facility with a smaller capacity than expected demand. Doing so may result in lost market opportunities, but it may also free capital resources for use elsewhere in the organization.

A major consideration in determining capacity is demand. A company operating with fairly constant monthly demand might build a plant capable of producing an amount each month roughly equivalent to its demand. But if its market is characterized by seasonal fluctuations, building a smaller plant to meet normal demand and then adding extra shifts during peak periods might be the most effective choice. Likewise, a restaurant that needs 150 seats for Saturday night but never needs more than 100 at any other time during the week would probably be foolish to expand to 150 seats. During the rest of the week, it must still pay to light, heat, cool, and clean the excess capacity.

Facilities

● **facilities**
The physical locations where products or services are created, stored, and distributed

Facilities are the physical locations where products or services are created, stored, and distributed. Major decisions pertain to location and layout.

● **location**
The physical positioning or geographic site of facilities

Location   **Location** is the physical positioning or geographic site of facilities; it must be determined by the needs and requirements of the organization. A company that relies heavily on railroads for transportation needs to locate close to rail facilities. As described earlier, GE decided that it did not need six plants to make circuit breakers, so it invested heavily in automating one plant and closed the other five. Different organizations in the same industry may have different facilities requirements. Benetton Group SPA uses only one distribution centre worldwide, whereas Kmart Corp. has several distribution centres in the United States alone. A retail business must choose its location carefully to be convenient for consumers.

● **layout**
The physical configuration of facilities, the arrangement of equipment within facilities, or both

● **product layout**
A physical configuration of facilities arranged around the product; used when large quantities of a single product are needed

Layout   The choice of physical configuration, or the **layout**, of facilities is closely related to other operations decisions. The three entirely different layout alternatives shown in Figure 21.3 help demonstrate the importance of the layout decision. A **product layout** is appropriate when large quantities of a single product are needed. It makes sense to custom design a straight-line flow of work for a product when a specific task is performed at each workstation as each unit flows past. Most assembly lines use this format. For example, IBM's PC factories use a product layout.

Process layouts are used in operations settings that create or process a variety of products. Auto repair shops and health-care clinics are good examples. Each car and each person is a separate "product." The needs of each incoming job are diagnosed as it enters the operations system, and the job is routed through the unique sequence of workstations needed to create the desired finished product. In a process layout, each type of conversion task is centralized in a single work-station or department. All welding is done in one designated shop location, and any car that requires welding is moved to that area. This setup is in contrast to the product layout, in which several different workstations may perform welding operations if the conversion task sequence so dictates.

The **fixed-position layout** is used when the organization creates a few very large and complex products. Aircraft manufacturers like The Boeing Co. and shipbuilders like Newport News use this method. An assembly line capable of moving a 747 would require an enormous plant, so instead the airplane itself remains stationary, and people and machines move around it as it is assembled.

● **process layout**
A physical configuration of facilities arranged around the process; used in facilities that create or process a variety of products

● **fixed-position layout**
A physical configuration of facilities arranged around a single work area; used for the manufacture of large and complex products such as airplanes

FIGURE 21.3 Approaches to Facilities Layout

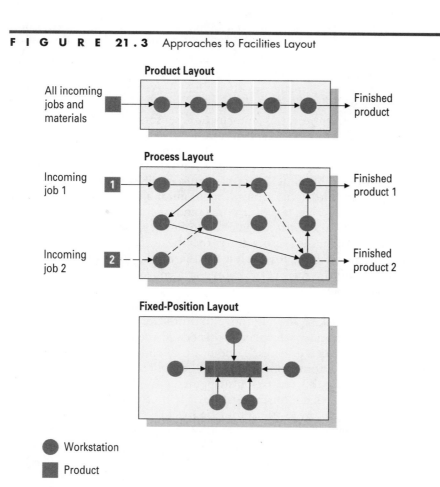

Product Layout

All incoming jobs and materials → ... → Finished product

Process Layout

Incoming job 1 → ... → Finished product 1

Incoming job 2 → ... → Finished product 2

Fixed-Position Layout

● Workstation
■ Product

When a manufacturer produces large quantities of a product (such as cars or computers), it may arrange its facilities into an assembly line (product layout). In a process layout, the work (such as patients in a hospital or custom pieces of furniture) moves through a variety of workstations. Locomotives and bridges are both manufactured in a fixed-position layout.

TECHNOLOGY AND QUALITY

technology
The set of processes and systems used by organizations to convert resources into products or services

A related element of operations management that affects quality is technology. In Chapter 3, we defined **technology** as the set of processes and systems used by organizations to convert resources into products or services.

Manufacturing Technology

Numerous forms of manufacturing technology are used in organizations. In Chapter 11 we discussed the research of Joan Woodward. Recall that Woodward identified three forms of technology—unit or small batch, large batch or mass production, and continuous process.[28] Each form of technology was thought to be associated with a specific type of organization structure. Of course, newer forms of technology not considered by Woodward also warrant attention. Two of these are automation and computer-assisted manufacturing.

automation
The process of designing work so that it can be completely or almost completely performed by machines

Automation **Automation** is the process of designing work so that it can be completely or almost completely performed by machines. Because automated machines operate quickly and make few errors, they increase the amount of work that can be done. Thus automation helps improve products and services, and it fosters innovation. Automation is the most recent step in the development of machines and machine-controlling devices. Machine-controlling devices have been around since the 1700s. James Watt, a Scottish engineer, invented a mechanical speed control to regulate the speed of steam engines in 1787. The Jacquard loom, developed by a French inventor, was controlled by paper cards with holes punched in them. Early accounting and computing equipment was controlled by similar punched cards.

Automation relies on feedback, information, sensors, and a control mechanism. Feedback is the flow of information from the machine back to the sensor. Sensors are the parts of the system that gather information and compare it to some preset standards. The control mechanism is the device that sends instructions to the automatic machine. These elements are illustrated by the example in Figure 21.4. A thermostat has sensors that monitor air temperature and compare it to a preset low value. If the air temperature falls below the preset value, the thermostat sends an electrical signal to the furnace, turning it on. The furnace heats the air. When the sensors detect that the air temperature has reached a value higher than the low preset value, the thermostat stops the furnace. The last step (shutting off the furnace) is known as feedback, a critical component of any automated operation.

Early automatic machines were primitive, and the use of automation was relatively slow to develop. The big move to automate factories began during World War II. The shortage of skilled workers and the development of high-speed computers combined to bring about a tremendous interest in automation. Programmable automation (the use of computers to control machines) was introduced during this era, far outstripping conventional automation (the use of mechanical or electromechanical devices to control machines).[29] The automobile industry began to use automatic machines for a variety of jobs. In fact, the term *automation* came into use in the 1950s in the automobile industry. The chemical and oil-refining industries also began to use computers to regulate production. It is this computerized, or programmable, automation that presents the greatest opportunities and challenges for management today.

The impact of automation on people in the workplace is complex. In the short term, people whose jobs are automated find themselves without jobs. In the long term, however, because of increasing production, more jobs are actually created than are lost. Nevertheless, not all companies are able to help displaced workers find new jobs, so the human costs are sometimes high. In the coal industry, for instance, automation has been used primarily in mining. The output per miner has risen dramatically from the 1950s on. The demand for coal, however, has decreased, and productivity gains resulting from automation have lessened the need for miners. Consequently, many workers have lost their jobs, and the industry has not been able to absorb them. In contrast, in the electronics industry, the rising demand for products has led to increasing employment opportunities despite the use of automation.

Computer-Assisted Manufacturing   Current extensions of automation generally revolve around computer-assisted manufacturing. **Computer-assisted manufacturing** is technology that relies on computers to design or manufacture products. One type of computer-assisted manufacturing is *computer-aided design (CAD)*—the use of computers to design parts and complete products and to simulate performance so that prototypes need not be constructed. McDonnell Douglas uses CAD to study hydraulic tubing in DC-10s. Japan's automotive industry uses it to speed up car design. GE used CAD to change the design of circuit breakers, and Benetton uses CAD to design new styles and products. Oneida Ltd., the table flatware firm, used CAD to design a new spoon in only two days.[30] CAD is usually combined with *computer-aided manufacturing (CAM)* to ensure that the design moves smoothly to production. The production computer shares the design computer's information and is able to have machines with the proper settings ready when production is needed. A CAM system is especially useful when reorders come in because the computer

● **computer-assisted manufacturing**
Technology that relies on computers to design or manufacture products

F I G U R E   21.4   A Simple Automatic Control Mechanism

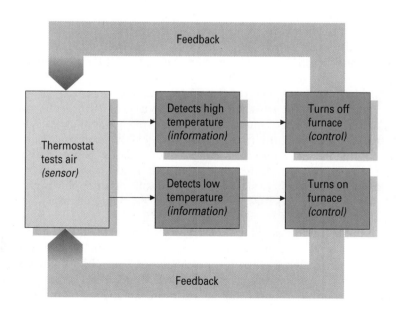

All automation includes feedback, information, sensors, and a control mechanism. A simple thermostat is an example of automation. Another example is Benetton's distribution centre in Italy. Orders are received, items pulled from stock and packaged for shipment, and invoices are prepared and transmitted with no human intervention.

can quickly produce the desired product, prepare labels and copies of orders, and send the product out to where it is wanted.

Closely aligned with this approach is *computer-integrated manufacturing (CIM)*. In CIM, CAD and CAM are linked together and computers adjust machine placements and settings automatically to enhance both the complexity and the flexibility of scheduling. All manufacturing activities are controlled by computer. Because the computer can access the company's other information systems, CIM is a powerful and complex management control tool.[31]

In *flexible manufacturing systems (FMS)*, robotic work units or workstations, assembly lines, and robotic carts or some other form of computer-controlled transport system usually move material as needed from one part of the system to another. FMS rely on computers to coordinate and integrate automated production and materials-handling facilities.[32]

These systems are not without disadvantages, however.[33] For example, because implementing them represents fundamental change, they also generate resistance. Additionally, because of their tremendous complexity, CAD systems are not always reliable. CIM systems are so expensive that they raise the break-even point for firms using them.[34] This means that the firm must operate at high levels of production and sales to be able to afford the systems.

Robotics One of the newest trends in manufacturing technology is robotics. A **robot** is any artificial device that is able to perform functions ordinarily thought to be appropriate for human beings. *Robotics* refers to the science and technology of the construction, maintenance, and use of robots. The use of industrial robots has steadily increased since 1980 and is expected to continue to increase slowly as more companies recognize the benefits that accrue to users of industrial robots.

Welding was one of the first applications for robots, and it continues to be the area for most applications. In second place and close behind is materials handling. Other applications include machine loading and unloading, painting and finishing, assembly, casting, and machining applications such as cutting, grinding, polishing, drilling, sanding, buffing, and deburring. Chrysler, for instance, replaced about two hundred welding jobs with fifty robots on an assembly line and increased productivity about 20 percent.[35] The use of robots in inspection work is increasing. They can check for cracks and holes, and they can be equipped with vision systems to perform visual inspections.

Robots are also beginning to move from the factory floor to all manner of other applications. The Montreal police recently used a robot to defuse a bomb planted at a pharmaceutical plant. At the Long Beach Memorial Hospital in California, brain surgeons are assisted by a robot arm that drills into the patient's skull with excellent precision.[36] Some newer applications involve remote work. For example, the use of robot submersibles controlled from the surface can help divers in remote locations. Surveillance robots fitted with microwave sensors can do things that a human guard cannot do such as "seeing" through nonmetallic walls and in the dark. In other applications, automated farming (agrimation) uses robot harvesters to pick fruit from a variety of trees.[37]

Robots are also used by small manufacturers. One robot slices carpeting to fit the inside of custom vans in an upholstery shop. Another stretches balloons flat so that they can be spray-painted with slogans at a novelties company. At a jewellery company, a robot holds class rings while they are engraved by a laser. These robots are lighter, faster, stronger, and more intelligent than those used

● **robot**
Any artificial device that is able to perform functions ordinarily thought to be appropriate for human beings

in heavy manufacturing and are the types that more and more organizations will be using in the future.[38]

Service Technology

Service technology is also changing rapidly. And it, too, is also moving more and more toward automated systems and procedures. In banking, for example, new technological breakthroughs have led to automated teller machines and increased the ease of moving funds between accounts or between different banks. Some people now have their paycheques deposited directly into a chequing account from which many of their bills are then automatically paid. And credit card transactions by Visa customers are recorded and billed electronically.

Hotels use increasingly sophisticated technology to accept and record room reservations. Universities use new technologies to electronically store and provide access to books, scientific journals, government reports, and articles. Hospitals and other health-care organizations use new forms of service technology to manage patient records, dispatch ambulances, and monitor vital signs. Restaurants use technology to record customer orders, order food and supplies, and prepare food. Given the increased role that service organizations are playing in today's economy, even more technological innovations are likely to be developed in the years to come.[39]

USING OPERATIONS SYSTEMS FOR QUALITY

After operations systems have been properly designed, they must then be put into use by the organization. Their basic functional purpose is to control transformation processes to ensure that relevant goals are achieved in areas such as quality and costs. Operations has a number of special purposes within this control framework, including purchasing and inventory management.

Operations Management as Control

One way of using operations management as control is to coordinate it with other functions. Monsanto Company, for example, established a consumer products division that produces and distributes fertilizers and lawn chemicals. To facilitate control the operations function was organized as an autonomous profit centre. Monsanto finds this effective because its manufacturing division is given the authority to determine not only the costs of creating the product but also the product price and the marketing programs.

In terms of overall organizational control, a division like the one used by Monsanto should be held accountable only for the activities over which it has decision-making authority. It would be inappropriate, of course, to make operations accountable for profitability in an organization that stresses sales and market share over quality and productivity. Misplaced accountability results in ineffective organizational control, to say nothing of hostility and conflict. Depending on the strategic role of operations, then, operations managers are accountable for different kinds of results. For example, in an organization using bureaucratic control, accountability is spelled out in rules and regulations. In a clan system, accountability is likely to be understood and accepted by everyone.

Within operations, managerial control ensures that resources and activities achieve primary goals such as a high percentage of on-time deliveries, low unit-production cost, or high product reliability. Any control system should focus on the elements that are most crucial to goal attainment. For example, firms in which product quality is a major concern (as it is at Rolex), might adopt a screening control system to monitor the product as it is being created. If quantity is a pressing issue (as it is at Timex), a post-action system might be used to identify defects at the end of the system without disrupting the manufacturing process itself.

Purchasing Management

● **purchasing management**
Buying materials and resources needed to produce products and services

Purchasing management is concerned with buying the materials and resources needed to create products and services. Thus the purchasing manager for a retailer like The Bay is responsible for buying the merchandise the store will sell. The purchasing manager for a manufacturer buys raw materials, parts, and machines needed by the organization. The manager responsible for purchasing must balance a number of constraints. Buying too much ties up capital and increases storage costs. Buying too little might lead to shortages and high reordering costs. The manager must also make sure that the quality of what is purchased meets the organization's needs, that the supplier is reliable, and that the best financial terms are negotiated.

Many firms have recently changed their approach to purchasing as a means to lower costs and improve quality and productivity. Rather than relying on hundreds or even thousands of suppliers, many companies are reducing their number of suppliers and negotiating special production-delivery arrangements. For example, one Honda plant negotiated an agreement with a local business owner, whereby he would start a new company to mount car stereo speakers into plastic mouldings. He delivers finished goods to the plant three times a day, and Honda buys all he can manufacture. Thus he has a stable sales base, Honda has a local and reliable supplier, and both companies benefit.

Inventory Management

● **inventory control**
Managing the organization's raw materials, work-in-process, finished goods, and products in-transit

Inventory control, also called materials control, is essential for effective operations management. The four basic kinds of inventories are *raw materials*, *work-in-process*, *finished-goods*, and *in-transit* inventories. As shown in Table 21.3, the sources of control over these inventories are as different as their purposes. Work-in-process inventories, for example, are made up of partially completed products that need further processing; they are controlled by the shop-floor system. In contrast, the quantities and costs of finished-goods inventories are under the control of the overall production scheduling system, which is determined by high-level planning decisions. In-transit inventories are controlled by the transportation and distribution systems.

● **just-in-time (JIT) method**
An inventory system in which necessary materials arrive as soon as they are needed (just in time) so that the production process is not interrupted

Like most other areas of operations management, inventory management changed notably in recent years. One particularly important breakthrough is the **just-in-time (JIT) method**. First popularized by the Japanese, the JIT system reduces the organization's investment in storage space for raw materials and in the materials themselves. Historically, manufacturers built large storage areas and filled them with materials, parts, and supplies that would be needed days, weeks, and even months in the future. Compared with the traditional approach to inventory management, a manager using the JIT approach orders

T A B L E   21.3 Inventory Types, Purposes, and Sources of Control

Type	Purpose	Source of Control
Raw materials	Provide the materials needed to make the product	Purchasing models and systems
Work-in-process	Enables overall production to be divided into stages of manageable size	Shop-floor control systems
Finished goods	Provide ready supply of products on customer demand and enable long, efficient production runs	High-level production scheduling systems in conjunction with marketing
In-transit (pipeline)	Distributes products to customers	Transportation and distribution control systems

JIT is a recent breakthrough in inventory management. With JIT inventory systems, materials arrive just as they are needed. JIT therefore helps an organization control its raw materials inventory by reducing the amount of space it must devote to storage.

materials and parts more often and in smaller quantities, thereby reducing investment in both storage space and actual inventory. The ideal arrangement is for materials to arrive just as they are needed—or just in time.

Recall our example about the small firm that assembles stereo speakers for Honda and delivers them three times a day, making it unnecessary for Honda to carry large quantities of the speakers in inventory. In an even more striking example, Johnson Controls makes automobile seats for Chrysler and ships them by small truckloads to a Chrysler plant 120 kilometres away. Each shipment is scheduled to arrive two hours before it is needed. Clearly, the JIT approach requires high levels of coordination and cooperation between the company and its suppliers. If shipments arrive too early, Chrysler has no place to store them. If they arrive too late, the entire assembly line may have to be shut down, resulting in enormous expense. When properly designed and used, the JIT method controls inventory very effectively.

SUMMARY OF KEY POINTS

Quality is a major consideration for all managers today. Quality is important because it affects competition, productivity, and costs. Total quality management is a comprehensive, organization-wide effort to enhance quality through a variety of avenues.

Productivity is also a major concern to managers. Productivity is an economic measure of how efficiently an organization is using its resources to create products or services. The United States still leads the world in individual productivity.

Quality and productivity are often addressed through operations management, the set of managerial activities that organizations use in creating their products and services. Operations management is important to both manufacturing and service organizations, and it plays an important role in an organization's strategy.

The starting point in using operations management to improve quality is to design appropriate operations systems. Major areas of concern are product and service design, capacity, and facilities.

Technology also plays an important role in quality. Automation is especially important today, and numerous computer-aided manufacturing techniques are widely practised. Robotics is also a growing area. Technology is as relevant to service organizations as to manufacturing organizations.

After an operations system has been designed and put into place, it serves a critical role in quality control. Major areas of interest during the use of operations systems are purchasing and inventory management.

DISCUSSION QUESTIONS

Questions for Review

1. What is quality? Why is it so important today?
2. What is productivity? How can it be improved?
3. What is the relationship of operations management to overall organizational strategy? Where do productivity and quality fit into that relationship?
4. What are the major components of operations systems? How are they designed?

Questions for Analysis

5. How might the management functions of planning, organizing, and leading relate to the management of quality and productivity?
6. Some people argue that quality and productivity are inversely related; as one goes up, the other goes down. How can that argument be refuted?
7. Is operations management most closely linked to corporate-level, business-level, or functional strategies? Why or in what way?

Questions for Application

8. Interview local managers in different kinds of organizations (business, service, religious) to determine how they address issues of quality and productivity.
9. Consider your college or university as an organization. How might it go about developing a TQM program?
10. Go to the library and locate information on several different organizations' uses of operations management. What similarities and differences do you find? Why do you think those similarities and differences exist?

BUILDING EFFECTIVE DIAGNOSTIC SKILLS

Exercise Overview

As noted in this chapter, the quality of a product or service is relative to price and expectations. A manager's diagnostic skills—the ability to visualize responses to a situation—can be useful in helping to best position quality relative to price and expectations.

Exercise Background

Think of a recent occasion in which you purchased a tangible product. For example, think about clothing, electronic equipment, luggage, or professional supplies that you subsequently came to feel to be of especially high quality. Now recall another product that you evaluated as having appropriate or adequate quality and a third that you felt had low or poor quality.

Next, recall parallel experiences involving purchases of services. Examples might include an airline, train, or bus trip; a meal in a restaurant; a haircut; or an oil change for your car.

Finally, recall three experiences in which both products and services were involved. Examples might include having questions answered by someone about a product you were buying or returning a defective or broken product for a refund or warranty repair. Try to recall instances in which there was an apparent disparity between product and service quality (that is, a poor-quality product accompanied by outstanding service or a high-quality product with mediocre service).

Exercise Task

Using the nine examples you just identified, do the following:

1. Assess the extent to which the quality you associated with each was a function of price and your expectations.
2. Consider whether the quality of each can be improved without greatly affecting price. If so, how?
3. Consider these questions: Can high-quality service offset only adequate or even poor product quality? Can outstanding product quality offset only adequate or even poor-quality service?

Total Quality Management at Xerox Canada

Xerox Corporation, originally named the Haloid Company, was founded in 1906 in Rochester, New York. Initially, the company manufactured and sold photographic paper. It has since widened its range of products as well as its international presence. In 1953, Xerox established a Canadian subsidiary, it first foray abroad. Today, the company is one of the premier document-processing businesses in the world, offering a wide array of consulting services and products such as publishing systems, copiers, printers, scanners, fax machines, and document-management software.

In the 1970s and 1980s, Xerox was faced with a host of business problems and challenges, including product maturity, rapidly changing markets, relentless foreign competition, and an explosion of available technology. In fact, Japanese competition so eroded the company's market share that Xerox faced a crisis that could have resulted in its demise, with profits plummeting $1 billion in one year alone. In just five years, the Japanese had captured 40 percent of the market. In 1983, Xerox Canada made a conscious decision to improve the company's bottom line through total quality management (TQM). The program, which was build according to a blueprint called Leadership Through Quality, was divided into several concrete elements.

First, Xerox Canada intensified its training efforts. It discovered that under its original training program, which concentrated on selected individuals, trained employees did not disseminate their acquired knowledge and skills. In the TQM program, the objective was to spend four years training every employee through its LUTI (Learn, Use, Train, Inspect) system. Once an individual was trained, he or she returned to work and used the tools and processes learned to train co-workers and inspect their work; the co-workers, in turn, trained other workers. The snowball effect this arrangement created fuelled a total cultural transformation, one that emphasized quality improvement.

Xerox Canada's TQM also emphasized specific tools and processes, including competitive benchmarking. To find a way out of the crisis in the 1980s, Xerox Canada turned to its affiliate Fuji Xerox, which was not experiencing the same problems. By using Fuji Xerox as a role model, Xerox formulated a strategy that emphasized employee involvement and competitive benchmarking.

The company also ensured that consistent and constant communication of corporate priorities and goals cascaded through the work groups. Formal media such as magazines, newsletters, corporate videos, and internal TV broadcasts, as well as informal vehicles such as staff meetings, were used to communicate the company's strategy. Xerox Canada's TQM program also involved rewarding (through promotion, for example) employees who modelled Leadership Through Quality behaviour.

Top-management support was critical to the success of the TQM program. Management priorities had to be shifted from an internal orientation to the satisfaction of external customer requirements. This was accomplished through intensive management training in quality techniques. The new corporate structure chart showed an upside-down pyramid that placed the customer, not senior executives, at the top of the corporate flow chart.

The practice of TQM at Xerox Canada seems to have yielded tangible benefits. During the 1980s, despite the recession and ferocious international competition, the company managed to cut its time to market by 50 percent, reduce the number of its suppliers from five thousand to five hundred, double the size of its business, regain market share lost in the 1970s, increase sales by introducing 125 new products, keep operating costs under control, and dramatically increase customer satisfaction. As Xerox Canada adapts to its changing environment, the company plans continue to emphasize employee training, teamwork, a focus on customers, and a commitment to improved quality.

Questions

1. What are some of the similarities between Xerox Canada's TQM strategy and TQM strategies discussed in this chapter?

2. In view of the globalization of competition, do you think Xerox Canada will continue to be a successful company? Why or why not?

3. What is the role of top-management support in a TQM program?

References: Dianne McGarry, "Playing on Both the Home and Away Teams," *Business Quarterly*, Winter 1994, pp. 81–88; Carolyn Green, "Remaking Xerox Canada," *Marketing*, April 5, 1993, p. 1; Richard Barton, "Business Process Re-engineering," *Business Quarterly*, Spring 1993, pp. 101–103; David McCamus, "Critical Quality Levers: TQM at Xerox Canada," *Business Quarterly*, Summer 1992, pp. 99–104; and "Beyond Quality," *Business Quarterly*, Summer 1992, pp. 89–136.

CHAPTER NOTES

1. "Chrysler Mounts Campaign to Cut Defects," *The Wall Street Journal*, January 27, 1994, pp. B1, B6; "Bug Control at Chrysler," *Business Week, August 22*, 1994, p. 26; and "Chrysler's Quality Crusade," *Business Week,* April 17, 1995, pp. 76–77.

2. Rhonda Reger, Loren Gustafson, Samuel DeMarie, and John Mullane, "Reframing the Organization: Why Implementing Total Quality Is Easier Said Than Done," *Academy of Management Review*, Vol. 19, No. 3, 1994, pp. 565–584.

3. "Quality—How to Make It Pay," *Business Week,* August 8, 1994, pp. 54–59.

4. Ross Johnson and William O. Winchell, *Management and Quality* (Milwaukee: American Society for Quality Control, 1989). See also Carol Reeves and David Bednar, "Defining Quality: Alternatives and Implications," *Academy of Management Review*, Vol. 19, No. 3, 1994, pp. 419–445.

5. Based on information available at the National Quality Institute Web site (http://www.nqi.com).

6. W. Edwards Deming, *Out of the Crisis* (Cambridge, Mass.: MIT Press, 1986).

7. David Waldman, "The Contributions of Total Quality Management to a Theory of Work Performance," *Academy of Management Review*, Vol. 19, No. 3, 1994, pp. 510–536.

8. Joel Dreyfuss, "Victories in the Quality Crusade," *Fortune*, October 10, 1988, pp. 80–88.

9. Barbara Spencer, "Models of Organization and Total Quality Management: A Comparison and Critical Evaluation," *Academy of Management Review*, Vol. 19, No. 3, 1994, pp. 446–471.

10. James Dean and David Bowen, "Management Theory and Total Quality: Improving Research and Practice Through Theory Development," *Academy of Management Review*, Vol. 19, No. 3, 1994, pp. 392–418.

11. Edward E. Lawler, "Total Quality Management and Employee Involvement: Are They Compatible?" *The Academy of Management Executive*, Vol. 8, No. 1, 1994, pp. 68–76.

12. "Quality is Becoming Job One in the Office, Too," *Business Week*, April 29, 1991, pp. 52–56.

13. Jeremy Main, "How to Steal the Best Ideas Around," *Fortune*, October 19, 1992, pp. 102–106.

14. James Brian Quinn and Frederick Hilmer, "Strategic Outsourcing," *Sloan Management Review*, Summer 1994, pp. 43–52.

15. Thomas Robertson, "How to Reduce Market Penetration Cycle Times," *Sloan Management Review*, Fall 1993, pp. 87–95.

16. Brian Dumaine, "How Managers Can Succeed Through Speed," *Fortune*, February 13, 1989, pp. 54–59.

17. Ronald Henkoff, "The Hot New Seal of Quality," *Fortune*, June 28, 1993, pp. 116–120.

18. Micro-Economic Policy Analysis Branch, "Canada Is Losing Ground in Productivity," (http://www.strategis.ic.gc.ca), October 11, 1996.

19. John W. Kendrick, *Understanding Productivity: An Introduction to the Dynamics of Productivity Change* (Baltimore: Johns Hopkins, 1977).

20. "The Productivity Payoff Arrives," *Fortune*, June 27, 1994, pp. 79–84.

21. Based on information available at Organization for Economic Co-operation and Development (OECD) Web site (http://www.oecd.org).

22. OECD Web site.

23. Statistics Canada, "Productivity, Hourly Compensation and Unit Labour Cost," *The Daily*, June 5, 1997, p. 5.

24. Micro-Economic Policy Analysis Branch, "Canada Is Losing Ground in Productivity."

25. David Wright and Paul Brauchle, "Teaming Up for Quality," *Training and Development*, September 1994, pp. 67–75.

26. Paul M. Swamidass, "Empirical Science: New Frontier in Operations Management Research," *Academy of Management Review*, October 1991, pp. 793–814.

27. "Sectoral Contribution," *OECD in Figures* (http://www.oecd.org).

28. Joan Woodward, *Industrial Organization: Theory and Practice* (London: Oxford University Press, 1965).

29. Paul D. Collins, Jerald Hage, and Frank M. Hull, "Organizational and Technological Predictors of Change in Automaticity," *Academy of Management Journal*, September 1988, pp. 512–543.

30. "Computers Speed the Design of More Workaday Products," *The Wall Street Journal*, January 18, 1985, p. 25.

31. Robert Bonsack, "Executive Checklist: Are You Ready for CIM?" *CIM Review*, Summer 1987, pp. 35–38.

32. M. Sepehri, "IBM's Automated Lexington Factory Focuses on Quality and Cost Effectiveness," *Industrial Engineering*, February 1987, pp. 66–74.

33. "Computers Speed the Design of More Workaday Products."

34. "How Automation Could Save the Day," *Business Week*, March 3, 1986, pp. 72–74.

35. Otto Friedrich, "The Robot Revolution," *Time*, December 8, 1980, pp. 72–83.

36. Gene Bylinsky, "Invasion of the Service Robots," *Fortune*, September 14, 1987, pp. 81–88.

37. "Robots Head for the Farm," *Business Week*, September 8, 1986, pp. 66–67.

38. "Boldly Going Where No Robot Has Gone Before," *Business Week*, December 22, 1986, p. 45.

39. James Brian Quinn and Martin Neil Baily, "Information Technology: Increasing Productivity in Services," *The Academy of Management Executive*, Vol. 8, No. 3, 1994, pp. 28–38.

Managing Information and Information Technology

22

OBJECTIVES

After studying this chapter, you should be able to:

● *Describe the role and importance of information in the manager's job.*

● *Identify the basic building blocks of information technology.*

● *Discuss the basic factors that determine an organization's information technology needs.*

● *Describe the basic kinds of information systems used by organizations.*

● *Discuss how information systems can be managed.*

● *Describe how information systems affect organizations.*

● *Identify recent advances in information technology.*

OUTLINE

Texas Instruments is a world leader in the use of information technology. Using state-of-the-art technology allows workers such as this one to stay abreast of what their colleagues around the world are doing.

Texas Instruments (TI) has operations around the world. While the firm's operations are concentrated in the state that is its namesake, TI also has facilities in more than thirty countries scattered across Europe, Asia, and South America.

The firm has long been a leader in integrated global design. Until recently, however, global design teams were relatively inefficient. Days at a time were lost as detailed engineering drawings travelled between countries. Even facsimile technology did not help greatly, because the images were often blurred and the drawings were very large—drawings were sometimes cut into small pieces, each piece was faxed separately, and someone on the other end taped them together.

Eventually, the firm began to transmit images and other data electronically through integrated computer information networks—*intranets*—linked by satellites. This new technology, increasingly referred to as rapid manufacturing,

> **"In two or three years rapid manufacturing will be on everybody's lips." (TI executive)**

allowed TI engineers in facilities around the globe to work on the same project simultaneously—to communicate just as easily as if they were sitting in the same room. Almost immediately after this system was implemented, the time needed to develop a new calculator dropped by 20 percent. Later improvements shaving another 17 percent off development time soon followed.

In some parts of the world, TI has had to go to great lengths to get its information technology in place. For example, the firm wanted to set up a satellite dish at its Bangalore, India, facility so that its engineers there could interface with TI engineers in other locations. The only way to get the dish to Bangalore was to haul it in by oxcart, but it appears to have been a worthwhile investment. Engineers there are now able to uplink with their counterparts in the United States and Japan and have made numerous contributions to the development of new forms of microchips.

One TI group that has taken special advantage of information technology and rapid manufacturing has been the Texas Instruments Registration and Identification System (Tiris) group. This group is managed in England, develops products in the Netherlands and Germany, and produces those products in Japan and Malaysia. The TI communication network has made it easier than anyone might have imagined for these engineers to work together, to communicate, and to coordinate their efforts. Indeed, Tiris management strongly feels that the system has given them a significant competitive advantage.

The system has also allowed the firm to expand the boundaries of its workday by taking advantage of different time zones. A U.S. financial exchange recently asked TI for a price quote on some new equipment. A group of managers in Dallas started work late in the afternoon; at quitting time they forwarded the files to their counterparts in Tokyo. Managers there took up the project, spent their day on it, and then passed the task on to managers in Nice, France. Managers there finished the job and sent the information back to Dallas. Within twenty-four hours of getting the request, TI could show the customer the price quote—and a computer-generated image from rapid manufacturing of exactly what the product would look like.[1] ●

exas Instruments is aggressively using the latest technology for competitive advantage. And increasingly, that technology is helping firms like Texas Instruments better manage the information that is so vital to their daily operations and strategic management. Information comes in a variety of forms and in large quantities. If organizations aren't careful, they can lose control of how they manage the information they need to conduct business efficiently and effectively. Consequently, in recent years businesses like TI have recognized that they need better ways to manage their information.

This chapter is about advances made by organizations in information management. We describe the role and importance of information to managers, the characteristics of useful information, and information management as control. We then identify the basic building blocks of information systems. We discuss the general and specific determinants of information system needs. We next examine the primary kinds of information systems used in organizations and describe how these information systems are managed. Finally, we look at the impact of information systems on organizations and highlight recent advances in information management.

INFORMATION AND THE MANAGER

Information has always been an integral part of every manager's job. Its importance, however, and therefore the need to manage it continue to grow rapidly. To appreciate this trend, we need to understand the role of information in the manager's job, characteristics of useful information, and the nature of information management as control.[2]

The Role of Information in the Manager's Job

In Chapters 1 and 18, we highlighted the role of communication in the manager's job. Given that information is a vital part of communication, it follows that management and information are closely related. Indeed, it is possible to conceptualize management itself as a series of steps involving the reception, processing, and dissemination of information. As illustrated in Figure 22.1, the manager is constantly bombarded with data and information (the difference between the two is noted later).

Suppose that Marie Dufour is an operations manager for a large manufacturing firm. During the course of a normal day, Marie receives a great many pieces of information from both formal and informal conversations and meetings, telephone calls, personal observation, letters, reports, memos, and trade publications. She gets a report from a subordinate that explains exactly how to solve a pressing problem, so she calls the subordinate and tells him to put the solution into effect immediately. She scans a copy of a report prepared for another manager, sees that it has no relevance to her, and discards it. She sees a *Globe and Mail* article that she knows Sara Ferris in marketing should see, so she passes it on to her. She sees yesterday's production report, but because she knows she won't need to analyze it for another week, she stores it. She observes a worker doing a job incorrectly and realizes that the incorrect method is associated with a mysterious quality problem that someone told her about last week.

An essential part of information-processing activity is differentiating between data and information. **Data** are raw figures and facts reflecting a single aspect of reality. The facts that a plant has thirty-five machines, that each machine is capable of producing one thousand units of output per day, that current and projected future demand for the units is thirty thousand per day, and that workers sufficiently skilled to run the machines make $25 an hour are data.

Information is data presented in a way or form that has meaning. Thus summarizing the four pieces of data just given provides information—the plant has excess capacity and is therefore incurring unnecessary costs. Information has meaning to a manager and provides a basis for action. The plant manager might use the information and decide to sell four machines (keeping one as a backup) and transfer five operators to other jobs.[3]

A related term is **information technology**, or **IT**. Information technology refers to the resources used by an organization to manage information that it needs to carry out its mission. IT may consist of computers, computer networks, and other pieces of hardware. In addition, IT also consists of software that facilitates the system's abilities to manage information in a way that is useful for managers.

The grocery industry uses data, information, and information technology to automate inventory and checkout facilities. The average Zehrs store, for example, carries 50,000 items. Computerized scanning machines at the checkout counters can provide daily sales figures for any product. These figures alone are data and have little meaning in their pure form. Information is compiled from this data by another computerized system. Using this IT system, managers can identify how any given product or product line is selling in any number of stores over any meaningful period of time.[4]

● **data**
Raw figures and facts reflecting a single aspect of reality

● **information**
Data presented in a way or form that has meaning

● **information technology (IT)**
Refers to the resources used by an organization to manage information that it needs to carry out its mission

F I G U R E   22.1   Managers as Information Processors

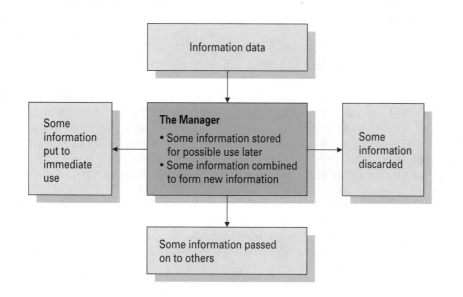

Managers who receive information and data must decide what to do with it. Some is stored for possible later use, and other information is combined to form new information. Subsequently, some is used immediately, some is passed on to others, and some is discarded.

Characteristics of Useful Information

What factors differentiate information that is useful from information that is not useful? In general, information is useful if it is accurate, timely, complete, and relevant.

Accurate   For information to be of real value to a manager, it must be accurate. Accuracy means that the information must provide a valid and reliable reflection of reality. A Japanese construction company once bought information from a consulting firm about a possible building site in London. The Japanese were told that the land, which would be sold in a sealed bid auction, would attract bids of close to $250 million (U.S.). They were also told that the land currently held an old building that could easily be demolished. Thus the Japanese bid $255 million (U.S.)—which was $90 million (U.S.) more than the next-highest bid. A few days later, the British government declared the building historic, preempting any thought of demolition. Clearly, the Japanese acted on information that was less than accurate.[5]

Timely   Information also needs to be timely. Timeliness does not necessarily mean speediness; it means only that information needs to be available in time for appropriate managerial action. What constitutes timeliness is a function of the situation facing the manager. When Marriott was gathering information for its Fairfield Inn project, managers projected a six-month window for data collection. They believed that this would give them an opportunity to do a good job of getting the information they needed while not delaying the project. In contrast, Marriott's computerized reservation and accounting system can provide a manager today with last night's occupancy level at any Marriott facility.[6]

Complete   Information must tell a complete story for it to be useful to a manager. If it is less than complete, the manager is likely to get an inaccurate or distorted picture of reality. For example, managers at one supermarket thought that house-brand products were more profitable than national brands because they yielded higher unit profits. On the basis of this information, they gave house brands a lot of shelf space and centred a lot of promotional activities around them. As the supermarket's managers became more sophisticated in understanding their information, however, they realized that national brands were actually more profitable over time because they sold many more units than house brands during any given period of time. Hence, while a store might sell 10 cans of house-brand coffee in a day with a profit of 25 cents per can (total profit of $2.50), it would also sell 15 cans of Maxwell House with a profit of 20 cents per can (total profit of $3).

Relevant   Finally, information must be relevant if it is to be useful to managers. Relevance, like timeliness, is defined according to the needs and circumstances of a particular manager. Operations managers need information on costs and productivity, human resource managers need information on hiring needs and turnover rates, and marketing managers need information on sales projections and advertising rates. As Wal-Mart contemplates countries for possible expansion opportunities, it gathers information about local regulations, customs, and so forth. But the information about any given country isn't really relevant until the decision is made to enter that market.[7]

Information Management as Control

The manager also needs to appreciate the role of information in control—indeed, to see information management as a vital part of the control process in the organization.[8] As already noted, managers receive much more data and information than they need or can use. Accordingly, deciding how to handle each piece of data and information involves a form of control.[9]

The control perspective on information management is illustrated in Figure 22.2. Information enters, is used by, and leaves the organization. For example, Marriott took great pains to make sure that it got all the information it needed to plan for and enter the economy lodging business. Once it gathered this preliminary information, it needed to make sure that the information was available in the proper form to everyone who needed it. In general, the effort to ensure that information is accurate, timely, complete, and relevant is a form of screening control. Finally, Marriott wanted to make sure that its competitors did not learn about its plans until the last possible minute. It also wanted to time and orchestrate news releases, public announcements, and advertising for maximum benefit. These efforts thus served a post-action control function.

F I G U R E 22.2   Information Management as Control

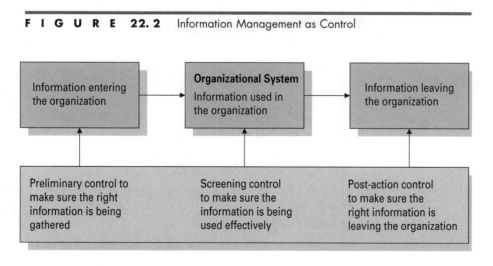

Information management can be a part of the control system via preliminary, screening, and/or post-action control mechanisms. Because information from the environment is just as much a resource as raw materials or finances, it must be monitored and managed to promote its efficient and effective utilization.

BUILDING BLOCKS OF INFORMATION TECHNOLOGY

Information technology is generally of two types—manual or computer-based. All information technology, as well as the systems that it defines, has five basic parts. Figure 22.3 diagrams these parts for a computer-based information technology system. The *input medium* is the device that is used to add data and information into the system. For example, a supermarket's optical scanner enters point-of-sale information. Likewise, someone can enter data through a keyboard.

The data that are entered into the system typically flow first to a processor. The *processor* is the part of the system that is capable of organizing, manipulating, sorting, or performing calculations or other transformations with the data. Most systems also have one or more *storage devices*—a place where data can be stored for later use. Floppy disks, hard disks, magnetic tapes, and optical disks are common forms of storage devices. As data are transformed into useable information, the resultant information must be communicated to the appropriate person by means of an *output medium*. Common ways to display output are video displays, printers, other computers, and facsimile machines.

Finally, the entire information technology system is operated by a *control system*—most often software of one form or another. Simple systems in small organizations can use commercial software. Microsoft Windows, DOS, and OS-2 are general operating systems that control more specialized types of software. Microsoft Word and WordPerfect are popular systems for word processing. Lotus 1-2-3 and Excel are popular spreadsheet programs, and dBASE III is frequently used for database management. Of course, elaborate systems such as those used by large businesses require a special customized operating system. When organizations start to link computers into a network, the operating system must be even more complex.

Computer-based information systems generally have five basic components—an input medium, a processor, an output medium, a storage device, and a control system. Noncomputer-based systems use parallel components for the same basic purposes.

F I G U R E   22.3   Building Blocks of a Computer-Based Information System

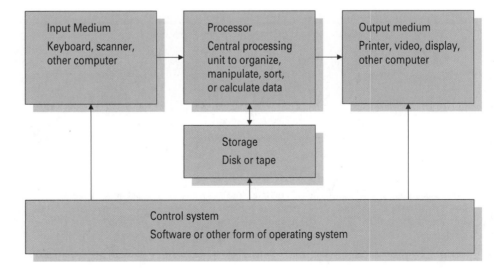

As we noted earlier, information technology systems need not be computerized. Many small organizations still function quite well with a manual system using paper documents, routing slips, paper clips, file folders, file cabinets, and typewriters. Increasingly, however, even small businesses are abandoning their manual systems for computerized ones. As hardware prices continue to drop and software becomes more and more powerful, computerized information systems will likely be within the reach of any business that wants to have one.

DETERMINANTS OF INFORMATION TECHNOLOGY NEEDS

What determines whether an organization needs an information system, and how do these factors help define the organization's information technology needs? In general, the major factors that determine these needs fall into two categories: general determinants and specific determinants.[10] These are illustrated in Figure 22.4.

General Determinants

Two general factors help define an organization's information technology needs. These factors are the environment and the size of the organization.

Environment   In Chapters 3 and 11, we noted that the environment of an organization affects that organization in many different ways. Still another way that the environment affects an organization is as a determinant of its information

---

F I G U R E   22. 4   Determinants of an Organization's Information-Processing Needs

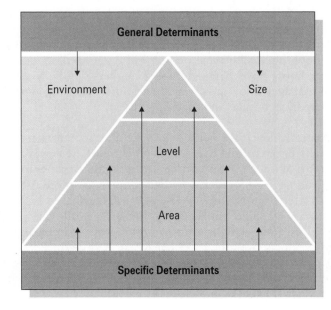

Information processing needs are determined by such general organizational factors as the environment and the organization's size and such specific managerial factors as their area and level in the organization.

technology needs. In general, the more uncertain and complex the environment, the greater is the need to formally manage information. Given that virtually all organizations face at least some degree of uncertainty, it can be argued that all organizations need to worry about managing their information. However, an organization like Corel or IBM that operates in an extremely uncertain environment has very strong needs for elaborate information technology.

Size   Size is another general determinant of an organization's information technology needs. The larger an organization is, the greater are its needs to manage its information systematically. Thus General Motors has greater information technology needs than does its Cadillac division alone, and each has greater needs than does a single Cadillac dealership. The effects of organizational size can also be either slightly constrained or greatly accentuated by the complexity of the organization. A large organization that is essentially a single division, for example, has less need for sophisticated information technology than does a firm of the same size that comprises several different divisions.

Specific Determinants

Two other factors serve to define the information technology needs of an organization. These factors are the area and level of the organization.

Area   By area, we mean basic functional areas like finance, operations, marketing, or human resources. Each of these areas has its own unique set of information technology needs.[11] Human resources, for example, needs complete demographic data on all current employees, job-grade information, employment equity, statistics, and so forth. Marketing needs data on current prices, market share, and advertising expenditures.

Another important ingredient is the extent to which the various areas within an organization work in an integrated and coordinated fashion. If each acts totally on its own, with coordination handled by the managerial hierarchy, each area can survive with its own information system. But if different areas are expected to coordinate their activities, then their information systems need to be coordinated. For example, the marketing system may be updated to include a projection for 10 percent more sales next year than previously expected. An integrated information system could use that information to let the operations manager know how much additional output will be needed, to let the human resource manager know how many additional workers will be needed, and to let the financial manager know how much additional working capital will be needed to support higher wage and materials costs.

Level   Organizational level also helps determine the information technology requirements of the organization. Managers at the top of the organization need broad, general kinds of information across a variety of time frames to help them with strategic planning. Middle managers need somewhat more specific information with a shorter time frame. Lower-level managers need highly specific information with a very short time frame. For example, the vice president of marketing at McCain Foods might want to know projected demand for eight different potato products over the next five years. A divisional sales manager might need to know projected demand for two of those potato products for the next one-year period. A district sales manager might need to know how much of one product is likely to be sold next month.

BASIC KINDS OF INFORMATION SYSTEMS

Organizations that use information systems, especially large organizations, often find that they need several kinds of systems to manage their information effectively. The four most general kinds of information systems are transaction-processing systems, basic management information systems, decision support systems, and executive information systems.[12]

Transaction-Processing Systems

Transaction-processing systems were the first computerized form of information system adopted by many businesses. A **transaction-processing system**, or **TPS**, is a system designed to handle routine and recurring transactions within the business. Visa uses a TPS to record charges to individual accounts, credit payments made on the accounts, and send monthly bills to customers. In general, a TPS is most useful when the organization has a large number of similar transactions to process. Thus most forms of customer billings, bank transactions, and point-of-sale records are amenable to this form of information system. The automated scanners at Sobeys that record each unit sold and its price are a form of TPS.

A TPS is especially helpful in aggregating large amounts of data into more manageable forms of information summaries. For example, a bank manager probably cares little about any given Visa transaction recorded for any single cardholder. More useful is information about the average number of purchases made by each cardholder, his or her average daily balance, average monthly finance charges assessed, and so forth. In general, a TPS is most useful to lower-level managers. Even though this approach was the earliest, it is still of considerable use and relevance to many organizations. Many of these organizations, however, have also found developing more sophisticated systems necessary.

● **transaction-processing system (TPS)**
A system designed to handle routine and recurring transactions within a business

Basic Management Information Systems

The next step in the evolution of information management is generally called the **management information system**, or **MIS**. An MIS is a system that gathers comprehensive data, organizes and summarizes it in a form valuable to functional managers, and then provides those same managers with the information they need to do their work. Figure 22.5 shows how such a system might work.

An MIS for a manufacturing firm might develop a computerized inventory system that keeps track of both anticipated orders and inventory on hand. A marketing representative talking to a customer about anticipated delivery dates can "plug into the system" and get a good idea of when an order can be shipped. Likewise, the plant manager can use the system to help determine how much of each of the firm's products to manufacture next week or next month.

A variation on the standard MIS is called an electronic data exchange, or EDE. The EDE system allows a company to tie directly into the computerized inventory system of a customer to check current sales levels and stock on hand. The customer can then transmit new orders directly into the supplier's system, and managers there are already geared up to start working on it. Use of EDE effectively can cut delivery times and increase sales.[13]

● **management information system (MIS)**
A system that gathers comprehensive data, organizes and summarizes it in a form valuable to managers, and provides those managers with the information they need to do their work

F I G U R E 22.5 A Basic Management Information System

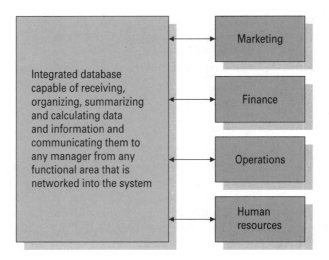

Decision Support Systems

● **decision support system (DSS)**

A system that automatically searches for, manipulates, and summarizes information needed by managers to make specific decisions

An increasingly common information system is called a **decision support system**, or **DSS**. A DSS is both very elaborate and quite powerful: it can automatically search for, manipulate, and summarize information needed for specific decisions. A DSS is much more flexible than a traditional MIS and can help cope with nonroutine problems and decisions.[14]

A manager might be interested in knowing the likely effects of a price increase for a particular product sold by the firm. Thus she might decide to query the DSS to determine the potential outcomes for price increases of 5, 7, and 10 percent. The DSS already knows the pricing history for the product, the prices charged by competitors, their most recent price changes, the effects of price on sales, sea–

Electronic banking systems help people and organizations complete complex transactions efficiently and quickly.

sonal variations in demand and price, inflation rates, and virtually any other relevant piece of information that might have already been determined. The system then calculates projected sales, market share, and profit profiles for each of the potential price-increase levels and provides them to the manager.

Decision support systems are very complex. They take considerable time and resources to develop, to maintain, and to teach managers how to effectively use them. They also seem to hold considerable potential for improving the quality of information available to managers as they make important decisions. Which and Why for Windows, developed by Montreal-based Arlington Software Corp., is a tool designed to improve and accelerate managerial decision making. It follows a template model listing weighted factors to be considered in making a decision; the user inputs relevant information and a best choice is recommended. This software assists managers in making purchasing, leasing, and hiring decisions.[15]

Executive Information Systems

Executive information systems are the newest form of information system. An **executive information system**, or **EIS**, is a system designed to meet the special information processing needs of top managers. Because many top managers lack basic computer skills and because they need highly specialized information not readily available in conventional systems, many executives were reluctant to use their organizations' information system.

An EIS is constructed to be very user-friendly (that is, technical knowledge is not necessary to use it). Instead, such systems generally use icons and symbols and require very few commands. The information they provide allows managers to bypass details and get directly to overall trends and patterns that may affect strategic decision making. It summarizes information for managers, rather than providing specific details. It also tailors the information to the specific needs of the manager.[16]

● **executive information system (EIS)**
A system designed to meet the special information processing needs of top managers

MANAGING INFORMATION SYSTEMS

At this point, the value and importance of information systems should be apparent. There are still important questions to be answered, however. How are such systems developed, and how are they used day to day? This section provides insights into these issues and related areas.

Establishing Information Systems

The basic steps involved in creating an information system are outlined in Figure 22.6.[17] The first step is to determine the information needs of the organization and to establish goals for what is to be achieved with the proposed system. It is absolutely imperative that the project have full support and an appropriate financial commitment from top management if it is to be successful. Once the decision has been made to develop and install an information system, a task force is usually formed to oversee everything. Target users must be well represented on such a task force.

Next, three tasks can be done simultaneously. One task is to assemble a database. Most organizations already possess the information they need for an information system, but it is often not in the correct form. In the United States, the Pentagon is spending large sums of money to transform all of its paper records into computer records. Many other branches of the U.S. government are also working hard to computerize their data.[18]

While the database is being assembled, the organization also needs to determine its hardware needs and acquire the appropriate equipment. Some systems rely solely on one large mainframe computer; others are increasingly using personal computers. Equipment is usually obtained from large manufacturers like IBM, Compaq, and Sun Microsystems. Finally, software needs must also be determined and an appropriate operating system obtained. Again, commercial packages may work, although most companies find some customization necessary to suit their needs.

The actual information system is created by integrating the database, the hardware, and the software. Obviously, the mechanics of doing this are beyond the scope of this discussion. However, the company usually has to rely on the expertise of outside consulting firms along with the vendors who provided the other parts of the system to get it all put together. During this phase, the equipment is installed, cables are strung between units, the data are entered into the system, the operating system is installed and tested, and so forth. During this phase, system controls are also installed. A control is simply a characteristic of the system that limits certain forms of access or limits what a person can do with the system. For example, top managers may want to limit access to certain sensitive data to a few key people. These people may be given private codes that they must enter before the data are made available. Ensuring that data cannot be accidentally erased by someone who happens to press the wrong key is important.

The next step is to develop documentation of how the system works and train people in how to use it. Documentation refers to manuals, computerized help programs, diagrams, and instruction sheets. Essentially, it tells people how to use the system for different purposes. Beyond pure documentation, however, training sessions are also common. Such sessions allow people to practise using the system under the watchful eye of experts.

The system must then be tested and appropriate modifications made. Regardless of how well planned an information system is, there will almost certainly be glitches once the system is operational. For example, the system may be unable to generate a report that needs to be made available to certain managers. Or the report may not be in the appropriate format. Or certain people may be unable to access data that they need to get other information from the system. In most cases, the consultant or internal group that installed the system is able to make such modifications as the need arises.

The organization must recognize that information management needs change over time. Hence, even though the glitches get straightened out and the information system is put into normal operation, modifications may still be needed in the future. For example, Domtar and Cascades announced plans to merge their corrugated fibreboard divisions in January 1998, but because their information systems were incompatible they did not anticipate a computer plan for the merged unit until the fall of 1999.[19] Information management is a continuous process. Even if an effective information system can be created and put into use, there is still a good chance that it will need to be occasionally modified to fit changing circumstances.

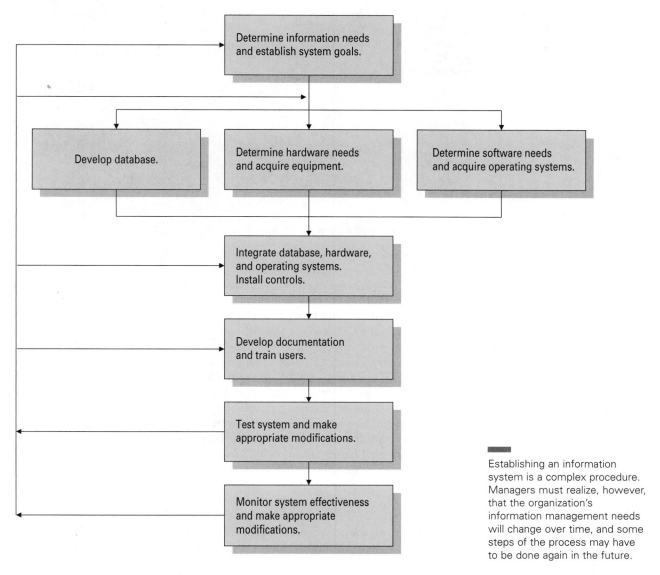

Establishing an information system is a complex procedure. Managers must realize, however, that the organization's information management needs will change over time, and some steps of the process may have to be done again in the future.

Integrating Information Systems

In very large and complex organizations, information systems must also be integrated. This integration may involve linkages between different information systems within the same organization or between different organizations altogether.[20] Within an organization, for example, the marketing system and the operations system probably need to be able to communicate with one another.

Linking systems together is not easy.[21] A company might install its first information system in operations using a Sun Microsystems package. A couple of years later, it might put a system into marketing but decide for some reason to use IBM equipment. When a decision is made still later to integrate the two

Most organizations continue to adopt and use the latest forms of information technology. To maximize the benefits of new information technology, however, firms must make sure that employees are properly trained in the uses and capabilities of hardware, software, and network linkages.

systems, differences in technology and operating systems might make such integration difficult or even impossible.

This problem can be overcome in two ways. One is to develop everything at once. Unfortunately, doing so is expensive, and sometimes managers simply can't anticipate today exactly what their needs will be tomorrow. The other solution is to adopt a standard type of system at the beginning so that subsequent additions fit properly. Even then, however, breakthroughs in information system technology may still make changing approaches in midstream necessary.

An example of a vast, integrated information system that links businesses, schools, and individuals is the **Internet**, known as the **information superhighway**. The Internet is changing the way people communicate. Every day, more and more people tie into the Internet to access information about such wide-ranging things as weather, sports, business information, hobbies, and leisure activities. The *Environment of Management* box discusses some of the emerging issues associated with the Internet.

● **Internet (information superhighway)**
An emerging integrated information system that can be accessed by anyone with a computer and a modem

Using Information Systems

The real test of the value of an information system is how it can be used. Ideally, an information system should be simple to use and nontechnical—that is, one should not have to be a computer expert to use the system. In theory, a manager should be able to access a modern information system by turning on a computer and clicking on icons in response to menu prompts. The manager should also be able to enter appropriate new data or request that certain kinds of information be provided. The requested information might first be displayed on a computer screen or monitor. After the manager is satisfied, the information can then be printed out on paper by a standard printer, or the manager can store the information back in the system for future use or for use by others.[22]

At Toronto's Hospital for Sick Children, X-rays and CT scans can be viewed at a patient's bedside by members of the pediatric critical care team. In the past, X-rays and CT scans were viewed either in the radiology department or at a special viewing station. In 1996, the Hospital for Sick Children received a Canadian Information Productivity Award of Distinction for the new system. The system converts high-resolution images into low-resolution images that are transmitted through the hospital's computer network to bedside terminals.[23]

THE IMPACT OF INFORMATION SYSTEMS ON ORGANIZATIONS

Information systems are clearly an important part of most modern organizations. Their effects are felt in a variety of ways. In particular, information systems affect performance, the organization itself, and people within the organization. Information systems also have clear limits to what they can do.

Performance Effects

Organizations install information systems because they think they will make the organization more effective and efficient. Globally, information technology is a $10 trillion industry, and in Canada this sector contributes approximately $40 billion to the GDP while employing 300,000 workers.[24] These figures are expected to rise significantly in the future.

Has the expenditure been worthwhile? Some experts say yes, but others have their doubts. The problem is that although information systems can speed up an organization's ability to crunch numbers and generate documents, measuring whether the increased speed is justified in light of the enormous costs involved is difficult. Many organizations, including Xerox, the Royal Bank of Canada, and Shoppers Drug Mart, claim that their information systems have contributed to their success. Indeed, consensus seems to be growing that information systems do pay for themselves over time, although an organization needs to recognize that the system may take years to pay its own way. Acadia University firmly believes that its commitment to information systems has paid huge dividends.

Other universities and businesses also believe that they have gained huge dividends from their commitment to information systems. The Relais system at the University of Alberta library electronically delivers the contents of more than six million books and journals to students and professors in dramatically less time than traditional libraries. At Air Canada, a waybill for every piece of cargo must be kept for seven years. In the past, waybills were occasionally misplaced, but now these slips are scanned into an indexed database that makes it possible to locate a piece of cargo within two minutes via telephone. The University of Alberta and Air Canada are only two of a growing number of organizations that are reporting productivity gains from improved information systems.[25]

Organizational Effects

Information systems affect the organization's basic structure and design. These effects generally happen in two ways. First, most organizations find creating a separate unit to handle the information management system useful; some even create a new top-management position, usually called the chief information

E-Mail Privacy

As of 1999, it was estimated that more than 100 million people are on the "information superhighway" (also known as the Internet); this number is expected to grow 500 percent by 2002. Most Internet users exchange e-mail (short for *electronic mail*) messages, sometimes many times each day. Evidence suggests that there is a significant gap between employees' perceptions of e-mail privacy and the rights of employers under the law to monitor and read workers' electronic messages. To promote a positive, productive work environment and to avoid potential legal liability, organizations need to develop and effectively communicate exactly what the organization's policies are with regard to e-mail privacy and monitoring.

Such policies are necessary expecially in light of no clear Canadian legislation on e-mail privacy. The situation is somewhat different in the United States. Although some legislative efforts are under way to change the situation, as of early 1995, the U.S. Electronics Communications Privacy Act of 1986 prohibits the interception of e-mail messages by third parties (someone other than the person sending or receiving the message) not part of the sender's organization. It does not so prohibit third-party interception, however, if the third party is a manager within the sender's organization. Thus your boss can read your e-mail.

Two employees of a Nissan Motor Co. subsidiary were reprimanded for what they were saying about a supervisor through e-mail. They filed a grievance arguing that their privacy had been violated. They were fired. Taken to court, Nissan was able to argue successfully that the company owned the computer system and, hence, could legally read anything on it. Many similar cases have established the organization's right to read employees' e-mail. Some jurisdictions have restricted an organization's right to eavesdrop on private conversations and telephone calls but e-mail has few clear rules.

Some computer users have taken to using encryption software. Such software is provided by a variety of companies, and shareware (free for test use with nominal fees to registered users) versions exist, too. If both sender and receiver have the same encrypting codes, they can send and receive with little concern about others reading their mail. A problem with encrypting codes is that they slow things down. Before sending a message, it must first be encrypted, and before reading it, it must be decrypted. For highly confidential materials encryption may be worth the effort but, for many routine messages, it is hardly worth the time and effort.

Good managers, of course, should not read, scan, or snoop into employees' e-mail indiscriminately. To do so suggests that an organizational culture of distrust exists that is hardly consistent with good management. Rather, well-managed organizations should issue policies explaining that although they have the legal right to read e-mail, they will do so only under certain circumstances, such as the suspicion of crimes like theft or espionage. With a clear policy and an atmosphere of trust, potential problems can be minimized.

References: Bonnie Brown, "Is E-Mail Private or Public? Companies Own E-Mail and Can Monitor It," *Computerworld*, July 27, 1994, pp. 135, 137; Corey L. Nelson, "Is E-Mail Private or Public? Employers Have No Right to Snoop Through Mail," *Computerworld*, July 27, 1994, pp. 135, 137; Betsy Simnacher, "Put Your E-Mail in an Envelope," *America's Network*, June 1, 1994, pp. 62–66; Philip Elmer-Dewitt, "Who's Reading Your Screen," *Time*, January 18, 1993, p. 46; James J. Cappel, "Closing the E-Mail Privacy Gap," *Journal of Systems Management*, December 1993, pp. 6–11; Cricket Liu, Jerry Peek, Russ Jones, Bryan Buus, and Adrian Nye, *Managing Internet Information Sources*, Sebastopol, Calif.: O'Reilly & Associates, 1994, pp. 5–6; and Michael Smith, "Who Owns the Internet" *Report on Business Magazine*, September 1998, pp. 90–98.

officer, or CIO.[26] This manager and her or his staff are responsible for maintaining the information system, upgrading it as appropriate, finding new uses for it, and training people in its use.

The second way in which information affects organizations is by allowing managers to eliminate layers in the managerial hierarchy. As discussed in Chapter 10, information systems allow managers to stay in touch with large numbers of subordinates, thereby eliminating the need for hierarchical control.

IBM, for example, eliminated a layer of management because of improved efficiencies achieved through its information management system. Some experts have suggested that in the future managers will be able to coordinate as many as two hundred subordinates at one time.[27] The *Managing in a Changing World* box also discusses how information technology is changing organizations.

Behavioural Effects

Information systems affect the behaviours of people in organizations. Some of these effects are positive; others are negative. On the plus side, information systems usually improve individual efficiency. Some people also enjoy their work more because they have fun using the new technology. As a result of computerized bulletin boards and electronic mail (e-mail), groups can form across organizational boundaries.

On the negative side, information systems can lead to isolation as people have everything they need to do their jobs without interacting with others. Managers can work at home easily, with the possible side effects of making them unavailable to others who need them or removing them from key parts of the social system. Computerized working arrangements also tend to be much less personal than other methods. For example, a computer-transmitted "pat on the back" will likely mean less than praise delivered in person. Researchers are just beginning to determine how individual behaviours and attitudes are affected by information systems.

Information System Limitations

Recognizing the limits of information systems is also necessary.[28] Several of these are listed in Table 22.1. First, as already noted, information systems are expensive and difficult to develop. Thus organizations may try to cut corners or install a system in such a piecemeal fashion that its effectiveness suffers.

Information systems are not suitable for all tasks or problems. Problems requiring human judgment must still be addressed by humans beings. Information systems are often a useful tool for managers, but they can seldom actually replace managers. Managers also may come to rely too much on infor-

---

TABLE 22.1 Limitations of Information Systems

1. Information systems are expensive and difficult to develop and implement.

2. Information systems are not suitable for all tasks or problems.

3. Managers sometimes rely on information systems too much.

4. Information provided to managers may not be as accurate, timely, complete, or relevant as it appears.

5. Managers may have unrealistic expectations of what the information system can do.

6. The information system may be subject to sabotage, computer viruses, or downtime.

Although information systems play a vital role in modern organizations, they are not without their limitations. In particular, information systems have six basic limitations. For example, one major limitation of installing an information system is cost. For a large company, an information system might cost several million dollars.

The Changing Office

Offices are changing. The people in offices are no longer all white men, the technology has moved from "low tech" to "high tech," walls have been replaced by partitions and low barriers, and now the office seems to be disappearing altogether as the virtual office emerges.

A computer with a high-speed modem can enable an office worker to telecommute, or work at home and send the completed work to an office miles away. An organization with large numbers of telecommuters could have a lower investment in buildings, parking, and services. Employees who use personal communication systems and call forwarding can create a virtual office, one in which all employees in the office are actually working at home or at a remote location but the customer is unaware of it. The customer calls a central number and is routed to or enters an extension number to reach the person with whom they should interact. Although the customer may believe that the person is behind a desk in a central office, he or she may be almost anywhere. Companies such as Procter & Gamble, IBM, and Compaq have to varying degrees adopted the virtual office concept in field sales and customer service.

Although adding beepers or cellular phones (or both) extends the contact for the virtual office, the employee still needs to use his or her computer to perform the required tasks. But with portable computers, even that element of the office can be taken almost anywhere. Thus the virtual office can also become the portable office. A major limitation, at present, is batteries. A laptop computer, modem, cellular phone, data adapters along with necessary software, a portable fax machine, and a portable printer is a lot of interconnected hardware to run off of just batteries. In the future, devices will become available that incorporate all of those in one machine that will enable greater battery life. You may be able to carry your office around with you.

There is, however, a downside to the virtual office. Having the technology to be in touch with the office no matter where you are means that your office can also be in touch with you no matter where you are. Indeed, some telecommuters feel that they are not so much linked to their offices as they are shackled to them. They cannot get away from the beepers, modems, portable computers, and other technology that created the virtual office in the first place. As with any technology, it can be used and abused.

References: Tim Clark, "Chiat 'Virtual Office' Swells," *Advertising Age*, August 1, 1994, p. 44; Rosalind Resnick, "Cyber Execs," *World Trade*, June 1994, pp. 42–46; Bart Dahmer, "It Ain't Heavy; It's My Computer," *Training and Development*, June 1994, pp. 58–60; Jeff Ubois, "Plugged in Away from the Office," *Working Woman*, June 1994, pp. 60–61; Allison Sprout Jr., "Moving Into the Virtual Office," *Fortune*, May 2, 1994, p. 103; Dennis H. Pillsbury, "Supporting the Virtual Office," *Rough Notes*, February 1994, pp. 50–52; Diane E. Lewis, "Modem Can Link, or Chain, Worker to Office," *Boston Sunday Globe*, July 18, 1993, pp. 1, 12; Philip Elmer-Dewitt, "A Portable Office That Fits in Your Palm," *Time*, February 15, 1993, pp. 56–57; Malia Boyd, "Chiat/Day," *Incentive*, October 1993, p. 2; and Thomas Davenport and Keri Pearlson, "Two Cheers for the Virtual Office," *Sloan Management Review*, Summer 1998, pp. 51–65.

mation systems. As a consequence, the manager may lose touch with the real-world problems he or she needs to be concerned about.

Information may not be as accurate, timely, complete, or relevant as it appears. There is a strong tendency for people to think that because a computer performed the calculations, the answer must be correct—especially if the answer is calculated to several decimal places. But if the initial information was flawed, all resultant computations using it are likely to be flawed as well.

Managers sometimes have unrealistic expectations about what information systems can accomplish. They may believe that the first stage of implementation will result in a full-blown Orwellian communication network that a child could use. When the manager comes to see the flaws and limits of the system, she or he may become disappointed and as a result not use the system effectively. Finally, the information system may be subject to sabotage, computer viruses, or downtime. Disgruntled employees have been known to deliberately enter false data.[29] And a company that relies too much on a computerized information system may find itself totally paralyzed in the event of a simple power outage.

SUMMARY OF KEY POINTS

Information is a vital part of every manager's job. For information to be useful, it must be accurate, timely, complete, and relevant. Information technology is best conceived of as part of the control process.

Information technology systems contain five basic components. These are an input medium, a processor, storage, a control system, and an output medium. Although the form varies, both manual and computerized information systems have these components.

An organization's information technology requirements are determined by four factors. Two general factors are the environment and size of the organization. Two specific factors are area and level of the organization. Each factor must be weighed in planning an information system.

There are four basic kinds of information systems—transaction-processing systems, basic management information systems, decision support systems, and executive information systems. Each provides certain types of information and is most valuable for specific types of managers.

Managing information systems involves three basic elements. The first is deciding how to establish information systems. Of course, this step actually involves a wide array of specific activities and steps. The systems must then be integrated. Finally, managers must be able to use them.

Information systems affect organizations in a variety of ways. Major influences are on performance, the organization itself, and behaviour within the organization. There are also limitations to the effectiveness of information systems. Managers should understand these limitations so as to not have unrealistic expectations.

DISCUSSION QUESTIONS

Questions for Review

1. What are the characteristics of useful information? How can information management aid in organizational control?
2. What are the building blocks of information systems? How are they related to one another?
3. What is a management information system? How can such a system benefit an organization?
4. What is an expert system? Do such systems have any significant potential for use by business organizations? Why or why not?

Questions for Analysis

5. In what ways is a management information system like an inventory control system or a production control system? In what ways is it different from those?

6. Some have said that the information revolution now occurring is like the industrial revolution in terms of the magnitude of its impact on organizations and society. What leads to such a view? Why might that view be an overstatement?

7. Can the chief information officer of an organization possibly become too powerful? If so, how might the situation be prevented? If not, why not?

Questions for Application

8. Interview a local business manager about the use of information in his or her organization. How is information managed? Is a computer system used? How well does the information system seem to be integrated with other aspects of organizational control?

9. Your college or university library deals in information. What kind of information system is used? Is it computerized? How might the information system be redesigned to be of more value to you?

10. Go to the library and see if you can locate a reference to the use of an expert system in a business firm. If you can, share it with the class. Why might this be a difficult assignment?

BUILDING EFFECTIVE TIME-MANAGEMENT SKILLS

Exercise Overview

Time-management skills refer to the manager's ability to prioritize work, to work efficiently, and to delegate appropriately. This exercise focuses on how time management and information technology may relate to one another.

Exercise Background

One of the biggest implied advantages of modern information technology today is time management—modern technology is supposed to make us more productive and more efficient and make it easier to communicate with one another. At the same time, most people acknowledge that information technology can also get out of hand.

Here are five forms of information technology. Start this exercise by thinking of ways that each form can both save and waste time.

1. Cellular telephone
2. E-mail
3. Voice mail
4. Internet
5. Facsimile machine

Exercise Task

With the preceding background information as context, do the following:
1. Describe what a manager can do to capitalize more on the advantages and minimize the disadvantages of each form of information technology in terms of time management.
2. Some managers have argued that they have become more efficient by turning off one or more of these information technology devices. Critique this idea from a time-management perspective.
3. Identify two other forms of information technology you use and characterize them in terms of time management.

Imagine an office in which all machines and equipment—dictating machines, computers, printers, fax machines, telephones, copiers, scanners, calculators, and all the other devices that comprise the modern office—were interconnected in such a way that the need for actually having a "hard" copy (i.e., a piece of paper) virtually disappears. This "paperless" office may not be far away.

The paperless office is being pursued by many different companies. Adobe Systems' Acrobat Exchange allows documents to be exchanged regardless of compatibility differences in software or hardware that developed them. A similar product is No Hands Software's Common Ground. Pinnacle Micro's Paperless 1 imaging system scans, stores, and distributes documents across networks. Bull HN Information Systems Inc. developed IMAGEworks, a document image processing system that can be linked to its mainframe computers. Computhink's The Paperless Office combines the power, flexibility, and speed of sophisticated document management systems with the convenience of Microsoft's Windows (95, 98, and NT) and Novell Netware. The program enables users to find and retrieve documents easily. Similarly, Edmonton-based Shana Corporation's electronic form software achieves cross-platform functionality, allowing users to work with forms on both Windows and Macintosh operating systems.

These and other programs have made it possible for organizations to substantially reduce the use of paper. The development of a paperless online billing system by Newstar Technologies of Toronto has been viewed with much interest by Canada's major banks. Canada Post and Sebra, a subsidiary of the Bank of Montreal, are developing the Electronic Post Office for bills and other mail. Since 1996, the University of British Columbia, the University of Victoria, Simon Fraser University, the University of Northern British Columbia, and the British Columbia Institute of Technology have been accepting admission applications from around the world via the Internet. The Information Management Branch and the Financial Management Branch of the federal Department of Natural Resources have piloted an imaging project that will provide employees of the Accounting Unit with access to scanned documents on their desktops and allow them to conduct verification and payment electronically.

Just as privacy is an issue with electronic mail, privacy and security are issues with the paperless office. For instance, how does one know whether a signature on a fax is genuine? Clearly someone who intercepts a file with a signature in it could copy it and use it for all sorts of purposes, both good and evil. Could privileged personal information about employees be more easily obtained and shared? Could offensive photographs, stories, or both be circulated more easily? These and related questions dealing with privacy, security, ethics, and morality will need to be carefully addressed as the paperless office of the future emerges.

Questions

1. What are the advantages and disadvantages of the paperless office?

2. Are certain types of information more readily amenable to digital processing in a paperless office than are others? If so, why; if not, why not?

3. How might book publishing change as the technology of the paperless office continues to develop? Will books become obsolete? Why or why not?

References: Christy Fisher, "An Interactive Stamp of Approval," *Advertising Age*, June 20, 1994, pp. 22, 25; David H. Freedman, "The Paperless Office Revisited," *CIO*, April 15, 1994, pp. 42–50; Joel Shore, "Pinnacle Provides Paperless Office," *Computer Reseller News*, February 14, 1994, pp. 2, 70; "Can Xerox Duplicate Its Glory Days?" *Business Week*, October 4, 1993, pp. 56–57; "Paper, Work, and Groups," *Macworld*, September 1, 1993, p. 51; Thomas McCarroll, "Ending the Paper Chase," *Time*, June 14, 1993, pp. 60, 65; "The Paperless Office" (http://www.computhink.com); Shana Corporation (http://www.canarie); "Imaging Pilot Project: Finance Records Office Accounts Payable Unit" (http://www.nrcan.gc.ca); "UBC Admission Application on the Web" (http://www.studentservices.ubc.com); and Amber Veverka, "Now Your Bills Going Out Online, *The Toronto Star*, January 15, 1999, p. C18.

CHAPTER NOTES

1. Gene Bylinsky, "Industry's Amazing Instant Prototypes," *Fortune*, January 12, 1998, pp. 120B–120D; Thomas Stewart, "Managing in a Wired Company," *Fortune*, July 11, 1994, pp. 44–56; *Hoover's Handbook of American Business 1998* (Austin, Tex.: Hoover's Business Press, 1998), pp. 1294–1295.

2. William B. Stevenson and Mary C. Gilly, "Information Processing and Problem Solving: The Migration of Problems Through Formal Positions and Networks of Ties," *Academy of Management Journal*, December 1991, pp. 918–928.

3. Lynda M. Applegate, James I. Cash Jr., and D. Quinn Mills, "Information Technology and Tomorrow's Manager," *Harvard Business Review*, November–December 1988, pp. 128–136.

4. "At Today's Supermarket, the Computer Is Doing It All," *Business Week*, August 11, 1986, pp. 64–66.

5. Carla Rapoport, "Great Japanese Mistakes," *Fortune*, February 13, 1989, pp. 108–111.

6. Brian Dumaine, "Corporate Spies Snoop to Conquer," *Fortune*, November 7, 1988, pp. 66–76.

7. John Huey, "Wal-Mart—Will It Take Over the World?" *Fortune*, January 30, 1989, pp. 52–61.

8. Peter Drucker, "The Information Executives Truly Need," *Harvard Business Review*, January–February 1995, pp. 54–63.

9. N. Venkatraman, "IT—Enabled Business Transformation: From Automation to Business Scope Redefinition," *Sloan Management Review*, Winter 1994, pp. 73–84.

10. See Jesse B. Tutor Jr., "Management and Future Technological Trends," *Texas A&M Business Forum*, Fall 1988, pp. 2–5.

11. Richard Boland, Ramkrishana Tenkasi, and Dov Te'eni, "Designing Information Technology to Support Distributed Cognition," *Organization Science*, August 1994, pp. 456–467.

12. V. Thomas Dock and James C. Wetherbe, *Computer Information Systems for Business* (St. Paul, Minn.: West, 1988).

13. "Believe in Yourself, Believe in the Merchandise," *Forbes*, September 8, 1997, pp. 118–124.

14. F. Warren McFarlan and Richard Nolan, "How to Manage an IT Outsourcing Alliance," *Sloan Management Review*, Winter 1995, pp. 9–24.

15. Darryl Taft, "Arlington Ships Decision Tool," *Computer Reseller News*, November 27, 1995, p. 165.

16. Jeremy Main, "At Last, Software CEOs Can Use," *Fortune*, March 13, 1989, pp. 77–83; see also, "Cyberspace," *Business Week*, February 27, 1995, pp. 78–86.

17. See George W. Reynolds, *Information Systems for Managers* (St. Paul, Minn.: West, 1988), for a detailed description of developing information systems.

18. "Computerizing Uncle Sam's Data: Oh, How the Public Is Paying," *Business Week*, December 15, 1986, pp. 102–103.

19. Yan Barcelo, "Power Surge," *CA Magazine*, October 1998, pp. 28–33.

20. "How Do You Build an Information Highway?" *Business Week*, September 16, 1991, pp. 108–112.

21. "Linking All the Company Data: We're Not There Yet," *Business Week*, May 11, 1987, p. 151.

22. David Kirkpatrick, "Why Not Farm Out Your Computing?" *Fortune*, September 23, 1991, pp. 103–112.

23. Piali Roy, "Information at Their Fingertips," *Canadian Business Technology*, Winter 1996, p. 80.

24. "She Said It," *Royal Bank Business Report*, November 1996, p. 7.

25. Charles Mandel, "Prometheus On-line," *Canadian Business Technology*, Winter 1996, pp. 79–82.

26. Michael Earl and David Feeny, "Is Your CIO Adding Value?" *Sloan Management Review*, Spring 1994, pp. 11–20.

27. Jeremy Main, "The Winning Organization," *Fortune*, September 26, 1988, pp. 50–60.

28. See Reynolds, *Information Systems for Managers*.

29. "Computer Headaches," *Newsweek*, July 6, 1987, pp. 34–35.

P A R T   VI   CTV Video Cases

ⓒⓉⓥ   The Controlling Process

NEWS ITEM:
TTC Attempts to Rebound from Crash (1996, 3:30)

One year after the subway crash that killed three transit riders, the Toronto Transit Commission continues to try to address the problems that led to the disaster. Not only are they dealing with the blow to their previously excellent reputation, but they are finding themselves fighting for the funding that will allow them to make the necessary changes.

Questions:

1. If safety is paramount, as stated in the video, then why is the TTC having difficulty acquiring the funds to make the necessary improvements?
2. According to the inquest, where does the TTC need to implement better controls?

NEWS ITEM:
Generation X Is Changing the World of Work (1998, 2:15)

Managers are quickly realizing that young Canadians now entering the workforce have different attitudes toward work than previous generations. While some managers see young Canadians as very demanding, or perhaps as holding unrealistic expectations, others maintain that Gen Xers are perfectly willing to work hard, but are simply asking for their work to be fulfilling. Gen Xers want to be given a sense of ownership about the work that they do and be able to have time for a life outside of the workplace.

Questions:

1. Despite the intense competition for jobs, researchers say that Gen Xers are likely to be more choosy and demanding about their work than older employees. Do you agree? Why or why not?

NEWS ITEM:
Canada Victim of "Brain Drain" (1998, 2:30)

Many young Canadians are finding the lure of job opportunities in the United States too hard to resist. Although they would like to stay in Canada—and lament the fact that so many of Canada's best and brightest are leaving the country—they also realize that the career opportunities being offered in the States, particularly in high-tech and computer industries, are too good to pass up.

The Controlling Process (Continued)

Questions:

1. What can American firms offer that Canadian firms canít? Conversely, what can Canadian firms try to do to influence Canadians to stay or, in turn, to lure workers from other countries?
2. Should the Canadian government, industry, or universities and other institutions play a role in trying to keep these bright people in Canada? What steps might they take?
3. Would you consider moving to another country? What factors would influence your decision to leave?

Tools for Planning and Decision Making

This appendix discusses a number of the basic tools and techniques that managers can use to enhance the efficiency and effectiveness of planning and decision making. We first describe forecasting, an extremely important tool, and then discuss several other planning techniques. Next we discuss several other tools that relate more to decision making. We conclude by assessing the strengths and weaknesses of the various tools and techniques.[1]

FORECASTING

To plan, managers must make assumptions about future events. But unlike wizards of old, planners cannot simply look into a crystal ball. Instead, they must develop forecasts of probable future circumstances. **Forecasting** is the process of developing assumptions or premises about the future that managers can use in planning or decision making.[2]

Sales and Revenue Forecasting

As the term implies, **sales forecasting** is concerned with predicting future sales. Because monetary resources (derived mainly from sales) are necessary to finance both current and future operations, knowledge of future sales is of vital importance. Sales forecasting is something that every business, from Petro-Canada to a neighbourhood pizza parlour, must do. Consider, for example, the following questions that a manager might need to answer:

1. How much of each of our products should we produce next week, next month, and next year?

2. How much money will we have available to spend on research and development and on new-product test marketing?

3. When and to what degree will we need to expand our existing production facilities?

4. How should we respond to union demands for a 15-percent pay increase?

5. If we borrow money for expansion, can we pay it back?

None of these questions can be adequately answered without some notion of what future revenues are likely to be. Thus sales forecasting is generally one of the first steps in planning.

Unfortunately, the term sales forecasting suggests that this form of forecasting is appropriate only for organizations that have something to sell. But other kinds of organizations also depend on financial resources, and so they also must forecast. The University of Montreal, for example, must forecast future provincial aid before planning course offerings, staff size, and so on. Hospitals must forecast their future income from patient fees, insurance payments, and other sources to assess their ability to expand. Although we continue to use the conventional term, keep in mind that what is really at issue is **revenue forecasting**.

Several sources of information are used to develop a sales forecast. Previous sales figures and any obvious trends, such as the company's growth or stability, usually serve as the base. General economic indicators, technological improvements, new marketing strategies, and the competition's behaviour all may be added together to ensure an accurate forecast. Once projected, the sales (or revenue) forecast becomes a guiding framework for a variety of other activities.

---

forecasting
The process of developing assumptions or premises about the future that managers can use in planning or decision making

sales forecasting
The prediction of future sales

revenue forecasting
The prediction of future revenues from all sources

Raw-material expenditures, advertising budgets, sales-commission structures, and similar operating costs are all based on projected sales figures.

Organizations often forecast sales across several time horizons. The longer-run forecasts may then be updated and refined as various shorter-run cycles are completed. For obvious reasons, a forecast should be as accurate as possible, and the accuracy of sales forecasting tends to increase as organizations learn from their previous forecasting experience. But the more uncertain and complex future conditions are likely to be, the more difficult developing accurate forecasts is. To partially offset these problems, forecasts are more useful to managers if they are expressed as a range rather than as an absolute index or number. If projected sales increases are expected to be between 10 and 12 percent, a manager can consider all the implications for the entire range. A 10 percent increase could dictate one set of activities; a 12 percent increase could call for a different set of activities.

Technological Forecasting

Technological forecasting is another type of forecasting used by many organizations. It focuses on predicting what future technologies are likely to emerge and when they are likely to be economically feasible.[3] In an era when technological breakthrough and innovation have become the rule rather than the exception, managers must be able to anticipate new developments. If a manager invests heavily in existing technology (such as production processes, equipment, and computer systems) and the technology becomes obsolete in the near future, the company has wasted its resources.

The most striking technological innovations in recent years have been in electronics, especially semiconductors. Home computers, electronic games, and sophisticated communications equipment are all evidence of the electronics explosion. Given the increasing importance of technology and the rapid pace of technological innovation, it follows that managers will grow increasingly concerned with technological forecasting in the years to come.

Other Types of Forecasting

Other types of forecasting are also important to many organizations. Resource forecasting projects the organization's future needs for and the availability of human resources, raw materials, and other resources. General economic conditions are the subject of economic forecasts. For example, some organizations undertake population or market-size forecasting. Some organizations also attempt to forecast future government fiscal policy and various government regulations that might be put into practice. Indeed, virtually any component in an organization's environment may be an appropriate area for forecasting.

Forecasting Techniques

To carry out the various kinds of forecasting we have identified, managers use several different techniques. Time-series analysis and causal modelling are two common quantitative techniques. Several qualitative techniques are also popular.

Time-Series Analysis   The underlying assumption of **time-series** analysis is that the past is a good predictor of the future. This technique is most useful when the manager has a lot of historical data available and when stable trends and patterns are apparent. In a time-series analysis, the variable under consid-

● **technological forecasting**
The prediction of what future technologies are likely to emerge and when they are likely to be economically feasible

● **time-series analysis**
A forecasting technique that extends past information into the future through the calculation of a best-fit line

FIGURE A.1 An Example of Time-Series Analysis

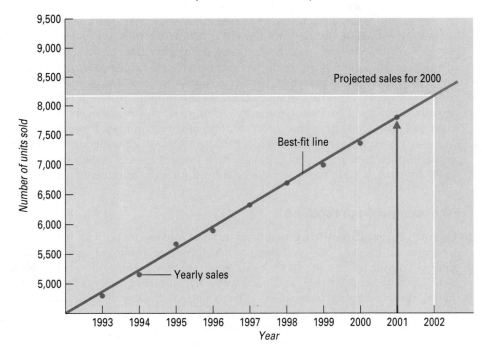

eration (such as sales or enrollment) is plotted across time, and a "best-fit" line is identified.[4] Figure A.1 shows how a time-series analysis might look. The dots represent the number of units sold for each year from 1993 through 2000. The "best-fit" line has also been drawn in. This is the line around which the dots cluster with the least variability. A manager who wants to know what sales to expect in 2000 simply extends the line. In this case, the projection would be around 8,200 units.

It is important to recognize that real time-series analysis involves much more than simply plotting sales data and then using a ruler and a pencil to draw and extend the line. Sophisticated mathematical procedures, among other things, are necessary to account for seasonal and cyclical fluctuations and to identify the true "best-fit" line. In real situations, data seldom follow the neat pattern found in Figure A.1. Indeed, the data points may be so widely dispersed that they mask meaningful trends from all but painstaking, computer-assisted inspection.

● **causal modelling**
A group of different techniques that determine causal relationships between different variables

● **regression model**
An equation that uses one set of variables to predict another variable

Causal Modelling   Another useful forecasting technique is **causal modelling**. Actually, the term causal modelling represents a group of several different techniques.[5] Table A.1 summarizes three of the most useful approaches. **Regression models** are equations created to predict a variable (such as sales volume) that depends on a number of other variables (such as price and advertising). The variable being predicted is called the dependent variable; the variables used to make the prediction are called independent variables. A typical regression equation used by a small business might take this form:

$$y = ax^1 + bx^2 + cx^3 + d$$
where
   y = the dependent variable (sales, in this case)

$x_1, x_2,$ and x_3 = independent variables (advertising budget, price, and commissions)

$a, b,$ and c = weights for the independent variables calculated during development of the regression model

d = a constant

To use the model, a manager can insert various alternatives for advertising budget, price, and commissions into the equation and then compute y. The calculated value of y represents the forecasted level of sales, given various levels of advertising, price, and commissions.[6]

Econometric models employ regression techniques at a much more complex level. **Econometric models** attempt to predict major economic shifts and the potential impact of those shifts on the organization. They might be used to predict various age, ethnic, and economic groups that will characterize different regions of Canada in the year 2005 and to further predict the kinds of products and services these groups may want. A complete econometric model may consist of hundreds or even thousands of equations. Computers are almost always necessary to apply them. Given the complexities involved in developing econometric models, many firms that decide to use them rely on outside consultants specializing in this approach.

Economic indicators, another form of causal model, are population statistics or indexes that reflect the economic well-being of a population. Examples of widely used economic indicators include the current rates of national productivity, inflation, and unemployment. In using such indicators, the manager draws on past experiences that have revealed a relationship between a certain indicator and some facet of the company's operations. Moore Corporation Limited, for example, can predict future sales of its business forms largely on the basis of current GNP estimates and other economic growth indexes.

● **econometric model**
A causal model that predicts major economic shifts and their impact on the organization

● **economic indicator**
A key population statistic or index that reflects the economic well-being of a population

T A B L E A. 1	**Summary of Causal Modelling Forecasting Techniques**
Regression models	Used to predict one variable (called the dependent variable) on the basis of known or assumed other variables (called independent variables). For example, we might predict future sales based on the values of price, advertising, and economic levels.
Econometric models	Make use of several multiple-regression equations to consider the impact of major economic shifts. For example, we might want to predict what impact the migration toward the West Coast might have on our organization.
Economic indicators	Various population statistics, indexes, or parameters that predict organizationally relevant variables such as discretionary income. Examples include cost-of-living index, inflation rate, and level of unemployment.

Managers use several different types of causal models in planning and decision making. Three popular models are regression models, econometric models, and economic indicators.

● **qualitative forecasting technique**
One of several techniques that rely on individual or group judgment rather than on mathematical analyses

Qualitative Forecasting Techniques   Organizations also use several qualitative techniques to develop forecasts. A **qualitative forecasting technique** relies more on individual or group judgment or opinion than on sophisticated mathematical analyses. The Delphi procedure, described in Chapter 8 as a mechanism for managing group decision-making activities, can also be used to develop forecasts. A variation of it—the *jury-of-expert-opinion* approach—involves using the basic Delphi process with members of top management. In this instance, top management serves as a collection of experts asked to make a prediction about something—competitive behaviour, trends in product demand, and so forth. Either a pure Delphi or a jury-of-expert-opinion approach might be useful in technological forecasting.

The *salesforce-composition* method of sales forecasting is a pooling of the predictions and opinions of experienced salespeople. Because of their experience, these individuals are often able to forecast quite accurately what various customers will do. Management takes these forecasts and combines and interprets the data to create plans. Textbook publishers use this procedure to project how many copies of a new title they might sell. The *customer evaluation* technique goes beyond an organization's salesforce and collects data from the organization's customers. The customers provide estimates of their own future needs for the goods and services that the organization supplies. Managers must combine, interpret, and act on this information. It is important to recognize that this approach has two major limitations. Customers may be less interested in taking time to develop accurate predictions than are members of the organization itself, and the method makes no provision for including any new customers that the organization may acquire. Wal-Mart helps its suppliers use this approach by providing them with detailed projections regarding what it intends to buy several months in advance.

Selecting an appropriate forecasting technique can be as important as applying it correctly. Some techniques are appropriate for only specific circumstances. For example, the salesforce-composition technique is good only for sales forecasting. Other techniques, like the Delphi method, are useful in a variety of situations. Some techniques, like the econometric models, require extensive use of computers, whereas others, like customer evaluation models, can be used with little mathematical expertise. Selection of a particular technique depends on the nature of the problem, the manager's experience and preferences, and available resources.[7]

OTHER PLANNING TECHNIQUES

Of course, planning involves more than just forecasting. Other tools and techniques that are of help for a variety of planning purposes include linear programming, break-even analysis, simulations, and PERT.

Linear Programming

● **linear programming**
A planning technique that determines the optimal combination of resources and activities

Linear programming is one of the most widely used quantitative tools for planning. **Linear programming** is a procedure for calculating the optimal combination of resources and activities. It is appropriate when an objective must be met (such as a sales quota or a certain production level) within a set of constraints (such as a limited advertising budget or limited production capabilities).

To illustrate how linear programming can be used, assume that a small electronics company produces two basic products—a high-quality cable television tuner and a high-quality receiver for picking up television audio and playing it through a stereo amplifier. Both products go through the same two departments, first production and then inspection and testing. Each product has a known profit margin and a high level of demand. The production manager's job is to produce the optimal combination of tuners (T) and receivers (R) to maximize profits and use the time in production (PR) and in inspection and testing (IT) most efficiently. Table A.2 gives the necessary information to use linear programming to solve this problem.

The *objective function* is an equation that represents what we want to achieve. In technical terms, it is a mathematical representation of the desirability of the consequences of a particular decision. In our example, the objective function can be represented as follows:

Maximize profit = $\$30X_T + \$20X_R$
where
R = the number of receivers to be produced
T = the number of tuners to be produced

The $30 and $20 figures are the respective profit margins of the tuner and receiver, as noted in Table A.2. The objective, then, is to maximize profits.

However, this objective must be accomplished within a specific set of constraints. In our example, the constraints are the time required to produce each product in each department and the total amount of time available. These data are also found in Table A.2, and can be used to construct the relevant constraint equations:

$10T + 6R \leq 150$
$4T + 4R \leq 80$

(that is, we cannot use more capacity than is available), and, of course,

$T \geq 0$
$R \geq 0$

TABLE A.2 Production Data for Tuners and Receivers

Department	Number of Hours Required per Unit		Production Capacity for Day (in Hours)
	Tuners (T)	Receivers (R)	
Production (PR)	10	6	150
Inspection and testing (IT)	4	4	80
Profit margin	$30	$20	

Linear programming can be used to determine the optimal number of tuners and receivers an organization might make. Essential information needed to perform this analysis includes the number of hours each product spends in each department, the production capacity for each department, and the profit margin for each product.

The set of equations consisting of the objective function and constraints can be solved graphically. To start, we first assume that production of each product is maximized when production of the other is at zero. The resultant solutions are then plotted on a coordinate axis. In the PR department, if $T = 0$ then:

$$10T + 6R \leq 150$$
$$10(0) + 6R \leq 150$$
$$R \leq 25$$

In the same department, if $R = 0$ then:

$$10T + 6(R) \leq 150$$
$$10T + 6(0) \leq 150$$
$$T \leq 15$$

Similarly, in the IT department, if no tuners are produced,

$$4T + 4R \leq 80$$
$$4(0) + 4R \leq 80$$
$$R \leq 20$$

and, if no receivers are produced,

$$4T + 4R \leq 80$$
$$4T + 4(0) \leq 80$$
$$T \leq 20$$

Finding the solution to a linear programming problem graphically is useful when only two alternatives are being considered. When problems are more complex, computers that can execute hundreds of equations and variables are necessary. Virtually all large firms, such as General Motors, Texaco, and Sears, use linear programming.

FIGURE A.2 The Graphical Solution of a Linear Programming Problem

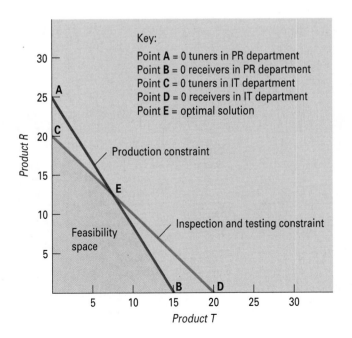

Key:
Point **A** = 0 tuners in PR department
Point **B** = 0 receivers in PR department
Point **C** = 0 tuners in IT department
Point **D** = 0 receivers in IT department
Point **E** = optimal solution

Production constraint

Inspection and testing constraint

Feasibility space

Product R

Product T

The four resulting inequalities are graphed in Figure A.2. The shaded region represents the feasibility space, or production combinations that do not exceed the capacity of either department. The optimal number of products is defined at one of the four corners of the shaded area—that is, the firm should produce 20 receivers only (point C), 15 tuners only (point B), 13 receivers and 7 tuners (point E), or no products at all. With the constraint that production of both tuners and receivers must be greater than zero, it follows that point E is the optimal solution. That combination requires 148 hours in PR and 80 hours in IT and yields $470 in profit. (Note that if only receivers were produced, the profit would be $400; producing only tuners would mean $450 in profit.)

Unfortunately, only two alternatives can be handled by the graphical method, and our example was extremely simple. When there are other alternatives, a complex algebraic method must be employed. Many real-world problems may require several hundred equations and variables. Clearly, computers are necessary to execute such sophisticated analyses. Linear programming is a powerful technique, and it plays an important role in both planning and decision making. It can be used to schedule production, select an optimal portfolio of investments, allocate sales representatives to territories, or produce an item at some minimum cost.[8]

Break-even Analysis

Linear programming is called a *normative procedure* because it prescribes the optimal solution to a problem. Break-even analysis is a *descriptive procedure* because it simply describes relationships among variables; it is then up to the manager to make decisions. We can define **break-even analysis** as a procedure for identifying the point at which revenues start covering their associated costs. It might be used to analyze the effects on profits of different price and output combinations or various levels of output.

Figure A.3 represents the key cost variables in break-even analysis. Creating most products or services includes three types of costs: fixed costs, variable costs, and total costs. Fixed costs are costs that are incurred regardless of what volume of output is being generated. They include rent or mortgage payments on the building, managerial salaries, and depreciation of plant and equipment. Variable costs are costs that vary with the number of units produced, such as the cost of raw materials and direct labour used to make each unit. Total costs

● **break–even analysis**
A procedure for identifying the point at which revenues start covering costs

FIGURE A.3 An Example of Cost Factors for Break-even Analysis

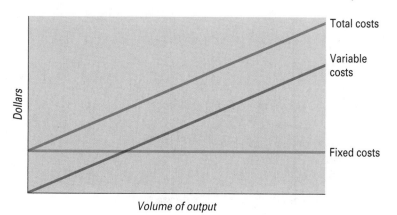

To determine the break-even point for profit on sales for a product or service, the manager first must determine both fixed and variable costs. These costs are then combined to show total costs.

are fixed costs plus variable costs. Note that because of fixed costs, the line for total costs never begins at zero.

Other important factors in break-even analysis are revenue and profit. Revenue, the total dollar amount of sales, is computed by multiplying the number of units sold by the sales price of each unit. Profit is then determined by subtracting total costs from total revenues. When revenues and total costs are plotted on the same axes, the break-even graph shown in Figure A.4 emerges. The point at which the lines representing total costs and total revenues cross is the break-even point. If the company represented in Figure A.4 sells more units than are represented by point A, it will realize a profit; selling less than that level will result in a loss.

Mathematically, the break-even point (expressed as units of production or volume) is shown by the formula

$$BP = \frac{TFC}{P - VC}$$

where

BP = break-even point
TFC = total fixed costs
P = price per unit
VC = variable cost per unit

Assume that you are considering the production of a new garden hoe with a curved handle. You have determined that an acceptable selling price will be $20. You have also determined that the variable costs per hoe will be $15, and you have total fixed costs of $400,000 per year. The question is how many hoes must you sell each year to break even. Using the break-even model, you find that:

$$BP = \frac{TFC}{P - VC}$$
$$BP = \frac{400,000}{20 - 15}$$
$$BP = 80,000 \text{ units}$$

After total costs are determined and graphed, the manager then graphs the total revenues that will be earned on different levels of sales. The regions defined by the intersection of the two graphs show loss and profit areas. The intersection itself shows the break-even point—the level of sales at which all costs are covered but no profits are earned.

FIGURE A.4 Break-even Analysis

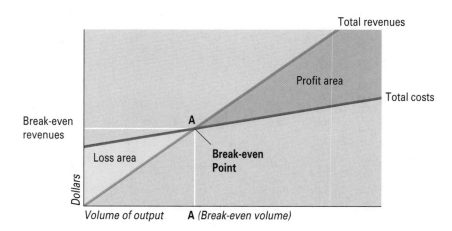

Thus you must sell 80,000 hoes to break even. Further analysis would also show that if you could raise your price to $25 per hoe, you would need to sell only 40,000 to break even, and so on.

Break-even analysis is a popular and important planning technique, but it also has noteworthy weaknesses.[9] It considers revenues only up to the break-even point, and it makes no allowance for the time value of money. For example, because the funds used to cover fixed and variable costs could be used for other purposes (such as investment), the organization is losing interest income by tying up its money before reaching the break-even point. Thus managers often used break-even analysis as only the first step in planning. After the preliminary analysis has been completed, managers use more sophisticated techniques (such as rate-of-return analysis or discounted-present-value analysis). Those techniques can help the manager decide whether to proceed or to divert resources into other areas.

Simulations

Another useful planning device is simulation. The word *simulate* means to copy or to represent. An **organizational simulation** is a model of a real-world situation that can be manipulated to discover how it functions. Simulation is a descriptive rather than a prescriptive technique. Northern Research & Engineering Corporation is an engineering consulting firm that helps clients plan new factories. By using a sophisticated factory simulation model, the firm recently helped a client cut several machines and operations from a new plant and save more than $750,000 (U.S.).

To consider another example, suppose that a city was going to build a new airport. Issues to be addressed might include the number of runways, the direction of those runways, the number of terminals and gates, the allocation of various carriers among the terminals and gates, and the technology and human resources needed to achieve a target frequency of takeoffs and landings. (Of course, actually planning such an airport would involve many more variables than these.) A model could be constructed to simulate these factors, as well as their interrelationships. The planner could then insert several different values for each factor and observe the probable results.

Simulation problems are in some ways similar to those addressed by linear programming, but simulation is more useful in very complex situations characterized by diverse constraints and opportunities. The development of sophisticated simulation models may require the expertise of outside specialists or consultants, and the complexity of simulation almost always necessitates the use of a computer. For these reasons, simulation is most likely to be used as a technique for planning in large organizations that have the required resources.

PERT

A final planning tool we discuss is PERT. **PERT**, an acronym for Program Evaluation and Review Technique, was developed by the U.S. Navy to help coordinate the activities of three thousand contractors during the development of the Polaris nuclear submarine, and it was credited with saving two years of work on the project.[10] It has subsequently been used by most large companies in a variety of ways. The purpose of PERT is to develop a network of activities and their interrelationships to highlight critical time intervals that affect the overall project. PERT has six basic steps:

- **organizational simulation**
A model of a real-world situation that can be manipulated to discover how it functions

- **PERT**
A planning tool that uses a network to plan projects involving numerous activities and their interrelationships

1. Identify the activities to be performed and the events that will mark their completion.

2. Develop a network showing the relationships among the activities and events.

3. Calculate the time needed for each event and the time necessary to get from each event to the next.

4. Identify within the network the longest path that leads to completion of the project. This path is called the critical path.

5. Refine the network.

6. Use the network to control the project.

Suppose that a marketing manager wants to use PERT to plan the test marketing and nationwide introduction of a new product. Table A.3 identifies the basic steps involved in carrying out this project. The activities are then arranged in a network like the one shown in Figure A.5. In the figure, each completed event is represented by a number in a circle. The activities are indicated by letters on the lines connecting the events. Notice that some activities are performed independently of one another and others must be performed in sequence. For example, test production (activity a) and test site location (activity c) can be done at the same time, but test site location has to be done before actual testing (activities f and g) can be done.

The time needed to get from one activity to another is then determined. The normal way to calculate the time between each activity is to average the most optimistic, most pessimistic, and most likely times, with the most likely time weighted by 4. Time is usually calculated with the following formula:

$$\text{Expected time} = \frac{a + 4b + c}{6}$$

where a = optimistic time
b = most likely time
c = pessimistic time

● **critical path**
The longest path through a PERT network

The expected number of weeks for each activity in our example is shown by the orange numbers along each path in Figure A.5. The **critical path**—or the longest path through the network—is then identified. This path is considered critical because it shows the shortest time in which the project can be completed. In our example, the critical path is 1-2-3-6-7-9-10-11-12-13, totalling 57 weeks. PERT thus tells the manager that the project will take 57 weeks to complete.

The first network may be refined. If 57 weeks to completion is too long a time, the manager might decide to begin preliminary package design before the test products are finished. Or the manager might decide that 10 weeks rather than 12 is a sufficient time period to monitor sales. The idea is that if the critical path can be shortened, so too can the overall duration of the project. The PERT network serves as an ongoing framework for both planning and control throughout the project. For example, the manager can use it to monitor where the project is relative to where it needs to be. Thus if an activity on the critical path takes longer than planned, the manager needs to make up the time elsewhere or live with the entire project's being late.

TABLE A.3 Activities and Events for Introducing a New Product

Activities	Events
a Produce limited quantity for test marketing.	**1** Origin of project.
	2 Completion of production for test marketing.
b Design preliminary package.	**3** Completion of design for preliminary package.
c Locate test market.	**4** Test market located.
d Obtain local merchant cooperation.	**5** Local merchant cooperation obtained.
e Ship product to selected retail outlets.	**6** Product for test marketing shipped to retail outlets.
f Monitor sales and customer reactions.	**7** Sales and customer reactions monitored.
g Survey customers in test-market area.	**8** Customers in test-market area surveyed.
h Make needed product changes.	**9** Product changes made.
i Make needed package changes.	**10** Package changes made.
j Mass produce the product.	**11** Product mass produced.
k Begin national advertising.	**12** National advertising carried out.
l Begin national distribution.	**13** National distribution completed.

PERT is used to plan schedules for projects and it is particularly useful when many activities with critical time intervals must be coordinated. Besides launching a new product, PERT is useful for projects like constructing a new factory or building, remodelling an office, or opening a new store.

DECISION-MAKING TOOLS

Managers can also use a number of tools that relate more specifically to decision making than to planning. Two commonly used tools and procedures are payoff matrices and decision trees.

Payoff Matrices

A **payoff matrix** specifies the probable value of different alternatives, depending on different possible outcomes associated with each. The use of a payoff matrix requires that several alternatives be available, that several different events could occur, and that the consequences depend on which alternative is selected and on which event or set of events occurs. An important concept in understanding the payoff matrix, then, is probability. A **probability** is the likelihood, expressed as a percentage, that a particular event will or will not occur. If we believe that a particular event will occur 75 times out of 100, we can say that the probability of its occurring is 75 percent, or .75. Probabilities range in

● **payoff matrix**
A decision-making tool that specifies the probable value of different alternatives depending on different possible outcomes associated with each

● **probability**
The likelihood, expressed as a percentage, that a particular event will or will not occur

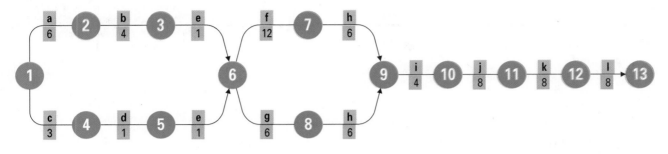

The blue numbers and letters correspond to the numbers and letters used in Table A.3.

The orange numbers refer to the expected number of weeks for each activity.

value from 0 (no chance of occurrence) to 1.00 (certain occurrence—also referred to as 100 percent). In the business world, there are few probabilities of either 0 or 1.00. Most probabilities that managers use are based on subjective judgment, intuition, and historical data.

● **expected value**
When applied to alternative courses of action, the sum of all possible values of outcomes from that action multiplied by their respective probabilities

The **expected value** of an alternative course of action is the sum of all possible values of outcomes from that action multiplied by their respective probabilities. Suppose that a venture capitalist is considering investing in a new company. If he believes that there is a .40 probability of making $100,000, a .30 probability of making $30,000, and a .30 probability of losing $20,000, the expected value (EV) of this alternative is:

$$EV = .40(100,000) + .30(30,000) + .30(-20,000)$$
$$EV = 40,000 + 9,000 - 6,000$$
$$EV = \$43,000$$

The investor can then weigh the expected value of this investment against the expected values of other available alternatives. The highest EV signals the investment that should most likely be selected.

For example, suppose that another venture capitalist is looking to invest $20,000 in a new business. She has identified three possible alternatives: a leisure products company, an energy enhancement company, and a food-processing company. Because the expected value of each alternative depends on short-run changes in the economy, especially inflation, she decides to develop a payoff matrix. She estimates that the probability of high inflation is .30 and the probability of low inflation is .70. She then estimates the probable returns for each investment in the event of both high and low inflation. Figure A.6 shows what the payoff matrix might look like (a minus sign indicates a loss). The expected value of investing in the leisure products company is:

$$EV = .30(-10,000) + .70(50,000)$$
$$EV = -3,000 + 35,000$$
$$EV = \$32,000$$

Similarly, the expected value of investing in the energy enhancement company is:

$$EV = .30(90,000) + .70(-15,000)$$
$$EV = 27,000 + (-10,500)$$
$$EV = \$16,500$$

And, finally, the expected value of investing in the food-processing company is:

$$EV = .30(30,000) + .70(25,000)$$
$$EV = 9,000 + 17,500$$
$$EV = \$26,500$$

Investing in the leisure products company, then, has the highest expected value.

Other potential uses for payoff matrices include determining optimal order quantities, deciding whether to repair or replace broken machinery, and deciding which of several new products to introduce. Of course, the real key to effectively using payoff matrices is making accurate estimates of the relevant probabilities.

Decision Trees

Decision trees are like payoff matrices in that they enhance a manager's ability to evaluate alternatives by making use of expected values. However, they are most appropriate when there are a number of decisions to be made in sequence.[11]

Figure A.7 illustrates a hypothetical decision tree. The firm represented wants to begin exporting its products to a foreign market, but limited capacity restricts it to only one market at first. Managers believe that either France or China would be the best alternative to start with. Whichever alternative is selected, sales for the product in that country may turn out to be high or low. In France, the chance of high sales is .80 and the chance of low sales is .20. The anticipated payoffs in these situations are predicted to be $20 million and $3 million, respectively. In China, the probabilities of high versus low sales are .60 and .40 respectively, and the associated payoffs are presumed to be $25 million and $6 million. As shown in the figure, the expected value of shipping to

● **decision tree**
A planning tool that extends the concept of a payoff matrix through a sequence of decisions

FIGURE A.6 An Example of a Payoff Matrix

		High inflation (Probability of .30)	Low inflation (Probability of .70)
Investment alternative 1	Leisure products company	−$10,000	+$50,000
Investment alternative 2	Energy enhancement company	+$90,000	−$15,000
Investment alternative 3	Food-processing company	+$30,000	+$25,000

A payoff matrix helps the manager determine the expected value of different alternatives. A payoff matrix is effective only if the manager ensures that probability estimates are as accurate as possible.

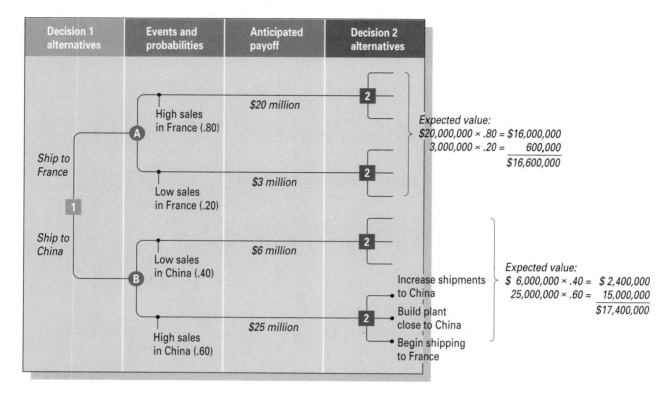

A decision tree extends the basic concepts of a payoff matrix through multiple decisions. This tree shows the possible outcomes of two levels of decisions. The first decision is whether to expand to China or France. The second decision, assuming that the company expands to China, is whether to increase shipments to China, build a plant close to China, or initiate shipping to France.

France is $16,600,000, whereas the expected value of shipping to China is $17,400,000.

The astute reader will note that this part of the decision could have been set up as a payoff matrix. The value of decision trees, however, is that we can extend the model to include subsequent decisions. Assume, for example, that the company begins shipping to China. If high sales do in fact materialize, the company will soon reach another decision situation. It might use the extra revenues to (1) increase shipments to China, (2) build a plant close to China to cut shipping costs, or (3) begin shipping to France. Various outcomes are possible for each decision, and each outcome will also have both a probability and an anticipated payoff. Computing expected values back through several tiers of decisions all the way to the initial one is therefore possible. As it is with payoff matrices, determining probabilities accurately is the crucial element in the process. Properly used, however, decision trees can provide managers with a useful road map through complex decision situations.

Other Techniques

In addition to payoff matrices and decision trees, a number of other quantitative methods are also available to facilitate decision making.[12]

Inventory Models   **Inventory models** are techniques that help the manager decide how much inventory to maintain. Target Stores uses inventory models

● **inventory model**
A technique that helps managers decide how much inventory to maintain

to help determine how much merchandise to order, when to order it, and so forth. Inventory consists of both raw materials (inputs) and finished goods (outputs). Polaroid Corp., for example, maintains a supply of the chemicals it uses to make film, the cartons it packs film in, and packaged film ready to be shipped. For finished goods, both extremes are bad: excess inventory ties up capital, whereas a small inventory can result in shortages and customer dissatisfaction. The same holds for raw materials: too much inventory ties up capital, but if a company runs out of resources, work stoppages may occur. Finally, because the process of placing an order for raw materials and supplies has associated costs (such as clerical time, shipping expenses, and higher unit costs for small quantities), minimizing the frequency of ordering is important. Inventory models help the manager make decisions in such a way as to optimize the size of inventory. New innovations in inventory management such as **just-in-time,** or **JIT,** rely heavily on decision-making models. A JIT system involves scheduling materials to arrive in short batches as they are needed, thereby eliminating the need for a big reserve inventory, warehouse space, and so forth.[13]

Queuing Models **Queuing models** are intended to help organizations manage waiting lines. We are all familiar with such situations: shoppers waiting to pay for groceries at Loblaws, drivers waiting to buy gas at a Petro-Canada station, travellers calling Canadian Airlines for reservations, and customers waiting for a teller at CIBC. At Loblaws, if a store manager has only one checkout stand in operation, the store's cost for checkout personnel is very low; however, many customers are upset by the long line that frequently develops. To solve the problem, the store manager could decide to keep twenty checkout stands open at all times. Customers would like the short waiting period, but personnel costs would be very high. The manager could use a queuing model to help determine the optimal number of checkout stands: the number that would balance personnel costs and customer waiting time. Target uses queuing models to determine how many checkout lanes to put in its stores.

Distribution Models A decision facing many marketing managers relates to the distribution of the organization's products. Specifically, the manager must decide where the products should go and how to transport them. Railroads, trucking, and air freight each has associated shipping costs, and each also follows different schedules and routes. The problem is to identify the combination of routes that optimizes distribution effectiveness and distribution costs. **Distribution models** help managers determine this optimal pattern of distribution.

Game Theory **Game theory** was originally developed to predict the effect of one company's decisions on competitors. Models developed from game theory are intended to predict how a competitor will react to various activities that an organization might undertake, such as price changes, promotional changes, and the introduction of new products.[14] If the Bank of Montreal were considering raising its prime lending rate by 1 percent, it might use a game theory model to predict whether the Bank of Nova Scotia would follow suit. If the model revealed that the Bank of Nova Scotia would, the Bank of Montreal would probably proceed; otherwise, it would probably maintain the current interest rates. Unfortunately, game theory has not yet proved as useful as it was originally expected to be. The complexities of the real world combined with the limitation of the technique itself restrict its applicability. Game

● **just-in-time (JIT)**
An inventory management technique in which materials are scheduled to arrive in small batches as they are needed, eliminating the need for resources such as big reserves and warehouse space

● **queuing model**
A model used to optimize waiting lines in organizations

● **distribution model**
A model used to determine the optimal pattern of distribution across different carriers and routes

● **game theory**
A planning tool used to predict how competitors will respond to different actions the organization might take

theory, however, does provide a useful conceptual framework for analyzing competitive behaviour, and its usefulness may be improved in the future.

● **artificial intelligence (AI)**
A computer program that attempts to duplicate the thought processes of experienced decision makers

Artificial Intelligence   A fairly new addition to the manager's quantitative tool kit is **artificial intelligence (AI)**. The most useful form of AI is the expert system.[15] An expert system is essentially a computer program that tries to duplicate the thought processes of experienced decision makers. For example, Compaq Computer has developed an expert system that checks sales orders for new computer systems and then designs preliminary layouts for those new systems. Compaq can now ship the computer to a customer in components for final assembly on site. This has enabled the company to cut back on its own final assembly facilities.

STRENGTHS AND WEAKNESSES OF PLANNING TOOLS

Like all issues confronting management, planning tools of the type described here have a number of strengths and weaknesses.

Weaknesses and Problems

One weakness of the planning and decision-making tools discussed in this appendix is that they may not always adequately reflect reality. Even with the most sophisticated and powerful computer-assisted technique, reality must often be simplified. Many problems are also not amenable to quantitative analysis because important elements of them are intangible or nonquantifiable. Employee morale or satisfaction, for example, is often a major factor in managerial decisions.

The use of these tools and techniques may also be quite costly. For example, only larger companies can afford to develop their own econometric models. Even though the computer explosion has increased the availability of quantitative aids, there is still some expense involved, and it will take time for many of these techniques to become widely used. Resistance to change also limits the use of planning tools in some settings. If a manager for a retail chain has always based decisions for new locations on personal visits, observations, and intuition, she or he may be less than eager to begin using a computer-based model for evaluating and selecting sites. Finally, problems may arise when managers have to rely on technical specialists to use sophisticated models. Experts trained in the use of complex mathematical procedures may not understand or appreciate other aspects of management.

Strengths and Advantages

On the plus side, planning and decision-making tools also offer many advantages. For situations that are amenable to quantification, they can bring sophisticated mathematical processes to bear on planning and decision making. Properly designed models and formulas also help decision makers "see reason." For example, a manager might not be inclined to introduce a new product line simply because she doesn't think it will be profitable. After seeing a forecast predicting first-year sales of 100,000 units coupled with a break-even analysis showing profitability after only 20,000, however, the manager will probably change her mind. Thus rational planning tools and techniques force the manager to look beyond personal prejudices and predispositions. Finally, the computer explosion is rapidly making sophisticated planning techniques available in a wider range of settings than ever.

The crucial point to remember is that planning tools and techniques are a means to an end, not an end in themselves. Just as a carpenter uses a handsaw in some situations and an electric saw in others, a manager must recognize that a particular model may be useful in some situations but not in others that may call for a different approach. Knowing the difference is one mark of a good manager.

APPENDIX NOTES

1. Anirudh Dhebar, "Managing the Quality of Quantitative Analysis," *Sloan Management Review,* Winter 1993, pp. 69–79.

2. See Wayne W. Daniel, *Essentials of Business Statistics,* 2nd ed. (Boston: Houghton Mifflin, 1988), for an overview of basic forecasting methods.

3. R. Balachandra, "Technological Forecasting: Who Does It and How Useful Is It?" *Technological Forecasting and Social Change,* January 1980, pp. 75–85.

4. Charles Ostrom, *Time-Series Analysis: Regression Techniques* (Beverly Hills, Calif.: Sage Publications, 1980).

5. See John C. Chambers, S.K. Mullick, and D. Smith, "How to Choose the Right Forecasting Technique," *Harvard Business Review,* July–August 1971, pp. 45–74, for a classic review.

6. Fred Kerlinger and Elazar Pedhazur, *Multiple Regression in Behavioral Research* (New York: Holt, 1973).

7. Chambers, Mullick, and Smith, "How to Choose the Right Forecasting Technique"; see also J. Scott Armstrong, *Long-Range Forecasting: From Crystal Ball to Computers* (New York: Wiley, 1978).

8. Nicholas A. Glaskowsky and Donald R. Hudson, *Business Logistics,* 3rd ed. (Fort Worth, Tex.: Harcourt Brace Jovanovich, 1992).

9. Glaskowsky and Hudson, *Business Logistics.*

10. Everett Adam Jr. and Ronald J. Ebert, *Production and Operations Management,* 5th ed. (Englewood Cliffs, N.J.: Prentice-Hall, 1992).

11. Robert E. Markland, *Topics in Management Science,* 4th ed. (New York: Wiley, 1993).

12. Adam and Ebert, *Production and Operations Management.*

13. Ramon L. Alonso and Cline W. Fraser, "JIT Hits Home: A Case Study in Reducing Management Delays," *Sloan Management Review,* Summer 1991, pp. 59–68.

14. "Businessman's Dilemma," *Forbes,* October 11, 1993, pp. 107–109.

15. Beau Sheil, "Thinking About Artificial Intelligence," *Harvard Business Review,* July–August 1987, pp. 91–97; and Dorothy Leonard-Barton and John J. Sviokla, "Putting Expert Systems to Work," *Harvard Business Review,* March–April 1988, pp. 91–98.

Index

Photo Credits

Part One

top left: Luisa Salerno; bottom: Glen Allison/Photodisc.

Chapter 1

p. 3, Ryan Remiorz/Canapress; p. 4, courtesy of S.B. Leclair; p. 13, Luisa Salerno; p. 23, David Portnoy/Black Star.

Chapter 2

p. 31, Luisa Salerno; p. 33, N.A.C. (C–033945); p. 43, AT&T Archives; p. 50, Luisa Salerno.

Part Two

p. 64, Luisa Salerno; p. 64, Al Harvey.

Chapter 3

p. 67, Frank Gunn/Canapress; p. 70, Tony Caldwell/*Halifax Daily News;* p. 74, Phil Snel/*Maclean's*; p. 88, David Fields/Onyx.

Chapter 4

p. 97, Peter Bregg/Canapress; p. 98, Kevin Frayer/Canapress; p. 105, Canapress; p. 115, Luisa Salerno.

Chapter 5

p. 125, Pablo Bartholomew/Gamma Liaison; p. 129, Fred Chartland/Canapress; p. 136, Ballard Power Systems; p. 143, Bob Edme/AP.

Part Three

p. 154, Luisa Salerno; p. 154, Al Harvey.

Chapter 6

p. 157, Kevin Frayer/Canapress; p. 158, Robert Wallis/SABA; p. 164, Louis Psihoyos/Matrix; p. 175, Luisa Salerno.

Chapter 7

p. 185, Luisa Salerno; p. 187, Bob Wilson/Canapress; p. 190, Forrest Anderson/Gamma Liaison; p. 198, Natural Resources Canada.

Chapter 8

p. 215, David Young-Wolff/PhotoEdit; p. 217, Andy Freeberg; p. 224, Jacques Boissnot/Canapress; p. 228, Ray Giguere/Canapress.

Chapter 9

p. 239, courtesy of Jacques-Whitford Group; p. 242, Joe Sohm/Stock Market; p. 247, Luisa Salerno; p. 254, Tom Hanson/Canapress.

Part Four

p. 266, Bob Daemmrich/Stock Boston; p. 266, Marc Romanelli/The Image Bank.

Chapter 10

p. 269, John Lehmann/Canapress; p. 273, Andy Freeberg; p. 275, Andy Freeberg; p. 287, Mike Thompson.

Chapter 11

p. 297, Phil Snel/*Maclean's*; p. 299, Todd Korel/*Maclean's;* p. 303, Robin Mayer; p. 308, Fred Chartrand/Canapress.

Chapter 12

p. 325, Mike Thompson; p. 327, courtesy of Chapters/Globe; p. 334, courtesy of *SHIFT* Magazine. p. 338, Tom Stewart.

Chapter 13

p. 353, John Madere; p. 356, Fred Chartrand/Canapress; p. 366, Luisa Salerno; p. 377, Larry Wong/*Edmonton Journal*.

Chapter 14

p. 385, Luisa Salerno; p. 387, Louise Bilodeau; p. 392, Luisa Salerno; p. 399, Paul Henry/Canapress.

Part Five

p. 410, Luisa Salerno; p. 410, Frank Gunn/Canapress.

Chapter 15

p. 413, courtesy of CAMI; p. 416, Al Harvey; p. 419, Staff/Canapress; p. 430, Tomasz Tomaszewski.

Chapter 16

p. 439, Luisa Salerno; p. 440, Vellis Krooks/Canapress; p. 444, Dan Callis; p. 453, Bob Daemmrich.

Chapter 17

p. 467, courtesy of ATCO; p. 471, John Lehnmann/Canapress; p. 476, Canadian Armed Forces; p. 485, Colin McConnell/*Toronto Star.*

Chapter 18

p. 497, John Abbot; p. 499, Jose Goitia/Canapress; p. 502, John Abbot; p. 509, Photodisc.

Chapter 19

p. 525, courtesy of 3M Canada; p. 530, Canapress; p. 535, Todd Korol/*Maclean's;* p. 537, Robin Nelson/Black Star.

To the owner of this book

We hope that you have enjoyed Griffin and Singh's *Management* (0-17-607400-7), and we would like to know as much about your experiences with this text as you would care to offer. Only through your comments and those of others can we learn how to make this a better text for future readers.

School _____ Your instructor's name _____

Course _____ Was the text required? _____ Recommended? _____

1. What did you like the most about *Management?*

_____
_____
_____

2. How useful was this text for your course?

_____
_____
_____

3. Do you have any recommendations for ways to improve the next edition of this text?

_____
_____
_____

4. In the space below or in a separate letter, please write any other comments you have about the book. (For example, please feel free to comment on reading level, writing style, terminology, design features, and learning aids.)

_____
_____
_____
_____

Optional

Your name _____ Date _____

May ITP Nelson quote you, either in promotion for *Management* or in future publishing ventures?

Yes _____ No _____

Thanks!

You can also send your comments to us via e-mail at
college@nelson.com

PLEASE TAPE SHUT. DO NOT STAPLE.

TAPE SHUT

TAPE SHUT

FOLD HERE

Nelson

TAPE SHUT

TAPE SHUT

0066102399-M1K5G4-BR01

NELSON, THOMSON LEARNING
MARKET AND PRODUCT DEVELOPMENT
PO BOX 60225 STN BRM B
TORONTO ON M7Y 2H1